SDS

KIRKPATRICK SALE

RANDOM HOUSE   NEW YORK

Harcourt Brace Jovanovich, Inc.: From "To Posterity" by Bertolt Brecht, from
Selected Poems of Bertolt Brecht, translated by H.R. Hays. Copyright 1947 by Bertolt
Brecht and H.R. Hays. From *Young Radicals* by Kenneth Keniston. Copyright ©
1968 by Kenneth Keniston.

The Saturday Evening Post: Statement by Phillip Abbott Luce, "Why I Quit the
Extreme Left" from the article "The Explosive Revival of the Far Left," May 8, 1965,
issue. Copyright © 1965 by The Curtis Publishing Company.

Library of Congress Cataloging in Publication Data

Sale, Kirkpatrick.
  SDS

  1. Students for a Democratic Society—History.
2. Radicalism—United States.   I. Title.
LB3602.s8363s24   322.4'2   72–12647
ISBN 0–394–47889–4

Manufactured in the United States of America
9 8 7 6 5 4 3 2
First Edition

This Book Is Dedicated
to Faith
in the Future

CONTENTS

SDS

1

A DECADE OF DEFIANCE

Sometime during the week of March 2, 1970, a group of perhaps seven or eight young men and women moved into an elegant townhouse at 18 West Eleventh Street in a quiet, handsome section of New York's Greenwich Village. The house was a four-story, 125-year-old, Federal-style building still with its original molding and glass, said to be on the market for $255,000, and it belonged to James Platt Wilkerson, a wealthy radio-station owner then away on a lengthy vacation on St. Kitts in the Caribbean. On the morning of March 6, a cloudy Friday typical of a Manhattan spring, a white station wagon double-parked in front of the building while several heavy boxes were unloaded, carried into the cellar, and placed near a workbench which Wilkerson used occasionally to refinish the antique furniture which decorated his house. Late that morning Cathlyn Wilkerson, twenty-five, the owner's daughter and a 1966 graduate of Swarthmore College, and Kathy Boudin, twenty-six, who had graduated from Bryn Mawr in 1965, were together near the front of the house, perhaps asleep in one of the expensively furnished bedrooms or in the sauna bath which was among the house's many luxuries; Ted Gold, twenty-three, who got his degree from Columbia University in 1969, was in the wood-paneled study amid James Wilkerson's prized collection of metal, wood, and china birds; several other people went about their business in the rear of the house. Downstairs, bent over the workbench, Terry Robbins, twenty-one, a Kenyon College dropout, and Diana Oughton, twenty-eight, a 1963 Bryn Mawr graduate and Peace Corps veteran, were at work fastening some doorbell wire from a cheap dimestore alarm clock through a small battery to a blasting cap set in a bundle of dynamite. Near them, on the floor and on open shelves, were more alarm clocks and batteries, additional wire, perhaps a hundred other sticks of dynamite, a number of already constructed pipe bombs and "antipersonnel" explosives studded with roofing nails, and several more blasting caps. A few minutes before twelve o'clock, one of the wires from the bomb they were assembling was attached in the wrong place, completing the electrical circuit.

The explosion rocked the entire block, shattered windows up to the sixth floor in the apartment house across the street, blasted a curtain from the front window onto a railing forty feet away, and punched a two-story hole, twenty feet in diameter, through the wall of the house next door. Within moments two more blasts erupted and the gas mains in the cellar caught fire. The interior of the house disintegrated and collapsed in a cloud of dusty debris, leaving only the back and front walls temporarily intact, and then flames roared up through the opening, leaped out the blasted windows, and an enormous cloud of gray-black smoke billowed into the street.

Out through the back garden, with its pebbled walks and rococo fountain, at least three people stumbled, coughing and partially blinded, then made their way over the walls into adjoining gardens; they immediately disappeared and were never identified. In the front of the house, Wilkerson, dressed only in a pair of blue jeans, and Boudin, naked, scrambled through the rubble and out of a front window, faces covered with dust, glass cuts on their bodies, dazed and trembling but apparently composed. Two passers-by helped the women out and Ann Hoffman—who lived in an apartment right next door to the Wilkerson house and whose husband, the actor Dustin Hoffman, had ironically become a symbol of youthful discontent through his recent movie, *The Graduate* —grabbed a curtain blown from the windows to cover the naked Boudin. Susan Wager, the former wife of actor Henry Fonda who lived a few doors down the block, ran up and helped pull the women away as more flames licked up the front wall and a part of it crumbled and collapsed; she quickly guided the two women to her own house, showed them the upstairs bathroom where they could wash and mend themselves, grabbed a few old clothes and dropped them outside the bathroom door, then returned to the burning house to see if anything more could be done. Behind her, Wilkerson and Boudin, hardly waiting to get clean, quickly put on the clothes and left the house, telling the housekeeper they were only going to the drugstore for some medicine; they, too, vanished without a trace and have never been seen in public again.

Inside the demolished house, three people lay dead. Ted Gold's body, recovered late that night, was crushed and mangled under the century-old beams, a victim of what the coroner called "asphyxia from compression." In the basement the torso of Diana Oughton was found four days later, without head or hands, riddled with roofing nails, every bone in it broken, and it was not until seven more days that she was identified, through a print taken from the severed tip of a right-hand little finger found nearby. The body of Terry Robbins was so thoroughly blown apart that there was not even enough of him left for a formal identification, and his identity was learned only through the subsequent messages of his companions.

Thus, starkly, amid ruins, did an era come to an end. For the inhabitants of that townhouse were not idle troublemakers or crazed criminals but members of a group of dedicated revolutionaries called the Weathermen who represented the last bizarre incarnation of the Students for a Democratic Society. And the Students for a Democratic Society was the force, beginning in the spring of 1960 exactly ten years before, which had shaped the politics of a generation and rekindled the fires of American radicalism for the first time in thirty years, the largest student organization ever known in this country and the major expression of the American left in the sixties. The explosion on West Eleventh Street was the ultimate symbol of SDS's tragic and ominous demise, and of the decade which had shaped it, a decade perhaps as fateful as any the nation has yet experienced, a decade marked by political and cultural upheavals still reverberating through the society, a decade of sit-ins and pickets, teach-ins and mass marches, student uprisings and building takeovers, ghetto rebellions and the destruction of property by arson and bombs, a decade notable for setting a considerable part of its youth against the system that bore them, against its traditions and values, its authorities and its way of life. A decade of defiance.

This book is the story of that decade. It is a story roughly divided into four periods: the first, the period of Reorganization from 1960 to 1962 when SDS takes a new name and lays the basis for the shape it was to assume; the second, the period of Reform from 1962 to 1965 when SDS tries to make American institutions live up to American ideals; the third, the period of Resistance from 1965 to 1968 when SDS spreads out from coast to coast with open confrontations against these institutions; and the last, the period of Revolution from 1968 to 1970 when SDS sets itself consciously for a thorough—and, for some, violent—overthrow of the American system. (The roots of SDS, going back to the first national student organization at the turn of the century, and a description of SDS's immediate predecessors placing the organization in its twentieth-century context, are covered in an appendix.) It is a story which above all tries to explain how in ten years an organization could transform itself from an insignificant band of alienated intellectuals into a major national force; what that force meant to the universities, the society, and the individuals it touched; what happened to undo it just as it appeared to reach the height of its power; and what legacy it left behind.

I was never a part of SDS—I graduated from college in 1958 when SDS's predecessor, something called SLID, was a campus joke and when we had to take the job of confrontation into our own hands—and so all of what follows is a reconstruction, albeit a careful reconstruction, of what SDS went through in that decade. It is based upon more than three steady years of work, interviewing former SDSers important and obscure, reading all of the nearly two hundred issues of SDS's paper, New Left Notes, and the hundreds of pamphlets put out by SDS, traveling to countless universities, and going through the cartons of letters, minutes, files, and other debris that have been collected in the SDS archives in Madison, Wisconsin. I have not tried to be omniscient, pretending to present verbatim those conversations and speeches I never heard or to record unpublicized events in private rooms I was never near; each quotation is from an actual source (cited at the end of the book), either a letter, an interview, a tape recording, a newspaper account, or some similar document; and each description is derived from independent sources such as contemporary witnesses, photographs, documentary movies, and multiple newspaper and magazine articles. Which is not to say that there may not be a mistake within these pages somewhere, but rather that what follows is history, not novel-as-history or memoir or tract, and it is intended to be as accurate a record as possible of what went on during these crucial years.

Though I was never a member of SDS, my interest in the organization stems from the fact that I was, like most people I know, considerably changed by the events and processes of the sixties which SDS helped to fashion. For most of this time I was either out of the country trying to bring changes to other societies or else more sedately boring from within the institutions of this one—yet I came to share the same animus that motivated the shapers of SDS, the same sense of dislocation from the nation that inspired those still on the campuses, ultimately even the same radicalization that SDS generated not only in the universities but throughout so many levels of the society. And I came to feel that the history of SDS would provide more than just an account of those who had been its formal members, more than a portrait of the student generation, but an explanation of what was happening to us all. SDS stood as the catalyst, vanguard, and personification of that decade of·defiance.

SDS was of course only a part of the political phenomenon known as "the Movement" and the Movement only a part of the larger process of cultural upheaval of the time, but it was the organized expression of that Movement, its intellectual mentor and the source of much of its energy, the largest, best known, and most influential element within it for a decade. SDS was also, to be sure, contradictory and chaotic, loosely and sometimes perilously structured, bewildered and timid and arrogant by turns, and it made countless mistakes, avoidable and otherwise, throughout its history and right up to its eventual mad disintegration, but it nonetheless left an impressive record of accomplishment which it is appropriate to review.

SDS was responsible for building much of the student support for the Southern sit-ins as the decade of the sixties began, and over the next four years it developed into the invaluable counterpart of the Student Nonviolent Coordinating Committee in the early civil-rights battles, battles which eventually opened a nation's eyes and led to the *de jure* elimination of segregation over much of the country. It was the group that produced the pamphlets and research in the early years of the decade that brought such issues as automation, poverty, disarmament, and the bankruptcy of the Cold War to the attention of at least the politically minded in the nation's colleges. It provided—chiefly through *The Port Huron Statement* of 1962—the intellectual and analytical tools which helped many students to fashion a political underpinning for their sense of cultural alienation, producing what was fairly called "the New Left," the first really *homegrown* left in America, taking its impulses not from European ideologies and practices (at least not until the end), but from dissatisfactions and distortions in the American experience. It established, even before the federal "war on poverty," one of the most ambitious social experiments ever undertaken by American youth on their own, the Economic Research and Action Projects of several hundred young men and women working in the ghettos of a dozen cities to improve the lot of the poor through direct action and "community unions"; this in turn later helped to generate a variety of political organizations, from the National Organizing Committee to the Young Lords Organization, run by the poor themselves. It was the first, and for some time the most important, organization to mobilize Americans against the war in Vietnam, supplying not only much of the analysis by which a generation came to understand the evils of that war and the system behind it, but also most of the techniques and shock troops for the marches, teach-ins, and confrontations, until ultimately a President was forced to resign and three-quarters of the country declared themselves against the official military policies of their government in a time of war. It was initially responsible for opening up the left spectrum of politics in this country, introducing successively the concepts of participatory democracy, corporate liberalism, local organizing, student power, the new working class, revolutionary consciousness, and imperialism, with the eventual effect of not only pushing the liberal canon to the left but establishing socialism as at least a possible political alternative for a considerable segment of the population.

SDS led the initial campaigns of students against the draft when conscription came down upon the campuses in 1966, and, though initially slow to lead the draft-resistance movement, it provided many of the earliest draft-card burners and later played a part in the agitation that led to major changes in the draft laws and the commitment of the federal government to an all-volunteer army. It was the inspiration and in many cases the supplier of talent for a wide range of "alternate institutions," such as the free universities, underground press, Movement "think tanks," guerrilla theater groups, free health clinics, alternate political parties, and collectives and communes, many of which lasted well into the seventies. It was among the earliest critics of the postwar university system, galvanizer of the student power movement, organizer of much of the student protest that was endemic from 1966 on, and directly or indirectly responsible for a wave of reforms and restructurings that have considerably changed the face of American colleges, from the grading and types of courses to the social and sexual lives of the students to the composition of the boards of trustees. It was the first to raise the issue of university complicity and expose connections between the academy and the government, leading to organized national campaigns against the Dow Chemical Company, draft boards, the Institute for Defense Analysis, university research and investments, and above all against ROTC (in a drive that by 1970 had eliminated thirty units, made eighty-three voluntary, and reduced enrollment by 56 percent from 1966).

SDS taught the mechanics of political organizing and protest to an activist segment of the student population and restored the legitimacy of mass dissent to the national scene, leading eventually to such direct political consequences as liberalized laws (with respect, for example, to abortion, marijuana, homosexuality, community control, and the rights of blacks, women, and the young), the reorganization of the Democratic Party and the nomination of George McGovern, and the extension of suffrage to eighteen-year-olds. It was the seedbed for the women's liberation movement—sometimes, to be sure, as much by inadvertence as intention—and supplied many of that movement's initial converts, and it played a part both formally and informally in other kinds of political broadening such as high-school organizing, GI resistance, trade-union agitation, the Venceremos Brigades to Cuba, and "radical caucuses" in the professional societies of almost every branch of the academy. It was part of, and sometimes the leader of, the use of symbolic violence as a political weapon, beginning with aggressive confrontations at the time of the Pentagon march in 1967 and escalating through "trashing" and bombing, contributing to what must have been one of the most violent periods in American history since the labor struggles of the 1890s and leading *Life* magazine to declare that "never in the history of this country has a small group, standing outside the pale of conventional power, made such an impact or created such havoc." It was thereby at least one of the causes for the vastly increased machinery of state repression that developed in the sixties—agents and informers, surveillance and harassment by FBI and police "Red Squads," computerized files on millions of citizens, expanded teams of federal prosecutors—and that may be one of the decade's most enduring monuments. Its early international contacts with representatives of the National Liberation Front of South Vietnam, the Republic of North Vietnam, Cuba, European Communist parties, and assorted Third World guerrilla groups were important in forging an international perspective for the Movement in its later stages, and the worldwide impact of the Movement was hailed by organizations from the Chinese Communist Party (citing it as one of the reasons for reopening contacts with the United States) and the NLF to the student movements of France, Germany, Czechoslovakia, and Japan.

SDS produced a remarkable series of leaders and thinkers, some of the best of the generation—Al Haber, Tom Hayden, Rennie Davis, Todd Gitlin, Carl Oglesby, Carol Glassman, Carl Davidson, Paul Booth, Marge Piercy, Jeff Shero, Jane Adams, Greg Calvert, Bernardine Dohrn, and literally hundreds of others —who continued to work in the forefront of political change, writing, speaking, organizing, researching, traveling, even after graduating from SDS and even after its demise, well on into the present decade. And perhaps more than anything else it touched the lives of millions of young men and women, both formal members and many more on the fringes, teaching them a new way of regarding their nation and its heritage, penetrating for them the myths and illusions of American society, providing for them (for the first time in the history of the American left) a new vision of personal, social, and cultural relations—in short, *radicalizing* them, until at the end of the decade various national surveys could point to more than a million people just within the universities who identified themselves as avowed revolutionaries, and one academic observer could declare that "radical, and indeed revolutionary, consciousness has rarely if ever had so substantial a numerical base or so much activist energy in this society as it now has."

What all of this adds up to, beyond the specific and immediate accommodations and reforms, is a quite considerable and perhaps permanent alteration of the American landscape over a remarkably short space of time. What all of this will mean for the future is more difficult to say, for certain elements have already faded, others have become exaggerated, still others endure in quiet and unnoticed ways. But if SDS, and the Movement of which it was a part, has been successful in just one thing, the creation of a permanent left in America, it will have served its times invaluably; and if the lessons of its history, its mistakes as well as its success, its entire ten-year transformation, are not forgotten, there may be even a newer and higher movement of challenge and change. It is for that reason that this book was written.

The explosion in the townhouse on West Eleventh Street marked the end of an era, but in this sense perhaps also a beginning.

REORGANIZATION
1960-1962

SDS is an educational association concerned with building a responsible and articulate left in the universities and to extending the influence of this community into the political life of the society more generally. The last year has been one of rebuilding, and the organization now is at that point where a lot of loose threads are being brought together, personal associations are being transformed into organizational responsibilities and program is being put on a firm base both of intellectual content and competent people to carry it forward. The synthesis continually in our mind is that which unites vision and relevance.

—AL HABER, mimeographed letter to
SDS and friends, December 4, 1961

2

SPRING 1960

As the decade of the sixties began, the Student League for Industrial Democracy—SLID, as it was known—gave no sign that it would grow into the most important student organization in the country's history. It had a part-time headquarters in a lower Manhattan office building, a single regular officer who had more or less dropped from sight, and a budget of no more than $3500 a year. It had, at best, a few hundred members, most of whom were once-a-year activists and many of whom were well past their undergraduate years. It had only three chapters—at Columbia and Yale, where both were known as the "John Dewey Discussion Club," and at Michigan—and they operated on their campuses with scant attention from the student body. Its activities consisted of sending occasional speakers to Eastern colleges, sponsoring a week-long summer "institute" to discuss the burning liberal problems of the day, and putting out occasional newsletters and pamphlets devoted to such questions as unionism and the Cold War. Its policies, if that is not too grand a word for the aimless whiffs of belief that floated around its offices, were approximately those set forth in the preamble to its constitution: "The Student League for Industrial Democracy is a non-partisan educational organization which seeks to promote greater active participation on the part of American students in the resolution of present-day problems."

And yet SLID was not without virtues. It could trace its history back to the formation of the nation's first student political organization in 1905 and through the two high points of twentieth-century radicalism in the 1910s and 1930s. It had a parent organization, the League for Industrial Democracy, which in many ways was a decrepit social-democratic holdover from another age but which did give the student department a few thousand dollars each year, some office space and equipment, and an occasional pamphlet or speaker to put through its mill. It had that legacy of skills essential for all struggling organizations of the political outer-world, a capacity for chapter building, pamphlet mongering, and conference holding, plus the quintessential ability to keep going with a shoestring budget and a horsecollar load. It had the distinction of being one of the few student organizations in the land at a time when events on the campuses suggested that something was struggling to be born:* the formation of a student party called SLATE at Berkeley in 1957, a three-thousand-strong student-power demonstration at Cornell in 1958, a ten-thousand-strong march for school desegregation in Washington the same year and another march with twice as many people the next, the founding of the pacifist Student Peace Union in 1959, and the first issue of the proto-Marxist *Studies on the Left* in the same year. And it had a small nucleus of people who discerned this imminent birth and were prepared to be its midwives, young men and women who, on looking at the campuses, wrote, "We sense a growing climate of insecurity in the land, a growing inclination to probe and question: What is happening to us, where are we going, what can we do?"

It was a measure of the new restlessness on the campuses that the members of SLID decided early in 1960 that the time had come to change its name. The stated reasons were simple—"industrial democracy" was too narrow an idea, it made the organization sound too labor oriented, it was too hard to recruit on college campuses with an antiquated and cumbersome name—but the overriding reason was that SLID felt, perhaps mostly unconsciously, the need to dissociate itself from the old and tired leader-

*Others were the National Student Association, the Student Peace Union, the Students for Democratic Action (offshoot of Americans for Democratic Action), Young People's Socialist League (youth wing of the Socialist Party), a tiny Communist Party youth organization, and various apolitical religious groupings.

ship of the League for Industrial Democracy in response to the
new college mood. A poll among members the previous July had
shown "Student League for Effective Democracy" and "Students
for Social Democracy" to be the strong favorites for the new title,
with the milder "Student Forum" and "Student Liberal Union"
—wisps of the McCarthyite fog of the fifties still lingered even in
those days, especially around LID—coming in not far behind. An
October meeting of the SLID leaders had debated "National Student Forum" without being able to engender much enthusiasm,
but a month later a new choice, "Students for a Democratic
Society," emerged as the clear favorite: it was dignified without
being stuffy, explicit without being precise, and it had the ring of
freshness. In January 1960, with some trepidation as to how the
elders in LID would take it, the young leaders of SLID made the
switch.

    As a name change, it was important only to a handful of
people around the New York office—but it was symbolic of a new
attitude within the organization, a new awareness that the American studentry was getting ready to shed its apathy for a resurgent
life of activism and that a student organization like SDS could
help it on its way.

    There was in 1960 no Tocqueville to warn, as the count did
in 1830, that "we are sitting on a volcano," though the universities
were stuffed with people whose specialty it was to predict, or at
least give a glimmering of, how human beings might behave.
There was no presidential commission, no professorial committee,
no scientific assembly foretelling what was to come. Academics
were preparing no books on students as the harbingers of a revived
left—their attention was still on juvenile gangs, or the dangers of
apathy. And yet the volcano was there, and smoldering.

    The reasons for the renaissance of student activity in the
1960s are generally familiar but they bear reexamination because
they help to explain why there was a new mood at this time, why
it was felt particularly among the young, and why it so directly
affected the student population.

    The first reason for the resurgence of the student left was that
the American system by 1960 had reached a point of serious—
though disguised and usually unadmitted—crisis. The *social* fab-

ric of the nation was clearly tattered: families were no longer the places where the young learned their values or the old sought their solace; marriages collapsed at a greater and greater rate, or were artificially sustained after the life had left them; sexuality was seen, and used, as a commodity; organized religion had lost its purpose and many of its followers; alcohol was accepted as the necessary basis for much social and economic converse and many familial arrangements, to which drugs ran a close second and were to increase; crime was abnormally high and on the verge of a three-fold jump; cities were choked with an excess population they could not cope with, becoming behavioral sinks in which neither air nor relationships could be cleansed.* The *economic* structure that had begun to crack in the thirties and had since been sustained by artificial means (government intervention, a permanent military economy, aerospace boondoggles, colonial investment, overseas monopolies, racial and sexual subjugation, waste, pollution, advertising, planned obsolescence, and inefficiency) began to show new signs of deterioration: high and unstoppable unemployment (especially among the young and the blacks), permanent poverty for a third of the nation, runaway inflation, recurrent dollar crises leading to devaluation, and minority control of much of the economy through vast new conglomerates, monopolies, and investment funds. The *political* life of the nation as it sank in its postwar doldrums was increasingly seen to be characterized by corruption, inefficiency, giant federal bureaucracies, identically

*To take just a few of those social ills measurable statistically: the median duration of marriages in the sixties was only six years, with the divorce rate climbing by 33 percent in the decade; the number of people in mental hospitals rose to 1 million by 1965, twice as many as in 1955, and mental outpatients increased from half a million in 1960 to 1.3 million in 1969; alcoholism rose steadily since World War II, affecting perhaps 5 million people in 1960 and between 9 and 15 million by 1970; drug consumption was the highest in the world, with an estimated third of all adults taking mind- and mood-affecting drugs, and 166 million prescriptions written for mind-affecting drugs in 1965, up to 225 million by 1970; there were some 18,000 suicides in 1955, rising steadily to 19,000 in 1960 and up to 22,000 in 1970; illegitimate births were two and a half times more frequent in 1960 than they had been before the war, and grew rapidly each year of the sixties; serious crimes were up 100 percent between 1950 and 1960 and were to go up another 148 percent by 1970, and the number of known murders increased similarly, going from 9,000 in 1960 to 15,000 in 1969. (For sources, see notes.)

rigidified parties, favors for the rich, apathy among the voters, power among the special interests and lobbies, and general unresponsiveness and remoteness—ultimately moving toward a profound swapping process in which the populace passively agreed to sacrifice certain individual rights and freedoms (privacy, speech, political belief, social mobility) for government promises of personal security, material comfort, and national quietude. And the *international* position of the nation, tied to a Cold War ideology, involved an acknowledged practice of foreign intervention (covertly through a massive secret "intelligence" system assuring regimes bought, coerced, or overthrown to our liking, overtly through economic penetration and military occupation) and the production of a vast system of planet-destroying armaments, rattled from crisis to crisis with an effect especially debilitating for the young. Taken together, all of this evidence argued persuasively that the nation's systems were severely strained and distended— and this was felt by many people, but particularly the young, as the decade opened.

The second and related reason for the troubles of the sixties was that the crisis of the system was accompanied by the crisis of belief. Becoming aware, even if subliminally, of the unworkability and distortions of many institutions, millions of Americans began to question those institutions—and many, dissatisfied with the answers, grew to distrust and reject them. The evidence is abundant that perhaps a half of the population—and certainly such sensitive minorities as the media, the intelligentsia, the blacks, and the young—were coming to have serious doubts about the nation's course: the staid National Committee for an Effective Congress later in the decade reported bluntly that "at all levels of American life people show similar fears, insecurities, and gnawing doubts to such an intense degree that the country may in fact be suffering from a kind of national nervous breakdown." For many this led to what the sociologists called the "delegitimization" of authority and the "deauthorization" of the entire system. The media played an important role in this, uncovering at least the surface deceit and corruption in the belief that by exposure the institutions would be self-correcting, and so too did the universities, inheritors of the strong tradition of skepticism in Western scholarship and stocked with a professoriate whose jobs had given them special knowledge of the weakness of national institutions. The young were most particularly affected, in part because they were confronted every day with disbelievers in their classrooms and on their ubiquitous television sets, in part because as youth they were predisposed to challenge and criticize parental institutions, and in part because they had had less time to become molded by the dominant culture and its values. They reacted initially with a sense of loss and a feeling of betrayal, then with a youthful moral outrage, and finally with an outburst of protest; Lewis Feuer is probably right in arguing that "every student movement is the outcome of a de-authorization of the elder generation."

The third reason for protest by the young was that for the first time in the nation's history they occupied a distinct and powerful position in society. It was not just that there were more people below the age of twenty-five than ever before (27.2 million between fourteen and twenty-four in 1960, growing to 40 million by 1970) and more in proportion to the rest of the population (15 percent in 1960, growing to 20 percent by 1970). It was not only that they were better educated than any previous American generation—there were more than twice as many high-school graduates in 1960 as in 1940, and more than 20 percent of the college-age population in universities (compared to 10 percent in 1920), growing to nearly 50 percent by 1970. More important was that, especially among the middle class and upward-reaching, the young of this generation had been specially invested by their parents with the opportunity of living out lives of money, education, mobility, ease (and presumably therefore happiness) that the parents themselves had been deprived of by the Depression and war years—and this is the central reason for the permissive upbringing, and the popularity of Dr. Spock, during the postwar period. Additionally, because these youths were thus allowed more money than earlier generations, and because there were so many of them, an economy continually in search of artificial stimulants immediately made them into a "youth market," accountable for no less than $40–45 billion by 1970; for the first time whole businesses catered to the young, designing clothes, music, foods, cosmetics, movies, and paraphernalia specifically for them. And the youth market did more than supply the young, it eventually *defined* the group, economically and socially, establishing a consciousness in society

at large (and particularly among the young) of their separateness
—so, just as *adolescence* had been culturally created in the early
part of the twentieth century as an "inevitable" human stage, now
youth came to be regarded as a distinct developmental stage, with
its own special needs and attitudes to go along with its own special
clothes and music.

Particular to this generation, too, was a new psychological
position that accompanied its new socioeconomic one, a position
highly directed toward protest. This generation, going through
early childhood in the postwar years of (generally) permissiveness
and child-oriented families, was uniquely caught in the tension
between *initiative* (independence, self-expression, aggressiveness
toward parents) and *guilt* (brought on by that independence and
aggressiveness); it turns out now, according to a number of psychologists (Erik Erikson prominent among them) that the type of
personality which goes through this tension at the ages of four and
five is likely to become both "anti-authoritarian" (from the emphasis on initiative) and "hyper-moralistic" (brought on by guilt).
Thus the adolescents of college age in the sixties were inclined to
protest not just out of the blue, but rather because they were likely
to be the products of a psychological upbringing predisposing
them to distrust and resist authority and to emphasize moral
values, especially those lacking in the parental generation. They
were, moreover, joined with thousands of others on the college
campuses who shared these traits in a setting where there was little
dilution from other social influences. Protest is the almost inevitable result: it would be so in a world disinfected of faults, it is
doubly so in a nation so fertile with them.

The final reason for protest in the sixties is that students were
gathered together in greater numbers than ever before and—as the
products of a university system which was now absolutely vital for
the functioning of the nation—had more power than ever before.
The sixties began with 3,789,000 people in institutions of higher
education and ended with 7,852,000 enrolled. In the sixties, for the
first time in the history of any nation, there were more students
than there were farmers—indeed, in any year after 1962 there were
more people engaged in formal studies than employed in transportation, public utilities, construction work, mining, or farming.
But it was not sheer numbers—students (as graduates) were also

crucial now to the maintenance of the highly complex technology on which the society had come to depend, to the functioning of such areas as government bureaucracy and the service industries which were now vital to the artificial economy, and to the transmission of the dominant culture in such expanding professions as teaching, reporting, social work, and the arts. Universities in fact now occupied a quite central position in American society: they were indispensable helpmeets of the federal government in the production of weapons, the development of scientific processes, the maintenance of the economy, and the study and manipulation of foreign cultures; they accounted for expenditures of nearly $7 billion in 1960, which was to rise to $22.7 billion by 1970; and they were the most important part of an $80-billion "knowledge industry" which accounted for as much as 29 percent of the Gross National Product in 1962 and 40 percent of it in 1970 and which employed some 43 percent of all American workers as the decade opened, more than 50 percent when it closed. Clark Kerr, one of the first to understand the new importance of universities, stated it best:

> The university has become a prime instrument of national purpose. This is new. . . . What the railroads did for the second half of the 19th century and the automobile for the first half of this century, the knowledge industry may do for the second half of this century: that is to serve as the focal point for national growth. And the university is at the center of the knowledge process.

And the students, be it not forgotten, were at the center of the university.

That, then, is the basis for protest in the sixties: the severe dislocations of the American system that by 1960 were beginning to produce a crisis of function and a crisis of belief, combined with a massive new generation which was coming to occupy a new position in society and which, at the university level, was starting to have a new importance in the workings of the system at the same time that they were disposed to challenge those very workings. It had never happened before.

SDS began the decade prosaically enough, planning a conference to be held at Ann Arbor that spring on "Human Rights in the North." Proposed by the 1959 convention, the conference looked as if it would be just one more of those speechified meetings characteristic not only of SLID/SDS but of student organizations in general, in which the grim seriousness of the problems discussed is outweighed only by the grim seriousness of the discussion itself. But this conference was to be different: on February 1, 1960, four black students walked into the Woolworth five-and-ten-cents store in the little town of Greensboro, North Carolina, sat down at the previously whites-only lunch counter, and ordered four cups of coffee.

The four black students were well aware that what they were doing was dramatic and different, but they could have had no idea what a change they were to bring. Before the month was over sit-ins were held at segregated restaurants in twenty cities throughout the South, by the end of that spring students at perhaps a hundred Northern colleges had been mobilized in support, and over the next year civil-rights activity touched almost every campus in the country: support groups formed, fund-raising committees were established, local sit-ins and pickets took place, campus civil-rights clubs began, students from around the country traveled to the South. The alliance-in-action between Southern blacks and young Northern whites, founded on a principle that was both morally pure and politically powerful, gave the student movement a strength that it had never before experienced.

The birth of the civil-rights movement also gave SDS its initial cause and the fortuitous Ann Arbor conference gave SDS its initial identification with that cause. The conference, held May 5–7 at the University of Michigan, was a clear success, at least on the scale of those days. There was wide attendance from civil rights leaders—Bayard Rustin, James Farmer (a former full-time organizer for SLID), Marvin Rich and James McCain from CORE, Herbert Hill from the NAACP, Michael Harrington from the Young People's Socialist League—and from the newly active students—SDSers from the Midwest, representatives of a new group called the Student Nonviolent Coordinating Committee, and two people later important in SDS, Bob Ross, a recent graduate of the prestigious Bronx High School of Science and a student-government leader at Michigan, and Tom Hayden, then the editor of the *Michigan Daily*. Nothing very grand was decided, but important friendships were formed, a new sense of commitment to civil-rights action was cemented, and SDS was set on a path of civil-rights support that provided it with much-needed visibility in the years ahead.

Then, in the wake of this conference, came a second fortuitous stroke, a grant to SDS of $10,000 from Detroit's United Automobile Workers Union, the *deus ex* (literally) *machina* whose largesse was periodically visited upon the student group over the next few years. And because of this grant SDS was able, for the first time in five years, to hire a full-time national officer with the responsibility of strengthening and energizing the organization. The position was to be called Field Secretary and the man selected was Robert Alan Haber.

Haber, then a graduate student at the University of Michigan and the Vice President of SDS, would prove to be the indispensable element in SDS's initial success. A short, balding, scholarly, introspective type, he had grown up in an academic atmosphere in Ann Arbor—where his father, an LID member in his younger days, was then a professor at the University of Michigan—and he was familiar with the university world; in addition, he had been a campus leader at Michigan, where he majored in sociology, a participant in leftish student politics from 1956, and for the last two years an increasingly active figure in SLID. Not only was he close to the student movement at a time when few even knew it existed but he was perceptive about its depth and direction. "I wish I were able better to convey," he wrote to the LID elders after he assumed office, "the enthusiasm and optimism that the young feel for a new movement on the campus. I wish I could give to you a sense of the energy and vitality that is going into it." And again, "I know that if any really radical liberal force is going to develop in America, it is going to come from the colleges and the young. Even baby steps toward our vision of a 'social transformation' are going to have to be [taken] on campuses."

But more than that, Haber also had the consequential perception of how SDS could capitalize upon this new mood and become a central part of it. First, he argued, SDS should play down the old SLID idea of establishing its own little chapters for its own little purposes at various campuses and concentrate instead on forming alliances with the *existing* campus groups that had al-

ready come into being in response to their own local needs—
student political parties, single-issue organizations (peace committees, civil-rights clubs), and *ad hoc* action groups built around
civil-rights picketing, sit-in support, and the like. Second, he said,
SDS could play its most valuable role by trying to coordinate these
groups and service their needs on a national scale, publishing
newsletters, sending literature, organizing conferences, keeping
the leaders in touch with one another, giving them a sense of
participating in a wider movement beyond their particular campuses. Third, SDS should involve itself as much as possible with
direct social action—support for and participation in pickets, sit-
ins, freedom marches, boycotts, protest demonstrations—rather
than limiting itself, as it had in the past, to strictly educational
work. And finally, SDS should abandon the ideological line-toeing
that had characterized SLID, work with any groups that were
genuinely involved in seeking social change, and content itself
with giving them a nonsectarian vision of the totality of the
American system and the connections between the various single-
issue maladies.

This last point is crucial. It is a vision which Haber felt must
lie at the heart of any organization that is truly *radical*—that is,
any organization that seeks to understand, make connections between, and operate on the *root causes* of present conditions; as
Haber put it later that year:

> In its early stage, student activity is neither very radical nor very
> profound social protest. It generally does not go beyond a single
> issue, or see issues are inter-related, or stress that involvement in one
> issue necessarily leads to others. It does not, in short, seek root
> causes. . . . There is no recognition that the various objects of protest
> are not *sui generis* but are symptomatic of institutional forces with
> which the movement must ultimately deal. . . .
>
> The challenge ahead is to appraise and evolve radical alterna-
> tives to the inadequate society of today, and to develop an institu-
> tionalized communication system that will give perspective to our
> immediate actions. We will then have the groundwork for a radical
> student movement in America.

This vision—of a group which connects, and operates on, otherwise isolated issues—accounts for much of SDS's early success.
Philosophically, it is a kind of proto-ideology, a way of linking

otherwise disjointed problems so that they can be seen to rise from a single set of national conditions and thus can be held in the mind, examined, dealt with. Psychologically, it satisfies the search for ideology which, as psychologists point out, is a crucial element in adolescence, especially for the moral young, and accounts for the enlistment in SDS right from the start of a group of very smart but heretofore undirected youths who had not been able to find a way to synthesize their dissatisfactions with the system and who became excited and energetic once they could. And strategically, it is a way of bringing together a number of disparate single-issue clubs and *ad hoc* groups on different campuses and of easily admitting or working with new causes as they arise; this is important for an organization that has to grow both *geographically* (so that its chapters can vary from campus to campus, giving expression to a wide variety of issues of student discontent) and *chronologically* (so that it can take on a succession of shifting causes from the bomb to civil rights to the war to imperialism).

Shortly after Haber was installed in the New York office with his new responsibility and his new perception, the first convention of SDS was held, on June 17–19, 1960. No longer the drab union halls and YMCA auditoriums of the fifties—now the meeting took place at the Barbizon-Plaza in New York. No longer the subdued and somewhat defeated attitude of conventions past—now, as one student put it, there was an awareness of "the widespread emergence of new student thinking on social issues" which the convention symbolized by holding a reception on behalf of students jailed and expelled from Florida A & M for a civil-rights sit-in. No longer the perfunctory panels on remote issues of "Freedom for the Captive Nations" and "The Need for Agricultural Price Supports"—now the convention started with a panel on "Student Radicalism: From the Close of World War I through the McCarthy Period" (with the unspoken assumption that it had not quite been reborn yet) and the discussion was so animated it was carried over to the next day (suggesting that it soon was likely to be). All that seemed to remain of the past was the sorry attendance —only twenty-nine members from nine universities—but among them were some people who were to be instrumental in the future: Sharon Jeffrey, a Michigan student whose mother was a Democratic Party committeewoman with close ties to the UAW; Jesse Lemisch, then at Yale and soon to make a mark as a major revisionist historian; Jonathan Weiss, an activist at Antioch; and Michigan junior Bob Ross. The largest number (eleven) came from Michigan, where Haber had done his spadework well, others from Columbia, Yale, and Wisconsin, and an additional fifty or so were guests, including Murray Kempton, Norman Thomas, trade unionist Don Slaiman, James Farmer, and banquet speaker Dwight Macdonald, whose topic was "The Relevance of Anarchism." Haber was elected President, his strong Michigan contingent coming through; Weiss, Vice President; and Yale student Eric Walther, International Vice President.*

It all seemed a fitting, a propitious, ending to the spring's first flush of student activism. Haber, reviewing what had been accomplished on the campuses and what had happened to his organization, concluded:

> We have spoken at last, with vigor, idealism and urgency, supporting our words with picket lines, demonstrations, money and even our own bodies. . . . We have taken the initiative from the adult spokesmen and leadership, setting the pace and policy as our actions evolve their own dynamic. Pessimism and cynicism have given way to direct action.

*The National Executive Committee consisted of Bob Craig (from Wisconsin), Eldon Clingan (Columbia), Sharon Jeffrey, Barbara Newman (Queens), Michael Rosenbaum (Columbia), Richard Weinert (Yale), and Carol Weisbrod (Columbia, and also SDS's part-time National Secretary).

3

FALL 1960-FALL 1961

By the fall of 1960, though some of the excitement of the spring had been forgotten on the campuses, the new mood of activism was still very much alive. *Operation Abolition,* a film distributed on the campuses by the House Un-American Activities Committee in which FBI Director J. Edgar Hoover accused students who had disrupted a HUAC hearing in May of being Communist-controlled, was greeted by college audiences with open derision and seemed mostly to encourage Student Davids in the notion of challenging the Establishmentarian Goliath. Civil-rights activity continued apace, though often now directed at less dramatic targets like off-campus housing discrimination and fraternity exclusion clauses; antibomb rallies and meetings still drew student audiences, and the Student Peace Union began one of its more successful years; campus groups to support the Castro revolution in Cuba, led in many cases by students who had returned from summertime visits, were formed at several of the larger schools. And in many places campus political parties were established or renewed: at Michigan, a new group called VOICE began, largely through the ministrations of Tom Hayden, who had spent the summer in Berkeley soaking up both the experience of SLATE and the politics of the left ("I got radicalized," Hayden has said: *no one* is born that way); at Oberlin, Rennie Davis and Paul Potter were organizing a Progressive Student League; at Chicago, Clark Kissinger was instrumental in POLIT; at Harvard, Todd Gitlin was active in TOCSIN; Paul Booth, only a freshman, was trying to initiate what later became the Political Action Club at Swarthmore. (It is more than a coincidence that all of these people should later occupy leading roles in SDS.)

Al Haber, meanwhile, operating out of the dingy SDS office downstairs from the LID headquarters at 119 East Nineteenth Street in New York, worked day and night to fashion the new student organization to capitalize on that mood. He felt then that civil rights was still the primary cause for student activists and that SDS could be, as he put it at the time, the organization for the "national coordination of student civil rights which seems so necessary." He established a civil-rights newsletter which by the end of the year had a circulation of more than ten thousand (including two thousand to Southern students, four thousand to Northern supporters, and three thousand to twenty-five of the most active campus civil-rights groups); he laid plans (never realized) for a second civil-rights conference for the spring; he established contacts, largely around the civil-rights issue, with several hundred colleges; and he pushed the SDS image at any civil-rights meeting that came along. Largely through his efforts, membership straggled up to 250 or so, with the most active people gathered around VOICE at Michigan; there were also formal though sporadic chapters at Syracuse, Western Reserve, Yale, Chicago, Brooklyn, Oberlin, and Harvard.

Herschel Kaminsky, then a graduate student at Minnesota, recalls meeting Haber at a SNCC meeting that October:

> I was very, very impressed with Haber. SLID had always represented to me the worst State Department kind of socialism, and to meet someone who was talking about turning what had been SLID into a multi-issue organization that did more than just attack the Soviet Union was a surprise. To find someone like Haber in there, who was very open and flexible on all sorts of questions and was talking about building a student movement in the United States that wasn't just a lot of abstract rhetoric about the taxes on the peasants of Tierra del Fuego or something, interested me and at that time really excited my imagination.

And Haber's view of SDS was also appealing. "At Minnesota we could get protest going, but we couldn't sustain it," Kaminsky says, "and I thought of SDS as being the kind of organization that could." And so it seemed to many others just then.

But before Haber could get the new SDS untracked and pointed in the direction he felt it had to go, he had to confront the immutability of SDS's parent organization, the League for Industrial Democracy. The LID had been through a great deal in its forty years as a vaguely social-democratic clearinghouse for liberal and left-liberal (and even a few protosocialist) ideas and causes, and it had emerged from its battles with Communists in the thirties and forties and from its alliances with trade unions in the forties and fifties with certain fundamental beliefs: a strong attachment to anti-Communism, a commitment to the American labor movement, a faith in Cold War liberalism, and a dedication to the apparently successful meliorism of the American welfare state. Concomitantly, through years of experience with its various student departments—one of which had even broken away to form an alliance with a Communist-influenced youth group in the thirties—the LID had settled upon a form for its student group assuring that it would keep its chapters free from Communist taint, confine its campus activities to seminars and speakers, hold its politics to a kind of Fabian do-gooderism, and devote its energies to educating younger generations through pamphlets, newsletters, and an occasional conference. Moreover, the present leadership of the LID, men who had stayed with the organization through all these not very enlightened years, were growing old and increasingly rigid: Nathaniel M. Minkoff, a power within the International Ladies Garment Workers Union—an intractable foe of leftism and the chief source of LID's financial support—was Chairman of the Board; Frank Trager, a conservative professor of sociology at New York University, was head of the Executive Committee and its major link with the student department; on the Board of Directors sat, among others, such familiar Cold Warriors as Daniel Bell, George S. Counts, Louis Fischer, Victor Reuther, John Roche, and Clarence Senior; on the National Council, a kind of advisory group, were men like Arnold Beichman, James B. Carey, the Reverend Donald Harrington, Sidney Hook, Alfred Baker Lewis, and Harry A. Overstreet. It is little wonder, then, that the LID elders, not terribly disposed to welcoming the awakening student mood in the first place, became positively alarmed as Haber elaborated more and more of his particular vision for SDS's future. They were especially worried about the student organization's overstepping what they regarded as its basic educational role and going into overt political action that was at odds with the LID's superrespectable image, and which might endanger its all-important tax exemption besides.* They were genuinely troubled by Haber's interest in linking up with any of the newly active campus groups and working alongside any of the responsive national organizations—outfits like SNCC, for example, or, worse, YPSL—for fear that this might embroil the LID in relations with Communist or quasi-Communist organizations, a fate worse than promiscuity. And, finally, they were faced with a serious drought in contributions—funds on hand in the fall did not exceed $2,000, and even the usual trade union sources in New York were not coming forth with the $40,000 or so a year that the LID demanded—so they were little inclined to pour a lot of money into an ambitious student organization with all the conferences, picket lines, protests, staff, and subsidies that Haber seemed to want.

The conflict came to a head in early 1961, after months of what Haber, in a lengthy and bitter letter to Trager, called the "backbiting, the hostility and the vicious pettyness." After several meetings the Executive Committee finally voted on March 23 to fire Haber; three days later, in an uncharacteristic fit of submissiveness, Haber sent in a letter of resignation saying he was off to join the National Student Association; and two days later Nathaniel Minkoff accepted the resignation and tossed in $100 as a severance gift, adding with unknowing prescience that he hoped Haber would "continue your warm interest in the student movement."

But then an extraordinary thing happened. Haber did not budge. He stayed on in New York, avoiding the office but carrying on correspondence from his apartment, weighing his weariness and his anger against his vision and his hopes, debating past and future, work accomplished and work undone. Finally he decided

---

*As a (distinctly) nonprofit organization, the LID was entitled to certain tax-exempt benefits—the kind that were essential to attract any sizable donations from wealthy patrons—so long as it did not engage, nor allow its various departments to engage, in direct political action in favor of any political party or legislative cause.

he was unwilling to give it all up, after all, and he wrote a six-page single-spaced letter to Trager declaring his intention to stay and fight. He acknowledged that he had little support in the New York office, but, with thinly disguised blackmail, he pointed out that most of the members elsewhere were on his side:

> I am president of the organization and will preside at the next student convention and can there present my case. I have the votes, as the saying goes . . . the membership of SDS would almost certainly support me.

He also knew that it might be possible to take this membership into something new:

> I would be free to initiate discussion in student and adult circles regarding the possibility of . . . the kind of radical democratic organization I have projected. . . . Many friends of the LID might well see a more aggressively dynamic youth organization closer to their interest.

The LID came to have second thoughts. Trager, especially, urged reconsideration of the case. Some of the less rigid LIDers were enlisted in the battle for the first time, and sided with Haber. Haber's father, who had dropped his LID contacts some time before but was still friendly with the elders, wrote long, warm letters to both Trager and Minkoff. To Minkoff he pointed out the virtues of the current young:

> I happen to be living on a college campus, an exciting and vital group of 25,000. They are students coming out of their shells; they are talking about ideas and ideals . . . are thinking beyond the vocational purposes which brought them to a college or university campus.

To Trager he said of his son:

> I am sure he has a deep sense of responsibility and he has a deep sense of mission. In all fairness, you and I had it at his age and we cannot be too hard on young people who exhibit it at their age.

By May the LID signaled that it was willing to reconsider. An Executive Committee meeting on the ninth of that month thrashed out the whole education-activist debate once more,

finally deciding "to see whether the student conflict can be resolved during the coming week."

At that point Haber made concessions of his own. In a
lengthy memo to the Executive Committee he modified his image,
drew in his horns, and tried to placate their fears. He toned down
his grandiose organizational plans, proposing a staff of four, a
modest series of mailings, and a small city-wide conference. He
played up his anti-Communism and the job SDS could do "as an
effective democratic counter-force to the . . . activity and influence
of Communist oriented youth," not to mention how it could of
course "represent the aspirations, problems and programs of the
labor movement to the current student generation." He played
down his activism and stressed how SDS could "serve as a clearing
house for publication, information and research on the left" with
"primarily an education program" that should cause "no difficulty
with our tax status." He agreed to LID demands that there be no
convention that year, just to smooth everything over and lessen
the chances for a youthful revolt. And he stressed how invaluable
he himself could be, not only for running the SDS office at a pace
no one had seen before but—and here was the clincher—for un-
dertaking personally the responsibility to raise the money for the
student program. The one thing he would not compromise on, and
he made no bones about it, was the necessity for the student group
to have "a greater flexibility in the kinds of membership and
chapter relations" than before and to develop "relations with as
many other democratic issue and action groups as possible"—in
other words, no anti-Communist hysteria from the elders. The
LID, to its credit, bought it. Trepidations there were, and even
some dark predictions. But there was also the frank recognition
that the LID itself had fallen on somewhat scabrous days—not
only were contributions diminishing, not only was the leadership
generation growing old and rickety, but the whole purpose of the
organization in the context of the sixties seemed blurry and uncertain: it had not been uncommon for people at board meetings to
raise the question of just what was the LID's current reason for
being, and in fact a series of committees had recently been established to determine exactly that, each successive one failing to
provide an answer. The strong feeling now was that if there were
to be new blood and energy and life in the LID, it would have to

come from the SDS; and if there was to be any life in SDS, it would probably have to come from Haber.

Haber was rehired.

Flush with his considerable victory, Haber chose the first opportunity to cement it. At the August convention of the NSA in Madison, he broadcast the virtues of the new SDS from every stump and platform, the start of a process of using this particular forum for publicity and recruitment that would continue for the next four years. An unlikely forum it may have seemed: the NSA was composed of student-government types, many of them churchly do-gooders who, for the most part, stood politically somewhere to the right of Adlai Stevenson, and it was being financed—though no one but the top leaders knew it at the time —by the Cold War moneys of the State Department and the CIA in their attempt to create a safe, not-too-liberal, uncritical weapon in their propaganda arsenal. But Haber knew that the convention was one of the few student meetings that attracted people from all over the country, it was well covered by the media ballyhooing it as the voice of the nation's campuses, it did attract a number of serious politically minded students who had no place else to go and who proved susceptible to the SDS position, and it was a convenient way for SDSers to meet and talk, to establish the lines of communication that during the rest of the year tended to become blurred and overextended.

At the 1961 NSA meeting SDS established a formal caucus with the Campus Americans for Democratic Actions—Campus ADA was the closest thing to SDS in those days, though acknowledged to be to its right—which was known (with caution characteristic of the time) as the Liberal Study Group. For the next three years the Liberal Study Group proved to be SDS's vehicle both to argue left-liberal positions in the convention itself and to publish mimeographed papers on current political topics with which to propagandize the participants (papers that later became the bulk of SDS's literature list during the rest of the year).

With the beginning of the 1961–1962 school year, "SDS" began to be a set of initials heard of, at least by the political fringe, at a growing number of campuses. It was essentially only a two-

man operation: Haber, in what was called the National Office in
New York, coordinated the meetings, made the contacts, wrote
the letters, gave the speeches, attended the conferences, and
mimeographed the pamphlets; and Tom Hayden, who had just
graduated from Michigan and been hired by the LID to be the
SDS Field Secretary (at a munificent $12 a day), worked out of
Atlanta, involving himself firsthand in the burgeoning civil-rights
movement. It wasn't much—"Tom was SDS's project and Al was
SDS's office," as Paul Booth says—but with the two of them
operating at full and dedicated pace it slowly became the liveliest
and most interesting student organization at work then, and the
ripples began to go out in rings from the active center. By mid-fall
SDS claimed a membership of 575 and twenty campus chapters.

Haber was of course the indispensable element, for it was his
vision, his enthusiasm, and his energy (Booth says, "Haber slept
underneath the mimeograph machine") that kept everything moving. But his choice of confederate was a stroke of happy genius.
Thomas Emmett Hayden was a charged and vibrant person, with
heavy dark eyes and a beaker nose on a striking face chiaroscuroed
by gentle acne scars on the cheeks, a lopsided cleft in the chin, and
angular dimples at the sides of the mouth; he would stand with
shoulders slumped and slightly hunched, as if keeping himself on
guard, somehow always wary but polite, interested, listening. He
had been born in 1940 of middle-class Irish parents (his father was
an accountant) in Royal Oak, Michigan, a suburb of Detroit; they
were Catholic—though later divorced—and his early schooling
was in parochial schools. He had gotten to the University of
Michigan on a tennis scholarship in 1957, was an English major
as well as editor of the paper, and graduated the previous June.
Now he thought of himself primarily as a journalist, though of the
involved rather than the "objective" kind, and was writing articles
not only for SDS but for such publications as the SDS-affiliated
Activist run by Jonathan Eisen at Oberlin, the Socialist Party's
New America, Liberation in New York, and even *Mademoiselle;*
the next year he would go on to be a graduate student in journalism—at least formally—at the University of Michigan.

Hayden, blessed with an instinct for being in the right place
at the right time, and carrying out Haber's civil-rights strategy for
SDS, operated in the South with the SNCC voter-registration

drive, sending back periodic reports which the National Office mimeographed and distributed to the campuses. Quietly, dryly he reported on the beatings, the murders, the harrowing lives of the SNCC youngsters trying to organize black voters in redneck country, "in more danger than nearly any student in this American generation has faced." These were practically the only writings coming out about the SNCC drive at that time, and they carried the unquestioned authenticity of one who had not only been there, but had been beaten (in McComb, Mississippi, in October) and jailed (in Albany, Georgia, in November). Through the SDS—chiefly in a twenty-eight-page pamphlet called "Revolution in Mississippi" sent out late that fall—and through other student publications such as the *Activist* (which carried a vivid photograph in one issue showing Hayden getting beaten), Hayden's writings reached a considerable campus audience. Betty Garman, a Skidmore graduate then working for the NSA, repeats what others have said, "These reports were very important to me: that's really the reason I went into SDS."

It is significant that Haber chose civil rights as SDS's initial emphasis and that Hayden was able to manifest it so dramatically, because it meant that SDS was able to make a reputation and an impact which it might not if it had chosen, say, antibomb activity, peace research, academic freedom, poverty, or university reform, all of which were current issues and any one of which might have seemed the "inevitable" trigger to student activism. Civil rights was the one cause with the greatest moral power, eventually the greatest national publicity, ultimately the strongest national impact, and having Haber's mind and Hayden's body so evidently on the line redounded to SDS's benefit. It was one measure of how accurately SDS was to read the student pulse, and profit thereby.

But SDS was also alive to the wider student mood from which the civil-rights activities sprang, as Hayden indicated in an essay in the *Activist* in the winter of 1961 called (in conscious imitation of C. Wright Mills) "A Letter to the New (Young) Left." It is not a profound essay, and its ideas are jumbled, half-formed, tentative, but it had the essential virtue of expressing much that was in the reaches of the student mind. Hayden shared some of the ground-rock liberal values of the time—he railed against the bomb, the "population problem," the "threatening future of China," "an incredibly conservative Congress," "the decline of already-meager social welfare legislation"—and expressed them in a litany that would have fit comfortably into the pages of the *New Republic*. But he also sensed, largely from his university experience, the inadequacy of liberal thought in either grasping the problems or suggesting anything but slippery welfaristic solutions, and its plastic-like susceptibility to distortion and subversion in the hands of people like Daniel Bell, Richard Hofstadter, and Arthur Schlesinger, where it simply became conservatism with a high forehead and a smiling face. In this acceptance of traditional liberal ends and simultaneous awareness of traditional liberal bankruptcy, Hayden was expressing what many of his generation were feeling; not only among the left but also among the right, the sham and shabbiness of the liberal tradition in which they all had grown up was slowly coming to be felt.

Hayden's solution to liberalism is "radicalism," by which he seems to mean—the difficulty is with his language, which is abstract and rhetorical—first an understanding of the underlying "real causes" of the problems of present society and then "a practice" that demands living outside that society ("the decision to disengage oneself entirely from the system being confronted"); in short, radicalism is the SDS style of making root connections plus the growing practice of operating on those connections in the real world beyond the campuses. Not to be overlooked here is the unspoken notion that inevitably one will lead to another, that an accurate analysis of root causes in America will inevitably create disgust, disenchantment, disengagement, and, ultimately, a willingness to change them. Hayden's radicalism, of course, is not very radical—what he wants is a kind of reformism "drawing on what remains of the adult labor, academic and political communities, not just revolting in despair against them"—and its ends go no further than the need to "visualize and then build structures to counter those which we oppose." It is, perhaps not surprisingly, a gut radicalism, a negative radicalism, what Hayden himself saw as "an almost instinctive opposition," for the times seemed to demand that the primary battle be *against* the easy acceptance of the system in power rather than *for* any particular alternative to it. Whatever its failings, and to an extent because of them, this kind of radicalism was an acute expression of the attitudes of many of the young of the period. Students read Hayden's essay; he began to become a "figure."

With the ongoing successes of the fall, and with the LID compromise still unshaken, Haber and Hayden felt that the time had finally come to formalize the new vision of SDS in a fresh organizational form. Accordingly, they planned a small conference for "reflection on our total effort, past, present and future," to be held in Ann Arbor over the Christmas vacation. Haber, the chief organizer of the conference, saw it as a meeting which would define, at least for the coming year, what role SDS could play in servicing and coordinating the wide variety of campus political parties and *ad hoc* groups that had now been established. He asked campus activists to come up with ideas for a national program that these groups could unite behind and SDS could run for them, and in the event almost every conceivable political notion of the time was put forth, most of them in lengthy papers that sat in deep piles in the University of Michigan Student Activities Building that weekend.

Robert Walters, an SDSer in Pennsylvania, noted that students other than those in the hard core of radicals are induced to join campus actions because they want "to do something *new*" and argued that *poverty* was the perfect issue (this was a year before Michael Harrington's *The Other America*): an obvious problem, something to be against, capable of enlisting liberal and union support, and involving the federal government. Bob Ross and Mark Chesler (a Cornell SDSer) pushed for *university reform* (three years before the Free Speech Movement at Berkeley), urging "that the university make itself relevant to the social order," allow students to "act as citizens within their communities," get rid of *in loco parentis,* and enlarge the power of students as against administrators. Curtis Gans, an early SDSer, then at North Carolina, wrote a paper with Haber suggesting a Southern Political Education Project to hold conferences to educate Southern whites and develop a black-and-white Southern cadre for *civil-rights action.* Jean Spencer, a Michigan senior, suggested a two-year project to establish *peace* centers on at least ten campuses for "discussion and communication" of war-related issues. Others urged action on civil-rights projects, Northern support of voter registration in the South, disarmament, and arms control, electoral action for peace candidates, and much other social detritus.

The program suggestions are revealing, imaginative, well developed, and analytically shrewd. But useless. The Ann Arbor conference foundered on this multiplicity of rocks, one group wanting to steer one way, one group another. Haber had known that the various campus groups were each searching for a national program to unite behind, but he forgot that each one had its own favorite, or at least wasn't prepared to submerge its interests in somebody else's favorite. The plain fact of it is that Haber had forgotten his own first principle. Knowing originally that single-issue orientation was wrong, that only a broad radical consensus could draw student militants together, he had been tempted by the initial impact of the fall civil-rights campaign to want to put SDS unreservedly behind a single project. But naturally enough no one could agree on which one. Paul Booth calls the meeting "a disaster, politically": "We couldn't settle on a specific political notion through which everyone would be SDS as well as whatever else they were into."

But this Ann Arbor meeting was, in spite of all that, no disaster. It was the first of what were to be a steady series of enormously congenial gatherings among sympathetic people, a process wrought by some mysterious chemistry of those early SDS days that no one has ever structurally analyzed. Many of those present had been at the NSA meeting that summer, most had been receiving the letters Hayden was sending from the South, and in getting together they found a real identity of interests and attitudes. There was among them a shared style, a kind of open Bohemianism filtered through the Beats that put a premium on honesty and naturalness; there was, too, an undercurrent of distinctly non-Beat urgency, a youthful passion and intensity, a sense that times were changing; and there was a common feeling about the horrible inadequacies of the present system and the real possibilities for altering it and finding something new. Betty Garman recalls the excitement she felt after one informal meeting during the conference:

> We talked about a new life, a new world—no one had ever put down
> on paper what this would look like, though we all had a notion

about it. We talked about the Cold War and its being over, how we all rejected both sides, both the Russian bloc and the American bloc, and how we all felt how rotten the American system was, without being able to put a name to it all. It was a terribly stimulating thing.

Paul Booth says simply, "It was all very convivial, we had a great time."

At the end of several days of this Haber had drawn enough like-minded people together to form the substructure of a new organization. A National Executive Committee was set up, with Haber as chairman, Bob Ross as vice chairman, plus Mark Acuff (from the University of New Mexico), Rebecca Adams (a Swarthmore senior), Booth, Donald Freeman (who had been organizing for SDS in Ohio), Sandra Cason Hayden (Tom's recent wife, a SNCC worker, known as Casey), Sharon Jeffrey, Timothy Jenkins (a Howard graduate and SNCC founder, then at Yale Law School), Daniel Johnston (Drake Law School), Steve Max (a young New York City activist who never bothered with college), Jim Monsonis (a Yale graduate working with SNCC in Atlanta), and Bob Zellner (from Huntingdon College, also a SNCCer). Among those serving as regional representatives were Nicholas Bateson (an Englishman then at North Carolina), Peter Countryman (a New England pacifist), Michael Locker (Earlham College), Robert Walters, and Houston Wade (the University of Texas). Paul Potter was to act as the official liaison with the NSA, and Richard Roman withYPSL, whose chairman he was. Hayden, of course, continued as Field Secretary.

At the end of the Ann Arbor meeting Haber also had come to see where he had gone wrong. He realized that what was important was not a single national program but the shared view of the world, and so at one late-night meeting he came up with the suggestion that SDS's real job should be to work creating a manifesto that would enunciate these basic feelings, and maybe thereafter could come an agreed-upon program around which an organization like SDS could function; as Hayden was to put it, "We have to grow and expand, and let moral values get a bit realigned. Then, when consciousness is at its proper state, we might talk seriously and in an action-oriented way about solutions." Hayden and a couple of others were given the task. SDS would collate their work, send out their drafts for comments, and when the manifesto was formulated, another meeting, perhaps, might debate and refine it.

And so was conceived what would become *The Port Huron Statement,* not only the crucial document for the reestablishment of the Haber-Hayden SDS but also, for part of a generation at least, its expression-on-paper. Those at the New Year's Eve party which ended the Ann Arbor conference could not then have imagined it, but the slightly sardonic words at the bottom of their conference schedule would prove to be prophetic:

"JANUARY 1st—The new left goes forth."

4

SPRING 1962

"Where," Tom Hayden said in a letter to the SDS membership, "does one begin thinking about manifestoes?" There was little for the generation of the sixties to turn to for guidance in setting out its politics, for the left tradition in this country had been strangulated by the forties and fifties and the left tradition in other nations was never applicable. It was faced with the enormous task of creating a political philosophy almost in a void.

Hayden plowed into the task undaunted nonetheless and spent most of his energies on it throughout the spring. Retired now from the Southern battlefields, he steeped himself in political philosophies, reading omnivorously, comparing, sifting, searching, constructing. He pored over works by C. Wright Mills, on whom he had written a dissertation in college, and by Harold Taylor, whose educational humanism he found congenial. He looked into Camus, Michels, Fromm, into David Riesman, Robert Nisbet, Michael Harrington, into Iris Murdoch, Sheldon Wolin, Norman O. Brown, William Appleman Williams, into *Studies on the Left* and the British *New Left Review*. He examined himself, his student generation, the awakening activists, the Southern black students with whom he had traveled; he looked at the professors he had known, the schools, the classes, the texts, the universities. He began putting things on paper: "We are the inheritors and the victims of a barren period in the development of human values." . . . "Strangely, we are in the universities but gain little enlightenment there—the old promise that knowledge and increased rationality would liberate society seems hollow, if not a lie." . . . "The liberation of this individual potential is the just end of society; the directing of the same potential, through voluntary participation, to the benefit of society, is the just end of the individual." . . . "The role of the intellectuals and of the universities (and therefore, I think, SDS) is to enable people to actively enjoy the common life and feel some sense of genuine influence over their personal and collective affairs." . . . "I am proposing that the world is not too complex, our knowledge not too limited, our time not so short, as to prevent the orderly building of a house of theory [the phrase is Murdoch's], or at least its foundation, right out in public, in the middle of the neighborhood." Slowly a set of ideas, a frail kind of ideology, a house of theory, did begin to appear.

In March, preparing for a speech he was to give at the University of Michigan, Hayden sharpened his critique of the American society:

> We must have a try at bringing society under human control. We must wrest control somehow from the endless machines that grind up men's jobs, the few hundred corporations that exercise greater power over the economy and the country than in feudal societies, the vast military profession that came into existence with universal military training during our brief lifetime, the irresponsible politicians secured by the ideological overlap, the seniority system and the gerrymandered base of our political structure, and the pervasive bureaucracy that perpetuates and multiplies itself everywhere: these are the dominators of human beings, the real, definable phenomena that make human beings feel victimized by undefinable "circumstance." Sadly, the university in America has become a part of this hierarchy of power, rather than an instrument to make men free.

Shortly afterward, in the early months of the spring, he sent out three "convention documents" in mimeographed form to the entire SDS mailing list, setting out his tentative thoughts about "values"—a concept very much on his mind—about the nature of democracy (complete with a bibliography), and about the ways in which students can make their politics felt. None of them was particularly inspiring—with the exception of a phrase or two, none has the life and clarity that would eventually mark the final manifesto*—nor did they elicit the massive membership response that they were designed to. But they were the first attempts at putting the vision of student activists into public form, and invaluable for that.

While all this was going on, Hayden was still traveling, visiting the chapters, absorbing thoughts (and sometimes writing them down verbatim) from all manner of people on and near the campuses—". . . not much letter-writing," as he put it, "but MANY DISCUSSIONS with people all around the country." One of the most formative came, somewhat unexpectedly, at a meeting of the National Executive Committee (and friends) at Chapel Hill, North Carolina, in May. At that meeting Hayden outlined his thinking to date in some detail, and suddenly ran into fire from a New York contingent consisting of Steve Max and James Brook, leaders of a struggling New York chapter growing out of a group called the FDR-Four Freedoms Club, and Harlon Joye, a New School SDSer and formerly editor of a defunct SDS magazine called *Venture*. Max, a dark, good-looking, serious, and intense young man, was a true "red-diaper baby"—his father was a former editor of the *Worker*—and he had been a member of the Communist Labor Youth League until he broke with the CP in 1956 while still in his early teens; he had graduated from high school but chose not to go on to college, devoting himself chiefly to political work and a few odd jobs. In a curious way he represented the Old Left rather than the New, an Old Left that had abandoned (as had the Communist Party) the sectarianism of the early thirties for what was in the sixties being called "realignment" —a reorganization of the Democratic Party into a party of liberals, blacks, poor, and those in the churches, labor unions, media, and universities; an Old Left that not only chose to work through conventional machinery (political parties) for immediate ends (electoral victories), but did so with a minimum of moralizing (willingness to compromise and work with imperfect others), a disdain of utopian theorizing, and (especially characteristic of the young New York City leftists) a knowledge of the theories and

*With the exception of two paragraphs in the first document and some phrases about "participatory democracy" in the second, none of the wording in these documents was used in the final statement.

experiences of the left of the thirties. Max, though young enough
to feel the stirrings on the campuses and sensible enough to see
that SDS might turn them to good advantage, was more or less
tied to this tradition and he was profoundly disturbed by what he
heard from Hayden about the manifesto. With a skill developed
by years of political infighting on New York's sectarian left, he
attacked Hayden's ideas for being insufficiently concrete, overly
utopian, weak on practical politics, and impossibly full of mysterious talk about "relevance" and "values." He urged instead a
document with a more political cast, related to practical politics,
which would "advocate political realignment and orient SDS to
bringing realignment about"—a document, by coincidence, which
his friend Brook just happened to be in the process of writing.
Hayden, no mean debater himself, argued just as vigorously that
a "political" analysis would produce too much of a "sectarian
political line" for a broad-based group to follow, and smack too
much of the discredited Old Left; and, he added, SDS "should
have no single strategy such as realignment," since that would
keep it from being open-ended and "receptive to new ideas."

    With the support of most of the NEC, Hayden managed to
vote down the Max–Brook attack, but it was an important indication nonetheless of an incipient split in SDS ranks. It was generally
conceived as a right-left split as time went on, with the "realignment" people regarded as rightists and the "value" people thought
to be on the left, but at this point it was really more a difference
in styles, in strategies, in emphasis, and, though little love was lost
between the two factions, the difference was livable with. Still,
Hayden came out of this conference more convinced than before
of the need to set out a broad definition of common values rather
than a lot of narrow statements about this or that political or
economic policy, which he was now convinced was hopelessly
outmoded. Throughout the month of May he worked on the
manifesto, refined it, and buttressed it, and then on the first of June
it was mimeographed at the New York headquarters. A week
before the convention itself, more than a hundred copies of the
final draft were sent out across the country.

    Meanwhile, SDS was gathering itself for the convention.
It had gotten a little publicity for joining an antitesting march

of some five thousand people led by the Student Peace Union
in front of the White House that February—one of the first
strong manifestations of the new student spirit but which at
the time got attention from the press largely because President
Kennedy chose to send out coffee and cocoa to warm the protesters. It held a conference at Oberlin in April, organized by
Oberlin student leader Rennie Davis, drawing over 120 people
to discuss the form and purposes of campus political parties. It
was also continuing to get attention with its civil-rights activity, chiefly through a conference in Chapel Hill just before
the NEC meeting which was designed to enlist Southerners
into the SNCC voter-registration cause. (The Chapel Hill meeting was a superficial failure in that it attracted very few Southerners, but it was another of those remarkable meetings where
a lot of basically like-minded people got together, talked
warmly, and felt themselves in union.)

At this point SDS had about two thousand people on various
mailing lists, about eight hundred or so who were considered
members, of whom more than half had paid their dollar-a-year
dues: evidence of some growth, though hardly spectacular, during
the Haber tenure. Chapters of, as Haber put it, "varying degrees
of success and constitutionality" were functioning at Michigan (a
hundred members), Oberlin, Columbia, Swarthmore, Temple,
Johns Hopkins, Syracuse, Vassar, Earlham, and Central State (a
small black school in Ohio which Don Freeman had enlisted); the
New York City "at-large" membership was put at 198. The National Office now had thirty-odd mimeographed pieces of literature on hand, though the speed and reliability with which they
were sent out to those who asked for them was open to considerable fluctuation. (In fact the condition of the New York office led
Haber to write at one point that spring, "I've lost all confidence
in central office functioning," and to add at the bottom of one
letter which was mailed two weeks after it was dated, "SDS screws
up again.") The budget was now up to $10,000 a year, and appar-
ently was being met by the LID, which in the preceding months
had enjoyed its own good fortune with a variety of gifts—$7500
from the American Federation of Labor, $5000 from the estate of
Mrs. Loula Lasker, $4000 from the ILG—and had experienced its
own minor revivification as Mike Harrington and trade unionist

Emanuel Muravchik were added to the Student Activities
Committee, Harry Fleischman became Executive Committee
Chairman, and Vera Rony, who had directed the liberal-labor
Workers' Defense League for the last six years, became Execu-
tive Director.

SDS was, in fact, one of the most promising student groups
going—though, given the still-modest strength of the student
movement, this wasn't saying much. (The Student Peace Union
probably had 3000 members at this point, Campus ADA about the
same, Turn Toward Peace perhaps half that, the Communist Party's Progressive Youth Organizing Committee was virtually defunct, YPSL had degenerated into a permanent floating faction
fight, and there was very little else on the scene.) In fact Norman
Thomas, as Michael Harrington remembers, was telling young
people who asked his advice to go into SDS instead of YPSL so
that they would avoid sterile faction fights and find something
"more native, more healthy."

It was somehow typical of SDS that two weeks before its
scheduled convention it didn't have a place to hold it. The National Office had begun by looking for places in the Midwest, since
the Michigan chapter was by far the largest in the country, but had
scoured Pennsylvania and New York as well looking for something remote and cheap, and hadn't come up with a thing. Just
fifteen days before the convention was to start Robb Burlage, a
young activist from Texas then doing graduate work at Harvard,
wrote to Haber, "I look forward to hearing from you further
about . . . such details as WHERE THE HELL IS IT GOING TO
BE?"

Finally settled on, reluctantly and at the last minute, was the
$250,000 FDR Camp belonging to the United Automobile Work-
ers at Port Huron, Michigan, some forty miles north of Detroit
at the southern end of Lake Huron; it was, by an unconscious bit
of historical appropriateness, the same camp where SLID members had gone in the late forties and early fifties to be staff members
for UAW summer retreats. According to SDS figures, 59 people
attended some or all of the five-day session from June 11 to 15,
though only 43 of them were full-fledged members with constitutional power to cast votes, and no more than 35 showed up at most

of the working sessions.* The biggest delegations of voting members were from New York City (13) and Michigan (5), but there were also representatives from chapters at Oberlin (3), Johns Hopkins (3), Swarthmore (2), and Earlham (1), while the Vassar chapter was represented by proxies and the Bowdoin group by an observer; no one attended from the chapters at Temple and Central State, and the Syracuse chapter hadn't made it through the spring intact. A number of voting members were unaffiliated with chapters or came representing other youth groups such as SNCC, Young Democrats, Campus ADA, Student Peace Union, NAACP, YPSL, and CORE. Three groups had nonvoting observers: the Young Christian Students, the National Student Christian Federation, and the Progressive Youth Organizing Committee. From the LID came Harry Fleischman, Michael Harrington, now generally regarded as the LID's "link to the youth," and Harold Taylor, former president of Sarah Lawrence College and a member of the Executive Committee. (There was at least one foreign visitor, Michael Vester, a member of the German SDS—Sozialistischer Deutsche Studentenbund, or League of German Socialist Students—who had been observing the American SDS for the previous few months.) Gary Weissman, former student body president at Wisconsin and a graduate student there, was elected chairman; Maria Varela, from Emmanuel College in Boston, was the secretary.

Some idea of the thoroughly staid and unregenerately middle-class nature of the delegates is given by a look at those elected to the National Executive Committee—consisting of the President, Vice President, and fifteen members elected at large—at the end of the conference. All but five of them had already graduated from college (and of those five all but Max were going to school), and all but Robb Burlage (from Texas) had attended colleges east

*Among those present: Paul Booth, Jim Brook, Robb Burlage, Judith Cowan, Richard Flacks, Don Freeman, Al Haber, Casey Hayden, Tom Hayden, Peter Henig, Sharon Jeffrey, Tim Jenkins, Tom Kahn, Mike Locker, Steve Max, Chuck McDew, Jim Monsonis, Ted Reed, Richard Roman, Bob Ross, Maria Varela, Monroe Wasch, Gary Weissman, and Bob Zellner.

Among older participants, LIDers, and outside observers present were Harry Fleischman, Roger Hagan, Michael Harrington, Jim Hawley, Arnold Kaufman, Herschel Kaminsky, Michael Liebowitz, Don Slaiman, Harold Taylor, and Michael Vester.

of the Mississippi. Four of the NEC officers were from the University of Michigan, two from Swarthmore, two from Wisconsin, two from Howard. Seven of them had been in elected positions in student government and four had gone on to work for the NSA.*

The Port Huron meeting was essentially a drafting session, directed primarily to putting together a final document on the basis of Hayden's last version of the manifesto. The bulk of the work was done in small study groups into which the conference divided, one for the "values" section, one for economics, one for domestic politics, one for foreign affairs, and so on. These study groups made recommendations which were reported to the convention at large, and these were then debated upon according to a formula of "bones-widgets-and-gizmos," under which bones (essential matters) could be given an hour's debate, gizmos (effluvia) only ten minutes, and widgets (of medium importance) something in between. Whole sections of the original draft were thrown out, the economics section was rewritten entirely, the values section was (in a shrewd stroke) moved up to the front, and many modifications suggested from the floor were adopted. The manifesto was such a growing document that the delegates couldn't even get through the business of approving it all by the last day and gave it over to a special committee headed by Hayden to produce a final statement. In fact, they left the manifesto-drafting convention without seeing the manifesto itself, which was not produced in full (and final) form until a full month later.

What emerged from all this was a document not so much written as stitched together, with inevitable hallmarks of the committee system. It was heavily derivative of all those authors Hayden had been absorbing over the spring, especially C. Wright Mills, and it was heavily sprinkled with the rhetoric, often the

*The NEC members were Tom Hayden, elected President, Paul Booth, Vice President, and Rebecca Adams (Swarthmore), Robb Burlage (then at Harvard), Ann Cook (Sarah Lawrence graduate, then at the Fletcher School), Judith Cowan (Wisconsin), Richard Flacks (Michigan graduate student), Betty Garman (Skidmore, then at Berkeley), Al Haber, Timothy Jenkins (Yale graduate student), Tom Kahn (Howard), Steve Max, Theodore Reed (Oberlin), Dick Roman (YPSL), Bob Ross (Michigan), Gary Weissman (Wisconsin), and Bob Zellner (Huntingdon, then SNCC).

jargon, of sociology. It was unabashedly middle class, concerned with poverty of vision rather than poverty of life, with apathy rather than poverty, with the world of the white student rather than the world of the blacks, the poor, or the workers. It was set firmly in mainstream politics, seeking the reform of wayward institutions rather than their abolition, and it had no comprehension of the dynamics of capitalism, of imperialism, of class conflict, certainly no conception of revolution. But none of that mattered. For *The Port Huron Statement* so thoroughly plumbed and analyzed the conditions of mid-century American society, and so successfully captured and shaped the spirit of the new student mood, that it became not only a statement of principles for the few hundred students around SDS, not only a political expression for the hundreds who were to come into the organization in succeeding years, but even more a summary of beliefs for much of the student generation as a whole, then and for several years to come.

Nearly four-fifths of the final document is taken up with a thoroughgoing critique of the present American system in all its aspects—political parties, big businesses, labor unions, the military-industrial complex, the arms race, nuclear stockpiling, racial discrimination—coupled with a series of suggested reforms—party realignment, expanded public spending, disarmament, foreign aid, civil-rights programs, and increased welfare. On foreign policy, it seeks an end to the Cold War through "universal controlled disarmament" by careful stages, the downgrading of NATO, "denuclearization" of the Third World, "national inspection systems," and it calls for the acceptance of "neutralism as a tolerable principle" and of "authoritarian variants of socialism" in undeveloped countries; in domestic matters, it argues for greater democracy through a political realignment producing "two genuine parties" (including "the shuttling of Southern Democrats out of the Democratic Party"), the establishment of citizens' lobbies, increased "worker participation" in business management, an expanded "public sector" within the economy subject to popular control, and it urges a vastly expanded welfare state that would undertake a "program against poverty," and improve housing, medical care, social security, mental hospitals, prisons, schools, and farms. A good deal of this, of course, is fairly familiar reformist politics in the traditional mold of enlightened liberalism as represented by, say, the ADA—but what gave it a particular strength was its radical sense that all of these problems were *interconnected*, that there was a total system of America within which its multiple parts functioned, and that social ills in one area were intimately linked to those in another, so that solutions, too, had to be connected. Each part of the document is informed with the same over-all vision, a vision of how men and communities can and should behave, and each subject that it takes up is measured against this vision and criticized accordingly. The initial importance of the manifesto, therefore, is that it shapes and gives coherence to the awakening political sense of this generation of students.

Even more important, however, is the other one-fifth of the document, for this is the part that supplies the analysis from which the critique stems, enunciates the vision against which it is measured, and provides, for the new generation, the strategy by which it can be altered—in short, nothing less than an *ideology*, however raw and imperfect and however much they would have resisted that word. And it does so, moreover, with a power and excitement rare to any document, rarer still to the documents of this time, with a dignity in its language, persuasiveness in its arguments, catholicity in its scope, and quiet skill in its presentation.

The *analysis* of the present system begins with the inescapable facts of militarism and racism ("the presence of the Bomb . . . the permeating and victimizing fact of human degradation"), which it sees as only the two most glaring symbols of an America gone wrong:

> America rests in national stalemate, its goals ambiguous and tradition-bound instead of informed and clear, its democratic system apathetic and manipulated rather than "of, by, and for the people." . . . The American political system is not the democratic model of which its glorifiers speak. In actuality it frustrates democracy by confusing the individual citizen, paralyzing policy discussion, and consolidating the irresponsible power of military and business interests. . . . America is without community, impulse, without the inner momentum necessary for an age when societies cannot successfully perpetuate themselves by their military weapons, when democracy must be viable because of

the quality of life, not its quantity of rockets. . . . Americans are in withdrawal from public life, from any collective effort at directing their own affairs.

The *vision* of a future system rests on a set of "social goals and values" that are quite simple, even classical, in isolation and quite potent in synergy. There is humanism:

> We regard men as infinitely precious and possessed of unfulfilled capacities for reason, freedom, and love. . . . Men have unrealized potential for self-cultivation, self-direction, self-understanding, and creativity.

Individualism:

> The goal of men and society should be human independence. . . . The individualism we affirm is not egoism [but the] kind that imprints one's unique individual qualities in the relation to other men, and to all human activity.

Community:

> Human relationships should involve fraternity and honesty. Human interdependence is a contemporary fact; human brotherhood must be willed, however, as a condition of future survival and as the most appropriate form of social relations. Personal links between man and man are needed.

And, as the medium for all the rest, participatory democracy:

> We seek the establishment of a democracy of individual participation, governed by two central aims: that the individual share in those social decisions determining the quality and direction of his life; that society be organized to encourage independence in men and provide the media for their common participation. In a participatory democracy, the political life would be based in several root principles: that decision-making of basic social consequence be carried on by public groups; that politics be seen positively, as the art of collectively creating an acceptable pattern of social relations; that politics has the function of bringing people out of isolation and into community, thus being a necessary, though not sufficient, means of finding meaning in personal life; that the political order should . . . provide outlets for the expression of personal grievance and aspiration [and] channels should be commonly available to relate men to knowledge and to power so that private problems—

from bad recreation facilities to personal alienation—are formulated as general issues.

And the *strategy* for getting from the present to the future is rooted in the awareness that students, academics, and intellectuals can forge a *new* left for America, using not the legislatures or the factories or the streets but the universities as the "potential base and agency in a movement of social change":

1. Any new left in American must be, in large measure, a left with real intellectual skills, committed to deliberativeness, honesty, reflection as working tools. The university permits the political life to be an adjunct to the academic one, and action to be informed by reason.

2. A new left must be distributed in significant social roles throughout the country. The universities are distributed in such a manner.

3. A new left must consist of younger people who matured in the post-war world, and partially be directed to the recruitment of younger people. The university is an obvious beginning point.

4. A new left must include liberals and socialists, the former for their relevance, the latter for their sense of thoroughgoing reforms in the system. The university is a more sensible place than a political party for these two traditions to begin to discuss their differences and look for political synthesis.

5. A new left must start controversy across the land, if national policies and national apathy are to be reversed. The ideal university is a community of controversy, within itself and in its effects on communities beyond.

6. A new left must transform modern complexity into issues that can be understood and felt close-up by every human being. It must give form to the feelings of helplessness and indifference, so that people may see the political, social and economic sources of their private troubles and organize to change society. In a time of supposed prosperity, moral complacency and political manipulation, a new left cannot rely on only aching stomachs to be the engine force of social reform. The case for change, for alternatives that will involve uncomfortable personal efforts must be argued as never before. The university is a relevant place for all of these activities.

And there is the special and inescapable importance of *The Port Huron Statement:* it gave to those dissatisfied with their

nation an analysis by which to dissect it, to those pressing instinctively for change a vision of what to work for, to those feeling
within themselves the need to act a strategy by which to become
effective. No ideology can do more.

It was not only in drafting this new statement, however, that
the Port Huron convention made a break with the past. In other
ways as well it undertook a process, in some ways unconscious,
of umbilicus-cutting, of separating themselves permanently from
the politics—so starkly represented by the LID—of the postwar
years.

The convention began with a symbol of this break. Jim Hawley, the delegate from the Communist Progressive Youth Organizing Committee, had come along to the convention and asked to
be seated as an observer. The people from YPSL, who had done
furious battle with the Communists often enough in the past,
objected, especially YPSL officers Roman and Kahn. But most of
the SDSers, not veterans of these particular internecine battles and
somehow not convinced that one Communist, acting as an observer, was going to push the organization into the Soviet camp,
took a what-the-hell-let-him-sit attitude. " 'Observer' status was
mere recognition that the PYOC member was there," the SDS
leadership said later. "It implied no expression of fraternity or
approval or even acceptance of him as a member of our 'community.' " Hawley was seated.

As the convention continued, it became even clearer that
SDSers were no longer going to play the anti-Communism tune
that, like a Musak melody, had been so depressingly standard in
the political offices of the fifties. The statement itself explicitly
attacked that past:

> An unreasoning anti-communism has become a major social prob-
> lem for those who want to construct a more democratic America.
> McCarthyism and other forms of exaggerated and conservative
> anti-communism seriously weaken democratic institutions and
> spawn movements contrary to the interest of basic freedoms and
> peace. . . . Even many liberals and socialists [read: LID members]
> share static and repetitious participation in the anti-communist cru-
> sade and often discourage tentative, inquiring discussion about "the
> Russian question" within their ranks.

It disputed the received Cold War view of the monolithic evil of
the Soviet Union—"Our basic national policy-making assumption
that the Soviet Union is inherently expansionist and aggressive
. . . is certainly open to question and debate"—and specifically
blamed the United States for continuation of the Cold War:

> Our paranoia about the Soviet Union has made us incapable of
> achieving agreements absolutely necessary for disarmament and the
> preservation of peace. . . .
>
>   There is, too, our own reluctance to face the uncertain world
> beyond the Cold War, our own shocking assumption that the risks
> of the present are fewer than the risks of a policy re-orientation to
> disarmament, our own unwillingness to face the implementation of
> our rhetorical commitments to peace and freedom.

Now none of this of course implied any particular cordiality toward the Soviet Union or conviviality toward the doctrines of
Communism. On the contrary, disclaimers—sincere ones, too, not
meant to deceive—abound: "Such a harsh critique of what we are
doing as a nation by no means implies that sole blame for the Cold
War rests on the United States," "There is Russian intransigence
and evasiveness," "As democrats we are in basic opposition to the
communist system," "The communist movement has failed, in
every sense, to achieve its stated intentions of leading a worldwide
movement for human emancipation," Russian and Chinese forced
economic expansion is "brutal," the Berlin wall represents "in-
humanity," and so on. But the other sentiments were sure to ruffle
some feathers in New York.

And in drafting a new constitution the convention went further in its break with the past, making several sweeping changes
in the basic document that with only a few alterations had been
the guiding light of the organization since 1946. It voted to scrap
the original preamble:

> Students for a Democratic Society is a non-partisan educational
> organization which seeks to promote greater action participation on
> the part of American students in the resolution of present-day prob-
> lems. It is hoped that such participation will contribute to their
> awareness of the need for the establishment in the United States of
> a cooperative commonwealth in which the principle regulating pro-
> duction, distribution, and exchange will be the supplying of human

needs, and under which human rights will be protected and extended.

In its place was put this formulation (which had been devised by Haber several months before):

> Students for a Democratic Society is an association of young people on the left. It seeks to create a sustained community of educational and political concern: one bringing together liberals and radicals, activists and scholars, students and faculty.
>
> It maintains a *vision* of a democratic society, where at all levels the people have control of the decisions which affect them and the resources on which they are dependent. It seeks a *relevance* through the continual focus on realities and on the programs necessary to effect change at the most basic levels of economic, political and social organization. It feels the *urgency* to put forth a radical, democratic program counterposed to authoritarian movements both of communism and the domestic right.

The earlier version, as Haber told the group, smacked too much of the " 'we have a panacea' impression or the impression that the Utopia is defined solely by an economic principle," it was too explicitly limited to students rather than the university community at large, and it was too vaguely oriented to some kind of bland "participation." The new preamble was broader, unafraid of such words as "left" and "radical," and held to that humanism-in-sociologese which was characteristic of the manifesto itself.

The convention also threw out the exclusion clause that had been the special pride of Harry Laidler, for most of its existence the guiding hand of the LID:

> Advocates of dictatorship and totalitarianism and of any political system that fails to provide for freedom of speech, of press, of religion, of assembly, and of political, economic, and cultural organization; or of any system that would deny civil rights to any person because of race, color, creed, or national origin are not eligible for membership.

In scrapping this as too negative and too "redbaiting," the delegates voted on a simpler, indeed rather a neat, formulation:

> SDS is an organization of democrats. It is civil libertarian in its treatment of those with whom it disagrees, but clear in its opposition to any totalitarian principle as a basis for government or social

organization. Advocates or apologists for such a principle are not eligible for membership.*

The convention also made other modifications in the constitution, which, though having nothing to do with anti-Communism, also signaled the new organization's independence. For one thing, it put into the charter Haber's conception of loose affiliation with campus groups: SDS would recognize not only formal chapters (which now needed only five members rather than the ten required heretofore) but also "associated groups" of independent campus clubs and "fraternal organizations" such as NSA and Campus ADA; and these chapters would no longer be required to adhere to the national organizational line or to report their independent stands to the NEC. For another, it established a new body, the National Council—composed of the seventeen national officers and delegates from each chapter—which was to meet regularly to establish policy on specific issues, freeing the annual convention for broad outlines and general orientation, and which was to become a kind of periodic town-meeting-of-the-college for quick and accurate readings of the campus pulse. Finally, it decided to spell out *de jure* the independence from the LID which Haber had won *de facto* the year before: "The SDS shall be autonomously constituted though its policy and functioning shall be within the broad aims and principles of the LID."

There was no confusion among the Port Huron delegates as to the dimensions of their departure from the past, and if there had been it would have been dispelled on the convention floor itself,

*In later years even this was seen as too exclusionary, but for Haber, its primary creator, as for many others of the early SDS generation, it was a way of asserting a genuine revulsion to authoritarianism and at the same time avoiding anti-Communism. As Haber explained in an essay on "exclusionism" three years later, "SDS rejects the formulation of anti-communism implicit (and explicit) in the exclusionist position. This rejection should not, however, be confused with an acceptance or tolerance of authoritarian or totalitarian values." (SDS paper, 1965, excerpted in Massimo Teodori, *The New Left: A Documentary History*, p. 218.)

Ironically, just four years after that, "anti-communism" was carefully employed by SDS, though in a completely reversed way: the members of one SDS faction expelled the Progressive Labor Party faction because PLP was held to be "anti-communist," while they themselves were the "true" communists.

where a number of the older participants made it abundantly clear that they thought it an unrelieved tragedy. Chief among them were Michael Harrington, a veteran socialist who had done many battles with Communist groups during the days of the fifties when the issue of how many Lenins could dance on the head of a pin divided the tiny forces of the left into more factions than there were Lenins, and Donald Slaiman, a veteran trade unionist who was working as an executive for the unremittingly anti-Communist AFL-CIO, and between them they carried on a vigorous floor fight against the new changes. Harrington was appalled by much of the manifesto draft—especially the sections which he felt were calculated to infuriate liberals, upon whom his realignment politics depended, and the parts taking a bland and insufficiently critical attitude toward the Soviet Union and other authoritarian regimes—and he didn't hesitate to make this clear to the younger delegates with all his considerable powers of argumentation and oratory. But the new generation found an unexpected defender of its policies in Roger Hagan, a liberal who had been active in the peace-oriented Committee of Correspondence of the period and who shared their sense of the futility of earlier Cold War formulations. "Hagan was a very important figure for us," Paul Booth recalls; "he was like an elder statesman, and he gave people a lot of confidence" in standing up to Harrington. The debates between the two, perhaps the most vivid clashes of the convention, ended with the draft formulations more or less intact, and the constitutional changes unaltered.*

The delegates left Port Huron after just five days together with a clear sense that they were starting something new, something fresh, something different from all that had gone before. Paul Booth says:

> We were exhilarated at the end—it was a tremendous experience. We were physically at the end of our rope—the last session went all night—but we really thought that we had done a great job. We *knew* we had a great document.

*Maria Varela recalls her attitude—and possibly that of the majority of the delegates—to that battle: "I couldn't figure out why Harrington and his buddy [Slaiman] were so upset at Huron and found out later it was because the Statement didn't take an anti-Stalinist stand . . . and even when I found that out it didn't make any sense to me." (Letter to author, February 15, 1970.)

Max, who remembers this euphoria as "more like grogginess"—
"when we saw that sun come up on the last day, I think we were
all pretty fuzzy-headed"—also remembers the sense that for the
first time a bunch of like-minded people got together and "really
got something done," coming away with a sense that, "if there are
so many of us who feel the same way, we can form a real organization." Perhaps Bob Ross says it best: "It was a little like starting
a journey."

5

SUMMER 1962

It is not difficult to feel that the Port Huron convention was a pristine example of, in Lewis Feuer's phrase, the conflict of generations. The umbilicus-cutting need not have been a wholly conscious act on the part of the delegates, but the effect of the convention nonetheless was to put the world, and the LID, on notice that something new had been born, and with all the talent of the newborn for making noise beyond any calculation of its size.

The LID was bound to react, and, as Mike Harrington among others had told the convention time and again, the reaction was predictable: "They'll go through the roof." They did, and Harrington was among the first into the shingles. The morning of the next to last day he returned to New York and gave the LID a blow by blow report of what the convention had wrought. The LID called SDS onto the carpet.

Of course the LID leaders realized that with the concession made to Haber the year before it was inevitable that SDS would continue to assert its independence from the parent organization in various ways. Indeed, SDSers all year long had been talking about their independent position, and Haber himself had had a long meeting with Student Activities Committee Chairman Emanuel Muravchik in the middle of May at which he tried to get the SDS position across. But the elders apparently never expected the treachery of Port Huron, and it was not long before they began to feel very much like a corporate Dr. Frankenstein.

On Thursday, June 28, some two weeks after the convention,

the LID held the first meeting with SDSers. Harry Fleischman and Vera Rony heard firsthand what Port Huron had done, and they were horrified. "To our amazement," as Rony put it just afterward,

> . . . the SDS convention adopted a policy statement which placed the blame for the cold war largely upon the U.S. . . . The students placed the blame for the present impasse on nuclear disarmament largely upon the U.S. and bitterly scored our foreign policy as a whole, while making the merest passing criticism of Soviet actions in this sphere. In addition, Communist youth observers were seated at the convention and given speaking rights. . . . After these events, the LID Executive Committee met to decide the position of the adult organization. It was the general view that we could not countenance a student body which disagreed with us on basic principles and adopted a popular front position.

And so Haber, still the National Secretary, and Hayden, the new President of the organization, were summoned to a "hearing" to "discover whether or not the officers of the SDS acted and plan to act in accordance with the basic principles of the parent organization. Until that time no materials, manifestos, constitutions, or other publications having to do with policy in any way, shape or form whatsoever may be mailed or distributed by the students under the identification of SDS." SDS, by the tone of the summons, was clearly condemned in advance.

At three o'clock on Friday, July 6, the hearing began. The LID was represented by Fleischman, Rony, Harrington, Roman, and Muravchik, the SDS by Haber, Hayden, and NECers Tim Jenkins, Robb Burlage, and Betty Garman, with a dozen other SDSers waiting nervously in the SDS office downstairs. The LID case, though more often sputtered than reasoned, was based largely on the issue of anti-Communism, but the hearing began with the argument that the convention was neither valid nor representative. As Harrington put it to the students:

> Let's get to the broad problem. There *is* no SDS as a functioning organization with a political life. It does not exist. So how can you get a representative convention from a nonorganization? Besides, this document of cosmic scope was *given* to the delegates—that's

obviously not representative. It would require a year's discussion to
get a really representative document. This can't even try to express
the view of the people who were there—even *that's* not possible in
such a short meeting. A founding convention should take ten days
to two weeks and a year of discussion.

Hayden answered that there *was* an organization, there was a
convention, and "SDS will grow as an organization to the extent
it has a political position—and for *that* it must draw up a large
statement first." As to the statement, it's not meant to be a manifesto—"We identify it not as that, but as the beginning of a dialogue, as it says right on the cover."

Then the attack began in earnest, starting with the seating of
the PYOC observer:

RONY: "Do you think that the LID would allow a commu-
nist-front group to be seated at a convention? Do you think you're
trying to run SDS within LID as the elders would?"

HARRINGTON: "There is a basic clash here between SDS's
and LID's concept of how to deal with other groups. . . . PYOC
is the *youth* group of the CP!—it's not a front group. There's a
tradition, and a good one, not to give it a voice or vote in the
community."

HAYDEN: "But we just allowed him to be seated, without any
declaration implying support or condemnation."

HARRINGTON: "We should have nothing to do with those
people."

FLEISCHMAN: "Would you give seats to the Nazis too?"

HARRINGTON: "United frontism means accepting reds to
your meeting. . . . You knew this would send LID through the
roof. This issue was settled on the left ten or twenty years ago—
and that you could countenance any united frontism now is incon-
ceivable. And you voted down the authoritarianism section [of the
constitution], too."

HAYDEN: "United frontism is a slanderous charge. We're not
supporting these groups but merely stating our opinions procedur-
ally."

And then the statement's alleged "softness on communism":

RONY: "We too are critical of the U.S., but we believe the

U.S.S.R. is clearly morally as vulnerable, or more so. This position [in the document] makes it impossible to talk to the American people as a whole. There's no mention of Russia breaking the test ban—*no reference*—the American public *must* notice this."

FLEISCHMAN: "It is the feeling of the Executive Committee that there is a 'single standard' lacking—this lambastes the U.S. and taps the Soviets on the wrist."*

RONY: "Hungary is dismissed. The Berlin Wall. You don't even mention *their* faults. Testing. Hungary. . . ."

HAYDEN: "We are not blind toward the Soviet Union, just *read* the sections. And just *read* the values section—there absolutely aren't double standards—we use a single standard. You have to *look* at the document."

HARRINGTON: "Document shmocuments. Slaiman and I said that this was antithetical to the LID and everything it's stood for."

HAYDEN: "There was no notion at Port Huron that these differences were irreconcilable. The document doesn't confuse community and fraternity."

And so it went, for better than two hours. The LID brought out other arguments, too. They objected to the fact that Steve Max had been chosen as a Field Secretary for the fall—his father was a Communist, you know, and wasn't he a Communist himself once? They harked back to a demonstration earlier that year at which SDS had joined other groups including PYOC in demonstrating against a rally held by the right-wing Young Americans for Freedom. They objected to the convention's sending greetings to a Japanese "World Conference Against Atom and Hydrogen Bombs and for the Prevention of Nuclear War," led by a pro-Soviet group (though in fact the greetings were sent by Haber rather than the convention and were by no means uncritical).

The hearing eventually disintegrated into isolated cocoons of anger. Both sides were so deeply involved, in a sense so disappointed in the other, that they could no longer hear. Haber ended the meeting by saying that the LID reaction was based on premature evidence and that Harrington's and Slaiman's arguments at

*The Student Peace Union's constitution embodied the LID's idea: "Members . . . are willing to apply to both East and West the same standards of criticism."

the convention itself had been "taken to heart" in drafting the final version; he suggested the meeting adjourn until the following week, when he hoped to have the final statement ready for the LID to read with care. The SDSers left.

It seemed like a temporary truce. It wasn't. An hour later Rony called Haber to say that the Executive Board had made several decisions: the elections which took place at the convention would be allowed to stand, but the staff members—Haber and Hayden—were off salary from that moment; the LID would have to have final approval over all documents for the time being; the LID would eventually appoint a secretary for the student division who would be responsible not to SDS but to the LID Executive Committee. What she didn't say was that the LID had cut off all funds for SDS, was hoping to confiscate the mailing lists so that no appeals could be directed over its head, and was in the process of changing the lock on the SDS office door. This last act, which SDSers didn't discover until Monday morning, was particularly galling to the students—more than anything else during the whole dispute it served over the next few years to symbolize what they saw as the petty-mindedness, the decadence, even the totalitarianism, of the LID: "Well," they would say more than once, "they locked us out of our own office, you know."

On July 1, 1962, some fifty people meeting at the Hotel Diplomat in New York City established a new political organization on the left. Its fourteen-member coordinating committee consisted entirely of people who had been members of the Communist Party and quit or were purged in late 1961 and early 1962 for being "ultraleftists" and "agents of the Albanian party"—i.e., "Maoists." Among them: Milton Rosen, who became chairman of the new group; Mortimer Scheer, vice chairman and head of West Coast operations; Fred Jerome, the editor of the group's five-month-old magazine; and Bill Epton, a black man. The name of the organization: the Progressive Labor Movement.

The enormity of the gulf between the two generations only slowly dawned on the SDSers, who had expected at most a little sniping but nothing like this barrage. Except for Haber, they didn't know the LID leadership well, and their experience with such LIDers as Harrington and Harold Taylor did not prepare them for the assault. Their reaction was seething anger.

Thirteen of the top nineteen officers (President, Vice President, NEC, and staff) came into New York, prepared for battle. Bob Ross recalls, with excusable synecdoche, "All of us felt our careers were going to be ruined, and America's best liberals were on the lip of red-baiting us out of existence. We knew we weren't communists, but the idea that our parent organization thought we were, was Kafkaesque."

Steve Max, in whose apartment the SDSers gathered to debate what to do next, remembers the fear of a McCarthyite attack: "We knew the LID would spend its energies trying to blackball us and make us some Communist organization if we broke with them." Paul Booth says, "They were vicious, personally vicious." Hayden took it especially hard. He had been fairly close friends with Harrington, who had sent him one of the first copies of *The Other America,* and they had drunk, traveled, and communed together. In fact, he had had a vision of a career not unlike that of Harrington's—a Catholic boy from the Midwest coming to New York to be a writer, to play a part in the liberal-socialist intellectual community—and he assumed that he would be accepted easily there, or, if there were disagreements, that they would be debated freely in the left community known for its democratic traditions and civil libertarian stands. To find that this community was petty, rigid, and mean was a blow. He told Jack Newfield, the *Village Voice* writer, then also in SDS, "It taught me that social democrats aren't radicals and can't be trusted in a radical movement. It taught me what social democrats really think about civil liberties and organizational integrity."

The SDS leaders met almost continuously Sunday and Monday in Max's apartment. (On Friday they had, with foresight, taken the mailing list from their offices, assuring for themselves what is, in the print-oriented world of the left, a most powerful weapon.) Shock and hurt eventually gave way to determination, a determination that may in the end have been as important as the Port Huron meeting itself in solidifying the fragile young organization.

There was considerable sentiment to split from the LID entirely, but there were several practical reasons against it.

Primarily, SDS relied heavily on LID income, office space, and equipment, which would be enormously difficult to replace at any time, but almost impossible if SDS were to be branded as a pro-Soviet, popular-fronting, Communist-infiltrated organization. Moreover, some argued, a student organization cut adrift from the liberal community would probably have no means of building wide political support and no means of enlisting that community on its behalf, things that all SDSers agreed then was crucial to any real change in the country. Finally, many of them thought it would be possible, if the present trouble could be weathered without any substantial compromise, to end-run the LID in the fall and carry on at the colleges as if nothing had happened; the LIDers would be too tired and too busy to spend very much time finding out what was going on from day to day, anyway.

The decision of the NEC, therefore—with one negative vote and one abstention, presumably the two YPSLites, Roman and Kahn—was to make a vigorous and uncompromising appeal to the LID Board. Hayden was set the task of compiling a statement of appeal to be presented to an emergency LID Executive Committee meeting called for July 12, and for the next three days SDSers worked almost around the clock. On the morning of the twelfth they came up with a twenty-seven-page single-spaced document whose completeness, honesty, and lack of compromise, if nothing else, must have impressed the LID elders.

The appeal document began by complaining about how the LID handled the crisis: "We have been maligned by deliberate anti-democratic procedure." It assailed the LID's firings without a proper hearing, its use of financial sanctions, and its unilateral interference with SDS staff: "Such meddling is at all times alien to the effort to honor and stimulate internal democratic mechanisms in a developing organization." It dismissed the charges of popular frontism as "a splicing of falsehood, exaggeration and slander," and carefully and methodically quoted from *The Port Huron Statement* to show that, though the analysis was hard on America, it was by no means pro-Soviet. And, throughout, it put forth a case for SDS's independence from the parent group without censorship or control, and, with more ingenuousness than straightforwardness, suggested that any conflicts resulting from this would merely "provide the basis for dialogue between well-

defined adult traditions and a new and inquiring student tradition.
. . . Friction between the generations represented in the LID is
both necessary and proper—and a spark of hope for change in our
times."

The emergency meeting was inconclusive. The LID had
cooled to the point where they were looking for ways to save the
relationship rather than cut SDS adrift, but they were still worried
and threatened by the creeping New Leftism, and they wanted to
be able to assert some control. They gave the office back, agreed
to give Hayden and Haber a special hearing and consider the
question of severance pay for them, and, having taken the time to
read it, they found that the revised manifesto really wasn't so bad
as they had at first supposed and agreed to let it be issued.* But
they still demanded a "regular review" of the major SDS papers
and of the groups with which SDS wanted to cooperate, and they
still wanted an LID-paid Student Secretary to oversee National
Office work, in the ancient tradition of the forties and fifties.

The cutting edge for SDS within LID councils was Harold
Taylor, and he apparently played a crucial role in modifying LID
rigidity, helped by young Andrew Norman and old Norman
Thomas. As he was to say several years later:

> In the debates and difficulties which ensued [from the convention],
> . . . I was impressed not only by the intelligence and forcefulness
> with which these young men of twenty-two made arguments which
> were essentially my own, but by the fact that they showed more faith
> in the power of democracy and in what they could do with it in
> political action than did their elders in the parent organization.

In the series of informal meetings between SDS and LID which
occupied most of July this support for the students proved valuable in forcing the LID Board members to reconsider, especially
coming from one who not only was a well-known educator but

---

*Harrington has acknowledged (in an interview with the author) that he made
two serious mistakes in reacting to the convention: he judged it on a preliminary
document, which in its final version was toned down to meet some of the
objections he had made on the floor, and he let his personal anger at what he
felt was a betrayal of true radicalism by this new breed of leftists interfere with
his basic sense that the students should be educated into the realities of politics,
not shunted off and excluded from them. Not long thereafter he publicly recanted
and apologized for the form, if not the substance, of his objections.

who also had been financially generous to the LID in the past.

As talks between the two factions continued, tempers faded and both began to see the wisdom of compromise. Gradually it became clear to the SDS that the basic work of the convention— the manifesto, officers, and constitution—would be allowed to stand, and that the LID would settle for the imposition of its own National Secretary and a few meaningless bows to "dialogue" and "cooperation"—nothing that couldn't be gotten around. The LID elders just didn't have the staying power, or even the same passionate concern, that the SDSers did, nor was their own organizational house that much in order. By the end of July it was apparent that they were willing to settle the affair with a few face-saves: Haber was to leave the New York office, and in his stead Jim Monsonis was to serve as the LID-paid National Secretary; the LID would draw up a "statement of principles" for all to see and abide by; a "dialogue" was to continue between the students and the Student Activities Committee; and that committee would have the nominal right to review SDS documents issued in the name of the organization (which were few, since most papers SDS sent out were written by and credited to individuals).

SDS, sadder, wiser, but organizationally pretty much unscathed, agreed. In late July Hayden scribbled a note to Burlage: "Things are 'patched.' Monsonis hired; LID without $$, still trying to write their 'statement of principles.'" The next month Muravchik, Fleischman, Thomas, and Harrington flew out to Columbus to cement things with the SDSers at that year's NSA meeting, and their attitude was genuinely conciliatory, expressive of their desire to keep the student division. Port Huron stood intact. But the post-Port Huron experience was a searing one for the young radicals. The awakening as to how political affairs are conducted in the real world, at least by those of the Old Left, was sharp, but all the better remembered for its sharpness. Increasingly they came to see the LID as a temporary convenience, cynically feeling that they would use it, but no longer trusting it. Increasingly, too, they came to feel their own strength, their own unity, their own distance from the past. The events of that summer shaped a new kind of organization, gave reality to a new movement.

The impact of *The Port Huron Statement of the Students for a Democratic Society*—its official name by the time of the final mimeographing in July—was remarkably swift, considering the times. It was handed out at the NSA meeting, instantly became the object of heated discussions, and right then and there won over a handful of NSA delegates into SDS ranks. One NSAer, Vivian Franklin from the University of Texas, was so taken with the document that she spent hours discussing it with the SDSers around and, as she wrote to Robb Burlage:

> By the time I started home, I felt a very real identity with the group, and found myself rather sad to be leaving them. . . . Upon arriving here, I went over *The Port Huron Statement* in detail and now find myself enthusiastic over the vision put forward therein to the point of effervescing these ideas to anyone even faintly inclined to have a comprehending ear.

A month later she was an SDS member, two months later she was asking for more copies of *The Port Huron Statement* to give her friends, and three months later she was the organizer of a successful SDS civil-rights conference in Dallas. As soon as school opened in the fall, other people had similar reactions. SDS chapters quickly distributed the statement around—often the National Office's slowness in reproducing copies meant that one tattered document passed through the hands of a dozen students—and found that arguments and adherents were produced with surprising regularity. By November the New York office was completely out of copies and trying to find time to mimeograph more. In the next two years no fewer than twenty thousand mimeographed copies (sixty-six single-spaced pages) were sent out from the National Office; in late 1964 another twenty thousand copies were printed as a small sixty-four-page booklet, which also was sold out after two years, and in the fall of 1966 still another twenty thousand copies were printed up: *The Port Huron Statement* may have been the most widely distributed document of the American left in the sixties.

The Port Huron Statement marks the end of SDS's period of reorganization and the beginning of SDS's serious, though as yet limited, impact on the campuses. It sets the tone for the years ahead. Its stated appeal to the privileged student—"bred in at least modest comfort, housed now in universities"—attracts the brighter, the consciously intellectual, youths at the best and most prestigious colleges, those of middle-class background or aspiration who were the leaders of the "postscarcity" generation. Its spirit of (in Todd Gitlin's phrase) *radical disappointment* in America and its liberalism strikes a chord among those who had come to feel that a nation of lofty ideals had become perverted by militarism, racism, apathy, materialism, and cynicism. Its visions of reform energize those who have newly awakened to activism and seek to reassert America's values, regenerate its institutions, reorganize its priorities.

The Port Huron Statement, as it stresses in its introduction, is "a beginning": "in our own debate and education, in our dialogue with society," in the establishment of a new organization, in the creation of a new ideology, in the development of a new student movement and a new left. It marked, Harold Taylor was to observe some years later, "a turning point in American political history, the point at which a coalition of student movements had become possible and a radical student movement had been formed. It also marked the coming of age of the new generation."

REFORM
1962-1965

*In the summer of 1963 the SDS National Convention saw America enter-
ing a New Era, an era marked by insurgency against both the tokenism
of the New Frontier and the conservatism of the traditional Right, and by
a growing demand for a society free from war and poverty.*

*Since that summer much has happened to justify those who saw this
insurgency as only a beginning: the development of mass movements based
around economic issues in cities like Chester, Pennsylvania, a March on
Washington linking the demands of full employment and civil rights,
cooperation of students and workers in demanding jobs and justice for the
unemployed in cities like Hazard, Kentucky, and the rapid growth of SDS
itself.*

*But with the new possibilities for a radical movement in America
must come new questioning—about the sort of society we are trying to
create, about the ways to achieve that society.*

> *—In which American institutions are the potentialities for radical
> action the greatest?*
> *—How must American institutions be reshaped to create a true
> democracy?*
> *—Around what issues is a genuine movement of the poor most likely
> to be created?*
> *—What steps can be taken to move the American middle class in a
> radical direction?*
> *—What attitude should community organizers take toward electoral
> action?*
> *—What useful roles are there for radicals who cannot be full-time
> activists or organizers?*
> *—What should be the program of SDS in 1964–65?*

—INVITATION TO THE SDS
NATIONAL CONVENTION, May 1964

6

FALL 1962–SPRING 1963

From October 22 to October 29, 1962, the SDS office at 112 East Nineteenth Street was in a turmoil. The phones were occupied at all hours, the ancient typewriters clacked incessantly, the new $300 multilith machine, the organization's proudest symbol of becomingness, churned out broadsheets and announcements far into the night. Little knots of people would gather at any time of day and start talking animatedly about bold action, or sudden trips to Canada and Sweden, or at least some kind of protest right here in New York City. And in the center of this storm, Jim Monsonis, who had been National Secretary for just three months, did his best to cope—he would talk on the phone to distant colleagues, take phone calls from SDSers in Michigan and Georgia, hold impromptu meetings—but there was little he could do.

This was not a sudden deluge of memberships, or another lockout by the LID, or an unexpected collapse of the leadership. This was the Cuban missile crisis.

It was a searing event in the lives of people everywhere, one of those few what-were-you-doing-when moments of history, but the terror of it went especially deep into those under twenty, who had grown up never knowing a world without nuclear annihilation: "It's remarkable," recalls Steve Max, who was around the SDS office at the time, "how many people thought they were going to die in the missile crisis—really remarkable." But for many the event held more than terror; it showed that the United States government was, for all its talk and all the energies of the peace movement, prepared to use nuclear weapons when it chose to, and it showed that the majority of the population, including many of those trumpeting themselves as liberals, was quite willing to let it. Those SDSers who still had liberal scales on their eyes were prepared to shed them now.

It was clearly a moment for action, but SDS did not know how to act. There was no machinery in the organization for swiftly organizing a national protest in the face of an unforeseen event; there was not even any provisional mechanism by which SDS could officially issue a press release—written by whom? approved by what?—or officially approve a joint march or statement. SDSers spontaneously ignited local protests at such places as Cornell, Michigan, Texas, and New York, but when they called the National Office to find out what the SDS position was or what SDS as an organization was going to do, Monsonis could tell them nothing. As he ruefully said later, "That's one of the problems in the way we're currently set up." One of the problems that would nag.

Monsonis did at any rate keep his wits. In a letter he sent out during the tense first week when Russian ships were steaming to Cuba, he wrote, "We're all ready to head to the nearest ILGWU local—if radical change is going to come to our society (e.g., a bomb), the ILG will be the last place to change."

The National Office—the NO, as everyone called it—was obviously incapable of responding to crises with anything more than wry humor, but it was nonetheless the core of the SDS operation during the 1962–1963 school year. It wasn't much—a few desks, some wooden chairs, typewriters that worked fitfully, telephones, piles of paper, and file cabinets in uncertain order—but when everyone returned to school that fall and the Port Huron euphoria wore off, it was still the only real manifestation of the new organization.

In a sense—a sense that even SDSers of the time subliminally realized—the NO was a contradiction. A student group that wants the growth of decentralized communites where participatory democracy can operate has at its center a single, centralized office. People who bridle at rigidity, bureaucracy, form filling, and parietal rules establish an office with all the inevitable trappings of the system they condemn. Burgeoning anticapitalists express themselves through a classic capitalist organization, the Home

Office. Utopians cluster around a dystopian organizational form.

And the organizational form is not merely trivial, lightly to be circumvented. Organizations are shaped by the societies in which they live, and they shape even those who ostensibly control them. Mid-century American organizations partook of their culture as the maggot partakes of the corpse. SDS almost without even thinking of it became an organization of officers at the top and bureaucratic administrators below, constitutions and bylaws, parliamentary meetings and points of order, conventions and committees, mimeograph machines and official documents, letters in triplicate and bills paid monthly, lists of members and calculations of dues, accounts receivable and payable, mailing lists, files, phones, a central office. Plus all the attendant habits and characteristics that this suggests: the dominance of males, especially those who can talk and manipulate (sexually or politically) best; the emphasis on form, legality, precedent, rules; the unconscious division into those who lead and those who follow, those who talk and those who listen, those who propose and those who do, those who write the pamphlets and those who mimeograph them.

It was not that the NO didn't try. The three officers—Monsonis, National Secretary, Don McKelvey, Assistant National Secretary, Max, Field Secretary—were diligent, active, dedicated people. But neither their long hours nor short pay nor selflessness could overcome the fact that they were organizationally trapped.

Monsonis was a serious, hard-working, rather colorless type who had gotten interested in SDS through his work with the National Student Christian Federation and SNCC and retained an essentially wide-eyed social-worker attitude—it was his apparent moderateness that made him so attractive to the LID when they were searching for a "safe" National Secretary. He was not without a sense of politics, but he had neither the solidness of a Haber nor the bite of a Hayden: he complained at one point, for example, that *The Port Huron Statement* failed to make any mention of class but at the same time he wondered why the statement didn't take account of the work of organized religions. He was nothing if not earnest: as he put it a couple of months after taking over the job, "I'm gradually getting acclimated to a sixteen-hour day, no money, and lots of problems." And for the earthly reward of $300 a month ($54 of which went for his Lower East Side apartment), and that was paid sporadically.

McKelvey was quite a different type. A 1960 graduate of Haverford, he was somewhat older than the others, and, he says today, a Maoist even then (though he managed to disguise it neatly enough at the time). A chubby, sloppy, personable fellow, he was always regarded as something of an oddball. He undertook the job of being a part-time office worker for SDS in the fall of 1962 because he had read and liked *The Port Huron Statement* and because the people he knew in YPSL and the Student Peace Union had told him the SDSers were dangerously radical: "My friends all told me you'd better stay away from Hayden and Haber, so naturally I went to them first." The part-time job turned out to take upwards of ten hours a day, at $28 a week, and it lasted two years—"a real martyr," someone said of him later, "but a real worker."

The third stalwart was Steve Max, whom the LID had reluctantly agreed to let SDS have as Field Secretary, though they refused to pay him a salary because they were still suspicious of his Communist background; the NEC at its meeting after the NSA convention in Columbus decided that individual members would pledge themselves to keep him alive with monthly donations out of their own pockets, but inevitably these materialized only occasionally and Max was kept alive mostly by guile and petty cash. Max was a tireless traveler, up and down the East Coast, though most of his work that fall was concentrated around the Boston area, where he not only had a girl friend but (quite consistent with his realignment politics) could also infiltrate the Senatorial campaign of H. Stuart Hughes.

To a remarkable degree, these three *were* SDS after things settled down that fall, and remained the nucleus throughout the year. Haber had been shunted off to Ann Arbor, where he occupied himself in graduate work, "savoring a return to the books," as he put it after two years away; and Hayden did a lot of traveling as SDS President—visiting several chapters in the fall, speaking to a university-reform conference in December, to the NSA in January, to Michigan-area colleges in the spring—but at the same time he was going to school at Michigan, was involved with personal problems in part having to do with his wife, who went south to join SNCC, and was doing a lot of rethinking about his future in the wake of the LID blowup. The burden on the NO was

enormous: at one point during the year, in what seems a fairly
typical letter, McKelvey wrote to Burlage: "Am tired and have
feeling of doing little except little grubby things like writing letters
(which I've been doing all night) . . . however, will plug along and
occasionally, hopefully, will try to get some thinking in edgewise."
But the organization had set up nothing else to take the place of
the NO, or to shift or decentralize the burden of work. A proposed
scheme for greater regional autonomy that was passed by the
Columbus NC never came about, despite faint moves toward
regional organizations in New England, Michigan, and Texas.
The NO remained practically the only visible manifestation of
SDS as a live national organization.

Visible but barely.

For one thing the LID, which was supposed to pay the salaries of the National Secretary and his assistant, as well as the rent,
utilities, and phones, was broke. Monsonis told the NEC in a
confidential memo, "LID has been just about out of money since
we returned from Columbus, not even paying salaries to their own
staff. . . . no money has been available for executive mailings,
shipping of material, etc." The ILGWU, as usual, was hit for "a
few thousand dollars," but it was only temporary sustenance and
a month later Monsonis reported, "The LID is totally broke, even
has been borrowing to pay my salary and hasn't met the payroll
upstairs [in the LID offices] for two weeks." *The Port Huron
Statement,* which was found to be an essential aid in the formation
of new chapters, was sent out only sporadically because there
wasn't enough money for stamps, and by the middle of November,
when the NO first ran out, there wasn't even enough cash on hand
to get more copies mimeographed. SDS went progressively into
the red: $173.57 by February, $183.85 by March, $241.32 by April.*

---

*The budget for March 23 through April 16 (from the April 16 "worklist"
mailing) gives a small sample of the difficulties:

Income		Outgo	
Memberships	$29.00	Postage	$48.05
Contributions	3.00	Mimeo paper	130.50
Literature	14.15	Mimeo ink	36.75
Supplies purchased	10.00	Office supplies	12.40
Unaccounted for	11.44		
	$67.59		$227.70

The irregularity of LID paychecks to the office staff produced its own complications, which Haber at one point described as "the feeling that you can't go to a movie without jeopardizing the next mailing." And as it became clear that SDS would never reach the $19,000 budget which it had projected at its Columbus meeting, many of the more ambitious plans—a university-reform study center in Berkeley, regional conferences in Michigan and New York, a "Center for Research in Southern Politics" (CRISP)— had to be scrapped. The heavy cloud of penury hung over the organization for the entire first year of its new life.

It wasn't only the lack of money, though. Communications simply weren't kept up. The Columbus NC had mandated the publication of a regular bulletin to keep members informed and give them a place for the regular percolation of ideas, but it didn't mandate anyone to *do* it, and mostly it fell to an already over-worked McKelvey. So the first *SDS Bulletin* of eight pages didn't get out until December; there were only two more during the entire spring (though the March–April one, it should be noted, was no less than seventy-eight mimeographed pages long, her-alded by SDS as the largest student publication ever produced). To supplement this somewhat infrequent journal the NO started to put out less formal mailings to a selected eighty or a hundred of the top people, but they were not exactly regular: the first of these "Work-list Mailings," which was supposed to be out in September, eventually appeared in November; the second ap-peared in February.*

The result was that people had to depend upon occasional conferences or visits from national officers to find out what their organization and its separate parts were doing. Monsonis would travel to as many meetings as his budget would allow—he saw his role as one of courting other organizations into the SDS orbit— and Max would go up and down the East Coast, concentrating on existing chapters. He describes his effect:

*There was even an *International Bulletin* planned to inform the membership on foreign affairs, but that never managed to come out at all. Its chief distinction was that in its prospectus in December 1962 Bob Ross set out SDS's position on Vietnam: "As long as we are involved in a commitment to support men like Diem in South Viet Nam, we will be forced to face revolution and discontent."

I went around mostly to campuses where there was already a chapter, trying to convince them SDS was a *national* organization. This
was very important for all of them—showing them the presence of
a national official, bringing them documents from the National
Office. You've got to remember this was before the media picked up
on us, and talked about us—when they did that you could read in
the papers and find out you were a member of a big organization,
but until then you didn't have any real way of knowing. So that's
what I did.

But that just wasn't enough, not for an organization with visions
of communality and collective action. Campuses where there were
only one or two people who had joined SDS tended to be ignored,
and several of the smaller chapters languished; as Barbara Gerson,
a Vassar SDSer, complained:

> If we go around urging people to set up chapters whose raison d'être
> is *not* an ongoing thing but is the program of SDS itself then some
> constant stimulus *must* be provided for these chapters. . . .[But] SDS
> sends its chapters no unifying program suggestions or reports.
> . . . Yes, if we had some sense we'd do stuff on our own, besides listen
> to lectures. But we don't have sense; that's why we formed an SDS
> chapter, if you get what I mean.

By January there were only nine chapters—Brandeis, Hunter,
Johns Hopkins/Goucher, Oberlin, Michigan, New York (the
FDR–Four Freedoms Club), North Texas State, Swarthmore,
Vassar; several places which had had chapters before Port Huron
—Central State, Earlham, Temple, and Syracuse—were floating
adrift, uncontacted, unorganized. McKelvey would shoot off late-
night letters at the slightest pretext urging distant strangers to
form SDS chapters at Mount Holyoke, Bowdoin, Wheaton College, Findlay College, even (for the first time, presaging a later
SDS impulse) Lexington High School; but once the gauntlet was
thrown nobody stayed around to see if it ever got picked up. Little
was done to bring in new members in any systematic way or to
follow up on the contacts Max and Monsonis made on their
various trips. There were only 447 paid-up members by January
—plus another 500 or so who considered themselves members in
everything but dues—and it was only happenstance that brought
in the slim trickle of new official members—19 in February, 35 in

March, 36 in April—that swelled the organization to perhaps 1100 (600 paid) by the end of the school year.

Not all the fault was the NO's, of course. Rennie Davis, spending that year at the University of Illinois, described bitterly how difficult it was to organize there:

> Our efforts for the most part this first semester have been to move people cross-grain against the horrific pressures for *anomie* and create the basis for some sort of intelligent political grouping (community, maybe). We suffer in extreme form all the usual political illnesses of American collegiate institutions: single issue groups generating their own Madisonian art for check and restraint of political-social action by pig-headed faction wars among themselves, a student leadership of "nice-guys" but frankly half-men without vision, a university administration opposed to academic freedom in principle and boasting of a vision of which the hallmark is bureaucracy and good business practices, and a terrestrial lay-out that is truly freakish in its stultification of the human mind.

Then, too, on several campuses, administrations put barriers in the way of people trying to get university recognition for their chapters (which was often necessary to get campus rooms, invite speakers, hold rallies). There was trouble at Boston University, at Hunter, at North Texas State, and others, but the crowning (though rather charming) example occurred at Georgia State College, where Dayton Pruitt, the one-member "chapter," reported the attitude of the dean of men: "He is going to 'approve our Constitution,' but warns us that Jimmy Hoffa and Communists will not be allowed to speak at our university and that—would you believe it?—if we picketed the school *in our underwear* he would take appropriate actions against our club—he was serious, too."

The tensions that were experienced during a period of near bankruptcy, incommunicativeness, and inactivity surfaced at the National Council meeting at Ann Arbor over the Christmas vacation. It was, as all NCs were to be, a freewheeling affair, not very carefully planned, with some thirty-five of the faithful present to share in a mixture of chaotic meetings, friendship renewals, lots of politics and gossip, a few love affairs, and beer drinking. This one, however, was unusually acerbic.

The meeting was dominated by discussion of a letter which

Haber and Barbara Jacobs (soon to be married to Haber) had sent
out to top SDSers on December 15 complaining about SDS's failures; specifically it charged that "the basic work isn't getting
done" by the NO, that there is no "program that is directed to
local organization" or even "an operating consensus on what it
means to have an SDS group somewhere," and that "we are
setting out on adventures beyond our physical and intellectual
capacities." It was a presumptuous letter, Haber having generally
retired from SDS affairs and therefore remote from the ongoing
problems, and bore certain marks of one who had retired from
office convinced that he was irreplaceable. The New York staff
workers, certainly, took it that way, and throughout the four days
of the meeting had their backs up; the camaraderie which had
characterized so many other meetings just wasn't there. Jacobs, in
a letter to Burlage, though asserting that it was good to get SDS
problems "out on the table, talked about, and maybe even thought
about," acknowledged that

> . . . the meeting has left me with a sour taste that is still quite strong.
> I am glad that some of my ideas are getting recognized and used
> because I think they are good. But I feel demoralized by the kinds
> of inter-relations that occur when, even in as fine a group as SDS,
> someone rocks the boat. I am discouraged by what I perceive to be
> a kind of arrogant resistance to the "new people," and a sincere
> belief on the part of some members that they, and SDS, have "the
> Word" and that their ideas can't be improved upon. I am not
> disturbed by this tendency only because I am affected by it, or
> because of some abstract egalitarian notions I have, but also because
> *my* experience tells me that there *is* more to be learned—particu-
> larly from people whose life experience, and particularly educa-
> tional experience has been different from the "important people" in
> SDS. In short, I think that incest is beginning to lead to inbreeding,
> with all its defects, and that new characters are needed on the scene.

What became clear at the meeting was that SDS could not
simply rest on Port Huron, no matter how diligent and official that
was. On the simplest level, what was needed was a lot of plain dirty
fund raising and a lot of laborious chapter organizing, but on a
deeper level something more obviously was wanted, though no
one could yet put a name to it. Somehow the organization had to
overcome the limitations imposed on it by—by just *being* an

organization; somehow it had to work outside of the institutions formed by the very society it criticized so bitterly. The question was—and it was asked by growing numbers that spring—how?

Partly as a result of its organizational malfunctioning, SDS remained relatively quiet during this school year. On the peace front, it did succeed in establishing a Peace Research and Education Project (PREP), which was to be a kind of leftish clearinghouse for gathering and publishing research on peace, disarmament, and foreign policy and was kept going largely by Dick Flacks, the balding, bespectacled graduate student who operated chiefly out of the basement of Tom Hayden's Ann Arbor house. But PREP confined itself to quiet academic research, avoiding action like the radioactive plague, and SDS itself made no effort to draw in the considerable numbers of students who might have been attracted to a multi-issue organization that fall after the disillusioning experiences of the government's hawkery in the missile crisis and by the complete failure of peace candidates at the polls in November. The Student Peace Union, for example, which had perhaps four to six thousand members at the start of the fall, was on the brink of collapse by December, and its followers might easily have been attracted to an organization which gave them some explanation for their failures and an ideology by which to revive their energies; but SDS never pressed the point and only a few of the better—and most bitter—peaceniks made the switch to SDS then.

On the civil-rights front, SDS began the year largely by trying to enlist support for the Northern Student Movement, itself a support group formed in 1961 to raise money for SNCC but which took an initiative this school year in establishing tutorial projects, mostly in Northeastern cities, to educate ghetto blacks; SDS joined NSM for an Election Day fund-raising appeal at the polls in November, but through halfhearted organization managed to collect no more than $3000. Individual SDSers were intimately involved with SNCC in the South—Betty Garman, Casey Hayden, and Bob Zellner prominent among them—but SDS as an organization provided little financial or ideological weaponry, and the Council of Federated Organizations established that winter to unite the voter-registration groups in the South functioned entirely without SDS assistance. By the spring, however, SDS chapters had thrown themselves once again energetically into civil-rights action: Martin Luther King's Birmingham march woke up the campuses again (not to mention the white press and the Washington establishment) and direct-action confrontations (in Danville, Albany, Cambridge, and elsewhere) drew widespread student support, in spite of the more than twenty thousand arrests made in the course of the year. SDSers at Swarthmore joined the Political Action Club's initial efforts at community organizing blacks in Cambridge and Chester; the Baltimore chapter was instrumental in "stand-in" civil-rights demonstrations at which several were arrested, VOICE demonstrated and leafleted in downtown Detroit; other chapters tried meetings, leaflets, and fund raising.

Aside from this, most of the life of SDS during these months was around Boston, largely thanks to Robb Burlage. Burlage was a bright young man—a professor of his at the University of Texas had called him one of the three best students he ever taught—who had been the editor of the *Daily Texan* and, through contact with Haber, became an early recruit to SDS ranks around civil-rights issues; he was then a graduate student in economics at Harvard (though the tug of his Southern roots was soon to prove too strong, and within a year he was to return to the South and get involved in less academic enterprises). Personable, charming, energetic, with sparkling eyes and a strong sense of humor, he became a natural focus for SDS activities in the Northeast that year.

In September Burlage began holding meetings with interested students, mostly those around the peace-oriented club TOCSIN and the Harvard/Radcliffe Liberal Union, an ADA affiliate. During October, when the peace dreams of these groups were shattered by Kennedy's missile-rattling, he began (with help from NECer Ann Cook at Tufts, and visits from Hayden and Max) to swing them around to SDS's more radical vision. The next month he began a series of "discussion groups" whose radicalism was limited to Paul Goodman, C. Wright Mills, Herbert Aptheker, Gandhi, the Fabians, and David Riesman, but which succeeded in drawing a lot of the bright young troubled people of the area and lasted enthusiastically through the spring. Max and others in

New York kept pressuring for a full-fledged, card-carrying chapter, but Burlage wanted to work slowly, through TOCSIN and the Liberal Union, adding individual members but not forcing the creation of an official chapter: "Harvard, man, is hard to crash." It was the right way. Before the year was over he had enlisted a dozen top-flight people, including three who were to prove important in the organization: Todd Gitlin, a Harvard senior and president of TOCSIN, Richard Rothstein, a leader of the Liberal Union, and Lee Webb, a peace activist and a senior at Boston University.

Burlage also was instrumental in organizing the only two important SDS conferences of the year, both around still another issue then faintly beginning to make itself felt on the nation's campuses: university reform. The first, on "The Role of the Student in Social Change," was held at Harvard at the end of November. There were a number of perceptive speeches—Roger Hagan on the need for a "revolutionary consciousness" among students; Noel Day, a young black politician in Boston, on racism; and Hayden on the manipulative "postideological" society—but the most important was given by Paul Potter, who had just gotten through his term as NSA vice president and was getting ever closer to the SDS mainstream.*

Universities, Potter maintained, are inextricably part of the world around them, and always have been, their job being to buttress "the vagaries of nationalistic concerns," perform "the truncated examination of the methods of manipulating existing institutions," engage in the "task of creating the men who will lead the *existing* system," and so on. Those who can get to see this

> . . . stand in a fundamentally different tradition from the vast majority of students and professors in the country; we recognize that we cannot accept their terms of analysis, that we demand a more fundamental, systematic and humane approach to the problems of mankind. We recognize that the Universities are currently concerned with the development of none of these approaches and are in fact, because of their historic commitments to the nourish-

*Monsonis reported shortly afterward that when he sent tapes of the speeches to a friend of his to be transcribed, she wrote back "saying that she's listened to them over and over and is now absolutely convinced that she must leave school and *do* something."

ment of the existing system, a commitment intensified ultimately by the Cold War, in some sense in opposition to their development. And we recognize that the only course for us is to stand outside the existing traditions and on our own intellectual, economic, political and human resources develop alternatives to the system so compelling as to obtain basic concessions from it.

And the alternatives will have to be quite far removed from anything now being suggested. They will involve totally new models, totally new behavior:

> We must . . . begin to search for a revolutionary model which is dynamic enough to extricate us from the continually narrowing concentric circles which define the limits of change within the established political power structure. . . .
>
> In order to develop a revolutionary model, concerned faculty and students will for the most part have to move outside the University-defined spectrum of lectures, seminars and officially sanctioned research. And more importantly . . . they will have to move outside the societally defined spectrum of what is relevant since relevance is defined today as that which is directed at *adjusting* the current power structure.

The point is profound: recognize that the universities are as corrupt as their settings—how could they be otherwise—and leave them before they corrupt you. What makes this so especially important is that it stands in polar opposition to *The Port Huron Statement*'s ideas of what universities and students can be and do —and the tension between these two impulses will continue throughout the decade to be faced by each wave of activist students: Is the university "a potential base and agency in a movement of social change" (*The Port Huron Statement*) or is it "ultimately committed to the nourishment of a national and international system in which the Cold War is inextricably rooted" (Potter)? Is the university the nest for those who can create real social change, or the hothouse for those who would resist it? Are students operating within the university truly agents of social change, or must they leave the campuses and operate in the "real" world outside? Are the universities bases from which assaults can effectively be made on the social system, or are they bastions of that system producing instead its minions? The former impulse leads to the Berkeley Free Speech Movement, to student power, to the explosive rebellions of the campuses; the latter leads to SDS's ghetto-organizing projects, to the "free universities," to the "dropout" culture of the youth ghettos, and more.

The second conference, at Brandeis in March, was an even more ambitious one on "University Reform." Eighty people showed up, and there were speeches by Paul Goodman, Herbert Marcuse (then teaching at Brandeis), and Hayden, three pretty incandescent stars even then. Goodman attacked the university for its handmaiden role with the Establishment and, possessed of a faith in the young that he was to abandon in not too many years, argued that it was the students who could turn the university around to "become a new center of initiative for our society." The contradiction in this—universities are supposed to be isolated from social and governmental influence on the one hand, yet to partake in social and political transformation on the other—was underscored by Marcuse, who wanted to have it both ways: "In the first place, the university should have nothing to do with the Cold War; in the second place, insofar as it does have to do with the Cold War, its purpose ought to be to end it." Hayden was perhaps wisest in recognizing that the only way to resolve it all was to change the society, for "the university cannot be reformed without a total social revolution."

The Brandeis conference was important in raising the university-reform issue almost two years before the Free Speech Movement at Berkeley forced it upon the attention of the country. But it also raised certain problems, as noted by Shelly Blum, an SDSer at CCNY who reported on the conference for *Common Sense:*

> At several different occasions, effective critiques were made of various aspects of the university experience by both students and faculty, but responses to the "what can we do?" question left much to be desired. . . . While personally useful, such discussions did not get even then to the question of what it is that we ought to be doing within the university today to create the kind of educational experience which is what we are led to expect from the liberal rhetoric regarding education. . . . It became clearer than at most previous discussions that we don't know just what it is that we are trying to construct and how we think it can be done. So much more must be done on the constructive as well as critical level.

The 1962–1963 school year was such a difficult one for the fledgling SDS that it might have seemed remarkable that SDS continued to exist, to command such fierce loyalties from its members, and, slowly, to grow. The thing that kept it alive was the special quality of its vision, combined with the special quality of its people.

SDS was, for many young collegians, the only organization anywhere, young or old, which enunciated the things they wanted said. Todd Gitlin, who had gravitated toward SDS at Harvard in the spring of 1962, became a confirmed follower around the time of the Cuban missile crisis, when the politics he had been following with TOCSIN became "completely discredited" and there were only a few people around during those days who "integrated their political and personal salvations at once"—and they were SDSers: "The way the SDS people operated was commensurate with the enormity of the problems of the society." Once he got to know them, he was also struck by "the whole thing about interrelatedness—that made a lot of sense to me then." By Christmastime he had resigned the chairmanship of TOCSIN and was, without being an official member, philosophically an SDSer.

This same quality was mentioned by another young student, from Piedmont College, who said, "I just decided that these are the best human beings around, and figured it is with them I should make the good fight. That way, even if you lose, you gain something very valuable." Another SDSer, quoted in Kenneth Keniston's *Young Radicals,* put it this way:

> Bill Westbury came and sort of complimented me for what he felt was a good job that I had played. . . . He said, "SDS is holding a series of seminars this year, and would you like to get involved?" I said, "I would love to," because I really felt the need for intellectual stimulation. . . . At the time, I was for peace, I was for dissent, I was for civil rights, and then sometimes, if the situation presented, I would wind up arguing for socialism. But I would also argue for better Medicare, higher minimum wages, or something like that. I considered myself a sort of liberal. A very militant political liberal. . . . [He went to an NC.] I heard several people whom I was unimpressed with, but it was [Clarkson] who just overwhelmed me with his mind. He didn't turn me on and say I should become involved or anything like that. I was just impressed with his mind

and his grasp of politics. So I decided at that point that I wanted to become part of that. That was what I was going to do, to be a part of, because I could learn a hell of a lot. And they were nice, they were good people. And I had a lot to learn. So what I did for the next year and a half, was just to listen. . . . I didn't say a word, I never even opened my mouth. I took notes, and I'd come back at night and study them and try to remember what was said. I read all the literature. . . .

The thing that I was thinking about was what was I going to do with my life, what kind of job am I going to have? And I wound up feeling that I might want to go to graduate school, but I never applied. . . . I wanted to learn, I wanted to learn how America was organized and I wanted to find out more about myself. I figured that these guys and publications and the books that they read could help me to do that. . . . Another thing I felt was kind of the ideology of the alienated: "The old values have been destroyed; the old structures and institutions of the past no longer fit our needs; therefore we must rebuild." That's how I personally connected into it.

Still another reaction comes from Jeremy Brecher, who was a freshman at Reed College when he first ran into SDS:

When I went to my first SDS NC meeting it was like, here is exactly what I'd been looking for for three years, all the things I believed in. It was unlike anything I'd been in before—an enormous sense of dynamism—a feeling of expansiveness—"*Dynamism*" is the only word for it. The other great thing was you had a feeling of breaking out, that SDS *was* becoming a mass movement, it was on the verge of relating to much broader groups on campus: the same way you can tell between a crowd ready for civil disobedience, ready to fight the police, and one that isn't, a whole different stance and attitude.

The feelings of many were perhaps best and most simply put by Douglas Ireland, a high-school student in the Boston area, who wrote after a few meetings with Burlage and his friends: "I feel at home in SDS."

It is possible to make some cautious generalizations about these early SDSers which help to explain some of their rather extraordinary effect. They were, for a start, often extremely bright and, more than that, *intellectual,* having gotten good grades in high school, moved on early to the best universities, proved themselves then among the top ranks academically, and many were planning (or engaged in) graduate work and professorial careers;

they were diligent readers, active thinkers and talkers, and, as the later literature lists of SDS will show, prodigious writers. They tended to come from middle-class and upper-middle-class (often professional) homes—there are no exact figures on this, but it was acknowledged often enough (and sometimes worried about) by the members themselves—with parents who could give them money, security, often a stable family life, and usually the more enduring middle-class values and ethics, often combined with that vague liberal perfectionism that is characteristic of the American middle class.* They were overwhelmingly from the East and generally from the cities (although there was a sizable minority from the Midwest), and many (perhaps a third) were Jewish, all of which went to produce a kind of sophistication, a cosmopolitanism, and a grounding in urban traditions. And they were often from families whose parents had had some contact with the left, usually during the thirties—a couple which was young during the thirties would tend to have children by the early forties, and these would be of college age by the early sixties; probably only a handful of the early SDSers were true "red-diaper babies"—Flacks, Max, and Ross among them—but since more than two million people went through the ranks of the Communist Party at one time or another in the thirties, and since there were millions more who moved in or near the other eddies of the left, it would not be surprising if a number of SDSers had some brush with the ideas and the ideals of the left during their upbringing.

They were, indeed, a remarkable group of people. They were committed, energetic, perceptive, political, and warm; they had a vision and they backed it up with unstinting if not always successful work; they were—not unimportant—personable, charismatic,

---

*Not all the early SDSers were prototypically middle class: Hayden's father was an accountant, Potter's a farmer, Ross's a garment worker, Webb's a laborer, and Max's an impoverished political functionary. But most did come from middle- and upper-middle-class environments—Booth's father was a federal civil servant and then a professor, Davis's father a federal economist and adviser to Harry Truman, Rothstein's father was also a federal civil servant, Brecher's parents were successful writers, Burlage's and Haber's fathers were university professors, Garman's was a corporation executive, Gitlin's a high-school teacher, Jeffrey's mother a political and labor leader—and those who did not usually came from "upwardly mobile" homes where they drank deeply of the middle-class ethic and moved from the better high schools to the elite universities along a familiar enough middle-class path.

articulate, and (many) good-looking; they were serious in a time that called for seriousness, yet still deeply and often self-consciously human, friendly, warm, working daily at knocking down the egocentric barriers their society had taught them to construct and trying to open themselves to others. Jack Newfield, who was of them and among them during all these early days, says simply: "The finest political people I have ever seen—and that includes those around Bobby Kennedy and anyone else—were those in the early days of SDS."

The school year ended with the annual convention, this time held June 14–17 at Camp Gulliver, a summer camp near Pine Hill, New York. It was some measure of the success of the organization that more than two hundred people showed up, representing thirty-two colleges and universities. The main business of the convention was to draft another general statement of principles— in the early years, conventions were supposed to set organizational principles and the quarterly National Councils were supposed to set specific programs—and for that Dick Flacks had prepared a paper over the spring (with considerable help from the theoretical apparatchik: Booth, Haber, Hayden, Ross) called *America and the New Era*. When he presented it to the convention it quickly became known as "Son of Port Huron."

America and the New Era is less impressive than *The Port Huron Statement*, in part because it comes after, but also because of its narrower focus. *The Port Huron Statement* is more visionary, more philosophical, more theoretical, while this is concerned more with the tangible aspects of American policy and immediate ways to change it; *The Port Huron Statement* surveys a wide range of problems, from overpopulation to parietal rules, while *America and the New Era* says almost nothing about foreign policy, is only secondarily concerned with the Cold War, and concentrates its attention almost wholly on an analysis of broad contemporary economic and political problems of the United States.*

*One of the reasons for the absence of a foreign policy section is that the conventioneers couldn't come to any agreement on what stands to take on all the various international problems—they were not yet ready to see them collectively in terms of imperialism, as a small minority wished—and so they agreed on a policy of "principled agnosticism" to avoid angry divisions. As Todd Gitlin

But there are two central perceptions in *America and the New Era,* and their enunciation by the Pine Hill delegates marks a step forward for SDS and the student movement of which it is a part.

The first is that America has reached a point of crisis, that considerable new forces are at work within it, that it stands teetering on an unknown brink: in short, "that a new era is upon us, and the simple categories and grand designs of the Cold War no longer serve." Internationally, the "conception of an American Century" has been shattered; a colonial transformation has taken place; the Communist bloc is no longer a monolith; Western Europe is challenging American power; the strategy of eyeball-to-eyeball deterrence has outlived its usefulness. Domestically, all the attempts "to manage social conflicts" are beginning to come unstuck, poverty is a stain that can no longer be ignored, the racial crisis is coming to a peak, government complicity with business —what is called here for the first time "corporate liberalism"— has resulted in a stalemate for both; and new voices in labor, the media, the middle classes, minorities, and even in Congress are beginning to be heard:

> The structure of quiescence is beginning to break down. The development of the civil rights movement and other centers of independent insurgency has for the first time since the war created centers of power outside the university to which intellectuals could turn for creative as well as political involvement. The beginning of a breakdown in the American consensus provides the possibility for genuinely critical and independent participation of intellectuals and students in national life. The bureaucratic and ideological structures of American institutions of liberal education have been penetrated.*

The second perception, which follows directly from this, is that there is in response to this new crisis "a new discontent, a new

---

remembers it, "We had a sense, even that early, that these issues would only be divisive; that we should agree on what we wanted for the U.S. rather than what we wanted elsewhere. Sometimes I think we would have done well—against all odds, especially the heightening of the war—to have sustained that attitude." (Letter to author.)

*Todd Gitlin says that for many people he knew the previous spring marked a significant turning point in their personal lives—"everyone broke apart in those last few months"—and this may have added psychological validity to the political analysis. (Interview with author.)

anger . . . groping towards a politics of insurgent protest"—a "new insurgency":

> There seems to be emerging a collection of people whose thought and action are increasingly being radicalized as they experienced the events of the new era. Moreover, the radical consciousness of these individuals is certainly representative of wider currents of urgency and dissatisfaction which exist in the communities from which they come. The militant resolve of Negroes North and South, the urgency and dedication of middle class peace advocates, the deepening anxiety of industrial workers, the spreading alienation of college students—this kind of motion and discontent in the population has given new stimulation to the development of radical thought, and is leading to a search for new forms of insurgent politics.

It is hardly an accident that SDS itself will very shortly come to take on one of these new forms, following the almost inevitable consequences of its analysis.

One immediate response to the sense of a new insurgency was a decision by the convention to amend the constitution so as to give more power to individual chapters and local members at national meetings; it was decided that chapters should elect delegates to the convention on the basis of one for every five of its members, with each delegate having two votes, and that chapters with more than twenty-five members might elect two representatives to the National Council. Another response was to put new and younger people into the leadership of the organization: though Hayden had been a successful president and was still perhaps the most powerful single figure in SDS, it was felt that he should not continue in office and that a regular rotation of the national officers allowing for new blood was necessary to insure true "participatory democracy." It was an understandable decision, perhaps inevitable, and one sanctioned by SDS's (and SLID's) history of annual turnovers, but it was to have two serious consequences: for one, the previous year's officers, despite their considerable organizational skills, were mechanically prevented from exercising continued leadership or else had to exert power from behind the scenes through informal and hidden personal manipulation; for another, the values of continuity, political experience, and cohesive politics were inevitably denied the organization, forcing it to reshape its national machinery each year, a process which later on would serve to lessen SDS's impact and efficiency and eventually threaten its ability to carry out any national programs at all. An SDS in which Hayden, Haber, Booth, Davis, and others continued to exercise formal leadership year after year throughout the sixties, instead of retiring to the sidelines and then dropping out entirely, would have been a far different, perhaps a more powerful and enduring, organization than what actually evolved.

One immediate consequence of this second response was a long scramble to find someone to replace Hayden, the difficulty of which might have suggested its artificiality. None of the old leadership wanted to go against the insurgent tide and keep the reins in practiced hands—Burlage, Davis, and Potter all were nominated for the presidency and all shied away—and finally the convention had to settle on Todd Gitlin, able and personable but still very new to the national organization. Gitlin recalls how, though trepidatious, he came to take the job:

> Davis and Potter both wanted me to accept, and the three of us ended up walking on the lawn outside. I don't exactly remember what we talked about. All of us were going to be in Ann Arbor the next year—I was going because I wanted to be *around* all this commotion—and they all had personal agendas that seemed more urgent than mine. What came through my mind was a paper, "Five Characters in Search of a Vision," I had written at Harvard just before, about what makes a person choose commitment, choose to become a radical, and that was *it,* I said yes. I was so stunned and overwhelmed that when I came out to give the acceptance speech I don't know what I said.

For National Secretary the convention chose Lee Webb, fresh out of Boston University and equally as inexperienced in the ways of national organizations, and though some continuity was kept— Booth was again elected Vice President, Max continued as Field Secretary, and McKelvey as Assistant National Secretary—the impulse toward the new insurgency was clearly dominant.*

*The NEC was abolished as a separate body, but fourteen "national officers" were elected to serve as the nucleus of each National Council, and these became known as the National Council members. Elected this year were Burlage, Davis, Flacks, Garman, Hayden, Jeffrey, Steve Johnson (Harvard), Max, Monsonis, Kimberly Moody (Johns Hopkins), Sarah Murphy (University of Chicago), Potter, Varela, Monte Wasch (CCNY). The National Secretary was also established as a "national officer" and a member of the National Council.

The Pine Hill convention ended with ritual, begun in nascent form at Port Huron, that would continue to mark SDS conventions, and many National Council meetings, for the next several years. It was called, usually, the "fund-raising orgy," and it followed something of the pattern that Dick Flacks later described:

> The scene might have been written by Genet; it was worthy of filming by Fellini. A young man, well clothed and well groomed but with his shirt collar open now, and his tie pulled down, shouted to the audience like an old-fashioned revivalist.
>
> "Come up," he cried, "come up and confess. Put some money in the pot and be saved!"
>
> And they came. The first youth, clutching the green pieces of paper in his hand, recited for all to hear: "My father is a newspaper editor. I give twenty-five dollars." His penitence brought cheers from the assembly. The sin of the next young man was a father who was assistant director of a government bureau. He gave forty dollars. "My dad is dean of a law school," confessed another, as he proffered fifty dollars for indulgence.

Few other SDSers recall these affairs as being as full of peccancy as all that, but there was certainly a sense of liberation, of kicking over, about them, as the young delegates emptied their pockets and made their pledges. Clark Kissinger, a former Chicago University student, recalls the sense of euphoria that clung to that final day: "The convention closed with a tremendous feeling of solidarity and comradeship," not the least of which was that "$1700 was donated to SDS by the delegates on the last evening, and notable personalities were ceremoniously tossed into the lake."

7

ERAP: FALL 1963-SPRING 1964

It was as if the American students of the 1960s had heard the words of one Pavel Axelrod, of the University of Kiev, in the 1870s:

> He who wishes to work for the people must abandon the university, forswear his privileged condition, his family, and turn his back even upon science and art. All connections linking him with the upper classes of society must be severed, all of his ships burned behind him; in a word, he must voluntarily cut himself off from any possible retreat. [He] must, so to speak, transform his whole inner essence, so as to feel one with the lowest strata of the people, not only ideologically, but also in everyday manner of life.

For, just as Axelrod and the Russian students had done a century before, a whole body of students now left the universities and went to become one with the lowest strata of the people.

It was an incredible movement. Nothing like it had ever been seen before in American life—not the Populist movement of the 1890s, not the settlement-house movement at the turn of the century, not the Unemployed Councils of the Communists in the thirties. Thousands of students turned from theory to action, from classrooms to slums, going south to register voters in impoverished black communities, organizing unemployed workers in the decaying inner cities, running tutorial projects for black high-school students through the North, even joining government-approved VISTA projects, poverty-planning centers and cooperatives, or simply dropping out to work and live among the people. It was, as many pointed out at the time, very much like the Russian Narodnik movement of the 1860s and 1870s, with much of the same mixture of idealism, guilt, asceticism, moralism, selflessness, and hard work, and though it seems to have run its course much quicker, seems to have been more swiftly changed into other impulses and other drives, it has in a certain way ended with the same results: revolt and repression.

SDS was only a part of the wider neo-Narodnik spirit of the sixties, but it was one of the first organizations to awaken to and capitalize on the new spirit, the only one to make a direct assault in the ghettos, where the worst of the problems festered, and one of the few to sustain its action beyond a summer's spasm, to enshrine its doing with theory and ideology, and to enlist a solid band of people who would continue on in political life. That its movement ultimately failed in its grand objectives—quite a dismal failure on its own terms—or at best counted a few latecoming victories, does not lessen the quite searing mark it put on so much of the generation of the time.

Tom Hayden was among the first to feel the new restlessness. As early as March 1963, having been told that the UAW was a likely source of money for student work around economic issues, Hayden wrote to Walter Reuther asking in general terms if maybe there wasn't something SDS could do that would qualify and hinting at something in the neighborhood of $7500.* No promises were made, but the UAW expressed interest. Hayden began thinking. In the "President's Report" in the March-April *SDS Bulletin* he gave an indication of where his mind was turning: "SDS is not growing locally with enough speed to be a major social movement in the near future. SDS is not thinking radically, and with consciousness of the organization as a weapon, about political objectives." He rejected the idea of turning the organization into a

---

*No doubts apparently were ever felt at this point about approaching either Reuther or his brother Victor, though they were known even then as having been ardent Cold Warriors and were perfect representatives of the liberal community SDS was ostensibly rejecting; four years later, at the time of the CIA disclosures, the closeness of the Reuthers' link with Cold War subversion became documented.

"think center" or uniting it with ineffective liberal bureaucracies:

> The people working in liberal causes at the grass roots, however, *are* distinguishable from the Establishment—by at least their discontent, albeit their political outlook is still maturing. Perhaps these nearly invisible actors, existing in every community, are the points of energy to which we should look—rather than to Geneva negotiators, or the heads of the labor movement, or the other entrenched liberal organizations.
>
> What we may need is a way to transform these invisible rebellions into a politics of responsible insurgence rooted in community after community, speaking in comprehensible terms to their felt needs. . . . Can the methods of SNCC be applied to the North? . . . Can we spread our organizational power as far as our ideological influence, or are we inevitably assigned to a vague educational role in a society that increasingly is built deaf to the sounds of protest?

Hayden was not alone in feeling the need for action, the call to some kind of "responsible insurgence." Throughout the organization dissatisfaction with the limitations of SDS was expressed. SDS had succeeded in establishing for itself a solid reputation as the most intellectual student group around, the place where the leaders and ideologues of other organizations went from time to time to forge their separate swords in the fires of debate and intellectuality; by the end of the 1962–63 school year it had a literature list of nearly twenty papers—Hayden on the role of students in universities, Burlage on the South, Haber on labor, Booth on electoral politics, *The Port Huron Statement*—that were popular on campuses with the types who read. But it was not known for *doing* anything on its own, either as a national group or (with few exceptions) in its chapters. That, combined with the organizational limitations of the National Office, chafed increasingly on a number of the SDS in-group, and they began searching for new drives and programs that would energize the membership and circumvent the NO.

America and the New Era encapsulated this growing impulse into the phrase, as much prescriptive as descriptive at that point, "the new insurgency":

> The new insurgents are active generators of a wide variety of political activities in the neighborhoods and communities where they are

located. Local insurgent actions include: mass direct action and voter registration campaigns among Negroes, political reform movements directed against entrenched Democratic machines, political action for peace, tutorial and other community based attempts to reach underprivileged youth, discussion groups, periodicals and research aimed at analysis and exposure of local political and economic conditions. Barely begun are efforts to initiate organized protest in depressed areas and urban slums, to organize non-union workers, to focus reform political clubs and candidacies on issues and programs directly relevant to the urban poor, and to involve slum-dwellers directly in political efforts.

The outcome of these efforts at creating insurgent politics could be the organization of constituencies expressing, for the first time in this generation, the needs of ordinary men for a decent life. . . .

The political insurgency, the rebirth of a populist liberalism, would upset existing American priorities and could rewrite the nation's agenda. . . .

A concerted effort to abolish poverty, unemployment, and racial inequality will be a prelude to the effort to bring into being a participatory democracy.

The idea of "the new insurgency" combined several strands. First, there was the growing dissatisfaction with university life and the growing realization, as Potter had expressed it at the Harvard conference, that universities might not be the agencies for change after all. By 1963 many SDS undergraduates had begun to feel the need to escape a university system which they saw ever more clearly as an unyielding and uncaring bureaucracy which turned them into holes on the edge of an IBM card, and which they came to realize was an intertwined and equally culpable part of the national system. And those in graduate school—including such influential members of the SDS in-group as Burlage, Davis, Flacks, Gitlin, Hayden, Haber, McEldowney, Potter, Ross, and Rothstein—faced the equally bleak prospect of continuing on for degrees they came to regard as pointless union cards or getting compromising jobs in a rat race they saw as deadening and meaningless. "The university," as Gitlin said, "begins to feel like a cage."

In their search for some way to live which would not violate the way they believed, most of the young activists looked to the civil-rights movement. That movement was a group of people acting on their principles, not sitting on them, taking part in "the real world" outside of the classroom, helping to shake the nation awake. That movement—especially SNCC—had shown as nothing had before that the poor and the downtrodden were remarkably savvy people withal, generous beyond understanding, shrewd in a most basic sense, forgiving, tough, decisive, committed, friendly: all of which ran counter to the myths the middle class had absorbed. It had also shown that the way to work with such people was not with top-down liberal paternalism but bottom-up identification and the sort of self-effacing, nonideological, with-the-people, leaderless, and nonmanipulative organization SNCC had developed. The SNCC mystique was powerful: blue work shirts, jeans, and army boots come into fashion, and the patterns of speech, the gestures, the argot of the SNCC fieldworkers come to be adopted.

And just at this time there also developed a sweeping economic analysis that gave intellectual justification for a concern with the poor and hence found a willing audience among the SDSers. It held basically that the nation was headed for an economic recession of major proportions and that there would soon be an army of discontented unemployed, as automation destroyed jobs, the postwar economy shrank, international economic competition grew stronger, and military-defense expenditures decreased. One of the earliest formulations of the analysis came at a conference in Nyack, New York, in June 1963, from which there grew a National Committee for Full Employment, guided by a brilliant young New York radical, Stanley Aronowitz, and designed precisely to meet the coming economic collapse. At the conference, attended by many SDSers, the most influential paper was one by Ray Brown, then working for the Federal Reserve System—and who should know better?—called "Our Crisis Economy: The End of the Boom":

> The labor force will expand by a million and a half each year in the coming decade. Add to this demand for jobs the number of jobs destroyed each year by automation (estimates range from one to one-and-a-half million), and the problem takes on monumental proportions. . . . The result is [by 1970] 11 million unemployed.

And that doesn't even count the part-time and marginally employed nor the millions who never make it into official job statistics. What more natural, then, than to make this enormous reservoir of human beings into an agency to change the system that has treated them so cruelly? It is obvious that the working classes care nothing for serious changes in the system that has bought them off with such apparent success, and no one could ever count on the middle classes for such a fight; only the poor have the numbers, the geographical distribution, the anger, and the will to press, along with the studentry, for radical change. As Gitlin was to say a year later, "The poor know they are poor and don't like it; hence they can be organized so as to demand an end to poverty and the construction of a decent social order."*

The economic analysis is not without support elsewhere. Other reasons for SDS to move among the poor seem equally compelling. America was swinging to a rightward racism—witness the rise of Goldwater and the John Birch Society—and if this was to be prevented, it would only be by awakening poor whites, the common fodder of such a swing, to their own subjugated position and their ultimate shared economic identity with the blacks. The "Other America," which Harrington had portrayed so movingly and John Kennedy had deigned to notice, was becoming less invisible, and the time seemed ripe to uplift the poor, now that they had been seen. Then, too, since it was obvious that corporate liberalism had failed, the alternative, following on from *The Port Huron Statement*'s call for "truly democratic alternatives to the present," was the creation of "counter-communities," anarchistic units where participatory democracy could be tried out firsthand.

Finally, there are some explanations for the impulse to the

*It does not matter, of course, that this analysis of growing unemployment turns out to be all wrong: with the system's vast ingenuity a whole new series of economic and military props (Vietnam, the moon) becomes created in the second half of the sixties to forestall economic crisis and keep people occupied, and with its vast capacity for self-deceit means are developed to ignore those who are not so kept. The analysis was developed by sophisticated and capable people of many political views, and held to by such distinguished men as (for example) W. H. Ferry, Michael Harrington, Gunnar Myrdal, Robert Theobald, Linus Pauling, Robert Heilbroner, and Ben B. Seligman (all signers of a document embodying this analysis called "The Triple Revolution," published the following year in *Liberation,* April 1964). What matters is that it was enormously influential at the time.

new insurgency beyond those stated and acknowledged at the time. These things are mixed up in it: a subliminal desire to escape from the bureaucratic and programed world into something explicity "irrational" and "inefficient," fundamentally, even disturbingly, antiestablishmentarian (Hayden: "The Movement is a community of insurgents aiming at a transformation of society led by the most excluded and 'unqualified' people"); a restless need of students to break out of the constrictive social mold in which they have dutifully spent their lives and to thumb their noses at it (Hayden: "Working in poor communities is a . . . position from which to expose the whole structure of pretense, status and glitter that masks the country's real human problems"); a drive to do something that gives meaning to a person's life (Hayden: "Students and poor people make each other feel real"); an ingrained American belief that action, confrontation, and putting bodies on the line is what really matters, where intellectuality and passivity and book-larnin' is too sissified (Hayden: "These problems [of organizing the poor] will be settled, if at all, more by feel than theory and mostly in immediate specific situations"); a very deep-seated wish to be selfless, to do for others instead of having everything done for you, to work out in demonstrable ways the moral fervor inside (Hayden: "Working in poor communities is a concrete task in which the split between job and values can be healed"); and finally a psychic drive to identify with someone else who is, as you wish to be, outside of the system, is by circumstance nontechnical, nonmoneyed, nonmanipulative, alienated and powerless (Hayden: "Radicals then would identify with all the scorned, the illegitimate and the hurt"). SDS's new strategy arises, then, because it is a healthy impulse in the most basic sense, for it allows, as psychologist Kenneth Keniston says in discussing Movement work in general, "a new harmony . . . between will and conscience, between ego and superego, between self and principle."

By the summer of 1963, the cause therefore seemed clear: organize the poor and the unemployed. The means seemed to have been given: a SNCC-inspired movement. The agents were to hand: the dissatisfied students of the university. Even the money was available: early in August, the UAW gave SDS $5000 for "an education and action program around economic issues." (Hayden wrote to Gitlin: "It is time to rejoice. We have the $5000—more than that . . . Maybe we're beginning to move. Pacem in terris.")

All that was needed was a mechanism, and it was to this that the SDSers now bent themselves.

Hayden's first notion was that the best way for SDS to make itself felt was by aligning with what was statistically the most deprived and at the same time what seemed the most militant and approachable segment of the poor: unemployed black and white youths. After a full day and half a night knocking the idea around with Gitlin and Booth (then both in Washington, D.C., at a Peace Research Institute) in July and then testing it out with some people in New York who had had slum-organizing experience, Hayden was ready to propose it formally to the September National Council meeting that was to be held after the NSA convention that year in Bloomington, Indiana. But one thing intervened: several SNCC workers at that NSA, including one by the name of Stokely Carmichael, were beginning to develop the rudiments of a black-power ideology, and were pushing the idea that the blacks could do the job in the South and that what young whites ought to be doing was organizing whites. SDS's target, obviously, should then be unemployed *white* youths. The NC, pressed by its most articulate leaders—Hayden, Webb, Gitlin, and others—welcomed the idea and the money that made it possible, and then and there established a program for the fall. A young white University of Michigan sophomore, Joe Chabot, would drop out and go organize, somehow, the unemployed white youths of Chicago; at the same time, not to get too far away from the intellectual tradition, a central office would be established in, say, Ann Arbor, away from the ghettos themselves, and run by some scholarly, dedicated soul like, say, Al Haber. And the program would be given a name having to do with the economy, to please the UAW, with education, so as to continue the SDS tradition, and with organizing, to suggest the new thrust: The Economic Research and Action Project, conveniently acronymed to ERAP (*Ee*-rap). That September ERAP officially began.

But something was wrong. The first three months of ERAP didn't work out at all the way they were supposed to. Haber seemed to be spending a lot of money in Ann Arbor, but nothing much seemed to be coming out of it other than a fancily printed brochure designed to raise money from rich liberals and a few pamphlets on economic matters written by SDS academics. Nor was Chabot's work in the real world any more promising. He spent the fall on the near northwest side of Chicago, a white working-class area fast decaying into slums, trying to talk with the teen-agers hanging around the street corners. But it turned out that he had no alternatives to offer the street youths, who never could figure out just what he was after, and he had no organizational support within the community, not even a storefront to work from. Early in November he sent this gloomy report back to the National Office:

> I have had [a] little experience on the streets with the unemployed fellow[s] around 19. I tried to enter into associations with these fellows by way of the settlements as they were my best source of introduction to the community, but I have not been accepted by any group of older teenagers of this neighborhood. They don't understand me. They are suspicious of me as well as everyone else who tries to have anything to do with them. . . . Communication is very difficult on every level—almost impossible when I try to ask direct questions of how a fellow thinks about anything in particular. Just to understand the slang would be a matter of probably six months. If I try to be accepted by some gang, it would probably be a process involving at least a year, and needless to say I don't have time for any such luxuries. . . .
>
> It is glum if it sounds that way. There is nothing to make them think socially at this time and nothing to give them confidence that in action their lives can improve. The kids feel totally at sea when an idea of joining together to press your demands is raised. They accept their state although dissatisfied and in revolt at the moment they have no leaders and no program. And at this point it is disenchanting to know that I've not met one fellow in the age group I would like to work in who is thinking socially.

By the end of December the ERAP treasury was more than half empty: over $500 had been spent in the National Office, almost $1000 went to keep Chabot functioning in Chicago, and more than $1500 was used up for Haber's operations in Ann

Arbor.* And nothing to show for it. Steve Max—never much disposed to ERAP anyway—limned the problem:

> The SDS program is considered too vague. We are always compli-
> mented on having the best critique of the political and economic
> situation, but when it comes to what we want and how we are going
> to get it, we start losing people. . . . It is simply not enough to tell
> our members to go and be locally insurgent. Our people already
> want to be insurgent; that is why they are in SDS. What they want
> to know is how and where.

Ironically, it was not in Chicago or in Ann Arbor that the ERAP idea bore fruit first but, of all places, in Chester, Pennsylvania.

Chester in 1963 was an economic and political sinkhole of some 63,000 people, 40 percent of them black, controlled by a Republican machine. It was fortunate in one thing: three miles away was the campus of Swarthmore College—small, Quaker, and leftish—and there a group of some thirty to fifty people in the Swarthmore Political Action Club, SDSers and those who had been influenced by SDS, were ready to engage themselves in the problems of just such a city. Many of the young SPACers had gotten interested in the integration movement in Cambridge, Maryland, in the spring of 1963 and had worked there with SNCC and its local affiliate during a formative summer of black organiz-ing, mass marches, red-neck violence, National Guard tear-gas-sing, and ultimately a compromise victory wrought by Robert Kennedy in Washington. When they returned to school in the fall the SPACers were ready for more action, and it wasn't long before they joined up with a black mobilizing committee in nearby Ches-ter. From November 4 to 14 nearly 100 Swarthmorians and Ches-ter blacks picketed, marched, sat-in, petitioned, and pressured the city hall and the local school board on a broad range of demands, and in the course of it some 57 students were arrested—the first large-scale violent action by any white campus-based group in the North. On the fourteenth the city caved in, all the demands were

---

*Haber's comparative extravagance was not resented by the other SDSers, who figured it was little enough considering the starving years he had already put in for SDS and the fact that the LID still owed him a chunk of money he was never likely to see.

met and charges against all the demonstrators were dropped. And still the movement went on: in the next two months three large community groups were organized and a concerted drive for economic improvement and political control was launched among the blacks.

The leader of SPAC was a tall, thin, blond named Carl Wittman, a shrewd young politician and SDSer whom Lee Webb called "brilliant, just brilliant" in the Chester actions. The SDS National Office worked with him during much of it, and Webb himself, chafing at office routine in New York and discovering that he wasn't really cut out to be a National Secretary, spent several days a week in Chester through the fall, seeing firsthand what a community-organizing project actually might look like and feeding this sense back to others in the organization. Meanwhile, rent strikes and similar community actions took place under the noses of SDSers in Baltimore, New York, Cleveland, and Chicago that fall, largely led by blacks, and this too suggested a new militancy and a new means for operating among the urban poor. Finally Wittman and Webb went out to Ann Arbor to talk to Hayden— he was still nominally a journalism graduate student—and for the first time since the summer, Webb remembers, Hayden "really got interested"; before their weekend was over they had hammered out a whole new idea for a revivified ERAP and determined to make the upcoming December National Council the battleground for its adoption.

The new idea was embodied in a paper called "An Interracial Movement of the Poor?" that Hayden and Wittman wrote in the next few months to sell the membership on the new ERAP idea. Long, discursive, and well-nigh unreadable, it nonetheless had an impact on many in SDS circles. Its main argument, a product of Wittman's Chester experience, was that whites could work together with blacks to mobilize a community, and that the job of organizing ought to be directed toward *all* the poor, black and white, young and old, and around *any* issue that moves them, not simply the question of jobs. Organize, the authors say, [around]

> ... *demands for political and economic changes of substantial benefit to the Negro and white poor.* Examples of these include improved housing, lower rents, better schools, full employment, extension of

welfare and Social Security assistance. They are not "Negro issues" per se; rather, they are precisely those issues which should appeal to lower-class whites as well as to Negroes.

And this organizing can't be done either with research centers or street-corner strangers—it needs people willing to live among the poor: *"We are people and we work with people.* Only if conscious *cooperative practice* is our main style will our ideology take on the right details; only then will it be tested and retested, changed, and finally shared with others."

At the December 1963 NC some seventy people—the largest number so far at an NC—met in New York with a sense that big things were going to happen. Paul Booth recalls, "By that time we were *it.* We were the wave of the future." Perhaps this feeling was heightened by the presence at the NC of two diametrically differ-ent people who both touched resonant chords among the SDSers: Bob Dylan and Alger Hiss. Dylan, who had just finished "Blowin' in the Wind" and was already a celebrity among the college gener-ation, dropped by the hall and was persuaded to say a few words, which Jeremy Brecher remembers as being something like: "Ah don' know what yew all are talkin' about . . . but it sounds like *yew* want somethin' to happen, and if that's what *yew* want that's what *Ah* want." Hiss had come by to deliver a message to one of the SDSers and as soon as it was known that he was in the back of the hall, a number of people insisted that he be introduced; he was, and to cheers: it was as much his outcastness, his defiance, as his politics that impressed the delegates, and he was for them a symbol of all their closely held anti-anti-Communism.

Webb, as he now admits, "staged" the meeting so that it would be heavy with those, especially from the Swarthmore area, who shared the into-the-ghetto view; he even had Jesse Gray, leader of the Harlem rent strike then going on, and Stanley Arono-witz, whose National Committee for Full Employment was by then a reality, come down to propagandize. Against them were ranged the realignment faction (Max and cohort) and an assort-ment of others, led chiefly by Haber, who thought "ghetto-jump-ing," as they put it, was remote from the needs both of students and of the nation as a whole. The result was the long-remembered

"Hayden-Haber Debate," at which SDS as an organization took a decisive turn.

Haber, quiet, bespectacled, somewhat older, opened by presenting a report on the first three months of ERAP under his egis and urging its continuation on the same essentially academic lines. ERAP, he held, should be a place for research and writing about the problems of the poor, an "independent center of radical thinking," formulating the programs around which *other* people organized for themselves. Students should concern themselves *as students,* avoid the "cult of the ghetto," and use their own problems and talents to organize around, on the campus. If SDS spread itself from campus to ghetto, it would be spreading itself too thin.

Hayden, intense, charming, casual, seemed to have been at his most winning. SDS, he said, has to be *relevant,* has to leave all the academic crap behind it, has to break out of intellectuality into contact with the grass roots of the nation. ERAP, by getting off the campuses and into the ghettos, would get to the grass roots, get to where the *people* are. There we can listen to them, learn from them, organize them to give voice to their legitimate complaints, mobilize them to demand from the society the decent life that is rightfully theirs. ERAP can be the insurgent action that would truly propel SDS on a "revolutionary trajectory" (as *America and the New Era* had put it). *Here at last was something for SDS to do.*

The vote when it came was lopsided: the Hayden position won twenty to six. There were still to be campus programs of research and education around poverty and civil rights, there was still to be work in peace, disarmament, educational reform, and electoral politics—but the main energies of the organization would now go into ERAP. Henceforth, as someone put it jocularly that day, SDS would operate on the principle of "Social Emergency: Local Insurgency."

It now remained to put the plan into effect, and for that the NC picked Rennie Davis to replace Haber in the ERAP headquarters. Davis, installed somewhat surreptitiously in the building of the University of Michigan's Center for the Study of Conflict Resolution, was the man most responsible for ERAP's success.* He was a serious, dedicated, indefatigable, ingrown person who had been born in Michigan in 1940, grew up in Virginia in a small rural town, and had gone on to Oberlin, where he was a political science major and a cofounder of the campus political party there; he had just completed, as we have seen, a frustrating year trying to organize students at the University of Illinois while he was doing graduate work, he had transferred to the University of Michigan for more studies, and he was now eager to push into something more tangible and by all odds more exciting. "ERAP under Rennie was a swirl of activity," Gitlin remembers, and Webb says he was "a great organizer" that spring: "He was able to excite people, get people going, handle organizational things— *and* be confident. He's never received his proper recognition: he was one of the very important people in SDS." Webb should know, for he handled the New York end while Davis was in Ann Arbor, and the two of them did most of the ERAP planning that spring. The phrase they used at the time was "organize with mirrors"—give people the illusion that ERAP was a real thing before it was. "The whole thing," Webb recalls, "was to translate SDS very very quickly from an intellectual research center to an aggressive expanding *political* organization." They formulated the notion of having projects of ten to twenty students in a dozen cities during the summer vacation which, if successful, might be continued in the fall. "I went out to Ann Arbor," Webb says, "and Rennie was there with two girls he had recruited. We bought the census tracts, got a book about cities from the library, and we sat down and wrote the proposals for all the different cities." They picked Chicago because Chabot was already working there, Newark because Aronowitz's Full Employment committee was interested in helping, Hazard, Kentucky, because a Committee of Miners was already at work there, Cleveland because a friend of Wittman's named Ollie Fein wanted to start one there, and so on. Then in a series of preparatory conferences at Hazard, Ann Arbor, and Urbana they spread the word, enlisted recruits, talked over the problems, hammered out their idea. Organizing with mirrors

*It was, incidentally, his clipped pronunciation of "ghetto" as "get-toe" that other SDSers kiddingly adopted and used regularly at ERAP meetings from then on.

or not, it worked. Before the spring was over they had firm projects set for no fewer than ten cities, and several hundred applications in from students all over the country who wanted to be part of ERAP Summer.

It was not all roses. The remaining money from the original UAW grant went very quickly, and by April 1964 ERAP was down to $700. Davis, in his phrase, "blitzed" the East trying to get money from unions, the few liberal foundations (such as the Kaplan Fund—later named as a CIA conduit—and the Stern Family Fund), and some sympathetic individuals like Harold Taylor and Victor Rabinowitz, the New York lawyer; but he warned ERAPers in April that each project itself would have to raise $50 per worker.

Then, too, the project farthest along—Chicago—was having serious problems. All had seemed promising as the new year began. Following the new strategy, Chabot had given up on white youths and turned to the white unemployed in general, and in February opened up a storefront office strategically placed just down from the unemployment compensation office. The Packinghouse Workers Union was sympathetic to the project (the ILG, incidentally, had turned it down), gave some money and help, and set up with SDS an organization called JOIN, whose initials stood for the thrust of that particular project, Jobs Or Income Now. Davis even recruited more staff—Dan Max, Steve's younger brother, came out from New York, and later Lee Webb himself, who had been granted Conscientious Objector status by his draft board and joined a religious group in Chicago for his alternate service, devoted full time to JOIN. But the project faltered. A few jobless people came in, there were meetings sometimes with as many as thirty people, some marginal successes were won in fighting the bureaucracy of the local compensation office—but there was no solid organization, no sense of community-building, no real getting through to the people, and the money ran out so fast that at one point there wasn't even enough to put up a bracket so that they could install a sink in the office. By late spring Chabot got discouraged and eventually simply left, taking the project's only car and $115 that had accumulated besides, arguing that it was little enough considering the hours he had put in; Davis agreed. And after the remaining staffers had put all their energies into a symbolic apple-selling demonstration in the Loop in late May, enticing only two dozen locals to join them, Davis wrote bitterly: "Hell, we've been working at this now since September and finally spring 25 guys into the streets."

ERAP was also causing serious tension in the organization. The ERAPers began to feel that SDS should give itself over almost entirely to community organizing, that people should drop out of school and that it might even be necessary for SDS to *become* ERAP. As Hayden and Wittman had put it in their winter paper, "We must be prepared to radically change, or even dissolve, our organization if conditions someday favor a broad new movement." Don McKelvey, unsympathetic to ERAP, gloomily discussed this tendency as personified by Hayden and Gitlin in a letter to Steve Max that spring:

> Tom, as Todd recounts it, thinks SDS should *be* community projects in the ghetto, that the campus program should be gutted. Todd's analysis is more moderate and more dangerous, from our point of view, viz: that social change originates with the most dispossessed and that other classes will cluster around the dispossessed as they organize, since they are the most dynamic. Now, the fault is not with that analysis . . . but with the notion that SDS *is* the movement rather than a particular sector of it with a particular thing to do—i.e. get middle-class students into politics in a meaningful, long-term way. I'm afraid that Todd has a too exploitative attitude toward the campus—and, in fact, he said it in one letter—that we mustn't allow the campus program to fail because it was necessary to the ghetto program. This is the wrong emphasis.

Haber, too, added his fire, in a blistering article in the March–April *SDS Bulletin:*

> I am highly critical of the substance of such community work because it has been without radical direction, clarity of goals, or significant differentiation from liberal reform. And I am critical of its organizational role because it diverts us from more important things, ignores our role as a *student* organization and has become the base for an unfortunate anti-intellectualism in SDS. . . .
>
> The "into the ghetto" enthusiasm has become linked with an anti-intellectualism, a disparagement of research and study, an urging of students to leave the university, a moral superiority for those

who "give their bodies", etc. "In the world" has come to mean "in the slum." Beside being slightly sick, this suggests a highly perverted analysis of American Society. . . .

The cult of the ghetto has diverted SDS from the primary and most difficult task of educating radicals. . . . As an organization for students, SDS will have failed. It will have people deny what they are, and hence never learn how to apply their values in what they do.

And a lonely warning was added from Jim Williams, a big, soft-spoken Kentuckian who had been instrumental in organizing the University of Louisville chapter the fall before. He tried to point out in SDS circles that ERAP was not likely to be any more successful than the Narodnik movement which it was imitating. "But they just thought that was something *old,*" Williams recalls with a smile. "I was known to have *old* thoughts."

As Gitlin put it in describing the April 1964 NC meeting to the membership, "Debates of major proportion are arising among us concerning organizational direction and emphasis." And that was an understatement: for the first time it began to appear that SDS wasn't broad enough to encompass all its divergencies.

By the time of the 1964 summer convention, held again at Camp Gulliver in Pine Hill, New York, from June 11 to 14, these divergencies had solidified into roughly three factions: the *realignment group,* which concerned itself with electoral action and reform politics, led by Steve Max and Jim Williams and made up of a number of New Yorkers connected with Max through the reform movement in the city, plus a number of new student members who were uncomfortable with the idea of going into the slums; the *campus-organizing group,* in which Dick Flacks and Clark Kissinger (the new National Secretary, who replaced Webb in May) were prominent—Haber is by now so disgusted he doesn't even *attend* the convention, for the first time in seven years—and which drew support from the more conventional student delegates and those in colleges relatively untouched by the SNCC mystique; and the *ERAP group,* including most of the old-timers and a strong Swarthmore contingent plus a number of younger members who were beginning to embody an apolitical protohippie attitude and were inclined toward the romance of living among the poor.* Since it was now a hoary tradition of fully two years that the job of summer conventions was to turn out programmatic papers like *The Port Huron Statement* and *America and the New Era,* each of these factions had come prepared with a document for the convention to enshrine.† This, it was thought, would resolve the factional dispute, for whichever paper was most popular with the convention would be the blueprint for the following year.

The papers were presented; the convention took just half an afternoon to reject all three. The solution was in the best existential tradition of the New Left—no program, no blueprint, nobody telling you what you have to do—and it kept the organization intact. The ERAPers could go off and do their thing—indeed, many of them were already in the projects—while those on the campuses could continue theirs. For form's (and Max's) sake the convention mandated the National Council to establish a Political Education Project (PEP) alongside of ERAP which would undertake the work of the realignment faction and participate actively in the upcoming Presidential-year elections—but even Max knew that it was a decision that did not reflect the dominant political mood of the organization as a whole, and certainly not of its leadership: "The dominant tone," he remembers, not without distaste, "was this thing about privilege, that we were the bourgeoisie and we should go out and work for the poor."

The elections on the last day of the convention reflected the divergent politics (given that student elections are swung on a lot more things than political positions), though the weight of the ERAPers was evident. All four nominated for President were ERAP supporters—Davis and Ken McEldowney, who were on the ERAP national staff, and Bob Ross and Paul Potter, who were going into ghetto projects, but Potter seems to have been elected because he wasn't as closely identified with the ERAP leadership. In a four-man race for Vice President, Wittman and Webb, strongly identified with ERAP, were rejected, as was Jeffrey Shero,

---

*It is only a coincidence, perhaps, but a similar range of political views appeared among the adult luminaries who attended the convention, including Roger Hagan, Simmons College Professor Sumner Rosen, *Studies on the Left* editor James Weinstein, the Reverend Malcolm *(Are you Running With Me, Jesus?)* Boyd, and a New York City lawyer and littérateur by the name of William Kunstler.
†There was a fourth, put out by a group called Touch and Sex, a fabrication born probably in the mind of Steve Max, which parodied what it called the romantic "feelie" politics of the ERAPers.

a University of Texas student at his first SDS convention who was being pushed by the realignment group; Vernon Grizzard, head of the Chester ERAP but also an undergraduate and not quite so identifiably of the in-group, was chosen instead. Elected as National Council members were solid ERAPers like Davis, Wittman, Webb, Ross, Egleson, Gitlin, and McEldowney, Sarah Murphy, Shero, and Tufts University undergraduate David Smith from the campus contingent, and Paul Booth, Jeremy Brecher, and Jim Williams from the realignment faction; the last member was Charles Smith, a motorcycle-riding Texan who introduced himself to the convention as a "Gandhian-Marxist-pacifist-anarchist," and whom no one could classify. Of them all, only six—Brecher, Egleson, Grizzard, Murphy, Shero, and David Smith—were still in school, a signal of the continuing division in the organization between a postgraduate leadership and an undergraduate following.

By the time the deliberations were over it was clear that the electoral-politics people were not a significant element in SDS, but that the other two factions were strong and that there was a real cleavage between them. For the moment the direction of the organization was decided in favor of the ERAP faction, because—in addition to the other general explanations for the attractions of local insurgency—ERAP was new, it was *doing* something, and it had behind it most of the traditional (and the more charismatic) SDS leadership. But the campus-directed element was strong, and growing. And the tension between those who wanted to go into the real world and build a Movement and those who wanted to stay and organize in the universities would continue to be felt in the organization in the years to come.

So the ERAPers, strengthened by a six-day training institute earlier in June and then by the to-each-his-own convention, set out to build an interracial movement of the poor.* As the summer began there were ten projects:

*Some notion of the character of the ERAPers can be gotten from a look at the kinds of colleges they came from. Of the 48 ERAPers at the 1964 convention, 14 of them came from Swarthmore and 14 from Michigan—the hotbeds of ERAP organizing activity—and one or two each from such prestigious schools as Bard, Bryn Mawr, Carleton, Harvard, Haverford, Williams, and others from American University, Boston University, CCNY, Illinois, Johns Hopkins, Louisville, MIT, and Wisconsin.

Baltimore: a project called (like Chicago's) JOIN, working to reorganize the unemployed in two communities, one of poor whites, one of poor blacks; ERAPers included Peter Davidowicz and former NECer Kimberly Moody;

Boston: organizing among suburban whites (chiefly in Bedford, Massachusetts) whose defense industry jobs would, it was held, soon be eliminated as the nation's economy went through a "conversion" from military to peace-oriented interests; Chuck Levenstein, a Tufts SDSer, was important here;

Chester: a continuation of the SPAC work in the black community; Grizzard was head of the ten-person project;

Chicago: an extension of the JOIN project which Chabot and Dan Max had started, working among the white unemployed; the fourteen-member staff included such heavies as Gitlin, Ross, and Webb;

Cleveland: a multi-issued project in a largely poor white community, planning actions around housing, rents, and welfare; ERAPers included Bryn Mawr SDSer Katherine Boudin, Ollie Fein and his wife, Charlotte, Michigan students Nanci Hollander and Dick Magidoff, Sharon Jeffrey, and Paul Potter;

Hazard, Kentucky: a joint project with the year-old Committee for Miners and Aronowitz's Full Employment Committee, chiefly organizing unemployed whites laid off from the mines; Steve Max joined it in the summer;

Louisville: a somewhat hazy venture instigated by local peace activists, designed to work almost exclusively with other local groups, chiefly in civil rights; Jim Williams led this project;

Newark: another multi-issued project, aimed for a racially mixed community and working with an existing neighborhood-improvement group; Hayden and Wittman were both here, with Swarthmorean Larry Gordon, Barry Kalish, and two invaluable Michigan SDSers, Jill Hamberg and Michael Zweig, among others;

Philadelphia: another JOIN project working among the unemployed in a mixed black-and-white area; the ten ERAPers were led by Nick Egleson;

Trenton: a multi-issued project directed toward high-school tutorials, urban renewal, and housing, chiefly among blacks; Swarthmorean Walter Popper was its director.

The ERAP leaders, though cold-eyed about the difficulties, were confident. They had raised what for SDS was the incredible sum of nearly $20,000, $5000 of that from the New Land Foundation and $5000 more from Joseph Buttinger, a *Dissent* editor and patron; they figured that it would last them well through the summer. They had enlisted as many students as they thought they could take on, starting out the summer with 125 enthusiastic people, and there were more behind them who could be used as replacements. They had gotten unexpectedly enthusiastic support from the adult community; to take one example, a letter signed by W. H. Ferry (of the Center for the Study of Democratic Institutions in Santa Barbara), A. J. Muste (the pacifist and leader of the Fellowship of Reconciliation), and I. F. Stone (the Washington journalist) was sent out in June to a variety of the left publications urging "moral, intellectual, and financial support" for ERAP:

> We want to inform your readers about a critical new development in the American political scene—the emergence of an organization of students and young people who are seriously committed to building a new American left. . . .
>
> The group we are referring to is Students for a Democratic Society, an organization which is about to celebrate its second anniversary by inaugurating a major new program. Their plan aims at creating interracial movements in key Northern and border-state communities around such issues as jobs, housing, and schools. Their strategy, like the strategy of the Southern civil rights movement, is to have students and young people serve as catalysts of protest in these communities. . . .
>
> . . . SDS has succeeded in attracting some of the best and angriest young minds now functioning, and has been able to put these minds to work in socially relevant ways.

ERAP seemed on its way to becoming the most important thing SDS had ever done.

Meanwhile . . .

8

FALL 1963–SPRING 1964

A photograph of the participants in SDS's National Council meeting in Bloomington, Indiana in the fall of 1963 has somehow managed to survive the generally haphazard file keeping and antihistorical inclinations of the organization. It shows what appears to be an ordinary band of young people gathered in front of one of those characterless modern buildings of which Midwestern universities make a specialty, smiling into the sun with a group-picture self-consciousness. The style of that time, the picture makes clear, was collegiate casual, the sartorial counterculture having not quite yet taken hold: hair is short, there are no beards or mustaches or beads or buttons, all the men are wearing ordinary summer shirts, and two of them even have on jackets; the women are in simple knee-length dresses or jeans. The only unusual thing about them is that all but two of them have their arms raised in a clenched-fist salute of the revolutionary left—the two nonconformists are, for their own mysterious reasons, Todd Gitlin, then just getting into his reign as SDS President, and Vernon Grizzard, the Swarthmorean who was to become Vice President the next year. (Paul Booth and Lee Webb, for *their* mysterious reasons, are the only ones signaling with their *left* arms.)

The photograph serves to put the organization in time, to remind one that SDS at this point, three years into the decade, is more potentiality than potency. This is an NC meeting with no more than thirty people—in later years several hundred would be common—reflecting an organization of less than seven hundred paid-up members with maybe that much again on the fringes who are members in spirit if not in card—which even so makes it one of the major groups in student politics, though still without a national image or reputation beyond the campuses. The style of the group is mainstream middle class—all of those in the picture are white, three-quarters of them male—and the very existence of a group picture suggests an outlook not so terribly far advanced beyond that of the campus club. Their spirit is more Gandhian than Guevaran and they see themselves more as proselytizers and propagandizers than organizers and mobilizers; they are, it is true, on the verge of pushing toward an action program (ERAP, authorized at this NC) but it is still formless and impulsive. SDS, in other words, does not yet have the strength to become the shaper and shaker of the student movement.

And yet those incongruous raised fists. They suggest the growing leftward restlessness of SDS, the power-that-might-be, the activism-that-is-to-come. They are, perhaps because of their incongruity, haunting.

While the "new insurgency" forces in SDS were gathering in the fall of 1963 and beginning to point in the direction of the ERAP that was to be, the National Office and those within its orbit continued to wrestle with the ongoing problems of organizational cohesion.

As the fall term began, the first and unmistakable crisis was one of leadership. Todd Gitlin, who was taking over the sizable presidential shoes of Haber and Hayden, had at that point neither the depth nor breadth to fill them. Gitlin, tall, light curly hair, glasses, and an air of *angst* about him, was unquestionably bright and earnest, but he was a bookish sort both by background and by training—his parents were New York City schoolteachers and his world until then had been essentially confined to the Bronx High School of Science (where he was valedictorian) and Harvard University; the challenge of leading an organization that needed to stamp itself vigorously on the campus world was somewhat beyond him. He was, moreover, registered as a graduate student in political science at the University of Michigan (on a scholarship), and though this put him in touch with one of SDS's most active centers (including Hayden, Haber, Davis, Potter, and the McEldowneys, plus the VOICE chapter, still the largest), it also tended to cut him off from both the National Office in New York and the other, less attractive, chapters. Then, too, he was only twenty, had been a member of SDS for less than a year, and was without much political experience; as he remembers it, "I was out of it for a long time. I had become President under such peculiar auspices, you know. I was bewildered. All of my anticipations were right: I wasn't prepared to be President."

Lee Webb, the new National Secretary, who, like Gitlin, had been recruited and pushed for national office by Robb Burlage, proved equally uncomfortable in his new job. The son of working-class New England parents, he had spent his winters in schools— Andover, then Boston University, both on scholarships—and his summers as a laborer, and had never worked in an office before in his life: the routine it demanded chafed, and he kept feeling that he ought to be out *doing* something with his life instead. He quickly discovered in the summer after his election that he had nothing politically in common with either Steve Max or Don McKelvey, with whom he had to work in the NO, and that much of what Burlage had told him about the size and activity of the organization was exaggerated: "That fall there were three or four SDS chapters, *functioning* chapters, and maybe five more paper chapters—which surprised me, because I'd heard that there were twenty or thirty." He says simply, "I was very, very bitter."

So Webb started traveling around the campuses, leaving the office routine behind, and very soon found the campaign of the Swarthmore people in the Chester ghettos a convenient excuse to stay away from New York. The trouble was that there was no one to take up the slack in the NO, and an already rigid office became inefficient as well. Ginger Ryan, who had been hired as a part-time assistant to keep some of the NO moving, wrote plaintively in one letter that October: "Our checking account gets smaller, smaller; none of the typewriters really work; where does money come from?"

In October the official ranks show 610 members, presumably paid up, in thirty-three states from Alaska to Georgia and five foreign countries, and at ninety-nine United States institutions, from Harvard to St. Cloud State College in Minnesota. Nineteen of them have enough members on paper to qualify as chapters (that is, five or more paid-up members of national SDS), but only the largest—Michigan (123), Vassar (26), CCNY (18), Harvard/ Radcliffe (17), Swarthmore (17), and Illinois (14)—have anything resembling a continuing program. Some other unofficial chapters, which had only a few national members, however—Hunter, Johns Hopkins, Oberlin, Rhode Island, Texas, Wayne State—among them managed to get a variety of activities started at their campuses without paying much attention to who was in SDS and who wasn't.

The NO did make one attempt that fall to launch a national program. The VOICE chapter had proposed in September that SDS use the occasion of a visit to Washington by Mme. Ngo Dinh Nhu, sister-in-law of Saigon tyrant Ngo Dinh Diem, for a demonstration against American involvement in Vietnam. *September 1963.* Gitlin heartily approved and invited the Student Peace Union, then reeling under factional disputes and the détente of the previous August's test-ban treaty but still the likeliest student group to care about the war, to join with SDS in staging the demonstration; the SPU, in need of a cause, readily agreed. Together they issued a call which was quite surprisingly prescient in its demands for United States withdrawal and its attack on the puppet regime, the use of chemical warfare, and the waste of American money.

But SDS couldn't rally its forces. Many of the older members felt that foreign affairs of any kind were essentially too remote from the basic interests of students, and this one especially so. Students, they argued, really care only about domestic issues, things like ghettos, the jobless, and organizing the poor. Gitlin, though helpful in planning a local demonstration in Ann Arbor, was unable to put together a national action; Booth, also interested, couldn't even get his friends at Swarthmore to go along; Webb had little interest in the subject. Eventually SDS had to give the real work of organizing the main demonstration over to the SPU and to concentrate instead on getting out some people for local protests.

The demonstration was held in Washington on October 18 and in the event, SDS did make it presence felt. Booth went down from Swarthmore to give a speech at a nighttime rally ("The Vietnamese have paid heavily for our folly. . . . This great nation [must] harness its human resources in behalf of causes which are just"), and two SDSers, Douglas Ireland and Ed Knappman, were arrested along with five other demonstrators for picketing in front of the Washington Press Club, where Mme. Nhu had been invited to speak. At a few campuses around the country joint SDS-SPU demonstrations were held: 400 attended a rally at Michigan, 400 more demonstrated at Wisconsin, 170 people at the University of Texas signed a petition calling for the end of United States aid to Saigon, 50 students picketed in downtown Detroit (one with a sign reading, DOWN WITH THE NHU FRONTIER), and 35 picketed a speech by Mme. Nhu at Howard University. This is not insignificant, given the date; but most of this was done without any real push from the upper levels of the SDS organization, and what might have been a dramatic political event was instead a back-page oddity.

As the ERAP blitz took over more and more of SDS's attention after the December National Council meeting and the whole balance of the organization shifted to ERAP headquarters in Ann Arbor, the organizational crisis in New York became worse. The December meeting tried to stave it off by halting Max's field trips and putting him into the NO full time, but Max found the job more and more burdensome as Webb was occupied elsewhere and political differences with McKelvey grew daily (McKelvey, after all, was calling himself a Maoist, while Max was working with reform Democrats). The December meeting had also decided that the NO should move out of the LID building to new quarters a few blocks down the street at 119 Fifth Avenue, making manifest the growing division between the two organizations which, though patched over successfully now for a year and a half, was still very real and still very acutely felt by the younger half; this meant lost files, delays, and more chaos than usual. Doug Ireland, another of Burlage's protégés, was brought onto the staff in February to restore some order, and he even came with enough money for his first three months' salary; but, though talented, he was both very young and very sickly, and that didn't help much either. The last straw was provided by the Selective Service System, which informed Lee Webb in April that he would be granted Conscientious

Objector status but would have to begin alternative service immediately, and being SDS's National Secretary didn't qualify. (Or perhaps that wasn't the last straw. Shortly thereafter it was discovered that there were mice in the new office.)

All of this was of course compounded by the fact that there wasn't any money. By the end of 1963 the LID was almost $8000 in debt, $5000 of which was incurred in the previous twelve months, when it had an income of $35,106 and expenditures of $40,477; it was meeting its SDS obligations, which it reckoned at about $4000 a year, only fitfully. SDS itself managed to limp along piling up debts slowly enough to forestall utter bankruptcy; through the bulk of the school year it was getting in around $600 a month from dues and contributions, and spending roughly $100 more—and every so often a generous donation would enable it to keep its head above water. Still, by late April, after the Fire Department inspectors ordered SDS to buy an extinguisher for the new office, Max confessed, "We can't afford it." And everyone in the NO was still living at a subsistence level—McKelvey on $28 a week, Max on whatever could be spared or borrowed—a fact which Max made a special point of trying to keep the ERAP people from forgetting; as he wrote wryly to Gitlin, "Think about dough for the office; as Mao says, 'If ghetto agitation means cadre starvation, in the long run the people suffer.' "

In March 1964 a conference of leading leftist student groups was held at Yale University to discuss what action could be taken against the war in Vietnam. A few SDSers participated, unofficially. The conference decided to hold a mass antiwar demonstration in May and to establish a national executive committee to make the arrangements. The majority of the members on the committee were members of the Progressive Labor Movement, a number of them unacknowledged. On May 2, 1964, 1000 students in New York City marched to the United Nations and heard speeches denouncing United States imperialism and the Saigon regime, while other meetings in Boston, San Francisco, and Madison similarly drew students into antiwar protests. Under the guidance of Progressive Labor, a student group named after those protests and called the May 2nd Movement (M2M) was then formed to focus student energy against the Vietnam war in particular and American imperialism in general. Its chairman was Haverford student Russell Stetler, who had been a member of SDS since the previous fall and was not a member of PL; among its chief operatives was Levi Laub, a PL member who had led a group of students to Cuba the previous summer and was planning a second student visit for this summer.

In a conference from April 15 to 18, 1964, the Progressive Labor Movement officially formed itself into the Progressive Labor Party. It claimed a membership of six hundred or so, but the number was not important. The open, hard militancy of the group, their free acknowledgment that they were communists, their heavy emphasis on organizing "Afro-American" workers in the ghettos, their bold student trips to Cuba in defiance of the government and their finger-giving attitude to HUAC upon their return, their imaginative analysis of the war in Vietnam as consistent with an American "imperialism"—these things made it noticed, and attractive, on the college campuses.

A few months later, at the September National Council meeting, SDSers officially took note of the new Progressive Labor Party with some amusement: "a strange and wonderful phenomenon," they called it.

___

And yet, ultimately neither the weaknesses of the leadership nor the inefficiencies of the National Office really seemed to matter that much. For there was now, more than ever before, a considerable strength in the chapters themselves. It was a time of heightened interest on the campuses, and most SDS people, not the types to sit around waiting for the NO to do their organizing for them, went out and did their own recruiting, wrote their own pamphlets, sent their own releases to the student paper, planned their own campus activities. In fact, chapters seemed to be growing all by themselves: at Reed, at Oklahoma, Northeastern, Kansas, Chicago, and even—tough territory for a latecomer to crack—at Berkeley. By April Max was saying, with some wonderment, "Chapters are forming so fast it's getting hard to keep up with it," and by the end of the 1963–64 school year there were twenty-nine honest-to-goodness chapters,* the membership had grown to al-

*Baltimore At-large, Berkeley, Brandeis, Chicago, CCNY, Delta State, Harvard/ Radcliffe, Hunter, Illinois, Kalamazoo, Kansas, Louisville, Michigan, Michigan State, New School, Northeastern, North Texas State, Oberlin, Oklahoma, Reed, Rhode Island, Rutgers, Swarthmore, Texas, Vassar, University of Washington, Wayne State, Wilson, Wisconsin. The strongest were said to be those at Illinois, Michigan, Rhode Island, Swarthmore, and Texas.

most a thousand, and the regular mailing list had fifteen hundred names. All proof that forceful energies in the organization were flowing from the bottom up.

What is at work, obviously, is the growing leftward spirit of the studentry, of which SDS, by its past as much as its present, is a beneficiary. Not by accident, during this same year there are also formed, in addition to the anti-war M2M, the PL-run Student Committee for Travel to Cuba, the reformist- and Communist Party-oriented W. E. B. DuBois Clubs, the Free Speech Movement at Berkeley, the Southern Student Organizing Committee (which will become affiliated with SDS), and the groups involved in Mississippi Summer. Amid all this SDS attracts because it is an established organization, it is a white outfit at a time of a growing black-power trend in SNCC, and it is (in both style and theory) part of the New Left and therefore free of the "ideological hang-ups" of M2M and the DuBois Clubs.

It takes no very special perception to discover the reasons for this leftward swing. In September 1963 four little black girls were blown to pieces in a dynamite blast of the Sixteenth Street Baptist Church in Birmingham, Alabama, signaling the utter unregener-acy of the South. In November John Kennedy, in whom many had placed lingering hopes in spite of themselves, was assassinated, and his alleged assassin was himself murdered: bloody and violent symbols of a bloody and violent country. He was followed into office by Lyndon Johnson, acknowledged by even his admirers to be the most glaring example of back-scratching, wheeler-dealing, arm-twisting corrupt Senate politics, and a rather boorish and ill-spoken Texas to boot. The aftermath of the Kennedy death produced a ream of different explanations, none of them terribly flattering to the Establishment and the most convincing of which suggested the complicity of the CIA, the Dallas police force, and Lyndon Johnson himself. The Vietnam maw had drawn to it enough soldiers—16,000 by mid-1964—to make it a national issue (Goldwater wants to send more, with nuclear warheads, Johnson promises that American boys won't fight an Asian war) and a depressing example of American adventurism, at the very least. The hopes of Mississippi Summer—and the dreams of peaceful change—were riddled in June 1964 by the blatant murders of SNCC workers James Chaney, Andrew Goodman, and Michael

Schwerner by law officers who clearly would never be punished. And then in Atlantic City, where the Democrats met in convention in August, the SNCC-inspired Mississippi Freedom Democratic Party, which expected to replace the racist official party delegation, was refused its seats and offered the "compromise" of sitting two at-large delegates instead; this compromise was made all the more distasteful by the fact that many of the most helpful supporters of the MFDP within the liberal community—people like the ADA's Joseph Rauh, upcoming politico Al Lowenstein, Martin Luther King, and LIDers Bayard Rustin and Tom Kahn —all urged its acceptance.

The wonder, really, is that *more* students didn't turn leftward *sooner.*

Now SDS itself at this point—mid-1964—was in certain ways not terribly far left. It did not have the imperialist analysis or the specifically anticapitalist stance of groups like M2M and the Young Socialist Alliance (the youth group of the Trotskyist Socialist Workers Party). It was not willing to declare itself socialist, though it had a number of people who thought of themselves that way and that was the clear if unstated implication of parts of both *The Port Huron Statement* and *America and the New Era.* (In May, Jim Williams complained, "In SDS . . . socialism is still 'the forbidden word.' Why is this when most of its leaders are socialists? Whom are we trying to fool?") It was not even ready yet to give up its basic sense that the institutions of the country, though their imperfections were glaring, were capable of reform, provided the citizens worked long and hard enough to bring that about. What SDS did have, however, was an analysis more in keeping with its time—the sense of making connections, of participatory democracy, of new insurgencies, of living one's life so that it did not contradict one's beliefs—that spoke to the student activists far better than the apparently discredited doctrines of the thirties. It had a sense of *moral* politics, of direct action, of putting bodies on the line, that made it more of an authentically left organization than the Communists with their popular-front politics, or the Progressive Laborites with their sectarian zeal.

Moreover, throughout the spring SDS made itself felt on the

campuses in concrete ways. Its *Bulletin,* several dozen mimeographed pages giving news of student activities and reports of
chapter goings-on, was appearing now practically every month
and reaching a primary audience of more than two thousand. The
literature list, probably the biggest of any student organization
and as sizable as any political group's, had grown to no fewer than
ninety-two papers and pamphlets (forty-nine by SDSers) on every
conceivable social or political issue, and the distribution of these
writings by SDS chapters, by other political clubs, even by teachers who assigned them to their classes, spread the organization's
reputation.* Gitlin began to grow into his job as the months went
on—he was "totally transformed," Flacks noted in February—
and began traveling, speaking, making contacts, visiting chapters;
in fact, as one SDSer is supposed to have put it, commenting on
Gitlin's renewed activity on the campuses and Hayden's in ERAP,
"Tom and Todd wait for no man." And a certain aura of solidity
and fashion accrued to the organization with increased support
from respected adults, such as the form letter which Harold Taylor and David Riesman sent out to academic and liberal circles on
May 1 with phrases like "SDS . . . is one of the important and
productive student groups" and "We respect the seriousness and
quality of their political analysis."

And at the campus level, SDS chapters and individuals
worked to make themselves felt. Often SDSers would join with
ongoing single-issue groups in support of particular actions relating to race, peace, elections, poverty, unions, indeed almost any
cause, liberal or not. One especially popular cause of the time was
the fight against bans on left-wing speakers on college campuses,
those relics from McCarthy days still in force at a remarkable
number of universities, particularly the state-supported ones; by
the simple act of inviting a Communist to speak, SDS chapters
could bring to campus attention a span of important issues having
to do with free speech, university authoritarianism, the univer-

---

*SDS becomes known, among other things, as the *"writingest"* organization
around, and the prolificity is, considering the obstacles, amazing. Some found the
verbiage too academic and too remote—SNCC people, for example, complained
that nobody could actually *read* these things and tended to groan at the sight
of them—but on the campuses, among intellectual youths searching for just this
kind of percolated knowledge, the impact was considerable.

sity's relation to political forces in the state, anti-Communism and the Cold War, and the nature of the American political system. SDSers used all kinds of recruiting and educational tools, one of the best proving to be debates with right-wingers, usually members of the Young Americans for Freedom who appeared with increasing frequency on the college scene, and who, one SDSer reported, "are usually the best recruiters to our cause." Chapters also frequently established study groups to do research on local problems like housing, discrimination, and poverty, and held meetings and seminars and discussion groups to try to get the growing numbers of disaffected students to make connections between national events, to put across the SDS vision, and ultimately to radicalize them.

All this produced a new strength in SDS that, for some, was almost euphoric. Dick Flacks, not normally given to elation, wrote that spring:

> We are in a new state. . . . It is tremendously exciting—one sign of it is that no one person can actually keep up with everything which is going on . . . another sign is the extent to which people are willing to commit themselves and the number and quality of the people who are attracted.
> "The times they are a-changing" and we are a part of it.

SDS's campus resurgence was assisted around the same time by the happy accident of selecting, for the first time, a National Secretary of surpassing organizational talents. After Webb's departure in March, Steve Max filled in as Acting National Secretary, but, as suggested, with something less than total success; the top people began looking everywhere for someone to replace him. At the April NC, they found Charles Clark Kissinger.

Clark Kissinger had been a student at Shimer College, in Illinois, transferred to the University of Chicago, where he majored in math and was active in starting the campus political party there, and after graduation in 1960 went on to work for an M.A. at Wisconsin, where he first joined SDS. When tapped for National Secretary, a job of limitless hours for the return of $75 a week, he was twenty-four, married, had a child, and was teaching math at Mundelein College, a small Catholic women's school in Chicago. From the sublime to the ridiculous.

Kissinger—high forehead, thin face, short-cropped hair, regular features—looked like a smooth and efficient administrator; he was. He kept the National Office intact during its most arduous year, and (with the considerable help of a new Assistant National Secretary, Helen Garvy) he got the letters out, the literature mailed, the books balanced, the files sorted, and the typewriters working, all at the same time. Arriving in New York in June, the first thing he did was empty out the office of so much trash that he had to pay $5 to have it carted away. He then got in two new file cabinets and had the floor swept; the next month he promoted a sickly second-hand air conditioner, some new chairs, and—the embourgeoisification is complete—a water fountain. He got new letterheads and membership cards printed up, and had a stamp made, the first SDS ever had, reading FILE COPY   DO NOT REMOVE   STUDENTS FOR A DEMOCRATIC SOCIETY. He initiated regular weekly mailings of two or three single-spaced pages to the hundred or so key people on the worklist, wrote them, and saw that they were sent out. He kept the bank account in order to the penny, instituted a new system of unified account-keeping for all the parts of the organization, and imported the extraordinary concept, heretofore unheard of around SDS, of "double-entry bookkeeping."

It is a mark of Kissinger's shrewdness that as one of his initial tasks he took it upon himself to try to establish smoother relations with the LID, which despite its own mounting debts (more than $10,000 worth by mid-1964), was after all still paying almost $400 a month to keep SDS going. He wrote polite self-introductory letters to Board Chairman Nathaniel Minkoff and Student Activities Committee head Emanuel Muravchik, both of which promised closer cooperation and communication with the LID. In June he told Tom Kahn, the young YPSLite who had just become Executive Secretary in place of Vera Rony, that he was "definitely interested" in distributing Kahn's new pamphlet, "The Economics of Equality," to SDS's full mailing list; in August he formally applied for admission to the LID, enclosing a membership check for $5. In drawing up the new SDS letterheads, he made sure that the phrase "The Student Department of the League for Industrial Democracy," actually appeared—this last had become a sore point with the LID since most of the literature going out of the office had somehow, Freudianly, forgotten to mention this relationship. Minkoff was snowed: "I should like to see," he tells Kissinger, "more of this spirit of affiliation and cooperation show."

But Kissinger was more than an automaton: he took the job in large part because he felt strongly that chapter organizing should be an essential balance in the organization to the ERAP emphasis and he saw an efficient NO as being important for this. As he said in his report to the membership:

> Perhaps the central preoccupation of the National Staff this summer is with preparations for the fall. We are in the process of creating a chapter organizing manual and stockpiling literature for distribution to chapters on campuses during the first few weeks of the fall semester. . . . In general, our potential is enormous—we have only to make the effort to carry our analysis and program to the American student. . . . Our task is now avoiding the temptation to "take one generation of campus leadership and . . . run!" We must instead look toward building the campus base as the wellspring of our student movement.

Here, then, was the other side of the tension in SDS: the strength and movement of the chapters. Though there was no question that the dynamic of the year had been ERAP, there was activity too within the universities. Sometimes it took the form of university-reform projects—one of which, a tentative program called the United States University Reform Project (USURP) was in fact mandated by the December 1963 National Council but came to naught; and sometimes the form of simple chapter-building, which Max and McKelvey especially emphasized and the latter put eloquently in a memo to the membership in January:

> We have a special position (which our analysis of society makes even more potentially effective) as people who can affect and attract college and university (and high school) students with two views in mind: the planting in their minds of seeds of doubt and thought which will bear fruit in their changing attitudes and actions with respect to social issues; the direction of an understandably smaller

group of students towards active involvement in social change, after they graduate and throughout their lives. *The actual work for social change* [i.e., ERAP] *must be subordinate to those two goals.*

This tension will continue to grow—not just for the next few months but for the entire life of the organization. The reason is simple. The inescapable problem was that *America had no left,* and for the activist student generation the essential quandary was: Is the job of students to build that left, to shuck their student robes and go into the world, building allies where they can, taking their message to anyone who will listen before it all collapses; or, is it rather to build the student part of this left, assuming that somehow the remainder will get built by those elsewhere reacting to their own felt needs, to stay behind the ivy walls to coalesce those who are known instead of presuming to proselytize those who are distant? Once aware, as the SDSers were by now, of how immense a task and yet how necessary to create that left, how wrenching then must be this question. Many, of whom the ERAPers are only part, felt that they must shoulder the whole burden themselves, that nobody gives a damn about students anyway—even if all the students were to lay down their books tomorrow, no one would notice—that the poor, or the working class, or the blacks (or all three) must be drawn in for any left to succeed, and if students don't do it, who will? Others, including the growing number of still-collegiate SDSers, answered that students (and sympathetic professors) are and can be a new force in society, with their own power to effect changes simply by acting on their own needs, that when the time comes for a united left in the nation the students had better have gotten their own constituency—say, a student union?—together; and that if the left is ever to come it will move —it will explode—from the campuses outward. The problem was made only more complicated by the fact of student transience, and the organizational transience of a student movement: those who have graduated, or dropped out, or forsaken higher education, and those who believed with Potter that the universities were hand-maidens of the corrupt society, tended to feel that the campuses were too limited and that it was the wider left that must be created; those who were still in school, or heading there, or working in the academy, and those who believed with the Port Huronites that universities were centers for social insurgency, tended to feel that the ghettos and the factories were too impenetrable and that it was the student left that must be made.

Consciously or subliminally, it was this quite monumental question that SDSers wrestled with; haltingly and yet with youthful recklessness, it was this that SDS as an organization tried to answer.

9

ERAP:
SUMMER 1964-SUMMER 1965

These are the voices of ERAP.

Up in the morning at 8 o'clock, to the office at 9, try to make a whole bunch of calls, go to people's houses, the people who've come into the office, setting up meetings for the night—that's the life style, *every single* day. . . . Nobody drank, I can't remember one kid having a bottle of beer that whole summer; we could have had the money, money wouldn't have been a problem—like, there was always enough money for Coke. . . . *No*body knew a thing about drugs, drugs were for nuts. No liquor, no drugs, no sex, and I think that was true like in all the projects. In a sense that summer was like the expression of a very significant quality of that generation—almost monk-like, or ascetic, or something like that. Because the whole ethic of community organizing was on the basis of those kinds of principles, you know: you *work.*

That's Lee Webb talking, describing the summer of 1964 with the JOIN project in Chicago.

Come you ladies and you gentlemen and listen to my song;
Tell it to you right but you may take it wrong;
I know you're busy, but take a little rest;
It's all about the organizers, work for SDS;
It's a hard time in the North, working for the SDS.

Oh, well, you go to your block and you work all day;
Til way after dark but you get no pay;
You talk about the meeting, the people say they know;

> You come to the meeting and three or four show;
> It's a hard time in the North, working for the SDS.
>
> You go back to the block and you talk some more;
> You're knocking on a door, it's on the second floor;
> Lady says who's there and who you looking for;
> I ain't got time, slip it under the door;
> It's a hard time in the North, working for the SDS.

That's a song (to the tune of "Penny's Farm") made up at the Newark Community Union Project (NCUP, pronounced *en*-cup).

> I went back to Louisville and struggled along with our ERAP project. We had an absolute *loon* who was running it, and there were a whole lot of people wandering around who were rejects from various groups, they were constantly shunted about. We limped along, we organized some street gangs, some young black guys, but we never *did* organize the unemployed. . . . It was peanut-butter and jelly, all those things. There were great competitions among ERAP projects to see which project could live cheaper than anyone else, and I think one week we *won,* not 'cause we were trying so hard, just 'cause there was about thirty dollars that week and that had to feed a dozen people or so.

That's Jim Williams, the University of Louisville SDSer, on the Louisville project.

> A primary difficulty is preventing the agents of the bourgeoisie from turning off our gas.

That's Charlie Smith, writing to the NO from the Baltimore ERAP project.

> The things SDS has done in Newark are valuable for our volunteers to be exposed to. We want to take advantage of their experience.

That's Frank Mankiewicz, then director of the Latin American operation of the Peace Corps, talking about NCUP.

> An organizer can spend two or more hours with a single individual. Through hundreds of conversations, slowly, clusters of unemployed contacts are made and identified on city maps. One person in a large unemployment area is approached about having a meeting: he agrees, but hasn't the time to contact neighbors. So the JOIN worker calls every nearby unemployed by phone or sees them in person. Thirty people are contacted; eight turn out. One is a racist,

but his arguments get put down by the group. One (maybe) is willing
to work and has some sense of what needs to be done. The others
go round and round on their personal troubles. The process is slow.

That's Rennie Davis, reporting on what it was like during the first
ERAP summer in the *SDS Bulletin*.

The organizer spends hours and hours in the community, listening
to people, drawing out their own ideas, rejecting their tendency to
depend on him for solutions. Meetings are organized at which people with no "connections" can be given a chance to talk and work
out problems together—usually for the first time. All this means
fostering in *everyone* that sense of decision-making power which
American society works to destroy. Only in this way can a movement be built which the Establishment can neither buy off nor
manage, a movement too vital ever to become a small clique of
spokesmen.

And that's Tom Hayden, writing in *Dissent* in 1965 on an old
dream, "the interracial movement of the poor."

ERAP was many things. When it began, during the summer
of 1964, it was already varied, but as it grew it sent out tendrils,
gathered new ideas, tried different tactics, and by the end, in late
1965, it was absolutely protean. Describing it is difficult.

The first ten projects managed to last through the first summer, and by then the difficulties of community organizing were
clear enough. There were the basic human problems that arise
whenever a dozen or two young people who may not have known
each other well try to live together, for an extended period, without any money or luxuries to cushion their contact, without much
in the way of sleep or diversion, driven by a sense of having to
accomplish something but seeing few victories. There were the
errors made through ignorance: of the cities they were going into
—Hayden and NCUP thought, for example, they'd be going to a
racially mixed area where the big problem was jobs, and they
found themselves in a black area where the concern was for better
housing; of the people they were living among, who were not
simply middle-class people with less money but startlingly and,
sometimes, uncomfortably different; and of the workings of a
foreign world of welfare, unemployment laws, city-run housing,

numbers, street violence, police harassment. There were the constant pressures from local establishments—all the projects were redbaited and beatnik-baited by city halls and local papers, and in the course of their existence countless arrests, raids, harassments, badgerings, and false accusations were made. (Hayden—short, dark—was once arrested in Newark on charges so preposterous that the chief witness for the prosecution pointed instead to Carl Wittman—tall, blond—as the perpetrator, and in Chicago the JOIN staffers were once arrested on the charge of keeping a "disorderly house" because men and women lived together there.)*

And then, of course, there was the insurmountable problem that the economy wasn't collapsing the way SDS had predicted it would; no depression was throwing people out of work to join an angry army of the urban unemployed. "Just as we got to Chicago," Lee Webb remembers, "lines at the unemployment compensation center started to get shorter." An economic boom period was beginning, to be accelerated by Vietnam expenditures, and Jobs Or Income Now was just not the issue around which people could be organized. All of the unemployment-directed JOIN projects (Chicago, Baltimore, Philadelphia) faltered, while the two projects (Newark and Cleveland) that tried to operate on *any* enunciated grievances of the community, from garbage collection to schools (that is, the multi-issue approach that Hayden and Wittman had put forth in "An Interracial Movement of the Poor?"), fared far better. For a while during the summer a running argument went on between the two approaches—Gitlin dubbed it the "GROIN-JOIN" debate, Garbage Removal Or Income Now *vs.* Jobs Or Income Now—but by the fall it was clear that JOIN would have to be altered, and all the projects that continued turned to the GROIN approach.

With problems, tensions, frustrations such as these, ERAP had to retrench. By the end of the 1964 summer Trenton, Louisville, and Hazard were dropped; Boston was given over to PREP; and Philadelphia and Chester were allowed to wither and drift

---

*Not only local establishments: in August 1964 Carl Wittman, with some trace of pride, reported a visit to NCUP from an agent of the Federal Bureau of Investigation, the first known FBI-SDS meeting in what was to be a close and steady relationship over the next five years.

into extinction by themselves. Baltimore and Chicago switched their emphasis to GROIN, and with Cleveland and Newark became the kernel of the ERAP operation as it headed into the new school year.

Despite setbacks, the ERAPers felt they had made considerable strides over the summer. Much had been learned: how to approach a strange neighborhood, how to live on forty-two cents a day, how to run meetings so that ordinary people are not bewildered, how to get people in a community to think about the community for a change. Much had been accomplished: lines were opened to people in the bureaucracy (unemployment compensation offices, welfare bureaus, city housing officials) who had never listened much to the poor before, small battles were won against red tape, landlords, police. In Cleveland, ERAPers were able to organize a group of poor white women into a Citizens United For Adequate Welfare, which in turn got through a free lunch program for poor children in the city schools; in Newark, NCUP managed to generate enough pressure to get a play street established, improve garbage collection somewhat, and force housing improvements out of landlords; in Baltimore, small victories were won against the Department of Public Welfare; in Chicago, like victories against the unemployment offices. This was not, of course, what ERAP had set out so grandiosely to do, and as Rennie Davis confessed at the end of the summer, "No project succeeded in giving life to our slogan, 'an interracial movement of the poor,' and certainly none 'organized a community.' " But what had been done was enough to convince a handful of people to stay on at each project after the summer and to press on during the winter. They had no illusions about the enormity of the job, and they knew they couldn't build a movement for social change in a few months.

In the summer of 1964, the Progressive Labor Party, then with perhaps six hundred members, was organizing in the slums of Harlem in New York City. It did not establish a permanent project; rather, it drew blacks into Marxist study groups and meetings to air their grievances against the city, and it led picket lines against "police brutality" and other local issues.

On July 18, 1964, Harlem blacks began an urban revolt over

the fatal shooting of a fifteen-year-old black boy by a white policeman, which the PLP newspaper, *Challenge,* supported editorially:
"There is no lawful government in this country today. Only a
revolution will establish one. If that is 'civil rebellion' let us make
the most of it." Bill Epton, a PLP organizer, and black, is reported
to have told a Harlem crowd: "We will not be fully free until we
smash this state completely . . . in that process, we're going to have
to kill a lot of cops, a lot of these judges, and we'll have to go up
against their army."

On August 5, Epton was indicted for "criminal anarchy" and
for advocating "the overthrow of the government of the state of
New York by force and violence." On December 20, 1965, after
a year of legal maneuverings, Epton was found guilty, largely on
the evidence of a police informer, of conspiring to overthrow the
government and conspiring to riot, and sent to jail. Some thirty
other members of PLP were subpoenaed by the New York Grand
Jury, and more than ten of them, including a City College student,
were convicted of contempt.

By the time of the December National Council, the ERAPers
knew that things were going badly, but also knew that they needed
more time and they managed to convince the rest of the organization that everything was fine—certain setbacks here and there, but
four projects at least were going ahead, with maybe fifty full-time
people in them, and who knew how many more might start before
next summer? Max and Williams tried to point out that it didn't
look as if an awful lot of *organizing* was going on—not many of
the community people seemed to be actually *involved* in the projects, doing the work along with the students—but those two had
just come from a bad experience with the Political Education
Project that fall, and no one paid much attention to them. In truth,
ERAP had failed noticeably in this respect—by its own estimates,
no more than thirty indigenous people in Newark had joined
NCUP and participated regularly in its meetings, and Cleveland
had twenty, Chicago maybe ten, and Baltimore only five—but the
ERAPers tried to make as little of this as possible.

Still, the ERAPers couldn't fool themselves, and the ERAP
meeting early in January 1965 after the National Council was over
was an agonizing period of self-questioning stretched over eight
days and nights. They all conceded that no interracial movement

of the poor was going to emerge in any foreseeable future, it proving hard enough to arrange even a uniracial Tuesday night meeting, and as for the notion of radicalizing the poor and launching them on a "revolutionary trajectory," well, that was hardly spoken of at all. The failure of ends caused people to concentrate on the inadequacies of their means, and whole days of the ERAP conference were given over to worried questioning. Do we have to have leaders at all? Don't leaders, by definition, manipulate, and aren't we fundamentally against manipulating? But aren't we all manipulating, just by being in the projects? Suppose you convince a man to come to a meeting—isn't that manipulating him? Isn't ghetto organizing an expression of snobbery, of paternalism? Would we be in the ghetto at all if we didn't think we had some superior wisdom which we needed to give to these people? Isn't that simply trying to co-opt these people into our way of doing things, our kind of movement?

There was no escape from the net of these questions, and the more the ERAPers struggled the more they became entangled. The young organizers were trying to find some way to build up the movement that would not violate its principles at the same time, but nothing in their summer's experience had really proved successful in that. "The whole thing was very morose," Paul Booth recalls. Ultimately the organizers came to decide that they should just continue doing what they were doing *for its own sake,* unencumbered by theory or explanation or questioning: we can't second-guess the future, let us go on doing what we know we should do. This conclusion was, by no coincidence, the same kind of thing the SNCC organizers had also decided, and it was pressed upon the meeting by SNCC leader Ivanhoe Donaldson and a number of other SNCC people in attendance. One report afterward said:

> SNCC organizers were present at the staff meeting and they managed to impress ERAP with the image of an organizer who never organized, who by his simple presence was the mystical medium for the spontaneous expression of the "people." The staff meeting ended in exhaustion, with a faith that the spirit would decide, that an invisible hand would enable all to be resolved if honesty prevailed.

Or, as they sang it around SNCC, "Do What the Spirit Say Do"—all very well for the psyche, but not much help in organizing.

ERAP as 1965 began was at a low point. The staff people were now continuing to live in the ghetto more because there was no place else in the society to go than because they thought they were doing anything significant in the way of changing it. "By the winter of 1965," says Richie Rothstein, a central figure in the Chicago project, "if you asked most ERAP organizers what they were attempting, they would simply have answered, 'to build a movement.' " Nothing more precise.

The isolation of the projects grew as the ERAPers themselves grew inward. ERAP in fact soon came to regard itself as pretty much separate from SDS, the projects feeling their primary responsibility not to the campus constituency but to the individual communities. This divarication was intensified by the decision of the January ERAP conference to abandon the national headquarters and to abolish leaders like Rennie Davis who were regarded as superfluous in a movement that sought none at all. Davis made one final trip as national director, enticed $5000 out of the Rabinowitz Foundation in New York to keep the projects going through one more summer, and then dismantled the operation in Ann Arbor; he went to Chicago to live with the JOIN project, where he would continue to work for the next two years. In March ERAP was officially abandoned as a national organization, and henceforth individual projects went off without central direction or assistance of any kind: no two ERAP organizing staffs even sat down to compare notes from that time on. In theory this seemed sensible enough, since no two projects were alike and an isolated headquarters sending out newsletters or setting up conferences didn't do much to strengthen them. But later many came to feel that the national framework had at least prevented the projects from total isolation; as Rothstein put it:

> . . . in isolation, each project came to develop an exaggerated sense of its own importance. Not feeling itself to be part of an experimental tactically variegated movement, each project acted as though it bore the burden of history on its shoulders alone. . . . How could

a project experiment with factory organizing, or even with leadership training in such a context? . . . In the absence of a broader
structure, with the burden of movement-building borne subjectively
by each project, experiments could not be risked.

SDS's antiwar march on Washington in the spring of 1965,
though it drew its impetus from the campus, served to revivify
ERAP for the summer. New people heard about the organization
and wanted to do something with it over the summer; students
who felt the war was the all-important issue thought that ERAP
was a way to get ghetto people marching against it; and a number
of previously quiescent students, now suddenly angry over Vietnam, wanted something to do other than the usual "summer job."
New ERAPs were started all over: in Hoboken, in New Haven
(where SDSer John Froines, later of the Chicago Eight, worked),
New Brunswick, Oakland, San Francisco, Roxbury, Massachusetts, Champaign, Illinois, and even in Cairo, Illinois, a city which
the ERAPers had previously dismissed. But now there was no
central direction—each project was started on local impetus, organized where it wanted to, picked up the cause it found best. More
existential now, in the SDS tradition, the organizers would simply
go into a poor area and listen for a while, seek out the grievances
and try to organize around them: no more prefabricated theories,
or hunches masquerading as analyses.

Three times as many people worked in projects this summer
as the summer before, more than four hundred in all. Their life
styles were somewhat different from those of the previous summer. Communal living—men and women sharing the same apartment—was now accepted (the unusual success of black-white
relations among the Cleveland organizers was laid specifically to
that closeness), not least because it turned out to be cheaper all
around. Marijuana was beginning to be smoked—still with dire
worries about its illegality—though nothing stronger was used.
Some slackening of the previous summer's monastic isolation occurred, with unspoken disapproval from the veterans: 1965 NCUP
summer people would take off weekends and head for New York,
parties, friends, sleep, relaxation, a different world, something that
had not happened the summer before. But the essential asceticism
remained the same; Andrew Kopkind, then writing for the *New*

Republic, pictured NCUP that summer as "a wrenching experience":

> Hardly anyone on the "outside" can image the completeness of [the students'] transformation, or the depth of their commitment. They are not down there for a visit in the slums. They are part of the slums, a kind of lay-brotherhood, or worker priests, except that they have no dogma to sell. They get no salary; they live on a subsistence allowance that the project as a whole uses for rent and food. Most of the time they are broke. . . . Newark project workers have to call "friends in the suburbs" every so often for $5 or $10, so the necessities of life can continue. . . . They eat a spartan diet of one-and-a-half meals a day, consisting mainly of powdered milk and large quantities of peanut butter and jelly, which seems to be the SDS staple. Occasionally they cadge much more appetizing (and, presumably, more nourishing) meals from their poor local friends.*

But the 1965 ERAP people found the same problems their predecessors had—the thirteen projects at the start of the summer dwindled to nine, then seven, and by the late fall only five (Baltimore, Cleveland, Chicago, Newark, and Oakland) were left. Some of the would-be organizers left in frustration, some had turned instead to Vietnam activities, and the majority soon decided to return to school: even that seemed better, and less frustrating, than trying to organize the ghettos. One project worker recalls:

> The [SDS] kids who worked there . . . they didn't get along at all well, and there were a lot of feuds. I got the impression that a lot of that was because they had been so completely unsuccessful. . . . Personal feuds—somebody wouldn't wash the dishes. They never washed the dishes. A lot of them lived together in one apartment which was a bad deal—much too close, much too filthy. . . . They had gotten very discouraged and started being hesitant about going out and working. They would sleep late hours and waste a lot of time, and then they really felt bad because, "What the hell are we doing here?"

*This was one of the earliest articles written about SDS in a national magazine and it certainly helped launch it on the public with a favorable image; the NO, not unhappily, referred to it privately as "a snow job." (Kissinger memo, July 31, 1965.)

The isolated, difficult world of the ERAP projects of this summer
—and of later projects that would be started from time to time—
is suggested by this account of organizing in a little Appalachian
town in Pennsylvania called Bellefonte, where a group of Penn
State SDSers set up a project in the summer of 1967:

> The organizers were students . . . well-versed in theory . . . organiz-
> ing around unemployment, welfare and corruption in the borough
> administration while learning how to modify the tactics developed
> by urban projects to fit the needs of semi-rural Appalachia. But
> though theory prepared them for the real problems, nothing in their
> middle-class lives and training had prepared them for the real peo-
> ple. As a result, they were never able to make their actions conform
> to their analysis. . . .
>
> The students decided to combine communal living quarters
> and an office in a three-story house. Their decision rested on the
> assumption that they would be working with adults. . . . But the first
> people to be attracted to the house were not adults but little kids
> "who came to be around us as friends in an atmosphere that was
> devoid of authoritarian restrictions." . . . The organizers thought
> that the project's "open door policy" would reach out to the parents
> through their kids and establish a good relationship with the adult
> community. Instead, the older brothers and older friends of the
> original kids started coming in through the open door. These older
> kids were veterans of the reformatory. . . .
>
> As the organizers became more interested in these kids, the
> open door began to make trouble. First the neighbors began to talk.
> They were hostile to the house for harboring the town's troublemak-
> ers. And they began to gossip about the hours that the women
> associated with the project were keeping at the house. The students
> were shocked to find the low-income people they had come to work
> with identifying so fully with "bourgeois" values. But they realized
> that they had to make a decision: either maintain their original
> vision of organizing adults and abandon the kids who were coming
> to the house; or work with the kids and alienate the welfare recipi-
> ents. They decided to stick with the kids.
>
> The open door now created a new set of difficulties. The organ-
> izers had never made their purpose in Bellefonte clear to the kids.
> As a result, the kids saw the house simply as a place that was always
> available for a party—and they partied continually. . . . The situa-
> tion became a nightmarish cycle. The organizers would return from
> the twelve-hour shifts they worked to an ongoing beer party. The

combination of work and party exhausted them so that they couldn't think straight, let alone talk the problem through. And silence gave consent to yet another round of parties. Toward the end it was impossible even to sleep at night. . . .

To complete the project's rout, personal hang-ups were woven into political problems. In common with most new leftists, the organizers were committed to developing close personal relationships as a basis for effective work. They held frequent "soul sessions," where they talked frankly and personally about the problems the project faced. Unfortunately, friction which had existed before the students moved to Bellefonte was aggravated by the tension and closeness of the project. Because these old quarrels harmed the project the group tried to resolve them at their meetings. Instead, the people involved began to use the soul sessions as a cover for personal attacks. The bad feeling generated would have been enough in itself to cripple the project.

In August the Bellefonte project disbanded.

By the end of the summer of 1965, ERAP had proven itself to be a failure. Like the Narodniki before them, ERAPers found "the people" harder to organize than they had imagined and, like them, they tended to feel that some kind of increased militance and direct confrontation would be necessary to effect real change. Of the five projects left at the end of 1965, Oakland soon disappeared, and Cleveland and Baltimore quietly withered in the following year. Chicago and Newark lasted into 1967, but their permutations took them almost totally away from SDS and into the engulfing life of the community, and only a few of the original student organizers stuck it out. Hayden, Wittman, Steve Block, and two vital women, Corinna Fales and Carol Glassman, held on in Newark; Davis, Rothstein, Gitlin, Mike James, Casey Hayden, and one or two others in Chicago. With the exception of a few local attempts like a Minneapolis Community Union Project in 1966 and the Bellefonte project in 1967—and even these were abandoned after the summer of 1967—ERAP ceased to have any major effect on SDS after 1965.

The reasons for ERAP's failure were roughly three.

First, ERAP was never able to shake off the middle-class beliefs and expectations it started with. The ERAPers' postscarcity consciousness ran smack up against the scarcity reality, and the collision was painful. The students expected the poor to be natively intelligent, informed, angry at the circumstances of their lives, prepared to unite against a common enemy—"they sometimes expect the poor to act out the moral values of the middleclass radical who has come to the slum," as Michael Harrington tellingly wrote—and instead they found the poor (for reasons not of their own making, of course) ignorant, passive, atomized and fragmented, and with a whole set of quite different values. Moreover, the students expected the idea of community organizations to be a great deal more powerful and attractive than it was; Nick Egleson, working in the Hoboken project in the summer of 1965,* put it this way:

> We have [gained] a greater respect for people's perception of their own surroundings. If they don't think an organization will get them anywhere, it is not always because, as we thought in the past, they have no experience with community organization, but sometimes it is because they have had just that experience and sometimes it is because they perceive the smallness of the organization compared to the enormity of the problem much better than we, the hopeful organizers, can allow ourselves to do.

Then, too, the organizers brought a good deal of middle-class guilt with them into the ghetto, not simply from having privileged positions, or money, or an education, but from running away from their own real and palpable grievances, which at this point in time seemed illegitimate to acknowledge openly (it would take a few years before students could admit that they too felt trod upon by the society, in ways maybe not as obvious but just as pervasive as those used on the poor). "ERAP," Todd Gitlin has written, "was built on guilt. . . . Guilt and its counterpart, shame, are healthy and necessary antidotes to privilege, but the antidote taken in large doses becomes poisonous."

Second, ERAP never resolved the contradictions between wanting fundamentally to change the nature of the state and

---

*This project, with Helen Garvy, Vernon Grizzard, Jill Hamberg, Carl Wittman, and others, was an initial attempt of SDSers to work in factory jobs to organize among blue-collar workers; this kind of organizing would later, under PL auspices, become a full-scale summer program known as the "work-in."

building its projects around all the shoddy instruments of that state. Whether JOIN or GROIN, the projects sought to *improve* the governmental services of their neighborhoods, break the red tape at the unemployment center, force the traffic department to put up a light, see to it that welfare checks arrived when they should—and then the organizers would go home at night and talk about "transforming the system," "building alternative institutions," and "revolutionary potential." ERAP, for all the talk, did not build *parallel* structures out of its projects, it built *parasite* structures, which had to live off the crumbs of the Establishment and soon determined their failure or success according to how many crumbs they got. The projects were caught in the very machinery *America and the New Era* had warned them about: "a politics of adjustment" whose "principle function is a mediating, rationalizing and managerial one" so as "to manipulate and control conflict" and "prevent popular upsurge." In spite of themselves, ERAPers were manipulated and handled by the state they had set out to change.

Third, ERAP was never able to escape the fact that the poor are not "the agents of change" in American society, whether there be massive unemployment or not. The poor, as the ERAPers found out to their sorrow, want leaders, they do not want to lead; the poor are myth-ridden, enervated, cynical, and historically the least likely to rebel; the poor are powerless, without even that small threat of being able to withdraw their bodies that workingmen and labor unions have, and at best they can only embarrass or discomfort, not threaten, the powers that be. After more than a year in the Newark ghetto Tom Hayden came to acknowledge this:

> Poor people know they are victimized from every direction. The facts of life always break through to expose the distance between American ideals and personal realities. This kind of knowledge, however, is kept undeveloped and unused because of another knowledge imposed on the poor, a keen sense of dependence on the oppressor. This is the source of that universal fear which leads poor people to act and even to think subserviently. Seeing themselves to blame for their situation, they rule out the possibility that they might be qualified to govern themselves and their own organizations. Besides fear, it is their sense of inadequacy and embarrassment which destroys the possibility of revolt.

ERAP, then, suffered from the incurable disease of having the wrong kinds of organizers with the wrong choice of methods operating in the wrong place at the wrong time. Marya Levenson, a Brandeis graduate who joined ERAP in Boston, said it all: "People ask why SDS's Economic Research and Action Projects (ERAP) disappeared. It's because we didn't know what the hell we were trying to do and that always caught up with us."

But was it only a failure? In one sense, yes: no beginnings were made toward the creation of an indigenous left of students and the poor, no army of ghettoites ever rose to challenge the state, or align blacks and whites together to demand their rightful share, nor were there even potent organizations of the poor pressing reforms upon the cities. But it had its other effects.

Of absolutely prime importance is the effect of the ERAP experience on those youths who passed through it. "Radicalization" is an often misused word, but it describes perfectly the experience of so many of the ERAP organizers. Testing some of the reformist hypotheses of the *The Port Huron Statement* and *America and the New Era* in concrete and specific ways, they found those assumptions in error; working with the instruments of the state, they found those instruments insufficient, or, worse, corrupt and evil; trying in the only way they could see to make the American dream a reality for the lowliest citizens, to keep the promises about equal opportunity and economic betterment they had heard so often from the nation's leaders, they found that goal impossible and the leaders indifferent. They tried the system, and found it wanting. Richie Rothstein has said:

> Those of us involved in ERAP . . . are now enemies of welfare state capitalism, with little faith or desire that the liberal-labor forces within this system be strengthened vis-a-vis their corporatist and reactionary allies. We view those forces—and the social "reforms" they espouse—as being incompatible with a non-interventionist world policy and as no more than a manipulative fraud perpetrated upon the dignity and humanity of the American people.
>
> We owe these conclusions in large measure to four years of ERAP experience.

Many who went through that experience sought more than community unions next time out—they were ready not to challenge the institutions of the system but to resist them.

There was a positive side to that experience, however, that also rubbed off, and that was the chance to try participatory democracy within the project itself. It was imperfect, of course—personal antagonisms surfaced, the more articulate dominated, males tended to outweigh females—but still the ERAP people did try to run their projects by putting their deepest beliefs into practice. Leaders *were* played down, and found to be often dispensable; meetings *could* be run without *Robert's Rules of Order* and elaborate procedures, and decisions *were* arrived at, often, through consensus; grand ideologies *could* be dispensed with, without everyone floundering, and daily work proved often enough to be its own reason for being. Rothstein again:

> In many cases the students who did short term tours of duty on ERAP staffs returned to their campuses to lead university reform and Vietnam protest movements. They were, as a result of their contact with ERAP, reinforced in their radical impulses. The democratic, "participatory" tone of all ERAP projects has, in this respect, contributed to the emergence of a new popular movement.

Perhaps no more than a thousand people ever went through this ERAP experience, but a great many of them ended up with the conviction first expressed on an NCUP button and then adopted as the motto for all of SDS: "Let the People Decide." They saw a little part of the future, and it worked—and they did not want to settle for less, in their next meeting, their next Movement job, their university, their country.

ERAP had its effects, too, on the organization whence it sprang. In general they were salutary, for during a most critical period before an active student movement was born, it gave SDS a sense of purpose and a reputation for doing something other than talking and mimeographing. Indeed, many came to see ERAP as the best expression of SDS, an example of the seriousness with which the young took their ideas, even as a potential key to real social change; Kopkind wrote, "There is no other movement, no other source of action in the US that is so doggedly exploring methods of social change, and putting them into practice." It is not an accident that Frank Mankiewicz and then Sargent Shriver himself, when they were at the Office of Economic Opportunity in charge of the "domestic Peace Corps," saw ideas and tactics worthy of emulation in ERAP—Mankiewicz even paid to have Hayden visit Washington to explain NCUP to his staff and several ERAPers served as well-paid consultants to VISTA in 1966 and 1967—for this was the opinion of many who came in contact with the projects. Whether or not this was all exaggerated (as it was), it did much to give the organization a sense of legitimization and purpose within, and an image of dynamism and seriousness without.

With the collapse of ERAP, generally acknowledged by the end of 1965, other less happy consequences for the organization came to be seen. Some bitter individuals soured by ERAP were simply lost to SDS altogether or participated in activities just enough to depress everyone within earshot. A number came to feel that it was too early to *do* anything in this society and turned instead to the development of theory, often ending in fetid Marxist bogs totally removed from the rest of the organization. More important, the absence of the ERAPers from SDS affairs in the period from 1964 to 1965 came to be felt: they were, after all, some of the best talents, the brightest minds, the most committed souls in the organization, and there they were, off in almost utter isolation, rarely participating in ongoing SDS business. As a result, younger people coming into SDS had fewer mentors, and with an increasing number of these people in 1965 the whole problem of "internal education"—passing on the original radical perceptions of the organization and infusing others with its open style and political-personal unity—became acute. From the summer of 1965 on, these early characteristics of SDS would begin to fade.

The most difficult effect of ERAP to judge is the one it set out to accomplish: changing the lives of people in the cities where it operated.

The experience of JOIN in Chicago is perhaps most instructive. By the end of the summer of 1965, when most of the students had returned to school, a half-dozen of the older organizers who remained decided, after prodding by the radicals, that greater reliance had to be placed on the local people rather than the student influx. An Organizing Committee of the staff members and the most active community members of JOIN was established, to give the latter a greater voice. Early in 1966 JOIN was formally incorporated, with a Board of Directors made up of Harriet Stulman and Richie Rothstein from the staff and Mary Hockenberry, John Howard, and Dovie Thurman from the local community: in fact as well as in legality, more of the thrust of JOIN now came from the locals. In September, JOIN was formally separated from SDS entirely, and in the next year split off into several separate groups, all organized by local people, for welfare action, publishing a newspaper, youth work, and ultimately organizing in other communities. By the end of 1967 the ERAP organizers were more or less pushed out of the project, having succeeded to some extent in making themselves superfluous, which after all was the idea from the start: organizing was now in the hands of the organized.

The spirit that lay behind this process is reflected in a statement one of the poor white community people made to Todd Gitlin and Nanci Hollander (for a time, married to Gitlin), whose book, *Uptown,* describes the people of the project:

> See, like it used to be you'd walk from Clifton to Wilson and somebody said, "Oh, there's one a those JOIN Communist people." It's not like that any more. People know JOIN's there. And if they have any problem they try to get in touch with JOIN. I'm known as JOIN in the neighborhood. It's nice to walk down the street and know that I'm known as JOIN and people are not callin you Communist.
>
> I feel more dedicated than when I started cause things are startin to happen and I was partly responsible for buildin things that happened. . . . It all causes things to happen, it causes people to get together. People know it's urban renewal tearin down the neighborhood and they know they're gonna be kicked out and that's a good feelin when they start organizin to do somethin about it. You get a great feelin when you see a group a people standin around demanding stuff that is rightfully theirs. I mean it's theirs and they never had it before and they want it now. It makes me feel good that after a year and a half the neighborhood has changed like that. And it seems to be throbbin with excitement of people wantin to do stuff, about the stuff we've been talkin about for a year and a half, and the things they've been listenin to and checkin up on. They wanna do it now, a lotta people around there.

So I can't drop out now, cause for one I don't want to. Things are in such a state where you have to fight em through and maybe eventually come up with an organization of people who control the community.

This is the kind of achievement impossible to measure, but clearly the ERAP experience has entered into this man's life, into the lives of others in his neighborhood. Directly traceable to this are the development in the sixties of a kind of poor-white "nationalism" in the JOIN area that in turn leads to the establishment by young whites of the Young Patriot Party (which became part of the "Rainbow Coalition" with the Black Panther Party and the Young Lords Organization) and the creation of Rising Up Angry, a group of young whites out of a "greaser" background (motorcycles, leather jackets, gangs) who adopted a revolutionary ideology in the late sixties. What the ultimate effect of this "nationalism" will be on the city's power structure is impossible to say, but it can't hurt.

Newark, similarly, touched the future. The project there also lasted well beyond the formal collapse of ERAP and until local people started acting on their own. At the end of the summer of 1965, the project staff dwindled to a half-dozen, still with Hayden and Wittman as the guiding forces, but it was estimated then that as many as 150 local people participated in its various programs and meetings. Over the next year, the tools which the NCUPers had developed—rent strikes, picketing of slumlords' homes, block meetings—began to spread to other parts of the city, not with any extraordinary success, to be sure, but perhaps with enough mixture of anticipation and frustration to have ultimately led to the anger that exploded in the urban revolt in the summer of 1967. That summer proved to be the death of NCUP, for it was the fourth summer of black rebellion and it (along with the whole growth of black power) finally convinced the young whites that they were unwanted and unneeded in the black ghettos. A few of the white ERAPers stayed on in Newark, however, getting jobs in the city and occasionally surfacing to organize, as for example during the two-week student strike at the Essex County Community College early in 1970. And a number of blacks who had been mobilized and radicalized by NCUP went on to help in the mayoralty campaign of Kenneth Gibson, who finally ousted the corrupt white regime in the summer of 1970 and became the city's first black mayor.

The effects of ERAP, then, are diffuse, and they lead out in rays almost impossible to track down. But for hundreds of heretofore untested young collegians, for hundreds of heretofore ignored blacks and white poor, ERAP had a clear impact—caused them, as the Chicago slum people put it, to become "turned around." Like malaria, or a war, it was something that no one who went through would ever forget. Whether it made anything significantly better, whether it seriously improved the lot of any individual, whether things would have been different without it, that is impossible to say. At the least, the ERAPers can say, in the words of the Bertolt Brecht poem pinned on the wall of the NCUP office:

> In my time streets led to the quicksand.
> Speech betrayed me to the slaughterer.
> There was little I could do. But without me
> The rulers would have been more secure. This was my hope.
> So the time passed away
> Which on earth was given me.

> For we knew only too well:
> Even the hatred of squalor
> Makes the brow grow stern.
> Even anger against injustice
> Makes the voice grow harsh. Alas, we
> Who wished to lay the foundations of kindness
> Could not ourselves be kind.

> But you, when at last it comes to pass
> That man can help his fellow man,
> Do not judge us
> Too harshly.

10

FALL 1964

Paul Potter, in one of his first President's reports to the membership in the fall of 1964, was unknowingly prophetic when he wrote: "The arena in which students today see themselves acting has not only expanded, it has qualitatively changed to include a different idea about the kind of questioning and action that is appropriate." Little did he know. Before the school year was out, students would be thrust on the consciousness of the country as never before and the phrase "student rebellion" would be common currency.

As the school year began SDS was remarkably diverse. It had, by a decision of the fall National Council meeting in Philadelphia, a new system of Regional Organizers, some ten students and ex-students who operated in different regions of the country, living on a few handouts from the National Office and whatever they could cadge from their own sources, keeping regional chapters in contact with one another, organizing conferences, traveling to new campuses, making the SDS presence felt.*It had a National Office staff of four and in Kissinger a director who actually saw to it that the worklist mailings, the bulletins, and the literature orders got out with something approaching regularity. And it had not only ERAP but two other ongoing projects, a revivified Peace

---

*Archie Allen operated in the South, in cooperation with SSOC, Jeremy Brecher worked in the Northwest, George Brosi in Minnesota-Iowa, Peter Davidowicz in Maryland, Vernon Grizzard in Pennsylvania, Dick Magidoff in Michigan, Ken McEldowney in Ohio-Indiana, Jeff Shero in Texas-Oklahoma, David Smith in New England, and Lee Webb (with help from Bob Ross) in Illinois-Wisconsin.

Research and Education Project in Ann Arbor and a Political Education Project in New York. For all its still limited resources and its comparative smallness, it had a breadth of activity that no group on the left, neither student nor adult, could then duplicate.

The projects which lay at the heart of SDS just then give some indication of its multiplicity.

ERAP, as we have seen, came through its first summer considerably sobered, but it was still intact by the fall of 1964, with a national office in Ann Arbor and perhaps fifty people scattered among the six ongoing projects. It was, to be sure, somewhat remote now from the campus constituency, despite recurring but chiefly unsuccessful attempts to link individual projects with nearby campus chapters and despite a strong effort by Davis to have students act as research centers for the projects (demographic studies, combing city records for slumlords, and the like). But its very existence gave SDS a stature among a lot of students and helped to establish for SDS a reputation as an earthy, gutsy, home-truths outfit, a kind of SNCC of the North.

PREP was an entirely different operation, a two-man think-tank and and traveling lecture team. Dick Flacks, who had run PREP for the last two years and had managed to get out a series of (very serious, very dull) *PREP Newsletters* on peace and foreign policy issues, had gone to Chicago to take up a job as assistant professor of sociology at the University of Chicago, and his place was filled by Todd Gitlin and Paul Booth. These two—"the Bobbsey twins of peacenikdom," as someone called them—had just ended a summer of doing peace research with a Washington foundation and had managed to latch on to a rich Texas liberal named Joe Weingarten, who ran a World Institute for World Peace in Houston and who agreed to give PREP $7500 on the understanding that they would promote his institute on campuses around the nation. There is no evidence that they ever did any successful promotion, but the money served to send the two of them on a variety of campus-speaking trips whose main effect was to organize chapters for SDS, and apparently Weingarten was none the wiser.

Booth's specialty was what was called "conversion"—the study of how to get the economy from warfare spending to welfare spending without its collapsing in the process—and that fit in nicely with his essentially reformist politics. He pored over economics books, made speeches, wrote articles for little peace-oriented publications, and tried to be a one-man research department for the Boston ERAP project, which, unlike the others, had been involved in actual conversion work around defense industries in the Boston suburbs and had therefore been put under PREP direction by the September NC. Gitlin, meanwhile, concerned himself with the draft, and put out a long paper on that subject which PREP distributed in the fall. His initial visits to campuses in the fall suggested that this could be a major SDS weapon—"What grassroots soundings I've been able to make," he wrote in October, "leave me convinced that this can be a powerful organizing issue" —but two months later he had come to see that "its potential was highly overrated"; Booth, traveling in the East, wrote him that there was absolutely no interest in the subject, even at Cornell, which was to be a major center of antidraft activity after the escalation of the war. Gitlin concluded that the effort was premature: Vietnam was not yet a reality to Americans, and the students were snug in their 2-S cocoons.

In addition to all the academicism, PREP did lay the groundwork for one successful action later on in the spring. Someone around Ann Arbor noticed in the paper that certain loans which U.S. banks had made to the government of South Africa after the Sharpeville massacre in 1960 were about to be renewed. Gitlin got interested. Working inductively from the premise that South Africa was bad, he slowly came to see how important were those bank loans in bolstering the government, and then to see how important U.S. investments were in general in supporting the regime; with Christopher Z. Hobson, a friend from Harvard, Gitlin looked into it a little and soon discovered which banks were involved in loans to South Africa, which American companies had accounts in those banks, and which corporations had additional ties to South Africa: when he laid it all out he found a surprising picture of the role of U.S. capitalism in the world. No one had expected this—there were no African experts around PREP, no economists, and no one who had had an imperialist analysis of American foreign policy. But when the entanglements were laid bare, the PREPers felt they had to do something, and something unusual. They decided that on March 19, two days before the fifth anniversary of Sharpeville, SDS would stage a protest in the form of a massive sit-in at the lower-Manhattan offices of the Chase Manhattan Bank, one of the prime movers in the loan agreements and a place where South Africa had regularly found a multimillion-dollar friend.* The sit-in was to involve civil disobedience and arrests were expected; in the words of Mike Davis—the son of a San Diego butcher, who later became the chief coordinator of the project—"Housing is being arranged by the New York City Police Department."

PEP, the last of SDS's projects that year, was the bone that had been thrown to the Max-Williams electoral-politics forces by the Pine Hill convention and reluctantly approved by the Philadelphia National Council. This was always a minority adventure within SDS ranks, and its famous slogan of "Part of the Way With LBJ," though often taken by outsiders to be a basic SDS position, was in fact the expression of a small group on what even then was considered the organization's "right wing."

In fact PEP represents SDS's first serious faction fight. The project was established largely because no one felt like denying the electoral-politics faction the right to do their own thing; "by that time," recalls Jim Williams, who became the PEP director, "it was clear that we had political differences with everybody and we didn't try to minimize that—we just said SDS has always been a multi-tendency organization and this is a tendency." But no one felt like giving it much of a chance, either. The PEP executive committee established by the National Council contained a full quota of those hostile to the whole thing—Garvy, Grizzard, Kissinger, Ross—and the project was launched with only $1000 from SDS, unlike ERAP, which took $5000 before it even got off the ground.

PEP managed to raise an initial grant of some $1300 from the Industrial Union Department of the AFL-CIO, on the understanding that it would distribute IUD's anti-Goldwater literature, which it did—fifty-seven thousand pieces of it, too. It also managed to distribute forty-five hundred copies of four election papers of its own, one by LID Executive Secretary Tom Kahn, one

*It was also, the students discovered with a certain cynical satisfaction, the place where the ILGWU, among others, kept a major account.

by Williams, one by Max together with Doug Ireland, and one by Robb Burlage. At several of the chapters, especially around New York and Boston and at the big Midwestern state universities, there was considerable response, but all action remained on a local level and it was up to local chapters to decide whether to pass out these papers, campaign against Goldwater, or sit on their hands.

The PEP position wasn't naive, and was shared by many people in the country if not in the organization. The PEPers knew that Johnson was untrustworthy and highhanded, but they had three ulterior motives in supporting him: to "fight against Goldwater and the ultra-right"; to push Johnson leftward and thus produce a real difference between the two parties, raising "the consciousness of the masses to a new level of political awareness"; and to try to keep the Democratic Party faithful to its party platform, "superior to any passed by a major national party since the first New Deal." "Keeping the limitations of the Johnson program in mind," they wrote,

> . . . we nonetheless realize what a Goldwater victory would mean.
> . . . Not only does the Goldwater program run precisely in the opposite direction from one which we would like to see pursued, but a Goldwater victory would, in fact, drastically alter the nature of political controversy in the country. No longer would the problem be one of how to further the detente with the Soviet Union, but rather how to achieve total victory over the atheistic-communistic menace. No longer would the question of the fight against poverty be open to consideration . . . rather, the issue would be how to remove slackers from the relief rolls.

This was the position known as "Johnson With Eyes Open."

The opposition to PEP took many forms. An increasing number of people coming into the organization greeted it with stony indifference, having outgrown electoral politics along with puberty some years before. Many of the old-timers joined in what Lee Webb now calls "an irresponsible campaign of political assassination" against PEP: Kissinger, for example, put a homemade poster over his desk, in plain view of the PEPers, reading, "Support the War in Viet Nam—Register Voters for Johnson"; that fall, for the first time in the history of SDS, he put a lock on a correspondence file to keep the letters he was writing about PEP away from PEP eyes (to which Max and Williams naturally responded by secretly making a key and reading everything he said about them). And then there were a number of other people who enunciated a principled political line against PEP. Al and Barbara Haber, for example, argued that SDS should actively urge people *not* to vote:

> To support Johnson is to support [his] move to the right and the de-issuization of presidential politics. The larger his victory, the stronger will be his mandate to continue leadership of a moderate coalition in which the left has no place. The larger his victory, the more resoundingly will the middle have defeated the edges—Goldwater's edge and our edge, too. The larger his victory, the more resoundingly will *our position* be defeated: "Extremism in pursuit of liberty is no vice, moderation in defense of justice is no virtue."

It is a measure of the amount of opposition to the PEP politics that dozens of boxes of the "Part of the Way With LBJ" buttons, which were regularly pushed on the membership, remained unsold after November.

With the lopsided Johnson victory, PEP was left floundering: not only had its analysis of the great Goldwater threat been proven wrong, but it was now stuck with a dislikable man who had a mandate to do anything he pleased. Max and Williams tried to argue to the PEP executive committee that "the Johnson landslide had produced many new possibilities for radical-liberal coalitions and campaigns for new, radical legislation," but as Kissinger reported in the minutes of that committee, "the analysis was received by the committee without comment." PEP then offered a new program of trying to put student pressure on Congress to get it to pass improved welfare legislation, but that too gained nothing more than offhanded support. PEP, it seemed, was dead, and it only remained for the December National Council meeting in New York to bury it.

PEP came into the December NC with a two-point proposal, the first to continue research into and promotion of progressive legislation to be pushed through Congress, and the second to set up a voter-registration program in Cairo, Illinois (community projects then being a big thing for SDS). "Max and I," Williams recalls, "went down to a Spanish magic shop and bought us some charms and hoped that would see us through." It didn't: the NC

gored them. "It was terrible—a bloodletting," Williams says. First
the elaborate legislative program was turned into a propaganda
effort on behalf of the Mississippi Freedom Democratic Party to
get it seated in Congress in place of the regular Mississippi delegation (an idea that had been only a small part of PEP's original
package); and then the Cairo project was taken away from them
and given to ERAP, which two days later decided that it should
be abandoned altogether. This was, as Paul Booth says, "the prime
example of sectarianism in SDS. We destroyed them."

Max and Williams knew they were beaten, and they didn't
bother to fight. "I just completely lost heart," Williams says,
sadly.

> It was a great disappointment . . . very traumatic for me. For a while
> after that I felt like a Cuban exile sitting at a table drinking coffee
> and waiting for the regime that kicked him out to collapse so that
> he can go back in; and then at one point you realize that it's not
> going to happen, and then you don't know what to do.

Max is more detached: "We failed to see the youth culture that
was coming up then, kids who were into drugs and the new culture
and who felt they were past electoral politics—we were trying to
show what was wrong with Congress and they already felt Congress was irrelevant to them." Williams looked around for a job,
and in February joined the International Brotherhood of Electri-
cal Workers in Washington (where he later started a short-lived
SDS chapter with SNCCer Phil Hutchings); Max, in an irony so
perfect that it is no longer ironic, joined the working staff of the
LID—by now they finally realized the identity of their politics—
though he would continue for several years more to be a participant in SDS affairs. The February 23, 1965 worklist mailing carried the PEP epitaph, a note from Max:

> Regretfully we announce that the Political Education Project is
> closing operations. . . . Of course Jim and I feel that an operation
> like PEP should be a major priority in an organization like SDS.
> Perhaps some of the funds now being used to build up large full-time
> community-work staffs could better be employed in research and
> education on the campus level. Unfortunately the organization has
> set its priorities in another way.
> It would be less than frank not to mention another considera-

tion that was in the back of our minds when we decided to close the projects. . . . For the most part there has been foaming at the mouth and cries of "sell out" whenever the words "New Coalition" [i.e., realignment] have been used. As a substitute for real debate, notions about plots against the organization and plots to organize a faction for the Convention have been circulated.

Let us hope that now with PEP dissolved and its staff scattered, there will be no further excuses for the lack of open and legitimate political differences in SDS, and that those who have dealt with the situation as a factional one will now be forced to come out and argue a real political position.

Needless to say, both Jim and I remain committed to SDS. . . . We should like to thank those friends who have stood by PEP during this fruitful, but often trying, experiment in organizational diversity.

This December meeting showed more than dissatisfaction over the Johnson election and electoral reformism. Max and Williams were victims of a new strain that was coming into SDS, produced by the cross-fertilization of two groups. The first was the older people, such as the ERAPers who had discovered a new approach to parliamentary democracy in their project meetings, plus a number of white SNCCers distraught by the Atlantic City compromise who turned to a superasceticism so apolitical that they were regarded as being drugged on a "freedom high"; the second was the younger college and high school people, also increasingly apolitical in traditional terms, members of an ever-more-alienated generation who had made their first appearance at the 1964 convention and who, it turned out, were little inclined to step-by-step arguments and structured political debates and were much given to such expressions as, "I feel alienated from this meeting."

It was one of Hayden's shrewd and apparently accidental political perceptions that he felt the alliance between these two groups, and he used the December meeting to express the new ghetto-hardened perceptions of the former while impressing them on the political *tabula rasa* of the latter. He would stand up in the middle of a heated argument, say something to the effect of "What if we were to stay here for six years and not come to a decision?"

and sit down, effectively sending the existential young women from the suburbs into a tizzy and drawing agreeing nods from the workshirted young men. "'Suppose parliamentary democracy," he would say, "were a contrivance of nineteenth-century imperialism and merely a tool of enslavement?" Or, "Suppose we rush through the debate and 'decide' to do something by a vote of 36 to 33. Will we really have decided anything?"

Williams, not unnaturally bitter at this point, remembers this as Hayden's "What-if-I-were-a-plum?" phase, and many of the NC delegates regarded this behavior as ill-mannered at best and anti-intellectual at worst, and a few passed it off as gut existentialism. But it was much more than that: it was the attempt to enunciate a politics *on the other side* of the parliamentary forms handed down from another era, to see if there was a way of carrying on the business of society without all the trappings of the society of business. Hayden saw that SDS was caught in the bind of trying to create a new world with the tools of the old.

That was what lay behind the debate between Hayden and Ray Brown which was one of the high points of the NC. Brown, author of the "crisis economy" paper that had helped push SDS into ERAP and projects with the unemployed poor, was there to give another speech on the direction of the economy, only this time he urged SDS to get into organizing the *working* poor. It was too much for Hayden. He got up and took Brown to task for his trotting out of theories about whom to organize. Look, he said in effect, we took your advice the last time and went into the ghettos —your theories turned out to be all wrong but we did it anyway and it turned out to be the right thing, an important thing for SDS and for those of us in the communities. And look: nobody could have given an analysis to Bob Moses proving that he ought to be organizing poor blacks in the most backward parts of Mississippi, but he did it anyway and *that* turned out to be the right thing. Theories don't mean a thing, there *is* no theoretical basis for doing what we're doing, and anyone who tries to tell you that there is is full of shit. We're *beyond* traditional theoretical premises. We're into something new.

It was a profound statement. Hayden was trying to warn SDS that if it was serious about changing the system it would have to abandon old theoretical approaches and worn-out techniques which that system had created for its own purposes, and try to evolve theories and techniques of its own: you don't try to kill a bee by piercing him with your stinger. The institutions, organizations, rules, theories and all the other taken-for-granted paraphernalia of twentieth-century America are not immutable and ordained, the inevitable products of human nature—they are the result of a particular social and economic system, and they are thereby tainted. One cannot use these products without the taint coming off on one's hands. There must be other ways to operate.

But SDS did not respond. Many were angered by the implicit arrogance in Hayden's remarks—after all, *he* didn't have any more answers than anyone else—and few saw the implications of what he was getting at; worse, Hayden himself was apparently not yet ready to do the hard work of pushing it across to the others. Creating a new organization, a new *form* of organization, in the midst of a society without models for it, without even the habits of thinking about it, was more than SDS could manage. Perhaps its ending would have been different if it could have.

The May 2nd Movement on November 7, 1964, renewed its dormant campaign to get male college and high-school students to sign a pledge stating that they would not fight in the war in Vietnam. Although a majority of the M2M steering committee were members of the Progressive Labor Party, which had advanced a clear imperialist explanation for the war, the M2M pledge itself did not incorporate such an analysis, and indeed was stanchly patriotic:

WE THE UNDERSIGNED,

ARE YOUNG AMERICANS OF DRAFT AGE. We understand our obligations to defend our country and to serve in the armed forces but we object to being asked to support the war in South Vietnam.

Believing that United States participation in that war is for the suppression of the Vietnamese struggle for national independence, we see no justification for our involvement. We agree with Senator Wayne Morse, who said on the floor of the Senate on March 4, 1964, regarding South Vietnam, that "We should never have gone in. We should never have stayed in. We should get out."

BELIEVING THAT WE SHOULD NOT BE ASKED TO FIGHT AGAINST THE PEOPLE OF VIETNAM, WE HEREWITH STATE OUR REFUSAL TO DO SO.

Even so, the pledge was regarded by many at the time as too extreme, and M2M, with fewer than two hundred members, was still too small to push it successfully at more than a few colleges. This was, however, the first of the "We Won't Go" statements and a precursor of the draft-refusal movement of later years.

The existence of the three SDS projects in the fall of 1964, however varied their success, was a sign that SDS was searching and experimenting, somehow organizationally aware of the flow of a new student mood without being able to find just the right channel for it, neither the romantic Narodnikism of ERAP nor the electoral legitimacy of PEP nor the analytical adventures of PREP somewhere in between. And because it was groping, it kept growing. Membership increased steadily to 1200 dues-payers by October, and then by December to 1365 people at 41 chapters and 37 states, the District of Columbia, and overseas.* Jeremy Brecher, the Regional Organizer for the Northwest, remembers that the SDS reputation had penetrated even into smaller colleges in his area: "They'd all heard about SDS and they were all really interested—no matter what little they had heard about it. SDS was the place to go."

And then, virtually out of the blue, SDS was blessed with its largest donation ever. Gitlin, working through Boston-area contacts, had managed after several months to talk million-heiress Anne Farnsworth into a donation of $25,000 to SDS that October (much of it intended for PREP, but in the event used by the organization as a whole, almost $10,000 going to ERAP). It was such a heady sum it caused the usually stolid Kissinger to draw up that November a budget for the next eight months of no less

---

*Kissinger, naturally, kept the tallies, and they can be presumed accurate. The chapters: Bergen County (New Jersey) High School, Berkeley, Boston At-large, Boston University, Brown/Pembroke, Bryn Mawr, Carleton, Chicago At-large, Chicago University, Cornell, Duke, Grinnell, Harpur, Harvard/Radcliffe, Illinois, Johns Hopkins/Goucher, Kalamazoo, Louisville, Maryland, Massachusetts Institute of Technology, Michigan, New York At-large, New York University, Oklahoma, Piedmont (North Carolina), Queens, Reed, Roosevelt, Rutgers, Sarah Lawrence, Simmons, Smith, Southern Illinois, Swarthmore, Texas, Tufts, Vassar, University of Washington, Western Kentucky State, Williams, and Wisconsin. Six of the chapters are west of the Mississippi, eight below the Mason-Dixon line (including Oklahoma and Texas).

than $66,000, ten times anything SDS had ever conceived of spending before. It also caused a few ruffled feathers, since it was mostly Kissinger and the in-group who decided how the $25,000 would be allocated, much to the displeasure of those who were not included in either the consultation or the distribution; and the Boston PREP people, who knew nothing about the money until it was in hand, were understandably peeved that their own sources of fund raising had been tapped without their knowledge. Still, $25,000 went a long way toward making everyone amenable.

Members, money—but the real measure of SDS's success was that it kept alive to its era. Because of that, it became the beneficiary of one of the most far-reaching events of this decade, the initial battle of the student rebellion.

The First Battle of Berkeley began on September 14, 1964, with an announcement from the administration of the University of California at Berkeley that organizing and soliciting funds for off-campus political action would henceforth be banned from the campus at the usual areas. It ended—as much as such things ever end—three months and twenty days later on January 3, 1965, with an announcement from the same administration that organizing and soliciting funds for off-campus political action would henceforth be permitted on campus at the usual areas. In the interim, students carried confrontation with authority to the point of spontaneously surrounding a police car for thirty-two hours to prevent the young man inside from being taken to jail;* the sit-in tactic was successfully transferred from Southern lunchcounters and Northern businesses to the halls of ivy on three separate occasions, first with 200 students, then with 400, and finally with 1000; the police were called in, for perhaps the first time ever at a major university campus, to arrest, with proven brutality, 814 students who had been engaged in a sit-in; undergraduates, joined by graduate students and a portion of the faculty, declared a successful strike of classes that went on for five days, the first time that tactic had been used at a single university; the university president,

*The man, it should be noted in passing, was Jack Weinberg, originator of the phrase, "Don't trust anyone over thirty," widely publicized by people over thirty in the media. On April 4, 1971, Jack Weinberg became thirty-one.

Clark Kerr (who had been a member of SLID—SDS's predecessor
—in his youth), a man nationally famed as the champion of the
super-efficient, technologically-perfected "multiversity," stumbled along from "non-negotiable demands" (a phrase he seems to
have been the first to inject at Berkeley, and thus into college life)
to redbaiting to amelioration, and finally confessed, "We fumbled,
we floundered, and the worst thing is I still don't know how we
should have handled it"; and the chancellor of the university was
forced out and a new, more lenient man put in his place. Here,
ab ovo, were all the elements of student protest that were to
become familiar at so many campuses in the next six years: the
sit-ins, strikes, police, nonstudents, arrests, mimeographed resolutions, bullhorns, committees, broken friendships, resignations, TV
cameras, headlines. Here was the university administration which
moves from blunder to blunder, with the trustees right behind, all
the while complaining with bewilderment that communications
have broken down and "normal channels" have not been followed;
here was the uncertain and essentially ostrichlike faculty which
initially acts as if it is discovering the students as people for the
first time and then reluctantly decides that they have a point and
finally sides with them; here was the studentry which is mobilized
by administration mistakes, is then sustained by a small core of
energetic, charismatic, disorganized, inefficient, joyful, impassioned, and sometimes brilliant leaders, and ultimately becomes
politicized in large numbers by watching the brutality of the police, the venality of the press, the superficiality of the faculty, and
the immorality of the administration.

  Berkeley had it all. And had it, moreover, in extremes: there,
at the central campus of the largest and perhaps best university
system in the country, was the most direct confrontation ever seen
in an American educational institution up to that time, with the
most police, the most arrests, the most students out on strike at
a single campus, and the most publicity. Sproul Plaza was Fort
Sumter, and this was the first shot fired in the war between Movement and University.

  But what was it, really, all about? Ostensibly the issue was
"free speech" and it was the *ad hoc* Free Speech Movement (FSM)
which directed most of the action. But though there were unquestionable angers and passions aroused over the administration's

limitations on political activity on campus, they could not by themselves have produced such a sustained confrontation, for the limitations were in fact quite minor, hardly distinguishable from other administrative clamps on political activity in the previous five years, easily capable of circumvention by those who cared, and an inconvenience to only a tiny percentage of the twenty-seven thousand students (and maybe three thousand nonstudents) on the campus.

Nor was the issue really the size and impersonality of the multiversity, although that explanation was by all odds the most popular, put forth by academic pundits, newspaper columnists, students at other universities, and, ultimately, as if to suggest how wrong it was, by Ronald Reagan himself.* This was the explanation which fit most readily into the liberal consciousness of the nation, for it conceded a problem, but a problem small enough to be admitted without a dislocation of one's political psyche and for which a variety of possible solutions could be imagined without a major reordering of society. And in fact it was to academic patching and pasting that many people at universities now turned, in order to "avoid a Berkeley" on their campuses. But though the deadening largeness of the major universities certainly did nothing to *resolve* the students' inner turmoil, and often helped to keep it alive by providing others among the mass who shared it, it was neither the cause for nor the sustenance of the protest. Most students *liked* the education they were getting (after a careful survey that fall, Berkeley sociologist Robert Somers concluded that "our data do not suggest that dissatisfaction with the educational process played any role at all"), a remarkably high percentage of the active protesters were transfer students who had come to Berkeley explicitly seeking this kind of mass education (perhaps as many as 49 percent of the FSM people were transfers, according to a study by the Berkeley Center for the Study of Higher Educa-

*In a speech before the San Francisco Commonwealth Club in June 1969, Reagan sympathized with students "being fed into the knowledge factory with no regard to their individualism, their aspirations or their dreams. Young men and women go to college to find themselves as individuals. . . . All too often they are herded into gigantic classes taught by teaching assistants hardly older than themselves. The feeling comes that they're nameless, faceless numbers on an assembly line." (Quoted by A. H. Raskin, *The New York Times Magazine,* January 11, 1970.)

tion), and demands for curricular change appear with only the slightest frequency in FSM statements during this period.

No, the basic source of the Berkeley protest was more involved than the desire for political activity or a restructured university, and more difficult to admit and deal with. It was of course, as we have seen underlying the whole impetus to student protest, the desire of young people to say something, to do something about the American society they lived in, the society that made them feel useless, exploited, guilty, paternalized, and consumerized, that allowed monstrous ills to be perpetuated. The Berkeley students were aware of the connection between their actions and the society at large right from the beginning. Political activity there for the last year had centered on civil-rights protests at Bay Area businesses (resulting in more than thirteen hundred arrests since November 1963), these protests had upset the right-wingers in the California establishment, and it was pressure from these right-wingers (chiefly William Knowland and his *Oakland Tribune*) that had forced the administration to clamp down on political activity in the first place. Once the battle had begun, the university was seen largely as a substitute for the society in which it functioned, and the students demanded of it the same humanity and justice they had demanded of the politicians of Mississippi, the bus stations of Alabama, the businessmen of San Francisco— only they expected more from the university than they did from most other institutions because of its own claims. During the course of the fight it was discovered that the university did not live up to its claims, but, more than that, neither did the police, the press, and the public, the very personifications of the society: the university proved not to be the home of fair and dispassionate reasoning, the regents showed themselves not to be wise statesmen above pettiness and vindictiveness, the press turned out not to be an unbiased and objective seeker after truth, the police proved not to be efficient agents of justice and servants of the people, and the public at large turned out not to be open to reason, to be willing to listen to another side of a story, to harbor sympathy. If anything, the society seemed to behave with savageness or callousness or duplicity. For the young men and women of Berkeley, this was innocence lost: tested, the society flunked. John R. Seeley, a sociology professor who was a sympathetic observer of the Berkeley events, captured this exactly:

> For what is now struck at is no longer this or that aspect of the University of California at Berkeley, or even the whole nine-campus monstrosity called the University of California. It is not even any longer the American University, but the American way of life. And not at its periphery but at its core. The students who wore placards saying "Do not bend, fold, spindle or mutilate," or "I am not the property of the Regents of the University of California," though they then thought themselves fighting a local and institutional battle, set in motion a train of thought, feeling, resolution and action that now addresses itself to the nation and the nation's basic orientation to itself and the world. The managerial society is being asked moral questions, and, failing credible answers is beginning to be choked of what is indispensable for its operation: the precursor of loyalty, the belief that, in general the society is right, or not wrong, or not seriously wrong, or not criminally wrong; and no longer in respect to an issue but in its fundamental form and character.

Berkeley 1964 was the first overt expression of this absolutely trancendental issue. And this is why there was such a reaction to it, with constant sensationalistic newspaper and television coverage, an immediate spate of literally dozens of articles in the periodicals, interminable academic studies, surveys, theses, and at least four books. Somewhere in its depths, the nation knew that Berkeley was more than an enlarged panty raid, was speaking, albeit haltingly, to something profound. The priests of the media ballyhooed Berkeley even as they condemned it, because it expressed their own liberal uncertainties about the new order which the nation found itself on the brink of, a new order which Clark Kerr himself had described as one where "the federal agencies will exercise increasingly specific controls and . . . greater external restraint will be imposed in most situations." The professors promoted Berkeley, not solely in the belief that it would promote them, because it was expressing truths about the nature of the academy and the kind of worldly thing it had become, which they had known for a long time but had not wanted to acknowledge.

It was not that anything so very wild had gone on (certainly nothing by the standards of a few years later): no deaths or major injuries, no bombs or fires, no serious damage to property (aside from the police car, which was used as a speaker's platform), no widespread violence (except for the police), not even a sustained picket line or strike. It was not even that this was the first major political disturbance on a university campus for thirty years, for there had been precursors of a smaller order at many universities and several at Berkeley itself. This relatively small event was made immense rather because Berkeley had been thought to be the triumph of the American dream, a public university acknowledged to be perhaps the finest in the country, the perfect postideological mixture of government, private industry, academia, computers, managerial skills, brains, and money—and the whole thing was being called into question. The young, upon whom the future of course would depend, were being given the American dream— *and they didn't want it.* More: they *attacked* it, with an innate challenge that reverberated through the entire society, striking at the premises and beliefs upon which it was founded. The Berkeley confrontation was a signal that a new generation had been born. America did not like what it had spawned.

With such an explosive reaction from the country as a whole, universities everywhere could not help being affected. Many administrations and faculties moved to redress long-standing student grievances and extensive probing and poking went on at most of the better schools, breaking open the lid of an academic Pandora's box out of which were to fly an immense variety of schemes and committees and curricula over the next few years. Many institutions moved to promote more freedom for students in political activity, greater faculty involvement in student conduct and academic reform, more flexible machinery in the administration to anticipate and handle student complaints, a stronger student voice in academic and nonacademic affairs, various schemes to "restructure" the university, more power to both students and teachers, and so on. And at many places this first taste of power proved exhilarating indeed.

Even the most moderate of the students sensed that life would be different after Berkeley, that they would no longer be regarded as frivolous stadium-fillers and that their lives and learning were of some concern to the outside world. The more active students did not take long to sense a new fragility in the university structure and to bring pressure to bear on faculty and administration for this or that real or pretended cause; they tended to realize, too, that people would now pay attention to them as they never had before and hence came to regard publicity as an elemental lever in their tactics, using wire-service reporters and television cameramen with a self-interest that heretofore had belonged only to politicians and entertainers. Finally, the already-committed students, like those in SDS, discovered that Berkeley began a period in which whole new possibilities opened up for, in their words, the "politicization" and "radicalization" of American students, specifically around their own grievances as students at first, but with the possibility now of having them relate those grievances to the world beyond and then sharing in the radical vision.

SDS saw immediately that the Berkeley events would be important, even before the immense publicity that was accorded them. In the October *Bulletin* it ran a front-page article—dull to be sure, and totally unhortatory—outlining the events up through the abandonment of the police car, and a wire of support was sent to the FSM soon after its formation the same month. (Not that SDS had much support to give, except through its local Berkeley chapter, and that turned out to be a rather weak and marginal group of people whose allegiances were directed elsewhere; still, the chapter was officially recognized by the university and it did make its presence known during the troubles by running a table to sell buttons with the SDS slogan, "A Free University in a Free Society.") Kissinger especially saw the value of Berkeley in directing SDS's attention back to campus affairs and away from the provinciality of the projects, and he pushed it hard. He "spent a fortune in phone calls to Berkeley," he confessed, then wrote and rushed out a special mailing early in the morning of October 3: "So far as I know," he wrote to Potter, "we are the only ones to respond at a national level—we really beat everybody on it." He pressed Berkeley chapter president Eric Levine to keep sending more information—used for articles in the *Bulletin* through January—and he managed to raid the coffers for money to fly Levine and one of FSM's most astute strategists, Steve Weissman, into the December NC meeting to tell the story first-hand. (Weissman was sufficiently impressed with the kind of people he met there that he agreed after the meeting to become a West Coast organizer for SDS.)

Kissinger was right: Berkeley was important for SDS. On the immediate level, it caused a lot of students to start thinking, to become alert to their own lives, own grievances, own power, and they often started looking around for an organization like SDS from which to get support so that they could express those things. SDS tried to emphasize in its organizing that it was like FSM on a national scale—a militant student group enunciating and taking action about campus grievances with the university and the world beyond—and tried to show how FSMs could grow on almost any campus if students started with an existing radical group like SDS. No other group on the student left at this point had anything like the geographical stretch of SDS, and no other had a system of Regional Organizers as effective. In spite of its comparatively small numbers (around thirteen hundred paid-up members) it was likely to have been heard of, likely to be nearby, to, and likely to have made contact with, students at any campus that wanted to take action; it was the natural organization to look toward. And in the months to come, as the Berkeley battle seeped into the awareness of students everywhere, SDS continued to draw the benefit. As Berkeley spurred the consciousness of the American student, so it spurred the growth of SDS.

But not even Berkeley would prove to be as decisive for SDS as the quite remote and then still modest war in Vietnam. A measure of the organization's alertness to the temper of its time —not to mention a certain simple luckiness—is that it kept alive to that issue, too.

At the end of 1964, 23,300 young American males were stationed in Vietnam through the courtesy of the U.S. Armed Forces. Their numbers were still comparatively small, technically they were there just to advise the South Vietnamese army, and they weren't really fighting a war since none had been declared—so most people back in their homeland tended to forget about them. The average man, the average college student, did not know where Vietnam was.

Actually, as we have seen, some antiwar sentiment began to surface among the student generation the previous year and had spread right along with the war: the Mme. Nhu picket in December 1963, the April 1964 meeting at Yale which launched the antiwar May 2nd Movement, the M2M spring demonstration and continuing marches through the summer, and in the fall the M2M "We Won't Go" petition. But even on the left this sentiment was never regarded with much importance, and M2M and like organizations remained small. SDS itself was always leery of paying too much attention to any single issue, especially one in foreign affairs. The farthest the PREP executive committee would go that November was a four-pronged program to prepare a "kit of materials" on the "Viet Cong," to determine if anyone was interested in some kind of "declaration of conscience" (à la the French intellectuals on Algeria in 1958), possibly to organize a "small conference" on Vietnam, and to "prepare a contingency plan of action in case of Vietnamese crisis," unlikely as that seemed. But they did agree that Gitlin could raise the issue at the December NC to see if there was any sentiment elsewhere for further action.

Gitlin and Booth invited journalist I. F. Stone to the December meeting, and on the night of the twenty-ninth he presented a lucid history of how America had become involved in Southeast Asia and a ringing declaration of why it should get out. For many SDSers, the Vietnam issue suddenly acquired a certain stature, and so when Gitlin finally introduced the subject during the course of his report on PREP activities, there was a debate beyond anything that had been expected.

It is around five o'clock on the afternoon of December 30, 1964, in a stuffy meeting hall of the Cloakmakers' Union in lower Manhattan, that the discussion of Vietnam begins. Gitlin, who has just finished outlining the plans for the Chase Manhattan sit-in, now suggests that SDS write and circulate to the college campuses a declaration stating, "I will not be drafted until the United States gets out of Viet Nam" and then campaign to get students to sign it. Jeff Shero, the Texas-area organizer, makes an alternate proposal: SDS should mount a campaign to raise medical supplies to send to the Viet Cong through the U.S. mails. Now the electoral-politics faction begins to get worried that things are going too far, that SDS will end up doing something too wild, too leftist, too pro-Communist. Jim Brook, an early SDSer and a friend of Max's from the early days, suggests that everyone stop for a while and think things over. The motion fails; the debate rages: Are we pro-Viet Cong, pro-North Vietnam? You can't get any antiwar support if you take a pro-Communist line. We must educate the campuses to the issues first, before we take any action. Let's give it all back to PREP to do. The war is taking lots of money away from poor people, now that's an issue. How can we support a corrupt regime?—and on and on. Dinner time is forgotten; those who care about such things duck out for sandwiches.

Finally, toward ten o'clock, Booth suggests and the meeting approves a two-minute limit on speeches for the rest of the evening, which in practice means no one can go on for much more than five minutes without a lot of catcalls. Gitlin valiantly tries to get back to his original antidraft petition. Brook, desperate now, and seeing that *some* kind of Vietnam action is going to be approved, counterposes the more modest idea of having SDS stage a protest march on Washington during the spring vacation (people had been marching on Washington for *years,* after all, and nothing very damaging can happen on a *march*). The idea seems attractive, and a number of people urge that it be done *along with* the petition. A debate rages again. Many ERAPers and the more alienated of the younger members oppose a march as too tame; others argue that the whole thing has too much of a single-issue focus to it and is not radical enough; while Kissinger and a number of campus-oriented people join with the PEP types in support of it because they see it as an effective way to organize among students and build up the organization on the campus level. Then, during a lull, a number of ERAPers leave the room. Kissinger, in the chair, calls for a vote on the march. It passes, with strong support from the chapter delegates, less enthusiasm from the NC members. The idea grows. Let's forget about the petition: that passes. Let's have the NO start organizing the march: that passes. A City College delegate, with a genius for ideological compromise, urges that the appeal be that "SDS advocates that the United States get out of Vietnam for the following reasons: a) war hurts the Vietnamese people; b) war hurts the American people; c) SDS is concerned about Vietnamese and American people": that passes. Steve Weissman, a lonely voice from the West, suggests that you can march and have a petition, too: that fails. Finally, at twelve-thirty A.M., David Smith moves for adjournment: that passes.

And so SDS found itself in antiwar politics long before there was any widespread interest, ahead of its time once again. Not that it anticipated that its march on Washington would be an over-whelming event—it would be, rather, one more example of SDS's multifacetedness, one more way to try to get its message across to the campuses. Not many could be expected to show up—maybe two thousand or so, that would be a good turnout, considering what M2M and others had been able to draw for similar events. Then in January, SDS got I. F. Stone and Ernest Gruening (who with Wayne Morse was the only Senator at that point forthrightly against the war) to agree to address the marchers, and the American Friends Service Committee endorsed the march. That was promising enough to cause Paul Booth to write: "All expectations are that it will be a big thing." What he meant was that maybe three thousand people would show up.

11

SPRING 1965

And then, escalation. In February the guerrilla fighters of the National Liberation Front of South Vietnam staged an attack against an outpost at a town called Plei Ku, and on February 7, 1965, Lyndon Johnson gave this as his reason for launching a major military response by the United States—for, in fact, an all-out war. He directed that American airplanes be sent to drop bombs on the territory of North Vietnam, presumed to be the invader of the South, and that the number of soldiers be increased rapidly (by 800 percent before the year's end)—from the ranks of the young through enlarged draft calls rather than from the rolls of the Reserves and National Guard in the population at large. With this single stroke Lyndon Johnson assured himself a prominent place in the history of infamy— and became the most successful recruiter SDS was ever to have.

Overnight the campuses became active. There were demonstrations, albeit confined to the hundreds of participants, at practically every major campus, and SDSers were prominent in leading actions at Brown/Pembroke, Carleton, Michigan, Minnesota, Rutgers, Baltimore, Boston, and New York, and in sponsoring a four-hundred-strong picket of the White House on February 20. Naturally the NO was swamped with calls for information and literature on Vietnam, and naturally it had nothing to give out other than a hastily drawn-up fact sheet and a few copies of a little PREP paper called "Vietnam, Symptom of World Malaise" written by David Arnold the previous spring; that "kit of materials" on the "Viet Cong" authorized by PREP in November had never quite materialized. All attention turned to the march, now set for April 17, which suddenly became the projected outlet for protest not just by the outraged students but by many of the older generation as well.

SDS operated in top gear. It hired more staff, at subsistence rates, until by the end of March there were nine full-time people, coordinated by Charles Capper and Martin Roysher, who had dropped out of school to handle the panoply of details. The NO installed a phone system with five separate lines (a hallmark of bureaucratic success), printed up 150,000 copies of the official march call, sent out 15,000 buttons advertising the march, and set up a separate Washington office with Paul Booth and Phil Hutchings to handle details there. The best energies of the organization now surfaced, and people who had been trained in campus organizing, those who had gone through the ERAP experience, veterans of the Free Speech Movement, all put their talents to work for the march; as Paul Booth puts it, "We just rolled over the whole antiwar movement—they had never seen anything like this."

By early April there was no longer any question but that the march would be successful, with optimists on the staff predicting ten thousand people. Everybody rallied to the event. Endorsements came in from Kay Boyle, James Farmer, Erich Fromm, W. H. Ferry, H. Stuart Hughes, Staughton Lynd, A. J. Muste, Mario Savio, Harold Taylor, Howard Zinn. All the peace organizations that had been floundering around for the last few years— Committee for Nonviolent Action, SANE, Student Peace Union, War Resisters League, Women Strike for Peace, Women's International League for Peace and Freedom—suddenly saw the march as the most important expression against the war, and started hovering around SDS clamoring for joint sponsorship; and all the new youth-centered organizations on the left—the DuBois Clubs, M2M, the Young People's Socialist League, and Youth Against War and Fascism (a small East Coast group formed in 1962 with ties to the Trotskyist Worker's World Party)—suddenly saw it as a springboard from which to launch their own organizational perspectives, and they pitched in to organize. Even liberal New

York unions, like the Drug and Hospital Workers Local 1199 and the Retail Workers Union District 65, and off-center political groups like the Bronx Reform Democrats, wanted to join in.

There was even money. Joan Baez sent in $2000, Pete Seeger contributed, a newly formed faculty group called the Universities Committee to Protest the War in Vietnam chipped in $1400 for a bus from Mississippi. Martin Peretz, a young teacher of political science at Harvard (and married to Anne Farnsworth, SDS's greatest benefactor to date), proved invaluable both as a donor and a dunner, and he and others in the organization now found considerable success fund-raising among polite liberals of wealth. Income in the month of March rose to nearly $5000, and shot up to $12,800 in April, more money in just two months than SDS had gotten in two *years* out of the LID. Of course SDS—nothing if not profligate—spent almost everything that came in on staff salaries, transportation, publicity, and all the other hidden burdens of political activity in America, and it ended the school year with only a few hundred dollars in the bank. Still, the fact that there was money at all was a welcome change.

And out on the campuses, SDS continued to reap the benefits of what Johnson had sowed. Students all over were drawn to SDS, and ten new chapters were created (making a total of fifty-two by the end of March), including Missouri,* Southern California, Stanford, Virginia, and, back after a hiatus, Wayne State. Regional Organizers used the impending march and the excitement over Vietnam to spread the SDS message: George Brosi established three new chapters in his Minnesota region; Robert Pardun, a Texas student and friend of Shero's who became suddenly active, reestablished the North Texas State chapter and laid the plans for a special march on the LBJ Ranch to coincide with the Washington march if Johnson tried to flee the capital; Lee Webb and Bob Ross, now through with the JOIN project, worked full time on campus organizing, eventually lining up enough people for Washington to fill nearly a hundred buses; and Steve Weissman, working both on the West Coast and in the South, helped in the

*SDSers there, in order to get approval from a cautious and conservative administration, told the dean in charge that SDS was, as its name implies, a bit like the Democratic Party. It got approved.

formation of four new chapters. And even those campuses where single-issue attitudes prevailed and there was no interest in formal SDS chapters, they started their own March-on-Washington committees to get students mobilized.

Not even *The New York Times* could fail to sense what was going on. On March 15 it ran its first major article on the New Left, an eight-column takeout largely concerned with SDS, quoting Tom Hayden, Bob Ross, Richie Rothstein, and Jeff Shero at length. It described the movement as "a new, small, loosely bound intelligentsia that calls itself the new student left and that wants to cause fundamental changes in society," listed SDS as among the "major groups" in this movement, went on to give six paragraphs to the organization's history and philosophy. "The New Student Left," ran the banner headline: "Movement Represents Serious Activists in Drive for Changes." Even the Establishment was taking note.

The May 2nd Movement also benefited from the new campus anger. Its "We Won't Go" petition had more than a thousand signatures by the end of February. Its own ranks increased to perhaps eight hundred. And it was encouraged to begin the publication of a regular newsletter, called *Free Student,* on whose editorial board were, among others, Les Coleman, a philosophy major at Harvard eventually to move to SDS, Jeff Gordon, a Brooklyn College student in PL and later PL's coordinator, Albert Maher, a Harvard graduate who was the son of a wealthy Texas businessman, and Richard Rhoads, an M2M organizer and PL figure in New York.

Meanwhile, SDS was having troubles back at the home front. Relations between the LID and SDS were at their lowest point since the Port Huron blowup, and getting worse. LIDers had in general looked askance on much of the student department's goings-on in the last two years—the moving into the ghettos, for instance, and the continued calls for action and demonstrations, not to mention the regular attacks which SDSers made in print and in person on the social-democratic tradition. (Why, in *The New York Times* article one of them, a mere twenty-one-year-old, had publicly discarded one of the LID's fundamental tenets: "We reject the idea," Richie Rothstein had said, "that you can bring change through getting elected to the legislature, and then handing down change from the top. Somehow, under that system, the poor still get treated poorly.") But they had looked especially dimly at the tendency of their junior colleagues to ally themselves with organizations of proven malefaction: SDS at local levels was known to have regularly cooperated with groups of all political stripes, including Communists and Trotskyists where they existed, on specific actions and causes; SDSers had joined in the planning of M2M's initial anti-Vietnam demonstration in May 1964 and SDS publications had urged membership support for it; and SDS had actually issued an invitation to the DuBois Clubs to send observers to its December 1964 National Council meeting. But all that paled to mere transgression in the light of the upcoming march on Washington: not only was it held in opposition to a war of undeniable anti-Communist intent, not only was it challenging a basic policy of "Communist containment" which the LID regarded as sacrosanct, but it actually *invited the participation of domestic Communist organizations.* The official SDS call said simply, "We urge the participation of all those who agree with us that the war in Vietnam injures both Vietnamese and Americans and should be stopped." That meant that such groups as the DuBois Clubs, M2M, and YAWF, and even the Communist and Progressive Labor parties themselves, might participate, and *that* meant that for the first time in more than fifteen years *Communists* would be marching publicly and equally with people from other parts of the political spectrum. The thought sent chills up liberal spines.

The LID had theoretically adopted a new image in the last year—Michael Harrington, thirty-seven, had been installed as Chairman of the Board, Tom Kahn, twenty-six, had become the new Executive Secretary, and people like Bayard Rustin, *Dissent* editor Irving Howe, sociologist Herbert Gans, and labor writer Thomas Brooks had been drawn around—but it was still dominated primarily by men who, as Harrington points out, were "trade-unionists from the New York needle trades who had been through the Communist fight of the 1920s when it was fought with guns and clubs, and who do not kid about these things." The march call precipitated the Port Huron fight all over again—charges of "united frontism," double standards, antiliberalism—but all the more virulent now because SDS was seen as becoming a force to reckon with. An when, despite pressure, SDS showed no signs of dissociating itself from the other groups or even of paying much attention to the objections of its elder colleagues, alarms went out from the LID to the liberal community that dangerous work was afoot. Kissinger, who only months before had bragged of having the LID "literally eating out of my hand," now felt it chewing more around the neck. Harrington himself was more or less out of commission, having been worn out trying to get his social democracy across to the New Left that wouldn't listen, but Kahn let it be known that the LID was strongly disapproving of SDS, not just for allowing Communists in the march but for refusing to repudiate them publicly. And Bayard Rustin even tried to dampen the march by keeping liberal friends and moderate civil-rights forces out of it.*

It was not only the LID which viewed the "frontism" of SDS with such horror. Many traditional liberals and peace groups got chills, too, and when it was rumored around that banners actually urging *withdrawal* from Vietnam were going to be carried and that marchers openly urging an *NLF victory* were going to be allowed in, these people moved to act. In Washington, Curtis Gans of the ADA (who had been, briefly, an SDSer in 1961–62) started redbaiting the organization among politicians, and eventually enough pressure was brought on Senator Gruening that he almost backed out of the ceremonies; only last-minute persuasion from Harold Taylor kept him in. (The Campus ADA, incidentally, eventually did boycott the march on the grounds that it let Communists in.) In Ann Arbor, the Center for the Study of Conflict Resolution, the outfit that had housed PREP since the fall, voted early in April to kick it out forthwith, on the extraordinary grounds that it "has developed into a research service organization to the action-oriented SDS." And in New York, in a statement issued just a few

---

*The LID could not have been too happy, either, about the kinds of sentiments represented by this item in an April worklist mailing, a parody of the spiritual "Oh, Freedom" written by Barbara Haber: "No strategic hamlets,/No strategic hamlets,/No strategic hamlets around me./And before I'll be fenced in/I'll vote for Ho Chi Minh/And go home to the North and be free."

days before the event, a group of prominent liberals including Robert Gilmore (a rich Turn Toward Peace leader, an LID board member, and a prime instigator of the statement), Stuart Hughes, A. J. Muste, Bayard Rustin, and Norman Thomas warned people away from the march because of its Communist taint. They too, they said, were worried about Vietnam, but there were limits: "In an effort to register such concern with our government and people, we welcome the cooperation of all those groups and individuals who, like ourselves, believe in the need for an independent peace movement, not committed to any form of totalitarianism or drawing inspiration from the foreign policy of any government." It sounded like Harry Laidler at his best. And then this group managed to get the *New York Post* to run a prominent editorial on the very eve of the march featuring this statement and going on to issue warnings about "attempts to convert the event into a pro-Communist production" and "a frenzied, one-sided anti-American show." By an ironic turn of history, the people responsible for this editorial attack on what was to become the most important student organization of the sixties were two of the top leaders of what was the most important student organization of the thirties: Joseph Lash, assistant editorial page editor of the *Post* and former executive secretary of the American Student Union, and James Wechsler, editorial page editor of the *Post* and former editor of the ASU's *Student Advocate.*

Some members of the liberal community were not so short-sighted. A letter from Phyllis ("Mrs. Gardner") Cox, and Anne and Martin Peretz, for example—three boosters of, and financial contributors to, the organization—took the statement-signers to task for having "gratuitously and unjustly evoked associations of the March with Communism" and for lending "their prestige to a foolish, divisive and destructive tactic"; subsequently Stuart Hughes and Norman Thomas apologized to SDS for having got sucked into it. And most traditional peace groups still wanted a hand in the march and kept pressing SDS for joint sponsorship so as to print their own stamp on it. This produced another crisis in those busy weeks. The peace groups suggested that SDS give over direction of the march to an *ad hoc* committee of leaders from the various peace organizations, that these have a bigger voice in selecting speakers, that banners favoring immediate withdrawal be forbidden, and that adults as well as students be urged to attend. Kissinger and Booth, doing most of the negotiating in New York for SDS, agreed that signs for immediate withdrawal could be banned if signs for *any* particular position would be forbidden as well—this was later abandoned in favor of a decision to ban only signs identifying particular groups in the line of march—and they agreed that adult groups could issue a second march call directed toward adults if they wished. But the issues of joint sponsorship and speaker selection, which hit at SDS's central role in the affair, were too important for individuals to decide and, in participatory-democratic tradition, had to be voted on by the National Council. On March 13, the NO sent out a ballot on whether SDS should go along with the peace groups (a ballot which, in classic SDS style, enumerated all the facts and then carried two equally impassioned sections, WHY THIS OFFER SHOULD BE ACCEPTED, and WHY THIS OFFER SHOULD BE REJECTED), and a week later the results were in: twenty-four for joint sponsorship, nineteen against, two abstentions.* SDS's single biggest planned action to date was on the verge of being totally transformed, the organization's own central role about to be overwhelmed. *But*—and this is also classic SDS—the majority refused to accept the victory. As Kissinger told the worklist, "Since, however, there were violent opinions on both sides, a number of votes were conditional, and the margin so close, a number of National Officers changed their vote from For to Against to avoid embarking on a radical change in plans without a clear organizational consensus." It was in the best democratic traditions of the organization—and it proved sound strategy as well. SDS told the peace groups it wanted to keep the sponsorship in its own hands but they were welcome to join in the march, and the peace groups, sensing by now that there was really no point in staging another and competing march, decided to go along anyway and urged everyone to join the SDS march. Not all

---

*The national officers' vote was: *for,* Potter, Grizzard, Booth, Brecher, Egleson, Kissinger, McEldowney, Ross, and Williams; *against,* Davis, Gitlin, David Smith, Webb, Wittman; Murphy, Shero, and Charles Smith were not heard from. Several chapters also voted, on the basis of one vote per chapter.

of them were happy about it,* and the two most conservative—
SANE and Turn Toward Peace—washed their hands of the whole
affair, but the eventual cooperation of the other peace organizations proved helpful.

Through all of this, be it noted, it was almost always SDS's
practice (admitting other left groups) rather than its *policies* (as
embodied in the call for the march) that upset people. The policies
were mild enough, the call representing more or less the lowest
common denominator after several weeks of letters, phone calls,
and informal discussion. The argument was simple: the government of South Vietnam is a dictatorship, so naturally the majority
of the people refuse to support it and want to overthrow it, and
U.S. presence there simply impedes (but of course cannot stop)
this process, and costs lives and dollars, and threatens a wider,
nuclear war; besides, the whole thing is immoral, and it kills
people. There was no mention whatsoever of a solution, neither
withdrawal nor negotiation nor pulling back to "enclaves," just
"end the war." There was no identification with Hanoi or the NLF
or "Third World" peoples in general, just "the people overwhelmingly want peace, self-determination, and the opportunity for development." There was no analysis of American foreign policy as
imperialist or interventionist, just "America is committing pointless murder." There were no attacks on the United States or the
Johnson Administration or corporate liberalism, just "this is a war
never declared by Congress." The call did challenge some basic
Administration assumptions—such as that the war was led by
China and Hanoi, that the country was a "domino" in China's
expansion game, that the Saigon government was legitimate and

*For example, David McReynolds, of the War Resisters League, wrote several
months later, "All of us were angered at finding out that S.D.S., with its 'participatory democracy,' had early on decided that we should all participate in the
March but that S.D.S. would make all the decisions. The adult peace movement
was asked to give up its own traditional Easter demonstrations in order not to
draw away from the Washington project. But, of course, S.D.S. would get the
full credit for the Washington project. Petty point? Right! The world is often
petty. But who proved more petty in the long run, the petty adult peace bureaucrats who gave way and helped get thousands of adults down to Washington, or
S.D.S. which did not give way, and which, in the midst of a grave crisis of foreign
policy insisted that S.D.S. be in a position to get full credit for the events of April
17th?" (*Liberation,* August 1965.)

popular—with a perception that was rare in those days, and it was quite outspoken in doing so, as befits a youthful organization. But this was by no means an extreme document, even for its times; less advanced, in fact, than most of *The Port Huron Statement* or *America and the New Era.*

SDS warmed up for its Washington march with the promised demonstration against the Chase Manhattan Bank for its loans to South Africa.

On Friday afternoon, March 19, 1965, some six hundred demonstrators clogged the streets in front of Chase Manhattan's gleaming offices in downtown Manhattan. Bank officials had gotten an injunction against an invasion of bank property and then closed down the offices to the public, so the demonstrators stood out front, singing freedom songs and holding hands with their arms crossed in front of their bodies in the old civil-rights gesture. After an hour, several dozen of them (including Potter, Gitlin, Booth, Hobson, and Arthur Waskow of the Institute for Policy Studies in Washington) sat down in front of the bank's entrance blocking part of the sidewalk, and continued singing. When the police finally ordered them on, they refused to move, locked arms, and waited to be arrested; when the police moved in, they went limp, and forty-three were thrown into waiting paddy wagons. It was SDS's first official act of civil disobedience.

Press coverage was slight, partly because in those early days SDSers knew so little about dealing with the press that they didn't realize Friday demonstrations get scant coverage because Saturday's paper is always the smallest. But the *Times* gave them some mention on the financial pages, slender stories moved over both AP and UPI wires, and there was some local television coverage. Around New York especially, where it was SDS's first public action of consequence, it attracted a good deal of attention in the colleges and enhanced the organization's reputation for action. But it remained, withal, a limited action on a moral plane. Though Gitlin and Booth, among others, were aware of the fundamentally imperialist nature of the bank loans and the U.S.–South African relationship—the PREP executive committee in fact had even proposed an expanded "program against American corporations" as having "more long-range potential than the crisis response program on Vietnam"—this awareness was never shared with the bulk of the demonstrators. The anticapitalist analysis and broader political implication that lay behind the bank loans was put abroad by neither hand nor mouth, and the sit-in remained essentially an isolated and one-dimensional act of outrage, as if Chase Manhattan were a Woolworth's with tellers.

The Chase Manhattan action, incidentally, marked the end of PREP. The South Africa issue seemed secondary to most SDSers in the face of Vietnam, and was left to other groups— chiefly religious organizations such as the Student Christian Federation and the Union Theological Seminary—to carry on while SDS looked elsewhere. The whole notion of "peace research," in fact, seemed somewhat ludicrous after the Vietnam escalation, and certainly no one was worrying much about how the country was going to manage its conversion to a peace economy. Gitlin moved on to the JOIN project in Chicago, Booth went into the National Office, and PREP was left to wither away.

While SDS was preparing for its first major antiwar action, another antiwar phenomenon was unfolding which also had a profound effect on the campuses. At the University of Michigan in the early morning of March 18, a group of teachers and students (including a large number of VOICE members) finally concluded their long night's discussion of how to demonstrate their opposition to the escalation of the war; their plan: get a group of experts on, and opponents of, the war to informally address and take questions from the university community *for an entire night.* The event would be called, following the rhetorical precedent of the civil-rights movement's main tactic, a "teach-in."

The University of Michigan teach-in was held on the night of March 24, 1965, and it was an astonishing success. The organizers expected five hundred people; perhaps as many as three thousand showed up during the evening. And it wasn't all boring lectures, either: there were teachers talking out of their own feelings to a mass of students they now regarded as citizens, not bluebooks, and there were folksingers and hecklers and bomb scares and coffee breaks and a torchlight parade—and it was all very exciting. "On that night," says Marc Pilisuk, one of the primary organizers, "people who really cared talked of things that really mattered." Most students found that refreshing.

Within days the teach-in idea swept the nation, and within the next two months more than a hundred colleges and universities participated—not just the expected ones like Wisconsin, Berkeley, Chicago, and Columbia, but surprising ones like Arizona, the University of Miami, Kent State, and Goucher, and unheard-of ones like Flint Junior College in Michigan, Marist College in Poughkeepsie, New York, and Principia College in Elsah, Illinois.* There was even a National Teach-in, in Washington, D.C., with professors from all over the country, radio hook-ups to 122 campuses, and full coverage by National Education Television for all twelve hours. And at the end of the school year, May 21-22, the largest and most outspoken of all the teach-ins was held, at Berkeley, of course, with an estimated thirty-five thousand people attending some or all of its thirty-six hours and a list of speakers ranging from liberals to representatives of the DuBois Clubs, the Progressive Labor Party, and SDS.†

Although SDSers participated in many teach-ins—a new SDS member at Michigan named Carl Oglesby spoke at the very first and SDS President Potter spoke at the largest—SDS as an organization never promoted them as a part of its over-all strategy. This was not only because the teach-ins were in the main faculty-led and faculty-directed, but because SDSers felt that these were essentially *apolitical* exercises whose best effect could be only to educate but not to radicalize. The basic assumptions behind the teach-ins—which perhaps reflected the somewhat snobbish and politically unsophisticated attitudes one would expect to find

*Not all colleges were enthusiastic, and not all professors. Among those who started a campaign to denounce the teach-ins was LID's Frank Trager.
†But perhaps the most famous teach-in was held at Rutgers, during which that university's Marxist historian Eugene Genovese, who was also the faculty adviser of the local SDS chapter, said, among much else, "I do not fear or regret the impending Viet Cong victory in Vietnam. I welcome it." This became a *cause célèbre* in that fall's gubernatorial race when injected by the Republican candidate to smear the incumbent Democrat; the Republican was defended by a long letter of some note in *The New York Times* claiming that "the victory for the Viet Cong which Professor Genovese 'welcomes' would mean, ultimately, the destruction of freedom of speech for all men for all time, not only in Asia but in the United States as well. . . . Any individual employed by the state should not be allowed to use his position for the purpose of giving aid and comfort to enemies of the state." The writer was New York lawyer Richard M. Nixon. (See *Teach-ins: U.S.A.,* edited by Louis Menashe and Ronald Radosh, Praeger, 1967.)

among physical scientists and psychologists, the dominant faculty groups in the movement—were that reason and truth would ultimately prevail in the present American society, that intellectuals and professors had special roles as beholders of that reason and tellers of that truth, and that the war in Vietnam was an isolated mistake of the American system rather than a logical extension of it. Most of those in SDS had by now rejected all three assumptions. They felt that the teach-ins would not draw people into a broader movement on the left and supply them with a radical politics for other occasions. Without ever even enunciating it or having to make an official decision, SDS indicated by its passive response that it had gone beyond the moderation of the teach-in phase of antiwar politics. It had by now learned bitter lessons about reformism, and it was coming to feel that only with the kind of confrontation and militancy a march represented could America be changed.

April 17 was one of those flawless Washington spring days: a cloudless sky, a gentle northeast breeze, temperature in the eighties. By nine o'clock in the morning, several thousand people were gathered along Pennsylvania Avenue, ready to head for the White House, and thousands more were still coming. Todd Gitlin recalls,

> Originally I was gloomy: I thought it would be good if we could get five thousand people. But it was so exciting. I took the bus with the Ann Arbor people, and we got out of the bus and there were already *thousands* of people there. It was really *so* exciting.

Buses began arriving from all parts of the country, as far away as Mississippi and Maine; a thousand people came from Boston, a thousand more from Philadelphia; three trains and fifty special buses pulled in from New York. At least fifty colleges and universities—and by one estimate more than a hundred—sent contingents from all the usual places (Ivy League schools, prestigious East Coast colleges, Midwestern state universities), but also from Tulsa, Iowa, North Dakota, Toronto, and British Columbia. By ten o'clock there were maybe eight thousand people walking slowly around the White House (Johnson himself was hidden away at his ranch in Texas, where four hundred SDS-led students picketed his front gate), carrying signs ranging from those which had been approved in advance like END THE WAR IN VIETNAM NOW, STOP THE KILLING, and I WON'T FIGHT IN VIETNAM, to homemade appeals such as WITHDRAW FROM VIETNAM and DEMOCRACY? THIS WAR IS MAKING THE WORLD SAFE FOR HY-POCRISY. And by two o'clock, when the marchers had gathered in the outdoor Sylvan Theater behind the Washington Monument, there were perhaps twenty-five thousand people.* It was the largest peace march in American history.

Sizable groups of nonstudents, both adults and blacks, were among the marchers, the former because of the peace groups, the latter because of SDS's conscious efforts to get a black turnout, plus the growing awareness in the black organizations that racism and militarism were linked—or, as one sign put it, ONE MAN ONE VOTE—SELMA OR SAIGON. Dress was for the most part informal, ties were in a minority, but not by much, and most of the women wore skirts; the large preponderance of the youths were clean-shaven and with short hair.

The program was an odd mixture, as befitted the time. There was a contingent of name folksingers—Joan Baez, Phil Ochs, Judy Collins—and a trio of SNCC amateurs. There were blacks—Bob Parris Moses of SNCC and Mrs. Iva Pearce of the Cleveland ERAP's welfare-mothers' organization—drawing the connections between segregation and defoliation and pressing home the urgent need for something to be done both in Vietnam and in the ghettos. There were the liberals—as I. F. Stone and Senator Gruening both identified themselves—who quickly established their distance from the dangerous Communists on the march (Stone by attacking the previous "generations of snotty Marxist-Leninists," Gruening by attacking China and its "expansionist" policies) and reduced everything to the issue of ending the war. And there were

* *The National Guardian* and one police spokesman estimated twenty-five thousand, SDS itself afterward spoke of twenty to twenty-five thousand, the *Washington Star* variously reported "up to 20,000" and "16,000," the *New York Times* said "more than 15,000." This begins a long succession of games-playing about crowd figures; police and conservative newspapers generally guessing as low as possible, march leaders and liberal newspapers trying to err on the upper side, and the truth impossible to discover even by various academics who have purported to analyze crowd photographs. Standard procedure on the left has become to take the police estimate and double it.

the radicals—SDS President Paul Potter and march chairman
Staughton Lynd, then assistant professor of history at Yale and
an editor of *Liberation*—who tried to put the war in a wider
context, to make connections. Lynd said:

> We are here to keep the faith with those of all countries and all ages
> who have sought to beat swords into plowshares and to war no
> more. We are here on behalf of millions of men and women through-
> out the world who are crying out, What has happened to the United
> States? We are here on behalf of Jean-Paul Sartre. And we are also
> here on behalf of those eight thousand miles from us for whom the
> Easter and Passover season brings death, not life. We are here on
> behalf of brave men who have been fighting for their country's
> independence three times as long as we fought for ours, and with
> much less foreign assistance. We are here on behalf of the American
> soldiers who do not understand the reason for the war in which they
> are dying.
>
> Above all we are here on behalf of the women and children of
> that land which we have turned into a fiery furnace, whose eyes as
> they look out at us from the pictures and the posters, ask us, Why?

Potter, who closed the rally, gave a speech even more poignant,
more impassioned, more radical. Potter, twenty-five, was in his
way a personification of SDS: he was bright and politically sophisticated, a graduate of Oberlin and a graduate student at Michigan,
a former national affairs vice president of NSA, a person of
ideology; but he was also a boy who had grown up on a small farm
in Illinois, was a champion chicken-judger at the age of twelve,
had gravitated to SDS chiefly because of its style and lived now
in the ERAP project in Cleveland, and, as his earlier university-
reform speech showed, possessed an original and individualistic
mind. ("Pure SDS," Gitlin says of Potter; "he doesn't get it out
of books—he has a remarkable ability to think for himself and not
pay attention to all the rhetorical shit whether academic or political.") Potter spoke for SDS, and for much of his generation:

> The incredible war in Vietnam has provided the razor, the terrifying
> sharp cutting edge that has finally severed the last vestige of illusion
> that morality and democracy are the guiding principles of American
> foreign policy.... That is a terrible and bitter insight for people who
> grew up as we did—and our revulsion at that insight, our refusal

to accept it as inevitable or necessary, is one of the reasons that so many people have come here today. . . .

But the war goes on; the freedom to conduct that war depends on the dehumanization not only of Vietnamese people but of Americans as well; it depends on the construction of a system of premises and thinking that insulates the President and his advisors thoroughly and completely from the human consequences of the decisions they make. . . .

What kind of system is it that allows good men to make those kinds of decisions? What kind of system is it that justifies the United States or any country seizing the destinies of the Vietnamese people and using them callously for its own purpose? What kind of system is it that disenfranchises people in the South, leaves millions upon millions of people throughout the country impoverished and excluded from the mainstream and promise of American society, that creates faceless and terrible bureaucracies and makes those the place where people spend their lives and do their work, that consistently puts material values before human values—and still persists in calling itself free and still persists in finding itself fit to police the world? What place is there for ordinary men in that system and how are they to control it, make it bend itself to their wills rather than bending them to its?

We must name that system,* We must name it, describe it, analyze it, understand it and change it. For it is only when that system is changed and brought under control that there can be any hope for stopping the forces that create a war in Vietnam today or a murder in the South tomorrow or all the incalculable, innumerable more subtle atrocities that are worked on people all over, all the time. . . .

I wonder what it means for each of us to say we want to end the war in Vietnam—whether, if we accept the full meaning of that statement and the gravity of the situation, we can simply leave the march and go back to the routines of a society that acts as if it were not in the midst of a grave crisis. . . .

There is no simple plan, no scheme or gimmick that can be

---

*This phrase, which later became famous in left circles, was taken by most people to suggest "imperialism" or "capitalism," and there were shouts from the crowd telling Potter to say those words. But Potter subsequently explained that "I did not fail to call the system capitalism because I was a coward or an opportunist. I refused to call it capitalism because capitalism was for me and my generation an inadequate description of the evils of America—a hollow, dead word tied to the thirties." (Potter, *A Name for Ourselves,* Little, Brown, 1971.)

proposed here. There is no simple way to attack something that is deeply rooted in the society. If the people of this country are to end the war in Vietnam, and to change the institutions which create it, then the pople of this country must create a massive social move-ment—and if that can be built around the issue of Vietnam then that is what we must do. . . .

But that means that we build a movement that works not simply in Washington but in communities and with the problems that face people throughout the society. That means that we build a movement that understands Vietnam in all its horror as but a symptom of a deeper malaise, that we build a movement that makes possible the implementation of values that would have prevented Vietnam, a movement based on the integrity of man and a belief in man's capacity to tolerate all the weird formulations of society that men may choose to strive for; a movement that will build on the new and creative forms of protest that are beginning to emerge, such as the teach-in, and extend their efforts and intensify them; that we will build a movement that will find ways to support the increasing numbers of young men who are unwilling to and will not fight in Vietnam; a movement that will not tolerate the escalation or prolon-gation of the war but will, if necessary, respond to the Administra-tion war effort with massive civil disobedience all over the country, that will wrench the country into a confrontation with the issues of the war; a movement that must of necessity reach out to all these people in Vietnam or elsewhere who are struggling to find decency and control for their lives.

The huge crowd sat still for a moment, then rose to its feet with the loudest and most sustained applause of the day.

After this speech, the crowd moved out from behind the Washington Monument and began a march down the huge mall toward the Capitol at the other end, there to present an end-the-war petition to Congress. The mood was in large part joyous and even exuberant, but there was an overtone of something darker. "We Shall Overcome," sung with the huge Capitol dome getting larger and the shadows lengthening across the mall, somehow sounded more menacing than it ever had before—"Deep in my heart/I *do* believe:/We *shall* overcome, some day"—and soon shouts of "Get Out, Get Out" and "End the War, End the War" drowned out the singing. Jack A. Smith, a *National Guardian* correspondent, and sympathetic, reported that it was "one of the

most impressive demonstrations this reporter has seen (including
the 1963 March on Washington with its quarter-million people).
Whatever there was of a picnic atmosphere before the walk to
Congress totally dissipated, replaced by a determination apparent
on every face." About 150 yards in front of the Capitol steps, the
marchers were supposed to stop so that a small contingent could
take the petition up to someone within the Capitol. But as the
front ranks slowed, a growing cry went up, "Let's *all* go, LET'S
ALL GO," and began spreading through the crowd. Staughton
Lynd recalls that moment:

> As the crowd moved down the Mall toward the seat of government,
> its path delimited on each side by rows of chartered buses so that
> there was nowhere to go but forward, toward the waiting policemen,
> it seemed that the great mass of people would simply flow on
> through and over the marble buildings, that our forward movement
> was irresistibly strong, that even had some been shot or arrested
> nothing could have stopped that crowd from taking possession of
> its government. Perhaps next time we should keep going, occupying
> for a time the rooms from which orders issue and sending to the
> people of Vietnam and the Dominican Republic the profound apolo-
> gies which are due; or quietly waiting on the Capitol steps until
> those who make policy for us, and who like ourselves are trapped
> by fear and pride, consent to enter into a dialogue with us and with
> mankind.

But 1965 was not yet a time of confrontation, of taking over the
buildings, and as the crowd approached the police cordon at the
Capitol steps the bulk of the crowd slowly halted. A few hundred
students moved across the cement walk and up the steps, calling
for the others to follow, but behind them SDS leaders were urging
people to stay and when they found they were alone, they stopped
and sat on the steps. Soon it was announced (incorrectly, as it
turned out, but effectively) that the petition had been "pasted to
the door of Congress" (actually it was handed to a Congressional
aide inside the Capitol) and the crowd cheered, relaxed, began
drifting toward the buses, and eventually, around six o'clock,
dispersed.

The response to the Potter speech and the apparent militancy
of a good number of the petitioners were signals of a growing
sentiment toward confrontation—as yet held, however, by a

minority. William A. Price, another *Guardian* correspondent, assessed the sentiment as being " . . . a search for greater unity, more
radical forms of protest. Clearly a frustration for many was the
dispersion of the march at the end of a long day without some
form of massive civil disobedience, for which many of the participants were ready." A few attempts were made to give vent to it:
there was a successful seven-man sit-in at the State Department;
a planned "mass civil-disobedience demonstration" of unspecified
nature that was even announced twice from the Sylvan Theater
stage but never came off because no one apparently knew how to
organize it and SDS chose not to; and a short-lived attempt at the
White House by about two dozen students to sit in and maintain
a vigil, the militant mood of which was expressed by Eric Mann,
an ex-CORE hand who was an ERAPer then and later became an
important activist in the Boston area: "This is not a political
demonstration. It is a personal witness and confrontation with the
power structure. We understand the need for a broad-based
demonstration, but in order to change a fundamentally rotten
system you have to take a fundamental decision." But the militance remained muted. For most, this was the first open declaration to the government of their opposition to the war, and the
belief that the government might listen, and respond, had not yet
dissipated.

The effects of the march on SDS were all things it would not
have expected three months before. For one thing, people noticed
it. Television coverage was only spotty (and David Brinkley with
his usual wry conservatism suggested they were all "loiterers"),
but there *was* some, and newspaper coverage was good, if unsympathetic. *The New York Times* ran the story on its front page, with
a picture and a three-column eighteen-point headline, but its tone
was distant and faintly amused:

> More than 15,000 students and a handful of adults picketed the
> White House in warm sunshine today, calling for an end to the
> fighting in Vietnam. Walking three or four abreast in orderly rows
> and carrying printed white signs, the students clogged the sidewalk.
> The principal occupant of the White House was at his ranch in
> Texas.

The *Times* story, as did all the coverage, emphasized both "beards and blue jeans" and the presence of a small band of Nazi and other right-wing counter-pickets, and substantially ignored the afternoon speeches and the petition. The Scripps-Howard papers ran an editorial calling SDS "highly suspect." And the now-defunct New York *Herald Tribune* stated that this "civil rights rally" was a "three-hour demonstration . . . organized at a cost of $100,000" —which happened to be wrong on all three counts: it was an antiwar demonstration, lasted closer to eight hours, and cost SDS perhaps $15,000 at most.*

Publicity of this kind disturbed a good many liberals, for whom marches and pickets were out of place and faintly embarrassing, and a lot of agonizing went on in LID circles. Murray Baron, a management relations consultant, for example, resigned from the LID Board of Directors the following Tuesday in protest over the "picketing Students for D.S." The following week, realizing the size of the gulf between the two generations, the Board itself voted to establish "dialogues" between SDS and the Student Affairs Committee (Harrington, Kahn, Brooks, Fleischman, and Howe, among others) "to explore, informally and in depth, various issues around which differences have arisen." One right-wing publicist, Arthur G. McDowell of a Council Against Communist Aggression, circulated a letter, primarily among the most conservative LID members, urging them all to resign, and arguing that:

> . . . the Communist apparatus had swung behind your Students for a Democratic (sic) Society. . . . S.D.S. had been the front for a maximum show of strength of a (for this project) united Communist turnout and mechanical operation. . . . The group you sponsor was the cover for a Communist mobilization against the President and Government of the U.S.†

---

*April NO expenses were $9,719.32, May's $6,880, largely but not wholly for the march; chapters and individuals, of course, had additional expenditures of their own. ("Financial Report" by Clark Kissinger, June 1965, SDS archives.)
†Harrington, it should be noted, quickly responded to this smear by circulating a three-page letter denouncing "Mr. McDowell's McCarthyite methods" and urging "open and friendly relations with SDS." But he was not very pleased with SDS, either, as he made clear, and one person in the NO remarked that with Harrington as a defender, "we don't need enemies."

In point of fact, the FBI itself had counted only seventy Communists during the whole affair.

It wasn't only the older generation that reacted, however.
Through its new publicity SDS was looked upon at college campuses now as the leading group, student or adult, in the burgeoning antiwar movement, and it was also coming to be seen as a
major force in what by then had been designated "the New Left"
as a whole. In the weeks following the march the formal national
membership increased by perhaps five hundred, until it was over
two thousand by the end of the school year. The number of
chapters increased to eighty, double the figure of the preceding
December.* Far more important, however, SDSers felt was the
"unsigned membership," the people who just began to gravitate
toward SDS, attend meetings, and join actions, both previously
apolitical youths and a number of articulate and talented people
on the fringes of other organizations who now found a place to
become involved. SDS was suddenly the place to go. Once there,
nobody paid much attention to signing them up officially— the
usual response even of Regional Organizers, whose job it is to
increase membership, was to draw up a list of the most active
people on any campus and regard them as SDS members whether
or not they were ever officially registered on Kissinger's lists back
in New York. As Kissinger put it that spring to one of the many
reporters then coming around, "We are, *de facto,* the largest
membership organization on the left [but] we don't stress signing
people up. We are not trying to make our organization bigger than
any other in the sense of organizational chauvinism [but] in the
sense that we have a viewpoint we hope many people will accept."
Either way, SDS had arrived.

Another happy effect of the march was a National Council
meeting right afterward that Kissinger called "one of the most

*Chapters began or were reestablished at Adelphi, Amherst, Antioch, Arizona
State, Bard, Brandeis, Brooklyn, Buffalo (SUNY), Central Missouri State,
CCNY, Columbia, Goddard, Indiana, Kansas, Kenyon, Long Island, Maine,
Massachusetts, MacMurray, University of Miami, Minnesota, Missouri, New
York High School At-large, North Carolina, North Texas State, Oberlin, Platts-
burg (SUNY), Princeton, Queensboro Community College, San Diego State,
Southern California, Stanford, Temple, University of the South, Vanderbilt,
Virginia, Washington, D.C. At-large, Wayne State, and Western Reserve.

pleasant and productive in recent SDS history." And why not? Everyone was flush from the unexpected success of the march and when the one hundred delegates got together on Sunday the ideas for what to do next were as plentiful as crumbs in an ERAP kitchen. There were several proposals for working on university reform and establishing "free universities": suggestions that the organization had better turn to its own internal education before it found an unbridgeable chasm between the old guard and the new influx; and recommendations that more blacks be systematically brought in to what was becoming an almost all-white SDS. But most of the suggestions concerned Vietnam. Kissinger proposed a strategy, quickly known as Kissinger's Kamikazi Plan, of sending SDS teams to military bases and induction centers to leaflet, picket, and otherwise persuade eighteen-year-olds not to register, draftees not to report, and enlisted men not to go on serving—all in violation of the 1917 Espionage Act, but which SDS would justify legally on the basis of the Nuremberg Doctrine. This was hotly debated but in the end turned out to be too strong for most of the campus delegates, and was shunted to a committee with the cautious reminder that "before the Kissinger plan can be put into effect the membership must be polled," something the organization had never done before. Another proposal—a visit to Hanoi by a left-wing American contingent—was also given over to a committee, an idea that would be implemented in time but by someone else. Hayden suggested a new Continental Congress —carrying the notion of alternate institutions to its logical extreme—made up of people who "really" represented America to meet in Washington over the summer and establish a new government right in the shadow of the old; that one was too bizarre even to go to a committee and was soon dropped, though it continued to lead an underground life on the left for the next several years. LID relations were discussed, with Kissinger proposing that SDS sever ties immediately and "get the hell out of New York City"; the NC only mandated Kissinger to "look into the possibility" of a permanent break but it agreed that moving the NO was desirable and authorized a transfer to the more central location of Chicago as soon as quarters could be found. Finally, Carl Oglesby proposed that a group called RIP (for research, information, and publications) be established to fill in the information gaps of the

members, especially with regard to Vietnam; Oglesby himself was
hired to put it into operation.

Carl Oglesby at that point was thirty years old, had a wife and
three children, and worked as a technical writer for the Bendix
Systems Division at $12,00 a year—not what one would call the
average SDSer. His roots were working class: his father had been
born in South Carolina and had left a patriarchal and unpleasant
family life on a farm there to get rich up North, ending up in the
rubber mills of Akron, Ohio; there he met Oglesby's mother, up
from Alabama, whom he married and later divorced. Oglesby
went through the Akron public school system, winning a national
oratory prize in his senior year with a pro–Cold War speech, and
went on to Kent State University, a place of surpassing dullness
in the early fifties which after three years he forsook for Greenwich Village and a life as an actor and playwright. He lasted a
year, returned to Kent State, married, and continued writing:
three plays, one produced in a small theater in Dallas and the
other two later put on at the University of Michigan, and an
unfinished novel. He worked at odd jobs for a while, then at the
turn of the decade moved to Ann Arbor to work for Bendix and
try to get a degree out of the University of Michigan in his spare
time. Though Hayden, Haber, and the VOICE chapter were then
active, Oglesby was far removed from the campus political scene
and never came in contact with them. Then in the summer of 1964
he happened to read D. F. Fleming's *The Cold War and Its Origins,* a skillful revisionist work showing American blame for postwar antagonisms, and the Cold War scales began to fall from his
eyes. That fall he wrote an article on the errors of America's Far
East policy that appeared in a campus magazine, the alert anten-
nae of SDS picked it up, and a few SDSers went out to Oglesby's suburban home to see if maybe he would become an SDS
ally.

> We talked. I got to thinking about things. As a writer, I needed a
> mode of action. . . . I couldn't just grumble and go off to the creative
> spider-hole and turn out plays. From what SDS said about the
> Movement, it sounded like a direct way I could deal with things.
> I had to decide: was I going to be a writer just to be a professional
> writer, or was I going to write in order to make change? I saw that
> people were already moving, so I joined up.

The first notion that fall was that Oglesby could help establish a "grass-roots theater" for SDS, and he was at work on that when the bombing moved into North Vietnam. Immediately he became active in SDS's Vietnam work, participating in the Michigan teach-in, writing (with Gitlin) a press release after President Johnson's Johns Hopkins speech on Vietnam that dissected it as designed for "conning Americans," and joining in pre-march organizing. But the National Council after the march was his first national SDS meeting, and he was impressed:

> A fantastic experience. For three days there was debate on various subjects, and I was absolutely convinced by each speaker. One would get up and defend a point, and I would be convinced. Then another guy would get up and refute the point so well I thought *he* was right. One after the other they got better and smarter. It was the first time I had seen debate when it wasn't an ego game. They were really beautiful people. Students! I had no idea until then that young people—anyone—could think so well.

And so Oglesby made the irrevocable decision to join the Movement and become a full-time "RIP" worker for SDS.

On May 8, 1965, the *Saturday Evening Post,* in a long article on "The Explosive Revival of The Far Left," carried a statement from one Phillip Abbott Luce under the headline, WHY I QUIT THE EXTREME LEFT. Luce, twenty-eight, had been a member of the Progressive Labor Party for more than a year and involved with PL members for more than two. He had gone to Cuba under PL auspices in the summer of 1963 and had been a member of the executive committee of a PL-led Student Committee for Travel to Cuba, which organized a second trip in the summer of 1964. He had been an organizer of a May 2nd Movement antiwar demonstration in August 1964 in Times Square during which forty-seven people, many from M2M, were arrested. He wrote:

> The more members of the Progressive Labor Movement I met [in 1963], the more impressed I became with the group. At first appearance and even later, I was attracted by the apparent openness of the movement. Here for the first time in my life I met a group of young Americans, many of whom openly called themselves Communists and forcefully preached the need for a revolution to end the evils in the United States. . . . In addition, nearly all of the members and

leaders that I met were young, vital, dynamic and extremely personable. They seemed to have a freshness of approach to political
problems and a frankness with each other that I had not seen or
heard of in other far-left parties. . . .

We set up the national executive committee of M-2-M in such
a way that Progressive Labor controlled it from its inception. At
present a majority of the national controlling body of 12 are members of P.L. But, as with the Student Committee for Travel to Cuba,
most of the P.L. members on the national governing body of M-2-M
are kept "secret" members.

We decided last January that M-2-M, although set up as a
"radical peace organization" specifically concerning Vietnam,
should also join in other campus protests, such as the one that led
to the riots at the University of California, in Berkeley. Although
emphasis is still laid on the need for American withdrawal from
Vietnam, the organizers for M-2-M are now busily trying to stir up
student grievances on various campuses including Brooklyn College, Adelphi, Harvard, University of Cincinnati and City College
of New York. The agitators claim that since the college administrations are the logical extension of the "power structure" (the Government), every student grievance should be the cause for a student
demonstration a la Berkeley. . . .

The philosophy behind all of this action among students—and
actually P.L.'s basic tactic—is to involve students in a direct confrontation with the power structure on any and all levels. Progressive Labor contends that any person can be made into a revolutionary if he is led into a fracas with some authority symbol, especially
the police. If he is arrested, or better still, beaten and jailed, the
chances are then good that he will begin to hate the police and the
court system. . . .

Luce left PL in February 1965, alarmed, he said, over plans for
terrorist activity by PL members, and began a career, familiar
from the thirties and forties, of warning people against the very
organization he had belonged to. Later that year he was a cooperative witness for the House Un-American Activities Committee,
and subsequently wrote a book with help from that committee.

In the weeks after the April march, SDS continued to set
itself on an inevitable path away from its old roots, its liberal
heritage, its period of reformism. Early in May it sponsored a
meeting at Swarthmore, directed by SDSer Patch Dellinger (son

of pacifist David Dellinger), which planned Vietnam antiwar committees which were to spend the summer in a variety of cities doing a rough mix of PREP propaganda work and ERAP community involvement. On May 12 it finally moved out of its New York City office—deliberately symbolic of a departure from the past—and set up headquarters at 1103 East Sixty-third Street in Chicago, just south of the University of Chicago campus in what SDSers made sure to point out was "the Woodlawn ghetto." On May 21 a number of Chicago-area SDSers and several of the NO participated in an antiwar sit-down in Chicago's Loop, during which forty people were arrested, the first time that SDS leadership was involved in massive civil disobedience against the war (and only the second time, including the Chase Manhattan sit-in, that it was organizationally involved in civil disobedience at all). SDS was even beginning to "name the system," albeit with the humor that it reserved for anything smacking of Old Left rhetoric: in one worklist mailing it ended a discussion of Vietnam and the Dominican Republic with, "Crush imperialism—the life you save may be your own."

The new spirit in SDS was the genie that April 17 let out of the bottle. It was imperfectly formed as yet and it would grow far larger, but it was even then unmistakable. Confrontations, such as the Washington march, seemed more desirable than committees; action, such as Berkeley represented, seemed more effective than agitation; alienation, such as the ERAPers had come to, seemed more inevitable than allegiance. SDS had spent five years, three of them with all the energy at its disposal, trying, in the old Quaker phrase, to speak truth to power; but power did not listen, power did not change. SDS had tried to wrest reforms in civil rights, in university governance, in economic distribution, in the inner cities, in the political parties, in the corporate institutions: PREP, ERAP, PEP, the vast literature production, the innumerable conferences, the meetings and seminars, the elaborate convention documents, the civil-rights protests and the antibomb marches, and even the march on the capital, all were infused with the belief that radical education and moral actions would change the ways of the system if the system would but heed them. Now, after the election failures, the civil-rights tokenism, the realignment collapse, the foreign adventurism, and the escalation of the war—

among much else—it seemed apparent that this just was not enough. Something more was necessary, and the next three years would be occupied with working out just what.

It is no accident that Carl Oglesby came to occupy a prominent place in SDS just as a new period in its life began. For although he was older and supremely intellectual, his very decision to give up a cushy suburban life for the uncertainties of radicalism portended the kind of commitment, the kind of alienation, the kind of uncompromising fixity, that the coming period of resistance would display. Oglesby was perfectly a man of resistance. In his literary way he expressed his own feeling, and the new spirit of SDS, in a note he wrote to Paul Booth that May:

> What gives you hope gives me bitterness—this balmy night, soft spring, sweet air. Life looks so little and death looks so big. You don't misunderstand me. What's worth working for is simply worth working for—on its own present terms, on the face value of what it *is.* I mean I'm not in the movement like a businessman's in business, waiting for the payoff on the investment. The value of my commitment is not *pending* anything, the commitment isn't waiting to be ratified by success or refuted by failure. Life is better than death, one sides with life always. . . .
>
> To the barricades!

RESISTANCE
1965-1968

Much of the anti-war movement, regardless of rhetoric, seems predicated on the assumption that existing power is legitimate and that the regular channels of political opposition are sufficient to end the war. For that reason it has concentrated on proving that there is substantial, growing public sentiment against the war (through large demonstrations, petitions, newspaper ads, referenda, etc.) and it has done this quite effectively. Its method has concentrated on anti-war propaganda and education and symbolic appeals to power. . . .

We are convinced that power throughout this society is illegitimate and will continue to be basically unresponsive to public opinion and normal political pressure. That conviction FORCES us to a conception of resistance—an effort to impede and disrupt the functioning of the military political machinery wherever it is local and vulnerable. We join a resistance movement out of no great optimism about its capacity to end the war; indeed we call this a resistance, not a revolution, because entrenched power is too strong to be broken. At best a resistance can delay and harass, strengthening the internal conflicts that make the war costly, aiding marginally the Vietnamese whose prosecution of the war is the most critical determinant of its outcome; at best a resistance sets seeds throughout the country of a movement aimed directly at imperialism and domestic exploitation.

—THE MOVEMENT, San Francisco, November 1967

12

SUMMER 1965

Almost as if it were aware that after the march on Washington it was becoming a new organization, SDS chose for its 1965 convention a site some distance from New York State, where the last two conventions had been held, and only two hundred miles from Port Huron, its geographical fountainhead. At Camp Maplehurst, near the tiny town of Kewadin, in the resort area of northern Michigan, some 450 SDSers met from June 9 to 13 in a convention that foreshadowed both a new style and a new direction for the organization.

For this convention, as those past, the life style was spare: delegates brought their own sleeping bags, often slept under the stars; the food, included in a $20 registration fee, was inadequate and unappetizing, and the nearest city of any size eighteen miles away; park regulations allowed no one in or out after 11:00 P.M. There were some familiar faces—a number of SNCC people showed up, the last convention they were to appear at before black power sent them in an irrevocably different direction; and observers came from all the groups on the left from the National Student Christian Federation to the Progressive Labor Party. Talk, as usual, centered around Movement gossip, Movement plans, and Movement rhetoric: "organize," "participate," "alienation," "consciousness," "moral," "relevance," "dialogue," "community," "initiative," "involvement."* But

---

*It is revealing that "Movement" by now had become the word the young left in America used to talk about itself, for it suggests sweep and action and drive, implies power without demanding precision, and can encompass civil rights as well as antiwar activists, small *ad hoc* demonstrations as well as SDS and SNCC.

it was clear that this convention would be like none before.

For now SDS was starting to become the home for a new breed of activist, a younger, more alienated, more committed student, part of that strain that had been growing in SDS over the last year and had increased even further with the escalation in Vietnam and the Washington march. They were new to national politics, had never before attended an SDS convention, knew the organization essentially as the caller of the April march, but when they looked around for a group that seemed to share their concerns, all that was on the horizon was SDS, and so they flocked to Kewadin—much to the bewilderment of the older SDSers, now irrevocably christened "the old guard." For the first time at a convention most of the people were unknown to each other, the proceedings were out of the hands of a group of old friends, the Port Huronites no longer dominated. "All sorts of things went on," Lee Webb says with some dismay, "all the traditions stopped." "It was an odd convention," Paul Booth recalls, "a *loony* convention: *every*one was loony." Looniness is in the eye of the beholder, but there is no question that SDS was changing, and Kewadin was a signal of that change. The period of resistance was taking shape.

The new breed brought to SDS a new style and a new heritage. For the first time at an SDS meeting people smoked marijuana; Pancho Villa mustaches, those droopy Western-movie addenda that eventually became a New Left cliché, made their first appearance in quantity; blue workshirts, denim jackets, and boots were worn by both men and women. These were people generally raised outside of the East, many from the Midwest and Southwest, and their ruralistic dress reflected a different tradition, one more aligned to the frontier, more violent, more individualistic, more bare-knuckled and callus-handed, than that of the early SDSers. They were non-Jewish, nonintellectual, nonurban, from a nonprofessional class, and often without any family tradition of political involvement, much less radicalism. They tended to be not only ignorant of the history of the left and its current half-life in New York City, but downright uninterested: they didn't know Dellinger from Dillinger, Rustin from Reston, Trotsky from Chomsky, *Liberation* from *Liberator,* the Socialist Workers Party from the Socialist Labor Party, and they didn't really care. Jack Newfield, surveying twenty-five of this new breed in 1965, found that

> . . . none had ever read Rosa Luxemburg, Max Weber, Eduard Bernstein, John Dewey, Peter Kropotkin, or John Stuart Mill. Less than five had actually read Lenin or Trotsky, and only a few more had ever read Marx. Almost all of them had read C. Wright Mills and Camus, and about half had read [Paul] Goodman, Frantz Fanon, and Herbert Marcuse. More had read *The Realist* than had read Mill's "Essay on Liberty," or the "Sermon on the Mount."

Not that they were all simply "anti-intellectual," the phrase with which many of the old guard and more of the Old Left dismissed them; rather, they were generally without exposure to this kind of learning, being underclassmen from mediocre colleges or conservative state universities; they were nervous and often inarticulate in public debates with well-versed old guard radicals; and they emphasized "morals" and "values," action and bodies-on-the-line, honesty and courage, not ideology and theory and what they called "Old Leftism" and "all that thirties horseshit." Their notions of politics had been formed *ab ovo* in the civil-rights struggle or with the impact of Vietnam escalation, so most of them had yet to make radical connections, to develop much beyond a moral view of race and war. Al Haber later in the year expressed the old guard's fear of the danger of these "moral activists" in SDS:

> The force of their energy and enthusiasm for action [ends up] preempting organizational resources and allowing no time for educational work. Why? Because self-education is hard; because it is slow; because they are not sure and secure in their beliefs; because the urgency of direct moral expression outweighs for them all other considerations.

In this he was prophetic—but he might just as well have tried to warn Detroit against having anything to do with the Model T.

The "energy and enthusiasm for action" which the new breed brought was accompanied by a sense of alienation, a bitterness, and a commitment that would help, in the next few years, to fuel the fires of resistance within SDS. As people often still in their teens, five, six, and seven years younger than the old guard, they had already experienced while still in high school the idealism-disillusion-revulsion syndrome that many of the older SDSers had gone through, they had lived through Selma, Dallas, Atlantic City, Santo Domingo, and Vietnam before they even came to SDS. For them, "We Shall Overcome" had already given way to "Blowin' in the Wind." They were in a sense more thoroughly anti-American than the early SDSers had been, quicker even than they to write off labor, liberals, the Democratic Party, reforms, and "the system" in general, emotionally inclined to plague both—all —houses. And they had made a break from their past more thorough than their predecessors; Texan Jeff Shero, spiritually a part of the new breed despite his year's experience in SDS, recalls:

> We were by instinct much more radical, much more willing to take risks, in a way because to become a part of something like SDS meant a tremendous number of breaks. If you were a New York student and became a member of SDS, it was essentially joining a political organization, which was a common experience. In Texas to join SDS meant breaking with your family, it meant being cut off —it was like in early Rome joining a Christian sect—and the break was so much more total, getting involved with something like SDS you had to be much more highly committed, and you were in a sense freed, 'cause you'd get written off. If you were from Texas, in SDS, you were a bad motherfucker, you couldn't go home for Christmas. Your mother didn't say, "Oh, isn't that nice, you're involved. We supported the republicans in the Spanish Civil War, and now you're in SDS and I'm glad to see you're socially concerned." In most of those places it meant, "*You Goddamn Communist.*" There was absolutely no reinforcing sympathy. . . . So we were strong, the commitment in those regions was stronger than it was in the East.

Finally, the new breed brought to SDS a kind of centrifugalism: a distrust of centralization, of leadership, of "top-down" organizations, and instead, an instinctive, ERAP-like reliance on small groups, locally based, operating individually. Most of the newcomers had joined SDS chapters on their campuses in the previous six months, largely around antiwar actions, and the success these chapters had during this time inclined them to reliance on this kind of local organization. Then, too, there was an under-the-surface antipathy to the national leadership, based in part on nervousness, awe, and unfamiliarity, in part on the remoteness and inaccessibility of the old guard. The newcomers were by heritage more individualistic, as well; some said at the time even "anarchistic"—something of the populist tradition clung to them, something of the distrust of the East, something of the frontier.

Though in numbers the new breed was not a majority at the convention—perhaps not more than two hundred—its energy was infectious and its style was evident throughout. Steve Max, not one to be sympathetic about it all, noted some of the effects:

> The role of chairman vanished; at this year's convention, full plenary sessions of 250 people were chaired by members picked at random with no regard to ability, while workshops debated having a chairman at all. Convention credentials went unchecked, and some key votes went uncounted. What constituted two thirds, a majority, or a quorum of the delegates remains a mystery to this day.

Beyond that, plenary sessions often deteriorated into mumbles and tangents, with people just as likely to be spending time out under the trees as in the smoky rooms. Workshops called to confront such issues as "The Political Program and Strategy of the Movement" or "Democracy and Organizational Structure" quickly turned into meandering discussions of whatever problems anyone wanted to bring up.* The effort to draw up a document

---

*One of the problems *not* discussed, according to firsthand accounts, was how to recruit and train young Americans for guerrilla warfare and service on the side of the National Liberation Front. This fabrication was put forth over the summer by right-wing columnist Fulton Lewis III, who was not there, subsequently repeated and embellished by the *New York Journal-American,* among other papers, and then picked up by *Reader's Digest,* which ran an article suggesting that the Kewadin convention was used for nothing but to entice youthful college students into the black-pajama force of the "Viet Cong." The story was widely publicized through a lengthy series in July sent out by United Press International, right-wing publications like *Human Events* and *U.S.A.,* and angry editorials in papers like the St. Louis *Globe-Democrat.* It sparked campaigns by some local rightists and hostile campus administrators to move against SDS chapters, but the effort by a group in Indiana to oust SDS from the University of Indiana, the best-publicized instance of this round of witch-hunting, was resisted by both students and administrators. The origin of all this appears to have been the presence of some young hangers-on—M2M people by one version, members of the Spartacist League according to the NO later on—who, as the NO phrased it, "were going around selling beer and talking about the 'International Brigade,'" an idea that gained no support there or after, and which was apparently treated with scorn by the SDSers. (NAC mailing, January 1966.) SDS at one point considered bringing legal action against *Reader's Digest* and other publications, but reluctantly concluded that neither the legal nor the publicity game would be worth the financial candle.

representing current SDS thinking was denounced as "statementism," and the more than twenty lengthy papers that had been submitted to the convention as drafts of the new *Port Huron Statement* were summarily discarded. An attempt to get the convention to agree to at least a unified position on foreign policy was similarly frustrated, and the resolution that finally passed ended up being a denunciation of foreign-policy resolutions. Efforts to fashion SDS into the leading organization against the war were sabotaged by old guarders resisting single-issueism and by newcomers resisting "top-down" unanimity. Attempts to centralize organizational direction in Chicago or give national officers additional power were similarly frustrated, the dominant attitude of the new breed being that the strength of SDS lay in the chapters, not in the NO. And when it came time to select national officers the new breed really made itself felt. In the first place, they almost managed to do away with national officers entirely. The plenary session debated for some time as to whether a truly democratic organization should have such a thing as a president, and at one point there was general agreement that the positions should be abolished—a move which was halted only by a decision to put the issue to the entire membership before taking action. (A membership referendum was held in the fall on this point, with Jeff Shero arguing for abolition, Paul Booth against, and the abolition move lost by about three to one—though fewer than six hundred people bothered to vote—but by then SDSers had had a whole summer to learn from.) When it came to the position of National Secretary, however—a position normally filled by the National Council people meeting after the convention—the centrifugal spirit *was* victorious, and not only did the delegates fail to find someone to fill Kissinger's shoes but they didn't seem to care very much. Max viewed these new-breed effects wryly, concluding, "To destroy formal structures in society is unfortunately no small task, but to do so in one's own organization is not only possible but easy." And when the delegates finally did agree to fill the top two positions, they filled each with a person distinctly *homo novo*.

The presidential race among Larry Gordon, Clark Kissinger, and Dick Magidoff of the old guard, and Carl Oglesby and Bob Pardun, more or less representative of the newcomers, was won easily by Oglesby. He was a fresh figure, the first President not from the old guard, a slightly remote person (by virtue of age and intellect) who could be counted on not to try to gather power or to play NO factional politics (about which he was presumed to be ignorant anyway, as a member for only half a year). He was also a non-Easterner, a country boy up from the mills of Akron, not (yet) versed in the ideologies of the Old Left, and a person whose obvious honesty and integrity appealed to the younger members ("Everyone felt a kind of intuitive trust in Carl," as one delegate put it). For Vice President, the convention chose Jeffrey Shero, a veritable symbol of the new breed.* Short, slim, bearded, with steady brown eyes and a gentle Texas drawl, Shero was Western rather than Eastern, his politics were instinctive rather than inherited, his style was shy and sensitive rather than articulate and probing, his manner was quiet, honest, bluntly—even naively—earnest. He grew up with a supportive mother and an unsympathetic stepfather (an Air Force colonel, no less), went through high school in Bryan, Texas, and then spent a checkered college career in and out of various universities, finding classes increasingly irrelevant in the face of the growing civil-rights movement. "I'd be going along," he recalls, "half putting up with it, sliding through, and then we'd have a civil-rights thing or a sit-in, which had immediate repercussions in human terms, and taking a test on

---

*One reason for his selection, as Shero himself recalls it, was that he had actually taken on Tom Hayden in debate. "Tom Hayden was the guru of SDS and we were in an Agents of Social Change workshop chaired by Robb Burlage, and Tom Hayden was arguing the classical ERAP theory about social change, and I didn't really understand who Tom Hayden was and wasn't too impressed by him—I thought he was a smart dude, but I wasn't in awe of him at all. So I started saying, Hey, I don't think that's right, I think the middle class is gonna move, et cetera, and I made up this big argument in defense of the middle class and students, and so, like, the workshop never came to a conclusion. So that night in the general plenary I was supposed to debate Tom Hayden on this, and after the workshop people began coming around saying, Well, you're a pretty good guy, Jeff, but you're gonna get chewed up tonight, I mean you're debating Tom Hayden, and I got a little scared. At any rate, that night I was supposed to speak first, so I talked, and I was waiting—I was kinda resigned, you know, to getting smashed—but then for some reason Tom decided not to argue: he got up and gave about a five-minute somewhat Zen speech, and sat down, and didn't come head to head against me. I got a certain amount of respect that night for taking him on." (Interview with author.)

Dickens' *Christmas Carol* in junior-level English literature seemed fucking ridiculous. And you could see on the one hand academic irrelevance if you spent the time on a test and on the other the real differences in people's lives." Shero was instrumental in making the SDS chapter at the University of Texas into a major civil-rights force in 1964 and 1965, leading one fight over the integration of bathroom facilities (for which the outstanding slogan was "Let My People Go"), establishing a tutorial program for ghetto high-schoolers in Austin, and working in several Southern states as a white support group for SNCC. His politics were formed here:

> Our sense of direct action and tactical sense came from the civil-rights movement. The civil-rights movement lent a whole plethora of tactics of direct action, confrontational in nature, which suited the psychology of people who had an idealistic sense of the country, its politics, and how institutions were supposed to be founded. Rage, and disillusionment, and a moral impulse to create something better —that was our background.

It was the background upon which the resistance movement would be built.*

The convention did agree on one substantive issue, to take the anti-Communist "exclusion clauses" out of the constitution. The preamble had said that SDS advocates "a radical, democratic program counterposed to authoritarian movements both of Communism and the domestic Right"; this was changed to "a radical, democratic program whose methods embody the democratic vision." The membership clause, adopted in 1960, had read:

> S.D.S. is an organization of democrats. It is civil libertarian in its treatment of those with whom it disagrees, but clear in its opposition

*The other national officers elected to the National Council were a fairly mixed bag, though the absence of ERAP types is noticeable. Chosen were Stanley Aronowitz, Paul Booth, Jeremy Brecher, Nick Egleson, Dick Flacks, Helen Garvy, Todd Gitlin, Al Haber, Ed Hamlett (a Southern Illinois University dropout, SNCC member, and SSOC founder), Clark Kissinger, Dick Magidoff, Carol McEldowney, Robert Pardun, Liora Proctor (who had been doing peace work with a Canadian group, the Student Union for Peace Action), and David Smith.

to any totalitarian principle as a basis for government or social
organization. *Advocates or apologists for such a principle are not
eligible for membership.*

The convention voted to change "totalitarian" to "anti-democratic" and "government or social" to "governmental, social, or
political," and to drop the last sentence entirely. These changes,
suggested by Kissinger, were opposed by some undergraduates
who had developed an antipathy to the tactics of the PL and the
CP—"If I'd wanted to [work with Stalinists] I'd have joined the
DuBois Clubs," one wrote, and another said, "I don't agree with
those people on principle, and I think we ought to say so"—and
by some who simply felt the need to "proclaim *some* standards"
and "have our politics up front." But they were approved by an
overwhelming majority of the delegates: the younger members
tended to feel that the clause was simply irrelevant—"The DAR
doesn't say that it excludes Communists, so why should we?"—
or unnecessarily divisive—"That's more of that old-left Red-baiting again, and we should be beyond that"; and the older SDSers
tended to view it as a way of making a clear break with LID politics and washing away the last stains of Cold War exclusionism.
    SDS thinking was summarized and defended in a long paper
later that year by Al Haber, who felt "nonexclusionism" was right
both pragmatically and politically. Exclusionism—or anti-Communism—had been destructive to the left in general in the past,
he argued, it was a waste of time and energy among people who
had limited resources of both, and it can't work in an organization
like SDS which has no very severe qualifications for membership
in the first place and has no clear-cut factions to expel even if it
wanted to. In the Movement, he said,

> people shall be judged by their behavior. If privately they smoke pot
> (or don't) or belong to YSA or the SP or the CP or DP or YAF or
> SDS or the Chamber of Commerce (or don't), that's their affair—
> with which others may agree or disagree, privately. When their
> public actions weaken the movement, or when they refuse to discuss
> and argue their beliefs with their colleagues, then they lose their
> right to speak in the Movement or for it.

That was to prove a somewhat optimistic assessment of the quality
of the Movement in the years to come, but it seemed logical

enough, and morally right, given the kind of organization SDS
was at the time.

Obviously the LID observers at Kewadin—shades of Port
Huron—were aghast. Tom Kahn spoke vigorously against any
constitutional change and warned that the LID elders would look
upon it as a further slap in their faces which, coming on top of the
move of the NO out of New York, the "pop-front" march on
Washington, and the already frigid relations, would likely lead to
a permanent break between SDS and its parent body. As it turned
out, LIDers certainly *were* upset at the news, and many responded
like venerable Harry Overstreet, who had been in the LID for fifty
years and a member of its National Council for most of that time:
in a series of angry letters he denounced SDS, warned of its
becoming part of a "foreign-based, world-wide force," and resigned forthwith. The majority in the LID, however, was not quite
ready to make the break with their younger charges, hoping once
again to keep them around long enough to realize the error of their
ways; to Harry Laidler, "Most of the [SDS] members are new and
naive. They are teachable." And so at its June meeting the Board
of Directors adopted, unanimously, a carrot-stick proposal reading:

> The League for Industrial Democracy in its long history has stood
> firmly, as a matter of uncompromising principle, against totalitari-
> anism of both the right and the left. We are therefore deeply trou-
> bled that the 1965 Convention of our student department, Students
> for a Democratic Society, removed from its Constitution and mem-
> bership card the long-standing reference to Communism as an au-
> thoritarian movement.
>
> We urge the SDS to carry on in the coming year a thoroughgo-
> ing discussion of the nature and function of democracy in society.
> We pledge our support, through literature and speakers at the cam-
> pus level, to aid SDS in these discussions.
>
> Toward this end, the Board seeks to continue and deepen the
> "dialogues" that have been initiated by the Student Activities Com-
> mittee. We seek a reaffirmation of SDS's adherence to the tradi-
> tional opposition of LID to totalitarianism of both the right and the
> left.

But things had gone too far for "dialogues," and 1962 was three
years ago. So little did SDS regard this emergency meeting that

not one of the four students who were members of the Board
bothered to appear. Tom Kahn, at least, was under no illusion
as to the SDS mood; in an angry letter to the NO in June he
wrote:

> I am . . . aware that there are those within SDS who have decided
> a split with the LID is inevitable and desirable. They are encouraged
> by others on the periphery of SDS who spend a great deal of energy
> attacking the LID and individual Board members as enemies and
> sell-outs. [If this continues,] the crossfire will intensify and pressures
> will be generated all along the line.

The effects of the Kewadin spirit upon SDS, however, went
far beyond the relations with the LID. In two quite crucial ways,
in program and in leadership, it sent SDS askew.

First, the Kewadin spirit meant that the organization would
have no effective strategies for the coming year, no ongoing projects, no programmatic plans. The whole emphasis was upon the
individual chapters, which were to be allowed to function as they
saw fit, pick issues as local conditions demanded, and operate as
much as possible without any national direction at all. This was,
of course, a continuation of the honored SDS tradition of the
Haberesque perception that SDS should build itself around the
strengths of ongoing campus groups rather than imposing national strategies, and of the SNCC and ERAP legacies that SDS
should avoid anything smacking of a powerful centralized organization. But it meant, in the short run, that SDS would flounder
in a sea of strategies over the next few months, and, in the long
run, that SDS would miss the opportunity, now at hand in the
wake of the April march, to point itself in the direction of building
a strong national organization, around either the war or the universities.

The decision not to make SDS into the leading organization of an expanded antiwar movement, which it could have
been, had many causes beyond simply the decentralizing attitudes of the new breed and what can only be called the bewilderment of the old guard. There was a fear that the war was
too much of a single-issue trap, too likely to make SDS into
some kind of peace organization where its tentacled radicalism
would shrivel up. There was a conviction that nothing could

really be done to end the war until there was, in the SDS
phrase, "a movement to change America" that would eradicate
the root *causes* of its war-making: "We must organize," the
usual rhetoric went, "not against *this* war but against the fifth
and sixth and seventh war from now." There was a traditional
antipathy to dealing with foreign policy issues at all as somehow remote from the immediate and overwhelming evils like
poverty and racism. And there was a suspicion that the whole
antiwar movement was fated to have as short an effective life
as the antibomb movements earlier—"Where would we be,"
the question was often asked, "if peace were to break out tomorrow?" Todd Gitlin, looking back, blames the old guard:

> Our failure of leadership—which was undeniable—was a reflection
> of the fact that our hearts were not on the campuses. . . . We were
> just plain stupid. . . . The leadership was already a closed elite, we
> didn't *understand* what an antiwar movement would be, we didn't
> have any *feel* for it. My own feeling then was that it was an abstrac-
> tion . . . because that kind of movement is so big, because I couldn't
> see what it would be, day to day. What we surrendered then was
> the chance for an anti-imperialist peace movement.

Or as Steve Weissman was to put it: SDS was guilty of "a consistent underestimation of the importance of the Anti-war Movement . . . to the creation of a permanent political force in
America." Here was that chance to build an American left, to go
beyond the students into the other strata of America, and SDS
didn't realize it.

Likewise SDS didn't see the possibilities of forging a massive
campus-based organization, something like a national union of
radical students, though that too may have been possible then.
Again, there were many causes. There was the lingering sense that
SDS's job should still be to build a multilayered left—as Dick
Flacks said in a position paper to the convention, "I want to see
us take seriously the possibility of radical workers, scientists, doc-
tors, city planners, economists, sociologists, poets and mothers"
—and not to fasten upon students alone. There was a perception
that, as Potter had noted, universities were so much a part of the
national sickness that they could not possibly be instruments for
national health; this blended neatly with the attitude of the new

breed that, as Shero had expressed it, the needs of the country were so great that it hardly made sense for students to continue academic lives (an attitude, incidentally, which animated the dropout phenomenon beginning now to lead young people away from the campuses and into the Movement offices, the youth ghettos of the cities, and the community projects). And there was a weariness among the old guard with the whole idea of student issues and student concerns, what Paul Booth called at the time, "a kind of shell-shock," a function "of too many years of campus experience, alienation and frustration: one only wants to get *out* —out of thinking about campuses, out of being on them or interested in them." Thus at the moment it might have played a cardinal role in fashioning this student generation into an ongoing political organization of national consequence, SDS chose not to.

The Kewadin spirit led SDS away from the assertion of national leadership and into a continued reliance upon local initiative. It was, in truth, perhaps the easiest and surest direction for the organization, then still young and small, and because of it SDS would be able to grow and prosper at the chapter level as no other campus organization had ever done. But for this, in the long run, it had to pay a price.

The second unfortunate effect of Kewadin was to turn the National Office into a shambles for the entire summer and to throw upon the organization a problem of leadership that would not be settled for more than a year.

The decision not to set a national strategy, coupled with the downgrading of the NO and the belief that SDS could get along without a National Secretary, wrought much trouble in Chicago. A cluster of people put in time in the National Office, but most were woefully inexperienced. Jeff Segal, an eighteen-year-old who had volunteered to do a little work around the place, found himself elected office manager by the rest of the staff (after a month he would take on the title of "Acting National Secretary"), but he was little known to the rest of the organization and new to the hurly-burly of Movement offices. Nor was there anyone around to give him, or anyone else, direction. Immediately after being elected Oglesby set off on a long swing through Cambodia, North Vietnam, and Japan to show American "solidarity" with foreign antiwar elements and didn't get back until August.* Shero, who had agreed to be editor of the *Bulletin* as well as Vice President, had disappeared without a word into the Southwest, thinking that his services wouldn't be required until the fall. It was, Paul Booth, believes, a distinct failure of the old guard:

> We didn't have enough of our heavies there because most people said, Aw fuck it. We didn't fully dominate it and other kinds of people—Segal, Shero, and the like—got into the NO and couldn't control it, couldn't do as Clark had done, which was to go his own direction and keep on top of things even though the heavies were elsewhere. And finally the thing got out of hand.

That's an understatement. With its newfound publicity— since the march a spate of newspaper articles and columns on SDS had appeared, and *The Nation,* the *New Republic, The Reporter,* and *U.S. News* all ran pieces in the early summer—SDS seemed to have attracted the attention of disaffected kids across the land. Letters poured in during the summer at a rate at least a hundred times greater than anything the NO had known before: "I saw an article on you and I wondered if you'd send me more information" . . . "I heard from a friend what kind of things you're doing, and I'd like to join" . . . "Please send me anything you have about the war" . . . "I don't make much, but maybe this five dollars can help." The office set up regional desks to answer the flood of mail, and most of the staff put in ten and twelve and sometimes eighteen hours a day, but even so correspondence fell way behind; classically typical of the confusion around the place was one letter sent

*Oglesby tells of meeting an airport attendant in Cambodia with whom he struck up a conversation in inept French: "Haltingly he asked me if I am an American. Quietly: oui. Then: am I a soldier? A man of the government? With what French gestures do I deny these guesses! A student, I say. A *radical* student. I felt compelled to spill the beans about myself. But how do you translate 'teach-in'? So finally I just blurt it out with all the French-sounding accent I can muster up: Pas un soldat! Pas un homme du gouvernement! Je suis un representif de la —teach-in! His head pops forward. His eyes go like pinwheels. "Teach-in?" he says—like that, as plain as anything. He takes my hand and nearly shakes it off. Oui, oui! he says. Teach-in. The marsh in Washington d'avril! The balloon in my chest pops. Some Cambodia! Some airport attendant!" (*SDS Bulletin,* Vol. 4, No. 1, Fall 1965.)

out in August which ended, "Thank you for your inconvenience." Literature orders were also cascading in, and they received even less attention than the letters. It seems that the
staffers, in a move to put into effect the kind of society they
were hoping to achieve, had decided that there would be no
"elitism" around the office and everyone would participate in
all the chores—"shitwork," as it was called—including mimeographing and mailing the literature; to achieve this egalitarian-
ism they instituted a system whereby the person who mailed
out the last copy of any pamphlet or paper would be the one
to mimeograph, collate, and staple new stacks of them. What
happened in practice was simply that no one sent out the last
copy of any item requested, and the literature shelves were pa-
pered with single copies undisturbed for weeks on end. By the
end of June almost no literature was going out at all, and only
a few worklist mailings trickled out from time to time.

And then the old bugaboo, money, reappeared. Kissinger's
final financial report for the 1964–65 fiscal year showed that SDS
had taken in the phenomenal sum of $65,147 ($50,000 from contributions) during the previous twelve months, the great bulk of it
since the April march: that was wealth beyond anything Max and
McKelvey could have imagined. Yet SDS had found no difficulty
in spending even that sum—$45,000 went for NO business, and
another $20,000 or so went to PREP and ERAP projects. By the
end of June SDS was broke. In July the phone was disconnected
for ten days—an ignominy that had not befallen the NO for two
years—and to top everything off the New York Consolidated
Edison company forwarded a bill for gas and electricity for May
and June, since no one had told them to disconnect the service in
the old New York office. Kissinger spent time on fund raising as
planned, but without much success; at the end of the summer one
staffer, wryly referring to the standard NO diet, joked, "Clark has
found a richy in Chicago who has agreed to provide the movement
with all the peanut butter it can use . . . one of the biggest peanut
butter magnates in the country. Clark is now working on jelly."
And when, in late July, $10,000 did come in, an anonymous dona-
tion from Anne Peretz, the NO managed to squander that with
truly remarkable facility. Most of it went into a "photo project,"

the brainchild of one D. Gorton, a friend of Shero's from the University of Mississippi (possible the *only* SDSer from there) and another representative of the new breed, who argued that nonverbal communications were the only effective way to reach the post-Gutenberg crowd on the campuses and somehow convinced the rest of SDS to endow him with a darkroom, enlarger, cameras, and various other photographic equipment. The paraphernalia, however, remained largely unused, the project floundered, and the next time anyone looked the money was gone.

Small wonder that Kissinger, a few months later, would refer to this summer as "the most dismal period in SDS history."

In the summer of 1965 the Progressive Labor Party held its first convention. The party had grown, by its own estimate to some fourteen hundred members, by other estimates to less than a thousand; its leaders judged the time ripe for a sharp new turn in policy and practice, which they spelled out for the party faithful during this meeting. Party chairman Milton Rosen, reviewing the decisions of that convention, wrote:

> The key ideological breakthrough of the convention was posing the question of having a serious party, or having more of the same. What differentiated the two was whether or not the party was to be a party of the working class, or whether it would preserve all the same middle-class aspects of the other new formations among Black and white student types. We chose to become a party of the working class. For PLP this was a profound decision. Because, to accomplish this meant not a partial transformation of the party, and the individual member of the party, but a total transformation of both.

Total transformation indeed: Rosen later admitted that of the two hundred people at that convention probably no more than four were workers. The convention also decided to stress the war as an organizing tool:

> At our founding convention we made certain political estimates. ... We pointed out that the U.S. war of aggression in Vietnam was part of a world-wide counter-revolutionary strategy of the U.S. We felt that the war was against the interests of most Americans and that opposition would surely mount as the consequences of the war were felt in the country.

Finally, PL named what it considered to be the enemy:

> We posed liberalism as the main ideological danger to the develop-
> ing radical movements. . . . We estimated that liberalism had re-
> ceived a crushing defeat and had lost a good deal of its potency.

It was with this basic strategy that PL worked for the next three
years.

It is not surprising that after Kewadin SDS was unable to
capitalize upon the antiwar spirit—it is only surprising that it tried
so hard. The mechanism was a project which operated out of the
National Office—totally without sanction, be it noted, from the
Kewadin convention, though in line with one of the resolutions
passed at the April NC—which tried to establish committees in
various cities to create and coordinate "grass-roots" sentiment
against Vietnam: "ERAPize the war," as one SDSer put it. Coordinators of the project were Dena Clamage, who had come into
the NO in January to help on the April march and wouldn't be
budged, and Mel McDonald, a graduate student at Texas who
dropped out after the bombing of North Vietnam, started organizing SDS groups at little Texas colleges, and finally drifted up to
the NO. Committees to End the War in Vietnam were established
over the summer in Chicago, Denver, Detroit, Madison, Milwaukee, New York, Oakland, and Portland, and SDSers began
working with the Berkeley Vietnam Day Committee in California.
Clamage and McDonald did their best to service and coordinate
these groups, chiefly by putting out several issues of a mimeographed *National Vietnam Newsletter,* the political character of
which is perhaps suggested by an unattributed map of Vietnam
printed at the end of the third issue, on which the "Enemy-
occupied areas" turn out to be places controlled by the U.S. and
South Vietnamese.

The coordinators, however, were never able to establish any
real national direction for the separate committees, largely because SDS had not established any national direction or any real
notion of what they wanted the committees to do. Their one
notable achievement over the summer was in enlisting a fairly
considerable turnout for an August antiwar march around an
Assembly of Unrepresented People—and here it was SDS itself

that messed things up. After the failure of the Kewadin convention to push SDS into becoming the coordinating antiwar organization in the Movement, a group of independent antiwar activists (among them Staughton Lynd, David Dellinger, Robert Parris Moses, and Stanley Aronowitz) got together to establish a National Coordinating Committee to End the War in Vietnam—the organization that, in many guises over the years, became the coordinator of most of the major marches of the decade—and its first action was the August march. Now SDS had determined at its June NC that it wanted to get out of the march business and had specifically chosen not to endorse the summer's action, all in line with the Kewadin spirit; but, not able to leave well enough alone, the NO went on to issue a statement (on what authority it is impossible to determine) just a few weeks before the Washington march dissociating SDS from it and effectively suggesting that SDSers had better things to do that weekend.* The statement came too late to halt the work of the city committees and many SDSers simply ignored it,† so there was a respectable enough turnout of five thousand on August 9; but the NO's gratuitous attempt to stifle the just-born antiwar movement rankled many activists, and feeling ran high against its "irresponsibility" and "divisiveness." Stanley Aronowitz, for one, was livid: "He never forgave SDS for that," Paul Booth says.

As it turned out, SDS got most of the blame for the march, anyway—at least in the halls of Congress. The Chairman of the House Un-American Activities Committee, Edwin E. Willis of Louisiana, first accused SDS of bringing all the rabble to town, and then, inspired by recent publicity given to a few war resisters

---

*"Participation in the symbolic Assembly on the 9th should be seriously questioned because of the likelihood of being arrested and facing trial, but more important, because the Assembly will not be real. . . . This so-called Assembly represents no-one except those participating and this is even in doubt at this point. No elections have been held, no plans are on the boards for creating a permanent counter-congress out of this Assembly, and last, there is no possibility of those participating achieving their desired goal of entering the House of Representatives en masse and declaring peace." (Worklist mailing, July 28, 1965.)

†Among the SDSers who had signed the call for the Assembly of Unrepresented People were Carl Oglesby, Dena Clamage and Mel McDonald of the Vietnam Project, Ed Hamlett, Bill Hartzog, Florence Howe, Paul Lauter, Staughton Lynd, Barry Weisberg, and Steve Weissman. (See, for example, *Liberation*, August 1965.)

who had burned their draft cards, went on to charge it with
plotting "a mass burning of draft cards" right there in Washington. Representatives Wilbur Mills and Mendel Rivers and Senator
Strom Thurmond introduced legislation making draft-card burners liable to a fine of $10,000 and five years in jail, which Congress
dutifully passed on the day after the march and which President
Johnson dutifully signed into law on August 30.

By the end of the summer it had become quite clear to the
SDS membership that the NO was in a shambles. Angry letters
poured in complaining of poor (or nonexistent) service, "absolutely inexcusable" membership mailings, and the failure to send
out the membership referendum on whether to have national
officers or not; typical was one missive beginning, "Dear National
Office (if we still have one)." Brecher remembers that the bitter
joke going around that summer was that the NO was divided into
two factions, "those that thought you should sleep in heaps and
those who thought you should sleep in mounds. That," he says,
"was the important issue in terms of where *they* were at." By the
end of August, the NO itself confessed its failure, the August 28
worklist mailing saying simply, "The National Office is in a general state of collapse and failing to perform the most rudimentary
functions despite the presence of 11 full-time staff members."

And finally the old guard rallied around. Kissinger reluctantly agreed to take charge of things until the next National
Council could pick a National Secretary, and his first move was
to get Paul Booth to leave the ERAP project he had been working
on in Oakland and come back to the NO. "Clark realized that we
had made a major blunder," Booth recalls, "in not taking charge
of the war movement, and he called me back to be National
Secretary. But by then it was too late, there was now another
vehicle, it was too late for us to be the antiwar movement, which
is what we should have been." Booth nonetheless accepted the
invitation, and with Kissinger, Gitlin, Rothstein, and a few other
SDS veterans began to try to find some new direction, to establish
some coherence, for the organization. And Al Haber, who had
been elected to the National Interim Committee in June after two
years away from the seats of power, played his usual role of angry,
insightful, slightly disappointed father figure; at the end of the

summer he shot off a list of complaints about SDS which seemed
to embody all the unhappiness that the old guard was feeling:

> SDS cooperates freely, and apparently uncritically, with groups like
> the May 2 Movement, the DuBois Clubs and Progressive Labor
> . . . yet there is little discussion as to the basis for cooperative action.
> . . . SDS seems to have a general hostility to the LID, our "parent"
> group, and to the intellectuals of the "democratic socialist" commu-
> nity. . . . Many former SDS supporters have left the organization
> or are deeply alienated from its present activity, organizational form
> and rhetoric. . . . Organizational involvement does not seem to
> produce, except for the leadership, a stable attachment to the radical
> community that lasts beyond college. . . . There is a certain hostility
> or intolerance to people whose vocation is not obviously "radical"
> and who pursue interests apart from the organizing objectives of the
> "movement." . . . There has been a deemphasis on the national
> organizational structure and leadership. Decisions are evolved
> rather than made.

Haber may not have been happy with it but SDS, in short, was
changing—adjusting, if imperfectly, to the new postreform movement it found itself in, groping for new forms, new methods, new
allies, new theories, new structures, and doing so with a new breed
of member. The old guard rallied around, but the organization
was inexorably changing even as it did so.

13

FALL 1965

Seeing the Chicago headquarters of SDS as the new school year began in the fall of 1965, it would be hard to imagine that this could be the center of an organization of national attention, much less national import. The office was located on the second floor of a dumpy, flaking building at 1103 East Sixty-third Street, a typically dreary byway in the black Woodlawn ghetto, huddled together with empty storefronts and beauty parlors and take-out joints, all of which would shudder when the elevated train passed by outside on its clattering way toward the Loop. Inside, in some ten ill-lit rooms, costing $225 a month, the paint peeling off the walls and plaster sifting from the ceiling, were a battery of typewriters, a mimeograph machine, some photographic equipment, phones, makeshift desks and rickety chairs, stuffed pigeonhole cabinets, and a plumbing system so bad that a sign above the sink read "Leaky pipe—do not use." And throughout, the flotsam of the Movement—an army cot, candy wrappers, jars of peanut butter, discarded clothes, piles of mimeographed papers, unopened mail, paperback books (Paul Goodman, Norman O. Brown, Ken Kesey), and on the walls an assortment of posters and messages including a dog-eared drawing of Eugene V. Debs, a Ben Shahn print, a poster of a sad-eyed Vietnamese child, a picture of a mimeograph machine with a penciled caption, "Our Founder," and two scrawls: "Burn, Baby, Burn" and "Make Love, Not War." Nor was the disarray only physical. The summer chaos had left its mark: summer workers had gone and new workers lasted only temporarily, money had run out, pamphlets were unprinted, literature orders were unfilled (and often as not unopened), even requests for membership and information lay unanswered for weeks.

Yet in the next four months SDS would come to be the object of intense publicity, the target of official government investigations, the beneficiary of a membership growth unlike anything it had ever seen, and the acknowledged center of the New Left: "the largest, most influential, most intellectual and most idealistic of the New Left organizations," in the New York *Herald Tribune*'s phrase.

Paul Booth was installed officially as National Secretary as the fall began, and to guide him in the National Office operations a special National Administrative Committee of Chicago-area people was established. The Booth regime, which lasted the entire school year, was the old guard's last fling. Booth himself proved not to be a popular figure with most of those of the new breed. His politics, which had always been in the careful center of SDS, hardly made him open or responsive to the new, often bizarre, usually romantic, always militant ideas coming up from under. His temperament turned him to the older members, whom he found much more congenial, personally and politically, so that when decisions had to be made he would more likely be on the phone talking with Webb and Gitlin and Potter than consulting the people around him in the office. And his style, with a flint-sharp mind, a skillful tongue, and years of infighting experience in political groups, was abrasive to the younger and less sophisticated people around the office. Jeff Shero, who finally made it to the National Office in the fall, recalls that he was "outclassed badly" by Booth and his "Eastern, verbal, intellectual tradition":

> I was destroyed by my first six months as SDS Vice President because I had come in with a vision and experiences about how people could relate to each other, like in the civil-rights movement. I was just kind of chewed up by the internal fighting, totally unprepared for that kind of thing, because I thought that if you had a disagreement with someone you just sat down and talked it out. I wasn't very able to deal with [Booth's] kind of stuff. By the time of the winter convention I was a psychological wreck.

But it was not just Booth himself: the whole structure of the
National Office worked, as it had shown in earlier years, against
those with ideas about a new life style. "Participatory democracy," wrote one Texas SDSer who had spent some time in the
Chicago headquarters, "is nonexistent within the national office
structure. [Working for SDS] is like getting saved by a traveling
preacher, who you later find out is a drunkard and beats his wife."
From within the confines of the NO, what seemed important was
not what the members as a whole thought or wanted, not what
priorities seemed important for the movement, not communication of ideas and strategies from one part of the organization to
the rest, but rather simply what would make the office itself function more smoothly. The result, as Kissinger reported to the membership, was that

> ... chapters, regional offices, and members find out what the organi-
> zation is doing by reading the newspapers. Important and useful
> information which the NO does get at the national level never
> makes it down to the local level. The membership is poorly serviced
> and hardly if ever drawn into community—much less decision mak-
> ing. And political knowledge is transmitted in SDS like folklore.

Life around the NO was all the more grating that fall because
at the same time that it failed to satisfy the yearnings for a liberated society it also failed to provide the comforts of a bourgeois
one. As in the summer, the twelve to fifteen office workers (there
was a fairly rapid turnover, as "Movement life" took its toll) lived
in a single large, and usually ill-kempt, $135-a-month apartment
(which also served as the hotel for SDSers passing through), so
that all of the abrasions of the day were carried home to be rubbed
again at night. Hours were erratic, but long, the concept of "weekend" forgotten; salaries were uniformly $12.50 a week, just enough
to make ascetic living unpleasant and not enough to indulge in
movies and records without feelings of guilt; responsibilities in the
office were confused, with priorities established by the crisis of the
moment and the arbitrary decisions of the National Secretary as
to what project was most desperate. Sam Bennett, who lasted just
two months as office manager, complained that fall: "I was like
a twentieth-century Alice: I had to shovel shit just as fast as I
could only to keep my head above it."

All of this might have been borne—indeed similar discomforts had been borne in the past and were to be in the future—had there been recurring evidence that all the sacrifice and effort was having a visible effect either on the gathering forces against the war or on the course of the Movement in general and its capacity to change a nation so askew. But the evidence was sparse, for as SDS went into the new school year it was as bewildered in strategy as it was in organization.

Clearly the Vietnam war was the dominant issue in America, the dominant issue for the left. Just as clearly, SDS still didn't know what to do about it. At the September National Council meeting, held at a park in Indiana on the September 7 weekend, an entire cacophony of strategies was put forward. Some in the organization urged negotiations, others demanded immediate withdrawal, still others wanted an outright NLF victory. Some wanted to emphasize the moral horror of the war, others concentrated on its illegality, a number argued that it took funds away from domestic needs, and a few even then saw it as an example of "American imperialism." Gitlin pressed for dramatic action by students, suggesting such things as sending American hostages to North Vietnamese targets so that U.S. planes would be afraid to bomb them and enlisting a mission of twenty-five to fifty people "to help rebuild a hospital or school destroyed by American bombings." Kissinger proposed an "International Student Strike" for later in the fall, during which students would boycott classes for a day or a week. Younger SDSers usually favored the idea of more marches and demonstrations, resisting the growing attitude that such tactics were fruitless and old-hat ("All right, you've been marching on Washington since 1957," one young SDSer complained, "but some of us have never even *visited* it, much less marched there.") And still others wanted to escalate into civil disobedience such as stopping troop trains (which the Berkeley Vietnam Day Committee was actually to accomplish that October) or organizing soldiers to resist or desert (the Kissinger Kamikazi Plan again). Many saw the draft as the natural antiwar tool since it struck at the very age group most receptive to radicalization, and they urged demonstrations against induction centers, mass registration for Conscientious Objector status, and even the

establishment of a Movement Church to ordain as ministers anyone who wanted to escape the draft that way. There was even a
sizable minority, including ERAPers and other old guarders, who
wanted to play down the whole concentration on Vietnam and to
have the antiwar movement, as Booth and Lee Webb put it in a
much-debated paper, "become a movement for domestic social
change" by developing "independent and mass constituencies for
democratic politics" out of "the immediate aspirations of the
poor, welfare recipients, trade-unionists, students, and others."

All of these proposals were presented, workshops spent hours
airing and attacking them, long debates raged about them for the
entire weekend, tempers grew heated and friendships cooled, and
at the end of it all SDS came flatly down in mid-air. The Kewadin
spirit still prevailed. The NC decided that it would give grudging
support to a third march on Washington, planned by the infant
National Coordinating Committee to End the War in Vietnam for
October 15 and 16, but it also went on record again as opposing
mass demonstrations: "We are for action that educates," the slogan went, "rather than action that demonstrates." It authorized
a limited program of building student antiwar sentiment through
campus education and local protest action: "Deepening the campus constituency will be the first priority during the coming
months"; it urged local chapters to adopt local strategies for action against the draft; and it dumped in the laps of the NO the job
of preparing *some* kind of national draft-counseling proposal that
would "mobilize opposition to the war among draft-age people"
—but with the proviso that this would have to be submitted in a
referendum to the membership for approval before any action was
taken.

As it happened, it was the last of these that was to draw the
greatest attention, though no one could have possibly foreseen
that, given the state of the NO. But by early October the NO
actually came up with a cautious, legal antidraft program focused
on three "visible expressions of protest":

   1. The act of filing for CO is, in itself, a gesture of personal
protest.
   2. On the campus, attempts should be made to stop the school
from turning over the class-rank information, to get professors to
refuse to hand in grades, and to organize campus strikes aimed

either at classes or exams. When recruiters appear on campus, they should be the focus of attention, challenged to debate, accused by picket signs of participation in war crimes. The same can be done at any time for ROTC officals, especially as part of a campaign to oust ROTC from the campus.

3. Demonstrations can be planned to expose or protest the nature and practices of the local draft boards.

These proposals were accompanied by a series of admonitions that draft organizing be continually related to "the broad context of the war in Vietnam" and "the undemocratic nature of our society," and by a caution that, though "filing for CO is strictly legal, unlike 'draft refusal,' " the government might see it as an obstruction of the draft and try to punish its instigators with five years in jail and a $10,000 fine. The package was just being made ready to be sent out to the membership for its vote, when a strange thing happened. SDS became a national villain.

By October, after eight long months, the antiwar movement finally touched a nerve in the body of the Establishment. The plans for the October 15–16 demonstrations had received considerable publicity in the early fall, the media having now dropped the attitude of amused scorn with which they treated the April SDS march and come around to the idea that there was a real protest movement afoot, and peopled by more than just a few crazy kids. The new movement against the draft, small though it was, became a particular delight of the newspapers, and CBS News ran regular reports of antidraft actions on its evening news program. In response the Administration and its allies were pressured into belittling the protesters and raising questions about their loyalty and patriotism. On October 13, two days before the planned demonstrations, Senator Thomas Dodd, an old line anti-Communist whose Senate Internal Security Committee had been looking into the antiwar protests, released a report asserting:

> The control of the anti-Vietnam movement has clearly passed from the hands of the moderate elements, who may have controlled it at one time, into the hands of Communists and extremist elements who are openly sympathetic to the Viet Cong and openly hostile to the United States. . . . This is particularly true of the national Vietnam protest movement scheduled for October 15–16.

On the same day elder statesman Dwight Eisenhower let it be known that he was "distressed and alarmed" by the antiwar movement and by the evident "moral deterioration" of America's youth.

And, because its reputation as the chief antiwar foe not only preceded but positively outran its actual workings, SDS was made into the prime target. On Thursday, October 14, Rowland Evans and Robert Novak, the syndicated columnists whose two most important outlets then were the *Herald Tribune* and the *Washington Post,* accused SDS of nothing less than treason. SDS, the columnists reported darkly, was mounting a major campaign to get American men to resist and evade the draft—"draft-dodging," they called it—and had even drawn up a "master plan" designed to "sabotage the war effort." This campaign, they said, "cannot be lightly passed off as an exuberant, youthful exercise of the right to dissent. It is a calculated effort to illegally undermine high national policy adopted by President Johnson and confirmed by Congress." Mississippi's John Stennis rose in the Senate the next morning to add his denunciation of SDS and bare its dangerous plans. "Workshops are being held by the Students for a Democratic Society," he said, "to devise ways to disrupt the necessary and normal operation of the draft system." Not only that, but they're planning to get people to file for CO status. "The purpose of this action is to jam the draft boards and to cause the Government to spend thousands of dollars in investigations and paperwork." This "deplorable and shameful activity," he went on, his anger mounting, makes it "imperative" for the government "to immediately move to jerk this movement up by the roots and grind it to bits before it has the opportunity to spread further."

Now the SDSers in Chicago were somewhat perplexed. The "master plan" so sinister to Evans and Novak was in fact a melange of proposals taken at random from the August issue of SDS's *National Vietnam Newsletter*—all of which had been specifically *rejected* by the September National Council. As to "workshops," this may have been a reference to one of the chaotic meetings at the NC, but the only place SDS was doing anything like that was in Los Angeles, where Mike Davis and some other SDSers had participated in weekly meetings with fifteen or twenty students who were trying to work out ways to spread draft information on local campuses. But in the face of such charges, Booth and the National Administrative Committee figured the best thing to do would be to get the real story out, and when a reporter from the Chicago *Sun-Times* came around after the Evans-Novak column they gave him copies of the actual referendum proposal. Much to their surprise, the *Sun-Times* splashed it across its front page on Friday, with the headline, "US-Wide Drive to Beat Draft Is Organized Here," UPI picked up the story for its wires, and a hungry press pounced upon it just as the weekend demonstrations were getting under way.

And on Saturday Attorney General Nicholas Katzenbach got into the act. At a Chicago press conference he announced that the government felt that antidraft activity "begins to move in the direction of treason" and it was watching the movement with great care: "There are some Communists in it and we may have to investigate. We may very well have some prosecutions." The Justice Department, he added, "has uncovered some persons working for the Students for a Democratic Society" who are possible Communists, and the student group was "one of many" organizations under examination. Though it seems that Katzenbach himself was trying to be judicious and careful, and never once accused SDS of specific wrongdoing, others at the press conference were not so circumspect. One, Northern Illinois Attorney General Edward V. Hanrahan, stated flatly that SDS was guilty of "treasonous activity" and declared that his staff had already begun a full-scale investigation. This was all the press needed: the stories went out with the clear implication that SDS was a subversive organization.

To top it all off, the weekend demonstrations were a surprising success. Upwards of one hundred thousand people took part —the *National Guardian* reported eighty thousand, a *Playboy* article estimated "nearly 100,000"—in more than ninety cities, the largest marches being in New York, San Francisco, Pittsburgh, New Haven, Cleveland, Detroit, Seattle, and Los Angeles. At least fifty SDS chapters participated, mobilizing people for the city marches and organizing demonstrations on many campuses— including a march on a chemical and biological warfare center at Fort Bragg by the University of North Carolina SDS, a death march on the state capital by the University of Texas chapter, a

teach-in by the fledgling Arizona State chapter, an Assembly of
Unrepresented People in Toronto by Buffalo SDS, and, in the first
action of its kind, a sit-in at the Ann Arbor draft board led by the
VOICE chapter, in which thirty-eight people, including VOICE
chairman Eric Chester and a young Michigan student named Bill
Ayers, were arrested. (This last demonstration got national publicity and became a *cause célèbre* over the next few months when
the local Michigan draft director thought up the idea of punishing
the men by reclassifying them from 2-S to 1-A, so as to put them,
in General Lewis Hershey's words, on "the belt that runs toward
the induction station.") Also over the weekend, David Miller, a
twenty-two-year-old Catholic pacifist, became the first person to
burn his draft card in defiance of the new federal law.

　　This was the largest antiwar demonstration to date and a
clear signal that the protest movement was real, and growing
larger daily. That provided little comfort in Washington. On Monday the Senate floor was awash with angry patriots; Thomas
Kuchel, Mike Mansfield, Spessard Holland, Richard Russell,
Leverett Saltonstall, William Proxmire, Frank Lausche, and Ever-
ett Dirksen all rushed to denounce the demonstrators, war protesters, and "draft-dodgers" en masse. *The New York Times*'s
Washington columnist James Reston allowed as how the protesters were damaging the country and "not promoting peace but
postponing it." And Johnson himself, hinting broadly at "investigations," let it be known that he was "worried" that "even well-
meaning demonstrators can become the victims of Communist
aggression."

　　In the following week, SDS hardly knew what to make of its
new-found fame. On the one hand, all the publicity had certainly
put the organization on the map, and membership soared. A
special *SDS Bulletin* noted: "Our Harvard organizer reports that
he walked into Harvard Yard with 30 membership cards and had
to go back for more ½ hour later. . . . He wasn't lying. We just
got 50 new membership cards from him special delivery." Students in the Chicago area poured into the NO to sign membership
cards, one of them saying, "If you are going to be redbaited, I want
to be on the list." In all, one thousand new two-dollar national
memberships were received, pushing the total national member-

ship over four thousand; the membership in individual chapters during this same period was thought to have doubled—the chapters in general kept only haphazard records of local members and the NO none at all, so it is impossible to tell—and SDS spokesmen now claimed a total of ten thousand local followers.

On the other hand, SDS was hardly able to capitalize on all the attention. After all, there *wasn't* any draft program, just a proposal that had been sent out to the members only that week and whose approval or disapproval would take weeks more to determine; and in any case no one in SDS had ever intended draft action to take top priority in the fall program. There wasn't even any official SDS position or program on the war itself. Furthermore, though being redbaited seemed to attract some college youths to the organization, it clearly disturbed and repelled many others—not to mention their parents, college administrators, and local patriotic types (in Nashville, for example, anti-SDS pressure grew so strong that Tennessee State SDSers had to close up shop), and some of the old guard wanted to squelch the "draft-dodging" image for fear that it might smear the whole antiwar effort. The NO tried to deal with the scores of press and television people who were traipsing up the creaking steps at Sixty-third Street by downplaying the draft and talking as best they could on the larger issue of the war, but there wasn't any document or statement or resolution they could point to and in the confusion the media continued to concentrate most on the draft proposal, generating the general impression that SDS was full of traitors. The consensus grew around the office that something had to be done, as Booth said, "to take the heat off."

Booth and Oglesby decided that the best thing would be to draw up a statement which would make SDS's noble intentions clear once and for all, and drop it in the laps of the press. They therefore arranged for a full-scale press conference in the Grand Ballroom of the National Press Club in Washington. They flew to the capital on Tuesday, and Booth worked arduously all through the night refining the statement, with help from Art Waskow and Jeremy Brecher, old-guard SDSers at the Institute for Policy Studies there, and Paul Cowan, a Harvard SDSer who happened to be in town; a few other friends of Booth's were consulted by telephone, but little was done to sound out anything like an SDS consensus. The next morning a bleary-eyed Booth faced a jam-packed press room:

> Students for a Democratic Society wishes to reiterate emphatically its intention to pursue its opposition to the war in Vietnam, undeterred by the diversionary tactics of the administration.
>
> We feel that the war is immoral at its root, that it is fought alongside a regime with no claim to represent its people, and that *it is foreclosing the hope of making America a decent and truly democratic society.*
>
> The commitment of SDS, and of the whole generation we represent, is clear: we are anxious to build villages; we refuse to burn them. We are anxious to help and to change our country; we refuse to destroy someone else's country. We are anxious to advance the cause of democracy; we do not believe that cause can be advanced by torture and terror.
>
> We are fully prepared to volunteer for service to our country and to democracy. We volunteer to go into Watts to work with the people of Watts to rebuild that neighborhood to be the kind of place that the people of Watts want it to be—and when we say "rebuild," we mean socially as well as physically. We volunteer to help the Peace Corps learn, as we have been learning in the slums and in Mississippi, how to energize the hungry and desperate and defeated of the world to make the big decisions. We volunteer to serve in hospitals and schools in the slums, in the Job Corps and VISTA, in the new Teachers Corps—and to do so in such a way as to strengthen democracy at its grass-roots. And in order to make our volunteering possible, we propose to the President that all those Americans who seek so vigorously to build instead of burn be given their chance to do so. We propose that he test the young people of America: if they had a free choice, would they want to burn and torture in Vietnam or to build a democracy at home and overseas? There is only one way to make the choice real: let us see what happens if service to democracy is made grounds for exemption from the military draft. I predict that almost every member of my generation would choose to build, not to burn; to teach, not to torture; to help, not to kill. And I am sure that the overwhelming majority of our brothers and cousins in the army in Vietnam, would make the same choice if they could—to serve and build, not kill and destroy. . . .
>
> Until the President agrees to our proposal, we have only one choice: we do in conscience object, utterly and wholeheartedly, to

this war; and we will encourage every member of our generation to object, and to file his objection through the Form 150 provided by the law for conscientious objection.

Thus was born what immediately came to be called the "Build, Not Burn" strategy. The wire services gave the statement extensive coverage, and most major papers carried stories. Though, inevitably, the slants varied—the *Chicago Tribune,* for example, tagged the story "Oglesby Tells Johnson Protesters' Terms"—most reports played up the humanitarian, not to say Boy Scout, cast of the statement and its clear alternative-service patriotism, and it seemed that in the battle of the headlines, SDS had won: it was off the hook and the critics of the antiwar movement were for the moment disarmed. Booth was quick to claim that "good effects were reported" on many campuses (at Vassar, he reported, the statement was mimeographed and used as an organizing tool), that in Washington "it bolstered our allies and compounded the embarrassment of the Katzenbachs," and that it "received an extremely favorable audience among church people."

But in the process Booth, and those around him, had made two serious errors, both of which tended to discredit the National Secretary, and by extension the NO, in the eyes of many in the organization and on its fringes.

The first error was political. In its attempt to dissociate SDS from the "draft-dodgers," the "Build, Not Burn" statement was actually more moderate than many in SDS would have liked. The NO was bombarded: a number of chapters launched formal protests and hundreds of individuals wrote in to complain. They argued that the statement did not attack the draft itself as an inequitable and undemocratic institution, but simply urged an extension of it into other areas; that it did not urge (as some groups in Berkeley and New York were already doing) opposition to the draft by any means possible, including outright evasion; and that it did not make any of the necessary connections between the draft and the war, showing them both as inevitable products of the American military-industrial state. The apologetic effect of it, especially, irritated many as being too defensive, too craven: Ken McEldowney and fifty others in the San Francisco region sent off a telegram: TONE OF STATEMENT DEPLORABLE. . . . READS LIKE

COPOUT TO KATZENBACH. Elsewhere people like Greg Calvert, then at Iowa State but eventually to be Booth's successor, felt the statement, as Calvert was to put it, was "the greatest formula ever devised for selling out the radical movement and playing into the cooptive hands of the establishment." And the May 2nd Movement from its own perspective said scornfully "This proposal creates illusions about the US government. It is as if the government has good agencies and bad agencies. The fact is that there is no democracy to do alternate service for." Small wonder that many SDSers soon started to put forth a counterslogan: "Build Not, Burn!"

The second error was procedural. Booth had, in effect, set SDS officially on a course of urging young men to file for Conscientious Objector status as a means of protesting the war, without having the slightest organizational support or justification for doing so. The National Secretary was not supposed to set policy, least of all on a program that was still before the membership and in defiance of the September NC vote giving campus educational work priority over any draft scheme. Shero, who all along had been a prime advocate of decentralization of SDS and a downgrading of the NO role, was particularly incensed, complaining bitterly about Booth's acting "unilaterally" to set policy for the entire organization; reporters, he said, should have simply been referred to local chapters which would tell them what was going on in any particular area, and the National Secretary could have stayed out of it completely. Others who resented reading in the papers about such a turnabout in national policy echoed Ken McEldowney's wry comment: "Participatory democracy begins at home."

Resentment against Booth for what he said was simply fueled by resentment that he said it at all. The disaffection that this produced, not only toward the National Secretary himself but toward the basic notion of a political decision-making central officer, would last.

On October 18 the May 2nd Movement announced its own anti-draft program:

> The opposition to the Vietnam Draft must be organized and political. One way is for people opposed to this draft . . . to organize

themselves into Anti-Draft Unions as the vehicle for draft opposition. These unions, as well as other groups, can—

1. Demonstrate at the induction centers. . . .

2. Expose and oppose college administration cooperation with the draft. . . . No ROTC on campus, No military recruitment on campus, No war research projects, can be demands. Organize STRIKES if demands aren't met.

3. Go to High Schools with leaflets, street meetings, ADU [antidraft union] organizing, etc. . . .

Such struggle cannot at this time prevent large numbers of young men from being forced into the Army. But it can bring many more people—particularly working class people—into the anti-war movement and thereby sharply increase the isolation of the government.

This same working-class rationale was reiterated by Jeff Gordon, the M2M leader, in an article in the M2M publication, *Free Student,* on November 27:

The key necessity for the peace movement is to broaden its base. If students remain isolated as the war goes on year after year they will be vulnerable to attack and discouragement. The erosion of rights and material conditions that the war necessarily entails provides the opportunity to involve other parts of the population, particularly workers. Recent strikes by thousands of defense workers give the lie to the idea that the war is in their interests. . . . We should oppose the draft in a way that all can participate. If we follow this up by organizationally approaching workers, as well as continuing our work on the campuses and in the communities, the movement will grow in size and in strength.

The issue of Communists in SDS, which the press and Senators made so much of during these October weeks—and which of course would continue to be an issue in the coming years—was not one which interested the SDSers themselves very much. It all seemed so irrelevant. True, the exclusion clause had been dropped, but that was more because there were no hordes of Communists asking to get in than because there were. The Communist Party itself was seen as a joke, a tired collection of middle-aged irrelevants who hadn't any idea of what the New Left was all about and certainly no means of taking it over. Not that SDS was the kind of organization that could very readily be taken over, even if anyone wanted to: "They can't take us over because they can't find us" was the standard joke. As to those with pro-Chinese or anti-imperialistic politics—the Progressive Labor and M2M people, for example—they were certainly allowed into the ranks but no one could figure out why they'd want to come if they had organizations of their own, and no one regarded their rather far-out ideas as likely to catch on with the bulk of SDSers. Carl Oglesby put the SDS stance best, in a speech to the *National Guardian* annual banquet that fall.

> SDS does not screen, purge, or use loyalty pledges. . . . We judge behavior. Those whose behavior runs athwart the deep SDS commitment to democracy just have no leverage over the democrats of SDS.
>
> And, in any case, SDS retains no detectives.
>
> Further, it is hard to see how a group could be "taken over" unless it has handles of power that can be seized, some "central apparatus" that can enforce orders. SDS has no such apparatus— only a beleaguered hot-spot in Chicago—and it is a main hard point with us that it never shall.

Nonetheless, there were many elders, especially liberal elders, who viewed the issue of Communist infiltration with utmost seriousness. The *New Republic,* for example, editorialized at the end of October:

> In our judgment . . . the Students for a Democratic Society do themselves and their aims a disservice by welcoming Communists in their ranks, and by making a virtue out of the indifference to the possibility of Communists becoming the dominant voice in their organization. . . . The SDS is "anxious to advance the cause of democracy." If they mean political democracy as we understand it, they will deal more realistically than they have with the fact of Communist participation.

And of course the people who took the whole question most seriously, and had for a year at least, were those in the LID.

Things, as we have seen, had not been going well between the LID and its offspring for some time. For a while during 1965 the LID tried to weather the storm, clinging to the idea of "dialogues" and hoping to keep the link to SDS both for reasons of principle (to educate the younger members away from wrong-minded positions, especially on the issue of Communism), and for reasons of pragmatism (to enjoy vicariously the attention and success of the student department and to have contacts with the important elements of the New Left). But it eventually became clear that the gulf between the two groups was unbridgeable; as Mike Harrington recalls it,

> . . . their whole style was increasingly one of screw-you. Their contempt for us was certainly coming through pretty loud and clear. . . . They were not simply having a more militant tactic on the war, but their attitude toward trade unions, toward liberal change, toward change in the Democratic Party—a whole spectrum of tactical issues which had once united us—were in the process of changing. It was around the war that this whole constellation of things came to a head.

Paul Feldman, a member of the LID Board of Directors, undertook to put the case against SDS in an *LID News Bulletin*. The basic trouble, he held, was the "new generation of radical youth" and their "ideological confusion, resulting from a visceral reaction to McCarthyism and a lack of political education." What had happened to SDS, he argued, was that it had fallen into the error of "agnosticism" on the question of Communism and it had failed "to judge the Communist side in the war by the same standards applied to the American role. A reactive anti-American establishmentarianism had been substituted for an analytical approach." That was bad enough, Lord knows, for "it clashed with our fundamental principles," but it also was tactically wrong, for it led "toward increasing isolation of the students from the very forces that are essential to democratic social progress"—and, incidentally, to the continuance of the LID—"the labor, civil rights, and liberal organizations." Clearly, Feldman argued, SDS had no rightful place in an organization whose "dedication to democracy placed it in principled opposition to Communism and all other forms of totalitarianism."

For most of those in SDS, this kind of argument was simple old-fogeyism. Some in the organization, it is true, shared the LID

worries—Haber, in particular, argued bitterly that SDS was falling into mindless association with "some of the Marxist anti-
American, anti-capitalist groupings"—and others wanted above
all to stay beneath the comforting protection of LID's tax-exemption shelter regardless of political differences. But the general
feeling was that the LID and the whole "democratic socialism"
of which it was a part simply represented the liberal wing of the
Establishment, a wing that had proven itself unworthy in every
challenge of the sixties, from civil rights to Vietnam.* This, combined with mounting anger at attacks on SDS and the New Left
from LID associates like Irving Howe and Bayard Rustin, and a
principled feeling that the two organizations no longer shared the
same basic philosophies, impelled the break from the student side.
Practical matters clinched the argument. SDS had discovered that
since the April march contributions were coming in at such a rate
that $3500 or so tossed its way by the LID was hardly important
to a $60,000-a-year organization; and the tax-exemption provi-
sions barring political activity increasingly grated on the students,
who ever since April had wanted to explore new and more militant
forms of political action which they knew would inevitably call
down the wrath of the IRS.

The tax-exemption issue made a convenient severing device.
SDS passed several resolutions urging the LID to drop its special
tax status, and the LID gave the matter cursory debate. But the
LID was hardly in a position to give up its educational role and
its tax windfall—what else, after all, did it have?—and at the end
of September it rejected the idea entirely. After some fruitless
negotiations on the subject, it seemed to all concerned to be a
convenient and graceful way to concretize the irremediable differences between the two organizations, and an "amicable severance" was at last agreed upon.

On October 4, 1965, an association that had lasted in one form
or other for more than forty years, and with roots going back to
the earliest part of the century, was dissolved:

*The ILG, pillar of this wing, had voted at its May convention to endorse
Johnson's actions in Vietnam and the Dominican Republic in strong terms, a fact
which a spring SDS worklist (May 27, 1965) had "noted in disgust." The same
worklist, be it added, referred to the LID as "our parent organization," apparently on the assumption that most SDSers didn't know what it was.

Acting under the instructions of the appropriate committees of our respective organizations, we have come to an understanding that Students for a Democratic Society shall cease to be the student department of the League for Industrial Democracy. . . . The reason for the separation is the desire of the SDS to engage in action programs which transcend the limits imposed by law on tax-exempt organizations. The League, on the other hand, has decided that it wishes to continue functioning as a tax-exempt educational organization.

Good form was kept—"The termination of SDS's status as the student department of the League . . . is not the consequence of political disagreement but an effort to preserve the interests and integrity of the two organizations"—but no one was fooled: politics, the basic politics of Old Left liberalism and New Left radicalism, was at the very heart of the sunderance. SDS now was on its own.

Having come into the spotlight during the October demonstrations, SDS had no desire to move into the wings. Nor could it, really, even if it had wanted to, for it was now seen by students as the leading antiwar organization in the land and the only vehicle through which their angered sentiments could express themselves. (The NCC, which had actually coordinated the demonstrations, was merely an administrative center, not a membership organization, as were most of the local *ad hoc* committees like the Fifth Avenue Peace Parade Committee in New York; none of the membership groups like M2M, the DuBois Clubs, or the Young Socialist Alliance had the energy, the publicity, the aura, or the stature of SDS.) So as attention turned to the next planned demonstration, a march on Washington which SANE had called for the Thanksgiving weekend, SDS was inevitably drawn in, despite its antipathy to mass marches in general and SANE's liberalism in particular.*

Campus interest in another demonstration was clearly strong, especially as a means of showing immediate defiance of the

*SANE had, after all, boycotted the April affair; and its Thanksgiving march coordinator, Sanford Gottlieb, had declared it as his objective to keep "kooks, communists or draft-dodgers" out of the Washington demonstration.

government's redbaiting attacks and support for "the right to dissent"; liberal friends of SDS urged it to join in so that the press and the Administration could not argue that the steam had gone out of the antiwar movement. But perhaps most persuasive, SOS, it turned out, had no other program of its own to follow. The draft proposal over which so much media commotion was made was *defeated* in the referendum, 279 to 243, with 35 abstentions, a vote which the NO regarded as expressing the membership's fear of legal repression but the small size of which (one-sixth of the 3139 people to whom ballots had been sent) probably indicated rather that most chapters wanted to go ahead with their own already functioning local programs—draft counseling in Austin, CO leafleting in Ann Arbor, draft-information booths at Los Angeles-area campuses, and so on—instead of getting involved in a national effort.

And so Carl Oglesby—this was again a unilateral decision of the NAC in Chicago, though one that seemed to have general support—began negotiating with SANE, and it was eventually agreed that in return for its participation SDS could issue its own call and add its own spokesman to the official program. The call was drawn up and 100,000 copies printed, considerably changing the tone of the demonstration—as well as the position of SDS from its April march:

> There must be an immediate cease fire and demobilization in South Vietnam. There must be a withdrawal of American troops. . . . All agreements must be ratified by the partisans of the "other side"— the National Liberation Front and North Vietnam.
> We are convinced that the only way to stop this and future wars is to organize a domestic social movement which challenges the very legitimacy of our foreign policy; this movement must also fight to end racism, to end the paternalism of our welfare system, to guarantee decent incomes for all, and to supplant the authoritarian control of our universities with a community of scholars.

Even more important, Oglesby himself agreed to be the SDS spokesman. Seeing in this chance to address a predominantly liberal audience an important opportunity to get across SDS politics, he bent himself (with help from Gitlin and Rothstein) to the task of writing a speech that would, as the NO people were saying, "tell it like it is." It turned out to be one of the most effective speeches any SDSer was to give.

November 27 was a raw, chill, overcast day, the kind that makes Washingtonians impatient for cherry blossoms, but by the *Guardian*'s estimate some forty thousand people showed up in the capital. By a prior agreement reached only after a brouhaha that almost split the burgeoning movement before the march even started, SANE agreed to relax its sign censorship and permit each group to carry its own signs; around the White House that morning, therefore, SANE banners for *"Negotiate Now"* vied with such slogans as *"Bring the GIs Home Now"* and *"Don't Negotiate—Evacuate,"* plus a large NLF banner that the SANE marshals tried to surround with American flags so the TV cameramen wouldn't notice. Shortly after noon the crowd was seated around the base of the Washington monument prepared for a long afternoon of speakers. Careful to emphasize its "respectable" tone, SANE had loaded the program with moderates who, as Oglesby was to say later, were so eager "to show their 'responsibleness,' to criticize 'both sides equally,' that some of their speeches would hardly have been wrong for a pro-war rally." The hour was growing late and nearly a third of the audience had gone to warmer surroundings when Oglesby, shunted away at the end of the program, rose to speak.

> The original commitment in Vietnam was made by President Truman, a mainstream liberal. It was seconded by President Eisenhower, a moderate liberal. It was intensified by the late President Kennedy, a flaming liberal. Think of the men who now engineer that war—those who study the maps, give the commands, push the buttons, and tally the dead: Bundy, McNamara, Rusk, Lodge, Goldberg, the President himself.
>
> They are not moral monsters.
> They are all honorable men.
> They are all liberals.
> But so, I'm sure, are many of us who are here today in protest. To understand the war, then, it seems necessary to take a closer look at this American liberalism. Maybe we are in for some surprises.

And slowly, laying American liberal Cold War errors at his listeners' feet, one by one, he provided those surprises. Support for Rhodesia, South Africa, Latin American dictators. The American-led overthrow of Mossadegh in Iran to the benefit of Gulf Oil; of Arbenz in Guatemala to the profits of United Fruit; of Jagan in Guyana to the satisfaction of the AFL-CIO; of Goulart in Brazil to the pleasure of State Department policy makers. The invasion of Cuba, of the Dominican Republic, planned and carried out by liberals, for liberals. The secret placement of nuclear weapons in West German hands. And Vietnam.

> This country, with its thirty-some years of liberalism, can send 200,000 young men to Vietnam to kill and die in the most dubious of wars, but it cannot get 100 voter registrars to go into Mississippi.
>   What do you make of it?
>   The financial burden of the war obliges us to cut millions from an already pathetic War on Poverty budget. But in almost the same breath, Congress appropriates $140 million for the Lockheed and Boeing companies to compete with each other on the supersonic transport project—that Disneyland creation that will cost us all about $2 billion before it's done.
>   What do you make of it?

Liberalism, of course, had tried to justify all these acts with "the ideology of anti-Communism."

>   Far from helping Americans deal with . . . truth, the anti-Communist ideology merely tries to disguise it so that things may stay the way they are. Thus, it depicts our presence in other lands not as a coercion, but a protection. It allows us even to say that the napalm in Vietnam is only another aspect of our humanitarian love —like those exorcisms in the Middle Ages that so often killed the patient. So we say to the Vietnamese peasant, the Cuban intellectual, the Peruvian worker: "You are better dead than red. If it hurts or if you don't understand why—sorry about that."
>   This is the action of *corporate liberalism*. It performs for the corporate state a function quite like what the Church once performed for the feudal state. It seeks to justify its burdens and protect it from change. . . .
>   Let me then speak directly to humanist liberals. If my facts are wrong, I will soon be corrected. But if they are right, then you may face a crisis of conscience. Corporatism or humanism;

which? For it has come to that. Will you let your dreams be used? Will you be grudging apologists for the corporate state? Or will you help try to change it—not in the name of this or that blueprint or ism, but in the name of simple human decency and democracy and the vision that wise and brave men saw in the time of our own Revolution?

And if your commitment to human value is unconditional, then disabuse yourselves of the notion that statements will bring change, if only the right statements can be written, or that interviews with the mighty will bring change if only the mighty can be reached, or that marches will bring change if only we can make them massive enough, or that policy proposals will bring change if only we can make them responsible enough.

We are dealing now with a colossus that does not want to be changed. It will not change itself. It will not cooperate with those who want to change it. . . . All the more reason for building [a] movement with a most relentless conviction.

There are people in this country today who are trying to build that movement, who aim at nothing less than a humanist reformation. And the humanist liberals must understand that it is this movement with which their own best hopes are most in tune. We radicals know the same history that you liberals know, and we can understand your occasional cynicism, exasperation, and even distrust. But we ask you to put these aside and help us risk a leap. Help us find enough time for the enormous work that needs doing here. Help us build. Help us shake the future in the name of plain human hope.

It was a devastating performance: skilled, moderate, learned, and compassionate, but uncompromising, angry, radical, and above all persuasive. It drew the only standing ovation of the afternoon. As reporter Ward Just was to say in the *Washington Post* the following week:

The speech was little noticed and all but unreported in the press, but in the post mortems following the recent March on Washington to End the War in Vietnam it was receiving the most attention of all speeches. . . . Leaders of the movement described the speech as a declaration of independence from the traditional thread of American liberalism on the one hand and a call to battle to alter the fundamental social, political and economic structure of the country on the other.

Perhaps old hat to the old guard, but to the audience in Washington, to much of the new campus generation, to many who were awakened to politics only with Vietnam, this was an eye-opener. The demand for reprints surpassed anything that SDS had known; within two weeks mimeographed copies were being run off in the NO and a Movement printing shop in Lawrence, Kansas, was preparing to reprint it by the thousands for SDS to distribute; the *Monthly Review* picked it up for its January 1966 issue; and for years afterward it would continue to be one of the most popular items of SDS literature.*

The Oglesby speech won SDS considerable respect in many quarters and proved to be the icing on the quite unexpected cake of success that fall. National media continued to focus on the organization: *The New York Times Magazine* ran a long and friendly piece by LIDer Tom Brooks; *Newsweek* did a special takeout on "The Demonstrators," featuring SDS; the *Nation* had a flattering profile by Jack Newfield; the *National Guardian,* whose circulation was now up to 28,000, gave steady weekly publicity to SDS doings; and SDSers even began to appear on occasional national television programs. Letters from students and sympathizers were coming in at the rate of more than a thousand a month—answered, of course, sporadically if at all—and nearly fifty student and youth organizations from more than twenty foreign countries sent official statements of support, newsletters, queries, proposals, and greetings.

*It is important to note, however, that the November 27 Oglesby speech, though more dramatic and more stylish, does not go beyond the April 17 Potter speech, delivered in the same spot on the same kind of occasion, in "naming the system." Both are talking about what will come to be called "imperialism" before another year is out, a phrase borrowed for want of a better from the Marxist groups whose influence in SDS, and the movement in general, was to grow; as Oglesby said two years later, his was "an attempt to describe imperialism without giving it that name, and to attribute imperialist policy to the structure of monopoly capitalism without pronouncing that term either. . . . Imperialism and monopoly capitalism were conceptions proper and necessary to the thorough critique of US policy, but they had been effectively drained of meaning by decades of strong, pervasive and subtle Cold War propaganda. . . . For most of the growing student movement in those days, these were still out-of-bounds terms." (Introduction to "Trapped in a System," Radical Education Project pamphlet, January 1969.) Nonetheless, SDS, it is clear, was able to talk about the fundamentals of the American state even when it had not been schooled in how to name them.

By the end of December SDS had grown to an estimated 4300 paid-up national members, at 124 chapters* in thirty-eight states and the District of Columbia (missing only Alabama, Alaska, Arkansas, Georgia, Hawaii, Idaho, Louisiana, Mississippi, Montana, Nevada, South Carolina, South Dakota, Utah, West Virginia, and Wyoming); no fewer than forty-four of the chapters had been started (or reestablished) that fall, some at places quite predictable (Los Angeles, Pennsylvania, Yale) and some quite unexpected (Iowa State, New Rochelle, Notre Dame—and there was even an attempt made at West Point). New regional organizations had been established, more or less spontaneously but growing out of the impetus to decentralization that had emerged at the June convention, in Boston, New York, Los Angeles, and San Francisco, and each had its own staff to put out its own mimeographed newsletters, contact local chapters, and set area strategies and programs quite independently of the National Office. Six chapters (Antioch, Indiana, Kansas, Michigan, Oklahoma, and Reed) were turning out independent newsletters for SDSers and friends in their own regions. Campus travelers made regular trips, generating interest at new campuses, solidifying it at the old; chief among them were Oglesby and Booth, plus heads of the Regional Offices, especially Ken McEldowney in San Francisco, Jane Adams in the Midwest, and John Maher (son of a wealthy Houston businessman, John F. Maher, and brother of Albert Maher, the M2M leader) in Boston. And to them were added the more informal

---

*New and renewed chapters over the last seven months included Ball State, Bennington, University of California (Davis, Los Angeles, Riverside, Santa Cruz), California State (Hayward, Los Angeles, Sacramento State, San Diego State, San Fernando Valley State, San Francisco State, San Jose State, Santa Ana), Chico State, Colorado State, Drake, Emmanuel, Florida, Goucher, Houston At-large, Hunter College (Bronx), Illinois (Urbana and Chicago Circle), Illinois State, Iowa, Iowa State, Kentucky, Kingsborough Community College, Los Angeles At-large, Macalester, Maine, Massachusetts, Michigan State, Milwaukee At-large, Missouri (at Kansas City), Nebraska, New Hampshire, New Mexico, New Rochelle, Newton High School, New York University (Downtown and Uptown), State University of New York (Albany, Buffalo, Plattsburg), North Carolina, North Dakota, Northern Illinois, Northeastern, Northwestern, Notre Dame, Oregon, Pasadena At-large, Pennsylvania, Piedmont, Pittsburgh At-large, Purdue, Rhode Island, Toledo At-large, University of Washington, Washington University, Wesleyan University, West Lafayette (Indiana) High School, Western Washington State, Woodrow Wilson High School (D.C.), Yale.

SDS wanderers—people in the old guard whose campus contacts were greatest, including some ERAPers beginning to feel that Movemental initiative had swung back to the universities.

Moreover, SDS was enjoying a steady and prosperous income for the first time in its history. More than $20,000 came in through contributions over the fall (after the October publicity, at the rate of about $250 a day), making up the bulk of the $24,600 total income for those four months. Expenditures, as usual, matched the income ($23,800), mostly for rent and office expenses. The NO could now project a budget of $75–80,000 a year, a far cry, indeed a shriek, from the early days.

Yet with all this the basic problems that had been wracking SDS since the Kewadin convention remained, and even as it rode the crest of its new success SDS turned its attention to them. Put schematically, there were four crucial problems:

Structure. Having no National Secretary had proven to be a disaster, but having one didn't seem to make anybody much happier, either in the Chicago office or out on the hustings. The NO was still functioning poorly, with rapid turnovers and chaotic operations. Participatory democracy was proving harder to implement in the burgeoning organization than anyone had imagined —membership referenda were obviously clumsy and ineffective, but arbitrary fiats from the National Secretary and NAC were obviously undemocratic. Some means had to be found to regulate the decision-making process.

Policies. As of December, SDS (though the news would have come as a surprise to many) had no official stand on Vietnam, on the draft, on university reform, or on domestic priorities, and no ready way to arrive at them. What general sense of shared ideology had been characteristic of the organization a year ago was no longer true, yet there were few papers being researched, speeches made, or letters written—as in the old days—to arrive at a new ideology. Known but a few months ago as a center for radical intellectuals, SDS was now regarded more as a place for antiwar activists.

Membership. Hundreds of new people had come into SDS, but they tended to be cut off from the old guard and given little direction, or education. There was little internal communication to them, other than sporadic worklist mailings concentrating on immediate news and crises, and almost no internal education. The older members were now regarded as an "elite," still the speech-makers and the decision-makers but often remote from the rank and file, with different concerns, different biases; there was much talk among them of starting a *new* organization, a *Movement* for a Democratic Society, for graduates and adults.

Strategy. SDS was still wrestling with the perennial problem of where to turn now, whether to build a larger movement or consolidate what it already had, whether to build alliances with the liberals or develop contacts with the Marxist left, whether to concentrate on students rather than ghetto dwellers or adult anti-war forces, whether to build solid bases on the campuses or try to forge an entirely new American left.

Now in truth these problems were so complex, tangled, and well-nigh insoluble that they would, in one form or another, re-main with the organization throughout its existence. But there was an assumption, especially among the old guard, that they had to be tackled, and immediately, and out of that assumption the idea for a special "rethinking conference" was born. What the old guard had in mind—unspoken, perhaps unacknowledged, but evi-dent—was the need to recreate Port Huron, to give SDS a second birth. The idea was logical enough, and touching: if some greater cohesion could be forged, members educated together, basic social theories agreed upon, internal communication opened up, and working democracy instituted, SDS could solve its major prob-lems and develop into a significant multigenerational, multidisci-plined, multi-issued, genuinely radical organization on the Ameri-can left. Indeed, if such an organization could have been created, it might well have been able to weather the disappointments and the successes, the factionalism and the radicalism of the next few years. But 1966 was not 1962.

The rethinking conference was duly held at the Illinois Uni-versity campus in Champaign-Urbana over the Christmas vaca-tion. Some 360 people from 66 chapters showed up, including a good number of those who had recently joined—among them a young Columbia student named John Fuerst and a gangling, mus-tached youth from the University of Nebraska named Carl David-

son, both of whom were to become prominent in the organization
—but the meeting was dominated by the old guard.* It was,
though they could not have known it, the last SDS conference they
would exert any appreciable influence on. For they were moving
off in a different direction from the bulk of the membership now,
concerned essentially with problems of postcollege activism that
little interested the new breed. And when they failed here to solve
the central problems, or to even make much sense out of them,
when they failed here to make SDS into an organization that
would express their concerns, they began to drift away and let the
younger hands take over.

For the meeting *was* a failure. None of the problems was
solved. Jonathan Eisen, writing in *The Activist,* called it "a
morass, a labyrinth, a marathon of procedural amendments, *non
sequiturs,* soul-searching and maneuvering, partying and arguing,
plenaries which went nowhere, proposals unheeded, undebated;
terminology which only the most in of the in-group could comprehend, much less care about; and a few who were too far gone
to participate in anything but getting girls. Pages and pages of
proposals, prospectuses, amendments, workshop resolutions,
recommendations, counter-recommendations, hasseling and
dancing to the Beatles." Gitlin more soberly confessed, "Almost
every person I talked to—while the meeting was going on, and
afterward—agreed that it was a disaster." And in a somber, bit-
ingly honest report to the membership he ticked off the failures,
failures not just of this meeting but of SDS as a whole:

> A dearth of ideological and strategic content to debates, where it
> would be appropriate. . . . Slogans and symbols replace analysis and
> hard thinking. . . . Elitism is and should be a matter of central
> concern. . . . Speechmaking . . . is the premium style. If you make
> a good speech, you're in; otherwise, you're out. . . . Our egos become

*Among those present, trying to recapture Port Huron, were Booth, Brecher,
Flacks, Garvy, Gitlin, Haber, Kissinger, Max, Carol McEldowney, Rothstein,
Ross, Webb, and Wittman. Hayden, with what is perhaps symbolic appropriateness, was not there: the Communist Party's Herbert Aptheker had invited him
and Staughton Lynd, as representatives of the New Left, on a "fact-finding" trip
to North Vietnam, the first American delegation to visit there. (See Hayden's
reports in *New Left Notes,* January 21, 1966, and the *Guardian,* January 29 and
February 5, 1966, and *The Other Side,* with Staughton Lynd; Signet, 1967.)

tied to our words, our proposals. We would sooner make speeches before the whole body than consult privately. . . . We would sooner split hairs than solve problems. . . . Out of exhaustion and/or common sense, everyone may agree to cut discussion short and move on to a vote [but] as often as not this resolution is purely arbitrary—the debate has produced little justification for either choice. . . . Aggressive sectionalism and snide anti-sectionalism . . . "the Texas guys," "those New York coalitionists," "the Chicago bunch."

Outside the plenary sessions, things were no better. A white member of the Texas delegation insulted a black at a party one night during the conference, there was a fight, and immediately the whole ugly issue of racism stalked the corridors. Black anger seethed, and white fear; there were fistfights, knives, threats: the Texas delegation was taken to task by angrier-than-thou whites for harboring racists, and it walked out en masse, charging reverse discrimination and liberal guilt-politics; black SDSers such as Carolyn Craven became convinced that SDS was irrevocably racist. It was a symbol, if symbol were needed, of how far SDS had come from those hopeful early days of the civil-rights movement.

Nor was the National Council meeting that followed any more successful. On the main political topics, the war and the draft, there was no resolution. A proposal to put SDS on record for immediate withdrawal of American troops was defeated, but no counterproposal could gain sufficient support either, and in the end the NC simply enshrined its disdain for "the Vietnam hangup" as national policy:

> We must be planning years ahead, rather than responding in every crisis. We should be prepared to reject activities that mobilize thousands of people but do not build constituencies. . . . We should be prepared to argue with the antiwar movement that the real lever for change in America is a domestic social movement. And, that the movement to end the war in Vietnam cannot end that war. Finally, we should also say that radicals have more important priorities than working simply to end the war.

True, all too true. But this restatement of the Kewadin spirit puzzled many of the newest members; as Helen Garvy later said, the younger people "just couldn't understand how SDS could vote against such a thing when there was a war going on."

On the draft, the conference rejected VOICE chairman Eric Chester's proposal for marches on army bases and induction centers to hold immediate-withdrawal rallies, and voted down several other proposals for actions against the draft, against university involvement in war research, against the 2-S deferment. All were regarded as too militant, unlikely to work on the newer and more remote campuses: "We can't even get beyond the teach-in level," one Nebraska delegate argued. The NC limited itself to approving the distribution of twenty thousand copies of a "Guide to Conscientious Objection," a breezy little pamphlet written mostly by Paul Lauter, an older SDSer working for the American Friends Service Committee in Chicago, which was not so much about how to be a CO as how to start thinking about becoming one; and to the launching of a "freedom draft" campaign, an idea of Jeremy Brecher's mixing Booth's "Build, Not Burn" with the M2M and DuBois Clubs' antidraft petitions of the year before. Chapters would get people to sign a special draft card ("I want to work for democracy. I do not want to fight in Vietnam, because the war is destroying our hopes for democracy both there and at home. I want to build, not burn. . . . "), one part of which would be carried by the signer, another sent to the White House, and the third returned to the NO for a grand tally.

As to internal problems, they too were mostly unresolved, but attempts were made to solve the most pressing. A Radical Education Project was to be set up in Ann Arbor to prepare and turn out analytical papers of the kind that SDS had once been famous for, so that newer members could be educated into the ideological sweep that had characterized the organization initially; this was the brainchild of Al Haber and bore the unmistakable marks of his belief, unchanged over five years, in the power of mimeographed papers to radicalize the nation. For internal education and general membership communication, the NC decided to give top priority to the establishment of a weekly bulletin or newspaper, another notion of Haber's. And, perhaps most significantly, the regional organizations that had grown up on their own in the last six months were given a seal of approval and other areas urged to start their own, as an attempt to deal with the problems of internal democracy and the NO administrative bottleneck.

Also raised among the internal problems was another issue that was enunciated here for the first time in SDS: women's liberation. A workshop on "Women in the Movement" (the first at any left meeting in this decade) produced a sharp call from a number of the women participants for greater "initiative and participation by women" in SDS and a greater understanding of the "woman question" by men in the organization. "Many women feel," the statement read, "that the problem of participation by women is a special problem—one that reflects not only inadequacies within SDS but one that also reflects greater societal problems, namely the problem of the role of women in American society today."

The December meetings were a touching symbol. Called by the old guard to reestablish the kind of SDS they had known and loved, it actually served to indicate that, inevitably, the organization was headed in new directions, the clock could not be turned back. The SDS that was family, that was shared assumptions and shared lives, was fading now, and something new and uncertain was growing in its place.

14

SPRING 1966

Nothing showed the distance between the old guard of SDS and the new breed better than their quite disparate responses to the most dramatic development of the spring of 1966: the decision of the Johnson Administration to draft students for the war in Vietnam.

Early in February, General Lewis B. Hershey, the director of the Selective Service System, announced that local draft boards would henceforth be free for the first time to induct into the armed services college students who were in the lower levels of their respective classes. Two methods would be used to determine this standing: university administrations would be asked to rank their male students by their past grade performance and give that information to the government, and a national draft examination would be given in May to all male undergraduates to assess their overall intelligence and achievement. The effect was electric. Suddenly on campuses all over the country, the war finally hit home. No longer was 2-S an inviolable sanctuary. No longer was fighting in Vietnam something that others had to do. The shock of what a war means began to sink in. The old guard, clustered essentially around the National Office in Chicago and hoping to use the NO as the instrument by which to push the membership into some concerted action programs on national issues, wanted to take advantage of this shock with an all-out effort, something as grand as the original march on Washington. The lack of a draft program (other than the "Freedom Draft Cards," which did not prove popular and were never even tabulated) had become an acute embarrassment and it was felt that SDS now had to come up with a concrete, dramatic, visible protest that would affirm SDS's place as the leading organization against the war. The notion finally settled upon, suggested by Lee Webb, was a national *counter*draft exam, giving SDSian questions and answers on Vietnam and American foreign policy, to be handed out by SDSers on the very day that students gathered for the Selective Service exam. The April National Council meeting at Antioch, guided by the old guard, approved the plan, which seemed to embody all virtues: it was simple, it avoided all questions of illegality, it had a built-in audience of students, and its appeal was intellectual rather than confrontational. (At the same time the NC refused to go along with a corollary proposal, pushed by Booth, that SDSers pledge not to take the draft exam themselves—and therefore be liable for induction—as proof of their "seriousness." The chapter people, arguing that this would "turn off most students" and put "a barrier between us and the 'crew cuts,' " refused to be pushed into something still so controversial; they demanded the issue be put to a mail ballot vote of the membership, where the idea was subsequently defeated, though in a vote so tiny—61–21—as to be meaningless.)

The NO moved into high gear. It expanded the Chicago staff from six to eleven, installed a special $200-a-month telephone line to coordinate printing and distribution, and farmed out contracts across the country for printing more than half a million exams. The exam itself was the result of weeks of consultations with Vietnam experts at more than a dozen campuses, coordinated by Mike Locker, Todd Gitlin, Staughton Lynd, and Paul Booth for SDS, along with several members of the faculty organization that had grown out of the teach-in movement, the Inter-University Committee for Debate on Foreign Policy. Its purpose, according to the instructions, was

> ... to allow you to check your understanding of the war in Vietnam.
> ... We believe in the importance in a democracy of putting the facts in the hands of every citizen to enable him to participate in decision-making. This is particularly true where the question is war and

peace, and where the citizens are the young men called upon to fight.*

Finally, on May 14, teams of nearly a thousand SDSers handed out 500,000 copies of the four-page printed exam at 850 of the 1200 SSS examination centers across the country. It was an operation, Paul Booth was to boast, "surpassing the April 1965 march."

It was also pretty much of a failure. True, at several exam centers students were impressed enough with the SDS material to get up and walk out entirely, and at campuses where Vietnam activity had been muted—especially in the South, where the SDS-affiliated Southern Student Organizing Committee gave the primary push—reaction was often favorable. But in general students were untouched: they read the SDS exam but they took the SSS one. No large protests took place, no hordes of suddenly awakened students swarmed to join SDS, no significant groups of people were moved to radicalism. Crowning ignominy of all: a press conference called on the steps of the Selective Service building in Washington drew just eight reporters, all local, and another press conference in Chicago drew none at all. Whatever else the exam was, it wasn't news.

Nor was it especially popular within the wider antiwar movement. Disappointment was frequently expressed with SDS for "copping out" on forging a militant program against the draft. In April Staughton Lynd voiced the feelings of many: "I am puzzled, too. I don't know why SDS decided not to emphasize an antidraft program. . . . The most obvious and tragic failure of the movement against the war in this last year has been its failure to develop a responsible program against the draft."

The response by the new generation of SDSers to the draft issue was altogether different: spontaneous, local, uncoordinated, growing out of the conditions of individual chapters and universi-

*Typical of the questions was this none-too-subtle sally: "Which of the following American military heroes has, in the past, warned against committing a large number of American troops to a land war on the Asian mainland: (A) Gen. Douglas MacArthur (B) Pres. Dwight D. Eisenhower (C) Gen. Matthew B. Ridgway (D) Gen. Maxwell Taylor (E) Gen. James Gavin (F) Gen. Omar Bradley? [Answer:] All have made such warnings."

ties—and infinitely more successful. The whole notion that university administrations were being used as the handmaidens of the Selective Service through the rank system came as a shock at many campuses, and various local movements were begun to keep the universities from releasing class ranks. At Harvard in February, at Wisconsin in March, at Cornell in April, local committees in which SDSers were prominent sought to block class ranking. Finally in May, just a few days before the exams, disruptions broke out spontaneously at a dozen different schools from Stanford and San Francisco State in the West, through Wayne State and Wisconsin in the Midwest, to City College, Brooklyn, and Columbia in the East. Not just disruptions, but for the first time a widespread adoption of the sit-in technique. The classic confrontation of this type was at the University of Chicago.

It was the SDS chapter at Chicago that initiated the antirank struggle there. The chapter had been a diligent one for the last year or so, under able leaders like Steve Kindred and Brent Kramer, but its membership had increased sharply during the fall of 1965, considerably helped by having around it some of the best SDS hands—not just those in the NO, located not far from the campus, but also junior faculty like sociologist Dick Flacks and historian Jesse Lemisch, and sociology graduate student Bob Ross. It was in early April—two months after the Hershey announcement—that SDS finally decided to make an issue over the question of class rank and university cooperation with the Selective Service System. The issue was a good one, SDSers felt, to awaken and politicize the campus because it could be fought at three different levels: as a protest against the war and the draft system that sustains it ("We feel that now is the time for a . . . courageous opposition to an immoral and discriminatory national policy"); as an attack on the university administration for its complicity with the government and the war ("the transformation of this University into a coding and classifying machine for the Selective Service"); and as a principled stand against tainting and distorting the educational process ("To rank is to change a community of scholars into a set of madly competing factions"). The combination was devastating, just as devastating as a similar combination had been at Berkeley a year-and-a-half before: an issue of high moral purpose (civil rights then, the war now), in which the liberal university administration took what could be seen as the side of evil (banning civil-rights organizing, cooperating with the draft), to the detriment of its own students and their free rights, thereby showing up the pernicious character of the university as the servant of a corrupt society. This special mixture of a broad national cause and local, felt grievances would continue to be the hallmark—usually over-looked—of all major student protest throughout the years of the sixties.

The rest of the scenario at Chicago had familiarities, too. Conventional attempts by students to get the administration to change its policy were met by the official "it's always been that way" and "it's out of our hands"; on April 12, the faculty commit-tee meeting to discuss the ranking issue turned away SDSers who asked to address the group with a curt "You're not welcome here." A week later SDS decided to start a petition of those who were against ranking, soon signing up some 800 students (out of an 8500-member student body) and another 20 faculty members. This also was ignored by the administration, which seemed con-tent to play down the whole issue in hopes that its *fait* would be *accompli* before too many students noticed. So SDS in some des-peration decided to form a single-issue *ad hoc* committee, to broaden support. Students Against the Rank (SAR) was born at a long and stormy session in front of the administration building on May 4, and at that time the idea of a sit-in was first suggested if the administration refused to change its stand. Seven days later, after continued university footdragging, the suggestion became a reality.

About four hundred people gathered in the rain in front of the administration building on the afternoon of May 11 and slowly began moving into the building for shelter; by four-thirty, almost quietly and without resistance from administration personnel, the sit-in was accomplished, the administration closed its offices and went home, and the four-story building was in the hands of the students.* For the next five days there took place what was later

*In his report to the Presidential Violence Commission in 1968, Jerome Skolnik, following a paper by Dick Flacks, calls this "the first successful closing of a university administration building"—overlooking the fact that the Free Speech Movement sit-in at Berkeley preceded it by seventeen months. (*The Politics of Protest;* Ballantine, 1969.)

acknowledged to be a memorable and moving experience. The students quickly established their own government, with scrupulous attention to participatory democracy and decisions-by-consensus; areas were set aside for eating, sleeping, studying, and talking; people walked around with the happy sense that they had just taken part in something historic. Paul Booth came over from the National Office to reiterate SDS support, and during the evening telegrams of support began arriving from student groups all around the country. As a later commentator was to write:

> Despite the fact that the students were taking a considerable personal risk in challenging the administration, most found themselves having a great time. . . . It was exciting and fun to get to know each other, to get acquainted and feel close in the unity of the moment. The sit-in was a five-day communal act, a deeply personal experience for those students involved.

The wire services were quick to send out reports, and coverage from local radio and television began that first night. The next day the Chicago papers gave the sit-in considerable publicity, with the *Chicago Tribune* running a long analysis on the front page and, on the editorial page, predictably blaming "a small minority of students, incited by a handful of experienced revolutionaries." Within days the national media were treating it as if it were another Berkeley.

It is worth pausing a moment to consider a study made of the Chicago antirank protesters, because it is one of the most revealing of such sociological examinations and one of the few to concentrate on SDS. It also shows results similar to other surveys of radical students, suggesting the general validity of its findings. And the fact that it was conducted by Dick Flacks, who could be presumed to have an intimate knowledge of the protesters and a built-in "control," makes it even more reliable.

The Flacks study reported that the grade average of the protesters was B to B-plus, slightly higher than a random group of nonprotesters, and most came from the top levels of their high-school classes. This is another confirmation of the point that activists in general did not protest their academic environments, in which they were succeeding remarkably well, but rather conditions beyond the university in which they felt the university was culpable. The protesters' families were likely to have high incomes (over $15,000), their fathers were mostly professional men, and their mothers had jobs of their own; individuality within the family, therefore, and a generally democratic (or egalitarian) home life were emphasized. Their upbringing was, by and large, permissive, and they tended to regard their fathers as lenient—70 percent of the males and 47 percent of the females rated their fathers "lenient" or "soft." The great majority of their grandparents were foreign-born and highly educated; a quarter of the grandmothers attended college. In general they supported the values of their parents—who were further to the left than their adult peers (only 13 percent of the fathers were Republican, against 40 percent of a sample of nonprotesters)—but they were likely to be politically more radical: 97 percent, for example, approved of civil disobedience, but only 57 percent of their fathers did, and 62 percent of them wanted the full socialization of industry, whereas only 23 percent of their fathers did. Nearly half of the sit-iners were Jewish by birth, though most said they themselves had no religion of their own. On a series of attitude tests they scored notably high on romanticism, intellectualism, and humanitarianism, and low on convential moralism (i.e., attitudes toward sex, drugs, and the like).

Campus activists of the SDS stripe, in other words, were likely to be among the brightest, most active, most concerned, and well-to-do, the comparative cream of the academic crop.

The Chicago administration, determined *not* to create "another Berkeley" by calling in the police, decided to just wait it out. It proved to be a shrewd decision, for while it did not diminish the import of the sit-in itself, on campus and elsewhere, it did prevent widespread disruption and student-wide support for the protesters' cause. Gradually, after days of fruitless negotiations with the administration and nights of long participatory-democracy meetings, the sit-iners began to tire. Three days after the initial takeover, when there was no sign their demands were being met, the group agreed to withdraw the bulk of the protesters, as a gesture of its faith in future negotiations, leaving only a token reserve to indicate that the demands were not being forgotten. The administration still would not give in, but a full faculty meeting was scheduled to meet in special session for the first time in the history of the university, and there were signs that a compromise would be reached. On May 16 SAR, heartened, voted to end its occupation completely.

The faculty meeting when it came was, much to SAR's surprise, a total rout for the students. By heavy margins the faculty voted to threaten harsh disciplinary action against future sit-ins or campus disruptions, and to put itself unshirkingly behind the administration policy with regard to ranking. The blow was severe, the students hardly believing that two months of work and negotiations and demonstrations and petitions and letters and arguments had produced not one single concession. But since the end of the school year was at hand, and regroupment was now impossible, there was little recourse. SAR had one last meeting, vowed to continue its fight in the fall, and disappeared into the mists of June.

In the short run, the Chicago sit-in had failed: the administration did not budge from its position, and the faculty supported its stand unhesitatingly. But in the long run the event was to have important repercussions.

In Chicago SAR, with more than a thousand members, was established as a political force among the students, and SDS shared in its glow; when it reactivated its protest the next fall, it was finally successful in getting the university faculty to agree not to give draft boards access to rank figures. At a dozen other universities rank protests were begun in the wake of the Chicago sit-in, among them: an SDS-led sit-in at Roosevelt University (where it was found that one of the trustees was the head of Science Research Associates, the firm that had drawn up the offending exams for SSS), a 50-strong sit-in at Cornell, a 7000-student march and subsequent sit-in at the administration building at Wisconsin, a sit-in and fast at the New York State University branch in New Paltz, a 110-member sit-in at Brooklyn College, and a demonstration at CCNY. Protests at San Francisco State led to a unanimous faculty vote to abolish ranking and at two other institutions—Wayne State and Haverford—led to decisions by the administrations to abandon class ranks that spring. And everywhere the issue of the draft became suddenly a legitimate subject of student controversy, which once ignited would continue to send

261   SPRING 1966

off sparks: whereas the draft occasioned not a single protest in the 1964–65 academic year, by 1967–68 it triggered demonstrations at fully a quarter of American colleges (and nearly half of the large public universities).

More than that. The demonstrations leading on from Chicago put the issue of the draft in the forefront of national issues. Two Presidential commissions were soon established, books were written, conferences were held, and politicians of all stripes came forward with reform proposals. The controversy grew to such proportions that within a year the Selective Service System abandoned both its ranking procedures and the examinations and the government was openly casting about for alternative systems. Among the public at large the connection between the draft and the war, only murkily understood before, was now made clearly, and among both radicals and liberals the idea of draft resistance was given a greater legitimacy.

The two most important consequences, however, the two that were to be integral to the new breed now showing itself in SDS, were the concepts of *complicity* and of *resistance*.

Complicity. The rank protests were the first to draw widespread campus attention to the link between universities and the war machine, and to the social and political function universities fulfilled even while styling themselves as ivory towers isolated from political concerns.* During this same spring first *Viet Report* and then *Ramparts* magazine appeared with issues showing how Michigan State University had been a witting partner of the Central Intelligence Agency in South Vietnam, carrying on various "counterinsurgency" tasks under the guise of impartial academic research; at Ann Arbor at the same time Mike Locker and Jill Hamberg did the research that allowed SDS to show up the activities of a member of the University's Board of Regents who was using his academic position to amass a private fortune; student researchers at a number of colleges began to examine the investment portfolios of their universities, only to find that extensive

*Isolated efforts had been made previously, but none had made this kind of impact. Among them were such SDS papers as Potter's "The University and the Cold War" (1964) and Oglesby's 1965 Washington speech; on individual campuses, SDSers had begun research on complicity as early as 1963, and Steve Weissman and Eric Levine had spent the summer of 1965 exploring the Univeristy of California's complicity role.

links with, for example, South African mining interests and Latin American commodity exploiters were common. Gradually, and with some shock, the notion of the independent and beneficent university began to be dispelled, and the extent to which the university was a culpable producer of social ills became clear: it talked of academic freedom but often punished professorial dissidents and stifled any student politics outside of a narrow range; it claimed to foster independent scholarship but was intimately tied to the federal government (mostly defense department) funding for two-thirds of its research work and to corporate and other governmental gifts for most of the remainder; it made much of its role of serving the American people, but tended to keep out blacks, poor people, and women from both the student body and the faculty, while its board of trustees was almost wholly filled with elderly males from mammoth corporations. All this was the beginning of a profound awakening for the New Left.

Resistance. For the first time in its history, SDS, at the University of Chicago, went up directly against a university administration in open confrontation, and if it could not really declare a victory, it certainly suffered no surrender. SDS had successfully taken over the administration building of a major university, it had taken direct action without any punishment, and it had publicized its cause beyond anything imaginable by other, less dramatic, methods. The lesson would not be lost elsewhere, and the sit-in technique would continue to grow in popularity: whereas there was one disruptive sit-in in 1964 (at Berkeley), and a half dozen in 1966, by 1967–68 it was the chief tactic in protest actions on at least sixty-five campuses, and by then resistance had become commonplace. Nor would the understanding of the weakness of the university be lost. Universities were now seen as vulnerable to confrontation, uncertain of how to deal with protest and disruption, inefficient when they were not simply maladroit, authoritarian when they were not simply ossified.

The realization of complicity on the part of the university, combined with a realization of how readily it could be confronted, was a crucial element in helping to turn attention back to the campus during the rest of the year. The awareness may have been only dim, and surely unconscious, but it was born now, never to be extinguished: the university could stand as a surrogate for the evils in society which it did so much to promote, and a surrogate who could be challanged directly and legitimately by those it had invited within its walls. Campus protest begins now in earnest.

In February 1966 the May 2nd Movement voted itself out of existence. The official reason was that it had done its job: when it was formed, it stated in its official obituary that May, "the existing student organizations represented a variety of unsatisfactory choices for many radicals who wished to take an active part in politics." Now, however, "an anti-imperialist perspective" had taken root, and "Students for a Democratic Society, the independent Committees to End the War in Viet Nam, the Vietnam Day Committees, and other groups have overcome some of the weakness imposed by the liberal-conservative leadership of past movements." To an extent that was true: SDSers like Oglesby and Gitlin had certainly accepted parts of an "imperialist" analysis, at least insofar as it applied to America's behavior overseas, and the kind of militancy that had been part of the M2M style was now fairly commonplace in SDS chapters. But a more telling explanation was simply that M2M's old-style rhetoric, reminiscent of the thirties, had failed to attract many of the new breed; membership was down to six hundred at most. Jeff Gordon, M2M's national coordinator, explained it to SDSers that M2M

> . . . had more or less atrophied. It had become a cadre organization and often merely recruited the most sophisticated people from the campus and separated them from the dynamic movement. They feel that SDS is a growing organization reflecting the movement and they want to add a new element to the movement by introducing their perspective.

As a consequence, a number of those from M2M immediately joined SDS. Gordon himself applied through the New York Regional Office on February 17, 1966; Sarah Murphy appended an ominous note to his application before she sent it on to the NO: "Note beflowered membership card of one Jeffrey Sheppard Gordon—and think about it."

A warning well given. For in fact the most fundamental reason for the dissolution of M2M was a shift of perspective on the part of the Progressive Labor Party, under whose influence it operated to the end. PL had been faced with real difficulties toward the end of 1965, partly as a result of the conviction of organizer Bill Epton in December on the charges, growing out of that 1964 Harlem uprising, of conspiracy to riot and to overthrow the state, and partly as a result of the defection of, and subsequent exposures by, Phillip Luce. It apparently decided to assert a new rigidity, tighten its ranks, reestablish what it called "cadre control," and guide its members and affiliates with a sterner hand. The New Left style that was coming to be associated with the hippies was held to be unpopular with the working masses and denounced as "bourgeois"; marijuana smoking and drinking were discouraged, couples living together were asked to get married, beards and long hair were frowned upon, casual blue-jean attire was renounced. At the same time, the tight rules of the party were reasserted: potential PL members had to undergo a three-month trial period, be approved first by two-thirds of the membership of their local organizations and then reviewed by the national bureaucracy, and agree to forgo membership in "organizations whose policies are objectively counter-revolutionary" or "having a discipline outside the party." Internal discipline was to be rigid: "No party member may make unconstructive statements publicly about the party, gossip about other party members, or disclose confidential information to nonparty members."

Under these circumstances it was felt that a loose and undisciplined student movement like M2M was more of a liability than an asset, and that PL would do better to recruit members from the ranks of such organizations as SDS. Of course few of the new breed emerging on the campuses could be counted upon to be attracted to the old-style discipline and working-class politics of a group like PL right from the start, but, newly awakened as they were, they were certainly likely material for eventual solicitation. And if the PL "perspective," as Gordon put it, with all its open avowal of communism and asserted militancy, could be put across, PL could draw new adherents gradually and carefully, with far more success than through any youth group of its own. Thus began what later SDSers were to call the invasion of the body-snatchers.

SDS viewed it all dispassionately: "A few Progressive Labor young organizers have recently sent in SDS membership cards," the membership was told in May, "as a result of PL's decision to dissolve the May 2nd Movement and recruit out of SDS (lucky us)."

Another example of the new-breed spirit, with which SDSers at many campuses were involved, was the growing "free university" movement which blossomed in the spring of 1966.

The roots of the movement go back to the "community of controversy" ideal set out in *The Port Huron Statement,* Paul Potter's inspired "Cold War and the Universities" paper, and the university-reform groups and meetings which SDS sponsored in 1962 and 1963. In the spring of 1964 a number of Berkeleyites actually began a New School, giving courses in "American History and the Growth of Empire," "Dream Politics and the Cold War," and "Problems of the City in Contemporary America," but that sputtered to a halt during the fall's turmoils. It was not until after the Free Speech Movement's successful sit-in, with their spontaneous seminars on everything in sight, and the teach-ins of the following spring that the idea of *alternative,* rather than merely reformed, universities began to be taken seriously. SDS organized a Free University Committee, under the direction of Rich Horevitz, in the spring of 1965, to push the idea on various campuses, and it was largely through its deliberations that the initial philosophy behind the free university movement was developed. Then, at the summer convention in Kewadin, several workshops spent long hours wrestling with the notion of what a "free educational atmosphere" would entail and setting out the basic features—open admission, "relevant" courses, unrestrictive curricula, community service, radical development—that future free universities were to adopt. SDS itself chose not to make the creation of free universities a national project—a lucky decision given the chaos that was to befall the NO in 1965—but it encouraged local chapters to "do their own thing" and it endorsed the idea of a "communications net" and campus travelers to maintain contact among those free universities that did develop.

By the fall of 1965, largely under SDS impetus, several free universities were in operation: in Berkeley, SDS reopened the New School largely through the efforts of SDSer Carolyn Craven, offering "Marx and Freud," "A Radical Approach to Science," "Agencies of Social Change and the New Movements"; in Gainesville, a Free University of Florida was established, and even incorporated; in New York, a Free University was begun in Greenwich Village, offering no fewer than forty-four courses ("Marxist Approaches to the Avant-garde Arts," "Ethics and Revolution," "Life in Mainland China Today"); and in Chicago, something called simply The School began with ten courses ("Neighborhood

Organization and Nonviolence," "Purposes of Revolution").

By the spring of 1966, the free-university movement was a live force, taking root in perhaps ten different cities. Though it took different shape in different places, it had a common impulse: to demonstrate in a concrete way what a radical and nonestablishmentarian educational experience might be. As a result, there were usually no grades, exams, or other forms of competition between students; anyone could attend (most schools asked only token fees if any at all) and almost anyone could teach; administration, such as it was, was in the hands of the students and the teachers, operating more or less on the theory of participatory democracy, with a premium upon flexibility and openness; no restrictions were put on subject matter (though at a few places, not by any means the majority, right-wing or pro-Establishment courses were discouraged) and the catalogues included numerous courses in Marxism and socialism, community organizing and movement building, Vietnam and the draft, Chinese politics and Latin American exploitation, film making and "guerrilla graphics," contemporary literature and "street poetry," body movement and karate, hippie culture and the student revolt, and even (put-ons, but not by much) "Zen Basketball" (at the San Francisco State Experimental College) and "Paper Airplanes and People" (at the Free University in Seattle). The whole idea, as those who started the Seattle school put it in 1966, was "to establish protest counter-institutions to the *un*free universities."

The appeal of the free universities was dual. To those, both students and teachers, who found the normal universities either insufficiently challenging, insufficiently radical, or insufficiently broad, these institutions offered a happy alternative, a kind of place where if the course they wanted wasn't in the curriculum they could always go and teach it themselves; as one of the founders of the San Francisco State Experimental College put it,

> We wanted students to take responsibility for their own education instead of having the institution believe it was supposed to meet the needs of students. We wanted it set up so students would come to meet their own needs and come to learn about their whole being, to learn how to think.

And to those who were interested in going beyond educational change to the forging of a wide left movement in the country, free universities seemed to be the perfect training schools; as Carolyn Craven of the San Francisco New School wrote,

> There is a vast amount of energy and talent in the Bay Area, and the rest of the country for that matter, among the professionals and intellectuals. There is a vast amount of work that needs to be done for the movement which could be done by these people operating in their own fields. The movement can also give these people the relevance they need in their lives. Hopefully through the New School, the courses and seminars, we will be able to involve and bring together different people and help them to find alternatives in their lives as well as contribute to the movement.

Such was the strength of these appeals that by the end of 1966 perhaps fifteen free universities had been established, several hundred more grew up in the following years, and by 1970 five hundred were estimated to be functioning. Not all of them were great successes—many were short-lived, some fell into the hands of entrepreneurs, others were absorbed into the fringes of existing universities, and a few became dominated by one special interest group or other; however, most of them began as bold embodiments of the idea of resistance to established institutions, and many of them retained that spirit to the end.

One of the most representative of the free universities, which opened with some thirty courses on February 1, 1966, was established on a $300 shoestring by SDSers at the University of Pennsylvania, using unoccupied university classrooms and reform-minded university teachers. Its purpose was to provide courses that were "too contemporary, controversial, broad or narrow to be part of the university curriculum," and its initial offerings included courses in black power, the New Left, contemporary education, and "American Youth in Revolt." Expecting maybe a hundred students to be interested, the organizers were astounded when more than six hundred students signed up for the first term's classes, and soon, without anybody's knowing quite how, the number of courses grew to nearly sixty. By the fall enrollment had jumped to more than a thousand, and both students and teachers started to come from off the campus—dropouts, community people, a couple of disciples of LSD-prophet Timothy Leary. Under the impetus of the free school, students began organizing projects in Philadelphia-area neighborhoods, putting pressure on the university itself for educational reform, and, perhaps most significantly, developing the facts to expose the university's complicity in the governmental war machine through its chemical and biological warfare research center on the campus.

But the Free University of Pennsylvania was a harbinger of the dangers that other free universities were to face. After its first year of operation, a number of the original SDSers graduated and increasing influence fell to the university faculty members, never especially politically advanced despite their interest in educational experimentation. Convinced by its early success that it should expand its operation and curriculum, it decided to cut off its connections with SDS and establish a broad-spectrum steering committee with a disparateness of political views. Enrollment grew further, and the range of courses broadened, but the radical vision and the militant politics which the SDSers had given it diminished; while two-thirds of the courses in the fall of 1966 had been political in content, only half of them were by the spring of 1967, and a bare fifteen percent by the following spring. Finally, the university itself, its eyes finally opened to the obvious appeal and success of the free university, decided to establish seminars of its own to be run along similar lines, and then, in the spring of 1968, moved to have the student government take over the whole operation. By then most of the original organizers, not to mention the original purposes, had gone, radical attention had turned back to the university itself, and FUP suffered its liberal swallow-up almost without a murmur.

Similar fates were to be suffered by other free universities. SDS began to sour on the ventures in early 1967 because, in Carl Davidson's words, they took many of the best people away from the campus, "enabling the existing university to function more smoothly, since the 'troublemakers' were gone," and because "they gave liberal administrators the rhetoric, the analysis, and sometimes the manpower to co-opt their programs and establish elitist forms of 'experimental' colleges inside of, although quarantined from, the existing educational system." Liberal student organizations like the NSA came to see that free universities were not threatening alternatives to a beleaguered educational system but, given different organizers and made less political, could become useful agents of reform within it; in the fall of 1968, the NSA was given a Ford Foundation grant of $305,000 to accomplish exactly that.

But the importance of the free-university movement as a vision, especially during its early years, cannot be gainsaid. For in its roots, in its original manifestations, in its early development, it embodied a new and significant notion for the left. The free universities were *alternatives* to the established order, and opposed to it, independent of (at least some of) the pressures of the surrounding society; those who founded them were not interested in working *through* the instruments of the society but *apart* from them, hoping as far as possible to remain untainted by them, trying by forging new shapes to avoid the built-in dangers inherent in even the best of the old. The new universities were part of a whole growing attitude that begins to be expressed now, the attitude that would shortly lead to the establishment of such alternative institutions as the underground papers, Liberation News Service, Newsreel, and the Movement Speakers Bureau; of research organizations like the African Research Group, North American Congress on Latin America, and the Pacific Research Institute; of various theater groups like the Bread and Puppet Theater and the San Francisco Mime Troupe; of local community-organizing groups in various cities, on the ERAP model; of new political groupings like the National Conference for New Politics, the Peace and Freedom Party, and the early Black Panther group in Lowndes County; and such professional organizations as the Medical Committee for Human Rights, Healthpax, and the New University Conference. These all mark the decline of reformism, and the start of revolutionary alternatives.

The influence of Progressive Labor began to be felt within SDS as early as this spring. Letters from PLers began appearing in SDS material ("There is only one anti-imperialist movement in the world. It is led by the Chinese Communists," etc.), and PLers like Jared Israel, at Harvard, Jeff Gordon, in New York, and Earl Silbar, at Roosevelt University in Chicago, played an increasingly visible part in SDS meetings. At the June NC it was the PL position paper on the draft that won the endorsement of the draft workshop. The paper, written by Silbar and Israel, took strong positions against class ranking and student deferments, for the "unconditional withdrawal" of U.S. troops from Vietnam, and for an end to the draft; but its special importance was its advocacy of something that now comes to be called "student power":*

> We are trying to build a radical student movement. The program we use must be based on the requirements of that general perspective at this time. As we see it, the job we've got now is to move the students who are presently opposed to the war into activities on the question of the war as concretely expressed in the institutions in which they study/live/work. We must develop struggles by these students on the campuses against the school administrations for student self-determination and against the war.
>
> This will mean broader base building. That is, we must take the anger that students feel against rank, 2S, etc., and turn it into opposition to the administration and the war. The war has in fact created the situation in which students are mad about rank; the administrations have compounded this anger by rendering the students powerless. We must learn how to combine these struggles to build a student movement against the war and fighting for university control. . . .
>
> We are trying to relate the war and general foreign policy issues which have created the present student militancy to the question of student power. . . . The crucial question here is to build student power against the administration on the basis of concrete issues important to our radical program.

SDS, however, was not yet ready to go so far. The NC as a whole rejected the workshop proposal, avoided the question of student deferments, ignored the whole question of student power, and voted down a position for SDS of "No rank, no test, no 2s, no alternate service, no draft, no army, no war." Student power, however, was now in the air, and it had only to bide its time.

The independent SDS-led draft and rank protests and the local SDS-influenced free universities in the spring of 1966 point

*This may be the first use of this term, following, of course, the "black power" paradigm laid down by SNCC.

to a crucial development in the growth of SDS: as the organization
gets bigger, its energies are expressed and its political directions
are determined more by separate campus chapters than by the NO
or the national meetings.

The number of chapters and members continued to grow
throughout the spring. By March there were 151 chapters, by
June (when 7 were dropped for inactivity but 28 new ones
signed on) there were 172. National membership rose to 5500,
and estimates of chapter membership were now being cited as
close to 15,000. A survey of the membership—the last one to
be done in such detail—showed that in March there were
chapters in 37 states, plus the District of Columbia, and members in all the states except Wyoming. Half the members
(2750) were concentrated, as might be expected, in the states
with the highest population—California, New York, Pennsylvania, Illinois, Michigan, Massachusetts, and Texas—and there
were fewer than 10 members in 17 states (Alabama, Alaska,
Delaware, Georgia, Hawaii, Idaho, Louisiana, Maine, Mississippi, Montana, Nevada, New Mexico, North Dakota, South
Carolina, South Dakota, Utah, West Virginia).

This same survey also determined, in a random sample of 5
percent of the membership, that less than half (40 percent) were
registered undergraduates and that they were outnumbered by
those who were graduate students or nonstudents (25 and 20
percent, respectively). At the same time, it was learned that fully
10 percent of the members were high-school students. (The status
of the remaining 5 percent was unknown.) If the sample can be
taken as accurate, it suggests several important developments:
first, that in the organization at this point there was a strong
influence of nonundergraduates, accounting in part for the lack of
interest by SDS in specifically campus problems and in building
a student left; second, that SDS influence was reaching down well
beyond the college level and beginning to have an effect on the
high schools, which were subsequently to become one of the major
targets for SDS organizing; and, third, that a sizable group of
people who weren't students at all—dropouts, hippies, political
professionals (e.g., the PLers), community people, organizers,
professors—had grown within the organization. This last development in particular was noted by Paul Booth who, in looking back,

believes that the National Council meeting that April was the last one run by students for students—"after that, the nonstudents took over, the pros and the organizers, and the NCs became fights between them."

Too much should not be made of the student-nonstudent dichotomy, for the figures indicate that still some 75 percent or so of the membership operated in university settings. But it is true that, certainly since the Booth regime, there had been a growing campus–off-campus split, with the National Office and national meetings preoccupied with different issues from those of the grass-roots membership. The rank protests, held without the slightest push from the NO, and the free universities, largely chapter-created, were two indications. The continued growth of regional organizations, with their own meetings, newsletters, presses, and programs, was another: this spring saw the addition of travelers and offices in the Midwest (Ohio, Indiana, Michigan), the Plain States (Iowa, Kansas, Missouri, Nebraska), the Niagara Region (upstate New York), the mid-South (Texas, Oklahoma, Arkansas, Louisiana), and the Northwest (Oregon, Washington). And the distance in life styles was still another, though less measurable indication—the new college people were the children of pot, LSD, "the Pill," off-campus "marriages," the Beatles, Fanon, Ken Kesey, Godard, long hair . . . and the NO stalwarts were not. One interesting example of this distance occurred in January, when several SDSers at the University of Oklahoma were arrested for possession of a matchboxful of marijuana, and the response of veterans like Steve Max and Clark Kissinger was shock and anger. Max, as a member of the National Administrative Committee, demanded an immediate investigation and urged SDS to outlaw all drugs; Kissinger, at his snidest, rejected the notion that drugs "are a part of the revolution we are fighting for":

> Perhaps. Yet while I personally may believe in sodomy, that doesn't mean that I implement the revolution by moving into the staff apartment with my sheep. That is, there are certain little pleasures I am willing to forgo until more important problems are solved (racism, the war, poverty, . . . things like that).

The chief instrument by which the NO tried to maintain contact with the growing number of chapters was *New Left Notes,* a (more or less) weekly newspaper which made its first appearance (with a box on the front page reading, "SURPRISE!") on January 21, 1966. It was a flimsy, four-page (later occasionally eight- and twelve-) tabloid, pasted up in the back rooms of the NO, never looking the same from one week to another, and regularly in the hands of well-meaning but inexperienced editors; but it had a kind of style to it, a snappiness, an enthusiasm, that made up for its obvious amateurishness. The front-page slogan—as it was to be for the next three years—was the NCUPers "Let the People Decide," and in terms of the paper itself that is exactly how it was edited. Almost any scrap of news, any letter, any essay or comment that came into the paper found its way into print: Hayden on his trip to North Vietnam, Cesar Chavez on the grape strike, Oglesby working out a theory of American "imperialism," Flacks worrying about "Whatever Became of the New Left?," and a variety of anonymous chapter people sending in reports on their latest actions, complaints about how meetings were run, paeans to the eye-opening quality of the New Left, and proposals for this or that future action. For SDS, and a movement that had very few other means of communication—*Liberation* magazine, a monthly, the *National Guardian,* a weekly but with other concerns as well, a few newsletters—*New Left Notes* was, for all its formlessness, sort of a weekly SDS convention, an invaluable and unduplicatable forum. Aside from those who complained about always getting it three weeks late, the only criticism making the rounds in those early days was that the name sounded like another rock group.

But a newspaper, however much energy was put into it—and the NO devoted top priority to it throughout the spring—could not bridge the gap. The NO, which had thought itself the tip of the SDS iceberg, found itself more of a floe instead, drifting off alone on its own currents while the main body went elsewhere. Its ballot mailings produced apathetic responses from the field, sometimes no more than a tenth of the membership bothering to vote; a referendum of the National Council on whether SDS should issue a statement of support for the Russian writers Sinyavsky and Daniel jailed by the Soviet government drew only twenty responses out of several hundred eligible (the vote was favorable, the statement sent). Its programs—such as the idea of a "national town meeting" to discuss Vietnam during the summer, passed by the April NC, or actions against South Africa, passed by the June NC—languished and eventually withered for a lack of nutrition from the ranks. Its projects, when they did emerge, were not sustained—an *SDS Labor Newsletter,* which the April NC authorized in a move to further an alliance of students and the labor movement, was edited for one issue by Lee Webb and then put in the hands of an SDS labor-support group in Boston, where it promptly died. Its all-out, last-ditch, "emergency fund-raising campaign," launched in April with the goal of producing a quick $10,000, produced all of $400 when it was abandoned in May: 268 individuals and 16 chapters had responded.

The financial crunch, in fact, was quite serious. Income, which had started out at around $9000 a month in January, had dropped to under $1000 by June. The debts mounted: SDS was $1750 in the hole in January, $2500 by March, $5000 by June. The April NC doubled the national dues to $4 a year, *New Left Notes* carried repeated warnings ("The picture is very bleak," "Things are desperate," "We are broke"), and a series of people from Judy Kissinger (Clark's wife) to Paul LeBlanc and Booth himself devoted considerable energy to bookkeeping and fund raising, but the slow descent continued. As one economy (not to mention sanity) measure, the NO gave up its staff apartment, although it then found it had to increase staff salaries to $30 a week so people could rent their own places. As another, the NO decided to move downtown, to 1608 West Madison Street on Chicago's crumbling, freeway-sliced West Side, where it was given a cheap second-floor office in a downtrodden building (over whose front door was chiseled, no one knew why, "Lomax") in a ragtaggle ghetto; the landlord was John Rossen, a one-time Communist Party functionary who owned a series of movie houses in the Chicago area and who still maintained a lively interest in the left. At the end of the school year, SDS had managed another of those penny-for-penny budgets,* and the organizational head was only a little above the fiscal waters.

One of the reasons for the money shortage was, of course,

*Fiscal income from June 1965 to July 1966 was $81,999.59 (major sources: contributions—$48,629, loans—$7126, dues—$6687, literature—$5691), expenditures were a close match at $82,697.26 (major allocations: utilities—$15,126, printing—$13,788, salaries—$11,992, projects—$7578, loans—$6123). (*New Left Notes,* September 23, 1966.)

that the LID tax shelter was no longer available; contributions
dropped sharply after the break (from $7067 in November to $895
in March). But another reason was the reluctance of many big
givers to get involved with an organization that was now under
the watchful eye of the FBI and publicly denounced by J. Edgar
Hoover himself. In a statement that February, Hoover said:

> One of the most militant organizations now engaged in activities
> protesting U.S. foreign policy is a student youth group called Stu-
> dents for a Democratic Society. Communists are actively promoting
> and participating in the activities of this organization, which is
> self-described as a group of liberals and radicals.

Hence, though Katzenbach had said nothing further about Justice
Department action against SDS, the FBI went right ahead,
launching a full-scale investigation. Agents made themselves
known around the NO—SDS responded by advertising in *New
Left Notes* for someone to "debug" the office telephones—and old
friends and employers of such SDS leaders as Booth and Hayden
were visited by agents. Students were secretly solicited to work as
FBI undercover agents infiltrating SDS chapters, presumably a
widespread activity but well documented in at least three cases:
William Divale has told how he was recruited to be an FBI agent
at Pasadena City College and was instrumental in forming an
unrecognized but successful SDS chapter there in the spring of
1966; Gerald Wayne Kirk told the House Internal Security Committee in 1969 how he had worked for the FBI within the SDS
chapter at the University of Chicago from the fall of 1965 on; and
Tommy Taft has written how he spied on antiwar elements at
Duke University for the FBI from the spring of 1965 at least to
the spring of 1966. Other agents approached college deans for SDS
chapter membership lists, a practice which was widespread
enough to come to the attention of Tom Kahn, who reported it
to Booth in Chicago. And when the student government at Wesleyan College protested these kinds of tactics, Hoover wrote, and
made public, an unusual, indignant letter of justification:

> The Attorney General stated publicly in October, 1965, that he had
> instructed the FBI to determine the extent of Communist infiltra-
> tion into the Students for a Democratic Society, which was estab-
> lishing chapters throughout the United States. . . . These

investigations are initiated in a straight-forward manner without apology to anyone and are conducted objectively, truthfully and impartially to determine the facts. . . .

Never was any attempt made to intimidate any student or official of the university. To say so is a misrepresentation of the matter. Your statement that the "FBI investigation is extremely hostile to the goal of academic freedom" is not only utterly false but is also so irresponsible as to cast doubt on the quality of academic reasoning or the motivation behind it.

Nor was the FBI alone. At the same time the U.S. Army's domestic intelligence agency, known as Continental United States Intelligence, or Conus Intel, was beginning secretly to send its agents to college campuses and collect papers and clippings on student activists.

On top of the financial crisis and the witch-hunting came a psychological blow. It is somehow symbolic that it was at this time that the Student Nonviolent Coordinating Committee, now with Stokely Carmichael as its spokesman, announced a new policy of "black power" that specifically sought to exclude whites from organizing in the black communities. It was the official pronouncement of the death of the dream, which of course was known to be dying, of multiracial organizing in multiracial communities for multiracial justice. And with it the generation of SDS leadership that had grown up inextricably entwined with SNCC and the civil-rights movement, the generation that had launched ERAP as the dramatic catalyst to an "interracial movement of the poor," the generation that had achieved its political consciousness through integration, found its past, like a rug in an old vaudeville routine, ripped from under its feet. Not that it came, really, as a surprise—Carmichael had been pushing the black-power idea for more than a year, and the ERAP experiences pointed in the same direction—but it was still, if only symbolically, a blow. SDS of course supported SNCC officially, and at a time when the liberal and media reaction was one of shock and outrage; the June NC went on record as feeling

> . . . a special urgency to restate our support. Let it be clear that we are not merely supporting SNCC's *right* to its views, we are welcoming and supporting the thrust of SNCC's *program*. . . . We must not simply *tolerate* this "black consciousness," we should *encourage* it.

But few of the old guard had any doubts that they were seeing the
end of an era.

All of this produced what Dick Flacks, in *New Left Notes*,
called "the malaise at the national level," and a renewed leadership crisis was inevitable. Booth was a lonely and frustrated figure,
trying to move an elephantine organization in a direction it did not
want to go. He did nothing to increase his popularity when he gave
an Associated Press reporter (duly printed by the AP) the impression that SDS was solidly behind the election-oriented National
Conference for New Politics and "already at work" for such candidates as Robert Scheer, running in the Democratic primary in
California.* In point of fact, SDS had never gone on record in
support of the NCNP and Berkeley SDSers, in general soured on
electoral politics and specifically down on the Democratic Party,
had not lifted a finger for Scheer; Berkeley SDSer Buddy Stein was
so outraged that in March he called for Booth's resignation:
"Your continuance in office means that you will preside over the
dissolution of democracy in Students for a Democratic Society."
The battle never came to a head, largely because Booth's term was
to be up in June, but the NAC, in an unprecedented move, reflected the growing disenchantment by directly forbidding Booth
to go to the NCNP meeting in May. Booth grew weary, then
disgusted; the lack of impact of the Vietnam Draft Exam, on

*Several SDSers of the old guard had engaged themselves in electoral activity
during the spring, the resurgence of the old realignment strategy now being
labeled "the new politics." The National Conference for New Politics (NCNP)
had been formed in the last half of 1965, primarily through the instigation of
Arthur Waskow but with significant support from Paul Booth, Bob Ross, Clark
Kissinger, Lee Webb, and even Tom Hayden, plus others of the SDS in-group,
and as the new year began it started to form local organizations for the 1966
Congressional election. Booth and Webb were on the national board of the
NCNP; Kissinger was the prime force behind a Committee for Independent
Political Action (CIPA) in Chicago's 49th Ward; Hayden and others in NCNP
worked to elect a local city councilman; Dena Clamage and Frank Joyce of the
Detroit Committee to End the War in Vietnam tried to drum up support for
peace candidates in the fall elections; Stanley Aronowitz and other SDSers in
New York attempted to run antiwar candidates on the upper West Side; Boston-
area SDSers gave support to the campaign of Thomas Boyleston Adams, a liberal
war-foe running for Senator. But all of this was at a far remove from the interests
of the bulk of the membership.

which he had worked so hard, left him further disheartened. Friends describe him at the end of the spring as being "totally burnt out"; to one of them he confessed that he was considering psychotherapy.

Finding someone to replace him, however, proved no easy task. Appeals for a successor in *New Left Notes* and in private correspondence produced no takers, and the April NC, specifically charged with finding a replacement, spent the whole weekend without turning up a single volunteer. Finally, at the June NC, Jane Adams, the Southern Illinois graduate and SNCC staffer who had already worked in the National Office and who had spent the last term organizing in the Iowa area, agreed to serve as a temporary National Secretary until the convention—which was to be held this year, for a change, at the end of the summer rather than the beginning. Her selection—the first time a woman occupied a top spot in the SDS hierarchy—and a crop of new people she brought in with her provided manifest proof that a new generation of leadership was coming to the fore in SDS to represent the new breed now dominant.

15

SUMMER 1966

It must have been with a sense of some dark humor that the new people in the National Office selected as a site for the 1966 annual convention a remote Methodist youth camp on the shores of Clear Lake, in north-central Iowa. Of course there were good practical reasons—they wanted a spot far from the old guard centers of power, and Chicago University SDSer Steve Kindred's father happened to be superintendent of the Methodist region where the camp was located—but the choice of *Iowa* must have seemed to them a delectable symbol.

Not that the people of Iowa were overjoyed about it all. As the Council Bluffs *Nonpareil* huffed, "The use of a Methodist church camp as a meeting place for a bunch of Communists, and a group of left-wing nuts who can't decide whether to work with the Communists or not, ought to be enough to make the Methodist lay people shudder, if not the hierarchy." And a number of local toughs, taking the cue, even went out to the camp to beat up on the Commies, only to find that most of the delegates were easily approachable, ready to talk, and glad to have the invaders stay and listen, which many did.

For the Clear Lake convention—some 350 delegates from 140 chapters meeting from August 29 to September 2—*was* symbolic. It marked the triumph, delayed for a year because of the collapse of the NO the summer before and the reassertion of the old guard, of the new breed in SDS, only a new breed grown overwhelmingly with a year's addition of thousands of new members. Leadership was now transferred from the original members to the newer ones, from the Eastern intellectuals to the middle-American activists, from those born in the left-wing traditions of the Coasts to those raised in the individualistic heritage of the frontier, from—as the Clear Lake rhetoric had it—the "politicos" to the "anarchists." It was the ascendance of what was now known in SDS as "prairie power."

The prairie-power influence was pervasive. On a blackboard in the main hall someone had written *"Revolt";* underneath it another had added *"The revolt has been scheduled by the Steering Committee."* Contempt for steering committees, chairmen, parliamentary procedure, "structure," "top-down organizing," and any other hint at rigidity was evident from the start. So many people walked out of meetings to carry on their debates under the trees or on the raft anchored in the lake that new SDSer Mark Kleiman was encouraged to issue a call denouncing "parliamentarianism" and asking "people who are interested in finding other ways" to contact him at the National Office. (It was an echo of a notable incident at the previous National Council meeting when one delegate publicly burned his SDS membership card as a protest against the "undemocratic" way the council was being run.) All calls for producing "a new Port Huron"—vigorously pushed by such old guarders as Clark Kissinger, who argued that SDS had to "lift its *de facto* ban on the written word"—were disregarded. Attempts to give SDS "a new ideology," though they tied up endless hours of debate, ended in unresolved tangles. When ERAPer Nick Egleson finally told the delegates to stop "overworrying ideology" and "overworking on a new theoretical document," the applause, *New Left Notes* reported, "boomed up from the floor."

Similarly with regard to a specific program for the coming year. Strong efforts were made for SDS to embark on a new antidraft program by forming local groups, like the M2M's antidraft unions, which would organize overt resistance to Selective Service, and there was enough raw sentiment behind this at one point to pass it with a lopsided 105–15 vote. But since it was felt, just as it had been a year previously, that this represented such a sharp departure from the past and a possible step into illegality, the delegates finally decided to submit it to a full membership referendum before going ahead; on this issue at least, SDS, like the Bourbons, learned nothing and forgot nothing. As a substitute measure the convention adopted an amorphous scheme, redolent with the very flesh of prairie power, of letting each area develop whatever projects it wanted, as long as they would "act on their own authority, raise their own funds, send out their own travelers, organize as they see fit, and be responsible for their activities without involving those SDS members who do not wish to share in their project." At the end of the convention only the blandest resolutions passed: support for the "Fort Hood Three" (three enlisted men who that summer had refused orders to go to Vietnam), further development of the Radical Education Project for internal education, changes in the constitution to remove all references to the LID, and the like.

However, prairie power did put its stamp upon the organization in positive, indeed quite pervasive, ways.

For one thing, the clear consensus of the convention was that SDS would develop what was called an "organizing thrust" toward the campuses, operating not with a national program but by energizing local people in local chapters around local grievances. The National Office would give this top priority by forming "an experimental program of full-time organizers committed to working on campuses" (in the words of the resolution presented by two leading prairie people, Jane Adams and Ohio SDSer Terry Robbins), but the bulk of the work would be done by individual SDSers on a chapter level—or, as Carl Oglesby put it, "Every member a radical organizer."

The convention also pushed for decentralization within SDS, downgrading the National Office in favor of regional and local organizations. More than simply an expression of the impulse anarchism of the prairie-power people, this was seen as an organizational necessity if SDS was to be flexible enough to adapt to whatever ideological levels it found at the nearly two hundred campuses where it now had chapters; the prairie people knew from their own experience that what went over at Michigan, say, would inevitably prove too extreme for Arizona State. But beyond that, the Booth operation and the failure of national programs in the last year had left a bad taste in the mouths of many SDSers, not only those in the prairie-power wing—to the point where at Clear

Lake the simple phrase "top-down" was enough to condemn almost any idea or program out of hand. There was a heated debate
on this issue—there were still enough old guarders around to put
up a spirited fight—but the majority clearly sided with prairie
people like Jeff Shero, who took the National Office relentlessly to
task:

> We have to create situations on campus or in the communities to
> reveal to people where they really are. Chapters should be strong,
> and we need organizers on the local level, *not* national visibility, to
> get over the feeling of isolation. Sending out NO literature is too
> impersonal a way of operating—I read *New Left Notes* on the pot,
> but I'd get off to talk to an organizer!

In the end, the constitution was changed to provide for regional
organizations with their own programs and their own operations,
and a motion was passed specifically directing the NO to give its
attention (and money) to campus organizing in the coming year.

The election of officers sealed the triumph of prairie power.
The old guard had been quietly sounding out candidates for several months, without success. Steve Weissman, for example, who
was asked to run for office that year, declined on the grounds that
SDS officers never had any real power, anyway; and it was only
at Clear Lake itself that they finally decided to push Lee Webb,
who had just finished his alternate service in Chicago and was free
for the coming year. Running against him for President were Bill
Hartzog, an Ohio-born college dropout who had been organizing
hospital workers in Topeka and who stood as the pure personification of prairie power, and Nick Egleson, who had been on the
fringes of the old guard but was sufficiently distant from them to
be regarded as a compromise candidate. On the first ballot Hartzog finished a poor third and was dropped,* and on the second
Egleson came out the clear favorite. ("Frankly," Webb recalls, "I
didn't have any supporters at the whole convention. There were
like maybe two or three people on my side, Booth and Ross and
a few others, and all these kids were *really* attacking me.") The

---

*He thereafter refused induction, stayed around as an SDS antidraft organizer
for a while, and then when things got hot was one of the first to go underground
as a means of avoiding the draft; according to Webb (interview with author),
"Nobody has ever heard from him since."

other elections were foregone: Carl Davidson, largely on the strength of a "student syndicalism" paper, was elected Vice President by the convention, and the next day, at the National Council, Greg Calvert, similarly identified with prairie power, was named National Secretary. The three officers were good representatives of the new SDS style.

Egleson, twenty-two, fit least into the mold—and would exert the least influence on the organization in the coming year—for he was an Easterner, decidedly dudish in appearance (thin, long neck, glasses, short and curly hair), a graduate of the select Taft School in Connecticut and of Swarthmore College, an ex-nuclear-physics major and a bookish type; as he analyzed it some years later, "My parents [were divorced], and their demands on my brother and me to share their hatred of each other, clearly drove me to run from all emotions. In my endless figuring out of how I should behave may lie some of the roots of my intellectualization." Nonetheless, Egleson had an undoubted honesty, and an unabrasive, soft-spoken manner. (When he accompanied Dave Dellinger to North Vietnam the following May, Dellinger reported that "Nick's natural SDS manner helped to break the ice" when talking with American prisoners of war there.) And his ERAP experiences in Philadelphia and Hoboken had led him to a kind of root anarchism and a commitment to local organizing not so different from that of the prairie people.

Carl Davidson, twenty-three, *looked* like prairie power: tall and lanky, slightly stooped in the shoulder, with longish brown hair and a Pancho Villa mustache, he gave off something of the air of a latter-day Daniel Boone—and he smoked a corncob pipe. He was born in Pennsylvania of working-class parents and went, because it was inexpensive, to Penn State, where he majored in, of all things, philosophy. ("The problem of calling oneself a socialist," he would tell the people at Clear Lake, is that "socialist is what philosophers call 'an essentially contested concept'—that is to say, a word which has so many definitions that you have to define it before you can begin to use it.") At Penn State in the spring of 1965 he helped to organize an *ad hoc* Committee for Student Freedom to fight the *in loco parentis* rules of the administration, giving him his first taste of campus organizing around local issues; there, too, he began his exploration of leftism, hung pictures of Eugene Debs on his walls, and joined the Industrial Workers of the World. After graduating in 1965, he took a job in the philosophy department at the University of Nebraska, where he continued to be active in student politics, operating as a traveler for SDS in the Plains Region and helping to organize a Campus Freedom Democratic Party at Nebraska in the spring of 1966.

Greg Calvert, twenty-eight, was older than many people in SDS, a dramatic kind of person, raw-boned, good-looking, self-possessed. Born of working-class parents in Longview, Washington, and raised in a middle-America district of Portland, Oregon, Calvert remembers "bumming around the Skid Row area" when he was a high schooler in the early fifties, and meeting burnt-out old Wobblies: "Some of us in the movement," he said many years later, "have wondered whether, after so much hope and so much life, we would end like some of those old Wobblies." He majored in history at the University of Oregon, graduated in 1960, and went on to Cornell for graduate work in European history in 1960–61, but he did not get drawn into the radical politics just then making itself felt. He spent some time at the University of Paris (there was even a strong rumor going around SDS circles that he had fought with the FLN in Algeria) and returned to teach European history at Iowa State. It was at Iowa State, where he had spent two and a half years, that Calvert finally became active in campus politics and increasingly involved with SDS. During the summer of 1966 he joined the National Office in Chicago, was made Acting Assistant National Secretary under Jane Adams in July and became the editor of *New Left Notes* in August; it was under his egis that a special thirty-two-page preconvention issue of *New Left Notes* was prepared (complete with ads from book publishers, left publications, and greetings from such other-generation supporters as New York lawyers Leonard Boudin—whose daughter Kathy was then on an ERAP project in Cleveland—and Victor Rabinowitz), the largest issue SDS ever produced.

None of the officers, be it noted, was a student or of student age. The same pattern held generally true for the National Council members elected by the convention. Five of the fourteen members (Jane Adams, Tom Condit, Mark Kleiman, Bob Speck, and Lee Webb) had spent much or all of the last year in the National Office; seven others (Carolyn Craven, Mike Davis, Roy Dahlberg,

Bill Hartzog, Mike James, Terry Robbins, and Jeff Shero) had been working full time as organizers and none was then a student; of the remainder, one was an undergraduate (Steve Kindred, a Chicago antirank organizer) and one was a graduate student (Nancy Bancroft, finishing up a master's at the Union Theological seminary). They were all, except Webb, associated with the prairie-power faction to one degree or another; it was a measure of the decline of the old guard that Bob Ross could do no better than tie for First Alternate. None was a student leader in the traditional sense, or a campus newspaper editor, or a student-council president; none was regarded as primarily an intellectual or was headed for an academic career; several had dropped out of college entirely before graduating, and none had dabbled in liberal student politics. It was an almost complete turnaround from the SDS leaders of, say, 1962.

Progressive Labor members showed up at the convention, and though, as Shero notes, "there weren't enough of them around yet for anyone to develop an anti-PL line," their presence was felt. Lee Webb, for one, remembers that they were among those opposing his presidency:

> PL were the ones who were really pushing the thing against me the hardest, because, I think, in a sense they saw me, or someone like me, as a threat to their attempts of really developing influence in SDS. . . . I wasn't at all sympathetic to them: I wanted to kick them out immediately, because I felt that they just weren't going to contribute anything to SDS and were just going to decrease the level of debate and discussion.

And John Maher, the Boston SDSer, felt concerned enough to precipitate a long, if somewhat disjointed, debate on "Communists in SDS." (His brother, as mentioned, was a PL functionary.) In a convention paper he pointed out the nature of "democratic centralism" in organizations like PL and the Communist Party:

> Party discipline in the PLP means that a member is obliged to carry out all the decisions of the Party, while in the CP a member is not obliged to carry out a decision with which he disagrees, though Party discipline will not permit him to work against it. Neither organization condones public criticism of the party line.

This practice, he felt, so foreign to the open individualism of the New Left, would cause difficulty in SDS ranks because you'd never know if you were debating with (or voting for) a person who had an open mind or was simply following some party order. His suggestion was that SDS require anyone who was a member of such a disciplined party to declare so before working with SDSers or running for office in the organization. But the motion gained little headway at Clear Lake: it smacked a little too much of redbaiting (especially coming after a summer in which various Congressional committees had run harassing investigations of "communist infiltration" of student groups); Communist Party members, of whom there were no more than forty or fifty in SDS, were in many cases known to the SDS leaders anyway, though they tended to keep their affiliations from the rank and file; and many PLers had no hesitancy in making their memberships—and their role as "the only true communists"—crystal clear. The National Council dismissed it with a 41–3 vote.

At this point the idea of a PL takeover or "Communist infiltration" was still regarded largely as a joke. The suggestion that Bettina Aptheker, Berkeley activist and CP member, had put forth at Clear Lake that the Communist Party was the logical force to lead the New Left was dismissed out of hand, Carl Oglesby being only the most eloquent in assigning it to the dust bin. The PLers were thought to have some good ideas, but their "Old Lefty phrasemongering," as it was called, and their general squareness of dress and attitude chilled most of the other SDSers; Mao and his little red book excited only laughter on the convention floor. The overwhelming attitude was still that the Old Left was old-fashioned and that SDS was too amorphous to get taken over by anything anyway.

The old guard took its defeat at Clear Lake stoically. Booth fired off one last letter to *New Left Notes* complaining that Clear Lake hadn't really agreed on *anything* for the coming year, and he even proposed one last "national action" of demonstrations against President Johnson, but when this was ignored he retired into silence. Webb moved on to Washington, where he started a fledgling D.C.-area region and began work for *Ramparts* magazine researching connections between the National Student Association and the CIA. Oglesby went back to Ann Arbor—where, incidentally, he was to meet, and influence, Bill Ayers and Diana

Oughton—to complete work on his examination of U.S. imperialism that appeared the following year in a volume called *Containment and Change*. Max, who had sat as chairman during the
plenary sessions, wrote a note to Jim Williams moaning that the
old guard had been vanquished and "there's nothing left of the old
people any more—it's just all these funny kids," and went back
to New York. Others moved off in their separate directions: Kissinger tried organizing in the Chicago area,* Gitlin concentrated
on writing a book about JOIN, Flacks, Lauter, Lemisch, Ross,
and others continued their academic careers; and though they
almost universally continued radical work, they did so now outside of the SDS framework.

An attempt was made at Clear Lake to establish an "adult
SDS" for these members who had "graduated" from SDS, along
with other nonstudent activists springing up among young professional workers in the larger cities. This idea of what was generally
called a "Movement for a Democratic Society," to be either affiliated with or the parent group of SDS, was a longstanding one,
kicking around SDS circles ever since it had become clear that the
LID was not the adult group SDSers wanted to graduate into. The
1964 convention mandated work on a "young adult New Left"
organization by Max, Burlage, and others, and a "Young Adult
Organizing" committee was actually established as early as the fall
of that year, with a big push from Hayden and Wittman. But at
that point the numbers of radicals were hardly sufficient for one
organization, much less two, and nothing materialized. The subject was brought up whenever movement people got together for
the next couple of years (Shero, for example, presented a working
paper on it to the Kewadin convention in 1965), and isolated
attempts were made at establishing individual MDS chapters:
several staffers at the Columbia University School of Social Work
actually formed an MDS in the fall of 1965, and early in 1966 starts
were made in Boston, San Francisco, Los Angeles, and Gary,
Indiana. By the time of Clear Lake many older members agreed

*Kissinger's efforts to run a radicalizing campaign with his Committee for
Independent Political Action in Chicago's 49th ward that fall were perhaps
symbolic of the old guard's success with electoral politics—the two candidates
CIPA put up were thrown off the ballot by Mayor Daley's Board of Elections
and subsequently kept off by Mayor Daley's courts.

with University of Pennsylvania faculty member (and SDSer) Edward Jahn, who wrote to *New Left Notes:*

> Students grow older; they graduate, get jobs, raise families. Many of them abandon radical politics as soon as they graduate—these are the Four Year Radicals. . . . But what about those who are still radicals after their four years are over—where can they go: SDS if it does not develop an organizational alternative for its older adherents . . . will die. The New Left must create an adult organization if the New Left is to survive.

But the call went unheeded, and those who did not want to devote themselves to the new "organizing thrust" simply went their own ways.

The Radical Education Project represented the closest thing to a continuing center for the old guard after Clear Lake. After sputtering through several false starts in the spring, REP finally had begun to take shape over the summer, and in July it was officially incorporated, with Haber as its president and Locker its secretary. It had been decided that REP had better have an existence formally separate from SDS, both because it could then put itself forward as a tax-exempt institution for fund-raising purposes and because it was clear that it was not going to get very much help or attention from the new influx of SDSers anyway. Doing some neat footwork, REP finally phrased it this way: "The RADICAL EDUCATION PROJECT is an independent education, research and publication organization initiated by Students for a Democratic Society, dedicated to the cause of democratic radicalism and aspiring to the creation of a new left in America." Just what that meant was spelled out in a lengthy, detailed, comprehensive prospectus:

> Democratic radicalism is renewing itself around a basically moral proposition: that people should have the opportunity to participate in shaping the decisions and the conditions of economic, political and cultural existence which affect their lives and destinies.
>
> This theme is not new. Indeed, it is deeply rooted in the traditions of utopian and scientific socialism, popular democracy and humanism. But it has acquired a new urgency and concreteness in the radical action movements of the last six years. It has become the unifying point of moral reference in the opposition to the corporate

state, in the anti-war movement, in the critique of authoritarianism and paternalism in the university, and in the freedom struggles of Negroes in particular and the American underclass in general.

If that sounds vaguely familiar, it is because this prospectus was no less than the attempted rewrite of *The Port Huron Statement* that so many of the old guard had been demanding, with much talk about "radical vision," "values and utopia," "man is the measure," "human potentiality and the good society," "potential agents of change," and so on. But it was a serious and ambitious document, it had a certain impact in academic circles, and it attracted immediate support from a number of well-known people on the left.*

REP began functioning, after a fashion, in Ann Arbor in the fall. The full-time staff included Jerry Badanes, Barry Bluestone, Mike and Evelyn Goldfield, Peter Henig, Jim Jacobs, and Steve Weissman, with help from Haber, Locker, Booth, and Magidoff. Yet by December not one piece of its own literature had been produced (other than three bibliographical "study guides" for radical seminars) and something like $6000 had been dribbled away. Attempts to reach the projected budget of $85,000 by barnstorming rich liberals and philanthropic institutions proved mostly futile.†

The concept of student power was of course inherent in much that had already gone on in the 1960s—in the campus civil-rights programs, the university-reform conferences, the Berkeley demonstration of 1964, the various campus political parties, the antiwar (especially the antirank) agitation, and the free universities. But it did not develop into a separate and self-conscious movement, with an enunciated strategy and an organizational

*Among the early REP sponsors were Philip Berrigan, Dave Dellinger, Douglas Dowd, Hal Draper, Norm Fruchter, Paul Goodman, Gabriel Kolko, Andrew Kopkind, William Kunstler, Paul Lauter, Staughton Lynd, Herbert Marcuse, Barrington Moore, Linus Pauling, Victor Rabinowitz, Marc Raskin, Harold Taylor, Arthur Waskow, William Appleman Williams, and Howard Zinn.
†One SDSer in *New Left Notes* (December 23, 1966) that fall described a disease endemic in Ann Arbor in which the "patient believes that we can get McGeorge Bundy in the movement if we would only write more grant proposals for the Ford Foundation." It was called REPatitis.

shape, until the Clear Lake convention. What it eventually became was something more than that encompassed by SDS, for it developed into the expression, at disparate campuses at different times for diverse reasons, of an entire awakening generation, many of whom had no interest in SDS or even in organized radical politics. But it would not have emerged when it did, and could not have taken the form that it did, were it not for SDS—and Carl Davidson.

Davidson's *A Student Syndicalist Movement: University Reform Revisited,* passed out in mimeograph form at Clear Lake, made an immediate impact. It was, startlingly, almost wholly free of the strangulating social-science rhetoric that made up the yeast of most of the early SDS papers; it was easy reading, with careful organization, lots of subheads, and concrete examples; and it was about half the length of the usual SDS position paper. But most important, of course, it enunciated an idea that many in SDS had begun to sense for themselves over the previous year.

Davidson's paper begins by restating the connections between universities and corporate liberalism:

> What we have to see clearly is the relation between the university and corporate liberal society at large. Most of us are outraged when our university administrators or their "student government" lackeys liken our universities and colleges to corporations. We bitterly respond with talk about a "community of scholars." However, the fact of the matter is that they are correct. Our educational institutions *are* corporations and knowledge factories. What we have failed to see in the past is how absolutely *vital* these factories are to the corporate liberal state.
>
> What do these factories produce? What are their commodities? The most obvious answer is "knowledge." Our factories produce the know-how that enables the corporate state to expand, to grow, and to exploit more efficiently and extensively both in our own country and in the third world. But "knowledge" is perhaps too abstract to be seen as a commodity. Concretely, the commodities of our factories are the *knowledgeable.* AID officials, Peace Corpsmen, military officers, CIA officials, segregationist judges, corporation lawyers, politicians of all sorts, welfare workers, managers of industry, labor bureaucrats (I could go on and on)—where do they come from? They are products of the factories we live and work in. . . .
>
> How did they become what they are? They were shaped and

formed on an assembly line that starts with children entering junior high school and ends with junior bureaucrats in commencement robes. And the rules and regulations of *in loco parentis* are essential tools along that entire assembly line. Without them, it would be difficult to produce the kind of men that can create, sustain, tolerate, and ignore situations like Watts, Mississippi and Vietnam. . . . *Our universities are already the chief agents for social change in the direction of 1984.*

And then Davidson posed the exciting question: "What would happen to a manipulative society if its means of creating manipulative people were done away with?" To which he answered: "We might then have a fighting chance to change the system!" How?

Obviously, we need to organize, to build a movement on the campuses with the primary purpose of radically transforming the university community. Too often we lose sight of this goal. To every program, every action, every position, and every demand, we must raise the question: How will this radically alter the lives of *every* student on this campus? With this in mind, I offer the following proposal for action.

That every SDS chapter organize a student syndicalist movement on its campus. I use the term "syndicalist" for a crucial reason. In the labor struggle, the syndicalist unions worked for industrial democracy and workers' control, rather than better wages and working conditions. Likewise, and I cannot repeat this often enough, the issue for us is "student control" (along with a yet-to-be-liberated faculty in some areas). What we do not want is a "company union" student movement that sees itself as a body that, under the rubric of "liberalization," helps a paternal administration *make better rules for us.* What we do want is a union of students where the students themselves decide what kind of rules they want or don't want. Or whether they need rules at all. Only this kind of student organization allows for decentralization, and the direct participation of students in all those decisions daily affecting their lives.

. . . The main purpose . . . is to develop a radical consciousness among *all* the students, in the *real* struggle yet to come against the administration.

And then, the possibility—a dream with a lineage going back to early SDS and the impulses of Kissinger and others of campus orientation—"to organize a mass radical base with a capacity for prolonged resistance, dedication, and endurance. With this in mind, it is easy to see why such a student syndicalist movement must be *national* (or even international) in its scope."

Davidson's debts are obvious: to the original syndicalists, to the Wobblies, to his own experiences at Penn State and Nebraska. But perhaps most profound is his debt to the SDS thinkers before him. The desire to work at different levels on different campuses is the same concept that animated Al Haber in the first few years of the organization. The recognition of connections between the authoritarian rigidity and dehumanization of the university and that of the society at large is the same that the whole first genera-tion of SDS had enunciated. The connections between the liberal state and the universities are the kind that Potter, Hayden, and Oglesby had made. The emphasis on students as the agents of social change, the idea of engaging people in "those decisions daily affecting their lives," and the importance placed on participatory democracy in a campus context are direct echoes of *The Port Huron Statement.*

In fact, in some ways *A Student Syndicalist Movement* is the new breed's own *Port Huron Statement,* a document for a new generation of SDSers who want once again to turn their attention to the campuses, once again to show the need for students to control the decisions that affect their lives, once again to get students to operate on their immediate felt grievances, once again to radicalize them by having them see the connections between these grievances and the national malaise. The first generation of SDS had started out by seeking its allies on the campus, but after a time turned from there to the ghettos, to the poor, to the black, and later still to the war, to the middle class, to the professionals. Now the second generation of SDS was bringing the organization back: build the student left first.

There were criticisms of the student-syndicalist approach, and they were voiced often within the next few months. The PL people scorned it for its lack of a "class analysis," its failure to see the need for students to join with the working class to carry out any revolution. Others argued that the idea of students' actually controlling their universities was, even if realizable, undesirable, since those universities still had to operate within and depend for their existence upon a corrupt system; if students were put in charge of universities, as Earl Silbar put it, "we would have to become the pimps of our dream." And many pointed to—as it was now regarded—the "danger of reformism" if the university administrations simply gave in on the most modest student demands (dorm hours, food prices, curriculum changes, and the like) and blunted the movement without altering the basic university structure.

But the time for student power was ripe. For one thing, there were now more people in the universities than ever before— 6,390,000, up from 3,788,000 in 1960, nearly 40 percent of the college-age population—and thus a larger pool from which to draw dissidents, and a larger group which could view itself self-consciously as a class. Not that all of them were committed radicals by any means—the best estimates put the activist ranks between 5 and 15 percent, or roughly 320,000 to 960,000—but many were certainly alienated, as the phrase went, disillusioned with much in the world around them, and ready to give vent to their anger, for which the university was at least the easiest target. The youth culture, too, had by now become firmly rooted, nurtured both by affluence and dissidence, and had brought forth its own special fruits in sexual behavior, the growing drug scene, the new styles of music, dress, literature, art, food, and philosophy; which in turn helped to sustain a now sizable group of people who, though not officially students, occupied the fringes of the universities in the burgeoning youth ghettos, more alienated still and far quicker to take the risks that direct action might bring. Apathy might still be the norm at many campuses—it is, after all, one of the intended products of the university environment—but it was nowhere near as pervasive as it had been ten years before, and now had to live side by side with the growing political awareness of many young people; students in the fall of 1966, we might remember, had already lived through six years of campus activism of one kind or another, six years of the war in Vietnam, six years of general political ferment within the nation.

Accompanying the heightened political consciousness was a growing change of attitude toward the university itself. The idea of complicity, inaugurated with the rank protests, and the impact of resistance, in the form of confrontations with the university power structure, were as yet imperfectly realized, but they unquestionably helped students to see campus governance in a new light. At the same time the universities came to be seen as important sources of power within the society—they were to the technological society what factories had been to the mechanical one—and thus potential levers for exerting influence on that society; students, especially as their numbers grew, could now think of themselves as a power bloc as legitimate as any other.

The time was ripe for student power within SDS as well. Much of it had to do with the kinds of people who now came to prominence in the organization. True, they were not students themselves and were in fact several years older than most undergraduates—but they had spent their college years as serious radical organizers (something that was not true of most in the earlier generation), and the experience, especially in the last year, had left them generally united in the idea that any chance for building a movement for change in America depended upon organizing and radicalizing the students. Also, many prominent members—Davidson, Shero, Adams, Kindred, Egleson, Robbins, Calvert—had been involved more in university politics and campus traveling than in such nonuniversity activities as antiwar marches, draft resistance, electoral politics, or labor support. They were also, coming from the prairie-power heritage, more comfortable with local actions than national programs and more concerned to have individual chapters operate on their own grievances than follow some national pattern.

But there is also the decisive fact that SDS saw no other avenues for effective radical politics. Vietnam was still thought to be too much of a single-issue protest, one, moreover, in which success seemed hopeless: marches, no matter how big or small, militant or docile, shaggy or clean-cut, had proved quite incapable of halting the war. Civil-rights work seemed hardly possible after SNCC's explicit rejection of white support; ERAP organizing seemed equally mistaken, given the now obvious failure of most ERAP projects and the explosive anger of the black ghettos that had been expressed in Watts. Draft resistance posed apparently insoluble poblems of illegality, elitism, membership support. Working with labor unions and unorganized workers was thought to be legitimate but basically old hat and unmilitant, while work-

ing with the middle class and professionals seemed somehow like
selling out. Campus organizing, in which all of these issues could
be raised but none had to be exclusively championed, seemed the
perfect answer.*

The choice was almost inevitable, an expression of all that
SDS had become. By this point SDS had to move on to some form
of resistance, both as an expression of the mood of its leaders and
as a means of creating an identity for itself in the absence of a
national program or national publicity. It needed to operate in a
decentralized and nonbureaucratic way, given both the natural
distaste for the opposites and its unfortunate experience in trying
them. It needed to orient itself around students, both because they
formed its logical and historical constituency and because other
constituencies were unavailable or unapproachable. And it needed
to keep pointing itself to the question of fundamental social
change rather than absorb itself in single issues and the reformist
dangers therein. Hence, student power.

And herein lies the paramount point about SDS and student
power. For while SDS now wanted to operate at the university
level, raising local grievances of individual campuses and building
its constituency among the students, it did so *not* to change the
educational system on the campus, *not* to achieve academic reforms, *not* even to get more power in the hands of students within
the university setting. It did so because it saw among the American studentry the possibility of creating a generation of committed
radicals, and thus to change the entire political and social structure of the country. Student power was merely a method, a tool,
a prod, a way to awaken students to the realities of the nation by
tuning them in to the realities of the campus, to make connections
between the demands for democratic control in the university and
the same demands in the body politic. Never lost was the cardinal
idea that students should be agents for *social* change: where pro-

---

*It should be noted that other organizations moved into the areas where SDS
left a vacuum. The Spring (later National) Mobilization Committee to End the
War in Vietnam was formed that fall to continue antiwar marches. A new group
called the Resistance, formally inaugurated the next spring, took up draft resistance. The Progressive Labor Party and the Communist Party both reaffirmed
in the fall their primary strategy of organizing among the working class, and the
latter specifically eschewed New Left organizing.

test took the form of picketing a Marine recruiter, the real target was the war and university complicity; where the protest was against dormitory hours, the real target was arbitrary authority and the nature of the Establishment's institutions. Student power, in short, was not educational but political.

Much confusion has reigned on this point. The media especially, more out of misunderstanding than malice, were unequipped to conceive of the best of the college generation as bordering on the verge of revolution and regularly saw protest issues in neat little vacuums. University administrators, not unnaturally, chose to regard protest as an educational problem, and thought (or hoped) that it could be meliorated by educational reforms, many of which, it was agreed, were long overdue.* Even students themselves sometimes regarded student power as a way of throwing off an unwanted rule or readjusting some glaring error; and on the smaller and more remote campuses where SDS chapters operated, students at various points over the next few years came to be attracted initially because they thought the organization was working merely for educational reform.

But of SDS's intention there never was a doubt. Davidson is quite explicit in his paper in talking about "sabotage" and "abolition" of universities, and his guiding idea is that, once exposed to student syndicalism, students would "never quite be the same, especially after they leave the university community." Calvert, in his report in *New Left Notes* on the Clear Lake convention, spelled it out further:

> There emerged a very clear understanding that SDS had repudiated any attempt to make itself a new version of older left-wing political parties in the United States or in Europe. Politically that meant a refusal to accept social-democratic or liberal-labor coalitionist images of our future. It meant that we were, as we have often said, dedicated to the building of truly radical constituencies in this

---

*At least seven universities (Berkeley, Brown, Colorado, Cornell, NYU, Oregon, and Wisconsin) established committees during the fall of 1966 to examine student conduct and student participation, and before the year was out most universities had some general reexamination of university rules, codes, governance, etc. By the end of the school year, 30 percent more universities than in 1965 had moved to make students part of various university committees. (Foster and Long, *Protest!*, p. 441.)

country. The establishment of a new group of SDS organizers was seen as the effective means of carrying that conviction to the American campus.

Student power, in other words, was meant to radicalize a generation, not to liberalize their education. Or, as Jeff Shero recalls, "We wanted to build an American left, and nothing less than that."

16

FALL 1966

Student power on the campuses: Jeff Shero describes the organizing process.

> When you'd go to organize a campus, you'd first have to find a
> contact, or meet some people, you'd have to have a lot of just
> discussions to figure out where people were at, and at some point
> you'd leave the group you'd found to talk to other kinds of people,
> to develop a sense of the campus. And you'd come back and you'd
> relate to different issues but put them in a coherent way. You'd try
> by the time you left to have an organizational meeting, try to sign
> people up in SDS, give them pamphlets to read to develop their
> analysis, and find the one issue they could begin to move on.
>   Organizers always understood how issues were related, and as
> soon as they got students into motion on one issue, as soon as they
> came in conflict with the authorities in the society, people would
> begin seeing the relationship to other issues, and the organizers
> could accelerate that process by explaining it. But it wasn't crucial
> which issues you began moving around: it could be racism in
> Florida, it could be the draft in New Mexico, it could be arbitrary
> university rules like smoking on campus in Utah. We had that
> dialectical sense that by getting people in motion and giving them
> an analytical overview, they would in a short period of time make
> all the connections.

The National Office worked hard to keep the motion going.
New Left Notes provided weekly coverage of campus actions,
cross-fertilizing the chapters with new ideas, issues, tactics. Litera-

ture production was stepped up with the reprinting of a number of the best-selling items, including a "Chapter Organizers Handbook," the Potter and Oglesby Washington march speeches, the "Guide to Conscientious Objection," Christopher Hobson's "Vietnam—Any Way Out?" and an additional twenty thousand copies of *The Port Huron Statement*. An elaborate survey of chapters was begun in an attempt to get a detailed profile of what the campus organizations really looked like and how they could best be served. Egleson, Calvert, and Davidson went on regular tours of the campuses, talking to chapter organizers and often—for SDS's reputation had now penetrated everywhere—drawing considerable crowds to public speeches and debates; Oglesby, too, was much in demand on the campus lecture circuit, and in at least one place (Colorado) his mere presence was enough to generate an SDS chapter overnight that remained active throughout the year. At the same time a half-dozen official campus travelers like Shero were working out of the Regional Offices, usually on salaries of no more than $30 a week, armed with piles of literature in the back seats of whatever cars they could cadge, servicing the chapters and spreading the SDS message to places where it had not yet taken hold; and a dozen unofficial travelers, committed SDSers who had dropped out or were giving only halfhearted attention to schoolwork, performed the same function with the same zeal.

All of this—combined, of course, with the continuing war, the rebellions in the black ghettos, the failure of the "war on poverty," the daily duplicity of the Johnson Administration, the lack of success of peace and liberal candidates in the Congressional elections, and the ongoing blague of American life—had its effect. The fall of 1966 was the beginning of active student resistance.

On many campuses the process began, as Davidson had envisioned, around strictly local grievances. At the University of Nebraska, for example, where Davidson's own influence lingered, SDS helped to form a left-wing campus party which organized on the issue of a student bill of rights and in the student-government elections managed to place three SDSers in power. At Penn State, the SDS chapter challenged the administration over its *in loco parentis* role, led a successful boycott of the campus elections, and after lengthy negotiations with a vacillating student government exposed its sandbox stature. At San Francisco State, students organized a boycott of the university eating facilities, complaining of high prices and inferior quality, and then went on to demand student control over the corporation that ran the cafeteria and the campus store. At New York University (downtown), SDSers organized a thousand-person rally against a proposed tuition increase, went on to hold a strike that was said to be 50 to 80 percent effective, and finally participated in a four-hundred-strong sit-in at the university's Main Building.

But by far the greatest number of student protests were directed at noncampus issues, usually the war, in which the university was involved; and here the protests were directed in classic fashion against the administration for its complicity with outside organizations. On many campuses (Antioch, Buffalo, CCNY, Columbia, Cornell, Oberlin, Michigan, and Wisconsin among them), SDS renewed its campaign against student ranking and the scheduled second round of Selective Service testing, again pointing to the role the universities were playing on behalf of the war machine; the Antioch drive was successful in getting the college to drop ranking. On several campuses, SDS devoted itself to exposing and protesting heretofore hidden university links: at NYU, SDSers wrote and distributed a document called "Who Controls the Board of Trustees?" which showed the connections between the university and various American corporations involved in overseas exploitation or the war in Vietnam, and at Pennsylvania, SDSers got nation-wide publicity for uncovering the extensive research in chemical and biological warfare the university was carrying on in secret. And at many universities the most significant issue of the fall was the recruiting of students on campus by Navy, Marine, CIA, or Dow Chemical Company recruiters—an issue particularly successful in galvanizing students because it blended so much: it exposed the university's complicity with the war, it showed up the administration's attitude toward free speech, and it allowed antiwar expressions in general a visible, tangible, local outlet. SDS led at least a half-dozen successful antirecruiting demonstrations that fall (at Brown,* Columbia,

*The Brown protest, on December 16, was only the second organized demonstration against Dow—the first was held in Torrance, California, in July—but the first at a college campus.

Kentucky, Maryland, Michigan, and Queens), but none was more striking than the one at Berkeley.

Yes, Berkeley—again. There a team of Navy recruiters put up a table in the student union at the end of November, despite a rule that only student organizations could use the hall, and the Berkeley SDS chapter seized the opportunity to set up its own table right next to it, distributing antiwar literature. Administration officials demanded that the SDS table be removed. SDS refused. SDSers and sympathetic students began a sit-in around the Navy table to prevent anyone from going near, and the administration called the police. More than a hundred local policemen swarmed on the crowd, and when one of the demonstrators was attacked by a heckling student, the cops moved in and started making arrests—of the demonstrators, not the hecklers. Ten people in all were carried off, including Jerry Rubin and Mario Savio, and SDSer Stew Albert. The Berkeley administration was reliving its past: by arbitrarily denying students freedom to speak and organize, by showing itself subservient to outside (and unpopular) interests, and then by calling in the police to arrest its own students, it once again radicalized a large part of the student body. That night a wide segment of the campus, including the teaching assistants, the National Student Association chapter, and the student government,* supported a call for a student strike. An administration spokesman tried to head it off by arguing that the student government had specifically recommended that Navy recruiters be allowed on campus; the student-government vice president rose and denied it flatly. The strike began the next day, with an estimated 75 percent success, and a prostrike rally at noon drew fifteen thousand: again the issue of calling the cops on campus proved to have swung general student support behind the minority activists. For five days the strike continued, with SDS pushing a wide range of demands, until December 6, when the faculty (apparently mindful of criticism of its role two years before) voted to support the administration, the administration agreed to appoint a high-level student-faculty commission to study governance of

---

*Whose president, no leftist, said, "We protest the general state of noncommunity on campus; we protest the hostility, distrust, and rampant disrespect which pollutes the university atmosphere; we protest the sickness pervading the university." (Bay Guardian, December 20, 1966)

the university, and student enthusiasm began to wane. Many of the students and most of the rest of the university chose to regard the crisis as an educational one; the student-faculty commission inevitably treated the issue as one of educational reform and eventually recommended a much greater role for students in both the educational and disciplinary machinery of the university. But SDS had made its point: the university was cooperating improperly with the agencies that were fighting the war, it was incapable of governing its own campus without recourse to the police, and it denied its students their proper voice in university affairs. From such acorns do radical oaks grow.*

Direct protest against the war also became a commonplace on the campuses now. At almost every school where there was an active SDS chapter (nearly two hundred), and many where there weren't, students organized against Administration policies: at places like Texas Western and Arizona State, SDS was generally confined to setting up tables in the student centers for the distribution of antiwar literature; at larger schools like Michigan and Wisconsin, it could organize the heckling of prowar speeches and disrupt Administration spokesmen; at a campus like San Fer-

---

*A careful study was made of the students who were active in this Berkeley protest, who were then compared with a random group of nonactivist students and with a sample of nonstudents from Berkeley's hippified youth ghetto. Compared to the other students, it was found, the activists' "fathers held higher status occupations and both parents were more highly educated"; three times as many were Jewish and twice as many (61 percent) professed no religious preference; they scored twice as high on a test measuring alienation; almost all expressed interest in national politics, compared to little more than a third of the nonactivists; they were more likely to discuss "intellectual ideas and politics" with their parents and were more likely to be in agreement with them. The study concluded that activists "were raised by highly educated, upper-middle-class parents which suggests a home atmosphere characterized by liberality and encouragement of continuing dialogue between parents and children" and by "considerable interaction and agreement on basic values." Compared to the dropout students, it was found, the activists were similar in many respects—in verbal ability, in nonprofession of religion, and in alienation—but here again they tended to come from higher-status homes and they were far closer to their parents. The nonstudents, the study concluded, were characterized by "family estrangement," were "more likely to feel that active confrontation on behalf of social change is futile and withdraw from restrictive, conventional society into a disaffiliated subculture," and "have made a more drastic departure from conventional paths to adulthood." (William A. Watts, Steve Lynch, and David Whittaker, *Journal of Counseling Psychology*, Vol. 16, No. 1, 1969.)

nando Valley State College, SDS even tried Kissinger's Kamikazi
Plan, speaking to National Guardsmen at a nearby base about the
war, and several dozen were arrested.* But the most successful—
and most publicized—antiwar demonstration of all was at Harvard.

Secretary of Defense Robert McNamara was invited by the
Harvard administration and its John F. Kennedy Institute of
Politics to give a lecture on November 7 to a select group of fifty
students. The Harvard/Radcliffe SDS chapter, demanding that
the university live up to its claims for free speech, proposed that
the Secretary engage in a debate with *Ramparts* editor Robert
Scheer, coincidentally there on the same weekend, or at least face
a public forum of antiwar questioners. Harvard refused. SDS then
circulated a petition calling for a public debate, which got sixteen
hundred signatures within a few days. Harvard refused again. SDS
vowed confrontation. Let *New Left Notes* take the story from
there:

> By 4 P.M., close to a thousand demonstrators (the *Crimson* said 800)
> ringed Quincy House, covering virtually all the exits. SDS heads ran
> a James Bond-type operation, with walkie-talkie equipped spotters
> on all sides of the building. After several false alarms and one
> attempted decoy maneuver, McNamara emerged in a police car on
> a narrow back street. While a dozen SDSers sat down around the
> car, others passed the signal over the walkie talkies around the
> block, and the thousand began running towards McNamara. Within
> moments, he was surrounded by what must have looked to him like
> a mob of howling beatniks; they were actually normal Harvard
> people, including faculty like Michael Walzer, delighted to have
> trapped the Secretary.
>
> McNamara told the crowd: "I spent four of the happiest years
> on the Berkeley campus doing some of the same things you're doing
> here. But there was one important difference: I was both tougher
> and more courteous." After laughter and shouts, he shouted vehe-
> mently, "I was tougher then and I'm tougher now!"
>
> The audience loved it. Mac was blowing his cool—unable to
> handle himself, quite possibly scared. The first question was about
> the origins of the Vietnamese war. "It started in '54–'55 when a

*Michael Klonsky, later SDS National Secretary, was one of the Valley State
SDS leaders.

million North Vietnamese flooded into South Vietnam," McNamara said. "Goin' home!" someone shouted. Mac countered "Why don't you guys get up here since you seem to know all the answers?" The next question asked for the number of civilian casualties in the South. "We don't know," Mac said. "Why not? Don't you care?" came the shouts. "The number of casualties . . ." Mac began, but was drowned out by cries of "*Civilian! Civilian!* Napalm victims!" A few PL-types in front were jumping up and down screaming "Murderer! Fascist!" Mac tried to regain his composure and said "Look fellas, we had an agreement . . ." A girl shrieked "What about your agreement to hold elections in 1956?"

Things seemed to be breaking up. The police moved in and whisked McNamara into Leverett House; an SDS leader,* fearing violence in the streets, took the microphone and ordered all SDS people to clear the area. The disciplined shock troops of the revolution turned and dispersed quickly, McNamara was hustled out through steam tunnels, and everyone went home to watch themselves on TV.

SDS was in the news again. *The New York Times* and the *Washington Post* carried the story on their front pages, as did most major newspapers, and all the network news broadcasts featured the event; conspicuously absent was any mention of SDS's prior attempts to arrange an organized public debate with the Secretary. The Harvard administration officially apologized, as did some twenty-seven hundred students; SDS did not. Three students wrote to *The New York Times:*

> We entered into this demonstration as our only means of expressing our repulsion to and disapproval of the war in Vietnam and those who propagate it. We consider any attempts to apologize on our behalf to be spurious. We do not apologize.

This adamancy, and the unusual means of confrontation, disturbed a number of Harvard students, perhaps the majority, but there was no question that SDS, again, had made its point: Harvard was shown to be high-handed rather than high-minded, devoted to free egress rather than free speech, dependent ultimately on the power of the police rather than the power of suasion—and

*Michael Ansara, who with David Loud was co-chairman of the chapter and was to continue to be active in SDS politics.

on top of it all apologetic to the chief architect of the Vietnam war.

From Berkeley to Harvard—it was happening all over, and on a scale never seen before in the history of American higher education. It is sometimes easy to forget what a remarkable development it all was, since within a few years the campus protest tended to seem as hallowed a university institution as the library, but in fact up to this point student disruptions (with the exception of Berkeley in 1964 and Chicago in the spring of 1966) were little noted nor long remembered. We must remember that it is only now that student protest becomes a part of American politics.*

Progressive Labor influence was noticeable throughout the fall. A number of articles in *New Left Notes* put forth PL lines. PLers, along with other varieties of SDSers, were important in running a Boston Labor Committee, doing strike-support work and general labor theorizing during the fall. PLers were persuasive in putting across their party's strong anti-imperialist line in a number of chapters, mostly in New York and Boston: on Vietnam, for example, the PL National Committee statement, published in the October–November issue of *PL*, read:

> To defeat imperialism we need the broadest movement possible around a clear anti-imperialist program: the demand for the United States to "get out of Vietnam, now." . . . This demand will expose the phony slogan of "negotiate now," with which the ruling class

---

*According to one survey of 78 of the most prominent colleges and universities, there were some 430 protests during this academic year, working out to roughly 6 per school. Another survey of 246 institutions of all types found that more than 50 of them had demonstrations both against Vietnam and against racial discrimination in which more than a quarter of the student body was involved; 90 percent of these universities had protests on administrative policies, and these involved over half the student body at more than 100 institutions. And the most comprehensive survey, by Richard E. Peterson of the Educational Testing Service in Princeton, New Jersey, found that the number of institutions reporting protests rose dramatically from 1964-65 to 1967-68: on the issue of the war in Vietnam the number rose from 178 to 327, on student participation in the formulation of university policies from 161 to 231, on administration racial discrimination from 42 to 155, on tests and grades from 76 to 107; and though no schools reported protests over war-related issues in 1964-65, 215 later cited protests over armed-forces recruiting, 213 over the draft, and 174 over Dow and CIA recruiting. In the 1964–65 survey 26 percent of the colleges reported the presence of New Left groups on campus, and in most cases the group was SDS. (Foster and Long, *Protest!* pp.365, 89 ff, 59 ff.)

is trying to control the peace movement and turn the mass discontent to their purpose.

By December, Brooklyn SDSer Sue Simensky wrote to Greg Calvert that PLer Jeff Gordon "represents the views of most SDSers" at Brooklyn College and that the PL position was winning adherents at New York regional meetings; traditional SDSers like Max, Ireland, Bob Gottlieb, Sue Eanet, and Sarah Murphy, she said, are loud talkers, but people find them "pretty much irrelevant." Calvert responded with what was presumably the National Office attitude at the time: Jeff Gordon may be a good guy,

> . . . but PL politics are not SDS politics and why is it no one can talk from an SDS perspective? . . . I know that cadre discipline is impressive, but I do not think that Maoism is the answer to our problems. . . . It just seems to me that if PL wants a delegate to the NC then they ought to become a fraternal organization of SDS like any other independent group and get their delegate openly and forthrightly.

National SDS basked in the light of that fall's student protests. Not that it was getting the kind of national publicity that had attracted attention to it before—there was practically no attention paid in the national press (*Reader's Guide*, for example, lists only one entry for the whole year) and the National Office went out of its way to avoid the Booth pattern of seeking publicity. Rather it was depending now upon interest generated on the campuses, where something new, active, visible, and immediate always attracts attention. Chapters were rejuvenated at several better-known schools (Amherst, Bard, Colorado State, Princeton, New Hampshire, Rochester, and Rutgers), and new chapters were formed during the fall at some eighteen other widely diverse places from Boston College to Bowling Green, University of the Pacific to St. Olaf. The total number of chapters on paper was now at least 265, of which the number of solid and active chapters, according to a mid-fall issue of *New Left Notes*, was somewhere around 175.* National membership rose to some 6000, while the total

*By the fall of 1966, these chapters had been formed in addition to those active in the fall of 1965: Albion, Baltimore At-large, Birmingham (Alabama) At-large, Boston College, Bowling Green, Bucknell, California (Humboldt State), Central State, Cincinnati At-large, Clemson, Cleveland ERAP, University of Colorado,

chapter membership was probably around 25,000*—though the
looseness of what this latter category meant is suggested by the
provision in the Brandeis chapter's 1966 constitution that "a person will be considered a member when he has attended two membership meetings."

Even finances were, after a serious drought, beginning to perk
up. The National Office began the school year $4300 in debt, and
operations for the five months from August turned a neat profit
of exactly $57.04 (largely thanks to contributions of more than
$9000 from SDS "alumni"). But by the end of the year Calvert had
launched SDS on an elaborate fund-raising drive, with 25,000
printed form letters of appeal ("Let's put our bread where our
hearts are, brothers!") and of thanks ("Your contribution is another link in building a true alternative to helplessness"), aimed
to supply an annual budget of $84,000 (or, as he figured it, $14
× 6000 national members). At the same time he made renewed
contacts with big givers—Anne Farnsworth was top on the list—
in the attempt to establish a system of small, regular contributions.
It is somewhat difficult to tell exactly how effective these fiscal
operations were, but something must have happened: by the end
of the year there was $2000 in the bank.

Although Nick Egleson was the first SDS President since

C.W. Post, Dalton High School (New York), Darrow High School (New York),
Delaware, DePauw, DeWitt High School (New York), Drew, Fashion Institute
of Technology, Finch, Franklin and Marshall, Free School of New York, Hart-
ford, Hawthorne (New Jersey) High School, Haverford, Hofstra, Illinois Insti-
tute of Technology, Iowa (Charles City) At-large, Kansas City At-large, Lake
Forest, Lawrence, Lewis and Clark, Lexington (Kentucky) At-large, Manhat-
tanville, Midwood High School (New York), Minneapolis ERAP, Moorhead,
Mount Holyoke, High School of Music and Art (New York), New School (New
York), New York (Cortland State and Stony Brook), Oakland University, Ohio,
Ohio Wesleyan, Oklahoma State, Penn State, Radical Education Project, St.
Cloud, St. Olaf, San Francisco Citizens for a Democratic Society, Seton Hall,
Stevenson High School (New York), Syracuse, Trinity, University of the Pacific,
Washington State, University of Washington, Weequahic (New Jersey) High
School, Wisconsin (La Crosse and Milwaukee), Yankton, Yonkers At-large. No
cumulative lists of active (or even nominal) chapters were being kept at this
point.
*Newsweek estimated SDS followers at 15,000, a study by three academics in
Protest! (Foster and Long, p.208) suggests 20,000 in 1966, and SDS itself in
December claimed 25,000.

Haber to live near and work out of the NO, he chose to spend the bulk of his time traveling the chapters. The dominant force in the office itself was Greg Calvert, who proved to be an able administrator as well as an effective campus speaker and a continuing source of organizational energy; he would close his letters with the Wobblies' "Don't mourn, organize"—and mean it. With Jane Adams, who became Assistant National Secretary, and also Calvert's steady companion, he directed an office staff of ten in an operation not structurally much different from that of Booth's, but with a much greater sense of camaraderie and purpose, which the success of their campus organizing strategy did nothing to diminish.*

It soon became clear that the prairie people around the National Office were revising their notions of just what should be done at a national level. It didn't take long before Davidson was urging SDSers to "work for better communications, internal education, and more thoughtful national programs," sounding for all the world like Paul Booth; and Calvert was somewhat petulantly berating those who "think that national programs are irrelevant": "Maybe we ought to refuse to be a national organization and decide that the only real problems are neighborhood problems and that involvement in anything larger is 'unreal' and that if we just hold on to each other hard enough in our little corners of this monster called America everything will be all right and straight and clean and decent until the bomb comes."

For Calvert especially the idea of an effective national organization was important, because he had a strong vision of what was

*A notion of Calvert's effect upon the office can be seen from a story he has related: "I can remember one of the most moving and unsettling events in the nine months I spent as national secretary of SDS. I had been out on the road for a couple of weeks, and during that time passed my 30th birthday. When I came back to the office, comrades younger than myself needed to assert their youthfulness in the face of my coming middle-age with something resembling guerrilla theater. In rummaging through my desk, they discovered an old passport photo of me from 1961, when I was leaving to go to Europe. I was dressed in a very straight suit, tie, and very short hair. I looked for all the world like what I was at the time, an Ivy League graduate student in history. They put next to it a picture from The New York Times of this rather scruffy looking, very tired, but younger-looking person—myself. They wrote underneath it, 'The good guerrilla in our society must know how to change his identity in order to fit all new situations.' " (Liberation, May 1969.)

needed now. In an extraordinary National Secretary's report in November he set that out—and, incidentally, spoke of SDS as "revolutionary" for the very first time. Responding to those who had despaired of SDS, and Movement work in general, because it had not lived up to their expectations of instant (or even gradual) bliss, Calvert wrote:

> In the face of frustration and confusion, our task—our revolutionary task—is not to purge ourselves of the desires, the vision, and the hope which brought us to the revolutionary movement. Our task is to examine ourselves and our movement and our work in order to sustain our revolutionary hope—in order that, despite the reality of frustration and despair, we might continue the building of the movement which we *know* is right because it corresponds to what we want for ourselves and what we understand to be necessary for the survival of the race.

The old guard of SDS, Calvert suggested, had been wrong in thinking that the organization could create among its members a truly free community, a "beloved community" as it was called, inside the pervasive and corrupting system:

> Let's quit playing games and stop the self-indulgent pretense of confusion. . . . We tried to get close to each other, we tried to create community in the midst of an anticommunitarian world, we tried to find love in the midst of lovelessness and it ended up as either a fruitless mutual-titillation society or as a disruptive self-destructive chaos. The results were catastrophic: let's face up to that.

What is needed, he argued, was not the abandonment of the ideal of freedom, but a new kind of organization to realize the goal:

> I am finally convinced that a truly revolutionary movement must be built out of the deepest revolutionary demands and out of the strongest revolutionary hopes—the demand for and the hope of freedom. I do not, however, believe that such a movement can be the beloved community; it can only be a revolutionary community of hope. . . .
>
> We are not the new life of freedom: but that does not mean that we cannot be the force which gives it birth. . . . Our freedom is not to be free but to be a force of freedom.

It was a clear call for a new level of struggle, a new perception of what SDS could do, and be. And inherent in it was the notion of revolution—not fully comprehended, perhaps, but ardently stated and openly sought, and no more shilly-shallying about it. SDS had the potential to be the crucible of revolution, and nothing less than that.

Nor was Calvert alone in feeling that SDS stood at the threshold of a new level. Davidson, too, argued that "the system must be fundamentally changed" and asserted that among the choice of weapons, "my own choice is revolution." Talk about the need for an ideology became increasingly common, references to Karl Marx were studded without apology through various pieces now, and regularly the idea of "socialism"—which no early SDSer could have used without embarrassment—was being championed, as in a long article by Steve Baum and Bernard Faber: "At this point, we in SDS must begin to write about and talk about socialist theory, so that we will be prepared to play a major role in developments, creating larger numbers of socialists, and developing socialist consciousness in all institutions in which we organize." Naturally, within this atmosphere certain of the Old Left ideas which had previously been scorned began to take on a new attractiveness, and both the International Socialists (a splinter from the American Socialist Party) and PL were quick to come forward with their own version of those ideas. It was too early for any significant change in policy by either national SDS or most of the campus chapters, but a new acceptance of the idea of revolution is visible now, and growing.

On December 17, 1966, the National Committee of the Progressive Labor Party adopted an official statement, "Road to Revolution II," the importance of which was meant to be suggested by the fact that it was named after the party's first major theoretical statement in March 1963. Though the bulk of it was taken up with a long, scornful, and blistering criticism of the Soviet Union and the American Communist Party for their "revisionism"—revising communism so as to fit in with their "imperialist" practices—the two most important elements were an attack on North Vietnam and a warning to PL members of dangers within their own ranks.

Hanoi was taken to task for accepting aid from a revisionist, reactionary power like the Soviet Union, since the Russians were really out to crush true revolutionaries: "There is no basis for

partial and temporary unity with the revisionists. Revolutionaries
should not enter into Soviet-inspired alliances. They are traps to
thwart the revolution." Revisionism, however, also exists closer to
home, in PL itself:

> It would be most naive of us not to recognize the danger of revision-
> ism in our party. . . . The main manifestation of revisionism inside
> our party at the present time is the continued isolation of too many
> members from the working people. . . . Revisionism is fundamen-
> tally the substitution of individual bourgeois interests for the inter-
> ests of the working class, and that is precisely what happens when
> members refuse to join the people.

Among the "numerous" examples cited are members who don't
want or don't try to get jobs, who get fired too frequently, or who
ignore their fellow workers, and one man who refused to go to a
party held by a fellow working-class tenant because he wanted to
go to a party given by some students instead.

> Among student members the idea of a worker-student alliance is
> advocated on paper, but to get some people to actually go out and
> meet the workers is like pulling teeth. . . . Essentially what these
> members—most of whom come from middle-class backgrounds—
> are saying is that working people are a drag. You have to spend time
> with them (because that's the line) but mainly others should do it.
> . . . That is revisionism. . . . If it is not fiercely opposed and overcome
> by our party, our party will never lead the working class, and no
> matter what these members might secretly wish, socialism cannot
> be achieved without the leadership of the working class.

The first concrete indication that SDS was heading toward a
new organizational level came at the Berkeley National Council
meeting late in December. And the issue that prompted it was, of
all things, the draft.

SDS, as we have seen, had been dragging its feet on the draft
issue for two years now. Earl Silbar, called "our man on the draft"
by *New Left Notes,* had been working out of the Chicago office
during the fall trying to generate some kind of program, but with
little success. The local draft unions proposed by Clear Lake had
come to nothing, and the membership referendum authorized at
that convention had produced only a little more than a hundred
votes by December. SDSers were now agonizing over the issues of

whether to denounce the 2-S deferment, which would be consistent with an antidraft position but would make them liable to induction, or whether to openly refuse induction, which would be more honorable than escaping to Canada or going underground but would expose them to penalties of five years in jail and a $10,000 fine, far harsher than anything they had had to face in the civil-rights days. Even many of those willing to take such personal risks—and there were a number in SDS—tended to acknowledge that this was more an expression of middle-class guilt, or a "politics of masochism," than an effective way to build up a mass antidraft organization.

In the meantime, however, a spontaneous antidraft movement was growing without any organizational direction at all, as draft calls now rose to some 40,000 a month. As early as July a group of eight young men met in New Haven with Staughton Lynd and signed a "We Won't Go" statement pledging to "return our draft cards to our local boards with a notice of our refusal to cooperate until American invasions are ended." The following month a larger meeting (which Calvert helped to organize) was held in Des Moines at which the idea of a mass draft-card burning was first mentioned, but not supported, and afterward a dozen or so men began traveling the campuses to get others to sign the pledge. At the same time, the case of the Fort Hood Three continued to attract attention and CO counseling by such groups as the War Resisters League in New York and the Quakers in Philadelphia continued to draw in several hundred men each month. The number of draft resisters indicted by the government rose to 680, nearly double the year before. In October SDSer Jeff Segal was sentenced to four years in jail for having refused induction in February 1965, the first time a major SDS organizer fell under the ax; and in December Peter Irons, a longtime SDSer and founder of the New Hampshire chapter, was sentenced to three years in jail for refusing military service. At the end of October a group of men around the Committee for Nonviolent Action and the *Catholic Worker* signed a statement refusing to "cooperate in any way with the Selective Service System," including registering, carrying a draft card, accepting deferment or exemption, or being inducted. In November several young men burned their draft cards outside a Boston courtroom where a draft protester was being tried; the next month Cornell SDS president Bruce Dancis, whose father had been a CO in World War II, became the first SDSer to destroy his draft card publicly, outside a meeting at which the Cornell faculty, with all deliberate speed, was discussing university policy toward Selective Service. And that same month a hastily organized conference at the University of Chicago drew a surprising five hundred people, thirty-two of whom—including SDSers Jeff Segal and Paul Booth—signed a "We Won't Go" pledge, the largest organized anti-induction protest to date. A week later *New Left Notes* publicly introduced the idea, in a proposal from Dartmouth SDSer John Spritzler, of having a mass draft-card burning by ten thousand young men.

The stage was set, therefore, for the Berkeley National Council. It was not only that the draft issue was hot—it was also that SDS was coming off a successful fall term of flexing its muscles, and feeling the power of confrontational politics on campus, and becoming aware of the need for a new organizational stance "beyond the beloved community"—but also, of course, the fact that the meeting was being held in Berkeley. For the first time everyone wanted to talk about the draft, and for the first time everyone wanted SDS to do something about it.

Not that anyone was sure what. In fact the debate on it, begun at two o'clock on the afternoon of December 27, went on for nineteen hours over two days before it was finally resolved. It was a debate typically SDSian. The tentacles of *Robert's Rules* had not been thrown off—there were regular votes on amendments to amendments—but at the same time no one hesitated to use any occasion to bring up almost any subject for discussion. In the middle of it all Carl Davidson announced that he had drawn up a proposal for an SDS antidraft program, but he didn't actually want to submit it until the National Council agreed that it would go into this area seriously; he was met by the argument that the NC couldn't very well go into it without knowing what kind of proposal the Vice President had to make. Davidson put it forward, and the fur started to fly. Does the NC have the power to commit the organization to draft refusal? Yes, because the membership referendum (which stood at 104–15 for refusal just then) gave a mandate, even if it represented only 1 percent of the membership. Should SDS have a national program at all, after having rejected the idea at Clear Lake? Yes, because, as Calvert put it, "a national draft resistance program would promote a . . . break of consciousness and force a re-examination of the assumptions that support the current system." But suppose the individual chapters aren't willing to go along, suppose they think that advocating an illegal program will turn away innocent freshmen who might be potential recruits? At this point Davidson, troubled now about the implications of a national program on an organization committed to decentralization, said he would withdraw the whole proposal. The parliamentarian told him that was impossible. Well, then, Davidson replied, the idea was really a mistake for SDS, so we should let some separate staff-oriented group handle it. Berkeley SDSer Mike Smith said no, SDS ought to make the effort, and it had to be an ambitious effort or else there was no point at all. But, the response came, the National Office can't handle an ambitious program (a point concurred in by several of the NO staff), having its hands full at the moment just getting out the paper and answering letters, and all you are proposing here "is a flight into the realm of fantasy," more "empty rhetoric" that will come to nothing. Nonsense, the National Office can do the job if we make it do the job, and besides we'll simply work twice as hard to see that it does. By the end of the first evening, after ten hours of wrangling, with the ranks dwindled and the remaining few bleary-eyed, it was decided to go ahead along the general lines of the Davidson proposal. Next day seven parts of the proposal, four subsections, and a stream of incidentals were voted upon, one by one; the final vote for adoption was lopsided: 53 to 10, with three abstentions. SDS was on record with the strongest antidraft program in the land.

The resolution was full of rhetoric about SDS's opposition to the "immoral, illegal, and genocidal war" and to "conscription in any form," with special subsections swiping at imperialism (though here called still "the economic system and the foreign policy of the United States") and paying homage to nonstudents ("poor, working-class, and middle-class communities"). But at its heart were these provisions:

> We maintain that all conscription is coercive and anti-democratic, and that it is used by the United States Government to oppress people in the United States and around the world. . . .

SDS opposes and will organize against any attempt to legiti-
mize the Selective Service System by reforms. The proposals for a
lottery or for compulsory national service would not change the
essential purpose of the draft—to abduct young men to fight in
aggressive wars. . . .

Since individual protest cannot develop the movement needed
to end the draft and the war, SDS adopts the following program:

SDS members will organize unions of draft resisters. The
members of these unions will be united by the common principle that under no circumstances will they allow themselves to
be drafted. The local unions will reach out to all young men
of draft age by organizing in the high schools, universities, and
communities. Courses of action will include (a) direct action
during pre-induction physicals and at the time of induction,
(b) anti-draft and anti-war education among potential inductees and their families, (c) demonstrations centering on draft
boards and recruiting stations, (d) encouraging young men
already in the military to oppose the war, and (e) circulating
petitions stating that the signer will refuse to serve in Vietnam
or submit to conscription in any form. National SDS will
coordinate the local unions on a regional and national level,
providing staff (including travelers), supplies, and financial
resources.

The resolution was important not only in what it said but in the
spirit that lay behind it—as Calvert put it (in a phrase that was
soon to sweep the Movement), SDS had moved "from protest to
resistance." In a report on the National Council in *New Left Notes,*
Calvert indicated why he felt the draft program was so important:

That program does not talk about politics or the taking of power.
It does not talk about the new society or the democratization of
decision-making. It talks about "resistance." And, finally, behind its
rhetoric and its programmatic details, it talks about the only thing
that has given life and creativity to "the movement." It talks about
the kind of struggle which has been most meaningful to the new left
—the revolutionary struggle which engages and claims the lives of
those involved despite the seeming impossibility of revolutionary
social change—the struggle which has the power to transform, to
revolutionize human lives whether or not it can revolutionize the
societal conditions of human existence.

. . . It offers no clear path to power, no magic formula for success, only struggle and a new life. No promise is made, only the hope that struggle and confrontation with the existing system of humanity will create freedom in the midst of a life-destroying society.

And, with a keen perception, Calvert understood what such a program said about SDS as an organization:

> At its present stage of development, SDS cannot be understood in terms of traditional political organization. Neither ideological clarity (as political analysis) nor organizational stability are fundamentally important to SDSers. What counts is that which creates *movement*. What counts is that SDS be where the action is. What counts is that SDS be involved in the creation of a cutting-edge in the freedom struggle.

"From protest to resistance"—and so it was. The drive toward resistance that had begun with the antiwar marches nearly two years before—bodies in file—and had gone on to the confrontation at the universities this year—bodies sitting-in—now found its first overt and programmatic form in the refusal to fight the war —bodies on the line.

It was a step from which there would be no retreat.

17

SPRING 1967

On a Saturday afternoon in the middle of February 1967 Greg
Calvert addressed some three hundred scholars and activists gathered in Princeton University's McCosh Hall for the first regional
conference of the Radical Education Project. His speech, which
had been hammered out with a number of the top SDS people over
previous weeks and which Calvert had stayed up all night to
polish, represented the conclusions of the new generation of SDS
after six months in power. "It is said," Calvert began,

> that when the Guatemalan guerrillas enter a new village, they do
> not talk about the "anti-imperialist struggle" nor do they give les-
> sons on dialectical materialism—neither do they distribute copies of
> the "Communist Manifesto" or of Chairman Mao's "On Contra-
> diction." What they do is gather together the people of the village
> in the center of the village and then, one by one, the guerrillas rise
> and talk to the villagers about their own lives: about how they see
> themselves and how they came to be who they are, about their
> deepest longings and the things they've striven for and hoped for,
> about the way in which their deepest longings were frustrated by the
> society in which they lived.
>   Then the guerrillas encourage the villagers to talk about their
> lives. And then a marvelous thing begins to happen. People who
> thought that their deepest problems and frustrations were their
> individual problems discover that their problems and longings are
> all the same—that no one man is any different than the others. That,
> in Sartre's phrase, "In each man there is all of man." And, finally,

that out of the discovery of their common humanity comes the decision that men must unite together in the struggle to destroy the conditions of their common oppression.

That, it seems to me, is what we are about.

Then, turning to the contemporary American scene, Calvert scornfully dismissed the theory, advanced by Old Left journalist Max Gordon the night before, that the desire for material goods was the impulse behind revolutionary movements. On the contrary, he said,

> there is only one impulse, one dynamic which can create and sustain an authentic revolutionary movement. The revolutionary struggle is always and always must be a struggle for freedom. No individual, no group, no class is genuinely engaged in a revolutionary movement unless their struggle is a struggle for their own liberation.

And then, the crucial distinction:

> The liberal reformist is always engaged in "fighting someone else's battles." His struggle is involved in relieving the tension produced by the contradictions between his own existence and life-style, his self-image, and the conditions of existence and life-style of those who do not share his privileged, unearned status. . . .
>
> The liberal does not speak comfortably of "freedom" or "liberation," but rather of justice and social amelioration. He does not sense himself to be unfree. He does not face the contradictions between his own human potential, his humanity, and the oppressive society in which he participates. To deal with the reality of his own unfreedom would require a shattering re-evaluation of his subjective life-experience.
>
> Liberal consciousness is conscience translated into action for others. . . .
>
> Radical or revolutionary consciousness . . . is the perception of *oneself* as unfree, as oppressed—and finally it is the discovery of oneself as *one of the oppressed* who must unite to transform the objective conditions of their existence in order to resolve the contradiction between potentiality and actuality. Revolutionary consciousness leads to *the struggle for one's own freedom in unity with others who share the burden of oppression.* . . . Our primary task at this stage of development is the encouragement or building of revolutionary consciousness, of consciousness of the conditions of unfreedom.

It may have seemed a very ordinary perception, this distinction between liberal and radical, but it was not. It was a sharp
pinpointing of where the Movement, and SDS, had come to—"the
struggle for one's own freedom"—as a result of having been told
by Black Power to consider their *own* problems, having been led
by student syndicalism to a concern with the student's *own* power,
and having finally seen in draft resistance the potential of young
men acting out of their *own* oppression. It was also a profound
realization of where the Movement and SDS were heading—a
"unity with others who share the burden of repression"—in the
move to create a community of identity beyond selfishness, a sense
of mutual need, a "revolutionary consciousness." Carl Davidson
a year later was to call the Calvert speech "a fundamental principal [*sic*] for the white new left," and he added, "No one can
understand the new left unless he grasps the dynamic of Calvert's
argument." For the next year SDS would live out the implications
of this new dynamic, as it moved consciously now from protest to
resistance.

Draft resistance depended ultimately upon young men making both a personal and a political decision of the kind that Calvert
described. It meant first a "perception of oneself as unfree" and
a willingness to act on that perception by declaring public opposition to the draft, giving up the 2-S sanctuary, refusing the conse-
quent induction, and then facing the real possibility of jail or exile.
It then meant forging "a unity with others" by writing, speaking,
leafleting, organizing. It was, in many ways, the perfect radical
process.

In January *New Left Notes* published an article that was as
instrumental as any other single item in promoting this process.
Peter Henig, who had been researching the draft for REP in Ann
Arbor, came across a Selective Service document that told with
embarrassing clarity just what the purpose of the Selective Service
System was:

> Delivery of manpower for induction, the process of providing a
> few thousand men with transportation to a reception center, is
> not much of an administrative or financial challenge. It is in
> dealing with the other millions of registrants that the System is

heavily occupied, developing more effective human beings in the national interest.

Chief among them are college students, and the document makes it clear that they are allowed to defer military service only as long as they seem likely to prove themselves useful—in the national interest, of course, not their own—in some other way. To channel them in these useful directions, constant pressure is necessary:

> Throughout his career as a student, the pressure—the threat of loss of deferment—continues. It continues with equal intensity after graduation. His local board requires periodic reports to find out what he is up to. He is impelled to pursue his skill rather than embark upon some less important enterprise and is encouraged to apply his skill in an essential activity in the national interest. The loss of deferred status is the consequence for the individual who acquired the skill and either does not use it or uses it in a non-essential activity.
>
> The psychology of granting wide choice under pressure to take action is the American or indirect way of achieving what is done by direction in foreign countries where choice is not permitted.

At last, "the American way" laid bare. It was, as Greg Calvert later noted, "at least in SDS . . . the first time anybody had bothered to read the material that came out of the Selective Service System," and it was a bombshell on the college campuses. The general response, as SDS printed it on a very successful button, was: NOT WITH MY LIFE YOU DON'T.*

In the first months of 1967 fledgling draft-resistance groups were started at several campuses, most notably at Wisconsin, Berkeley, and Cornell, where the groundwork had been laid as early as the previous fall. The existence of the Cornell group was largely due to former SDS regional traveler and chapter founder Tom Bell, who had now dropped out of school to work full time on draft organizing, and SDSers were prominent elsewhere as well. By March, according to Jeff Segal, then out on bail from his draft sentence and acting as SDS's national draft coordinator, there were maybe twenty-five groups on college campuses. At the same time there had sprung up parallel "We Won't Go" groups

---

*The line was taken from a Grade-B film running at the time, *Not With My Wife You Don't.* But what a difference.

of men who pledged themselves to refuse service in Vietnam (though not necessarily refusing service elsewhere or resisting the draft in toto), and who usually announced themselves in bold advertisements in the college papers. As the spring wore on, 350 students in the New England area signed such statements, some 300 at Stanford, 391 at Cornell, 150 at Wisconsin, 126 in Milwaukee, 110 in Portland, and 257 at various medical schools, plus smaller groups at campuses from Queens to San Francisco State.

The role of SDS in all this was mixed. SDS was not the shaper and shaker of the draft-resistance movement as clearly as it had been, for example, of ghetto organizing, the initial war protests, or campus protest. Primarily this was because draft-resistance organizing was basically so intimate a process, depending upon face-to-face conversations and a sense of close-knit community in the face of imminent danger, that no national organization, not even one as devoted to decentralization as SDS, could have molded it. But it was also true that SDS, coming in late as it did, found that much of the seedwork had been done, so that where it was successful this spring was largely in those areas where it joined with existing groups or previously committed individuals. Moreover, the enthusiasm for draft resistance as expressed in Berkeley turned out not to be universally shared among the membership and less than half the chapters chose to swing themselves over from student power or complicity campaigns to draft work.* And on top of it all, as the National Office underlings had predicted in Berkeley, the Chicago office had its hands full already with all the other operations of a large and growing organization.

But it is safe to say that without the impetus from SDS as a national organization, and especially from individual SDSers working on their own with all the skills they had learned from other political work, draft resistance would never have reached the proportions that it did. After initial uncertainty as to how to follow out the Berkeley resolution, the National Office began to devote considerable energy to general support and propaganda for

*A poll reported in *The New York Times* of January 11 indicated that some 80 percent of college students "prefer to retain their student deferments" (though a like number also wanted to see other changes in the draft law). It was this self-protectionism more than anything else that stood in the way of an all-out SDS effort.

the draft movement. Calvert and Davidson both made extensive tours on campuses pushing their conviction that the time had come to move from protest to resistance and urging draft refusal as one of those ways. Calvert, particularly, who had been in on the earliest days of draft refusal and who, despite the safety of his age (then twenty-nine), had returned his draft card to his local board with a statement that he wanted to "resign from your system," was an influential force: he played a pivotal role at a wide-spectrum student conference in February that ended up with a group of organizations from the Young Americans for Freedom to the DuBois Clubs supporting a surprisingly strong antidraft position, and he added his personal testament by joining a group of SDSers at his old Iowa State campus who chained the wheels and blocked the path of a bus carrying men for induction. The NO put out two buttons with wide popularity on the campuses—NOT WITH MY LIFE YOU DON'T and one reading simply RESIST—and cranked up the printing presses to grind out five thousand copies of the Berkeley resolution and ten thousand copies of the old "Guide to Conscientious Ojection." *New Left Notes* periodically ran a column of news and suggestions called "On the Draft," and on March 27 devoted a special twelve-page issue entirely to draft resistance and "We Won't Go" strategies which eventually sold ten thousand copies. In addition to Segal, who worked out of the National Office with considerable help from Assistant National Secretary Dee Jacobsen, SDS had eight full-time draft organizers: Levi Kingston, Doug Norberg, and Mark Kleiman in California, Morty Miller in New England, Bob Pardun in Texas-Oklahoma, Mark Harris at Antioch, Tom Bell in Ithaca, and Mendy Samstein in New York (though only the first five got NO salaries, of up to $30 a week, and then only sporadically). All of this was important in helping to crystallize those organizations which had been only tentatively formed before, and in pushing the idea of draft refusal to the foreground of student politics, where it was to stand for months as the touchstone of radicalism.

And it was SDSers who were largely responsible for the most propelling antidraft action of the spring, the mass draft-card burning in New York City during the April 15 Spring Moratorium. This was planned and led by the people around the Cornell draft-resistance group, inspired by SDSer Bruce Dancis's draft-card destruction in December, who argued that "powerful resistance is now demanded: radical, illegal, unpleasant, sustained," and issued a call in early March for five hundred people to join them in a mass "burn-in." As April 15 approached, however, it seemed that no more than fifty or sixty people could be found to declare their commitment: this explicit move from protest to resistance was condemned by many "moderate" groups, denounced even by the Spring Mobilization's steering committee, and feared by many young men who were otherwise actively against the war. The Cornell group, nervous and fearful, but determined now, vowed to go ahead anyway.

Just before the mass march was to begin in the late morning of April 15, several hundred people crowded onto a large knoll in Central Park's Sheep Meadow. A few people tried to speak above the excited hubbub, there was a song or two, and then as the first hesitant matches touched the first small cards in the center of the crowd a gasp and then a cheer went up, dissolving into a steady chant of "*Re*-sist, *Re*-sist, *Re*-sist." Twenty cards were aflame, then fifty, and soon men began pushing in from the fringes holding their cards above the waiting matches, cigarette lighters, and a flaming coffee can. Before it was over more than a hundred and fifty people—no one knows for sure since no one bothered to keep close count and the FBI and New York Red Squad agents made a quick scramble for the scraps—had put their lives "on the line" for their politics.* One of them, Martin Jezer, felt, he said, that "not to have burned a draft card on April 15 would have been tantamount to living in Boston in 1773 and not to have dropped tea in Boston harbor." It was an important symbolic moment for the antidraft movement. Combined with the beginnings of the West Coast group called Resistance, which was launched this same day with a call for the mass turn-in of draft cards in the fall, this was to reverberate throughout ivied halls around the country. *New York Times* columnist Tom Wicker was not alone in calling up visions of what the future might hold:

*Among them: Bell, Dancis (with a new card), the five Cornellians who signed the original call (Jan Flora, Burton Ira Weiss, Robert Nelson, Michael Rotkin, and Timothy Larkin), New York pacifist Martin Jezer, Don Baty (whose story is told by Anthony Lukas in his *Don't Shoot—We Are Your Children!*, Random House, 1971), one Green Beret (Gary Rader), several veterans, and a number of women who burned cards of absent friends or husbands.

If the Johnson Administration had to prosecute 100,000 Americans in order to maintain its authority, its real power to pursue the Vietnamese war or any other policy would be crippled if not destroyed. It would then be faced not with dissent, but with civil disobedience on a scale amounting to revolt.

By the beginning of summer, there was no doubt that on the draft front at least, resistance had begun. According to Jeff Segal and Martin Jezer, some sixty antidraft unions had been established by June and at least two thousand men had signed "We Won't Go" statements.* Other national groups—the DuBois Clubs, the Student Mobilization Committee, the Southern Students Organizing Committee—adopted draft-resistance programs; and several local organizations—the Boston Draft Resistance Group, New England Resist, CADRE (Chicago Area Draft Resistance), the Draft Denial in New York City—had sprung up to launch successful drives on a regional level. No one knows for sure how many young men were affected, but the Justice Department announced that it had just finished prosecuting 1335 draft cases in the fiscal year ending July 1, up from 663 in the previous fiscal year, and the figure would continue to mount. By now, in Staughton Lynd's words, "draft resistance was a cutting edge or growing point for the Movement as a whole."

Student protests in the spring of 1967 were another expression of the Calvertian "struggle for one's own freedom in unity with others who share the burden of oppression." This was not new— it had been embodied in the student power drive for several months now—but the feeling that the struggle was moving to a higher stage certainly was. Jack Smith, during a long profile of SDS for the *Guardian,* wrote that "virtually the entire leadership and most SDS activists to whom this reporter spoke maintain that a broad movement can be developed . . . based on a radical rejection of American life and culture and on resistance to the demands of society." Calvert and Davidson, who between them

*This may be an underestimate. Figures given in *New Left Notes* during the spring, in the May 27 issue of the *New Republic,* and Ferber and Lynd's *The Resistance* (1971) indicate that some 2262 young men signed "We Won't Go" statements, not counting those above draft age who pledged support, and this probably does not include signers at many small local groups.

visited more than a hundred campuses that spring, were heady with the success they found in reaching the students. Davidson, describing for Smith the "Guatemala guerrilla" approach he used with students, said, "You'd be astonished at the reception this gets, when people realize that they aren't alone, that the failures and the problems they ascribed to themselves stem in large part from the society in which they live and the images of themselves they accepted from society." And Calvert even saw "an indigenous revolt"—though as yet "impotent, personalized or evidenced by apathy"—among the young, a great many of whom, he felt, were "turned off on America." SDS's job was simply to perfect this process:

> For SDS, organizing people, in one sense, is detaching them from the American reality. When we break them out of that reality, that America, they begin to see their own lives, and America, in a new way. . . . The process, really, is to allow the real person to confront the real America.

Increasingly students, like draft resisters, having done with protest and negotiation, were "confronting the real America" and putting resistance into practice. By May, in a long front-page dispatch on student radicalism, *The New York Times* could say flatly: "The spirit of resistance and direct action constitutes perhaps the major attitude in the New Left today."

Resistance at Cornell (January 20): when the local district attorney tried to confiscate copies of the student literary magazine, he was met by an angry crowd of two thousand students who sold the magazine in open defiance of his authority; and when five students were arrested, they surrounded the police car and forced the DA to give up his prisoners. Resistance at Penn State (February 10): thirty-five SDSers began a three-day sit-in at the office of the president until he agreed to answer SDS's questions about university policy with regard to releasing student organization lists to the House Internal Security Committee. Resistance at the University of Wisconsin (February 27): eleven students were arrested for disrupting the recruiting efforts of a Dow Chemical Company representative, and several hundred others sat in at the administration building until the university president agreed to post a $1200 bond out of his own pocket for the arrested students and to call a faculty meeting to reconsider the university's blanket policy of open recruiting. Resistance at Columbia (March 13): a student strike was threatened if the administration did not abide by a student referendum that had voted 1333 to 563 against giving class ranks to the Selective Service, and, under pressure, the University Council voted two to one to go along with the student wishes.* Resistance at the New School for Social Research (April 13): an antiwar strike organized by SDS succeeded in keeping some 65 percent of the thirteen thousand students from attending classes, and angry students shouted both New School President John Everett and Senator Eugene McCarthy off stage that night when the two of them tried to circumvent the strike. Resistance at conservative Los Angeles City College (May 30): four hundred students defied a college ruling and the threats of administrators

*The building of resistance to the point where a chapter can threaten a student strike is not a happenstance. The Columbia experience suggests exactly what goes into the efforts behind the ultimate headline. SDS had started agitating against class rank from the time of the first SSS exam in the spring of 1966, but had not met much encouragement. With the escalation of the war and a statement from the Columbia *College* faculty in January 1967 urging withholding of rank, the Columbia student government proposed a referendum and SDS seized upon this as a convenient educational and tactical weapon. SDS, with something over a hundred members, held daytime rallies, passed out leaflets between classes, and sent its minions (including one Mark Rudd) out canvassing every floor in every dormitory on campus. After the referendum vote was in, the students showing themselves solidly against ranking, and the administration was still mute, SDS started pushing the issue of student power in leaflets and rallies and called for a strike if the administration didn't give in. Laboriously then it created links with other campus organizations (not all of whom were comfortable bedfellows) until six other groups, mostly nonpolitical, agreed to support the demands. Student strike committees were then established in each dormitory, with liaisons (usually SDSers) to a campus strike headquarters while SDS continued to grind out leaflets, became instrumental in turning out a flimsy newspaper called *Strike News*, visited sympathetic (or potentially sympathetic) faculty and administration members, and participated in endless strategy meetings. With others in the broad-based strike committee, SDS then held daily rallies, established phone links with off-campus students, held regular dormitory-floor discussion groups, organized an impromptu financial campaign, coordinated distribution and publicity, established a pool of voluntary manpower, arranged for tables to be manned regularly throughout the campus, planned a Strike Dance to raise money, and, in the midst of it all, set up plans for an alternate school (courses on Vietnam, Columbia and the Warfare State, etc.) when the strike came. And all of this, from referendum to victory, in less than a month. (*New Left Notes*, April 24, May 1, June 12, and June 19, 1967.)

to hear Carl Davidson and student speakers talk about student power, free speech on campus, SDS organizing, and the Vietnam war—and, with unheard-of boldness, twenty-five of them afterward marched on to the deans' offices to protest the threats. Resistance at the black colleges and universities: at Howard University (March 21), students prevented SSS director Lewis Hershey from propagandizing on stage and defied the administration when it tried to crack down; at Texas State, Jackson State, and Fisk University (May), student protests led to the invasion of local police, attacks by the police on the students, and, at Texas State, the killing of one policeman, presumably from a ricochet. And resistance even in DeKalb, Illinois (February 17-19), where SDS's Midwestern Regional Conference that spring ended with a feeling, according to Bill Murphy of the Northeastern Illinois University SDS,

> . . . that we are emerging from a period of disenchantment, of near despair, of disorganization, of relative inactivity. We have entered into a new spirit centered around the themes that ran thru the conference—namely: that we in SDS—involved in the radical movement—are participating in DEAD SERIOUS BUSINESS. We must open our eyes to the fact that resistance in one area is not enough. Our resistances must be total and absolute. This must lead to a revolution unlike any other in history. It cannot be solely political; it must be all encompassing—starting from within our own hearts and proceeding outward and upward.*

*Not that resistance looked like a revolution or even a bitter battle at every campus. At Texas it took the form of "Gentle Thursday," when people were asked to "be nice and gentle to each other" for one whole day and poets were invited to recite, singers to sing, artists to draw, and strangers to embrace. As Bob Pardun, the Texas regional traveler, described it in *New Left Notes* (February 3, 1967), "When Gentle Thursday arrived, we had a balloon seller on campus and a large part of the student body sat on the grass. One of my beatnik friends was invited out for lunch by two sorority chicks. People talked, flew kites, wrote gentle things on the sidewalks, buildings and the ROTC airplane. The general repercussions were very good. We did in fact begin to make inroads between us and the rest of the student body." And if the National Office would not have thought of this exactly as resistance, the Texas administration did. SDS was called before the Committee on Student Organizations, chastised, and disciplined. It was, Pardun said, "an excellent opportunity for us to get our newer members involved in confrontation with the administration." And it was soon picked up by other, usually conservative, campuses, among them Colorado, Iowa, Kentucky, Missouri, and New Mexico.

Resistance, clearly, was on the rise. And yet, though the scale of student protests escalated, the issues, on balance, remained the same. At many campuses student-power issues (parietal rules, curriculum complaints, arbitrary administrative authority) ignited protests; SDSers at a number of campuses (notably Cornell, Illinois, Michigan, Missouri, Princeton, Queens, and even Virginia's staid Old Dominion College) turned these into clearly political struggles. On a few campuses (Colorado, Iowa State, Indiana, Michigan, Michigan State, Northwestern, Stanford, and Wisconsin), SDSers and other self-named "radical" candidates won student government presidencies and used them to raise political demands. The war continued to generate some protests as an issue by itself (especially at Columbia, Florida, San Fernando Valley State, Stanford, and Texas), usually when a local politico, an administration figure, or one of the White House apologists appeared in public to proclaim its virtues.

But by far the greatest number of protests continued to center on the issue of complicity. There were referenda and demonstrations against the draft and the still persistent practice of class ranking (Columbia, Cornell, CUNY, Howard, Iowa State, San Francisco State, Stanford); protests against secret military research and big-business interference in university affairs (Chicago, Columbia, New York University, Pennsylvania, and Stanford); and sit-ins, pickets, and disruptions of recruiters from Dow, the CIA, and the armed forces (Brown, Columbia, Cornell, Iowa, Iowa State, Missouri, Nebraska, New Paltz, Northern Illinois University, Old Dominion, Pomona, San Francisco State, Toledo, UCLA, and Wisconsin). As the role of the universities became clearer with each passing month, the extent of their intertwining with the worst of America became similarly clear. And though there was little opportunity to protest it, the complicity anger was not diminished with the revelations that many college administrators were working on behalf of the FBI to spy on and send regular reports about students who were active in political affairs. In Berkeley during this spring the admissions officer admitted that in "three or four cases in the last few months" student records were given to the FBI; at Brigham Young University the president acknowledged that he had recruited students to spy on eight professors whom he regarded as too liberal, six of whom were forced to resign; at Duke University the administration admitted to compiling dossiers on the political views and social habits of each of its students, some of which found their way into FBI hands; at the coolest of all imaginable hotbeds, New York State College at Brockport, one administrator affirmed that there were no fewer than five people on the campus "in regular contact with the FBI" and said "surveillance work is occurring on every campus in the country"; and documented evidence indicated that at least six other universities—Illinois, Indiana, Kansas, Ohio State, Michigan State, and Texas—collaborated with the FBI. All this, as many students realized, could only be the visible tip of the clandestine iceberg.*

The complicity protests were for the most part local responses to national troubles, but insofar as they had any coherent national character it was due to SDS. There was almost no attention paid by the national media—the best, albeit accidental, source for coordinating national actions—and what there was tended to treat all campus disruptions as essentially about local educational issues. It was left to *New Left Notes,* and the regional travelers and chapter activists who learned from it, to spread the word. Though the circulation was only a little over five thousand at the time, careful work by editor Cathy Wilkerson, a Swarthmore SDSer who joined the NO in December, and cooperation from various campus correspondents made it into an effective coordinator of the whys and hows of complicity protests. During the spring it printed several exposures by diligent campus sleuths of ongoing projects where universities were involved with the government: "Project Themis," a $20-million program using fifty universities (out of 171 which wanted the job) for research relating to overseas "defense missions"; the Institute for Defense Analysis, a Department of Defense offspring linking twelve major universities in a $15-million-a-year program of classified (predominantly military) research; and a network of thirty-eight universities or university-

*Those were not the only signs of repression either, simply the ones where the university was most involved. During this year Army Intelligence officers owned up to a year-long investigation of one SDSer in ROTC at Washington University, and another SDS member at Iowa was told by an FBI agent that the bureau knows "all about the stunts which SDS pulls." (*New Left Notes,* February 20 and 27, 1967.)

connected institutions working on chemical and biological warfare. In addition, the paper gave steady coverage to complicity protests, giving the details of organization and follow-through, the assessments of victory, and, perhaps most important, the honest confessions of defeat, with the addenda of how to do better next time.

The unquestionable escalation in campus protests in the early months of 1967 was aided considerably by the reports by Harrison Salisbury of massive U.S. bombing of civilian targets in North Vietnam and the scalawaggery of the United States Congress in refusing to seat the duly-elected Harlem Representative, Adam Clayton Powell. But nothing shook the student world so much as the exposure of the National Student Association. On February 13, in advance of a story it was running on the NSA, *Ramparts* magazine took a full-page ad in several major papers to declare that it had uncovered information that NSA was funded by the Central Intelligence Agency. Ever since 1952, it seems—though more probably even since NSA's founding in 1948—the CIA had been paying substantial portions of the NSA budget, controlling its top positions, influencing its policies, recruiting its members into the spy business, and using the organization to promote its Cold War policies both within the country and in student affairs abroad. The handsome NSA building in Washington, the $500,000-or-so yearly budget, the delegations to this or that youth festival, the annual meetings—all had been provided by the CIA, and all with the knowledge and cooperation of most of the students who had been top NSA officials.

To most students, the news was a penetrating shock. Those who had dealt with NSA in any proximity, of course, had long suspected "funny money" somewhere—Tom Hayden, for example, knew that things weren't entirely above board when a lengthy civil-rights memorandum which NSA had hired him to write in 1961 somehow just never got printed; both Paul Booth and Paul Potter (NSA vice president in 1961–62, but never let in on the big secret) felt something was fishy when they were on the target end of mysteriously spontaneous redbaiting campaigns by NSA officials; and as SDS began to grow in the mid-sixties, a number of people starving their way through the NO had begun to wonder how an organization without even a campus constituency (NSA represents official student governments, not students) could keep going for so long, so lavishly. But most students had accepted the myth that NSA was pure and idealistic and believed that an American government would never stoop so low as to manipulate some of its own students to deceive the rest, and for them the revelations hit with special force.

SDS chapters were quick to circulate the news and hold meetings on its implications, often tying it in with past or impending visits from CIA recruiters. Nick Egleson, in announcing to the press SDS's disaffiliation from another CIA student front, the United States Youth Council (of which it had been a nominal member but was a year and a half in arrears in its dues), attacked CIA activities as "just one facet of a larger problem: the involvement of the government and the military in all aspects of American educational life."

> Not only must the CIA be uprooted from student organizations; the time has come to separate education from the military, learning from the processes of government. Secret military research in our universities not only compromises the integrity of our scientists and scholars, but also perverts the real education tasks of those institutions.

Ironically, another "moderate" student organization, the Campus Americans for Democratic Action, was going through its own troubles just at the same time. CADA, under chairman Claudia Dreifus (an SDSer at NYU in the early days), had split from the parent ADA over the latter's centrist and stuffy ways, but found itself isolated and crushed in the resulting melee. In February it disbanded. More ironically still, CADA and the NSA had been hatching grand plans for a "moderate left" national student organization that would rival and, they hoped, supplant SDS. With those two organizations in shambles, SDS, scruffy and long-haired though it may have been, seemed a white knight by comparison.

In the spring of 1967 the Progressive Labor Party suffered a serious lesion as a result of a dispute over the "Road to Revolution II" statement adopted the preceding fall and published in the February-March issue of its magazine, *PL*. Several PL groups on the West Coast, where the party had acquired an early strength among older leftists dissatisfied with the Communist Party, objected to both the manner by which it had been adopted and several key points it made. The statement, they pointed out, had not been fully debated within the party, had been published without the requisite "prior discussion" with local party groups, and had been approved by the party's National Committee only after it had appeared; one National Committee member who had expressed disapproval had been suspended. More serious than that, the statement's attacks on the "revisionist" Vietnamese put the party in opposition to one of the most dynamic forces for revolutionary change in the world and in isolation from virtually every other Marxist-Leninist party in existence. The Washington State PL group independently published newsletters in opposition to the statement, whereupon its chairman, Clayton Van Lydegraf, was expelled from the party by the New York leaders, and he left, taking several people out with him; the California PL group also raised objections, and some fifteen to twenty of its members were subsequently expelled or chose to disaffiliate. At the same time a group of PLers in Canada, many in the Vancouver area, began complaining about the leadership of Milt Rosen—one of them, Jack Scott, was suspicious about his "apparently unlimited source of funds" from Georgia land and Texas oil (this last a reference to Albert Maher)—and about what they regarded as the high-handed dealings of Phil Taylor, one of Rosen's chief operatives in Canada.

The result of this was more than just another split in an Old Left already splintered into an array of toothpicks. It meant that PL lost much of its heretofore supportive Western base—and, with it, many (if not most) of its nonstudent, nonintellectual, working-class and trade-union members, the very kinds of people it declared itself to be of and for. Party membership was thereby narrowed primarily to the group in and around New York, which had always been the intellectual center of the party, and to people who were PLers first and workers (because the party told them to get working-class jobs) second.

This, in turn, meant that PL had to search elsewhere for new support, and it saw in the burgeoning and increasingly militant student movement a natural—and for many, both cadres and leaders, a congenial—source of recruits. Jeff Gordon, in an article in the February-March *PL*, developed the idea, still new in PL circles, of a worker-student *alliance* as a means of tapping this source. "The student and intellectual movement," he wrote, "is simmering" but "activists on campus are turning inward, moving to secondary and often esoteric issues or doing nothing at all." The way to enlist students, he argued, was to get them to join with the all-powerful working class so that they will feel they have a good chance to win at least in the long run." This worker-student alliance, he felt, should engage in a variety of actions including support for striking workers, support for the demands of campus workers, and involvement of workers in antiwar actions. Thus was born a PL strategy, the worker-student alliance, that was to have important ramifications for SDS in the coming years.

Three months later, at the start of the 1967 summer vacations, PL announced another program to enlist students: a "Vietnam Work-In." This would be an effort to enroll students in summer jobs on assembly lines and in the shops, wherever the true working class might be found, and have them talk to their fellow workers about the war. "Thousands of students," PL announced somewhat optimistically, would be organized "to bring the ideas, the politics and the urgency of the anti-Vietnam war movement, among the workers on their jobs."

The most natural source of students for programs such as these, and for eventual recruitment into the party, was of course SDS. From this spring on PL redoubled its efforts to push its politics in and recruit its membership from the ranks of SDS.

The idea of a worker-student alliance was first put to the student organization at the April National Council meeting in Cambridge, a PL stronghold, but since *New Left Notes* had not found space to print the proposal beforehand and since many SDSers were innately suspicious of any new scheme coming from the PLers, no action was taken on it. It was not until the May 1 *New Left Notes* that SDSers at large learned about the idea. Al Greene, an SDS member, wrote that "the potential which exists for a radical worker-student alliance is very much apparent," and urged the official adoption of a policy by which SDS chapters (which he called "locals," adopting PL terminology) would support local strikes, unionize unrepresented employees, discuss the war and American politics among workers, and "cultivate at least the seeds of a real alliance between working people . . . and radical students." There was no identification of Greene as a member of PL or any mention of the worker-student alliance as a PL strategy.

The work-in proposal made its appearance four weeks later, in the May 29 *New Left Notes*. A page-one article, sounding for all the world like a Milt Rosen polemic, argued that

> . . . conscious and directed working-class opposition to the war is the most powerful anti-war movement imaginable. To be with, to move and move with American workers, we've got to work with them. To bring anti-war, anti-racism, and radical ideas to the workers we've got to know what moves them, what their attitudes really are; we've got to know where they live. This can best be done by sharing their work, their on the job problems.

It urged every SDSer to "go out and get a job" for the summer, "preferably in large industries or places employing many area residents." And it even, for perhaps the first time in serious SDS discourse, threw in a (not quite apposite) quotation from Lenin: "There can be no revolutionary practice without revolutionary theory." Of the twelve signers, all designated as SDSers, only three were listed as being members of PL; none of the ten regional work-in coordinators whom SDSers were asked to contact was identified as a party member.

Meanwhile, the general antiwar movement in the land continued to grow. Plans for the newest series of marches, on April 15 in New York and San Francisco, were laid by the largest popular-front organization to date, the Spring Mobilization Committee to End the War in Vietnam, which had grown out of the ashes of the National Coordinating Committee in the spring and summer of 1966. SDS, as usual, despite repeated blandishments, officially said it would have nothing to do with the organization, treating it with the same sympathetic scorn it had shown its predecessor: as ERAPer Mike James told the Mobilization high command, SDS policy was "Don't mobilize, organize." But in the early months of 1967, as the war in Vietnam escalated, American deaths approached the 9000 mark, and President Johnson seemed hell-bent on the leveling of North Vietnam, sentiment on many campuses shifted toward support. Debate riffled the pages of *New Left Notes* for some weeks, the "no-more-parades" people arguing against the "telling-truth-to-power" advocates, but slowly it became clear that most of the chapters were caught up in the mobilization idea, and the April National Council, meeting just two weeks before the marches, finally lent its grudging support.

On one level, the Mobilization was a singular success. Some 300,000 people gathered in New York and San Francisco, Martin Luther King made a dramatic speech appealing to the Administration to "save our national honor," and the whole thing, according to the organizers, represented "the largest demonstration of any kind ever held in the history of the U.S. for any reason." Many of those who marched did so under SDS banners, providing the SDS leadership with a bitter sense of its political distance from the chapter constituency and reinforcing Calvert's complaint that "in effect we have been used to make other people's political points and to help build others' organizations."

But on another level, the Mobilization marked for many the end of trying to change national policies through peaceful protest; and this time it was not only the SDS veterans who spoke of the futility of marches, but many of the younger recruits as well. To them it was clear that this mobilization, despite its size and now generally favorable press coverage, was as fruitless as the previous ones, a conviction which the subsequent increases in American troops and draft inductions did nothing to dispel. In the words of Dotson Rader, a Columbia SDSer who suffered the additional ignominy of getting his head beaten by New York City cops during the Mobilization:

> The meaninglessness of non-violent, "democratic" methods was becoming clear to us in the spring of 1967. The Civil Rights Movement was dead. Pacifism was dead. Some Leftists—the Trotskyites, Maoists, radical socialists, anarchists, some of the radicals in SDS, Stokely Carmichael, Rap Brown, Tom Hayden—knew it early. But it took the rest of us a while to give up the sweet life of the democratic Left for revolt.

"Revolt"—is that too strong a word? Perhaps, but not by much. For many others wrestled that spring with the feeling that there was something more, something stronger, that needed to be done, were led to their first real contemplation of what a revolt, a *revolution*—how odd it sounded, how dissynchronous, yet . . . —would mean. Now for the first time the people around SDS began toying with the idea of revolution. It was not seen in terms of students' taking to the hills or (in spite of a growing fad for Che

Guevara posters) of armed guerrilla warfare; it was something only tentative and experimental, a faint nibble at the forbidden fruit; and it was for the most part still meant jocularly, as in such *New Left Notes* lines as "We can't fight the revolution on an empty stomach," or "If you believe in the revolution, pay your dues." But it signaled a willingness, on the part of the most active SDSers at least, to confront the idea of a sweeping and total change in the institutions of America brought about through a conjunction of the forces for resistance and the attitudes of the alienated counter-culture. This is what Calvert meant when he spoke of building a "revolutionary consciousness."

The problem, as those of the SDS leadership saw it, was how to move more people from personal action to political commitment, how to raise the level of those who were so obviously potential recruits—the draft resister, the campus demonstrator, the antiwar marcher—to that of "revolutionary consciousness." Davidson put it simply: "We need to move from protest to resistance; to dig in for the long haul; to become full-time, radical, sustained, relevant. In short, we need to make a revolution. But again, how do we go about it?"

SDS came up with two answers that spring.

The first, the simplest, was as old as Haber's first memo to the LID: internal education. Only this time it was to have a new name, not noticeably chosen for its greater felicity: "institutes for teacher-organizers."

The idea of the "T-O institutes," as they became known, was a queer mixture of the familiar graduate-school seminar, the ERAP communal-living projects, and the political "cadre schools" that Old Left groups like the Communist Party used to run during the summers. SDS was to set up three summer-long institutes, in Chicago, Boston, and Los Angeles, where potential T-Os would live together, take seminars in subjects like political theory, community organizing, and Marxian economics, hold regular "round-table" sessions on the student movement and the state of American politics, and undertake short-term "field projects" with local students in summer jobs or attending school. At the end of the summer, it was hoped, there would be at least thirty regional travelers who would be equipped to go around to existing

chapters to push the political level of SDSers toward a revolutionary consciousness.

The idea was sensible enough, but somehow SDS and internal
education never could mix well. The National Office started the
project on the assumption that it could use the Radical Education
Project to run its seminars, and came in for a rude shock when
REP answered that it hadn't been a part of SDS since its independent incorporation a year ago and in any case had no intention of
giving up its independent research work to become a minor
figment in an SDS dream. Then the NO tried to raise $20,000 to
launch the projects, even putting out a small promotional brochure (showing pictures of the current campus travelers and laud-
ing them as "the backbone of the student movement"), without
getting so much as a nibble from the charitable foundations. Ultimately SDS was forced to set up its own education project and dip
into its own coffers for most of the money. But it went ahead,
selected the T-O trainees, enlisted some of its most experienced
people as project directors,* and on June 16, the T-O institutes
began.

The second answer that SDS came to was another old one,
the "need for an ideology." Now in truth SDS had never lacked
an ideology, and for most of its early life *The Port Huron Statement* and *America and the New Era* enunciated it; moreover, each
of its previous ventures—civil rights, university reform, ERAP,
Vietnam protest, the draft, student syndicalism—had been accompanied by comprehensive and radical theories, proto-ideologies
really, no matter what the critics said. But at this stage something
different and even more comprehensive was wanted, some unified
way of talking about the war, the military machine, imperialism,
complicity, university governance, corporate liberalism, and the
"postscarcity" economy, all in such a way as to develop that
"revolutionary consciousness."

There were a number of entries in the ideological lists in the
spring of 1967. Carl Oglesby's book, *Containment and Change*
(distributed in large numbers by the NO), had just been published
and circulated widely among SDS's theoretical types; its careful

*Egleson, Potter, and Hal Benenson in Boston; Pardun, Adams, and Jacobsen
in Chicago; Davidson and Norberg in Los Angeles.

and detailed construction of the methods of American imperialism offered the scaffolding of an original ideological analysis. A new quarterly, *Radical America,* was begun by Paul Buhle and other SDSers, the only theoretical journal of the American New Left now that *Studies on the Left* had disintegrated. And *New Left Notes* itself offered a monthly section called "Praxis" to present what Cathy Wilkerson called "the large number of longer, more 'theoretical' articles which come in" and to satisfy "the wide-felt need for a more current analysis."

But the most successful ideological contestant was a concept called "the new working class," which SDS this spring seized upon as the theoretical foundation for its new revolutionary ideology. The idea of the new working class was originally presented to SDS by three students at the New School for Social Research, Bob Gottlieb, Gerry Tenney, and Dave Gilbert, and it formed part of a long paper which they delivered to the Princeton REP conference, called, with conscious geographical parody, "The Port Authority Statement."* The concept, though presented at times in the most excruciating jargon and accompanied by self-conscious charts and tables and footnotes, was essentially simple. The new working class, unlike the traditional working class, is made up of those people with "technical, clerical, and professional jobs that require educational backgrounds" and of those in the schools and universities who provide them with those backgrounds. The new class "lies at the very hub of production" and is crucial for the operation of a highly industrialized, technocratic, computerized, and sophisticated society. Students, "in that they will by and large constitute this new working class, are becoming the most structurally relevant and necessary components of the productive processes of modern American capitalism"; they are, therefore, increasingly important "for the maintenance and stability of American society" and "socially necessary

*To be sure the concept was not original with SDS: it had been expressed in an early form by C. Wright Mills and, still more attenuated, by *The Port Huron Statement;* it had taken another form in Milovan Djilas and, following him, David Bazelon; and it found still later forms in such European Marxists as André Gorz, Herbert Marcuse, and Serge Mallet, the latter two of whom had dissected and debated it in the heavy pages of the *International Socialist Journal* the previous spring and summer. But it was SDS who introduced it to the broad American left.

for the functioning of the economic system." If the members of the new working class can recognize "their structural, technical role in maintaining, developing and rationalizing American capitalism," they will understand "their own power as a force for social change"—and in this process students can form the vanguard when they "begin to articulate demands of control and participation," first at the university and then on the job. This is what makes the whole movement toward student protest so important, important beyond the comparatively small numbers involved, for "the organizing of students on the campus around the questions of student control, the draft, and the universities' servicing of the military can develop a radical consciousness concerning the role and nature of their future work positions."

Here, in theoretical form, with the fillip of a class analysis, was an ideological formulation of considerable power. It explained why the Selective Service was forcing students into nonmilitary jobs valuable for "the national interest," it supported Davidson's idea of student power being used to transform the society by transforming the university, and it justified Calvert's instinct that students were right in operating out of the desire for their own freedom. It accounted for the new militance being shown by teachers, social workers, and hospital employees, for the growing support of such adult groups as REP and a Movement for a Democratic Society and a new "Radicals in the Professions" organization, and for the increasing numbers of people from the so-called middle class now to be found in the antiwar marches. Above all, it meshed with the mood of SDS just then, justifying the past and programing the future, and it did so in a way that any SDSer on any campus could grasp, and be led on to a revolutionary consciousness. It did, in short, everything a good ideological concept should do.

And Greg Calvert knew it instantly. After hearing the paper at the Princeton conference he stayed up much of the night to work it into his speech the next day. It was, he said, "a powerful tool":

It enables us to understand the special role of students in relation to the present structure of industrial capitalism. Students are the "trainees" for the new working class and the factory-like multiversities are the institutions which prepare them for their slots in the bureaucratic machinery of corporate capitalism. We must stop apologizing for being students or for organizing students. Students are in fact a key group in the creation of the productive forces of this super-technological capitalism. We have organized them out of their own alienation from the multiversity and have raised the demand for "student control." That is important: because that is precisely the demand that the new working class must raise when it is functioning as the new working class in the economic system. It is that demand which the system cannot fulfill and survive as it is. That is why it is potentially a real revolutionary demand in a way that demands for higher wages can never be.

. . . We can see that it was a mistake to assume that the only radical role which students could play would be as organizers of other classes.

Liberals operate out of other people's oppression; the radical operates out of his own.

During the quite considerable turmoils of this spring, the National Office in Chicago was operating with surprising energy and perhaps with more efficiency than it had ever shown before.

The three top national officers were especially diligent in their campus travels, the NO estimating at the end of the school year that they had "visited approximately 150 chapters and filled almost 200 speaking engagements." A nascent film library had sent out its five films for more than a hundred showings, some hundred thousand pamphlets and papers were printed and mailed, orders for three thousand bumper stickers, eight thousand posters, and ten thousand buttons were filled, and more than six thousand individual letters of organizational business were sent out. *New Left Notes,* after someone in the NO figured out the postal regulations, now actually got sent out the same week it was printed, and during the spring some 120,000 individual newspapers were addressed and mailed. The office itself, expanded now to the third floor of the Rossen building, had achieved a kind of efficient chaos; along one wall a five-shelf bookcase was stuffed with pamphlets and printed forms, neatly stacked and labeled; a twenty-eight-drawer file cabinet was filled with cards attempting to keep memberships and dues payments in reasonable order; the floors were swept, occasionally, and the random pop bottles, coffee containers, crumpled papers, and old lunch bags were removed with some periodicity.

Officially, by the end of June, SDS had 6371 national members, although of that number only 875 had paid their second-term dues—"the rest," NO staffer Jim Fite complained, "seem to think that the only thing they have to do is pay their dues once and then forget it. That is a lot of bullshit." But in addition there were perhaps five times that many people who counted themselves members, according to Davidson and Egleson after an extensive tour of the campuses. Davidson wrote:

> According to our modest, if not conservative, estimates, about 30,-
> 000 young Americans consider themselves members of SDS chap-
> ters. [This] is remarkable in two ways. First, we are much larger
> than we thought we were. Second, starting from almost zero, we
> have achieved that number in 7 years; we have grown *tenfold* in only
> 2 years.

The question of the exact number of chapters was somewhat murky, since chapters would fold as their activists graduated without letting anyone know, or they would sprout up with equal anonymity ("Hardly a week goes by," Davidson reported, "that the National Office doesn't discover an active SDS chapter somewhere that no one knew existed").* But after careful tabulation in December 1966, the NO figured they had exactly 227 chapters starting the new year, down from the figure of 265 it had been using; in the course of the spring 20 new or revivified chapters joined,† making a total of 247 by the end of the school year. Membership was still concentrated in New York, Massachusetts, Wisconsin, Michigan, Illinois, and California.

The bedrock problem of the NO during the spring was the

---

*A measure of the problem is suggested by Colorado. According to Tom Cleaver, the unofficial regional traveler there, there were five SDS chapters around the state as of February 1967, though only two of them, Colorado State University and Colorado University, were recognized by the NO. But the NO lists as of October 1966 show only one chapter, at Denver University, and only one chapter was added from the state in the spring, at Colorado State College. So, depending on who's reckoning, there were either four full-fledged chapters, none, two, or possibly five.

†Brooklyn Movement for a Democratic Society, California (Riverside), Colgate, Colorado State College, Columbia MDS, University of Denver, Fort Worth At-large, Loyola of Chicago, University of Maine, Mount Prospect College, New York (Albany), Orange (California) High School, Rutgers, Shimer College, Skid Row At-large (this was the NO's own chapter), Texas Tech, Wagner, Westside Chicago At-large, West Virginia, Wisconsin (Eau Claire).

old one, money. Income (mostly contributions) averaged a little over $100 a day at the beginning of the year, and rose somewhat during the spring as a result of the general upsurge in political activity and the three-part series in the *Guardian*. But it simply wasn't enough: by April SDS was more than $7000 in debt, with only the dubious consolation that it was now more in debt than the entire annual income of the organization had been in the early years. It seemed hardly inappropriate for one NAC report to read, "Current Financial Status: The grim financial situation was again reviewed; prayers were offered, beads rubbed, and a young white mouse (who had fortuitously wandered into the room) was offered as a sacrifice to the Gods of the liberal corporate establishment," or for Dee Jacobsen later to report that NO staffers sat around trying to figure out how to pilfer the coffers of the Brink's depository in East Chicago.

The April National Council meeting decided that the time had come for escalation. It voted to raise SDS dues to $5.00 forthwith, to impose an immediate chapter tax of $5.00 a head payable by June 1, to ask all SDS members with jobs to contribute 10 percent of their incomes over $4000 to the national coffers, and to go on a "binge" to raise $25,000 by September. Now the effect of this was really more ethereal than real—by the beginning of May only Columbia, Harvard, and Wisconsin had paid their chapter taxes, and there were no signs of any others rushing forward —but it apparently convinced the NO: in May it plunked down $2500 toward a $7000 justifier machine for printing *New Left Notes*, bought $4000 worth of composition equipment, and added a press, a camera, and a darkroom. As if that weren't enough, the NAC then decided to buy a *house* (apparently from their landlord, John Rossen), at the "extremely low" price of $11,500—with visions, in Jacobsen's words, that it would "provide enough space for two staff apartments (the rent from which will pay for the property in 10 years), an education center with a library and two offices, a conference and literature production room, a small apartment for teacher-organizers and visiting chapter people, a large storage room, and a cellar for housing a wine press and political prisoners." Small wonder, then, that by July SDS was $16,499 in debt. It was injury added to insult when one of the NO staffers came down with infectious hepatitis, the entire staff had to be given special serum shots, and the Chicago Health Department informed them that they'd have to fork out $100 to get treated since most of the serum, normally given free, had been sent off to Vietnam.

But, withal, the stalwarts of SDS did not lose their sense of humor. In April someone came across a cartoon showing dozens of little children, happy smiles on their faces, dashing out of the gates of a school, while six big angry guards with flailing nets raced after them in fruitless pursuit. By instant and common agreement, the cartoon was made part of the official letterhead on SDS stationery.

18

SUMMER 1967

The summer of 1967. It was the best of times: "For white radicals it was a time of politics of affirmation rather than a politics of guilt" (Staughton Lynd); it was the worst of times: "To be white and a radical in America this summer is to see horror and feel impotence" (Andrew Kopkind). It was the epoch of belief: "They were . . . sustained by the satisfactions they derived from their work, from their associations with friends in it, and from the deep, if usually unstated, conviction that what they were doing was politically and ethically important" (Kenneth Keniston); it was the epoch of incredulity: "It was a tough summer. . . . We had no idea of what to do with our lives" (Frank Bardacke). It was the summer of hope: "The new tone . . . is one of victory. A little premature perhaps, but inevitable victory nonetheless. And the beauty of it all is that it's happening everywhere" (Larry Freudiger); it was the summer of despair: "I am very pessimistic about the prospects of change, even of meaningful reforms, in this country. . . . I think violence is necessary, and it frightens me" (Michael Zweig).

It was not, one should hasten to add, really the beginning of a revolution, or at least not perceptibly so, but in many ways it was not so far from it. The American political scene, the new world of the youth, was a maelstrom of activity, swirling with the flotsam of every conceivable emotion and idea.

There was the emergence of the hippie movement into a

powerful and pullulating force in America. The pinnacles were in Haight-Ashbury in San Francisco and the Village byways in New York, but everywhere in between was the evidence of the new culture: bell-bottoms, workclothes, Army jackets, flowers, beads; guitars, theramins, amplifiers, transistors, hi-fis, light shows; runaways, dropouts, teeny-boppers, Yippies, Diggers, provos, groupies; marijuana, amphetamines, acid, Leary; be-ins, love-ins, camp-outs, orgies, pot parties, communes, panhandling; underground papers, records, psychedelic posters, buttons. A counterculture had hit America, for the first time in at least forty years, and it was real enough for the sociologists to study it, for the media to promulgate it, for the businessmen to make money off it, for the youth, a large segment of the youth, to live it.

There was Vietnam Summer, the left-liberal bell-ringing campaign that sent upwards of 20,000 people out into the streets to get community people, mostly from the middle class, actively behind the antiwar movement. Of liberal origins and of liberal sponsorship—primarily the Martin Luther King entourage and Spring Mobilization types (neither of whom advocated immediate withdrawal yet), probably with funding from Robert Kennedy— it was immediately suspect among most SDSers; Lief Johnson, a New York City SDSer, said it all in *New Left Notes:*

> Vietnam Summer is a liberal protest. It was initiated by top liberals, it acts upon liberal assumptions, it proceeds on liberal undemocratic methods of organization and leadership. The underlying purpose of this liberal strategy is to recapture leadership of the peace and civil rights movement, to blunt the awakening of our radical, anti-liberal identity, and finally to lay the groundwork for leading us into a coalitionist liberal-progressive third party movement.

But it was also broad enough, short enough, and single-issued enough to scoop up a whole fishnet of people, and among them were many SDSers: those, like Oglesby and Potter, who served on its steering committee; those like Lee Webb, who became its executive director, and John Maher and Marilyn Salzman (later married to Lee Webb), who served in its national office; and those, like the people in SDS's Niagara region, who became the bulwarks of the local operation.*

There was the revolt of the urban blacks, breaking out most noticeably in Newark and Detroit that summer, but with fulgurations in no fewer than fifty-seven other Northern ghettos as well. It was on a scale that had not been seen since the Watts rebellion of 1965, and the police and National Guard response was on a level that had not been seen anywhere in the sixties: at least twenty-four blacks were killed in Newark, forty-three in Detroit, and ten more in other scattered cities. One man who closely observed the Newark uprising wrote:

> This is not a time for radical illusions about "revolution." . . . But the actions of white America toward the ghetto are showing black people, especially the young, that they must prepare to fight back. The conditions slowly are being created for an American form of guerrilla warfare based in the slums. The riot represents a signal of this fundamental change.

That was Tom Hayden, who left Newark after that summer and in the face of that change, his dream of the interracial movement of the poor, even of a black community union, having altered considerably during the three years he worked among the black people of that city. But his sense of reality was still intact.

There was the "T-O" experiment which SDS bravely went ahead with, despite impoverishment, and it turned out to be remarkably successful—though for none of the expected reasons. The Los Angeles group disintegrated after a few weeks, the Chicago people spent more time worrying about harassment from the police than Marxist seminars, and the Boston collective went about its organizing work without much concern for the grand

---

*There would, in fact, have been no Vietnam Summer if there had been no SDS. The entire climate of opinion for such an operation was created by SDS's continued opposition to the war; the organizational style was copied from SDS (a "National Office," worklists, WATS lines, decentralized coordination); national leaders were drawn mostly from the SDS old guard ("I still considered myself SDS," Webb has said in an interview with the author) and local leaders from SDS chapters ("I hired a whole lot of SDS people so they could build the regions where they worked"); and the very idea itself is directly traceable to Tom Hayden, who had proposed something very much of this kind—for the summer of 1965.

plan of it all. But when it was over, several dozen people had gone through a communal experience that left its mark, and somehow their casual work for the Movement in the process committed them to the cause. The cadre-building notion suffered from the hippie-summer atmosphere—including a new indulgence in drugs, hallucinogenic and otherwise—so the seminars were seldom held, the books went unread, and the elaborate training never took place. Still, in the words of one California recruit, previously a hippie dropout for whom " 'Movement people' were always a bummer," the T-O experience taught something: "You become serious about the Movement if you're serious about your life, and the Movement is a healthy meaningful thing."

There was a spasmodic spate of conferences, a succession of week-long answers to where the left, or American politics, or Movement veterans, should go next. First there was the "Back-to-the-Drawing-Boards" conference organized by SDS old guarders in June, at which all attempts to forge a new political force were frustrated by a do-your-own-thing hippiness symbolized by the presence there of Abbie Hoffman and the "anarchist" Diggers from New York. Then came the Radicals in the Professions Conference, in Ann Arbor in July, drawing several hundred Movement alumni who were trying to solve the problem of how to hold down a job and be a radical without doing violence to either. Then there was the National Student Association meeting at the University of Maryland, where most NSAers went about blithely as if the CIA had never existed, and where a counter-conference organized by SDS served to challenge but not, as planned, dissolve the NSA forever. Last came the ballyhooed convention of the National Conference for New Politics in Chicago, which disintegrated into a bitter black-white feud, failed to inspire either side with its idea of middle-class electoral action, and soon thereafter brought down the whole NCNP organization around it.

There was, in the middle of all this, increased surveillance and harassment from the punitive branches of government, from the national level to the local, marking the beginning of the Establishment's stepped-up campaign of repression. Among the items: on June 20, sixteen blacks, said to be members of a Revolutionary Action Movement, were arrested in New York with the story that they were planning assassinations; on June 23, Los Angeles police violently broke up an antiwar demonstration cosponsored by SDS, arrested fifty-one and sent forty to the hospital; on June 26, SNCC chairman H. Rap Brown was arrested for incitement to riot; in July, President Johnson told city and state officials confronted with violence "not to analyze but end the disorder"; in the same month, on orders from Johnson and other high Administration officials, the Army's secret surveillance net, the Continental United States Intelligence, stepped up its spying operations on all dissident political groups, and made its information known to the FBI and local police and Red Squad officials; throughout the summer local police engaged in petty harassment of SDS groups in Norman, Oklahoma, Dallas, Los Angeles, and New York City; and in Chicago the National Office suffered open daily surveillance, arbitrary arrests of at least ten NO staffers for simply driving to the office (located in a black ghetto area), and the expenditure of more than $1000 for bond posting. Nothing on this scale had been seen since the darkest days of the McCarthy era.

And there was draft-resistance organizing, free universities, demonstrations against Johnson, working with California farm laborers, work-ins and strike supports, picketing and marches and sit-ins. REP and NACLA had summer programs for research on complicity, big business, and imperialism. ERAP was in the last summer of ghetto programs in Newark, Cleveland, Chicago, and Minneapolis. A "Revolutionary Contingent" was formed in New York to enlist young Americans to fight in guerrilla revolutions in Guatemala, Colombia, and Venezuela. A Southern Labor Action Movement was formed by SSOC to enlist young Southerners to start wildcat strikes and labor radicalizing in the South. Abbie Hoffman and a group of proto-Yippies showered dollar bills on the Stock Exchange in New York. Mario Savio and other Free Speech Movement activists went with much fanfare into jail in California on four-month sentences stemming from the 1964 demonstrations. Liberation News Service was established to provide Movement news to underground papers, and an Underground Press Service was begun to coordinate the twenty or so existing underground— or, more properly, counterculture—newspapers. In Sweden there was a summer-long tribunal, led by Bertrand Russell (and including SDS's own Carl Oglesby), to assess U.S. war crimes in Vietnam; and in Moscow there was one conference (attended by Jeff

Shero) to celebrate the fiftieth anniversary of the Bolshevik Revolution, while in Havana there was another to plan a new one for
the Third World.

That was the maelstrom of the summer of 1967: the explosion
of a real American left, of a true if youthful counterculture, onto
the American consciousness, unlike anything seen for thirty years
at least, and more probably for sixty.

At the core of it all was a new generation of Americans, the
youth of the sixties, and with the summer came the books, reports,
articles, and academic studies to try to explain them to a troubled
land.

Time magazine began it all by citing the new generation as
its "Man of the Year," proclaiming that "this is not just a new
generation, but a new kind of generation," and going on to determine that "today's youth appears more deeply committed to the
fundamental Western ethos—decency, tolerance, brotherhood—
than almost any generation since the age of chivalry." The *Nation,*
with an issue devoted to the class of 1967, took an almost antithetical tack, finding the young obsessed with immediate gratification,
dominated by emotions ("They often seem to throb rather than
think": Wallace Stegner) and mired in disillusionment ("The belief of the new generation that everything is SHIT": Karl Shapiro).
Erik Erikson, in that summer's issue of *Daedalus,* argued that
"more than any young generation before and with less reliance on
a meaningful choice of traditional world images, the youth of
today is forced to ask what is *universally relevant* in human life
in this technological age at this junction of history." Christopher
Jencks and David Riesman, in Columbia University's *Teachers
College Record* at the same time said that, "looking at undergraduate sub-cultures in historical perspective, we are inclined to
predict that the dissident minority will continue to grow." And to
cap it all, Paul Goodman, in *Playboy,* examined the souls of
radical students and catalogued

> . . . their solidarity based on community rather than ideology, their
> style of direct and frank confrontation, their democratic inclusive-
> ness and aristocratic carelessness of status, caste or getting ahead,
> their selectivity of the affluent standard of living, their effort to be

authentic and committed to their causes rather than merely belonging, their determination to have a say and their refusal to be processed as standard items, their extreme distrust of top-down direction, their disposition to anarchist organization and direct action, their disillusion with the system of institutions, and their belief that they can carry on major social functions in improvised parallel enterprises.

On a more scholarly level, there also appeared a series of works on student activists. A special issue of the *Journal of Social Issues* appeared in July devoted to "Student Activism and the Decade of Protest," the first such academic attention given to the New Left; in Boston, Yale psychologist Kenneth Keniston spent the summer interviewing the Vietnam Summer office people in depth, for his *Young Radicals;* and a detailed report on campus activism, by Joseph Katz of the Stanford Institute for the Study of Human Problems, was published by no less than the U.S. Office of Education. From these and other sources there began to emerge a rough picture of the activist of 1967.

The academic evidence painted a flattering—perhaps overly flattering—picture of the New Left. The activists were found to be brighter than average, usually academically superior, the best performers in high school, high in verbal (though not in mathematical) skills, and normally attracted to the best colleges and universities. They were seen to be psychologically "healthy," by whatever laboratory tests used to determine such things: high in self-esteem and a sense of autonomy, self-confident and self-expressive, socially mature, flexible, tolerant, and far better adjusted than their conservative colleagues or much of the nonactivist middle; "activism," reported one psychologist that year, "is, presently, a generally healthy aspect of the process of maturation." They were found to be from the "better" homes, predominantly from families with above-average income, education, and occupational status, where one or both of the parents were in the professions, and where parental values, overwhelmingly liberal and permissive, were emulated and extended rather than resisted and rejected. (So much for the generation gap.) They were judged decidedly moralistic, highly concerned with the right-or-wrong consequences of individual acts (and ready to condemn others—presidents and administrators not excepted—for transgressing them), though their moral codes were often at odds with those pronounced by society and they had very little concern for conventions about sex, drugs, marriage, and the like. And they were grouped in large communities where they numbered between 5 and 13 percent of the student bodies, thus being able to achieve a certain social cohesion and to exert a clear political influence (especially in a country where it is reckoned that no more than 1 or 2 percent of the adult population is politically active).

The activists, in short, the young men and women in the ranks of the campus protests, the antiwar marches, the draft-card burnings, and the SDS chapters, were found upon examination to be of the kind that America usually regards as its best. They were, moreover, precisely those that the nation depends upon for the propagation and development of its values, its culture, its traditions, its ideas—i.e., the intelligentsia. Whatever one might think of them, it seemed clear that they mattered.

What, then, of SDS in all of this? Where did it stand? What had it become? The summer of 1967 is a particularly good time to assess the organization, for it stood at one of its clearest points: suspended now between reform and revolution, between personal protest and political, between action and ideology, between local strength and national promise. And it is appropriate to examine a body in suspension.

The figures are easiest: a national membership of 6400, a total membership of perhaps 30,000, an annual budget of at least $87,-000 a year, a formal presence on 250 campuses (and influence on many more), eight regional travelers, off-campus projects in six major cities, and an established national office with a dozen or so full-time workers.

It was vast, containing multitudes: the old guard, the East Coast intellectuals, the prairie-power people, the hordes of the upper Midwest, the small-college and backwater students, the West Coast activists, the politicized hippies. The political range extended from naive liberals caught up by student power or marching against the war, through connections-making radicals without formal ideology, to red-book Maoists of the Progressive Labor stripe; as Carl Davidson assessed things in February: "We have within our ranks Communists of both varieties, socialists of all sorts, 3 or 4 different kinds of anarchists, anarchosyndicalists, syndicalists, social democrats, humanist liberals, a growing number of ex-YAF libertarian laissez-faire capitalists, and, of course, the articulate vanguard of the psychedelic liberation front." Davidson also gave his view of the various types of SDSers on the campus during these days:

> The bulk of the membership, about 85-90%, is made up of what I call the "SHOCK TROOPS." They are usually the younger members, freshmen and sophomores, rapidly moving into the hippy, Bobby Dylan syndrome. Having been completely turned off by the American system of compulsory miseducation, they are staunchly anti-intellectual and rarely read anything unless it comes from the underground press syndicate. . . . They are morally outraged about the war, cops, racism, poverty, their parents, the middle class, and authority figures in general. They have a sense that all those things are connected somehow and that money has something to do with it. They long for community and feel their own isolation acutely, which is probably why they stick with SDS.
>
> The second SDS type makes up about 5-10% of the chapter's membership. These are the "SUPERINTELLECTUALS." Most are graduate students in the Social Sciences or Humanities; a few are married. . . . They spell out grand strategies for the chapter's activities, but will rarely sit behind the literature tables. They talk a lot about power structure research, the need for analysis, and are turned on by the REP prospectus. They join most of the demonstrations, but rarely help make the picket signs. . . . Without a doubt some of the most brilliant young people in America today. . . .
>
> The third ideal type within SDS, the final 5%, are what I call the "ORGANIZERS." These are the people that keep the chapters going. . . . An increasing number are dropping out of school, but staying near the University community. Many more would probably drop out if it weren't for 2-S and the draft. They do the bureaucratic shitwork (reserving rooms, setting up tables, ordering literature, etc.) or see that it gets done. They are constantly trying to involve new people or reinvolve old people in the chapter's activities. . . . There is not much political analysis here. Most of the organizer's projects are experimental, spur-of-the-moment decisions. . . . Their politics tend to be erratic, changing whenever they finally get a chance to read a new book. . . . They are the people who try to attend the regional and national conferences.

Davidson is somewhat sardonic about the way these three types interact:

> The superintellectuals are intensely cynical toward the younger shock troops, especially the hippies. In retaliation the younger troops put the superintellectuals in the middle class bag along with their parents and the Dean of Men. . . . For the most part . . . our intellectuals view the organizer as a sloppy-thinking mystic with no sense of history. In return, the organizer often looks at the superintellectual as a new kind of Fabian Society opportunist who lacks the guts to break with the middle class. . . . The organizer's attitudes toward [the "shock troops"] are truly ambivalent, almost schizoid . . . likely to be the result of the fact that he is not too far removed from that whole scene himself. He certainly shares their pain. . . . When he is particularly worn out and burdened, he measures his exhaustion against their frivolity, feels cheated, and reacts with bitter harangues about bourgeois decadence. The younger troops' feelings toward the organizer are mixed as well. Sometimes there is a great deal of admiration and the resulting shyness, especially if the organizer is particularly charismatic. Sometimes, they feel guilty, because of their failure to be more involved in the chapter's daily work. But they often justify this by attributing a lack of sensitivity to the organizer.

All that is unduly grim, no doubt, but it also has the ring of truth to it. SDS was nothing if not diverse.

But what of its strengths?

SDS was without question the largest, best-known, and most influential student political group in the country, easily more important and dynamic than such preadamites as the Young Democrats, Young Republicans, or Young Americans for Freedom. It was now the only real student group on the left, M2M and the Student Peace Union having folded and the DuBois Clubs breathing their last, and such groups as the Socialist Workers Party's Young Socialist Alliance and the Socialist Party's Young People's Socialist League, though formally extant, being hardly noticeable. Though there were radical groups on various isolated campuses, and any number of *ad hoc* student organizations for single-issue politics, SDS was the only organization with a national presence. Its chapters instigated or participated in most of the campus protests, its strategies and tactics guided virtually every university action in some measure, and its newspaper, travelers, officers, and meetings were the source of much of the ferment that politicized campuses, left administrators sleepless, and raised the issue of campus governance for the first time in this century.

But SDS was more than that. It was the leading activist and most fulgent intellectual group in the entire left spectrum, old or new. The Old Left parties, though feeding off the resurgence of antiestablishmentarian politics, were still quite minuscule, and the ongoing pacifist organizations—War Resisters League, Fellowship of Reconciliation, and the like—still attracted only a dedicated few. The only potential rivals just then were the Spring (soon to be National) Mobilization and the draft-resistance movement, and both were essentially *ad hoc,* single-issue, uncohesive, non-membership coalitions, more temporary bases for action than permanent organizations. It was SDS, both collegiate and alumni, which was the wellspring of many, and transmitter of most, of the ideas that began to create a new consciousness among at least a minority of the college generation and the recently graduated professionals. It was SDS, though by no means alone, and often standing on the shoulders of others, which produced the developing analysis of the war, capitalism, imperialism, complicity—and, of course, their connections—that came to be fairly commonplace within the political arena in the next few years. It was SDS that people looked to for new theories about the agents of change, new literature on the glaring ills of campus and nation, new information about Defense Department contracts, Selective Service machinations, hidden university research. It was SDS, in short, more than any other single group on a national scale, which was pushing people left.

All that said, SDS was still an organization wracked by problems, pulled in different directions, containing the seeds of its own demise. What of its weaknesses?

The first, inevitable, perhaps unsurmountable, problem was of "distance," and it had many components. SDS was a national office that had a turnover of people and ideas at least once a year, a welter of varying chapters operating on their own, and very little in between. This resulted in a continual separation of the National Office from the interests of the chapters, a separation exaggerated during a time like this when the NO activists were trying to develop and push a heightened political consciousness on the rest of the organization. So, while Calvert and Davidson were worrying about building "revolutionary consciousness," the SDSers at Bowling Green were wondering how to answer redbaiting from the conservatives; while Davidson was trying to get a team of people to teach radical politics, the chapter at Arizona State wondered if it dared set up an SDS literature table in the student commons room; while the National Council scorned the idea of mass marches, kids in every SDS chapter went out and organized for them. Slowly the NO, and with it the veteran leaders and other friends in the inner circles, began to draw away from the constituency at large, but now with the growing feeling that it was harder and harder to bridge the gap.

One possible means across the gap might have been the SDS alumni, but they were generally neglected. SDS seemed designedly gerontocidal, changing its basic leadership with every convention and sending the older people, often with acutely developed skills and irreplaceable experience, out to fend for themselves in other pastures. After all, something like thirty-five or forty thousand people had gone through the SDS experience by now, and they had to be a resource worth tapping. But no. Though they did radicalizing work of inestimable value, they felt cut off from the life lines of an involving, meaningful movement; as Barbara and Al Haber expressed it that summer:

> On the one hand, many of us can no longer tolerate psychologically the demands of orthodox jobs or the training they require. Radical consciousness has produced a painful awareness of the personal emptiness and social evil of most traditional career patterns. . . . On the other hand . . . the alternatives which have been created by the movement, and the radical generations before us, are too narrow, too limited and too unsuccessful.

All of which tended to create among the alumni a sense of isolation from the new people, younger, with a new style, and new strategies, and even new politics. The Habers, again: "The most pervasive problem [is] the feeling of isolation from the mainstream of the movement. The movement people [are] remote physically and psychologically." So the alumni went off elsewhere, to their own concerns—they were not included, they were not used.

The distance problem was compounded by two others, not specific to SDS but found throughout the New Left—and of course throughout the entire society from which it springs—which now began to be named and confronted: "elitism" and "male chauvinism." Elitism is the tendency of a handful of top leaders—the "heavies," they were called, since "leaders" was a bad word—to dominate an organization by virtue of their elected positions, or manipulative skill, or oral felicity, or administrative brilliance. No matter how much an organization like SDS was aware of the problem—and its unwavering antipathy to leaders from the very start was evidence of that—it was unable to avoid the trap: good souls became active, activists became leaders, leaders became an elite.* Various chapters tried to deal with it by various means—rotating chairmen, governance by committees, conscious withdrawal of heavies—but the problem of course persisted. And it elided very easily into male chauvinism, since the leaders were usually men, or women who identified with and modeled themselves after men, and the followers, bearing the flags, at the mimeographs, in the beds, were usually women. But where elitism had been seen as a problem all along, it is only now, with a growing women's consciousness and self-identification, that male chauvinism takes on a special malevolence of its own and

*Marge Piercy once described the trap: "The typical Movement institution consists of one or more men who act as charismatic spokesmen, who speak in the name of the institution, and negotiate and represent that body to other bodies in and outside the Movement, and who manipulate the relationships inside to maintain his or their position. . . . Most prestige in the Movement rests not on having done anything in particular, but in having visibly dominated some gathering, in manipulating a certain set of rhetorical counters well in public, or in having played some theatrical role." ("The Grand Coolie Damn," *Sisterhood is Powerful*, Random House, 1970.) And Nick Egleson later confessed how it worked: "My high school . . . was a finishing school for men and it was meant to teach the sons of the rich how to rule the empire. . . . I ran most of the extra-curricular activities—debating, newspaper, press club, drama workshop—and hustled my way out of classes and required athletics. Only later did I see that it was I who had been hustled. I learned the hustling game. I am afraid that when my ideas shifted allegiance from nuclear physics to the Blacks and the Vietnamese that at first I shifted en masse all my ways of operating. I organized my corner of the movement the way I had organized the newspaper: top down, with regard for ideas and product but not for emotions of people: with structures that looked democratic but let hustlers with my traits, chiefly other men, rise to the top. Damn it all: family, school, and state, and damn the circus too." (*Liberation*, April 1970.)

that the special quality of sexism comes to be recognized—by the women, at any rate, if not yet by the men.

The earliest impulse to "women's liberation" in SDS was the paper presented at the December 1965 "rethinking conference," but in the time since then attention to the issue had grown enormously. Movement gatherings began including special workshops dealing with women's problems—a special session on the "role of women" had been part of the December 1966 draft-resistance conference in Chicago, for example (though, to be sure, concerned with their role in support of draft-resisting men)—and at a number of the traditionally active campuses women's groups began meeting in tentative examinations of sexism in American society. In SDS Jane Adams appeared to carry on the battle almost single-handedly. In an article, "On Equality for Women," in a January 1967 *New Left Notes,* for example, she argued that women must begin "demanding equality within the organization one is in, refusing to be intimidated by the male chauvinism which does exist, even within the movement"; three months later she added:

> And I don't see how we can build a strong movement for a free, democratic society as long as women are treated like "second-class citizens" and retain a submissive role. . . . As long as almost all the organizers and staff are male,* the fears that bind girls in chapters will be perpetuated; the habit of looking to men for leadership (by both men and women) will be continued. That has to be broken down by women assuming initiative and responsibility.

It is only a symbol, but one that would never have appeared before, that the cover of the convention issue of *New Left Notes* this summer showed a picture of a smiling young blond woman with a rifle in her hand, under the caption THE NEW AMERICAN WOMAN.

---

*At the time, the only women in major organizational roles in SDS were Adams herself, a regional traveler, Sarah Murphy, in charge of the New York office, and Cathy Wilkerson, editor of *New Left Notes.* Women were also prominent in ERAP projects (Kathy Boudin, Connie Brown, Carol Glassman, Carol McEl-downey, Jean Tepperman, and Peggy Terry, to name only a few), and at REP (Alice Fialkin, Evi Goldfield, Barbara Haber, and Kathy McAfee, among others). Of the elected members of the National Council, there were only three women out of twenty members and alternates (Adams, Nancy Bancroft, Carolyn Craven), and in the NAC, though it fluctuated, there were usually no more than two or three.

Problems and promises, SDS was at this point, whatever else, a force to be reckoned with by students in general, by the world of the left, by the universities where it was generally housed, by the society at large at which it was aimed. It was—perhaps it is all that need be said—the touchstone of American radicalism.

The mingle-mangle that was SDS in the summer of 1967 can be seen in relief at the SDS National Convention, held in Ann Arbor from June 25 to July 2.

The convention drew between two hundred and fifty and three hundred people, of whom maybe two hundred were voting delegates. Their appearance was now firmly hippiesque—men in longish hair, often with mustaches and occasionally with beards, and blue workshirts and jeans predominating; women tending toward long, straight hair, with eye make-up but not lipstick, usually in jeans, occasionally barefoot. Buttons were routinely worn by both: "sds," "Make Love Not War," "Resist," "October 16" (the last a reference to the Resistance's planned mass draft-card turn-in for the fall).

Though many old familiar faces were present—including both Steve Max and Jim Williams, probably the only left-liberals in the place—the majority of delegates were newer, many of whom had gotten caught up in the student power sweep of the last year and were attending their first convention, and this would prove a source of some tension throughout the week. Progressive Labor made a respectable showing—perhaps forty or fifty people—and distinguished themselves by shorter hair and a caucus-like discipline.* Also present were a number of young Communist Party people, cut loose from the nearly defunct DuBois Clubs and trying now to rebuild a base among the students by surreptitiously using SDS. A good number of people identified themselves as anarchists,

---

*Don McKelvey, whose politics were not so far from PL's but who was nonetheless quite independent, reported after the convention (in a *SUPA Bulletin,* August 1967): "PL people are quite active in SDS, the only 'ideological Left' people who were (or who were evident); they seem to be accepted; they certainly were, in general, at the convention. . . . I get the sense they were a 'semi-caucus' at the convention, and I expect they certainly made disciplined decisions beforehand about what they were going to do. But I got no sense whatever . . . that there was any attempt to 'take over'—they were simply pushing their politics, which were the only genuinely hard-line politics (i.e., definite and clear politics) there."

including one group with ties to the small IWW office still hanging on in Chicago.

SDS conventions were always bizarre affairs, part reunion, part student-government meeting, part cruising strip, part smoke-filled room, part serious politics. In one sense, by these days conventions never really changed much for the organization, since individual chapters went their own ways and determined for themselves what SDS would be during the year; this was what was being expressed by Jim O'Brien, a Wisconsin SDSer who went on to be one of the most dedicated historians of the Movement, when he reported after this meeting:

> If the national SDS convention just held in Ann Arbor showed anything, it was that SDS is not a national organization. Sooner or later, every new delegate learns this; when he does, he sits back, relaxes, endures the long debates and parliamentary hang-ups with a happy passivity. Occasionally he goes out for donuts or Blimpy Burgers without wondering too much what will be going on in his absence. The convention is a place to meet people and exchange experiences, and the formal resolutions are important only as they in some way symbolize those people and those experiences.

Not untrue, and fashionably cynical. And yet, in another sense, SDS conventions were extremely important: in bringing to the surface the problems and passions of the organization, in weighing and calculating the strengths and directions of the factions, in electing people who will establish the national presence over the next year, and in charting the actual direction and programs for the year ahead—or, equally important, failing to.

The "distance" problem surfaced at the very first plenary meeting on Tuesday night in the form of a separation between the Calvert-Davidson wing and the more moderate chapters. Of particular issue was a front-page *New York Times* article in May which had begun with a quotation from Calvert that "We are working to build a guerrilla force in an urban environment," and had gone on to warn menacingly that "the threat of violence in his words characterizes the current radicalization of the New Left." Now in fact the article was largely an unfounded scare story which depended for proof of violence on such things as Che posters and draft-card burning, and Calvert had subsequently explained to the membership in *New Left Notes* that he was opposed to violence and had been misquoted: "I felt that young Americans who worked for the radical transformation of this society were similar in many respects to guerrilla organizers in the Third World." But the quotation, and the wide circulation it was given by a press growing discomforted with the increasing tide of resistance on the nation's campuses, disturbed many in the campus constituency: not only was a national officer presuming to speak politically for the organization as a whole—shades of Paul Booth! —but he seemed to be setting policy for SDS on an issue that had never even been discussed, much less approved, at a national meeting, and one which alarmed most of the constituency, which shied from violence and was by no means ready for guerrilla warfare. Calvert did some fast talking that night. He acknowledged that, in the light of how exaggerated the whole thing had become, sitting for the interview "was a stupid thing, a trap," another example of the way in which the "capitalistic media" distorted events for their own ends; but, he argued, the membership had to understand that the national officers inevitably functioned in political roles just by virtue of their positions, that nothing in the way of real policy had been made at all by the quotation, and anyway this was no excuse to try to damage the national leadership. Ultimately he was forced to proclaim that the debate was "really a matter of who will control this convention," and upon that appeal the battle subsided and Calvert breathed easier. But it was clear to all that the problem of growing distance between national leadership and constituency was a real one, and not to be disposed of easily.

A "direction" problem also surfaced, inevitably, and that was less easy to solve. Workshops would meet for long hours during the day to hash out proposals to put before the plenary sessions at night, but as likely as not the workshop participants couldn't agree on any one proposal or else on one with such a low common denominator that it had little effect, and the plenaries were only worse. People were arguing lines by this point, not really listening to the other sides, trying to win an audience over to the correctness of their point of view, or scorning completely ideas that were too "reformist" or "liberal" or "wimpy." This was particularly true of the PL people, of course, because they not only had a line but were convinced of its holiness, but it also tended to characterize others who had made up their minds and the National Office people to some extent. Arthur Waskow believes that this convention marked a turning point:

> For the first time in SDS people were extremely hostile to any organizing except their own, for the first time they had a sense of real competitiveness and restricted options—that is, if people chose X they would not be able to choose Y, and if they did they were wrong. I don't remember that kind of feeling before that.

What this kind of "correct-line-ism," as it was called, meant for SDS was that it was almost impossible for it to agree upon strategies or programs for the coming year (a task which the convention had now assumed), and in general only the most uncontroversial proposals could be adopted. PL thought that new-working-class organizing was dangerous and wrongheaded, most chapter people thought PL's blue-collar interest was doomed to failure, chapters who advocated election work and third-party priorities were laughed at by the anarchists and the hippieized "cultural" radicals, and these in turn were scorned for their frivolity and lack of "politics" by the veterans and other heavies. Divisions were not homogenized as they so often were in the earlier years.*

So when a "relations with other groups" workshop proposed that SDS establish immediate fraternal relations with such leftist foreign youth groups as the German SDS and the Japanese Zengakuren, this was resisted by many, young and old, who thought it pointless and didn't know anything about the foreign organizations anyway. Dozens of elaborate suggestions were presented as to how SDS might join with and politicize the "cultural revolution"—the hippie counterculture—and all were ultimately discarded in favor of a simple resolution to join the Underground

---

*An interesting example of the growing tension in SDS took place after adjournment one night. As one correspondent wrote in *New Left Notes* (July 24): "The registration files were missing, and the rumor was that they had been sequestered away by a FBI/CIA agent. There was talk about a suspicious convention delegate: he had a red beard. After the NC was dismissed that night, the body marched off across the University of Michigan campus to confront the suspicious delegate, who had been trailed to his pad by some super-sleuth leftists with latent J. Edgar Hoover tendencies. The witch trial lasted but half a minute. Two hard-core Trot friends recognized and cleared the accused before the crowd of some self-appointed inquisitors. . . . If brother is going to accuse brother, then SDS is threatened."

Press Service and something called the Haymarket Riot Fan Club. On the draft, the convention agreed to some very sharp rhetoric over the objections of PL, which now wanted to mute the draft issue so as not to frighten away sons of the hawkish working class, but it would not settle upon any tactics for the year ahead beyond those already approved at Berkeley. And on the item which the NO had counted upon to provide the whole thrust of SDS for the year ahead—a mass student strike in the spring based on student issues but "united in the common demand for the immediate withdrawal of U.S. troops from Vietnam"—there was so much hostility from the chapter representatives, skeptical of its chances and fearful of ending up with egg on their faces if it failed, that the whole thing was put off to the December National Council with the specific proviso that at least ten chapters had to guarantee its chances of success before the NO moved.

The convention did find certain things to agree upon. It voted a statement of support for SNCC and the Revolutionary Action Movement, vowed to oppose government repression against "militant, radical, and revolutionary groups," called upon SDSers to support "ghetto rebellions" and "by direct action, including civil disobedience if called for," and authorized the Harvard chapter (more than half PL) to go ahead with a Labor Research and Action Program in Boston. It approved the establishment of a Radical Education Center, a scheme of Davidson's for carrying on internal education through a literature program and regular articles in *New Left Notes*. It also approved, with a few modifications from the floor and a great deal of uneasiness from the men, a report from the women's workshop calling upon women to assert their independence and men to deal with their "male chauvinism"; it was the first time the issue of male chauvinism had been joined in SDS, and the first time a New Left organization took a stand on it. Thus, in a significant sense, did the women's liberation movement begin.*

*The statement, drafted by Jane Adams, Susan Cloke, Jean Peak, and Elizabeth Sutherland, took a surprisingly strong position for its time: "Women, because of their colonial relationship to men, have to fight for their own independence. This fight for our own independence will lead to the growth and development of the revolutionary movement in this country. Only the independent woman can be truly effective in the larger revolutionary struggle. . . . People who identify with the movement and feel that their own lives are part of the base to bring about radical social change must recognize the necessity for the liberation of women.

On two other issues the convention passed statements but with so little general agreement on their implementation that they remained rhetorical flourishes without the guise of program. They are significant, however, in demonstrating the political development of SDS by this point, at least the development of the convention-going types. The first was the Vietnam war, the discussion of which was brought on by the prospect of still another Washington march in October, which the convention only grudgingly supported:

> We urge all SDS chapters which do participate in the march to support immediate withdrawal. Only such a position is commensurate with our recognition of the real role of the U.S. in Vietnam— not a mistake of any essentially good government, but the logical result of a government which oppresses people in the U.S. and throughout the world.

That passed almost without a murmur, and as if that weren't enough the convention then adopted by an overwhelming voice vote an additional statement put forth by a Rutgers PLer, Larry Poleshuck:

> SDS holds that the position of "Stop the Bombing" and "Negotiations Now" are not in the best interests of the Vietnamese or the American people. Allowing the National Liberation Front token representation in the government which has existed because of U.S. military involvement is no just solution to the Vietnam War. The U.S. has no right in any way to determine the future of the Vietnamese. Therefore we must call for an immediate U.S. withdrawal. The growing sentiment among Americans for an end to the war is a threat to the small minority who benefit from the domination of

---

Our brothers must recognize that because they were brought up in the United States they cannot be free of the burden of male chauvinism.

"1. Therefore we demand that our brothers recognize that they must deal with their own problems of male chauvinism in their own personal, social, and political relationships.

"2. It is obvious from this convention that full advantage is not taken of abilities and potential contributions of movement women. We call upon women to demand full participation in all aspects of movement work, from licking stamps to assuming leadership positions.

"We recognize the difficulty our brothers will have in dealing with male chauvinism and we will assume our full responsibility in helping to resolve the contradiction." (*New Left Notes,* July 10, 1967.)

Vietnam. Leaders like Bobby Kennedy who call for negotiations are
trying to channel legitimate desires of American people for peace
into a solution which is acceptable to the basic interests of that
minority. The anti-war movement must not unintentionally support
continued oppression of the Vietnamese. We must insist on an
immediate withdrawal of the U.S. from Vietnam.

Here was SDS's first official stand on Vietnam since the "end the
war" demand of the 1965 march and the "immoral, illegal, and
genocidal war" position of the 1966 antidraft resolution, and it is
quite a measure of how the organization, or at least its resolution-
passing wing, had come in just two years. It easily encompassed
the idea of imperialism and the link between oppression at home
and abroad, and it called for immediate withdrawal long before
that was a popular idea even on the left. Only a month before,
Arthur Schlesinger, Jr. had told his right-thinking countrymen
how scandalous that was—"No serious American," he wrote in
the *Times,* "has proposed unilateral withdrawal; and this, after
all, would be the only action which could hand the game to our
enemies"—and here were a bunch of America's "Man-of-the-
Year" kids proposing exactly that. Yes, and they would be joined
by a lot of serious Americans, and Arthur Schlesinger too, within
the next two years.

The second subject of rhetorical agreement was the draft:

SDS reaffirms its opposition to conscription in any form. We maintain that all conscription is coercive and anti-democratic, and that
it is used by the United States Government to oppress people in the
United States and around the world. . . . The draft provides a
manpower pool for an aggressive and imperialistic foreign policy.
Americans who cannot freely determine the shape of their own lives
are in turn forced to suppress those abroad who struggle for self-
determination. . . . A draft-resistance program must move beyond
individual protest to collective action. SDS reaffirms its call for the
formation of draft-resistance unions. Tactics such as civil disobedience and disruption of the Selective Service System are among those
advocated.

Nor was that all—Jeff Shero popped up from the floor proposing
an amendment that SDS help men already in the service "in
opposition and disruption within the armed forces" and give "aid
to servicemen who wish to terminate their association with the

armed forces by going underground." By a lopsided vote SDS went on record in favor of desertion from the military—and this was an organization which only two years ago couldn't even pass a mild resolution against the draft.

The failure of the 1967 convention to decide upon a course of action for the year ahead was serious—it had happened really only once before, in 1965, with unpleasant consequences—for it meant that chapters would tend to operate in isolation or take their direction from other sources, like the media. As Paul Booth later analyzed it, "Once they stopped passing programs and started arguing stupid lines—or however good they were—they lost the ability to set any course for the student movement, and then the course was set by *The New York Times* and the TV stations, so that whatever was most dramatic was then emulated, whether it was good or not." And when chapters *did* do imaginative and effective things on their own, there was no organizational way to communicate and duplicate them; as Booth says,

> During this whole period . . . there was a tremendous development of a lot of very healthy things—working-class community organizing, campus actions around community issues of a planned character—but there was no way to find out about them. For example at Cornell, where they fought and won a tremendous fight for low-cost public housing in Ithaca, done by SDS, and I never found out about it until I ran into a guy from there. There were a lot of these things, but *New Left Notes* became an organ for *lines* now rather than *news*, so you never knew about them. Independent of whether it was good politics or not, it was bad organizationally.

Added to this was a failure to come up with either the plan or the personnel for effective leadership. The process was begun when the NO introduced a long-awaited plan for the reorganization of national officers and the elimination of the presidency; the proposal was to replace them with three equal officers, a National Secretary in charge of the NO and responsible for implementing national programs, an Education Secretary for internal education and chapter communications, and an Inter-organizational Secretary acting as liaison with other political groups. The basic scheme was Calvert's and the basic motives were, as near as one can tell, ingenuous: to eliminate a presidency which had become largely a figurehead position, to allow the open election of the National Secretary where the real power had come to reside anyway, to eliminate a needless and antiegalitarian hierarchy within the NO (the kind that had produced frictions in the last several years), and to define clearly the specific administrative roles of each top official, which had always been murky in the past. The effects of it, however, as time was to show, were to concentrate even more power in the hands of the National Secretary, who could now operate almost without restrictions (the old National Secretary had been responsible, at least in theory, to both the elected national officers and the quarterly National Councils); to make the NO even more of a closed-off world, with officers who were virtually forced to move to Chicago and work full time in that potentially insulated environment; and, by allowing *de jure* power to coincide with *de facto* power, to concentrate forces almost beyond reach of any other organizational tendency or influence and to permit the leadership to go its own way virtually unchecked until the next convention. Apparently these effects, however, were unrealized at the time and the general egalitarian caste given to the whole thing seemed convincing enough to the delegates present: not one voice was raised in protest about the elimination of the presidency, the whole debate took scarcely an hour, and the reorganization was approved by even more than the two-thirds vote which the constitution required.*

*Little real attention was given throughout SDS's career to the organizational forms through which it expressed itself, though from time to time certain individuals conceded the problem to be important. One organizational form never considered, oddly enough, even when the question was in the air, was that of matching officers to a wide range of specific duties rather than concentrating power in three individuals, no matter what their titles were: a membership officer for chapter records, an editorial officer for the newspaper and pamphlets, a press officer for contacts with the media, an administrative officer for the office, a political officer for internal education, a personnel officer for travelers and regional staffs, an alumni officer for contacts with graduates, a finance officer for fund raising, and so on. Another plan apparently never seriously discussed was that of choosing among slates of officers according to the political programs they proposed for the coming year (rather than on the basis of personalities), with the administrative machinery then being obliged to carry out the membership mandate until the next convention. For additional consideration of SDS's organizational problems, see Rich Rothstein, *NUC Newsletter*, April 20, 1971, and *Liberation*, February 1972, reprinted as an NUC pamphlet, 1972; replies from Mel Rothenberg in the June *NUC Newsletter* and Bob Ross and Howard Ehrlich in the September issue; and Norm Fruchter, *Liberation*, February 1972.

The evening session, devoted to filling these three new posts, completed the leadership muddle. For the post of National Secretary there were nominated Jeff Segal, prominent because of his draft-resistance organizing during the spring, Eric Chester, the former VOICE leader now organizing for SDS in San Francisco, who had been vocal on the floor, and Mike Spiegel, prominent for nothing much other than being one of the first two Harvard SDSers to grab onto the bumper of McNamara's car during the December 1966 confrontation. Spiegel was elected with a clear majority on the first ballot. Spiegel was young (then just twenty), a bit over six feet, well-built, good-looking, with impelling dark eyes behind horn-rimmed glasses, short though somewhat bushy hair, and an SDSer's full, drooping mustache. Born in Portland, Oregon, he had been outstanding in high school, went to Harvard in 1964 as a sociology major, became politicized during the summer of 1966 while working in a Michigan auto assembly plant, and returned to Harvard to join SDS. He said later:

> I think I could have come as close as anyone with a name like Spiegel to becoming a member of the ruling class, but I have always had this thing about reality. I could never skirt things. I have to meet them head-on. This is why I went to SDS. No one else had an explanation for the reality.

The explanation, especially with regard to Vietnam, convinced and radicalized the young junior, and he went off to the national convention full of fire. But no one would have predicted his election, being so young and so unknown: only Paul Booth and Vernon Grizzard, of all the top SDS officers over the years, were undergraduates when elected, and only Booth, at nineteen, was younger; and both then had reputations of a sort, and the organization was a thirtieth of its present size. Moreover, no one would have predicted that the convention, just after having established the office of National Secretary as a politically powerful lever, would have put there in the flesh a man whose name was known only to a few—the issue of *New Left Notes* reporting his election called him "Spiegal"—and whose politics were known to fewer still.

This election was followed by one for the Education Secretary, and the muddle was compounded. Carl Davidson, who had been so involved with internal education, would have been a natural choice, and he was willing to run. But the nominees were Art Rosenblum, Texas traveler Bob Pardun, and New York organizer Sue Eanet, and Pardun won easily on the first ballot. Pardun, twenty-four, who had been born in Pueblo, Colorado, but migrated to Texas, was blond and tall, with a faint Will Rogers look about him, an unruly forelock, and a soft Texas drawl. He had already developed a reputation in SDS for his regional work and he had a strong Texas chapter behind him, "more close-knit," he says, "than the other chapters, we felt more like brothers and sisters." But he was the kind of person, one could have predicted, who was better off traveling the Southern plains than stuck behind a Chicago desk.

The last election was for Inter-organizational Secretary. This time Carl Davidson was nominated, he ran against VOICE delegate Mark Scher and West Coast organizer Bob Speck, and he won handily. It was the first time that a national officer repeated since Paul Booth had served two terms as Vice President (in 1962–63 and 1963–64) and one as National Secretary (in 1956–66) —but it still made only bizarre sense to put this student-syndicalist and chapter-oriented man into a job where he had to be nice to the Young Christians and decipher letters from the Zengakuren.*

And so the convention ended, without a national program, without even local directions, without a cohesive team in the National Office, with all its problems intact. Yet nothing could hold back SDS now, for it was an organization of resistance in a time of resistance, and oddly enough it was about to enjoy one of its most successful years.

*The final session of the plenary also elected new members of the National Council, which had been reduced from fourteen officers to eight, and was dubbed the National Interim Committee. Originally each was to have been from a different region, but the convention didn't accept that and instead selected Sue Eanet, John Fuerst, and Steve Halliwell from the New York region, Greg Calvert, Mike James, Jeff Segal, and Cathy Wilkerson from the "Chicago crowd," and Jeff Shero.

19

FALL 1967

On Monday morning, October 16, 1967, the thirty thousand students of the University of Wisconsin in Madison were met with a two-page mimeographed handout, without date or signature. "From Tuesday to Friday of this week," it began, "Dow Chemical Company will be recruiting on this campus. On Tuesday, this fact will be brought to the attention of the entire campus. On Wednesday, students will block Dow from recruiting." Just like that. The rationale that followed was simple, a straightforward presentation of the radical case: Dow was part of the war machine ("The work of the government cannot be separated from the daily operations of American corporations or universities. To end the war, it is necessary to comprehend its true nature, to understand the extent to which major institutions such as this university and Dow Corporation are committed to its continuation"), the war machine has not been halted even after two years of opposition ("On this campus, opposition has become 'in': Not one faculty member in a hundred will defend the government. But the war effort has not even slowed down"), and therefore to stop it something more must be done ("We must move from protest to resistance. Before, we talked. Now we must act. We must stop what we oppose").

Wisconsin was a campus with a history of protest—including a sit-in against Selective Service ranking in May 1966 and a demonstration against Dow in February 1967—but this promised to be on a different scale. On the one side were the students, many of whom had already become familiar with the university's complicity in war-making through previous SDS exposures* and who were already active in getting recruits for the upcoming march on the Pentagon; loosely formed into an Anti-Dow Coordinating Committee, with members of SDS and the Committee to End the War in Vietnam prominent among them, they had now explicitly warned of open resistance. On the other side was the administration, led by a newly appointed chancellor, William Sewell, who had vowed to protect the visit of any recruiter from anywhere and had made preparations with campus and local police to provide that protection; and behind him stood the company that profited from making jellied death, and the whole horror of Vietnam. It was all set for—the word of the day on the campuses—confrontation.

On Tuesday morning, October 17, some two hundred pickets walked back and forth in front of the Commerce Building, home of the business faculty and site of the recruitment interviews. They carried signs saying HEY, HEY, LBJ, HOW MANY KIDS DID YOU KILL TODAY? and HELL NO, WE WON'T GO, which turned out to be an unexpectedly all-purpose slogan. Students were allowed to come and go, no attempt at obstruction was made, and around noon the picketers dispersed. A lunchtime rally was held on the mall in front of the library, but it was sparsely attended.

Wednesday morning began quietly enough, with a regrouping of picketers in front of the Commerce Building. But, as promised, this time they moved from protest to resistance. At around ten-thirty more than a hundred picketers walked purposefully into the building, sat down in front of the office in which the Dow man was meeting with a student, linked arms, and notified the anxious officials standing around that there would be no more interviews that day. Within an hour the corridor on both sides of the office was blocked from wall to wall with milling students, perhaps 350 in all, while outside another 2000 of the curious and/or sympathetic gathered, sensing trouble as sure as any turkey buzzard. Administration officials inside pleaded and demanded that the

---

*One of which singled out the role of the Army Math Research Center on campus in performing logistical work for the Department of Defense; it was this center which, three years later, was bombed, accidentally killing a graduate student.

demonstrators leave; no one budged. Police from the university's office of "Protection and Security" and twenty more off-duty Madison policemen hired for the day took up places menacingly on the fringes; still no one budged. Nominally in charge was campus police chief Ralph Hanson, who had expected a docile crowd, the civil-disobedient pacifists he was used to, types who would move along when threatened or submit meekly to arrest. But this bunch seemed different: they were, Hanson reported to his superiors, "hostile." A little after noon, Hanson called the Madison police for more reinforcements, and shortly some thirty riot police showed up, ostentatiously donning their riot helmets and plastic faceguards, brandishing heavy riot sticks, and forming ranks outside the doors of the building.

Inside, tension and worries mounted. Hanson, seeking some way out, offered a compromise: if the students would leave, Dow would leave. The demonstrators quickly agreed, and dispatched a delegation to get confirmation of this from Chancellor Sewell. Sewell, however, would have none of it. The delegation returned to the ranks and warned that violence would be next; those who want to may leave, the rest should remove their glasses, take off sharp objects like earrings and buttons, and prepare to pull their coats over their heads for protection: "We are serious about this."

At 1:30 P.M., Hanson, on consultation with administration officials, decided to move in. Giving a final warning to the students that they faced arrest, he moved outside, gathered around him a force of fifty policemen, and charged the front entrance to the building. Suddenly, chaos. Hanson and the first ranks of cops were pushed aside by the students inside, but in their wake the Madison riot squad rushed wildly, flailing and pelting, using sticks and fists, without supervision—even (as Hanson acknowledged later) without any clear instructions about what to do. Students poured out of the building, their heads oozing blood, groaning and crying, limping and bruised. A young woman was hurtled out, stumbled, and fell unconscious into the arms of two students; a young man blinded by blood from his forehead and screaming with rage staggered about. In a matter of twelve minutes, by official estimate, the building was cleared.

Not so the area outside. There the thousands of students gathered were shocked at the brutality before them. Some called the university hospital, only to be told that it refused to send ambulances, and then ran into the street to stop passing cars to carry away the wounded students. Others milled about, pulling demonstrators out of the arms of police and sheltering them in the crowd, obstructing arrests, yelling and chanting. At one point when six students were hustled into a paddy wagon, the bystanders surrounded the wagon, began pounding on it with their fists, let the air out of the tires, and finally lay down in front of it; the police, stymied, took the names of their captives and let them free. More shoving, hitting, taunting, and then, tear gas—tear gas for the first time on a major college campus.

> There was no sudden pain [one student recalled], no hurt comparable to that of being hit or having a toothache or getting burned, nor any of the other pains one is used to in normal life. There is simply a sudden total change of consciousness . . . nothing matters but eyes and nose and throat. Burning, tearing, corrosive—all are inadequate words for it; tear gas does not hurt or cause pain, but it has an absolutism, an ability to take over one's whole being that is shocking at the same time and puzzling afterwards.

Several hundred students received this baptism of tears, gagged, retreated, assembled again, angrier now, and moved back toward the lines of police, only to be repulsed by another smoky wave of gas.

It was sometime in mid-afternoon during this tear-gas attack that the student crowd, reinforced now by indignant liberal and thrill-seeker alike, turned from defense to offense. It began to throw rocks from the campus gardens, bricks, even shoes, anything to try to respond to the brutality it had witnessed. Police retaliated with the next "crowd-controller" on their list, the nerve gas, Mace; it worked on immediate individuals—one young man writhed in agony on the ground for several minutes after being sprayed—but it failed to dispel the crowd. One policeman was struck in the face with a brick, and fell unconscious to the ground; another was hit in the leg by a rock, collapsed in pain, and was descended upon by students beating him with their fists and feet until scattered by a phalanx of cops. Then, reinforcements. The county sheriff's office sent in a squad of men with riot equipment and police dogs, and the student crowd, grown weary now, unused

to its own fury, losing adrenalin, sensing a victory, yet wanting to
lick wounds, gradually dispersed. By six-thirty the last of the
crowd had gone and the traces of tear gas were only faint whiffs
in the nearby trees. Seven policemen were treated in the university
hospital, three with broken bones; sixty-five students were treated,
several with serious injuries, one thought to be permanently
blinded.

Within an hour a mass rally was begun on the library mall
to fashion a student response to the invasion. An estimated five
thousand students and perhaps two hundred faculty members
showed up, and the mood was bitter, angry, militant: overwhelmingly they agreed not to attend any classes until recruiters from
the Dow Chemical Company were forever banned from the university. The student newspaper, the *Daily Cardinal,* supported the
strike, then the student government, finally even a right-wing
campus party. The student front was solid.

For the next two days the boycott of classes was nearly total,
despite outraged cries from the state legislators down the street
and a strong proadministration stand by the faculty. Over the
weekend attention was diverted to the Pentagon demonstration,
but the strike was still strong enough on Monday to prompt the
faculty into a second meeting to see if it could defuse the crisis.
That night it voted to establish a student-faculty committee to
look into the issues of recruiters on campus, student obstruction,
and the use of outside police, and that seemed to be enough to
satisfy the bulk of the student body, whose anger was now spent
and whose docility was being reasserted. By Tuesday the strike
had fizzled out, sixteen students had been suspended, three teaching assistants had been fired from their teaching jobs for joining
the strike, and Dow recruitment had been temporarily canceled.
None of the issues—recruitment, protest, police, complicity, or
violence—had been settled, but the lamina of sweet reasonableness
had been successfully applied, and the crisis was over. But though
the university was intact, it had been severely shaken, and for the
rest of the year the Dow issue would continue to nettle the campus; ultimately the administration decided to readmit the Dow
recruiters, though it was forced to do so at a remote point on the
campus heavily guarded by policemen—and at the end of the year
Chancellor Sewell resigned. The victory in the move from protest

to resistance was only partial, but the Wisconsin radicals felt that they had, at least, made their point; as one wrote:

> A demonstration earns its name when it demonstrates something, preferably when it demonstrates something in a context that is not normally seen. In a society such as ours, where advertising, education, public relations, group dynamics, operations research, systems analysis, and so on and so forth are all generally directed toward masking reality, demonstrations of reality are one of the most valuable institutions we have. At the University of Wisconsin, then, we have just had two of the most educational weeks in the university's existence.

Resistance came to American politics that fall with—literally —a vengeance. The process that had begun in the spring with the first widespread university confrontations now became absolutely polymorphic.

There was the spread of the Black Panther Party for Self-Defense through the ghettos of Oakland and the subsequent frame-up of its leader, Huey Newton, in October; the formation of the Committee of Returned Volunteers, ex-Peace Corps workers who had seen the fruits of imperialism firsthand and came home to do something about them; the establishment of the Committee to Aid the National Liberation Front, the first organized expression of the growing pro-NLF sympathies of the American left; the publication of a manifesto of open defiance to the government, "A Call to Resist Illegitimate Authority," signed by 158 (and later 2000) older supporters of draft resistance; the first use of the epithet "pig" to describe authorities, appearing in print in the September 25 *New Left Notes;* the arrest of a Kansas SDS leader, Charles V. Blackmon, on charges that he threatened to kill President Johnson; the creation of black student organizations at, among other schools, Cornell, Harvard, Howard, and San Fransisco State; the wishing-into-being of the Yippies (putatively the Youth International Party), joining provo, counterculture, and left politics in one mercurial lump; the formation of the Peace and Freedom Party to contest the 1968 elections with a left-wing slate, an antiwar platform, and a biracial leadership; the mass draft card turn-ins organized by the Resistance, in which more than 2000

young men publicly dissociated themselves from the draft during
the fall; the first raid upon a Selective Service office, at the Baltimore Customs House, where in October a group including the
Reverend Philip Berrigan destroyed draft records by pouring
blood on them; and above all, the swelling tide of confrontation
in the streets, on scores of campuses from coast to coast, even in
the nation's capital.

In the streets. On Friday morning, October 20, some ten
thousand people marched on the draft induction center in Oakland, California, prepared to do battle, and to win—and they won.
They had been organized by a loose and uneasy coalition of Berkeley leftists, of which the SDSers represented one militant wing,*
around the campaign to make October 16-20 "Stop the Draft
Week." They had just been through most of that week and each
tactic out of the past that they had tried had proved a failure: civil
disobedience and symbolic arrest on Monday turned out to be
fruitless, frustrating, and self-defeating when the sit-iners got
swiftly carted off to jail without more than a ripple of disruption;
unplanned violent confrontation on Tuesday proved suicidal when
the vastly more numerous and better equipped police force proceeded to flay and arrest the marchers without worry, provocation
or noticeable signs of mercy, leaving them in a shambles; and
peaceful picketing on Wednesday was seen by most to be sterile,
empty, and ultimately demoralizing when the draft inductees got
carted off anyway. So now on Friday they were back for more,
only this time the tactic was new: to be mobile not stationary, to

---

*Stuart McRae, of the Resistance, described the coalition this way: "The argu-
ment polarized into a debate between the traditional pacifists who envisioned the
usual kind of sit-in . . . and radicals, mainly SDS people, vicariously intoxicated
by the summer riots, who spoke at first clearly, but with increasing vagueness
of violent confrontation with the power structure, i.e. cops." It was here that
SDSers, and their comrades, developed perhaps the first rationale in the New
Left for the use of violence, one that would now be offered right down through
the Weathermen's "Days of Rage"; as their mimeographed handouts put it, "the
gentle, almost timid tone of peace demonstrations has left many young people,
black and white, feeling they have no place" in the antiwar movement and its
useless moral witnessing, whereas violence now offered "a way to speak to those
young people" and possibly "involving young people who are facing conscription: black people, high school students, the unemployed and young working
people." (by Ferber and Lynd, *The Resistance*, pp. 141-2.)

attack, disperse, and regroup, to be aggressive but not foolhardy, to come prepared with helmets and shields and signs mounted on serviceable plywood poles. Karen Wald, a Berkeley SDSer who had just finished a summer as coeditor of *New Left Notes,* reported back to the paper the feeling of that morning:.

> It was soon evident that there were more of US than THEM, and this combined with our mobility enabled groups of demonstrators to carry out actions unimpeded by the police. Trash cans and newspaper racks were pulled into the streets. Writing appeared on walls, on sidewalks: "Free Oakland," "Che Lives," "Resist," "Shut It Down." Soon, unlocked cars were pushed into the intersections, along with large potted trees and movable benches. The sanctity of private property, which had held white students back from this kind of defensive action before, gave way to a new evaluation. . . .
>
> The real change came about when one line of demonstrators, instead of simply backing up before a line of police, dispersed to the sidewalks—then quickly, instinctively, converged on the streets again behind the line of cops. The cops suddenly, uncomfortably, found themselves surrounded. . . . Nervous and demoralized, the cops stood there, shuffling their feet, looking worried and unhappy. . . .
>
> Word spread among the various bands of demonstrators who were now beginning to feel and even act somewhat like urban guerrillas. . . . For the first time demonstrators, unarmed, saw police lines retreat in front of them. It was our first taste of real victory. . . .
>
> Today we had tasted something different—we had taken and held downtown Oakland for the past four hours, we had seen the cops back away from us. . . . Not only the sanctity of property, and the sanctity (invulnerability) of cops had been destroyed that day; we had begun to establish new goals, new criterion [*sic*] for success in what were clearly the early battles of a long, long war.

Something indeed was different. Frank Bardacke wrote afterward:

> Stop the Draft Week changed the movement. We did not do anything as grand as "move from dissent to resistance," as some leaders claimed. But we went through a change—we became a more serious and more radical movement. . . . We did not loot or shoot. But in our own way we said to America that at this moment in history we do not recognize the legitimacy of

Amerian political authority. Our little anarchist party was meant
to convey the most political of messages: we consider ourselves
political outlaws. The American government has the power to
force us to submit but we no longer believe that it has the authority to compel us to obey.*

One month later, at the opposite end of the country, the
Foreign Policy Association held its fiftieth anniversary dinner,
with Secretary of State Dean Rusk as its featured speaker, at the
New York Hilton—a combination that was irresistible: the Foreign Policy Association was a collection of elderly, rich, powerful,
and influential Cold Warriors ("the architects of American imperialism," as New York Regional Office leader Steve Halliwell
put it in *New Left Notes*), Dean Rusk was the personification of
the soft-talking government committing genocide in Vietnam, and
the New York Hilton was the New York Hilton. A demonstration
was organized chiefly by the Fifth Avenue Peace Parade Committee, an ally of the National Mobilization Committee, but it was
clear in advance that many people in New York wanted to make
it more than a symbolic, peaceful, gentlemanly affair. The SDS
Regional Office worked to build it into a major confrontation, and
local chapters were alerted that plans were afoot to storm the
police barricades, create general disruption, make the evening
unpleasant for the dignitaries and, some hoped, stop Rusk from
speaking altogether. In the afternoon before the event the Columbia chapter of SDS, somewhat guilty about having been desultory in organizing previous demonstrations, held a rally on
campus where some two hundred people were exhorted by chapter
leaders Ted Kaptchuk and Ted Gold to take the battle into the
enemy's home ground and give them a taste of "direct action." As
Halliwell described the strategy, "The idea behind direct action is
disruption; that is to say, since picketing has proved completely
ineffectual in producing official response and is now carefully
enough controlled to prevent confrontations with the target group
or individual, people have begun to find ways to prevent events

*Frank Bardacke was among the seven men later indicted for conspiracy as a
result of this demonstration; his companions in the "Oakland Seven," all people
in and around SDS at the time, were Terry Cannon, Reese Erlich, Steve Hamilton, Bob Mandel, Mike Smith, and Jeff Segal.

from occurring or at least make those events the scene of enough disquiet to indicate the growing level of dissent to the public."

That night, November 14, a crowd of somewhere between five and ten thousand people—an accurate head count was impossible, since the area was crowded and most of the demonstrators never stood still for long—greeted Rusk and his fellow diners with banners, jeers, and appropriate obscenities as they made their way through the heavy police lines into the hotel. Those who tried to crash through the barriers were roughly pushed back, and a number were arrested. Then one group—New York police say it was Columbia SDSers—started throwing bottles, bags of red paint and cow's blood, and any available trash at the police and arriving limousines. Several people thought to be responsible were dragged from the crowd by the riot squads, roughed up, and arrested, but others managed to dart away, repeat the attack, then fall back again, eluding arrest. Soon knots of protesters were gathered at half a dozen intersections, yelling and jeering, overturning trash baskets, denting anything that looked vaguely like a posh limousine, pulling fire alarms—and then moving on to the sidewalks and down the side streets when police approached, only to reappear moments later farther down the avenue. For more than three hours the middle of Manhattan was chaos, the police befuddled by these new hit-and-run tactics (and in their befuddlement often taking it out brutally on the other demonstrators still massed peaceably), the mobile bands of demonstrators growing increasingly elated and increasingly uncontrolled, and the throngs of Times Square onlookers puzzled and angered by turns. When it was all over, sometime after eleven o'clock, forty-six people had been arrested, at least twenty-one demonstrators had been hospitalized, and five policemen had been treated for injuries. Despite the failure of the demonstrators to escape arrest entirely, and despite the arrest of Ted Gold, Mark Rudd, and Ron Carver of the Columbia chapter on potentially serious charges of "incitement to riot," most of the rank-and-file SDSers there were excited by the new escalation of tactics. "It was the first time we ever tried to take the offensive," one has said, "and, you know, it *worked.*"

The New York Times that week was somewhat less enthused. Assuming its most outraged perch, it accused the demonstrators of being "junior-grade stormtroopers," and added:

> The organizers of this sorry spectacle . . . apparently did not even attempt to discourage the militant minority, notably those led by the Students for a Democratic Society, who they surely knew would seek to stir up trouble. The leaders of both groups share a heavy responsibility for a disgraceful episode that only debases dissent, obstructing development of the national debate on Vietnam policy that is so urgently needed.

The *Times,* alas, understood neither the extent nor the rationale of the opposition to the Vietnam war, a poignant measure of the chasm between the Establishment and its children. The paper, even in the fall of 1967, had not come out in opposition to the war, still believed that there was room for "national debate" on the subject, and still imagined that the forces of the left were interested only in inaugurating such a debate. The circles around SDS had long discarded "debate," had tired of the peaceful "dissent" which finally had come to seem respectable to the *Times* editorialists, and were now on to something, the politics of resistance, that at least could make the policy makers sit up and take notice and maybe start to drag the country, kicking and screaming, to a position of honor.

On the campuses. Resistance was not new here, of course, but its extent, its militance, and the response to it were all at unexpected heights.

Though many of the milder demonstrations still involved demands against university administrations over purely student-power issues, those which moved on to resistance were in greatest part those relating to complicity. Complicity was understood by more students now—even liberals came to see the point—and radical researchers at hundreds of campuses, large and small, continued through the fall to produce papers and pamphlets exposing in detail the links, sometimes quite nefarious, between campus and government. And as these revelations grew, and the nature of the system became clearer, so the reaction to it all increased. In the words of Michael Kazin, a leader of the Harvard

SDS chapter at the time, "The level of tactics has changed because the analysis has changed."*

The means of attacking complicity were, as before, demonstrations against recruiters from the military services, the CIA, and war-connected industries such as Dow, plus for the first time a significant number of protests over the presence of units of the Reserve Officers Training Corps on campus. According to one survey, nearly a quarter of all institutions, and more than 60 percent of the large universities, had recruiting protests during the school year, and in another survey no fewer than 106 campuses acknowledged recruiter demonstrations during the fall months alone. Of the sixty largest and best-publicized demonstrations of the fall, forty involved recruiters (twenty of them Dow recruiters), six attacked ROTC, and six others were broadly against the war, while only eight attacked administrations for various local grievances. But what made this fall different was that student tactics

---

*To cite just a few exposures that fall: Columbia SDSers published proof of a $125,000-a-year contract between the CIA and Columbia's School of International Affairs, a link which the school's dean, Andrew Cordier, had repeatedly denied all along and was now forced to admit. VOICE exposed "Project Michigan," part of the University of Michigan's $21.6 million contract with the Pentagon concerned with developing infrared sensing equipment to be used in jungle fighting; VOICE members also forced Lee DuBridge, president of the war-connected California Institute of Technology, to defend publicly secret war research on university campuses: "Because," he said, "it is valuable." "Valuable for what?" cried one SDSer. "Valuable," he blurted, "for killing people." SDS's Southern California Regional Office unveiled the elaborate links between the University of California and various parts of the defense industry, and held a "University complicity teach-in" at UCLA in October. Penn State SDSers uncovered their university's research contracts with the Department of Defense for running an ordnance laboratory and developing the nuclear submarine fleet. MIT SDS put out a detailed twenty-one-page pamphlet showing that the university's involvement with defense contracts was so extensive it depended upon the government for 79 percent of its annual budget. Harvard SDS publicized the big-business connections of the university's trustees (13 corporation chairmanships, 8 presidencies, 108 directorships) plus heavy university investments in segregated businesses in the South and apartheid supporters like Chase Manhattan. *New Left Notes* (September 25) listed the fifty universities, from Hawaii to New York and Alaska to Florida, taking part in the Pentagon's "Project Themis" and publicized exposures in other newspapers showing up university complicity in a $30-million-a-year counterinsurgency project and in ongoing research in chemical and biological warfare. NACLA put out pamphlets detailing the Cold War roles of the nominally independent Institute for International Education and the prestigious Foreign Policy Association.

now tended to begin with obstructive sit-ins and go on up from there; as Carl Davidson, rejoicing on the sidelines, put it:

> No one goes limp anymore, or meekly to jail. Police violence does not go unanswered. Sit-ins are no longer symbolic, but strategic: to protect people or hold positions, rather than to allow oneself to be passively stepped over or carted off. . . . While the anti-recruiter sit-ins last Spring were primarily acts of moral witness and political protest, an increasing number of the sit-ins this Fall displayed the quality of Tactical Political Resistance. Their purpose was the disruption and obstruction of certain events and actions BY WHATEVER MEANS NECESSARY.

Thus at least twenty of the largest demonstrations involved sit-ins designed to imprison recruiters or prevent them from operating, and at three campuses the recruiters were chased right off the premises; according to a survey at the time no fewer than 45 percent of the recruiter actions (i.e., forty-eight of them) involved personal violence of one kind or another.* Administration reaction in at least twenty of the demonstrations was to call in the police, marking the first time that outside force had ever been used on college campuses on such a scale—Berkeley had sent for the cops twice and police had invaded a few black colleges in the South, but this was the first widespread use—and the inevitable result was simply to escalate the confrontation, create violence, and usually muster broad student support; again according to the survey of recruiter demonstrations, the level of the protest was expanded in half the cases where police were called in and 73 percent of the cases where students were arrested. At a half a

---

*Antirecruiting demonstrations against the CIA took place at Brandeis, Brown, University of Colorado, Kentucky, Pennsylvania, and Tulane; against military recruiters at Adelphi, Brooklyn, California (Irvine, Riverside, Santa Cruz, and San Jose), Colorado, Harvard, Iowa, Michigan State, Oberlin, and Pratt Institute; against Dow at Boston University, Brandeis, California (Berkeley, Los Angeles State, San Jose, San Fernando Valley, and UCLA), Chicago, CCNY, Connecticut, Harvard, Illinois, Indiana, Iowa, Minnesota, NYU, Pennsylvania, Rochester, Vanderbilt, and Wisconsin; and against the International Volunteers Service at Goddard College. Anti-ROTC actions took place at Arizona, Brandeis, Howard, Louisiana State (!), Rutgers, and San Francisco State. Antiwar protests occurred at Berkeley, Indiana, Princeton, Stony Brook, Washington University, and Yale. Anti-administration demonstrations were held at Berkeley, CCNY, Howard, Miles College, Missouri, Rochester, San Francisco State, and the University of Washington.

dozen campuses (including Brooklyn, Rochester, San Francisco State, and Wisconsin) the ultimate weapon of student resistance, the strike, was attempted, with varying degrees of success.

It is of particular notice that resistance should have focused so often just now on Dow, for that marks a growing sophistication among many students of the role of corporations in propagating the war and is a solid indication that at least a rudimentary understanding of imperialism was catching hold. Dow had been making napalm (among other war supplies) since 1966, and the evils of napalm in producing violent disfiguration and death among the Vietnamese civilian population were well enough known, but before this fall there had been only a few scattered attempts to use the presence of Dow's recruiters as occasions for protests against the war. During the 1967–68 academic year, according to the Dow people, its agents made 339 campus visits and were demonstrated against or prevented from recruiting at 113 of them. Connections were very clearly being made; as the Wisconsin demonstrators had put it, "We pick this week to demonstrate against Dow, against the university as a corporation and against the war *because they are all one.*"

It is also of notice that the strategy of resistance, though practiced with a flourish at the larger state universities and traditionally liberal colleges, extends to quite staid and remote campuses where there has been very little protest before. SDS is largely but not wholly responsible for this, since its influence and its chapters had reached many of the smaller schools by now; not every place that had an SDS group had a confrontation, of course, but almost every place that had a confrontation had an active SDS presence. At Indiana, for example, in what was that university's first major action, nearly a hundred students (including a large number of SDSers) surrounded the office a Dow recruiter was using and demanded a debate, only to be rebuffed by the recruiter, harangued by the administration, and arrested and beaten by the campus police and Bloomington riot squad, thus precipitating what the official faculty report on the incident called "a crisis in the life of the university." At Brooklyn College, a place not known for its radicalism, students were so shocked by the calling in of police to arrest Jeffrey Gordon and other SDSers for setting up a table next to a Navy recruiter's, and were so outraged at the

resulting blood and brutality, that they closed down the campus
for the next five days, until the college gave in to their demands
that the police would be summoned no more and the military
would recruit no more. Resistance came, too, to Adelphi, where
a Marine recruiter was locked up for four hours; to Goddard
College, where antirecruiting sit-iners were told by the administration, "When you come to college you lose your rights"; to Princeton, where thirty-one people were arrested during an IDA sit-in;
to Colorado, Arizona, Vanderbilt, Pratt, Kentucky, and Stony
Brook. . . .

   In the capital. At mid-afternoon on October 21 some one
hundred thousand Americans—students in the main, but older
people, dropouts, housewives, others, too—marched through long
lines of bayonet-ready soldiers and baton-wielding federal marshals toward the locus of American power, the Pentagon. They
had assembled where told to assemble, listened to the droning
speeches, sung the desultory antiwar songs, followed the usual
leaders—but now, it was clear, something new was about to happen. The front ranks ran up against a line of soldiers, paused,
backed off . . . a few moral protesters deliberately crossed the lines
and were arrested . . . leaders of the National Mobilization Committee, which had called the march, gave reassuring speeches
through their bullhorns . . . there was a tense pause . . . and
suddenly a group of young people—an SDS contingent and some
New York Yippies—made a breakthrough in the line of soldiers,
swept over the weather fences, ran past more startled troops, and
presented themselves directly to the walls of the Pentagon itself.
Several dozen people made a dash for a side door, assaulting the
war machine where it was apparently vulnerable, but they were
halted at the entrance by a group of young paratroopers, beaten
with rifle butts, hauled away, and arrested. By then, however,
several thousand more had come up behind them; troops and
marshals flailed desperately at the crowd, fired tear gas, used their
clubs, but still the demonstrators poured through, until finally
something between five and ten thousand demonstrators were
encamped on the Pentagon lawns, facing rows of bayonets and the
prospect of violence, but victorious still, and exhilarated.

An NLF flag was raised on a liberated Pentagon flagstaff, its gold star winking up at Secretary of Defense Robert McNamara and the other military brass observing from the windows over-head. A group of inspired hippies—"witches, warlocks, holymen, seers, prophets, mystics, saints, sorcerers, shamans, troubadours, minstrels, bards, roadmen, and madmen," according to the *East Village Other*—began their planned exorcism and levitation of the massive building with elaborate rituals and calls. One young man helped his woman over a barbed wire fence, lay down with her in front of a line of bewildered soldiers, and they proceeded, unper-turbed and undisturbed, to make love. Another man threw a rock and broke a window, the only overt act of violence by the demon-strators during the entire day. As evening approached, food ap-peared from somewhere, people began relieving themselves against the walls of the Pentagon, plentiful supplies of marijuana passed through the crowds, little knots of people sang, a few political types gave impromptu speeches, and then, quite without warning, a draft card was burned, and then another, and another, until perhaps a hundred little fires could be seen aloft throughout the crowd.

As the night wore on, the demonstrators tore up weather fences and movable benches to build bonfires against the whipping cold, waiting with some trepidation for the expected order at midnight that the rally permit had expired and the crowd was to disperse. SDSers were conspicuous among them—the police later claimed that "SDS played a very prominent role in prolonging and sustaining the actual siege of the Pentagon itself"—and when midnight came, the order was given, and the troops slowly moved toward the crowd. It was Greg Calvert who had the bullhorn; he spoke of the people who had made the war, the people who were now directing these troops against their fellow countrymen, and he told them: "The troops you employ belong to us and not to you. They don't belong to the generals. They belong to a new hope for America that those generals could never participate in." Fanciful as it may seem, perhaps someone was listening to that. For after a sweep by one line of troops down the right side of the mall, with no visible signs that the demonstrators were prepared to budge, the soldiers suddenly stopped, and re-formed their lines: apparently the chaos of confrontation, the battle of soldiers against countrymen, was not to be. Into the dawn, huddled around dying fires, embracing to keep warm, the demonstrators kept their vigil, while just feet away stood the weary soldiers, their lines intact but immobile.

Fully seven hundred people had by now been arrested, at least twice that number had been beaten and bloodied, tear gas and truncheons had been used and loaded guns were only feet away—and yet the demonstrators would not give an inch. Even when sparks of violence ignited during that night, and the threat of a full-scale explosion seemed very real, the reaction from the crowd was unflinching:

> An SDS girl from Boston was dozing about 2:30 A.M. in the morning [sic] about 15 feet and several rows from me. The guy next to her was grabbed by marshals and she awoke startled. In waking she must have brushed against a soldier—it isn't quite clear. She was then grabbed by a marshal, dragged through the line, whereupon the marshal started clubbing the hell out of her.
>
> We focused a spotlight and a camera on him. The look on his face could only have been that of someone having an orgasm. Pictures were taken. The girl, who ended up getting three broken ribs, was carried to a paddy wagon; the marshal came up to a line of soldiers, and with a sadistic look on his face, ominously held his club high towards the crowd. The crowd near the girl rose to its feet, started screaming, and had difficulty restraining itself from a suicidal assault into the several rows of readied troops.

Then, toward dawn, most of the demonstrators agreed that their point had been made, their attack on the headquarters of the American war machine (which no one would really have believed possible a week before) complete. At sunrise, the large bulk of the crowd marched down the Pentagon walkways to the parking lots and streets, and home.

It was, for all concerned, a truly educative experience. The government, on the one hand, bewildered and angry in turns, had for the first time used its own troops to threaten its own white middle-class children and had seen in this mild, containable form what a true revolt might possibly look like; for failing to predict and contain the Pentagon militance, according to *The New York*

Times, "senior officers caught what one source described as 'undiluted hell' from high political leaders, apparently including President Johnson," and began scurrying around inaugurating a whole series of intelligence and security operations designed to protect the government from its own citizens. The Movement for its part felt that it had moved right up to the brink of insurrection —and though it had shied away unprepared and unsure, it was left with the taste of resistance, defiant mass resistance, and it liked the taste; REPer Mike Goldfield, writing in *New Left Notes,* drew these conclusions:

> Symbolically . . . the invincibility of the greatest military power in the world was attacked. Hawks, and military men especially, have chided weak-minded university administrators about their inability to put the clamps down on unruly, sissy students. Yet several thousand of us outwitted the Pentagon plans for making us look silly, kept McNamara up all night, the government confused about what to do, and blatantly broke several laws in plain view of all (i.e., draft card burning, pot laws, defacing government property, and the obvious one of charging the Pentagon). . . . The move from protest to resistance has been made.

Even the Progressive Labor Party—which, as we shall see, was hardly receptive to the resistance strategy—found some of the confrontations that fall exhilarating. Milt Rosen, the party's chairman, wrote of the Brooklyn College demonstration:

> Very often a united front on one question can lead to a broader united front on other questions. This can lead to involving more people in struggle and winning more people to the more fundamental point. The recent Brooklyn College experience is very germane. At the school the united front—PL and SDS—were acting against some aspect of the war. The school attacked. The students defended the right of the united front to carry on its actions without harassment. The school called the cops. The focus of the united front shifted momentarily away from the war to "cops on campus and student-faculty control." . . .
> Ten thousand students supported the strike and the anti-war united front. Many of these students previously supported the war or were passive. Because of this broader involvement some changed their minds and some were won over from passiveness to opposition. The SDS grew, we will grow, opposition to the war will grow, and

opposition to the administration will grow. Naturally, there will be attacks and complications. But the action proved our basic premise that the majority of students can be won to struggle against the system.

The national leaders of SDS, though they had by no means planned or foreseen this explosion of resistance, were quick to pick up on it, promote it, and turn it insofar as they could into a kind of national program for the fall.*

Following the Pentagon, Carl Davidson evolved a new strategy for SDS called "Toward Institutional Resistance," which called for students to embark upon "the disruption, dislocation and destruction of the military's access to the manpower, intelligence, or resources of our universities" so as to produce "two complementary goals: 1) the weakening of the resisted dominant institution and 2) developing a consciousness of power among those resisting the dominant institution." His article was widely reproduced on the college campuses and proved very influential among a number of radical groups. SDS Regional Offices, now numbering five (New York City, upstate New York, Southern California, Boston, Washington), held regional conferences to find targets and occasions for resistance actions, put out newsletters telling what the campus demonstrations were, and sent campus travelers around to push the resistance theme.

In neither money nor efficiency was the NO notable. It

*Carl Davidson even went so far as to claim credit for the whole thing to SDS —"The idea of organizing a national movement to expel the military from the campus . . . formally became a major SDS national program at the June, 1967 National Convention in Ann Arbor, Michigan," he said in *New Left Notes* (November 13, 1967)—but that simply was not true. The convention had rejected all major national programs and its only reference to "the military on campus" was a passing aside in the tentative student-strike resolution. More than one observer has accepted the Davidson version. Richard Peterson of the Educational Testing Service, for example, later wrote: "Opposition to war-effort recruiters took place mainly at the public and independent universities. In large part these demonstrations were organized by local chapters of Students for a Democratic Society, in pursuance of a 'direction' approved at their national meeting the previous summer, and may be taken as a gauge of SDS's ability to override its cherished localism and mount a coordinated 'program' on a national scale." (Foster and Long, *Protest!* p. 66.) In truth, there was no direction, no overriding, and no coordinated program.

seemed that no matter how much came in by way of contributions the organization always found a way to spend it and be on the lookout for more. This fall, for example, Mike Spiegel inveigled a handsome $12,000 gift from an anonymous figure—it was, he agreed, "a charitable handout from the middle class which likes our libertarian ideas"—but a month later the coffers were virtually empty. Throughout these months income averaged around $1800 a week (mostly from contributions and literature orders), and expenditures (chiefly for printing supplies, salaries, and overhead of the NO) were about the same.* For the calendar year the NO filed a tax report listing a total income for 1967 of $70,698.85 ($33,931.00 from contributions), expenses of $68,754.47, and profit of $1944.38. Office organization was equally haphazard. The new three-secretary scheme and the new national officers did not work particularly well: Davidson was bored with his role as Inter-organizational Secretary and spent most of his time traveling and writing in his role as a semiofficial guru; Pardun, as Education Secretary, tried to keep up the elaborate file on chapter activities and contacts but felt rather more comfortable on the road; and Spiegel—well, Spiegel found himself a little out of his depth as a twenty-year-old National Secretary for an organization of national prominence, and his reaction was to spend his time on

*A fairly typical entry is this headed "Tale with a Tragic Ending," from the week of November 7 to November 13 (*New Left Notes,* November 20):

INCOME:		EXPENSES:	
Dues & Subscriptions:	$478.00	Petty Cash:	$5.20
Literature:	238.00	Travel:	240.00
Contributions:	146.50	Subsistence:	345.00
Pledges:	91.05	Office & REC supplies:	73.12
Sales:	92.16	Printing Supplies:	432.51
Miscellaneous:	85.00	Exchanges:	35.00
Exchanges:	35.00	Car Expenses:	9.00
NLN Ads:	00.00	Typesetting:	18.32
Printing:	324.75	Postage:	43.67
Loans:	00.00	Telephone (REC):	47.66
Chapter Tax:	00.00	Gas & Electric (REC)	34.01
Journal A:	−15.00	Rent (REC)	125.00
		Debts:	50.00
Total:	$1505.46	Miscellaneous:	−244.87
		Total:	$1703.36

quotidian minutiae while letting others take the spotlight.

But it hardly seemed to matter. This was another instance of SDS's being there, with good politics, experience, charisma, and a dedicated hard core of activists, when the general mood of the young, principally the campus young, needed it. And the SDS leadership, especially those around the National Office, felt itself in the vortex of a swirling movement whose momentum hardly depended upon financial or bureaucratic efficiency. Something crucial was happening now: SDS *began to feel itself revolutionary.* As Greg Calvert expressed it some time later, the feeling was that "in the resistance movement there is a truly radical and potentially revolutionary movement among whites." In an interview that December he said:

> I think that what happened in the last six months happened first in the ghetto rebellions and then it happened in a new wave of militancy in the white student movement. People began to identify themselves as powerful or as an historical force for the first time. Suddenly we were no longer the isolated bright-eyed utopians of America dreaming about a future which we really didn't think we could realize. . . . I think it's possible to realize a powerful organization linked together. It may be the first serious American revolutionary organization in 175 years.

This was pretty heady stuff, and its effects on the organization were quickly evident. For one thing, the SDS leadership, feeling that perhaps they could now realize that dream of forging a broad American left that had haunted SDSers from the beginning, turned swiftly away from the students-first idea that had energized the student-power strategy. The student movement seemed no longer sufficient: what was wanted was a broad alliance of young whites, blacks, the working class, the poor, all those ready for revolution. In a special issue of *New Left Notes* designed for wide campus distribution that September, NO staffer John Veneziale argued:

> Students as students, in my opinion, are not necessary for a revolution. The only reason even to attempt a campus movement is that students are useful and universities have a large concentration of young potential people whose middle class and bourgeois values are

not irreversibly entrenched; otherwise they are not worth the trouble. . . . If a person in the U.S. in 1967 considers himself or herself a student, he or she negates the meaning of being a revolutionary.

And in a most remarkable turnaround, Carl Davidson said in the same issue:

What can students do? Organizing struggles over domitory rules seems frivolous when compared to the ghetto rebellions. And white students are no longer wanted or necessary in the black movement. . . . Draft resistance tables in the student union building—the arrogance of it all. We organize students against the draft when the Army is made up of young men who are poor, black, Spanish-American, hillbillies, or working class. Everyone except students. How can we be so stupid when we plan our strategies?

Students are oppressed. Bullshit. We are being trained to be the oppressors and the underlings of oppressors.*

For another thing, as a result, the SDS leadership turned increasingly away from the student-oriented new-working-class theories that had surfaced in the spring. Those theories, and their defenses, because they had to be created new, seemed too hard to formulate and polish in the instant, especially in the face of attacks from people like the PL dogmatists and especially at a time when action brought its own rewards and resistance seemed enough to create visions of the revolution. SDSers involved in theory tended to give up the hard work of fashioning their own, of finding formulations that were new, particular to their time and place, valid for a postindustrial system, consistent with the Movement they had seen develop, true to their own experience, coherent with their own reality. They turned more often instead to something ready-made, something so all-encompassing that you needed only to consult its index to find the correct solution for your particular nagging problem. The feeling grew that what SDS lacked was a series of engraved ideological tablets along its organizational walls and a bearded nineteenth-century portrait over its hearth. And the inevitable result was a turn toward the traditional standby, Marxism.

* *New Left Notes* kept up the same drumbeat through the fall—see Steve Hamilton, October 2; Mike James, October 9; Bob Pardun, November 6; Thad Marty, November 20; Vernon Urban, December 4; and Les Coleman, December 11.

Now it may have been that this was simply the collective perception of an inevitable truth—as Che Guevara was fond of noting, "It's not my fault that reality is Marxist"—or it may have been a response to the ease and surety with which the new PL people (and behind them the Communist Party members) answered all questions by referring to the Marxist standards. But the more reasonable explanation was, as Oglesby later said, that when the SDSers began to be led by their own logic toward the idea of revolution, they found that *"there was—and is—no other coherent, integrative, and explicit philosophy of revolution."* He added:

> I don't think the American Left's first stab at producing for itself a *fulfilled* revolutionary consciousness could have produced anything better, could have gone beyond this ancestor-worship politics. It was necessary to discover—or maybe the word is confess—that we had ancestors in the first place.

Of course the acceptance of—or at least reading of—those ancestors who had been scorned by the New Left for so long came only haltingly and was still in its infancy here; but gradually quotations from Marx, then Lenin, and then the modern European Marxists found their way into SDS and other Movement literature. Carl Davidson was now talking easily about "class analysis" and "imperialism"— "Who among us today," he asked in November, "would argue that America is not an imperialist power?"—and when he went on to assert, in a discussion of whether Dow recruiters had the civil liberty to operate on campuses, that "to respect and operate within the realm of bourgeois civil liberties is to remain enslaved," he felt himself comfortably within the Marxist-Leninist tradition—as indeed he was.* These same burgeoning perceptions led many in the upper levels of SDS to relish the new contacts being made this fall with leftists and revolutionaries from other countries, especially North and South Vietnam: Steve Halliwell, for example, reported back to the SDS membership after meeting revolutionary Vietnamese in Bratislava that fall:

---

*But most of his constituency was not. Several people wrote in to *New Left Notes* to denounce Davidson for this opinion, and when he repeated it at a REP conference the same month he was attacked by several people including SDSers Eric Chester, Christopher Hobson (Chicago), and Michael Klare (Columbia). Thus grew the rift.

For those present, the manner of the people from both North and South who presented [their] information is of crucial importance, for their manner is that of men and women struggling in a society in revolution. . . . It is that total endeavor by a society in revolution that came across in the course of our conversations. Against a society demanding freedom and independence from an imperialist force, there is no weapon save destruction of every individual in revolt that will bring about any end other than victory for the liberation forces.*

Finally, the SDS leadership began to see itself more and more (in the Marxist phraseology) as a "vanguard" in the impending revolution, or at least as the core of that potential vanguard. The people around the NO itself became an increasingly close-knit group: a number of the staff lived and slept together in nearby apartments in a quasi-communal style; they shared drug experiences (marijuana mostly, but also LSD), out of which came, initially at least, a sense of closeness and unity; and they developed their political ideas together both through informal contacts around the office and in formal meetings which they held to "advance their political education," in the words of the National Administrative Committee. Davidson and Calvert (who still spent a good deal of his time in Chicago) were especially important figures, providing the solidarity of continuity that the NO had lacked since Haber's time, and acting as the centripetal force for many of the people around the NO who were several years younger. Then, too, there was the feeling of being a bastion against the forces of a repressive society, a feeling enhanced by the regular harassment of the Chicago police and by one destructive raid made upon the SDS building that fall by unknown attackers; in

*There were other contacts between SDSers and third-world revolutionaries at this time—Carl Oglesby spent part of the summer at Bertrand Russell's war crimes tribunal, Cathy Wilkerson and Carol McEldowney spent some time with NLF people in Cambodia in November, a meeting of North American and NLF students was held in Montreal, and Davidson, Tom Hayden, Todd Gitlin, and others traveled to Cuba at the end of the year. But the Bratislava meeting—which attracted such SDSers as Rennie Davis, Thorne Dreyer, Nick Egleson, Dick Flacks, Norm Fruchter, Carol Glassman, Hayden, Halliwell, Andy Kopkind, Robert Kramer, Carol McEldowney, Doug Norberg, and Wilkerson—was the most formative; Christopher Jencks noted in the *New Republic* (October 7, 1967) that "the most striking fact about the young radicals was the extent to which they identified with the Viet Cong."

response the NAC voted to put wire mesh on the office windows, to admit visitors from the street only by buzzer, and to station one of the staff each night in the office as a security guard (though it was decided he would not be armed unless someone could "procure some type of tear gas"). It was left to Greg Calvert to enunciate the new level of understanding, and he did so in a remarkable article in *New Left Notes* in December. Starting with the premise that "our organizational structure and style are proving inadequate to cope with the strains which the new upsurge of activity and the new political seriousness have produced," he proposed to scrap that old idea of participatory democracy: "The basic problem with participatory democracy lies not in its analysis or vision, but in its basic inadequacy as a style of work for a serious radical organization." What SDS needs, he said, is "responsible collective leadership," or a "steering committee . . . responsible for the development of long-range organizing strategies and programs which can be intelligently discussed and criticized by the members." Only with such a collective can SDS become a "revolutionary organization" capable of "serious analysis" and enlistment of "those elements in the society which can form the base of a mass movement." How far had SDS now come.

Or at least the leadership. For it should not be thought that all of SDS was swept up in the same celebration of resistance and anticipation of revolution. Many in the membership, and not alone the newest and most innocent members, complained about the new trends and the ever-more-obvious "distance" problem. *New Left Notes* was full of complaints from people asking what they were supposed to do on the day *after* resistance. What happens after a confrontation, no matter how successful, when the administration seems conciliatory, the faculty votes reforms, and the students end up not having seen the bedrock issue of complicity anyway? What happens when, as one Wisconsin SDSer put it, "the many liberal students and faculty members who struck against police brutality are still not convinced that Dow or the CIA should be thrown off campus. They don't believe the university is part of the corporate hierarchy that rules America; they don't even believe that a corporate hierarchy DOES rule America"? It is all very well for the NO to see and to relish a pattern of nation-wide events which to them forms resistance, but the realities on a single campus are different. If Davidson scorns the idea of SDS tables in the student-union building, that might make sense from his perspective—but, as one angry SDSer from the University of Nebraska told him, "In case you don't know, sitting behind an SDS literature table involves taking a very large step, if you happen to be a Nebraskan fresh off the farm and don't even know who Marx is." Of the national officers, only Spiegel seemed truly worried about the distance problem— "There is the inevitable tendency for the NO to become further and further alienated from the membership; it takes on an internal logic of its own"— but, he argued, it is up to the chapters to advance more rapidly, not for the NO to hold back:

> As SDS grows and assumes a more primary political role on the left, its internal structure must be examined. We cannot afford to become more mature politically while permitting a weak spot in our internal structure to continue to hold us back.

What really lies behind this continuous fissure is the absolutely crucial question of how to build a movement for rapid and wholesale change in America: by raising the level of confrontation so as to threaten the sources of power, or by educating and organizing to gain as wide a following as possible? Are more recruits brought in by militant action and a sense that things are happening, the enemy is weakening, the stakes are getting higher, and victories are being won? Or does this turn away potential allies, alienate those whose consciousness is not yet identical, serve to isolate and splinter the minority, and stiffen the backs of those in power? Is the task one of regular, sustained resistance, putting one's body on the line, acting out of one's felt anger and need, moving when and where possible with whoever is ready, building militance ever higher? Or is it one of long-range base-building, appealing to other segments of the population, holding one's own feelings in check so as to win new converts, waiting until the time is right, spreading the message ever wider?

Even in the flush of resistance, this issue began to trouble the organization. The national leadership, without a direct and

immediate constituency to worry about and with a perception
of the broad national effects of resistance, tended to favor the
resistance strategy. Many of the chapters—by no means all but
especially those which found their lances blunted after actions
of resistance or which found themselves coopted and isolated
in their immediate locales—tended to opt for base-building. In
the next year this tension will continue to grow, continue to
pose the most serious question for the continuance of SDS as a
national organization. It would have been small comfort for
SDSers, even if they had been aware of it, to know that this
question was one faced, and agonized over, by every revolutionary organization in history.

"We should have moved then." Steve Weissman, then in Ann
Arbor working for the Radical Education Project, has looked
back on these fateful months with the perspective of the old
guard:

> We should have done more to stop them when they took over in
> 1967. It was clear enough that a new Marxist group was taking over,
> and a new style, without a vote, nothing connected to the chapters,
> or to the organization as a whole. It was just a decision by a few
> people, the people around the National Office. The NO had always
> been its own separate organization, that's true, but it had always
> thought of itself as just trying to keep things going, nothing like this.
> Now it became a collective unto itself.

But the old guard did not move then. The older members
found little welcome, except as monuments, among the chapters or in the regional offices, and there was no regularized
way for national SDS to use their talents; they felt, moreover,
little inclination to assert themselves in a students' movement,
especially at a time when it seemed that the left could branch
out into other parts of the population. Then, too, there was
other work to occupy them—although the ERAP projects
were all but finished now (except for JOIN, and it had almost
none of the original people), there was REP, now producing
pamphlets by the thousands (some sixty different items by the
end of the year), organizing conferences (notably one on "the
university and the military" at Chicago in November), running

a speakers bureau,* and starting a "Radicals in the Professions" newsletter for communication among (mostly academic) Movement alumni; there was NACLA, moving into complicity research in a major way; there were left-wing publications like *Ramparts,* the *Movement,* the *Guardian,* and *Radical America,* plus a host of counterculture newspapers and several specialized media projects, such as Newsreel, for making and distributing Movement films. Haber and Flacks were teaching, Hayden and Davis spent much of their time traveling abroad, Oglesby was writing and lecturing, Booth was doing union work, Kissinger was living out his dream of an independent political party, Webb was enticed to the Institute for Policy Studies, Potter was organizing in the Boston area, Egleson and Grizzard were doing draft resistance in Boston—and so it went. The alumni had not left radical politics, but they had other tasks, and, thus isolated, with their own preoccupations, they were in no position to move anywhere in the new SDS.

Part of the strategy of the Progressive Labor Party after the defection of much of its West Coast membership—in addition to the emphasis on the student movement—had been an attempt to rebuild strength among the working class. The party reasserted stern discipline over its remaining members and saw to it that they worked in factory jobs and lived in working-class communities; party chairman Milt Rosen detailed the directive: "We have to have more discipline based on collectivity, based on understanding, people have to become more accountable to the party, people have to work, people have to go to school, people have to accomplish something in the community." At the same time PL thought

*The list of speakers that fall suggests both the central role played by SDSers in radical work at the time and the reliance upon old-timers rather than those brought in since student syndicalism. SDSers on the list included Jane Adams, Bill Ayers, Nancy Bancroft, Hal Benenson, Heather Tobis Booth, Paul Booth, Robb Burlage, Eric Chester, Rennie Davis, Dick Flacks, John Fuerst, Dave Gilbert, Nanci Gitlin, Todd Gitlin, Carol Glassman, Mike Goldfield, Bob Gottlieb, Dick Greeman, Barbara Haber, Steve Halliwell, Jill Hamberg, Tom Hayden, Peter Henig, James Jacobs, Mike James, Steve Johnson, Clark Kissinger, Chuck Levenstein, Mike Locker, Kathy McAfee, Carol McEldowney, Dick Magidoff, John Maher, Eric Mann, Carl Oglesby, Paul Potter, Bob Ross, Gerry Tenney, Harriet Stulman, Lee Webb, Steve Weissman, Jim Williams, Carl Wittman, Martha Zweig, Michael Zweig.

to pull in its horns, avoid the confrontational tactics it had used before, and present itself to the working public as a more moderate political force; Rosen said:

> In the past we put a lot of emphasis on open agitation. Our ability to grow from this has been very limited. People in the community are not generally ready to organize directly against the war, or under revolutionary banners, although huge numbers are opposed to the war, and some forces are deadly opposed to the system. Therefore, we must continually probe for the level around which people are ready to organize.

This process, in PL, became known as "base-building," and it stood in opposition to "resistance." "Without real base-building," Rosen told the members, "the party will shrivel up and die," and he added, "We reject tactics like 'resistance' because these tactics will not only isolate radicals from workers, but from other students and intellectuals that could be won." "Base-building" became the central watchword of Progressive Labor throughout 1967 and 1968, precisely at the time that resistance was at its height; thus neatly did PL assert its territoriality in the debate that was just beginning to emerge in SDS.

On the campus level, the new PL strategy took several forms. PL members argued against most confrontations, as at Harvard, on the grounds that they tended to alienate both the campus majority and the surrounding working-class community. PL chose tactics, as at Brooklyn College, which were calculated to appeal to liberal and moderate elements and thus, as Jeffrey Gordon put it, "win over thousands of other students to our position." PL avoided student-power issues which might strike the working class as elitist; California PL organizer John Levin wrote in the November–December issue of *PL*:

> Student power . . . tends to emphasize the individualistic nature of the student movement, that students are somehow a privileged class which is to be treated nicely. . . . Student power . . . tends to isolate itself and would eventually lead us into conflict with the workers of this country. It is most important that SDS take the lead in breaking the antiwar movement out of its isolation and bringing it into alliance with the working class.

Above all, PL put the finishing theoretical touches on its "worker-student alliance" strategy and prepared to launch it into the student movement with all its skill.

Though actual party membership seems to have remained well under a thousand this fall, the PL approach attracted a number of students into the PL orbit, especially in the strongholds of Boston, Chicago, and New York. Those who had early doubts about resistance, or who had been burned by unsuccessful confrontations, were sympathetic to the base-building idea, though often not to the specific notion of a working-class base. Those who had groped their way to radicalism through opposition to the war but had still to surround it with any developed analysis found an undeniable appeal in PL's ready-made formulas—and this was enhanced by the fact that there was little theoretical opposition, either from the old guard, represented by *The Port Huron Statement* and the REP prospectus,* or from the present SDS leadership, represented by a still-unpolished new-working-class position that was being totally ignored in the heat of resistance. And those who were simply young and easily swayed could be impressed by the PLers' open espousal of revolution, thoroughgoing anti-Americanism, unselfish devotion to the workers' cause, forthright declarations of communism—and, not least, their readiness to take on the hard jobs involved in running a chapter, a devotional task willed upon them by the party and applauded by all their fellows.

The SDS leadership was aware of these attractions, and aware, too, that PL was moving in a greater swath through the organizational fields. Jeff Shero recalls the PLers' impact at about this time:

> They'd raise questions that'd take up everybody's time, their theoretical Marxist questions, like every matter you'd debate they'd bring up their traditional political view of the working class, and you had to deal with it, and it skewered all debate—even if like eighty per cent of the people thought that it was nuts. They had an internally disciplined faction that could always keep up that pressure. . . .
>
> PL had a comprehensive ideological structure with which they could interpret the world, and at any time on any subject they could give a classical Marxist analysis of what the problem

*"The old guard," Steve Weissman said several years later, "failed especially in never getting anything down on paper setting out what they believed or figuring out how to make the younger people see what *they* saw. No one ever formalized the vision." (Interview with author.)

was and rally their solid support behind that. And then you'd
have the other people who were trying to debate and discover
what America was about, the American system and how it
worked, but were uncertain and needed to talk out things, and
had a lot of ambiguity. But there was no way to mobilize ambiguity and searching against a classical Marxist analysis. They
had an ideological tradition—and it was almost impossible to
solidify a counteranalysis to that.

PL couldn't be outmaneuvered or outdisciplined, and it couldn't
even be outthrown, for that would fly in the face of SDS's antiexclusionist tradition. It had, therefore, to be borne, with the hope
that SDS could rely upon the good sense of American college
students, the open traditions of the past, and the practices that had
so far brought such success.

The December National Council meeting, held in Bloomington, Indiana, over the Christmas holidays, was the first
chance for SDS to air the tensions that had been swirling
around since the first major outbreak of resistance on the Wisconsin campus, and no opportunity was lost to do just that.
There was a Southern caucus, the first organized and sizable
Southern contingent since the days of SNCC delegations,
which presented an endless document on Southern history and
traditions, condemned "the 'New Militancy' of the past six
months" in no uncertain terms, and came down on the side of
what it called "base-broadening." There was a strong gathering
of community organizers of the JOIN stripe who wanted now
to cut all student ties and move alone as a separate organization called the National Community Union ("We, as people of
the white working class, believe the course taken by SDS and
the Radical Movement is no longer relevant to what we consider to be our role in the movement"), a step which the NC
applauded and endorsed with $1000 besides. There was
Progressive Labor, advancing its old idea of a summer "work-
in" to get students into the factories, a notion that received little debate and less interest, but passed by a clear majority
because no one really cared. And there was, for the first time,
a vocal high-school contingent which wanted to set about officially organizing the more-militant-than-thou high-school set

and whose proposals for a team of national organizers and national publicity were endorsed almost without a murmur.*

But the basic tension that had to be aired in Bloomington was that between the resistance forces on the one hand and a variety of moderating forces (smaller chapters, the Southern caucus, PL, and the like) on the other. The lines were drawn over the question of the planned student strike for the spring.

It seemed to the national leadership and many of the large-university delegates that the time had come for a massive display of student resistance, a proposal which Carl Davidson and Greg Calvert spelled out for the membership in an article called "Ten Days to Shake the Empire." The basic premise was that the American empire was weakening:

> The crisis we are confronting is the disruption and dislocation of the political economy of imperialism in the face of wars of national liberation, of which Vietnam is only one front. The struggles of Third World movements abroad and black America at home have marked the beginning of the end of U.S. corporate capitalism. . . . The conclusion we must draw is that the primary task for the radical student movement at this time is to develop a political strategy of anti-imperialism.

The expression of this anti-imperialism would come during ten days in April when SDS would inaugurate a "program of actions in resistance to the war in Vietnam," selecting "a variety of targets for direct action on and off the campus," preferably "financial and corporate industrial targets." Nothing more definite than that was

---

*Bob Pardun, in his ironic way, took a somewhat dim view of all this perturbation. As he told the membership before the meeting, "If an anthropologist were to do a functional analysis of a typical SDS-NC he would come up with something like this: 'It appears that the primary activity of an NC is debating for long hours over issues of an intellectual-political nature. The time spent talking about implementing those decisions is usually very minimal. The debates usually go on for hours and their primary function seems to be the lowering of the frustration level of those involved so that they can then go home somewhat less tense than before. For those who do not take direct part in these discussions, and that is the majority of those attending, the function seems to be to get them into the halls or onto the grass where they can discuss their organizing problems, find out what others are doing and try to coordinate their activities. A secondary function is to discourage those who are new to the organization from ever coming to another NC.' " (*New Left Notes,* December 11, 1967.)

enumerated, but it was clear that the NO forces had discarded the whole notion of student strikes in favor of a more elaborate attack on the corporate structure which they saw underlying the empire.

The Progressive Labor contingent, which showed up at the NC in numbers surprising to the other SDSers (perhaps a quarter of the three-hundred-odd delegates), was naturally opposed to any scheme so dependent upon resistance, and one which was likely to involve factories and blue-collar workplaces as well: "We are for sharpening the struggle with U.S. imperialism," it announced, in a proposal drawn up by John Levin and Earl Silbar, "but only on our own grounds—where we come out stronger both ideologically and numerically." PL proposed instead a spring program which would stick to the campuses and concentrate on the issue of university complicity, possibly including a student strike.

The informal reception this proposal received as it was handed around before the plenary sessions indicated that it spoke more directly to the interests of the chapter delegates, but there was still a strong reluctance to follow any scheme laid down by the PL people and so three New York SDSers, Naomi Jaffe, Bob Gottlieb, and John Fuerst, hastily drew up a compromise scheme that still included ten days of resistance but would allow chapters to "develop tactics based on analysis of their own specific situation and in response to their own local needs." Anti-imperialism would still be the emphasis: but a kind of base-building among other groups would also be essential:

> The links we want to build are those which really unite fragmented groups because we experience similar problems and similar sources of oppression. These links have to be developed organically, not mechanically or on paper or in rhetoric about the "working class" but in terms of our politics and chapter programs.*

*David Gilbert, aligned with the authors of this proposal, later wrote that this motion "was offered to counter both the right opportunism of PLP and the empty (not particularly left) adventurism of the NO: right opportunist in that PLP withdrew into 'base-building' without understanding the necessity of linking up different constituencies around anti-imperialism . . . [and] their only form of constituency links was the mechanical 'worker-student alliance'; adventurist, because the NO talked about anti-imperialist politics without any sense of the concrete immediate issues that could relate such politics to a base." (Letter to NO, February 25, 1968, archives.)

When the issue finally came to a head at the last plenary session, it was quickly apparent that the Davidson-Calvert scheme was unpopular and that the national leadership had become, in the words of John Maher, "too remote from chapter work to know if this program or another makes sense for any area, much less for the whole organization." The NO people didn't even come forth with much support on its behalf, shrouding themselves in a cloak of "nonmanipulation" (Davidson, it should be noted, was absent on a trip to Cuba), and the delegates roundly expressed themselves as being against all such grandiose national programs and especially those with such overinflated rhetoric as "Ten Days to Shake the Empire." When it finally came down to a vote, the NO withdrew its plan in favor of the Jaffe-Gottlieb-Fuerst proposal, and that handily outdrew the PL scheme, 40 to 22.*

It was not so much that the National Council rejected the resistance strategy—resistance would continue to characterize the coming spring—as it sought to close the distance gap and slow down the movement of the national leadership toward ideas more militant than the membership was ready for. Mike Spiegel, in reporting to the membership on the NC, somewhat petulantly maintained that the Davidson-Calvert proposal had been rejected because "it is comprehensive only to that minority of SDS members who work at the national level and are in daily contact with the national demands. Those demands and the resultant perspective are alien to the political experience of the majority of members working at the chapter

---

*In passing, it should be pointed out that nothing more elaborate was contained in the final resolution than "a period of action [which] would extend over a ten-day period in April to allow chapters to carry out a schedule of education programs, joint actions and demonstrations aimed at a variety of institutions," and that no one—participants of all political stripes agree—gave the slightest thought to pinpointing where those actions would be concentrated. It was thus sheer nonsense for the *Reader's Digest*'s Eugene H. Methvin to claim, after the Columbia blowup in the spring: "Late last year, 300 delegates to the SDS National Council at Bloomington, Ind., decided to launch a national campaign they dubbed 'Ten days to shake the empire.' Secret caucuses picked Columbia for a 'beacon' demonstration whose flare would spark a nationwide conflagration." ("SDS: Engineers of Campus Chaos," *Reader's Digest,* October 1968.) There were no caucuses to pick "beacons," there were of course no "secret" caucuses, and if there had been it would be difficult to figure out who would have done any picking at the time.

level." That is possible; yet, as one woman from San Francisco State argued in *New Left Notes:*

> There is something wrong when the national officers in Chicago, untied to any base of their own, see different perspectives and national demands than the majority of SDS members. The success or failure of the movement and the revolution depends on the chapter people who do the daily organizing and on the correctness of their perspectives and analyses.

Note, however, that she, too, with all her emphasis on the chapters, is talking about revolution.

20

SPRING 1968

*"Monday, January 1. Breakfast in bed. Walk—E. Side."** Bernardine Dohrn had a late breakfast, spent the afternoon walking through New York's Lower East Side, and then returned to her Greenwich Village apartment to prepare for a three-week journey to Great Britain.

Bernardine Dohrn, twenty-five, was then assistant executive secretary of the National Lawyers Guild, an alliance of left-wing lawyers which for two decades had carried on legal defense for a variety of radical organizations, including the Communist Party, and was just then enjoying a new life as a center of legal advice and strategy for the New Left. Dohrn was herself a recent graduate of the University of Chicago Law School who had chosen not to take a bar examination and to concentrate instead on radical work; as she said later, plenty of other people could be lawyers but she could serve a better purpose directly involved in the Movement. She was a woman of undeniable attractiveness, of medium height, with long brown hair, vibrant brown eyes, sharp features, and an air of electric, no-nonsense energy about her. She was an activist, but not yet a militant; a radical, but not a socialist. In six

*In an apartment at 4943 North Winthrop Street, Chicago, investigators of the Illinois Crime Commission early in 1970 found a quantity of books and papers which had been left behind by the occupants sometime in the fall of 1969. Among the papers was a small appointment book for the year 1968, in which Bernardine Dohrn kept a record of her meetings and appointments and recounted in brief diary-like jottings the memorable parts of her days.

months' time, after the events of this turbulent spring, she would become a major national officer of SDS, a self-described "communist," and the symbol of SDS's final turn toward revolution.

"Tuesday, January 2. London—Air India. . . . Monday, January 15. . . . Quentin Hoare, New Left Review. LSE lecture, Stop It meeting." It was a pleasure trip, this visit to Britain, but it would be the rare American leftist who could go to London and not take pains to meet English counterparts. For 1968 was a year of growing international consciousness for the American Movement, following on from the tentative contacts of the previous fall.

While Dohrn was in London, other Movement people were in Cuba, the first of many junkets to that island in the next few years. Carl Davidson, Todd Gitlin, Tom Hayden, and Dave Dellinger were among the delegates to the International Cultural Congress in January; the next month, accepting an invitation from the Cuban Federation of University Students, SDS sent twenty more visitors;* in March a contingent of thirty-three more SDSers was sent; and in the summer several other organized trips were made, one of which Dohrn had planned to join. A few SDSers also made journeys to Southeast Asia, including one visit to Hanoi on which Vernon Grizzard was among those negotiating for the release of additional American prisoners of war. Much was made of these trips, of course, by witch-hunters in the media—Drew Pearson, for instance, would claim in June that "after extensive research this column is able to report that there is an international student conspiracy"—but at this point in fact only the most rudimentary contacts had been made, and most of what the international left knew about each other came from the world's press. Reports of the April uprising at Columbia University, for example, were greeted by French students with great enthusiasm, and accounts of the subsequent revolt by French students against the De Gaulle government proved an inspiration on many American campuses in May. Still, there is no question that the growing international consciousness of the young American left helped to turn it in a deliberately revolutionary direction.

"Friday, January 26. Rennie—lawyers meeting." The Na-

---

*Among them, Karen Ashley, Les Coleman, Joe Horton, Ed Jennings, Dick Reavis, Mark Rudd, Paul Shinoff, and Jean Weisman.

tional Mobilization Committee, having at last done with peaceful marches, was planning an all-out demonstration in Chicago during the Democratic Party National Convention in August, and it had enticed Rennie Davis and Tom Hayden out of their 1967 doldrums to coordinate that effort. As part of their preparations they planned a legal defense committee and for this they turned to the National Lawyers Guild. Dohrn convened the meeting on the night of January 26, and she and NLG executive secretary Kenneth Cloke pledged that night to offer their support and at least a month of their time to laying the legal groundwork in Chicago; as it turned out, by August Bernardine Dohrn had other things entirely on her mind.

"Monday, January 29. Spock rally—8. 14th-8th & 9th Ave." The action of the Federal government in indicting five prominent friends of draft resistance—Dr. Benjamin Spock, William Sloane Coffin, Jr., Michael Ferber, Mitchell Goodman, and Marcus Raskin—for conspiracy in "counseling, aiding, and abetting" young men to avoid and resist the Selective Service System was the first unmistakable signal that the left faced a serious threat of repression. The National Lawyers Guild was only one of many organizations which geared itself for the task of legal defense, and throughout the spring Dohrn would spend considerable time helping in the preparation of a variety of courtroom cases.

The stimulus for the government's campaign was the Pentagon demonstration, an event whose scope caught the Administration by surprise despite elaborate plans and extensive surveillance. In its wake agencies all over Washington began to move. The White House, with Lyndon Johnson making it known that he wanted "all aspects of civil disturbance matters" to receive "full attention," established a top-level Presidential team to coordinate government operations. The Department of Defense expanded its intelligence network—without, incidentally, the knowledge of the Attorney General, Ramsey Clark—until it had some one thousand agents filing reports for a massive two-volume compendium that recorded (and made available to state and local agencies) the names, pictures, locations, and political beliefs of upwards of eighteen thousand citizens; ROTC units were encouraged to enlist their student officers in additional surveillance of campus leftists. The Selective Service System issued a directive to local draft

boards that students involved in draft resistance were to be immediately reclassified 1-A and, if possible, packed off to Vietnam.*
(At the same time grand juries in at least six cities began handing down indictments against student draft-card burners and "We Won't Go" signers, and federal agents served subpoenas on students at more than two dozen campuses.) The FBI, which already had sixty-three hundred agents in the field—not including an unknown, but large, number of infiltrators—expanded its surveillance operations, openly visiting students and faculty members and successfully enlisting administration officials to spy on and submit reports about campus radicals. Both houses of Congress authorized special committee investigations of a variety of left organizations, including SDS, and in January President Johnson gave new life to the discredited Subversive Activities Control Board, which thereupon inaugurated a much-publicized investigation of the DuBois Clubs—a case of the blind chasing the halt if there ever was one.

Encouraged by such top-level sanction, local agencies—state police, city Red Squads, university administrations—joined the game. Oakland officials, with testimony from two undercover agents who had joined the Stop the Draft Week campaign, drew up their own mini-Spock conspiracy charges against seven Oakland radicals for their part in the October demonstrations; even Iowa City got into the act with conspiracy charges against seven University of Iowa students (including local SDS activist Bruce Clark) for an anti-Dow demonstration in December. Police departments set up surveillance of known SDS centers on a number of campuses—usually making little secret of their presence—and encouraged right-minded students to report on their fellows; a student government representative at Penn State estimated in February that there were no fewer than two hundred student informers operating on his campus, some doing their own private wiretapping. Undoubtedly the Texas state police were not unique in

---

*And not just full-fledged resisters; even SDS membership was grounds for reclassification in some cases. John Milton Ratliff, an Oklahoma University SDSer, was informed by his local board on November 13—the letter was reproduced on the front page of *New Left Notes* (November 20, 1967)—that "the local board did not feel that your activity as a member of SDS is to the best interest of the U.S. Government" and that he was to be inducted forthwith.

their operations, only the most embarrassed, when it became known that one of their undercover men was elected to the presidency of the University of Texas SDS chapter.

The response of the left to this high-level repression was initially disbelief, then uncertainty, and finally anger. By the time of the Spock indictments it was prepared for resistance. SDS immediately issued a call for demonstrations to be held across the country to show the strength of the left "in the face of this repression." John Fuerst, then traveling for SDS in Wisconsin, wrote an article for *New Left Notes* proclaiming proudly that "Dr. Benjamin Spock's crime has already been committed by thousands in the antiwar movement" and called for immediate defense not only of the five men but also "of the program they supported." The Spock rally in New York City was only one of many organized during January, and it was accompanied by renewed calls for draft resistance and a petition claiming equal guilt with the Spock defendants signed by no fewer than twenty-eight thousand individuals. Dozens of chapters organized marches and meetings, and a number, such as the New School chapter, immediately set up draft-counseling tables to carry on the Spock tradition in open defiance of the Justice Department.

"Wednesday, January 31. 1:00 Rutgers, Students & Draft. . . . Brass Rail, Guild dinner." And, nine thousand miles away, the National Liberation Front began its Têt offensive, the decisive military turning point of the Vietnam war. The general SDS reaction was captured rather neatly in *New Left Notes* five days later by two Associated Press pictures, one showing American Marines marching in classic Hollywood style across a bridge into Hue, the next showing them moments later running back under NLF fire with shock and terror on their faces. It was the NO's only comment on Têt.

"Saturday, February 10. SDS regional." Bernardine Dohrn slowly grew closer to the SDS people in New York during her year at the Lawyers Guild, and by the time of the February meeting of the New York region she was accorded a position as a leader, with New York SDSers Naomi Jaffe and Sue Shargell, of the workshop on women's liberation. It was a conference which, as it turned out, was symptomatic of all that was raging in the national organization just then.

In the first place, as the meeting tried to set plans for the April "Ten Days" action, the spectrum of political views that emerged was positively iridescent; SDS had always been marked by diversity, but now it looked as if it was actually *plagued* by it. There were those trying to work through third-party politics at the upcoming elections by supporting the Peace and Freedom Party, urging spring actions around canvassing and petitions. There were those who wanted to take student power to its logical extension by abandoning the sham of mere "student participation" and work instead for the outright takeover of universities by students. There were the Progressive Labor forces proposing, naturally, a worker-student alliance and campus actions built around support for local strikes, agitation against a proposed transit-fare increase, and development of a summer work-in program. There were the cultural radicals, pushing a "spring offensive" at the Museum of Modern Art to reveal "where the museum directors and patrons get their money (Venezuelan oil, South African gold)." There were the imaginative street-action people, loosely grouped around a new Lower East Side collective called the Up Against the Wall, Motherfuckers,* who were organizing a scheme to hold "a procession up 5th Avenue with everyone carrying their own garbage" and dumping it on the plaza at Lincoln Center. There were various groups emphasizing high-school organizing, draft resistance, women's liberation, alternate media, and practically every other cause in the left pantheon of the time. And there were those, emergent now in full array after the metamorphosis of the fall, who saw themselves as revolutionaries—not bomb planters or barricade fighters, or not yet, but people who had come to have a "revolutionary consciousness" and were putting that together with serious attempts to think about how to transform American society inside-out. For them the practice of resistance led inexorably to the building of a revolution; in the words of the SDS regional newsletter, *Firebomb:*

> An organization like ours takes a major step forward when it finally comes to understand that it is involved in a struggle against an

*The name was taken from the usual greeting police used on longhairs and blacks in the inner city when stopping them on the street. It was also used by LeRoi Jones (later Imamu Amiri Baraka) in a poem given much circulation that spring.

enemy and takes major steps toward confronting that enemy head-on. A serious organization consciously seeking to develop a revolutionary practice creates a life-or-death dynamic within the society it is trying to destroy and re-create.

But in the second place, these budding revolutionaries ran head-on into another group of "revolutionaries," the class warriors from Progressive Labor. The New York regional meeting was the occasion for the first open move by the Progressive Labor forces against SDS, and it coincided with the first open declaration of war between the PL and the national leadership. Progressive Labor, strong in New York, had become increasingly dismayed by the trend of the Regional Office toward resistance, and took the occasion of the regional meeting to assail it bitterly for such "adventurist" tactics as the Rusk demonstration in November and a botched-up march on the Whitehall induction center in December; then, tapping the RO at its weakest point and taking advantage of its acknowledged failure in recent months to service the surrounding chapters adequately, PL proposed the establishment of a "regional NAC," an administrative committee elected from SDSers at large to oversee the operations of the New York office. The RO stalwarts—chief among whom were Steve Halliwell, David Gilbert, Naomi Jaffe, Jeff Jones, Marge Piercy, and Ted Gold —were caught flatfooted; PL, led by Jeff Gordon, Richard Rhoads, and Charlotte and Gordon Fischer, and with heavy support from the chapters at Brooklyn College, City College, Fordham, and Rutgers, pressed its advantage and was able to push through the reorganization scheme before the RO people knew quite what was happening. In the subsequent election to the committee, PL lodged four of its members, the RO sat three, and the remaining three were people of indeterminate politics who could be counted on to side with PL from time to time. It was a clear victory for Progressive Labor and a foretoken of troubles to come.

And the national leadership, just at that moment, was in the middle of a tussle with PL in the pages of *New Left Notes.* On the front page of the February 12 issue appeared an article by three New England SDSers and PL sympathizers (including Alan Spector, who would go on to be a PL-SDS leader after the 1969 split) which took the NO to task for everything from lying about the results of the December National Council meeting, to supporting window breaking in preference to worker-student alliances, to running SDS with a dictatorial "top-down" approach. Carl Davidson answered for the NO people with an eight-column blast accusing the three of taking stands "uninformed at best, deliberately misleading at worst," lifting statements out of context, mounting "unwarranted and misleading" attacks, and making distortions so great that they "can only be a deliberate attempt to mislead, or a sign of stupidity." This was the first public signal of open warfare between PL and others in SDS, and a signal that the spirit of compromise and consensus so common in the early days of SDS was finally dead.

"*Monday, February 19. 7:30 Radical law students. . . . Wednesday, February 21. Yale Law School. . . . Friday, March 1. 4:00 Ken—me, NYU Law School. . . . Saturday, March 2. 9:30 Law Student Conf.*" Part of the work of the Lawyers Guild for the 1967–1968 school year was to try to get law-school students to work in draft resistance, both as counselors with some legal knowledge and as resisters themselves; the main brunt of the job fell to Dohrn, and much of the early spring was spent giving speeches and organizing committees in various Eastern law schools. Her impact was immediate. "She was an overwhelming personality," says a man who worked with her then:

> First of all there was her sex appeal. She had the most amazing legs —every draft resister on the East Coast knew those legs. People would come from miles around just to *see* her. But she was regarded as a good "political person" at a time when other women in the movement weren't given any responsibility at all. Students really turned on to her. She did a good job.

"*Saturday, March 9. Rad. in Prof. Conf., Boston.*" The Radicals in the Professions Conference held in Cambridge that spring was one of several still pursuing the question of what Movement "alumni" were to do with their lives. There were moves to establish a local Movement for a Democratic Society in New York, Cleveland, New Orleans, and Springfield, Massachusetts (Bob Gottlieb and Marge Piercy set forth a lively rationale for the MDS at the Cambridge meeting). There was continual pressure for using graduates for community organizing among the poor whites

—really, a new and more knowledgeable ERAP—following the example of the new National Community Union in Chicago and several independent efforts on the West Coast (where Mike Klonsky, Steve Hamilton, and Bob Avakian were among those trying this approach). There was an expansion of GI organizing and Movement veterans were involved in Resistance Inside the Army (RITA), the "coffee-house movement" establishing off-base centers to attract young soldiers, and various propagandizing efforts in army-base towns.* There was media action aplenty, the start of dozens of new newspapers, the production of the first half-dozen films by the Newsreel people in New York, and even the beginnings of a "Radio Free People" to start Movement radio stations and circulate tapes relating to radical politics. There was a spurt of interest in street theater, or guerrilla theater, with at least three dozen "RATs" (Radical Acting Troups) springing up across the country.

But the biggest alumni event of the spring was the establishment of the New University Conference at a meeting of some 350 academics in Chicago three weeks after the Radicals in the Professions conference in Cambridge. The list of sponsors suggests the heavy influence of SDS alumni—among them, Heather Tobis Booth, Jeremy Brecher, John Ehrenreich, Al Haber, Tom Hayden, Michael Klare, Jesse Lemisch, Kathy McAfee, Don McKelvey, Julie Nichamin, Lee Webb, and Michael Zweig—as does the fact that the keynote speakers were Dick Flacks and Staughton Lynd. Enthusiasm for a membership organization of Movement academics and intellectuals was considerable, and the foundations of it were laid that weekend, with Bob Ross selected as national director, Flacks, Mike Goldfield, and Dan Friedlander (a red-diaper alumnus of the

*Clark Kissinger was still pushing a somewhat modified version of his old "kamikazi plan" (New Left Notes, March 11), "a program directed at those thousands of students who will reluctantly and begrudgingly go into the Army" to get them to organize "resistance and propaganda" once they get there. To his own draft board, after they sent him a notice that he was being reclassified 1-A for his political work, Kissinger offered to be one of the first practitioners of the program. "I am currently employed doing full-time anti-war work among civilians," he wrote them. "If it is your desire, however, that I be transferred to doing anti-war organizing among the troops, I shall cheerfully report for induction." He was not drafted.

University of Chicago SDS) elected to the steering committee, and offices set up in Chicago. Its program:

1. Organize local chapters across the nation to help overcome the isolation and impotence now afflicting campus-based radicals [and] to: define their political roles on and off campus; engage in mutual support and self-criticism concerning teaching and intellectual activity; create centers for radical initiative on the campus.

2. Encourage the formation of radical caucuses within professional disciplines and associations.

3. Organize so that we may eventually be prepared to defend campus radicals against politically motivated harassment and firings.

4. Aid in establishing a new magazine of analysis and research for the movement.

5. Form alliances with student activists seeking to expose and dislocate university collaboration in war research and social manipulation, and join with black and white radicals who are demanding that the universities become responsible to the needs of the black communities which surround them and from which they now seek protection, not insight.

Within months, the NUC would start making itself felt, primarily through various "radical caucuses" in the academic associations, and in the coming years it would prove to be a strong, if limited, force for the left among university faculties.

"Friday, March 22. 7:45 United. Chicago. SDS draft meeting. . . . Sunday, March 24. Mom & Dad." Bernardine Dohrn's parents lived in Chicago, where both of them had grown up, and whenever she came through town she made a point of seeing them.

Bernardine Dohrn was born in Chicago on January 12, 1942. Her mother, who had been working as a secretary, was of Swedish descent; her father, then Bernard Ohrnstein, was a Hungarian Jew who later changed the family name to facilitate his career as a credit manager, a bit of melting-pot Americana that Bernardine later viewed with considerable disgust. When she was eight the family, now including a younger sister, moved to Whitefish Bay, Wisconsin, a suburb of Milwaukee, and there Bernardine spent a quite ordinary career in school, getting above-average grades, plowing into dozens of extracurricular activities, becoming editor of the high-school paper, joining Future Nurses, and the like.

After graduating from high school in 1959 she spent two years at Miami University, in Ohio, but she developed rheumatic fever and transferred to the University of Chicago to be closer to home, her parents having moved back to the city; though eddies of the New Left were aswirl at the time, they apparently left her untouched, for there is no record of her as a student activist at either university. Dohrn graduated in 1963, a history major, and spent the next year getting an MA in history in the Chicago graduate school, but the liberal-arts world seemed increasingly remote and in the fall of 1964 she switched to law school, planning a career as a liberal do-gooding lawyer.

For the next few years, while still in law school, her life took on the attributes of many liberal activists before her: she worked one summer in an antipoverty program in New York, became a volunteer aid in an unsuccessful Congressional campaign, joined Martin Luther King's crusade to push integration in the Chicago suburbs, and gave her legal services on behalf of rent-strikers in Chicago ghettos. (It was during the latter struggle in 1966–1967 that she met the young organizers around the JOIN project, making allies and friends that would continue with her for the next several years.) The fundamental failures of all these high-hope projects must have soured the young law student gradually, for by the time of her graduation in June 1967 she had given up the idea of becoming a lawyer and working within the courts, and opted instead for a full-time life in the Movement. That fall she joined the National Lawyers Guild, at quite some remove from the liberal Democrat, not to mention the Future Nurse, she had once been.

"Monday, March 25. Rennie & Tom." The unexpectedly strong showing by Eugene McCarthy in the New Hampshire Presidential primary on March 12—and the subsequent entry of Robert Kennedy into the Presidential race—raised a new problem for the Mobilization staffers preparing for the Chicago convention. It now seemed likely that a large number of liberal youths, supporters of the Democratic challengers, would be coming to Chicago to lobby for their candidates, a gesture which might blunt the antielectoral message which the Mobilization, and with them the Yippies, were trying to put across. Dohrn had lunch with Davis and Hayden while she was in Chicago, discussing this prob-

lem and the continuing plans for legal work around the demonstrations.

The Mobilization was not the only one to whom McCarthy
and Kennedy presented problems. SDS people on the campuses
noticed that suddenly there was talk about "one last chance for
the system" and "a real way to end the war," all of their careful
antielectoral radicalism seeming to fall on deaf ears. College students of many political descriptions rallied to McCarthy's gently
fluttering banner, canvassing and campaigning, clamoring to join
the election staffs, shaving and bathing themselves "Clean for
Gene," and some SDSers—the younger ones, usually, and more
single-issue—were among them. Things got so bad that at the
April National Council meeting a number of chapter representatives would be talking with some anguish about the defections
from radical ranks on the campus. The general SDS position, of
course, was never in doubt, and there was not even the slightest
hint of "Part of the way with EMcC" (or RFK); as a matter of
fact, the SDS line had been expressed with some neatness earlier
in the year in a fund-raising ad directed at liberals:

> WHY BE A DISSENTING DEMOCRAT? SO WE CAN GO THROUGH
> IT ALL OVER AGAIN WITH BOBBY? SOME FOLKS NEVER LEARN.
> OTHERS DO—THEY BECOME DISGUSTED EX-DEMOCRATS. . . .
> You can make a contribution to building a new America (rather
> than propping up the old one) by supporting Students for a
> Democratic Society. SDS works to change the system, not the
> personalities.

(The clincher in the ad was, incidentally, a dotted-line box for
donations beginning, "I noticed your office is in the slums of
Chicago, not Beverly Hills. Here is my check.")

"Tuesday, March 26. Women's grp." Since the first of the
year Bernardine Dohrn had been meeting with various women in
informal sessions, part of a growing movement of small women's
groups which were getting together now all over the country; the
SDS National Office estimated that thirty-five such groups had
been formed by the end of the spring. She also achieved a certain
reputation among these groups with the publication of a paper,
written with Naomi Jaffe, which was one of the earliest attempts
to see women's liberation in terms of imperialism and exploitation.

Reprinted in *New Left Notes* in March, it was Dohrn's introduction to the membership of SDS.

"Thursday, March 28. Drive to Lexington. . . . Friday, March 29. NC—Lexington, Ky." The Lexington National Council meeting was the first major SDS gathering that Bernardine Dohrn is known to have attended. It was the largest NC to date, a reflection of SDS's continued stature, with 102 official delegates and as many as 350 observers. The weekend session began with a collection of a meager $200 from the delegates—nothing like the orgies of the past—and pledges of additional money from nine chapters, plus promises from Carl Davidson to donate a dollar bill on behalf of the National Office staff and from the University of Maine chapter to send along a hundred pounds of potatoes to the NO; but, just to be sure, the NC added on an additional chapter tax to the unsuccessful one it had imposed the year before, a move which was acknowledged to be more in hope than in anticipation. Nineteen new chapters were admitted, bringing the number of recognized chapters to around 280 (the NO was claiming 300 at the time).* What was particularly striking about the new additions was that so many represented a constituency previously untouched—Louisiana State, Danville (Illinois) Junior College—and areas previously unpenetrated—Parsons College of Fairfield, Iowa, Bradley University of Peoria, Illinois; and while the growth of membership may have been encouraging, the obvious chasm

*There were 247 recognized chapters as of the 1967 convention, and the Bloomington NC had admitted 18—Albright College, Alice's Restaurant Marxist-Leninist (in truth the Los Angeles Regional Office), Bowling Green State, Chico State, Detroit At-large, Elmhurst College, Franklin and Marshall, Georgetown University, Grinnell College, Hank Williams Chapter (a group of Chicago JOINers), New Mexico, Millard Fillmore Memorial Chapter (the New York Regional Office), Ripon College, Southern Methodist, Syracuse, Swarthmore, Whitman College, Wichita State—and the Lexington NC an additional 18—Aunt Molly Jackson Chapter (Louisville activists), Bradley University, California State at Los Angeles, *CAW* magazine, Colonel Rex Applegate Memorial Kill Or Be Killed Chapter in San Francisco (Applegate was the author of *Crowd and Riot Control,* the standard police manual for subduing demonstrators), Danville Junior College, Defiance (Ohio) College, Fordham, Frank Rizzo Memorial Chapter (some Philadelphia SDSers commemorating a still-very-much-alive police chief), Haverford/Bryn Mawr, Owosso (Michigan) High School, Louisiana State, Parsons College, St. Louis University, Sarah Lawrence, Tulane, University High School (Los Angeles), and the Up Against the Wall, Motherfucker group in New York.

between the likely political level of these chapters and that of the national leadership suggested trouble unless the most careful steps were taken. It is not likely that those SDS veterans developing their "revolutionary consciousness" would have much identification with the problems of the Parsons College chapter, or that many delegates from church-run Defiance College would have much in common with the heavies from the Motherfucker collective.*

It would be logical to think that the Lexington meeting was devoted to putting the finishing touches on the "Ten Days" campaign that had so exercised the delegates to the previous NC and which had been set as the organization's top priority for the spring. Alas, it is logic that reckons without the vagaries of SDS politics. Between the two NCs, much had happened. The Student Mobilization Committee—the younger branch of the National Mobilization Committee which was pretty well dominated by youthful proto-Trotskyists associated with the Socialist Workers Party and other assorted left-liberals—had effectively coopted the student strike idea, planning a nation-wide walkout for April 26, while SDS was still trying to figure out just *what* it was going to do during those April days. Then, too, there was a certain amount of resentment still smoldering about the way the idea had been thrust on the organization by the NO, and Progressive Labor did what it could to fan those embers on the chapter level with talk about "top-down organizing," "manipulation," and the like. And the NO, waiting for feedback from the chapters and regions so that it would not be accused of manipulating the campaign, made little effort to instigate action where none was visible and even less effort to coordinate action where it was planned. The result was that by the time of the Lexington meeting, SDS was in poor shape to give any direction to the April actions, and the delegates realized it. Whatever local demonstrations had been conceived were already planned and organized for, and there seemed little point at this juncture to try to reestablish any national program; the Ten Days, therefore, was hardly mentioned at all.

*Except perhaps in appreciation of the Motherfuckers' antics—such as proposing, and getting passed, an amendment to a resolution supporting California grape strikers which suggested "that SDS drink more wine and do less talking."

Instead, in line with the leadership's new sense of revolutionary possibilities and its swing away from students, the NC involved itself with issues concentrating on other constituencies: the
poor, the working class, GIs, even high-school students. But above
all, blacks.

There were several strains running together to form the new
feeling that the cause of black America should become a central
concern for SDS. Black students, now lured to major white universities in increasing numbers and beginning to form themselves into
separate black student organizations, were thought to be ready to
move on the campuses and in need of supportive allies. The
Kerner Report announced its unequivocal conclusion that "white
racism is essentially responsible for the explosive mixture which
has been accumulating in our cities since the end of World War
II." Repression of black radicals had been stepped up, with the
multiple arrests of SNCC's H. Rap Brown, the jailing of LeRoi
Jones in Newark, the railroading of Texas State students on riot
charges, and above all the brutal, unprovoked murder of three
black students at South Carolina State College by South Carolina
state police just two months before. White radicals came to feel
that they might be next on the repression lists—as SNCC's James
Forman told SDSers, "All the equipment the city police forces
around this country say they are buying to use against us, the
blacks, can and will be used against white antiwar demonstrators." There was the inevitable element of guilt—for white racism
in general, for being white, middle-class, privileged students in
particular—which had been expressed steadily in issues of *New
Left Notes* condemning "white racism," "white supremacy,"
"white chauvinism inside the Movement," and "white-skin privilege." And many SDSers had the sense, after three summers of
ghetto rebellion, that black Americans were on the brink of a real
insurrection, perhaps a revolution, and those who were serious
about revolution should be standing at their sides.

The new shift of focus was expressed for the NC in a moving
and persuasive speech by Carl Oglesby, who told the young delegates that the job of SDS now was to turn from the issue of war
to that of racism. Radicals have done all they can now toward
ending the war, he suggested, and adventures like the Chicago
convention demonstration or schemes for involving working-class

communities around the draft were not really going to help much. Radicals now should turn to the questions of black liberation and white racism, fighting not only for the sake of the oppressed blacks but also because this struck a blow at one of the pillars of the system. The ghetto, in short, should replace the campus or the induction center or the factory as the locus of SDS's organizing activity.

The delgates responded. In a proposal adopted almost unanimously, SDS went on record as giving top priority to support for "the black struggle for liberation":

> We feel that we have to respond to the black struggle for survival because it is a struggle against imperialism and against a racist culture which we also are fighting. . . . We must give visibility to the black struggle for liberation. . . . We must make the State pay as high a price as possible for genocide. Part of this price is the presence of a white constituency in the coming rebellions. . . . We must institute programs of internal education on racism, the history of the black people in this country, and the history of the black liberation movement. . . . We should give physical and financial aid to those black people now the object of State repression.

And, specifically for expiation:

> We have a special responsibility to fight racism among our own white population. . . . We recognize that racism insinuates itself into both our personal and political attitudes. We are determined to fight it in our personal lives as we fight all the aspects of a racist culture that the system attempts to inject into us.

Ultimately, "We must see our job as one of moving the white population into a position of rebellion which joins the black struggle for liberation to make the American revolution."

Thus began a fateful process for SDS. Staughton Lynd saw it a year later as the start of "a politics of guilt": "During the last year SDS has been reverting to the very politics of middle-class self-flagellation which it charges to the Resistance; that is, that since the spring of 1968 National Council meeting SDS has asked white people again to play the role of auxiliaries to other peoples' radicalism." Similarly Greg Calvert, to whom the reversion to "fighting someone else's battles" seemed a serious setback for SDS, responded:

The reorientation of SDS in that spring of 1968 was to drop the draft resistance and resistance themology almost entirely, and to revert to, "We got to support the black movement, racism is our issue. Anti-racism is the radical position."

What you do to a white man in today's society when you tell him he's got to fight the anti-racism struggle is give him a struggle that doesn't have any outside to it. I do not want to deny that racism is a problem, as male chauvinism is a problem inside of us. But I wish to insist that the only way we can finally fight against racism effectively is to be fighting our battles for our own liberation, in alliance with black people fighting their struggle for their own liberation.

In a sense, this *was* a "politics of guilt," but it was also more than that, a politics (however imperfectly realized or expressed) of revolution. Calvert was right in seeing the decline of resistance, for what was coming in its place was a feeling that the battle had to be escalated beyond bodies-on-the-line to something more meaningful still, more capable of exerting real power upon the land. For this allies seemed to be necessary, and especially black allies, those who already seemed to be on the road to revolution. As Carl Davidson was to analyze it:

Put simply, SDS saw that the student movement could go in one of two directions from "where they are at." They could focus on limited on-campus issues "about their lives" and go in the direction of "student power." Or they could raise those issues about their lives that led them to form alliances with other oppressed constituencies beyond the campus, a direction leading to the growth of revolutionary class consciousness. . . . Calvert believes that [SDS's] approach to the problem of racism is the politics of guilt. Most of SDS believes that this is the cutting edge, the dividing line that separates revolutionary practice from reformist and reactionary practice in this country.

It was a turn that displeased a number in SDS. Calvert left the Lexington NC with a sense of dismay, and it turned to bitterness in the succeeding weeks as the NO plunged into what Calvert saw as an attempt "to grind out an elaborate analysis of racism, couched in the most abstruse and dogmatic language so that the line would be right at its national convention in June." (He also raised violent objections in the NO to the reprinting of a James

Forman speech titled "Liberation Will Come From a Black
Thing," calling it "wrong" and "obscene" for its implied slighting
of white resistance.) By the end of the spring Calvert had become
thoroughly disenchanted with the new politics, gave up on SDS
entirely and retired to the comparative placidity of Austin, Texas.
Behind him he left an organization ready for a new thrust.

The Lexington NC adjourned on Sunday afternoon, March
31, and the delegates returned home. That night American politics
took a dramatic turn.

*"Sunday, March 31. Pikeville. Flowers—porch. . . . Johnson
speech."* The withdrawal of Lyndon Johnson from the Presidential race and the concomitant start of peace negotiations with the
National Liberation Front was regarded, at least at the instant, as
a signal victory for the American left and the antiwar forces it had
unleashed during the last three years. The student left was jubi-
lant, and at many colleges there were victory parties in the dormitories, impromptu marches on the campus, celebrations in the
halls. "We knew, at least our analysis was, that getting rid of
Johnson didn't make that much difference," one SDSer said later.
"But just the thought that we wouldn't have to see that awful face
any more and hear those continual lies in that syrupy backwoods
drawl, and thinking we all had something to do with that, well
that was enough to give us an incredible high that night. I'll never
forget it."

"Wednesday, April 3. Resistance." For much of the spring
Bernardine Dohrn had been occupied with draft resistance, and
like many had looked forward with enthusiasm to the April Resistance meeting and the third round of draft-card turn-ins. The
Johnson speech changed things, very neatly deflating the war as
an issue and the draft as an organizing tool. As the New York
Resistance people analyzed the subsequent events in their own
obituary a year later,

> Resistance in larger cities began to lose steam. We had been success-
> ful in helping to move the middle class significantly: McCarthy and
> Kennedy entered the presidential race, the government was pushed
> into negotiations and Johnson was forced to step down. But it was
> precisely these events which pulled the political rug out from under
> us. . . . We had reached the point of "diminishing returns"—increas-
> ing the number of draft resisters would do little or nothing to move

people. Also, the "repressive tolerance" of the government and the selectivity with which it prosecuted resisters helped destroy the psychological momentum of noncooperation. The drama was taken out of it, and the media lost interest. While at one time, turning in one's draft card was the only example of a politics of risk, in the past year other groups have offered tactics that also involved risk— "streetfighting," campus confrontation, etc. People no longer felt a need for noncooperation as a means of personal radicalization.

Draft resistance, in short, died a single-issue death. Despite the considerable efforts throughout 1967 of SDS leaders and others who saw the connections and emphasized the politics, it was never to overcome its primary character as a moral instrument of protest to the Vietnam war.

SDS's own draft programs, though kept alive, likewise began to wither at about this time. Campus support never materialized after April, especially when it became clear that few students were actually being drafted; the Selective Service System after two years had finally learned a lesson and was calling up less than 20 percent of the college population,depending for most of its fodder on strata of the society that were less inclined to make a fuss about it. Off-campus draft work ran up against other harsh realities: most high-school kids did not regard the draft as a pressing issue in their lives, a sizable minority either had no aversion to the draft or actually welcomed it as an escape, draft-card burning and resistance in working communities was regarded as faintly cowardly and decidedly unpatriotic, and the unfortunately feeble alternatives of jail, underground, or exile stirred little enthusiasm among most potential recruits. Gradually the frustrations of unsuccess and the pressures from an unamiable society (jails, police, landlords, parents) left the draft resisters beaten and bitter, and most moved on to other tasks—and not a few came to decide that what was really necessary in this society was not the abolition of the draft but the abolition of the system.

Yet the Johnson withdrawal was proof at the same time of how much the draft-resistance movement and the SDS efforts had accomplished, and its successes should not go unrecorded. It is impossible to estimate how many men actually refused induction, burned or turned in their draft cards, or refused to register for the draft, but the figure is clearly in the tens of thousands, and perhaps as many as a million.* This obviously had an impact on the entire student generation, and the liberal community in general, as Walter Lippmann wrote (just a week, incidentally, before the President's announcement):

> The President is confronted with the resistance, open or passive, of the whole military generation, their teachers, their friends, their families. The attempt to fight a distant war by conscription is producing a demoralization which threatens the very security of the nation.

It also led to a turnabout in public thinking on the draft, so that by the middle of 1968 pollster Louis Harris figured that 36 percent of the public was against the system, a figure that would continue to rise as the war went on; so pervasive did the antidraft attitude become that even Richard Nixon announced his support for a draft overhaul, and the Congress of the United States showed so little support that it actually refused to renew the draft authority for a time in the middle of 1971. Few in Washington now doubt that there will be a thorough overhaul, or quite possibly the abolition, of the draft within the next decade.

"Thursday, April 4. . . . Law student meeting, King shot. Times Square." The assassination of Martin Luther King at a motel in Memphis, Tennessee, was a propelling moment for radicals both black and white: it seemed a signal, as if one were needed, that the old ways were finished, that whatever romance lingered from the civil-rights days was dispelled, that the time had come for more than nonviolence, more than working with the system, more than moral witness.

---

*Michael Ferber and Staughton Lynd have made the closest study of this issue, in their book, *The Resistance*. Their figures are admittedly uncertain, but even if their guesses are not perfect they indicate the scope of resistance: some 5000 men turned in draft cards publicly, "several times" as many probably have done so privately, between 10,000 and 25,000 draft-delinquent cases were reported to the federal government yearly from 1966 to 1969, Department of Justice prosecuted 3161 people in the high point of resistance between June 1966 and June 1968 (and would go on to prosecute another 6000 in the next two years), Canadian exiles number something close to 15,000, nonregistrants are estimated at between 50,000 and 100,000, COs grew in the two years after the Pentagon demonstration from 23,800 to 34,500, delinquencies from 15,600 to 31,900, and alternate service increased by 737,000. Resistance in some form, then, may have been practiced by at least a million young men in the years after the rise of draft resistance.

The ghettos exploded. As many "civil disorders" took place in the twenty-five days after King's death as in all of the previous year, with more arrests and more injuries. "Violence in varying degrees, ranging from minor disturbances to major riots, erupted in more than 100 cities," according to the ever-watchful J. Edgar Hoover. "The April outbreaks and the subsequent disorders resulted in more than 60 deaths, injuries to thousands of persons, and millions of dollars in property damage." Federal troops were called into Wilmington, Delaware, Baltimore, Chicago, and the nation's capital; in this single month more National Guardsmen (35,000) and more federal troops (23,700) were called into action than had been called in all of 1967, and that had been an eventful year. The usually phlegmatic Jerome Skolnik, in his report to the National Violence Commission, determined: *"Never* before in this country has such a massive military response been mounted against racial disorder."

SDS regarded the assassination as simply confirmation of the Lexington message, blatant evidence of the need to act against a system bent on genocide, and the NO issued an immediate summons for "a strong response from the radical community." It came. Some two dozen black colleges and universities and more than a hundred white institutions mounted protests led by SDS chapters in many places. SDS mounted or participated in demonstrations in several major cities: Rennie Davis, Clark Kissinger, Noel Ignatin, and others organized marches in Chicago; SDS chapters and Resistance workers led a massive rally in Boston; regional SDS people in Washington, D.C. picketed the White House until dispersed by club-wielding police; Detroit radicals, many from Wayne State SDS, held a memorial demonstration; and in New York a conglomerate of militants turned up in Times Square, treating the city to its first mild display of what was to be called "trashing" (window breaking, trash-can spilling, windshield smashing). Bernardine Dohrn was there. A friend remembers that night, when she first heard of King's death:

> She was really stunned. I must admit that I was fairly jaded by then, and I remember saying that with King dead, the Panthers and the other militants would have a clear field to lead the revolution. But Bernardine was sincerely moved, and she began to cry. She cried for

a while and she talked about Chicago, when she had worked with King. She said she hadn't always agreed with him, but she responded to him as a human being. Then she went home and changed her clothes. I'll never forget that—she said she was changing into her riot clothes: pants. We went up to Times Square, and there was a demonstration going on of pissed-off black kids and white radicals. We started ripping signs and getting really out of hand and then some kids trashed a jewelry store. Bernardine really dug it. She was still crying, but afterward we had a long talk about urban guerrilla warfare and what had to be done now—by any means necessary.

By any means necessary. Bernardine Dohrn was not the only person in the spring of 1968 led to the conclusion, finally, that violent measures would be necessary in the struggle of the American left. These months mark the emergence of political violence on a significant scale across the country.

Violence, the social scientists have determined, has been a hallmark of twentieth-century America, and it has been a formative preoccupation with those who grew up during the period marked by Auschwitz, Hiroshima, Southern terrorism, Vietnam, assassinations, urban rebellions, police riots, and governmental repression. Kenneth Keniston found that his Vietnam Summer interviewees were immersed in violence from earliest childhood: "In the lives of these young radicals, as in much of their generation, the threats of inner and outer violence are fused, each exciting the other" to the point where "the issue of violence is to this generation what the issue of sex was to the Victorian world"; another survey of SDSers in 1966 found a "special way in which they have experienced violence, both directly and vicariously" and determined that "this special and intense preoccupation seems to be a necessary element in comprehending the predominance of violent dystopian futures [projected in essays] among SDS youth."

But *originated* violence characterized none of the early activists; they were all victims. Hayden, Potter, and others beaten in the South, Gitlin, Grizzard, Booth, and countless others jailed for civil-rights demonstrations, ERAPers harassed and arrested by local police and vigilantes, antiwar marchers beaten and gassed, students at Berkeley, in several black schools, and elsewhere clubbed, kicked, shot at, and arrested by police. Even with the rise

of resistance, in the previous fall offensive violence was characteristic only of the Stop the Draft Week and Rusk demonstrations,
and then limited to minor property damage and bottle throwing;
the students at the Pentagon, at Wisconsin, Indiana, Brooklyn,
Oberlin, San Jose State, and the rest were initially victims of police
charges, Mace, and tear gas.

But resistance taught certain lessons. It showed that police
when given the chance know little restraint in exercising the brutality of their profession on unarmed and defenseless students,
that the government would move with all the powers in its arsenal
to jail, induct, spy upon, harass, and pressure youthful activists,
and that even universities were willing to resort to force to protect
their private property from demonstrators. It showed that the
forces running the society, the university as much as the government, were powerful, not to say ruthless, and that the press and
the public in general supported their exercise of both power and
ruthlessness. In a simple phrase, resistance exposed the nature of,
and erased the legitimacy from, the major institutions of the society.

But resistance also showed that at least a minority of the
people could be made to act, and act vigorously, in pursuit of
their goals; that there was energy to be tapped among the
young and discontented; that people in situations of confrontation will make rapid and consequential choices, taking a swift
lesson in the making of connections when a police club hits
them on the head in defense of a Dow recruiter and his university hosts. It showed that other people, heretofore quiescent
—moderates, liberals, faculty members, families, sympathetic
members of the public—can be prodded into various forms of
action and support, forced to draw lines and take sides, and
occasionally won over behind some radical demands. And it
showed that concessions could be wrested from these forces—
slowing the escalation of the war, holding off on draft calls, re-
forming campus governance, cutting ties to the corporate and
military machines—but only when (and by no means always
even then) they were confronted by large-scale, serious, militant, political disruption.

Out of resistance, then, there grew an understanding of

power, an appreciation of the values of confrontation, and thence a willingness to initiate violence. *Not* violence against people, it should be pointed out—it was the police not the demonstrators, the campus "jocks" not the radicals, the rednecks not the picketers, who generally started the fights; nor was it, in spite of the myopic media, violence on a scale remotely resembling "terrorism" or "bomb throwing" or "guerrilla warfare" or "revolution." It was violence against property and quite specifically property connected with a hated or complicit institution: benches in the Oakland streets, cars at the Hilton dinner, then draft records in Catonsville and Boston, finally, and dramatically, buildings on the campuses.

Between January and May of 1968 there were ten reported incidents of the bombing and burning of campus buildings related to political issues (half of them, however, directed at two buildings, the ROTC building in Stanford and the NROTC building at Berkeley).* It marked the first concerted use of such tactics of violence by the student left in this generation—indeed, the first use by students in the history of the country.† Compared to the vio-

---

*In January a bomb, proved later a dud, was found in a building at Howard University, and an arsonist caused $50,000 worth of damage to a Berkeley administration building; in February the Berkeley NROTC building was bombed, the Stanford ROTC building suffered a $35,000 fire, and the Oakland power lines leading to the nefarious Lawrence Radiation Laboratory were cut; in March the Stanford building suffered another fire and three weeks later the Berkeley building received another minor bombing; in April the ROTC building on the campus of Tennessee Agriculture and Industry University was burned to the ground; in May the Stanford ROTC building suffered still another fire with an estimated $60,000 damage, bombs caused minor damage at administration buildings on the campuses of Southern Illinois University and Wisconsin; and in June another successful attack was made on the power lines of the Pacific Power and Light Company in Oakland.

†The history of student protest in this country is sketchy, but the most violent previous incidents seem to have been things like college outbuildings set on fire and an "infernal machine" exploded in one hall at Harvard in 1814; possible firecracker-type bombs in 1823 in the Harvard yard; windows broken in Harvard rooms in 1834, and classroom furniture smashed; a fire on the University of Vermont campus green in the 1870s. The period of the Intercollegiate Socialist Society's growth after the turn of the century saw almost no student militance of any kind, and in the period of the thirties the students confined themselves to verbal threats, a few one-day strikes, and an accidental encounter or two with administrative authorities: nothing, so far as is known, in the way of bombing or burning.

lence of the state, this was a mite, compared to the violence of everyday public America, a snippet—yet it was a signal that times were changing, and rapidly, too.

SDS by no means embraced the new turn, the general sentiment seeming to be that violence was not defensible morally, not persuasive publicly, and not effective tactically. Carl Davidson took pains to dissociate the resistance people from " 'the Left adventurers,' or, simply, 'the crazies' "; Calvert added that "the New Left has its problems with the Left-wing adventurists who think that sabotage and terrorism will bring the socialist revolution tomorrow"; and the large bulk of the membership seemed to agree with a *New Left Notes* letter writer who argued simply, "We can't succeed with violence. . . . We cannot win an armed revolution—never." And yet it fascinated, the idea of violence, and as frustration grew, repression grew, the monumentality of the task grew, and its necessity, so did the possibilities of violence.

"Sunday, April 21. Days of Resistance." April began the escalation of student resistance that would mark this spring as the most explosive period up to that time in the history of American universities.

The Ten Days of Resistance (as it was now called), which had been thought of originally as SDS's dramatic escalation of activism, happened ironically without significant participation from national SDS. The reasons, as Bob Pardun recalls it, were two. First,

> . . . there was a lot of hostility to that program, an *incredible* amount of hostility. . . . PL had gotten itself strong in a whole lot of chapters, and being strong that meant they'd always bring up the whole thing about decentralism and NO coordinating from the top down, and all that bullshit. And when you'd say, What about *your* organization and "democratic centralism" and top-down, they'd say, PL is something different and as members of PL we have a right to organize any way we want, top-down or not, but as members of SDS we don't want *that* organization to be that way, SDS should be something else. That was always their excuse for hanging up action: the NO had conceived of it and therefore it was top-down and therefore it was bad and the local chapters shouldn't do it.

Second, the NO, smarting under the complaints from a number of chapters about its attempts to "go too fast" into resistance, shied away from mounting any kind of aggressive campaign and its staffers turned their backs. Pardun recalls:

> There were faults of individuals who were assigned to do certain things and didn't do them. Like the national coordinator [Greg Calvert] didn't do a thing, didn't coordinate *anything,* and as the Ten Days approached we had no idea what was to happen anywhere across the country. We knew stuff was supposed to happen in Chicago 'cause we lived there, and we heard rumors about Wisconsin, and Texas, but as for what was happening anywhere else, we just didn't know—because the founder of the plan, and coordinator of the plan, had flipped out and left.

What action there was during those days, therefore, was due to the energies of local SDSers who chose not to wait around for national direction and to the careful organizing done by the Student Mobilization Committee. At least fifty colleges and universities took part all across the country,* with rallies, marches, teach-ins, and sit-ins, climaxing in a one-day "student strike" on April 26. It was a demonstration of significant proportions—probably as many as a million students stayed away from classes that day as a protest against the war and the government propagating it—and yet somehow its impact on the public was slight. Most reports at the time tended to focus on Columbia, which was certainly the most dramatic event of that week but had nothing whatsoever to do with the nation-wide Ten Days actions, and when local protests were covered it was often with the implication that they were aping the events in New York. Few media accounts emphasized the simple fact that the first mass strike action since the 1930s and

---

*It is probably an underestimate, but it is the best that can be arrived at from a study of Senate documents, Student Mobilization Committee reports, and SDS records. Institutions involved were Alabama, Arizona, Berkeley, Biltmore, Brown, Bucknell, Chicago, CCNY, Connecticut, Drew, Florida, Indiana, Maine, Massachusetts, Memphis State, Minnesota, Moravian, North Carolina, Oberlin, Olympic, Patterson State, Penn State, Portland State, Purdue, Queens (North Carolina), San Francisco State, San Jose State, Simmons, Southern Illinois, Trinity, Virginia, University of Washington, Washington State University, Wayne State, Wellesley, Wilson; there were also city-wide marches with uncounted area colleges in Boston, Cleveland, Chicago, New York, and Los Angeles.

the largest student strike in the history of the country was taking place.*

"Thursday, May 2. . . . To NYC, Columbia." The rebellion of Columbia was ten days old by the time Bernardine Dohrn arrived from a Lawyers Guild trip through the South: the buildings had been occupied, communalized, and then forcibly emptied, the student demands had been hoisted, resisted, and then in part acceded to, the administration had been cowed, refortified, and then exposed in full complicity, the New York police had been called, tested, and found unbelievably brutal, and the whole thing had been broadcast, televised, written about, and pontificated at by every medium in every part of the country. Dohrn went right to work with other members of the Lawyers Guild to arrange bail and prepare cases for many of the 712 people arrested, while on the campus an all-out strike had just begun.

The sequence of events that has passed into the history of the sixties simply as "Columbia" has been told many ways, but perhaps most pertinent is to examine the central, though not necessarily controlling, role played by the SDS chapter. This is all the more pertinent because the history of the Columbia chapter is the history of many other SDS chapters of the time, writ larger, of course, and more flamboyantly, but in essentials the same.

Columbia SDS had several sputters in the early sixties, but the chapter began in earnest after the SDS march in the spring of 1965, largely around the efforts of John Fuerst, Harvey Bloom, and Neumann. In the spring of 1966 it was accorded recognition as an official campus organization, spending

*The American Student Union claimed (extravagantly) that five hundred thousand students stayed out during its one-day strike in May 1936. There is no way of knowing just how many students struck thirty-two years later, but, judging from the size of the places involved (institutions like Arizona, Connecticut, Southern Illinois, San Francisco State) and the greater national scope (from Arizona to Maine, Washington to Florida, whereas the earlier strike was almost entirely centered on New York colleges), probably at least twice that. *New Left Notes* (April 29) estimated that one million college and high-school students struck; the *Guardian* (May 4) figured "nearly a million." For the sake of precision it should be noted that both actions might more properly be called boycotts rather than strikes, since they were temporary, limited, and did not depend upon the meeting of demands by the target institution.

the term trying to build a membership; among the early converts were Ted Kaptchuk and Ted Gold, both sophomores at the time. SDS led a protest of some two hundred members and sympathizers against a CIA recruiter in the fall of 1966, its first real demonstration and one of the earliest attempts to organize around the issue of university complicity, and on the next day it took the (for Columbia) quite unheard-of step of marching into the administration building, to deliver a letter demanding the end of CIA recruiting; a week later, receiving no answer, the SDSers marched into the building again, this time cornering President Grayson Kirk and forcing him into a debate on university complicity at which the unprepared and stuttering president came off a decided second to the angry students. The confrontation, mild though it was, shattered Columbia precedent and established SDS as an important voice, certainly the leading radical voice, on campus, and its regular membership increased to something over one hundred, including a young sophomore from a New Jersey suburb by the name of Mark Rudd.

But the chapter leaders during the 1966–67 school year had no illusions as to power, and they bent themselves to methodical work at the mimeograph machines and with an occasional bullhorn, trying to establish broad student support, avoiding confrontations which they felt would only antagonize the campus. It was at this time that many of them became associated with the group of New York SDSers around the newly founded "Praxis" supplement to *New Left Notes* and fell quickly under the sway of the new-working-class theories; their campus work emphasized the university's role in producing the new technological society and they saw their mission chiefly as *exposing* university complicity (by research and writing if possible, by picketing and rallies if not), not *confronting* it. In fact, when the CIA recruiters returned again in February 1967, the chapter voted officially not to interrupt them, sensing that such a move was premature for the still-docile student body; and when eighteen students, many of them SDS members—including Tony Papert, a pre-med student and PL stalwart, and John Jacobs, known as "JJ" a onetime PLer turned free-lance radical—went and sat-in at the CIA office anyway, SDS leaders officially *disavowed* any connection. Instead, the chapter concentrated on the class-rank issue, full of meat for its complicity theorists, and swung its energies behind a student referendum on the issue which was inaugurated by the student government; it was only when the antirank position won by almost three-to-one and sizable student support was assured that SDS threatened a strike if the administration did not abolish ranking. After some footdragging, the university backed down and abandoned class rank, and SDS stock soared to a new high on the campus. Flush with success, SDS decided to go after the Marine recruiters, and though the demonstration ended up in violence, right enough, it was violence instigated by the conservative "jocks" of the campus, and served to enhance SDS's position as a "responsible" power on campus. And when SDS researchers went on that spring to present the campus with convincing proof of Columbia's involvement first with the Institute for Defense Analysis and then with the CIA, bringing complicity charges home in a way that even the most mole-eyed liberal could see, SDS seemed on the verge of becoming a major campus force.

Somehow it didn't happen. Throughout the fall of 1967, at a time when resistance was in the air everywhere, SDS at Columbia was quiet, confused, congealed: it was going through the doldrums that practically every chapter encountered at one time or another. Several of the former chapter leaders had graduated or dropped out. Drugs proved a more satisfying answer than politics for many, and certainly less frustrating. Progressive Labor members were gumming up chapter debates, turning the weekly meetings increasingly into battles between "correct lines" rather than forums to thrash out ideas. Elitism and male chauvinism turned away many potential recruits who could not find the in-group congenial, and lack of coherence and lack of action turned away still others. Membership fluctuated between two and three hundred despite organizing campaigns and dormitory canvassing. And above all sharp disagreements had grown up in the chapter between the moderate leadership, now dubbed, half-mockingly, the "praxis axis"—Kaptchuk, Gold, David Gilbert (a 1966 Columbia graduate), and others—and the resistance followers, who became known as the "action faction"—among them Jacobs, Papert, and Rudd.

When the chapter finally did decide to mount an all-out drive against military and corporate recruiting, it was effectively coopted (in a move of rare sagacity by the Kirk administration) by the university's decisions to ban all recruiting until the Columbia College student body had a chance to vote on the issue and to appoint a faculty committee to offer its recommendations. Columbia SDS, like the chapters at many universities, was hog-tied by the referendum tactic, for it did not start out with the majority of students on its side, as it had with ranking—most still did not see the connections between recruiting and complicity, and were told that recruiting fell under the unassailable mantle of "free speech" or "civil liberties" anyway—and it was given only a few weeks to persuade them. The student body voted three-to-one for "open recruiting," the faculty followed this with a similar recommendation, and SDS was out in the cold. The free election of the masters by the slaves was invincible. As David Gilbert was to put it: "SDS, which a few months earlier had successfully led the majority of students against class rank for the war, was already discredited on campus as both adventurist and do-nothing."

It was in the wake of this defeat in early 1968 that the action faction began to assert itself. Rudd, still new to radicalism himself but a man who knew what he liked, scored the praxis axis for putting " 'organizing' and 'base-building' above action and 'confrontation' " and chided their "various pieties about the necessity to build the base before you take action." It was the actionists who turned a planned picketing of Dow recruiters on February 23 into an outright sit-in, much to the dismay of Kaptchuk, who objected unavailingly, "A picket line has its time and place," and was answered, "Who are you going to alienate—some half-assed liberals?" It was they who attacked the site of the Columbia gym in February, the day after construction had begun. And it was they who, against an explicit thirty-to-one vote of the chapter, pulled an unusual bit of theater the next month in throwing a lemon meringue pie in the face of an SSS colonel come to sell Columbia on the virtues of the military life. Rudd later felt that this was a turning point—"in a criticism session held after the pie incident, members of the chapter began to learn the difference between the verbal 'base-building,' nonstruggle approach of the old leadership . . . and the aggressive approach of those who saw the primacy of developing a movement based on struggle"—for shortly thereafter Rudd was elected chairman of the chapter, Nick Freudenberg, another actionist and a sophomore, became vice-chairman, and the action faction held sway.*

The issues which the action faction seized upon that spring were obvious ones: racism, as represented by the university's usurping Harlem land and building a gym which would admit community people through the back door; imperialism, as symbolized by the university's close involvement with the Institute for Defense Analysis and its secret defense department work; authoritarianism, as embodied in the arbitrary and unilateral rulings of the administration, especially with regard to student demonstrations and discipline. As at many campuses where demonstrations took place, the issues were both important and irrelevant at

---

*The action-faction-vs.-praxis-axis dispute was going on in virtually every SDS chapter across the land; sometimes it took the form of Progressive Labor vs. "New Left" factions, sometimes veterans vs. newcomers, sometimes resistance vs. base-building, but the underlying tensions were the same. One of the most revealing descriptions of this kind of split appears in a report sent into the NO by an anonymous chapter correspondent from the University of Missouri sometime early in 1968, all the more interesting because it covers what must be regarded as an average, even a conservative, chapter: "A large majority of members make up the first category at any given time. These are the 'liberals.' They are generally, but not always, newer members. They think talk of revolution is silly and often recoil violently from the use of unorthodox tactics. They hope, someday, to convince a majority of the student body to clean up the campus and put an end to the war.

"The people in the second category call themselves 'kamikazes.' (Those in the first call them 'nuts.') Their view of everything is apocalyptic, and in fact it often seems that only the possibility of apocalypse allows them to breathe the same air as everyone else. The thinking of the 'liberals' enrages them; they would like to throw all the 'liberals' out of the chapter and then get down to the business of making a revolution. But on those rare occasions when votes are taken—on any issue—the 'liberals' always prevail and this drives the 'kamikazes' out on the campus to hold an unapproved demonstration which, in turn, enrages the 'liberals' afresh. . . .

"The third category is made up of the 'old-timers.' These are usually seniors or graduate students, and are nearly always the leaders, elected or *de facto,* of the chapter. They are leaders because of their experience in the movement, and past movements, and because of their connections with the movement in other parts of the country, but not necessarily because of any special aptitude for leadership. They may side with either the 'liberals' or 'kamikazes' in an argument, but probably go along with the former more often because they think there is less danger in that of destroying the chapter or permanently stunting its growth. Time goes by, the 'old-timers' grow easily bored by debates they have heard countless times before and they begin to avoid meetings." (Letter to NO, undated [1968], archives.)

the same time. They were important in that they spoke to major social ills beyond the campus, thus giving student protest that wider dimension that it always must have, and because they tied the university directly into those ills, giving protest the immediate reality it needs to be effective. But they were irrelevant in the sense that they were only a few, and not especially the worst, of many similar issues that could expose the nature of the university and thereby the nature of the system of which it was a part, and in that even a university sanctioned by the gods and governed by saints could be made a target by those who were really addressing themselves to the larger maladies of the society, for which the university stood as surrogate. Conservative critics were right, for the wrong reasons, when they argued that if the university had given in on these demands the radicals would have found three others just as urgent; or, in the words of a famous Berkeley slogan, "The issue is not the issue."

Once the action faction found the university's weak spots it began to push. On March 27 Rudd led a hundred-strong delegation into Low Library (the administration building) with an anti-IDA petition, an action which led to six of the chapter leaders—Rudd, Freudenberg, Gold, Jacobs, Ed Hyman, and Morris Grossner—being put on probation. Two weeks later he disrupted a pious university memorial service for Martin Luther King with a blunt speech suggesting that an institution taking over Harlem land, fighting the unionization of its own black workers, participating in an institution (IDA) doing research on "riot control," and punishing students for nonviolent demonstrations, had little place paying honor to Dr. King. And two weeks after that the chapter voted, despite strong resistance from the praxis people, to resist the university's moves against the six leaders by holding a rally and marching once again on the president's office; it even voted a "contingency" plan leading to "occupation and blockade" of the administration building, but hardly anyone took such an idea seriously and the vote was perfunctory. On the next day, April 23, the uprising began, surpassing anything that even the most militant of the activists had imagined.

During the early stages of the uprising—abortive marches around the campus, the occupation of one building by a black-and-white coalition, the holding hostage of a college dean—every-

thing happened so quickly and haphazardly that the chapter factions never had time to show. But after the whites were kicked out
of the occupied building and then in some disarray took over Low
Library itself, the cracks began to appear. In Low perhaps a
hundred or so white radicals heard the news that the cops were
coming, Rudd and several of the action faction opted for discretion, a vote was taken to abandon the building, and the actionists
scampered out the front windows to safety; Tony Papert, a few PL
comrades, and a number of other determined SDSers (close to
thirty in all) decided to stay, a move which succinctly made Papert
the *de facto* leader of Low in the days to come and surrounded
PL with a definite aura of respect. When the police "bust" turned
out to be unfounded, more students drifted back to Low and the
upper stories fell to the students. But the cracks kept appearing:
at an SDS meeting that same afternoon, Rudd and a few of the
action faction not occupying the president's office urged everyone
to join the Low contingent; he was voted down, seventy-to-three,
by the praxis people, who wanted to go slow, avoid "turning off"
the majority of students, spend the time canvassing dormitories
and holding discussion groups to build support before further
action. Rudd then proposed that SDS take over more buildings,
and was voted down again; in a white rage, Rudd shouted to the
meeting, "I resign as chairman of this fucking organization," and
stormed out the door. Behind him the vote was overwhelming to
try the base-building techniques of the praxis axis.

Within a day, however, it appeared that things had gone too
far for that: the campus was already, in the word of the day,
"polarized." Two more buildings were taken over by people who
were not associated with *any* faction of SDS, conservative students had organized and were preparing to try a little confrontation of their own, and the faculty had entered the fray. The SDS
forces regrouped, Rudd was accepted back as chairman without
ado, and both praxis and action alike found themselves in agreement that defiance in a time of crisis was necessary; indeed, both
sides were able to claim victories, the action faction showing that
building takeovers had succeeded in shaking up Columbia as
never before, the praxis axis saying that such student support as
there was to date would never have materialized without the
earlier months of base-building. That night SDS presented a solid

front to the faculty, and it was praxis leader David Gilbert who made a passionate and unflinching defense of the SDS tactics to the assembled professors. Later the same night, with the pro-SDS forces bulging the rafters at Low, SDSers took over still another building, Mathematics Hall.

For the next four days, with five buildings in the hands of some thousand students, the incredible adrenalin of victory and fear kept together what were by now dozens of political factions. A "Strike Central" was established in a neutral building, where Rudd, senior SDSers Lewis Cole and Juan Gonzalez, and other members allied to the action group held sway (most of them were to remain there when the bust finally came, avoiding arrest), and where the readiness of a cadre of PL people to keep the bureaucracy functioning gave PL still another red feather in its cap. Other PLers joined the crowd at Low, where Tony Papert held forth in the President's office, talking about class conflict and a prerevolutionary society and the necessity of revolutionary change, fresh and heady stuff for many of the young occupiers.* And in Math, where Tom Hayden and a melange of New York street radicals including some of the Motherfuckers had come to lend their support, all kinds of politics were represented but the communards turned out to be rather more concerned with "life styles" than rhetoric. The effective united front among all the variety of SDSers was neatly symbolized on Saturday night, when three SDS leaders addressed a crowd of antiwar marchers who collected outside the

---

*Also at Low, students went through administration files, pulling out and duplicating papers showing Columbia's behind-the-scenes roles in a variety of secret enterprises. Many of these were smuggled out and later reprinted in Jeff Shero's *RAT* (making the SDS operation complete). One document was a memorandum in which Grayson Kirk proposed planting a phony story in the *Times* to gain support for the gym; another showed how Kirk tried to avoid and squelch a local community group opposing the university's expansionism; a third was a letter from George Beadle, president of the University of Chicago and a director of the IDA, telling Kirk that they could work out a way to fudge radical student and faculty demands and still "allow the work of IDA to continue without interruption." Perhaps the most significant document, this from the files of vice-president David Truman, was a record of the official minutes of a high-level meeting of the CIA-funded Council on Foreign Relations at which the elaborate machinations of the CIA and various covert military forces—and the important role of American universities within them—were spelled out (for a fuller account, see Ruth First, *Power in Africa,* Pantheon, 1970).

university gates: Mark Rudd, Ted Kaptchuk, and Tom Hayden.

The police attack, coming on the eighth day of the occupations, and with the full approval of the Columbia authorities, was not extraordinarily brutal compared to the treatment dealt to ghetto minorities, the gunning down of unarmed students at Orangeburg, or even the precedents at Berkeley, Wisconsin, and Oakland. But the grim, methodical cruelty, the indiscriminate use of force on any nearby body, the injuries to more than two hundred young people, the mass arrests of more than seven hundred people, and the presence of reporters from every known media, combined to give it a special impact on the students involved, on the flabbergasted faculty, on campuses elsewhere, and on much of the nation beyond academe. It was one more example of students putting themselves on the defensive, in spite of the presumed lessons of the Oakland and Rusk demonstrations, a lesson that many would not forget.* It was also one more link in the chain of evidence—the police riot at the Democratic Convention would be another one —that active dissent would not be tolerated by the state and violent repression would be.

During the successful month-long strike which followed the clearing of the buildings, the paper began to peel from the cracks of the SDS chapter even as the bulk of the student body rallied to the cause. The majority wanted to stick to the hard line and see through the original issues of the protest, but there were many willing to modify the stance so as to insure greater campus participation in the strike. Most of the chapter supported the idea of holding "liberated classes" during the last weeks of the semester, where old teachers would offer new courses and new teachers would offer radical ones; but PL, for example, was vociferous in opposing the plan, arguing that the struggle had to be escalated against the real administration, not blunted by substituting an alternative, albeit "liberated," one. Some, supported by PL and a variety of other radicals who had already done work in the sur-

---

*The few tactics that were used to impede the police were notable failures: soap spread on the stairs of Mathematics halted the police only slightly, but made it easy for protesters' bodies to be slid down the steps at a ghastly clip, while at least one complicated barricade mounted against doors inside Low to withstand the police charge proved ineffective when it was found that the doors opened outward.

rounding community, wanted to take the battle off the campus and involve the people actually being squeezed by Columbia's slum-lordism; others, mostly praxis people, felt that the first job was on the campus, trying to demonstrate in a "liberated university" what it was that the radical vision was all about. And because the chapter as a whole had never faced up to these issues before, because it was no more united in goals than it was in tactics, differences such as these prevented it from joining ranks in the hour of its victory and pushing its advantage along a single front. SDS floundered. When the liberals, who were now by far the largest group supporting the strike, eventually came forward with an old-fashioned student-power line—"restructuring" and re-forming the university to give the students a larger voice, make classes more "relevant," and the like—SDS had no way to oppose them because it had no concept of its own of what it wanted the university to be, or do, or whether there should be a university at all. Within days, the liberals broke from the radicals, drawing most of the student body with them, and set to work making schemes for a nicer and more cosmetized university, much to the relief of the vested interests among faculty and administration, not to mention the Ford Foundation and other bulwarks of the *status quo* who came forward with $40,000 to help the liberal students along. Reform is what really won the rebellion at Columbia—as at many other places where radicals began the job but were either too inexperienced or too powerless to continue it—and the radical vision which animated the high moments of crisis proved chimeri-cal in the long days afterward.

But three momentous experiences which underlay the Co-lumbia rebellion did linger and did much to shape the revolution-ary politics that SDS was edging toward. The first was the experi-ence of those who encountered the communal life—thrown together with like-minded men and women, sharing, meeting, loving, eating, defecating, sleeping, talking, and deciding together, with no authority, no rules, no force to limit them, and making the decisions that affected their own lives. One man wrote, "This was the first event in most of our lives where we felt effective, where what we were doing belonged to us," and another, over-whelmed by "the satisfaction of acting together with others," concluded: "I wanted to organize my life around being and doing radical work partly because it was sexier and it made me feel smart and partly because it was freeing and it felt right inside." The second experience grew out of the alliance with black students— one of the earliest expressions of the Lexington National Council spirit and the first practical racial coalition since the civil-rights days—and the strength this gave to the white students' cause. The blacks were slow in joining the issues at Columbia (it was SDS, for example, which instigated the gym and Martin Luther King protests) and insisted on going their own way once they had (carrying on their own negotiations, breaking from the central strike committee, making their separate peace with the authorities), but their mere presence gave the rebellion legitimacy, confidence, and power. "We were spurred on," Mark Rudd said later, "by a tremendous push from history, if you will, embodied in the militant black students at Columbia." The third experience was the most complicated of all, for it had to do with students' taking a political view of themselves, and their university, and the society beyond, confronting the true implications of the old SDS slogan, "A free university in a free society." When one professor asked Mark Rudd on the third day of the takeovers whether he really wanted to destroy the university—"Doesn't the university have any redeeming features that merit your saving it?"—the SDS chairman was at a loss for an answer: he hadn't really thought about what he really wanted out of the university in the long run, what kind of reforms he expected from an institution which he knew to be so complicit and compromised; hardly anyone in the chapter had. But during the next days and weeks, as the administration and then the trustees and then the faculty showed themselves to consist of limited, rigid, compromised people (the liberals as much as the moderates), and as the liberal students deserted the SDSers for their own narrow concerns, it became clear to many SDSers in a very direct way that it was not the *reform* of the university that they really wanted, not the limiting of complicity, not the *restructuring* of the evil complex, but something much vaster, more significant, more, well, revolutionary. "To student rebels," wrote Dick Greeman, an SDS veteran and one of the few Columbia faculty members unflinching in his support for the radicals, the lessons of Columbia were that "allies must be sought in the black ghettos and in the ranks of labor, not on campus. It means that 'a free university' will only exist *after* we have won a 'free society.' " Many of the Columbia strikers made their break with the academy after these days, putting the dream of university reform and student power behind them forever; by commencement time neither Rudd nor most of the other SDSers had much doubt about how to answer the question of the university's "redeeming features."

The seeds of Weatherman are planted here.

Columbia 1968 was the most significant student rebellion to date, surpassing even Berkeley 1964 (an event with which it shared many characteristics), and, according to Carl Oglesby, "just as important, just as pregnant and portentous, as what happened in Haymarket Square" a century earlier. Not so much because it was extreme or unusual (there had been other building takeovers, other hostage-holdings, other massive police busts) as that it occurred in the media capital of the world, at a prestigious Ivy League university, at a time when campuses everywhere were roiled with demonstrations—and, like Berkeley, suggested that America's children had not only awakened from the American dream but were prepared to move on to actually destroying all it stood for. Columbia quickly became the symbol of all campus protest, and it energized the news media, angered the politicians, terrified the academics, and inspired the students. And it put SDS (whatever its deficiencies at Columbia or its difficulties nationally, SDS played some role in virtually every outbreak) on the front pages and news programs of the land, catapulting it to a prominence that no other student organization had enjoyed before or since. As *Fortune* put it, somewhat hyperbolically, "You can't argue with success: and S.D.S. has yet to lose a battle."

SDS, if not quite a household word yet, at least penetrated the living room. Grayson Kirk went on national television and denounced SDSers as "those who are out to wreck the university." Eric Sevareid and other television commentators delivered themselves of philippics against the unwashed and misbehaved. The Associated Press, whose headquarters sits on land owned by Columbia University, filed thousands of inches of copy daily, with pictures, interviews, and a special "backgrounder" that showed how Mark Rudd had planned the whole thing in diabolical detail since October.* The national news weeklies rushed into print with skeletal profiles of SDS, seeing it as the "prime mover" of campus revolts, full of "intellectual arrogance and a facile conviction that ends justify the means," and able to employ with "single-minded fervor" the "classic revolutionary techniques." *The New York Times,* in whose backyard the rebellion took place, gave especially prominent and lengthy coverage to Columbia and to SDS's role, though displaying its penchant for inaccuracy both in a myriad of everyday details and in the conclusions it drew.† In the eyes of the nation's leading newspaper, whose board chairman was a Columbia trustee and whose powerful assistant managing editor was an ardent alumnus, SDS engaged in the "rule-or-ruin tactics of a minority" and "substituted dictatorship by temper tantrum for undergraduate democracy," thus interrupting the work of a great university that should be allowed "to turn once again to its mission of teaching, research and public service"—written without irony, as if none of what SDS had been saying about the university's missions of slum-lording, war complicity, autocracy, and public disservice had reached its ears. The *Times*'s remedy for the problem was force: "Any society, academic or other, that lacks the will to defend itself against illegitimate disruption and takeover is crippled and, as a free society may be doomed"; and, "Even most sympathizers with the Columbia students . . . feel the line has to be drawn somewhere if an orderly society is to survive." Even the *Times,* however, was outdone by *Barron's,* the right-wing, surprisingly influential, weekly of Dow Jones & Company, which carried a front-page article full of foreboding:

*It was true that Rudd had drawn up plans in the fall for ways in which the action faction could operate in the spring, including a one-day sit-in and a student strike. What the AP forgot to mention was that no one at Columbia took the plans seriously and the chapter voted them down in October with a definite air of derision.

†No student at Columbia, no matter of what politics, was without serious complaints about the *Times*'s coverage. The moderate, even unadventuresome, United States Student Press Association found the paper's reporting so misguided that it issued a special statement: "The *Times'* treatment of the Columbia protest indicates clearly the need for an independent, tough college press. The commercial press just isn't going to report what is really happening on college campuses." (See also *Columbia Daily Spectator,* April 27 and May 10, and Jack Newfield, *The Dutton Review,* No. 1, 1970.)

> The siege tactics which disrupted Columbia and brought its normal
> activities to a halt represent the latest attempt by a revolutionary
> movement which aims to seize first the universities and then the
> industries of America. The rebels are members of Students for a
> Democratic Society. . . . Since SDS tactics have succeeded in crip-
> pling a great university, the next target can be a City Hall, the State
> Capitol, or even the White House. . . . The Columbia crisis vitally
> affects the life of every American.

So pleased was *Barron's* by its message that it took a full-page
advertisement in the *Times* four days later to reprint the article
in full. It was then only left for *Fortune* to set out for the Establishment the true nature of its enemy:

> These youngsters, organized in the Students for a Democratic So-
> ciety, (S.D.S.), are acting out a revolution—not a protest, and not
> a rebellion, but an honest-to-God revolution. They see themselves
> as the Che Guevaras of our society, and their intention is to seize
> control of the university, destroy its present structure, and establish
> the "liberated" university as the redoubt from which to storm and
> overthrow "bourgeois" America. This is what they say they are
> doing—they are the least conspiratorial and most candid of revolu-
> tionists—and this is what in fact they *are* doing.

The most ardently resistant SDSer couldn't have put it better—
and even he wouldn't have been so convinced.

In the weeks after Columbia, as protests continued throughout the country, the press was joined by the politicians. President
Johnson led the pack, with a speech at Texas Christian University
—one of the few campuses, it was said, where he would be safe
to go—accusing militant students of being "young totalitarians."
The House Un-American Activities Committee rushed forth with
a report (written by Phillip Luce, the one-time PLer now turned
witch-hunter) saying that radical and black groups "are seriously
considering the possibility of instituting armed insurrection in this
country" and citing SDS in particular as a group planning "guer-
rilla-type operations" against the government (a charge apparently based solely on Calvert's misunderstood remarks to the
Times reporter the previous May). At least half the state legislatures in the land received bills outlawing various radical organizations and withholding funds from disorderly students or
insufficiently hard-line administrators. The U.S. Congress went

even further, passing bills that would withdraw aid from students who "disrupt" universities, deny funds to universities that ban military recruiters (as at least twenty-two institutions had done by May), and allow the President to send federal troops, specifically exempted from sanctions on interfering with an individual's civil rights, anywhere in the country at his own whim. (This was in addition to a law passed in March—the one that would be used against the "Chicago Eight"—making the crossing of a state line to participate "in a riot or committing any act of violence in furtherance of a riot" a crime punishable by five years in prison and a fine of $10,000.) Meanwhile, in less public actions, the FBI instructed its offices to send out right-wing literature "anonymously to college educators who have shown a reluctance to take decisive action against the 'New Left' "—selecting for one of its innominate missives the *Barron's* article—and thereafter to report "positive results or comments by recipients." And at the Pentagon a so-called "domestic war room" was set up to examine files from the now-enormous army surveillance system and to prepare military responses to civil insurrections, guerrilla warfare, and whatever else the citizens might spring.

University administrations tended to interpret Columbia much as they had Berkeley, and just as Berkeley had triggered a series of academic changes under the threat of "another Berkeley," so now began a wave of concessions and reforms designed to frustrate the SDS slogan of "two, three, many Columbias."* Plans for "restructuring" began to appear everywhere, students were hastily placed on university committees, student-faculty-administrative forums were held, curriculum committees were set up, vice-presidents-for-student-affairs were installed; in all, according to one extensive survey, no fewer than 72 percent of American colleges and universities expanded and improved measures for student participation in campus governance during this school year, and it doesn't take much imagination to figure out when most of that happened.

And the students elsewhere—what of them? For reasons having as much to do with their own particular circumstances as the

*The phrase, initiated by the Columbia strikers and picked up by the NO as a national call, was of course modeled on Che Guevara's appeal for "two, three, many Vietnams."

example of Columbia, but clearly shocked, angered, inspired, and animated by those widely publicized events, they exploded. Columbia, and the Ten Days action which accompanied it, was like a detonator. More student protests took place during the following weeks than had ever occurred before, and they were of greater militance, concerned with more sweeping demands, and engaged in by a greater number of students. Significant demonstrations, with escalated tactics, occurred on at least forty campuses—there were building takeovers, for example, at Brooklyn College, Cheyney State, Delaware, Delaware State, Denver, Northwestern, Ohio State, and Stanford, and other forms of demonstrations leading to police attacks, violence, and the arrest of more than 150 students at Alfred, Brooklyn, Hawaii, Long Beach, Marquette, University of Miami, Ohio, Roosevelt, San Francisco State, and Southern Illinois. There is no way to measure exactly the number of demonstrations during these weeks, but several major studies at the time suggest the rough dimensions, and there is no doubt that this spring surpassed anything seen before; one of the surveys concluded succinctly, "College student unrest has escalated to the point where perhaps most officials responsible for the higher learning in America would now consider it their number one problem."

The surveys bear a somewhat closer look, for they suggest not only the quantity of student revolts but their quality, which were both little understood at the time. As to numbers, the National Student Association calculated that there were 221 demonstrations involving 35 or more people at 110 colleges and universities from January to June, with the bulk of them falling in April and May. A survey by the authors of *Protest!* indicated that during this period there were as many as 310 demonstrations (included in this definition are the circulation of petititions and the formal enunciation of demands by student groups). And a study by the Educational Testing Service, using an even looser definition, found no fewer than 3463 protests during the year, of which something like 2000 can be presumed to have taken place in the spring. As to the quality of student resistance, all three surveys are in general agreement. The protests were widespread, occurring coast to coast and in the South as well as the North, at small Catholic colleges as well as major state universities, affecting at least two-thirds of the larger institutions. The tactics were militant, perhaps as many as a third involving sit-ins, strikes, hostages, and takeovers, but all but a very few took place without violence (in the sense of bodily harm or serious property damage), and what there was tended to be instigated by the calling in of police. The greatest number of protests focused on the larger political and social questions— Vietnam and racism, predominantly—and only a few of the significant demonstrations had anything to do with student power, parietal rules, curricula, and the like. New Left campus groups, chiefly SDS chapters but also many *ad hoc* organizations, were instrumental in leading the protests, especially the political ones and especially the larger and more militant. And students in the great majority of instances won their battles, wresting administration concessions, promises, and reforms, while in only a few cases were they punished by arrest, suspension, or university discipline.

Two, three, many Columbias indeed.

"Tuesday, May 21. 5—Columbia . . . sit-in Hamilton—barricades." The events of the spring were making an impact on Bernardine Dohrn. The disappointments of draft resistance, the shock of King's death, the frustrations of the slow (and errant) grinding of American courts, the extraordinary explosion of the campuses—these must have wrought a slow metamorphosis. By the time of the second Columbia outbreak, Dohrn was there, literally at the barricades.

Columbia had traveled through warped space; Rudd called it a *déjà-vu*. Exactly four weeks after its first demonstration SDS led another rally on the campus—this time to protest disciplinary action against four of its leaders—moved into the very building it had begun with before, barricaded the doors again, and once more prepared for the police to come. The chapter had shaken down considerably by then, the actionists having carried the day and won new recruits in the wake of the police invasion and the SDS victories (an end to gym construction, withdrawal from the IDA, reorganization of student discipline, humiliation of the administration). The most virulent debates now were apt to come between the regular SDSers and the PL faction, the latter having won a good deal of respect during the April days and used its advantage wisely to draw in new recruits; but both were united in the need to act again in the face of further administrative threats and both were well represented at this new takeover. For most of them this round of the battle would be decisive: the university announced

that day that any student arrested when the police cleared the
building would be suspended, and the question of whether to be
full-time students or full-time radicals was posed irrevocably that
night. Juan Gonzalez defined the issue:

> It was a confrontation which showed how much we believe in what
> we were fighting for. If our goals went beyond the university, then
> we should have been willing to leave it if necessary. Were we stu-
> dents who were politically active, or activists who happened to be
> students?

For most of SDS, praxis and action alike, the answer was clear.
In the end seventy young radicals made their career decisions that
night, to which the actual calling-in of the police and the ensuing
brutality was secondary. Weatherman was beginning to take
shape.

"*Wednesday, May 22. Ct [court]—160 arrests. Tombs [the
Manhattan House of Detention], . . . Monday, June 3. Fly to Chgo.
. . . Great joy.*" Dohrn and others in the National Lawyers Guild
were important in handling the cases of many of the Columbia
students. After the initial court procedures were finished she made
a brief visit to Chicago to see her parents and some old friends,
and to check on the preparations for the Democratic Convention,
before going off to the SDS convention in East Lansing, Michigan,
where her life would be changed.

She was not the only one in Chicago feeling great joy those
days. The SDS National Office, as might be expected, was riding
high. Membership took a quick jump, at it always does in the wake
of widespread publicity when unaffiliated students get the sense
that there's something going on that they should be a part of—
national membership rose to perhaps seven thousand, and chapter
membership, according to Carl Davidson, to forty thousand. (It
seems possible that this latter figure is too low by a third, judging
from information uncovered by the Educational Testing Service
in its 1967–68 survey showing that student left groups, "mainly"
SDS chapters, have "something on the order of 2 percent of the
national student population," which would be approximately 140,-
000 people.) Chapters, too, were added at an accelerated rate,
Davidson again figuring more than 350 chapters by the end of the
spring (this estimate seems borne out by the ETS survey, indicating that there were left-wing groups at some 395 of the institutions

it contacted, and "these would mainly be SDS chapters").*

Finances, too, enjoyed the same upswing, though in the end it amounted to nothing more spectacular than enough to bring the organization to a happy breakeven point by the middle of June. The whole question of where SDS got its money became of much interest to the media just now, ironically at a time when *New Left Notes* was no longer making SDS finances public, and dark theories were invented to explain how this apparently ragamuffin organization, operating out of clearly church-mousian headquarters, could have the cash to finance a student rebellion. The *Chicago Tribune* was typical, declaring mysteriously, "Officers of the SDS seem to have abundant funds for travel, not only from campus to campus in the United States but also to Viet Nam, Cuba and other Communist countries," and noting that they "welcome and receive Communist support." No doubt the NO wished that such easy access to the Banco Habana and the Central Peking Bank really existed, but in fact the sources were much more ordinary: as the NO reported to the June convention, the total income for the 1967–68 school year was $115,094, of which $51,773 came from outright contributions† and $19,059 from dues and subscriptions,

---

*There are no longer any accurate or cumulative records kept by the NO of which universities and colleges had chapters, but among those chapters known to have begun during this period are Arizona, Eastern Michigan State, Hawaii, Loyola of Chicago, North Carolina, Portland State, Toledo, Nevada (the first breakthrough in that region), and (with important later consequences) Kent State University. The ETS survey also gives some indication of the kinds of places where chapters might be found—93 percent of the independent universities had "student Left organizations," 76 percent of the public universities, 52 percent of the independent liberal arts colleges, 44 percent of the public liberal arts colleges, 35 percent of Protestant-run institutions, 30 percent of the technical institutions, 27 percent of Catholic institutions, and 15 percent of the teachers colleges. (Foster and Long, *Protest!*, p. 80.)

†The Boston region raised the most money during the year, the NO reported, and though it gave no sources the obvious speculation is that they would include Anne Peretz, Abby Rockefeller (heir to part of the family's wealth, a radical, and a resident of New England at the time), perhaps John Maher, and certain unidentifiable scions of American wealth found in such profusion at Harvard. Two general membership dunnings during high days—the NO was shrewd enough to know when the mood was right—one in October and one in May, netted $5900. But it seems that the liberal sources of money were still shrinking, and the bulk of the income coming from $5 and $10 contributions from the dedicated few; as the NO put it in one of its printed thank-you letters of mid-1968, "Because we have made our politics clear and our positions firm, we must rely on our membership and people like you for money."

with the rest, if it followed the pattern of previous years, from the
sale of literature and buttons, and from outside printing jobs.
Expenditures were $114,642, with the largest outlay going for a
brand-new Heidelberg Printing Press purchased during the heady
days of June.

Columbia, and the outbreak of student protest which it symbolized, also had its effect on SDS thinking. It seemed first of all
to be the culmination of the period of resistance, proof that the
long months of SDS work were paying off, both in the targets
students were picking (war, complicity, racism, rather than dress
codes and dorm hours) and the tactics (sit-ins, hostages, takeovers, not petitions and pickets). Carl Davidson saw it as a major
turning point in SDS history:

> Since the Columbia Rebellion, SDS has been thrust onto a new
> plateau as a national political force. The importance of that event
> in our history should not be underestimated. More than any other
> event in our recent political past, Columbia has successfully
> summed up and expressed the best aspects of the main thrust of our
> national political efforts in the last two years.

But more than that, Columbia was a vivid demonstration that
students, though (as the general SDS analysis had it) still irrelevant insofar as they pressed for their own selfish ends, could be
a serious threat to the society when they acted for larger political
goals; as Tom Hayden felt it:

> The striking students were not holding onto a narrow conception
> of students as a privileged class asking for inclusion in the university
> as it now exists. . . . The Columbia students were instead taking an
> internationalist and revolutionary view of themselves in opposition
> to the imperialism of the very institutions in which they have been
> groomed and educated. . . . They want a new and independent
> university standing against the mainstream of American society, or
> they want no university at all.

Moreover, students, through their head-on confrontations with
some of the major institutions of the society (universities, police,
media), could expose the nature of those institutions, radicalize
the community of the young, and create new recruits to the cause
of total social transformation. *That* is what SDS meant by "two,
three, many Columbias." "The Columbia strike," wrote New England regional traveler Eric Mann, "more than any other event in

our history, has given the radical student movement the belief that we can really change this country."

"Wednesday, June 5. Kennedy shot." The death of Robert Kennedy came with a kind of fated resignation, another glaring symptom of the national malady.* Few in the upper levels of SDS had any special regard for Kennedy—though on the chapter level there were reports of SDSers willing to defect from radicalism if he became the Democratic Presidential candidate—but, as with the death of King, there was an undefinable sense of anguish, and it is said that Tom Hayden wept beside the coffin of Robert Kennedy as it lay open for final homage.

"Sunday, June 9. To East Lansing. Steve & Tom—off to write at Student Center." Bernardine Dohrn arrived at the SDS convention a little early, planning to write a position paper with Steve Halliwell, the New York organizer with whom she had been close throughout the spring, and Tom Bell, the Cornell SDSer who was now working as a Teamster and an MDS organizer in Springfield, Massachusetts. Their purpose was to put forth a program for the coming year that would embody the rudimentary new-working-class ideas, offset any worker-student program the PL people

---

*Sirhan Sirhan, the convicted assassin, had been on the fringes of the radical movement at Pasadena City College in 1964 and 1965, and he was good friends with several SDSers, particularly one Walter Crowe, a Communist Party member and an official delegate to the Bloomington National Council meeting in December 1967 from the UCLA SDS chapter. But Sirhan's particular brand of madness disinclined him from joining any group, and his ultimate act was unconnected to any known organization. (See William Divale, *I Lived Inside the Campus Revolution,* Cowles, 1970.)

The Kennedy assassination was, incidentally, predicted in a bizarre way by Greg Calvert in an article in *New Left Notes* (March 25) written more than two months before, in which he fantasized that Ethel Kennedy was reading a passage from a (presumably real) history of the Roman Republic: " 'In 133 BC, Tiberius Gracchus, the elder son of one of the new commercial families which had made their fortunes during the last Punic War, was elected Tribune on a platform of liberal reform measures. . . . Conservative opposition to the reforms was strong, however, and Tiberius Gracchus was assassinated. . . . A decade later, in 121 BC, Tiberius's younger brother, Gaius, got himself elected Tribune on a platform even more liberal than that of his elder brother. . . . Unfortunately for the younger Gracchus, the conservatives in the Senate reacted with the same blind hostility of the prior period, and Gaius was also assassinated in circumstances similar to those leading to his brother's death.' " The reaction, as Calvert imagined it: " 'No, Bobby, No! ' shrieked Ethel as she threw down her book and ran for the telephone."

would come up with, and turn the manifest revolutionary spirit of the spring into an organized force for the fall.

"Monday, June 10. SDS Convention. . . . Friday, June 14. Caucus. Elected." On Wednesday night of convention week open warfare broke out between Progressive Labor and the other factions in SDS. In response an alliance of disparate people—some actionists, some praxisites, some pro–working class, some campus-directed, but all troubled by PL—was formed into a rival caucus. The caucus put forth a slate of three officers to be presented to the convention, and for Inter-organizational Secretary it chose Bernardine Dohrn. On Friday night Dohrn faced the plenary to answer questions about her background and beliefs. In one of those answers, with only six words, she presaged the new direction that SDS would take in the final period of its history.

"Do you consider yourself a socialist?" someone in the crowd asked.

"I consider myself," Bernardine Dohrn said, "a revolutionary communist."

She was elected without opposition.

REVOLUTION
1968-1970

In SDS we believe that the only solution to the problems of imperialism is a socialist revolution. Liberal reforms which do not change the basic structure of society will not end the exploitation of working people by the rich. If we are to be free, the imperialist monster which totally controls our economic and social lives must be totally destroyed and replaced with socialism.

By a socialist revolution we mean the complete reorganization of America. Workers will control the goods and wealth they produce. Schools, transportation, housing, and all the other institutions of social welfare will be controlled by the people and not by the few rich men who now run America. Black and brown people will seize control of their communities and take back the culture which centuries of imperialist oppression has robbed from them. Women will break from the secondary roles they fill in capitalist America, and along with men will develop non-exploitative human relationships.

In the past, SDS has been an organization primarily made up of students, and at one time we even fought for reforms in universities that only increased the privileges enjoyed by students. But SDS is getting bigger, because to make a revolution in America we must build a youth movement that includes not only students but also the masses of young people who have been excluded from school. We are building a working class youth movement that understands imperialism and its ruling class as the main enemy and socialism as its main goal.

—THE FIRE NEXT TIME *(New Left Notes),* August 1970

21

SUMMER 1968

On the walls of the huge room in the Student Union on the Michigan State campus in East Lansing were pictures of Lenin and Trotsky and a few hammer-and-sickle emblems, on the stage were the red banner of communism and the black of anarchism, and on the floor were people with red armbands, large red and black flags, and "little red books" of Mao's thoughts. The young men and women cheered their colleagues and greeted photographers with the raised clenched fist of revolution—no longer seeming the least incongruous—and when lining up to cast votes they passed their time singing songs from an IWW songbook or renditions of the "Internationale" in which no one seemed quite certain of the words. Motions from the floor outdid one another in their claims to be "revolutionary," one calling for a "movement which plays a revolutionary role," another for "the destruction of this capitalist, imperalist, racist system," and still another for creating an organization of "professional revolutionaries." And in workshops and plenaries, in caucuses and informal meetings, on the floor and over the dinner tables, one theme predominated: in the words of one reporter, "throughout the convention 'the revolution' was the binding topic of conversation."

This was the 1968 convention of SDS, the organization's acknowledged, if somewhat tentative, step into the waging of revolution. Some eight hundred people gathered from June 9 to 15, perhaps five hundred of them actual delegates or voting members and the rest observers of every political stripe from

IWW to FBI.* There were postcollegians in their mid-twenties who were new to national SDS (people like Bill Ayers and Diana Oughton) and had been drawn to it by its reputation as the only serious revolutionary group around; there were many who had been drawn into SDS chapters during the spring confrontations (the Columbia contingent among them), looking to SDS to carry on that impetus on a national scale; there were quite a number of Progressive Labor Party SDSers, noticeable for their purposely straight dress, starched workshirts and coats-and-ties, fifties-short hair, and smooth-shaven faces; there were a considerable number of Old Left groups for the first time, Spartacists, Wobblies, Communists, International Socialists, Socialist Workers, and Lord knows what else, chiefly concerned with buttonholing likely recruits and hawking their books and pamphlets; there were several groups of politicized hippies (represented most dramatically by the Up Against the Wall, Motherfucker collective from New York) who were concerned to meld the cultural revolution with the political and were usually dismissed as "anarchists" by the more conventional; and there were in the interstices of all this many undefined people with various shades of revolutionary fervor attending the convention through habit, hope, or boredom. Nothing if not diverse, and even contradictory, but they went to East Lansing out of the pervading sense that SDS, coming off a triumphant year (its deficiencies unknown or overlooked after the success of Columbia), was the likely organization to be the cutting edge of the second American revolution.

In the year and a half since Greg Calvert first put forth the tentative notion of "revolutionary consciousness" at that Princeton conference, SDS—and with it much of the white Movement —had been heading inexorably toward thinking of itself, and feel-

*SDSers at this point fully expected surveillance and infiltration. One of the workshops, in fact, billed as devoted to a discussion of sabotage, was explicitly designed to attract all likely FBI and Red Squad agents so as to keep them away from the other, serious workshops. By all accounts, the stratagem worked: one agent who attended, from the sheriff's office of Jefferson Parish, Louisiana, had the perspicacity to realize that "everyone who didn't fit the mold, who appeared to be agents, undercover workers, Federal Bureau of Investigation, or local police intelligence units, all went to the sabotage and explosives workshop." (Senate hearings on "Riots, Civil and Criminal Disorders," Part 18, p. 3654.)

ing itself, revolutionary. By the middle of 1968 there were many
thousands of people who could, with no sense of hyperbole, agree
with the SDS convention paper which argued that "our movement
is an element of the revolutionary vanguard painfully forming
from the innards of America."

By no means a majority of the young shared this attitude, of
course, not even all of the politicized young. What is remarkable
is that so many did, and many more would come to in the course
of the next two years: university students, yes, but dropouts and
nonstudents, too, and academics and community organizers, the
denizens of the youth ghettos and hippies, kids still in high school
and in the community colleges, and Movement alumni and adults
along the left as well. (The numbers are impossible to reckon,
really, though one cautious survey in the fall of 1968 found approximately 368,000 people enrolled in colleges who considered
themselves revolutionaries and another in the fall of 1970 counted
no fewer than 1,170,000)—which suggests, given the character of
the left at the time, that there must have been something like twice
that many again who thought of themselves as revolutionaries and
were to be found *not* in the colleges but in the Movement organizations, high schools, and the streets. What they all meant by
"revolution," of course, was as varied as their lives. For many
there is little doubt that romantic and momentary impulses were
predominant and that the wellsprings of alienation were more
powerful than any tide of analysis or ideology. Still for many
others, and these the significant actors on the stage—the leaders
of SDS and the *ad hoc* campus groups, the Movement organizers
and communicators, the heavies and the in-groups—revolution
was precise enough to be a coherent and sensible goal, something
real enough for them to give their lives over to, day after day,
month after month. That this should have happened at all is
remarkable; that it should have happened in so short a time is
almost incredible.

Revolution: how had it come to that? It was a blend of many
things: bitterness, hatred, and alienation, hope, confidence, and
conviction, energy, passion, and need. It was the pattern woven
by all the threads of the sixties, the inevitable product of the
awakened generation as it probed deeper and deeper into the
character of its nation. At least as it applies to SDS, its leading

exemplar by the summer of 1968, the impulse to revolution can be explained, if oversimply, as follows.

There was a primary sense, begun by no more than a reading of the morning papers and developed through the new perspectives and new analyses available to the Movement now, that the evils *in* America were the evils *of* America, inextricably a part of the total system that gave them a home; and the eighteen-year-old now, if political at all, stood a good chance of already knowing this, starting with the analysis that it had taken the SDSers of the early period years to learn. Clearly something drastic would be necessary to eradicate those evils and alter that system: various reforms had been tried, confrontation had been tried, there had been civil-rights agitation, university pressures, antiwar marches, doorbell ringing, electoral action, student power, draft resistance, demonstrations, campus uprisings, even tentative political violence—all to little avail, not even when the ranks of protest grew larger, when broad segments of the young and the intelligentsia and the suburban middle classes became aroused. Worse: those who wanted peaceable change, who tried to work through approved channels, seemed to be systematically ignored, ostracized, or—as with the Kennedys and King—eliminated. More was necessary, and in the words of Bob Pardun, "What it came to that year was that people came to the conclusion that the only way to stop the war was make a revolution, and the only way to stop racism was make a revolution." "The monster"—that was the recurrent phrase now—could not be altered, deviated, halted: it had to be destroyed. And the time seemed to be ripe. The government had shown its weakness in the face of an aroused people— in one form, at the Pentagon, in a more important way, at Têt— and the departure of Johnson and the start of peace talks suggested that it might be beginning to run scared. The almost-revolution in France in May introduced the possibility of the radical overthrow of established regimes even in advanced industrial nations despite their armed might and domestic entrenchment. The almost-takeover of Columbia suggested that serious radical attacks upon American institutions had reached a new level and the feeling was abroad that, in Tom Hayden's words, "what is certain is that we are moving toward power—the power to stop the machine if it cannot be made to serve humane ends."

Dissident forces were certainly in motion: the blacks, as the ghetto uprisings of the last two years and the reaction to King's assassination had shown; the students, as the Pentagon, the Ten Days, and the aftermath of Columbia had shown; the Third World, as the tenacity of the Vietnamese rebellion, the rise of the Arab guerrilla movement, and the success of the Cuban revolution had shown; perhaps certain segments of the working class, as the subway strikes, telephone strikes, and a variety of wildcat walkouts had shown; and even soldiers, as the initial achievements of GI organizing had shown. The very fact of high-level repression was taken as a sign that the government felt seriously enough threatened by the rise of the left to resort to increasingly harsh and desperate means; as SDS traveler Neil Buckley put it, "as a political movement, we are on to something, and They know it." A multitude of feelings, in short, all pointing to the idea that revolution was not only necessary, but possible.

There were other and more subtle forces at work, too, promoting the impulse to revolution. The media, with a predictable measure of exaggeration and paranoia, began treating the New Left as if it were a developed and dangerous insurrectionary threat already, the effect of which was to convince many young people that they really *were* that, or should be, and to sanction all their first steps in that direction—often before they had bothered to think the whole thing through. The additional celebrations of youth culture by parts of the society, and the embracement of it by wide segments of the capitalist economy, also served to convince many that youth had significant power within America and that its expression in political terms might be as devastating as its expression in cultural ones. Within the Establishment, traditionally right-wing forces seized upon the bold proclamations of revolution and the tentative acting-out of those proclamations and trumpeted them before Congressional committees, businessmen's associations, and conservative organizations as justifications of their world view and excuses to increase their powers of control and repression. And within the Movement itself, the more-militant-than-thou dynamic that serves so often to push all kinds of groups to their logical fringes operated to make those unabashedly proclaiming themselves revolutionaries the ones increasingly listened to and emulated; within SDS chapters, for example, it became increasingly difficult for praxis-axis types to withstand the appeal of the action factions, or for the base-builders to hold on to student allegiances in the face of the confrontationists.

The SDS leadership, hoping to ride on the wave of this new political fervor, went into the East Lansing convention with a conscious desire to make SDS into a revolutionary organization. No one knew just how that was to be done, of course, but the paper that Bernardine Dohrn had written with Tom Bell and Steve Halliwell seemed to be pointed in the right direction, and by convention time the NO forces and their allies decided to make that their chief strategy. "The challenge at this juncture in movement history," the proposal said, "is to change the emphasis from *building* a radical movement to *using* the radical movement in the work of making revolution." To this end it offered two strategies which the national leadership saw as the chief priorities for the year ahead: first, to develop revolutionary organizations in the larger cities, perhaps based on university campuses but reaching out to wider constituencies beyond the campus where allies for any truly revolutionary movement would have to be found, including high-school and junior-college students, young workers and professionals, welfare workers and recipients, and Movement alumni;* second, to start laying "the groundwork for the development of a new left revolutionary organization" that would keep "SDS people who see themselves as life-time revolutionaries" in touch with one another and would be "capable of making detailed strategic decisions, committing resources in the most effective way, and keeping effective administration to assure detailed knowledge of how work is progressing"—in short, an SDS with muscles.

SDS just might have been able to start making this kind of an organization, one that would match the new seriousness of those who felt themselves revolutionary, in spite of the fact that its leaders were handicapped by a lack of agreed-upon analysis, a hazy notion of revolutionary history, and only a few brief weeks

*The concept of city-wide organizing was one which had been developed over the spring by Carl Davidson and which he had detailed in an article in the April 16, 1968, *Guardian.*

to put their ideas together. But it was never given the chance. For it was at the East Lansing convention that the Progressive Labor Party, carrying on the offensive it had begun at the New York regional meeting in February, made its first concerted move to impose its politics on SDS, and the resulting chaos produced a meeting that could hardly even agree upon a time to adjourn, much less an organization for revolution.

PL was present in surprising force, and was well-organized. Its fifty- or sixty-member contingent was enhanced by the fact that many bore five-vote delegate authorizations from their local chapters, giving them a weight at the convention far out of proportion to their actual membership; and it operated as a closed caucus, making binding decisions in advance about the proposals on the floor so as to establish a unified voting bloc of considerable power. Moreover, PL had abandoned its previous strategy of "swimming in the sea" of SDS, hoping to entice potential party recruits from the disgruntled and the bewildered; now it decided to push its politics at every opportunity, its members speaking up at every workshop, introducing counterproposals at every plenary, waving their little red books at every juncture. Bob Pardun recalls how PL began its attacks during the workshops that occupied the first days of the convention:

> What happened was that time after time, people who hadn't been in SDS too long, who couldn't handle the war, couldn't handle racism, couldn't handle empire too good—people who just came to SDS and were excited by SDS and came to a national meeting—ran into all of these SDS workshops that sounded really exciting but when they'd get in them and started talking, the PL line would come down *kavoom!: this is the PL line.* People would say, O.K., and try to take the PL line into account and figure out where their [PLers'] heads were at and what was going on—and the PL people would watch it happen and they wouldn't try to adjust or modify anything and they'd just push down the PL line again. And it got very frustrating because you could never *argue* with the PL people, you could never *convince* them of anything—especially if you didn't have the rhetoric or any of that stuff—so you were always at their mercy, especially if you were a young guy, facing a guy who came on like a teacher with a line that you couldn't really understand. People got very frustrated in their conversations, they couldn't take

these discussion groups as far as they wanted them, and they got very uptight about it and there was a lot of seething against PL.*

The seething spilled out on the floor of the convention with the first plenary session on Thursday night, when the SDS leadership formally presented the Bell-Dohrn-Halliwell proposal. It was, as it turned out, an unfortunate redoubt from which to do battle with PL: its prose was clotted and murky, virtually inaccessible to those newer SDSers who had not spent years in learning New Left mandarin; its ideas of how concretely to go about creating city-wide organizations or a new revolutionary SDS were frail to the point of vacuity; and its analysis was loosely based in new-working-class ideas (Halliwell, be it rememberd, was close to the original new-working-class formulators in New York) which had never been developed, tested, or substantiated for the majority of SDSers. PLers immediately recognized the weaknesses and, with jugular instincts, attacked mercilessly. They attacked the new-working-class ideas. They picked up a one-line quotation from Herbert Marcuse and ridiculed him for his "misunderstanding" of the working class. They made fun of the sloppy language, scoffed at the idea of trying to organize without the industrial proletariat, scorned the attempt to centralize SDS. And they pointed to the almost-revolution in France as an example of what could happen when students allied with the working classes, suggesting with a little historical sleight-of-hand that this was the model for serious American revolutionaries to follow. (Which evoked, among much else, a bit of impromptu theater from the Motherfuckers, who dressed one person up as "Student," another

*Pardun and the SDSers were by no means the only people to experience these troubles with PL at this time. John Cohen, who worked with Sam Melville and other New Yorkers who tried to keep the spirit of Columbia going throughout that summer, was but one of many with similar sentiments: "Our committee was a microcosm of the Movement. Throughout the summer we threw ourselves into action—rallies, marches, building seizures, picket lines. At first we grew in strength and energy; but as we did, Progressive Labor infiltrated, and began to push its ideological line onto us. Meetings twisted from close, friendly gatherings directed toward hope and trust into strident ideological battles. To deal with PL's destructive intrusion, we were forced to use just the kind of political manipulations we despised. By packing meetings and limiting voting rights we threw PL out; but we left ourselves disenchanted, sour and dispirited." (From an essay in *Letters from Attica*, by Samuel Melville, Morrow, 1972.)

as "Worker," and joined them into a "Worker-Student Alliance" in an elaborate marriage ceremony.) The PL attack was quite effective, and not even the polemical experts of the NO faction could blunt it: they didn't want to seem to be anti-working-class and they certainly couldn't play down the importance of the events in France. After what seemed to be interminable debate, PL carried the final vote against the proposal, 485 to 355, and the leadership's chief strategy lay in ruins.

At this point the regular SDSers became downright panicky. It was clear that PL had no more than a quarter of the delegates, but also clear that they were able to swing over to their side a great many of the uncommitted people impressed with their arguments, and their positiveness, on the floor. Anti-PL heavies decided to meet in a caucus of their own—not formally closed, but not exactly welcoming PLers, either, a fighting-fire-with-fire technique that signaled the end of part of the early SDS spirit of openness and camaraderie—but their choices were clearly limited. They couldn't kick PL out, since SDS was still proudly antiexclusionist and took a civil-libertarian, let-the-factions-contend point of view; they found it difficult to outargue PL, since most of them were still working out their own politics, still groping toward what it meant to be revolutionary, and hadn't their own red books and bearded prophets to refer to; and all that was left was to try to outmaneuver them. The NO caucus decided to concentrate its forces on reorganizing the national structure along the lines of a centralized "cadre" approach, which it hoped would put enough power in the hands of the traditional SDSers to either eliminate or curtail PL influence in the organization.

So the NO faction rallied behind a proposal originally drawn up by Jeff Segal and later modified by Neil Buckley which would replace the present ineffective National Interim Committee with a body of seventeen national officers—four National Secretaries in Chicago and fifteen Field Secretaries in the various regions—who would be full-time workers for SDS and who would meet regularly between national meetings to establish and carry out the basic policies of the organization. It was presented to the delegates as a matter of top priority—Pardun, for example, told the meeting that "if this group does not get together in the next two years, we'll be wiped out"—but the delegate response was hardly enthusiastic.

Progressive Labor and the other organized factions correctly saw it as an attempt to lessen the influence they were able to exert in the present freewheeling system—Jeff Gordon called it "a clear attempt at a power grab" by the NO group—and many of the chapter people regarded it as an unnecessary arrogation of control to the Chicago crowd, in defiance of all the traditions of SDS. The debate was long and acerbic, with lines sometimes ten to fifteen deep at the microphones set in the aisles for speakers from the floor, and when it became apparent that the NO scheme couldn't win a majority, everybody got into the act. Mike Klonsky suggested the creation of a "political committee" which would map out SDS's revolutionary policies while the rest of the organization went its way; the Motherfucker collective pressed its idea for "destructuring" SDS into collectives and affinity groups ("The duty of the revolutionary," read their handout, "is to make a revolutionary organization"); and finally PL itself came forth with a proposal designed to reduce the role of the National Office and strengthen the power of regional organizations. Debate on the reorganization schemes went on for more than ten hours—the watchword from the floor was, "If someone has something to say, let him say it"—with interminable caucuses, speeches, votes, proposals, and amendments, until the convention finally had to be extended into the weekend, the time originally set aside for the National Council meeting.* It was one of the longest debates on a single subject in the history of SDS conventions—and one of the most inconclusive. In the end not one of the proposals passed.

When at last it became clear that the NO faction was going to have a tough time getting *any* of its ideas through the convention—in fact going to have a tough time continuing SDS along its own lines in the face of the PL challenge—it finally decided to present the PL problem directly to the delegates, a highly unusual admission of factional turmoil. Pardun started things with a speech theoretically on "principle" inside Movement organiza-

*The National Council never did meet, leaving it up to Spiegel himself to give provisional recognition to the ten new chapters seeking admission (later approved officially): Duke, East Michigan, Falls Church (Virginia) High School, Memphis State University Larry Payne Memorial Chapter, Nevada (Reno), Portland (Maine) At-large, Solidarity Bookstore Louis Lingg Memorial Chapter (Chicago), South Woodstock (Vermont) At-large, Smith College No More Ugly Babies Chapter, Virginia.

tions, which in no time developed into an attack on Progressive Labor as an "external cadre," a group, he said, really *outside* the family of SDS which didn't really care about the survival of the organization and was using it simply for its selfish ends:

> We must demand that external cadre operate in a principled fashion. It's simply not principled to move into SDS in order to recruit members for another party. Your function should be to bring in ideas. It's not principled either to pack meetings in order to manipulate acceptance of a line or to tie up valuable time discussing issues that the collective does not wish to discuss.

It was a voice out of the past, and it affected PL not at all, but it did not fail to arouse an audible gasp among the assembled delegates—for it was the first open denunciation of PL at a national meeting, and it hinted that the sacred New Left principle of nonexclusionism was being stretched to its limits.

Pardun's denunciation was augmented by others in the debates that followed: no matter what the motion on the floor, NO sympathizers took the opportunity to condemn PL for its rigidity, its cadre discipline, its divisiveness in SDS, its anti-Hanoi politics, its working-class blinders, its short hair, and anything else anyone could think of. But the final gauntlet was hurled down by Tom Bell, who had obviously been brooding on the defeat of the paper of which he had been a proud coauthor. Bell, a longtime SDSer, one of the founders of the Cornell chapter, a Niagara region traveler, an early draft-resistance organizer, now with the MDS in Springfield, took the rostrum with visible anger: he had seen the move toward a revolutionary organization suffer an unexpected defeat, he had watched the NO proposals get clogged in PL glue in every plenary, and felt that SDS might be losing its chance to forge the revolution. Normally a quiet man—in fact his success in building the draft-resistance forces had been due to his low-key manner—he was shaking now. "We came openly and honestly to this convention in order to propose an SDS program," he declared. But the PL people had obstructed every move, descended with their unwavering and unlistening line at every meeting, and the result has been this endless, pointless, frustrating series of debates, with nobody learning anything, nobody deciding anything. "It isn't possible to have a debate on the floor," he charged, "because of the organized opposition of PLP." And unless SDS does something about it now, the organization will surely collapse. At that one PLer from the floor began shouting at the platform; Bell paused. Redbaiting, the PLer called, all you guys from the NO faction are simply redbaiting us because we're communists. Bell was stunned, his color livid, his voice quivering. "Redbaiting! *Red*baiting!? *I'm* the communist here, not you guys from PL!" In fact, he said, it's you guys from PL who are holding this organization back from being *really* communist, from *really* getting on with the revolution. "PL out," he shouted into the microphone, "PL OUT." The cry was taken up immediately on the floor— possibly spontaneously, but more likely by prearrangement among the NO people hoping to stampede PL off the floor and out of the organization: "PL OUT! PL OUT! PL OUT!" Feet stamping in rhythm, hands clapping, chairs banging, and finally people standing, fists raised, dancing about, yelling: *"PL OUT, PL OUT, PL OUT!"* The din went on for two full minutes, then three, and four, turning the huge hall into a maelstrom of bitterness. And in the middle, through it all, the PLers sat, impassive, unpanicked even if bewildered, recognizing a maneuver of desperation and refusing to be carried up in it. Soon the tumult faded: no more than two hundred of the delegates could be enticed into the outburst, and most of the rest just sat, apparently unconvinced by the NO arguments, embarrassed and confused by the tactics, shocked at the flouting of SDS's antiexclusionism, feeling themselves even sympathetic to PL on civil-libertarian grounds alone, ultimately deciding perhaps that however crazy the PL people might be in their adulation of the working class, the NO people had shown themselves fully as mad, and with a somewhat slimmer justification. NO staffer Tim McCarthy, in the chair, finally gaveled the meeting to a relative quiet, organized a long three-sided debate— pro-PL, anti-PL, and neutralists—and the evening faded into unmemorable bickering. No vote was ever taken, but it was clear that PL not only was not going to be stampeded out of SDS but that most of those in SDS simply didn't want them out.

Jeff Gordon, writing in *PL* after the convention, gave his side's response to the abortive expulsion attempt:

> The ideology of the NO/NWC [National Office/New Working Class] caucus was weak, confused, and easily shot full of holes. It

was under serious ideological attack by the increasing number of
people who are beginning to support an anti-imperialist, pro-work-
ing class perspective. The NO/NWC structural proposals were opposed by many who opposed top-down structure. Instead of responding with a political defense of their ideological and
organizational perspective, the NO/NWC caucus came up with the
old ace in the hole, the one weapon they hoped could unite their own
split ranks—anti-communism. They intended to use it as the main
political tool to push through their proposals and bludgeon down
any opposition. . . .

The main element of the attack against PLP was the charge
that its members in SDS are "external cadre." . . . The use by
the NO/NWC forces of such terms as "external cadre" is just
an attempt to confuse the issue of what are the correct revolutionary politics that must be followed! It is an appeal to narrow
organizational chauvinism and to anti-communism. "External
cadre" is no different than the term "outside agitator," which is
used by the ruling class to attack those it can't defeat by other
means. . . .

Another aspect of the attack is put this way: "PLers are
puritanical dogmatists. Just look at their short hair. They want to
stop us from doing our own thing." This is really an appeal to the
most reactionary aspects in people, the aspect that is most individu-
alist and the most decadent. It is an attack on our belief that freedom lies in collective, class struggle, not going off and doing your
own thing. If we are to become revolutionaries, "our own thing"
must be to struggle to build the revolutionary movement and make
the revolution. . . .

This appeal to anti-communism was set back at the SDS convention! . . . That was an important victory for the revolutionary
direction of SDS. But the struggle promises to go on; anti-communism must be met more sharply and decisively each time it raises
its ugly head. The future of SDS as a positive factor in the American
revolution is at stake.

The only real victory NO people were able to salvage at
the convention was the election of officers. The NO caucus,
fearful of PL inroads, decided to propose a slate for the three
top officers (the first time in SDS a single slate had ever been
presented): Mike Klonsky for National Secretary, Bernardine
Dohrn for Inter-organizational Secretary, and Les Coleman for
Education Secretary. Progressive Labor people protested the

tactic, but they realized that they did not have more than a quarter of the votes themselves and to put up a counterslate of their own would risk inviting defeat, ridicule, and perhaps a recurrence of the exclusionist explosion; they cast dissenting votes, but put up no candidates of their own. So Klonsky and Dohrn both ran unopposed (except for one Motherfucker who walked down the aisles with a wastebasket over his head while his friend yelled, "I nominate this trash can for National Secretary") and were elected decisively. But the spectacle of such rubber-stamping (unparticipatory, not to mention undemocratic) finally aroused the delegates and a contesting candidate, New England SDSer Fred Gordon, was nominated to challenge Coleman; Gordon was elected by a single vote, largely on the strength of the simple argument that the NO faction shouldn't dictate all the officers.

It was certainly an odd trio, befitting an odd convention. Klonsky, who had just turned twenty-five, was a blond and bony Californian, with straight, floppy hair, narrow eyes, a slight mustache, and a truly prognathous jaw that tended to give him the look of a slightly pugnacious longshoreman. He was a red-diaper baby—his father was a former organization secretary for the Communist Party in Eastern Pennsylvania and Delaware and later, after moving the family west, a member of the Southern California District Committee of the party—and he was one of the earliest recruits to SDS in California. He helped to organize the chapter at San Fernando Valley State College in the fall of 1965, and it became one of the most active and imaginative chapters in the area, among the first to try GI organizing and to attack Dow recruiters. Klonsky became active on the national scene early in 1967, writing a few articles for *New Left Notes* and the *Guardian,* working in draft organizing, and helping to run the Los Angeles Regional Office (where he met, was arrested with, and later married Sue Eanet, the former New York SDSer). In early 1968 he tried some ERAPoid community organizing among a poor-white and Mexican-American community in the Silverlake area of Los Angeles, and it was during this time that his primarily working-class politics took shape; as he said in *New Left Notes,* "I think we've got to break out of the bag of debate between Movement intellectuals about which is better, organizing or mobilizing, and develop a program which will make community and working-class organizing a reality." By the time of the convention he represented one of the largest of the new, proto-Marxist tendencies in SDS, non-PL people who nonetheless supported the working class and emphasized community and factory organizing. But there was nothing rigid about his politics: when asked during the convention if he was a Stalinist, he replied, "Having been a communist only a few months, I have difficulty understanding what you mean by that"—and by "communist," with a lower-case "c," he meant deliberately to distinguish himself from his father's politics, using a formulation that a number in SDS were using now.

Fred Gordon, twenty-four, short, dark, serious, clean-shaven, was a New Englander, born in Newton, Massachusetts, and a 1966 graduate of Harvard College. He was, as far as is known, a member of no particular political group—he had been friends with PLers in the Boston area, and with them helped run a series of student seminars in the summer of 1966 on such topics as socialism, labor, and imperialism, but he was not a PL member; he had studied for the last two years under Herbert Marcuse at San Diego State College, but gave no indication of associating with a new-working-class position; and he had been active in Southern California draft work, in fact planning a community-organizing draft committee in San Diego for the summer, but had not heretofore been identified with the community-organizing groups in SDS. At the time of his election his most evident political passion was no more than a desire to make the convention vote more democratic.

And Bernardine Dohrn, as we have seen, was a still different type of SDSer, a first-generation radical, campus-oriented, drawn more to the new-working-class analysis, sympathetic to the new youth culture, a supporter of the resistance strategies, and strongly behind the impulses to revolution as they expressed themselves during the spring.

The Klonsky-Dohrn election signaled the last-ditch triumph of the NO caucus, and it was solidified through the election of the eight national officers of the National Interim Committee, all of them generally associated with NO politics.* It was a slim consolation perhaps, but it did mean that the direction of the NO for the coming year would be in sympathetic hands, a not insignificant factor, and it did mean that these hands would be more or less bent to the task of shaping a revolution. Not that anyone among them even now had any sure ideas about how to bring that about, and certainly the convention had given them no guidelines whatsoever, refusing to pass any resolution with an explicit program. But in the course of the next year, as the country coughed up one disillusionment after another—the police riots in Chicago, the nomination of Humphrey and Nixon and the election of the latter, the stalemate of the Paris peace talks, the indictment of the Chicago Eight—and as the youth of America expressed their outrage as never before, the existence of a group of SDS officers unblushingly committed to revolution would have its effect.

The Progressive Labor Party's offensive within SDS in the summer and fall of 1968 was not a matter of accident or good fortune: it was a calculated political move based on a decision of the party's national committee to emphasize recruitment of new members into the party. The rationale had been announced by Milton Rosen, chairman of the party, in his speech to the May 1968 convention:

> How do we move the struggle from one level to another? . . . Sell
> magazines and our other literature, that may be the best thing you

*The eight: Bartee Haile, a veteran Texas activist, who had been traveling for SDS in the Texas-Oklahoma region and doing draft work there; Mike James, the Chicago JOIN organizer, who was elected to an unprecedented third term; Jeff Jones, a dropout from Antioch College who had been working with SDS in New York City; Eric Mann, the former NCUP worker and Newark teacher, then organizing in the Boston area; Charles "Chip" Marshall, a 1967 Cornell graduate and SDS traveler in the Niagara region; Carl Oglesby, back in the inner circle after a two-year absence; Morgan Spector, a San Francisco Regional Office leader; and Mike Spiegel, about to move to the Washington, D.C. Regional Office. Mark Rudd, who had become a symbolic media figure, was rejected for top office—"He's your man," one SDSer told reporters (*The New York Times,* June 16, 1968), "not ours"—but he was made an alternate to the NIC; Harvard PLer Jared Israel mustered enough votes to come in as second alternate. Oglesby was the oldest of all the eleven national officers, Spiegel the youngest; the average age was about 25, a continuance of the practice of having officers beyond undergraduate age but at this juncture prophetic of SDS's move off the campuses.

can do. You can't get the Columbia students to go and take over
City Hall; the workers won't shut down the factories now. Maybe
at Columbia or any place one of the biggest things you could do is
to recruit people into the party. Why? Because you will politicize
guys [sic] and you will have more forces to go among the masses
to politicize *them*, and try to improve them. The revolutionary
movement doesn't come out of the air. You have to raise political
ideas among a lot of people. That is the most important thing you
can do. It gives the revolutionary Left, our party, much more
strength and footing.

Now every scintilla of PL theory argued that it should direct its
recruitment efforts at members of the industrial working class, but
PL was honest enough with itself to recognize that its attempt at
working-class organizing, the acknowledged party thrust in the
last three years, was having almost no effect. Even the elaborate
work-in program of the summer of 1968, which (according to PL)
involved some three hundred fifty students, was to end without
any noticeable inclination by the students to stay on the production lines or by the workers to flock to Progressive Labor. As the
national committee was forced to confess:

> While we have concluded that the objective conditions are certainly
> ripe and full of class struggle out of which workers can be recruited
> to our party, . . . whom have we NOT been recruiting? Industrial
> workers (except in rare instances).

And so therefore PL was forced to look to the student ranks,
chiefly to SDS, where recruitment possibilities seemed much more
promising. The growth of a sizable number of people thinking of
themselves as "revolutionary" seemed to augur well, especially
since many of them seemed to be coming around to PL's emphasis
on the industrial proletariat. The fact that so many present PLers
were students or recent students meant that they would be able
to understand and infiltrate student groups far more easily than
they would the blue-collar ones. And PL's long-standing role in
SDS seemed to give it a particular vantage point there, particularly at a time when SDS was drawing in a lot of new and searching students and yet often failing to satisfy their needs. Hence the
stepped-up role by PL at all levels of SDS.

At places where PL was strong, or where PL had effective
control of the chapter, it was simply necessary to encourage membership in SDS and then select out of those people the ones who

seemed likeliest to be suitable "candidate members" of PL itself. But at places where PL was in a minority, or had no more than one or two members, PL chose to form "worker-student alliance" caucuses and under that rubric enlist sympathizers who might be prejudiced against PL itself or unwilling at the start to undergo the rigors and discipline of full-scale PL membership. The strategy of the worker-student alliance—or WSA, as it quickly became known—was pressed in full force when the fall term began: PLers made sure to bring it up at the initial chapter meetings, PL spokesmen built speeches around it at SDS rallies, PL literature both on the national and the campus level stressed it. PL SDSers drew up a lengthy pamphlet on their summertime work-in experiences which emphasized WSA politics ("We are convinced that strikes and economic demands must be supported, that a worker-student alliance must be built if SDS is going to become a viable and politically effective group"). One of the most forceful presentations was by Peter Bilazarian, a Harvard SDSer who addressed a fall rally in Boston:

> What I am proposing is that the student movement become *not* a separate interest group for students where students are able to "do their own thing," but that it adopt the strategy of *worker-student alliance*. . . .
>
> It is impossible for any basic change to come about in this country by the actions of students alone—no matter how radical or militant they may be. Just think—even if we could shut down every university in America tomorrow to protest the war, what would this do to seriously injure the war effort? How many factories would stop producing war materials? . . . If [students] expect to change things or even win some good reforms for themselves then they must ally themselves with other oppressed groups that have a common enemy, a common interest, and the potential *power* to change things. The only group which really fits all these conditions is the working class (and this includes black and white workers), and especially the industrial working class.

If the East Lansing convention was SDS's first step toward revolution, the Chicago convention was young America's. Because it was televised, because it occasioned the unmuzzled brutality of the Chicago police, because it displayed the bankruptcy of American liberalism, and because it exposed once again the decrepitude of the American two-party system, the Democratic National Convention in August was one of the most propelling and influential events of the sixties, becoming very quickly the symbolic watershed for the end of the resistance period.

It was ironic that so much of the organization of the demonstrations in Chicago should have been in the hands of first-generation SDSers—Davis and Hayden were project coordinators for the National Mobilization Committee, and they gathered around them such veteran SDSers as Kathy Boudin, Connie Brown, Corinna Fales, John Froines, Carol Glassman, Vernon Grizzard, Mike Locker and the NACLA people, Paul Potter, Jeff Shero, and Lee Webb—because the current SDSers opposed the venture from the start. The irony shows how transient SDS was, how much it had changed in such a brief time. Davis and Hayden were by no means reformers still, and they were as dedicated as anyone in SDS to the overhaul of American imperialism, but they retained a faith that speaking truth to power, and to the television-watchers under that power, was the means to that end: "Demonstrate that politicians do not speak for us," went the Mobilization call, "encourage and help educate discontented Democrats to seek new and independent forms of protest and resistance." The current leaders of SDS shared no such faith, had long ago assumed that people regarded politicians as frauds, and saw "discontented Democrats" as about the last constituency that anybody would want to organize into the ranks of the revolution. From the beginning SDSers opposed the Mobilization plans, rejecting as usual the idea of mass marches but doubly scornful of any project mired in electoral politics, and they gave only grudging cooperation to Davis and Hayden, whom they kept accusing of having either "old-fashioned politics" or no politics at all. No sooner had Mike Klonsky settled into the NO, for example, than he wrote scornfully that "whatever the politics of New Left oriented Hayden and Rennie Davis may be (it is still unclear to many of us), it probably doesn't even matter." Note, please, "New Left oriented" now used as a pejorative.

As August approached, however, and the Mobilization and the Yippies gained more and more publicity for the Chicago action, SDS began to have second thoughts. Though still opposing the demonstration, it could no longer ignore it. In July the NIC decided to take a middle position: though it would not encourage large numbers of SDSers to attend convention week, it would enlist a cadre of "organizers" to go to Chicago with the object of "educating and making contact with McCarthy kids during that week" so as to communicate "the style and juices of SDS politics and organization." A letter sent out to the membership on August 11 said:

> We hope SDS people coming here for the convention will come as organizers and not as cannon fodder for the MOB. That means we have to concentrate on getting our best organizers from around the country to come here and do what they can how they can to get the McCarthy kids out of their bag and into SDS chapters in the fall. . . . This will be an organizing job and not a picnic. Chicago is "pig-city" and they are up tight.

When convention week began SDS had perhaps five hundred people on hand for its propaganda blitz. It operated out of five "Movement centers," the chief one being installed in a church not far from Lincoln Park, where the bulk of the demonstrators gathered and the initial clashes with police took place. SDS distributed stacks of its regular literature, sold copies of a special issue of *New Left Notes* (including a dramatic "Open Letter" from Carl Oglesby to the McCarthy supporters), pasted up copies around the town of a daily wallposter called "Handwriting on the Wall," and passed out thousands of copies of a mimeographed MESSAGE TO FELLOW STUDENTS WORKING FOR MCCARTHY.* When the

---

*"We address you sincerely as brothers and sisters engaged in a vital, serious search to change today's reality, a battle we have been waging for 8 years now as a national student organization. . . . As we witness this Democratic National Convention coming to Chicago, our analysis tells us that the major decisions have already been made, or the reins are out of the electorate's hands. . . . We reject your candidate, not because he's yours, but precisely because he's *not*, because all he *can* do is make statements, a figurehead, mouthpiece, manipulated, just like the other candidates, by those who really hold power and make the decisions. . . . We are saying that electoral politics provides a chance for different *styles* of carrying out what we call imperialism, America's behavior as *logical extension* of its political and economic structuring, but it DOESN'T concern itself with ending it once and for all. And it makes no difference at all to the guy who's sent to fight against a foreign people, or against his OWN for that matter, *who* is sitting in the top chair at the time. Our analysis of power in this country tells us that Gene McCarthy would not be *able* to keep those boys home with their families and girlfriends, even *were* he able to get himself elected. . . . Our experience too has been one of frustration in attempting to effect Change. Where do we turn? Alone we don't possess power. But finding liberating solutions and *deciding* to possess power by joining forces with other oppressed people we can do. And the consciousness of the tremendous *possibilities* for man, of the liberating *potential* of technology and productive organization, is what keeps us going. . . . We share a common future. Join us!"

crunch came, however, it turned out that SDS had guessed all wrong. It was not the "McCarthy kids" who provided the energy of convention week, nor was it even the several thousand Movement people gathered from around the country—it was the young people from the Chicago area, black and brown and white, who made up the majority of the demonstrators and who proved by their militance that the young were prepared to take to the streets, imaginatively and forcefully, to express their civilized discontents. SDSers in Chicago were hardly dismayed at the turnabout—it confirmed their revolutionary vision—and they missed scarcely a beat in adjusting to it. Mike Klonsky took the bullhorn in Grant Park to celebrate the new militancy, denouncing the "reformism" of the Mobilization and urging people to find their politics in direct action. NICer Jeff Jones announced that Chicago was the beginning of the union of "youth power" and "black power," the prelude of revolutionary change. SDS organizers quickly turned from arguing the McCarthyites into radical politics to developing what they called "affinity groups" and "street guerrillas" capable of avoiding the mass police attacks and taking the battle into the streets of Chicago. (The fact that all this was done without specific membership sanction and at variance with the NIC directives seemed to bother the NO people not at all, but there was criticism of it at later NIC meetings.) "Handwriting on the Wall" concluded:

> Those of us who have been in the streets for the past five days didn't give a flying fuck whether McCarthy would win or lose; and now that he's lost, still don't. Only the youth of America and the Vietnamese will stop the war in Vietnam; and only the youth and the black people of America will create the new life. This, not a liberal Senator's political career, is our struggle.

In the end, though, nothing that SDS did, or could do, was as effective in making instant militants and potential radicals out of the demonstrators as what the police did. In a single week Chicago proved itself incontestably to be "pig-city," and with a vengeance that not even the NO anticipated. More than a hundred demonstrators ended up in local hospitals, an estimated 625 were treated by Movement medical centers, and easily that many again nursed their wounds on their own; some 668 people were arrested and one young man was shot to death by the police. Nothing impeded in the slightest the foregone nomination of Hubert Humphrey and the rout of liberal Democrats, but the proportions of that defeat, accompanied by the storm-trooper methods used to insure it, surprised, angered, and "radicalized" a good many people, young and old, during that turbulent week. The impact on the country as a whole was not quite so neat—every survey indicated that the public in general favored the response of the Chicago establishment against the Commie-hippie-freaks in the streets—but for many of those who experienced the brutality firsthand and for millions more who watched the agony on their television screens, Chicago 1968 provided the definitive push over the line into activism and radicalism.

For Progressive Labor, the Chicago actions were nothing but a childish outburst, a play-acting at revolution, more of the foolish "wild-in-the-streets" resistance that estranged the working masses and prevented the left from building a base among the American people. PLers lost no opportunity to denounce the whole affair, before, during, and after, and their organs ridiculed the Mobilization leaders, the Yippies, and the NO faction of SDS for getting involved. The September issue of *Challenge* was typical:

> The right-wing of SDS, via its control of the National Office and *New Left Notes*, echoed Hayden's [classless] line. Jeff Jones of the New York Regional Office put it forward in Grant Park Thursday when he claimed it was "Youth and Black Power in the streets" that would lead to revolutionary change. This after the events of the day before [when police openly beat up demonstrators] and the entire decade had so clearly demonstrated that youth and Black power in the streets, without the power of the working class, can never defeat the organized armed force of the imperialists.

For SDS, the lessons of Chicago were profound, and each of them seemed to confirm the rightness of the move into revolution. Chicago proved once and for all, for those still needing proof, that the country could not be educated or reformed out of its pernicious system, even by establishmentarian reformers like McCarthy. It showed that even resistance, open and defiant resistance, was not enough to wrest changes, for the institutions of American society, grounded in violence, would use violence in their own defense when the threat was regarded as serious enough. It indicated that there was a sizable constituency beyond the campuses—young blacks, high-schoolers, political young workers, street gangs, "greasers," dropouts, and the rest—willing to risk themselves in courageous and drastic ways to defy the system-in-being; "Chicago has shown us," Klonsky later said, "that young people in this country are not necessarily caught up in the bullshit that is the American electoral process." It proved that, temporarily at least, real victories for the left were to be won by people willing to act, that action in the streets was itself a kind of base-building. And it convinced the SDS leadership—kicking itself for failing to have seen the Chicago potential and to have led it from the beginning—that the time had come to discard its fears of being "too radical," of "alienating" potential recruits, and to take its new commitment to revolution directly to the youth of America.

22

FALL 1968

"There's a whole new set on campus," wrote Terry Robbins and Bill Ayers, the travelers for SDS in the Ohio-Michigan region at the start of the 1968–69 school year. "The Movement is opening up all over the place: the first generation of high-school SDS coming onto the campus, the no-choice election-fraud bullshit, Columbia, and Chicago all have contributed to a new atmosphere of optimism and aggressiveness and the possibility for continued, prolonged action." Both travelers, committed actionists, devoted themselves to pushing SDS within that atmosphere for all they were worth:

> We're saying to people that youth is the revolution . . . that politics is about life, struggle, survival. . . . We're saying that there ain't no place to be today but in the Movement. . . . And we're saying to kids all over the place that if you're tired of the Vietnamese eating napalm for breakfast, if you're tired of the blacks eating tear gas for dinner, and if YOU'RE tired of eating plastic for lunch, then give it a name:
> Call it SDS, and join us.

"Join us"—that was the slogan for SDS now: and it was as descriptive as it was hortatory. SDS grew in the first few months of that fall as never before. Students at hundreds of campuses flocked to SDS chapter meetings in record numbers—at major universities like Stanford and Colorado, where there had been only minimal chapters before, and at isolated schools like Mon-

tana and Cazenovia Community College, where there had been
neither SDS nor any other noticeable political groups before.
"Across the country," New Left Notes reported, "first SDS meetings have seen two, three, and four times as many" participants
as before: more than five hundred students attended the first chapter meeting at Stanford, which had been used to fifty people; four
hundred participated in the first meetings at Texas, which had
never had more than one hundred or so at any time before; more
than two hundred turned up to join SDS at such generally sluggish
campuses as Kent State, Penn State, and Trinity College; and up
to one hundred appeared at Case Western, Long Beach State,
University of Miami, Oklahoma, Pennsylvania, and Wyoming,
most of which had less than twenty interested people the year
before. At Princeton, 106 students out of the freshman class of 851
applied for SDS membership during their first week on campus.
At an East Tennessee high school one student passed around a
petition to see how many people wanted to start an SDS chapter
and it ended up with 150 signatures; a charter was duly granted.
A GI at Fort Hood, Texas, sent in $25 in dues from five soldiers
there who wanted to start a chapter. "I got my freshman orientation watching the Democratic Convention on TV," went one letter
sent in to the National Office. "Count me in." Five dollars was
enclosed.

At least a dozen new chapters were started in the first few
weeks of the term (including Georgetown and Missouri Universities and high schools in New Jersey, Louisiana, New York, Pennsylvania, and North Carolina) and dozens more were renewed
after fallow periods (including North Texas State, Swarthmore,
and Kentucky). But chapter applications poured in to the National Office so fast that Cathy Archibald, hastily put in charge
of such minutiae, reported that "we can't keep track of them all";
the best estimates were that before the term was out somewhere
between three hundred and fifty and four hundred chapters were
in existence, at least one hundred of which were new. Membership
figures were similarly chaotic—Archibald said that so many came
in "we just stopped counting"—but the NO claimed 80,000 chapter members by November, and Carl Davidson estimated 100,000
the same month, both of which are probably conservative figures.

At the same time, SDS was enjoying an extraordinary flush

of national publicity, based apparently on the media assumption that SDS was really at the bottom of all the nation's troubles. *Newsweek* carried a long back-to-school article on CAMPUS RE-BELS: WHO, WHY, WHAT, which declared SDS one of the prime "magnets for students who feel themselves alienated from 'the system,' " and acknowledged that "most serious campus activism begins with the SDS." *Life* presented a lavish twelve-page article profiling SDS as "the most vocal representative" of the Movement and featuring long and surprisingly sympathetic interviews with Oglesby, Spiegel, James, and other luminaries. This was matched by an even more sympathetic article from the other barrel of the mass-media shotgun, *Look* magazine, which named SDS as "the center of the vortex" of "campus explosions" and argued that "the idealists, visionaries and truncheon-scarred campus guerrillas of Students for a Democratic Society have shaken the American university to its roots." Its conclusion:

> Sometimes inspired, often chaotic, the Students for a Democratic Society represents an effort by a key minority of the Nuclear Generation to break out of a political and moral maze built by their elders. . . . What began on the campus may well prove educational for our entire society.

On the wings of such approbation, SDS's membership, and hopes, went soaring.

One further indication of "the whole new set on campus" was a survey taken for *Fortune* by the Daniel Yankelovitch company in October (and published in January). Though no obviously "revolutionary" types were included in the poll, the results showed clearly that young people in general, and in particular the opinion-making college students (what *Fortune* called the "forerunners") were farther to the left than most people had suspected. The "forerunners" showed an "extraordinary rejection of traditional American values," half of them holding that the U.S. is a "sick" society and refusing to support *any* political candidate, and more than two-thirds agreeing that the Vietnam war was a mistake and that both draft resistance and civil disobedience were justified under *any* circumstances; for them, Che Guevara was a more popular figure than Johnson, Nixon, Humphrey, or Wallace. Most surprisingly, more than one million youths identified themselves as part of the New or Old Left, including 27 percent of the "fore-runners," 8 percent of other college students, and 5 percent of noncollege youth. Fertile ground indeed for SDS.

The National Office was the focus of most of the new attention and of course was barely able to cope with it. The staff, in addition to the three National Secretaries, fluctuated between ten and fifteen people, anchored by Sue Eanet Klonsky, Cathy Archibald, and Assistant National Secretary Tim McCarthy. Salaries were only $15 a week—when there was enough money at hand —which didn't do much to lure additional workers to the revolution, and it even became necessary for National Secretary Mike Klonsky to moonlight: "I have a wife and kid and we can only afford to pay me $15 a week, which means that maybe a couple of days a week I'll have to go out and load trucks or pick up a part-time job on the side." On top of which the workload was prodigious—Klonsky spoke of working twelve to sixteen hours a day, seven days a week, and that seems to have been the general pattern throughout most of the year. Even so, it was impossible to keep up with the barrage of material: two to three hundred letters a day (most of which were answered with a form letter or some available pamphlet stuffed into an envelope with a note like "Hope this helps"), more than two hundred magazines and newspapers a week (four of which— The New York Times, Wall Street Journal, Time, Newsweek—were clipped and filed, though with increasing haphazardness as the year wore on), and an incredible variety of pamphlets, newsletters, bulletins, and press releases from organizations all over the world (most of which was addressed to Bernardine Dohrn—fully 90 percent of it with her name misspelled "Bernadine," a mistake made by most SDSers, too—since she was nominally in charge of interorganizational matters, but which piled up unopened in boxes near her desk). Literature production could not keep up with the demand—the NO announced at one point that it would need an immediate influx of $7000 to produce ten pamphlets in enough quantity to fill back orders—but the NO print shop did put out a considerable amount of material: a new eight-page introduction-to-SDS pamphlet, form letters on high-school organizing and forming new

SDS chapters,* and of course weekly issues of *New Left Notes,* usually of eight pages. In fact *New Left Notes* went through a change symbolic of the exciting period the organization was going through: under editor David Millstone it took on more the look of the counterculture papers, its small gray front-page logo replaced by a big stark one with "SDS" in 120-point type, huge cartoons and drawings in place of most of the type on the front page, and borders, designs, and photographs splashed liberally throughout.

Regional Offices enjoyed an influx of new life, too. New regional centers were established in Ann Arbor, Chicago, Dallas, Newark, Philadelphia, and San Francisco, joining those already functioning in Cambridge, Ithaca, New York, Los Angeles, and Washington.† Though still not the self-sufficient kind of organizations that SDSers envisioned, Regional Offices did put out newsletters, hold regional conferences, and coordinate interchapter activities; they also provided centers where area SDSers and other political people could gather, as in New York, where the RO— which the regular SDSers had wrested back into their own control, mostly by ignoring rather than besting the PLers—also became the headquarters of a newly formed Teachers for a Democratic Society, in which Ted Gold was intrumental. Regional Offices were augmented by the full-time travelers, including most of the NIC representatives, who regularly made the rounds of regional campuses. One of the most successful was Mark Rudd, still riding on the media wave, who became SDS's official traveling fund raiser and managed to round up more than $3000 by November through his appearances on college campuses from New York

---

*The high-school letter confessed, "We don't like form letters any better than you do," but added, "except that it means that we get to leave the office sometime."

†Among those working out of the Regional Offices were: in Ann Arbor, Ayers, Robbins, and Diana Oughton; in Cambridge, NICer Eric Mann, Mike Ansara, and Russ Neufeld (there was also a PL-operated regional office run out of the apartment of John Pennington); in Dallas, NIC representative Bartee Haile and his wife, Marjorie; in Chicago, Les Coleman and Chicago University graduate student Howard Machtinger; in Ithaca, NICer Chip Marshall and Cornellians Joe Kelly and Jeff Dowd; in Los Angeles, Ken Cloke; in New York, NICer Jeff Jones and Columbia SDSer Martin Kenner; in Philadelphia, Steve Fraser (ex-PLer, now of the Philadelphia Labor Committee); in San Francisco, NICer Morgan Spector; in Washington, NICer Mike Spiegel and Cathy Wilkerson.

to California.* His fund-raising style seems not to have been
wholly fraternal, however: the story has it that after one appearance at Kent State that fall, when he got into an argument with
a local SDS leader who wanted to keep a small part of the gate
receipts to defray local expenses, they ended up brawling in the
chapter house and Rudd went away with the whole take.

SDS seemed to be at its peak, acknowledged on every side to
be the dominant organization of the resurgent American left, and
its move into revolution seemed to be confirmed with every passing week.

SDS's optimism took formal shape at the fall National Council meeting, held at the University of Colorado, in Boulder, on the
weekend of October 11–13. Some 450 people were gathered, the
largest number yet at a fall meeting, and the general spirit among
them suggested that SDS was ready to take its place as a national
power in the promising days to come. The clearest expression of
this came in a proposal submitted to the NC by Bernardine
Dohrn, John Jacobs (her current inamorato), and Jeff Jones of the
New York Regional Office:

> We believe that now is a time when the national political situation
> calls for our vocal, demonstrative presence more than ever. SDS
> now has a national identity and the election period is the oppor-
> tunity to *both* inject the ideas of SDS into the political arena *and*
> to make that national image a local reality by simultaneously involv-
> ing thousands in militant regional actions all over the country.
>
> Because political conditions are very open right now, and may
> be increasingly repressive in the coming period, we should think in
> terms of what programs now will develop the seeds of revolution
> most broadly. "Developing the seeds of revolution" goes beyond
> having large numbers of people understand or agree with our ideas.
> What's also needed is to turn masses of people on to looking at their
> own role as active agents of change. What does this is for people to

---

*Rudd was valuable enough to SDS that when he was threatened by the draft
Klonsky felt moved to write a letter to the local draft board pointing out that
Rudd had openly admitted he was a communist and was likely to cause "havoc,
even anarchy inside the ranks." "In my opinion," he wrote (letter, November 28,
1968, archives) "Mr. Rudd would present a threat to the internal security of the
nation inside the army. . . . If Rudd is drafted, don't say I didn't warn you." He
wasn't.

decide for radicalism not in the abstract, but concretely through their own decisions to *act* in specific cases. Involving large numbers of people directly in decisive actions will make the difference between a movement which depends overly on its "leaders," and can be repressed easily, and one with resilience and depth which continues to multiply and grow under adverse conditions. The goal of regional mobilizations is, like the Red Guard movement,* to guarantee revolution by insuring the self-activity, involvement, and experience of masses of people.

The target of these mobilizations, they proposed, would be the November Presidential elections: they called for a two-day national student strike, the first day for on-campus teach-ins, guerrilla theater, and rallies, and the second for massive city-wide marches and demonstrations.

> The student strike is an important political statement by the student movement to the rest of the country. It is possible to expand the politics of Columbia, to denounce the universities and schools as an intrinsic part of the capitalist system, and to link that assault to the broader issues of the electoral apparatus and the political parties of racism and imperialism.

The Dohrn-Jacobs-Jones proposal ran into some predictable opposition from the PLers assembled—probably as many as a hundred of them—on the grounds that it looked like more of the old resistance strategy and was bound to alienate the working classes. But it clearly spoke to the enthusiasms of the majority of the delegates and it passed by more than four to one, while a PL proposal for a march on Washington on Election Day was defeated easily. The strike call was even given a slogan thought to be only slightly hyperbolic: "No class today, no ruling class tomorrow!"

As if that weren't ambitious enough, the NC also approved with similar enthusiasm an elaborate campaign to recruit high-school students into SDS and "organize in the high school to move students to overthrow [the] system by confronting the issues that directly affect them." This was an area with a long history in SDS. In 1966 SDS had printed five thousand copies of a booklet on "high-school reform" by Los Angeles high-school SDSer Mark

---

*This phrase was deleted in the final version of the proposal submitted to the NC.

Kleiman (which right-wing publicist Alice Widener at the time called "one of the most dangerous documents ever printed in the United States"); in 1967, at the Bloomington NC, and in 1968, at the Lexington NC, SDS had also approved programs for establishing high-school organizers in the regions, producing pamphlets on students' rights, and publishing a national high-school newsletter. But the subject was given special importance now because it had become obvious that student politicization was moving rapidly down the age ladder—high-school SDS chapters mushroomed in the fall, radical high-school organizations (like New York's High School Student Union) began to take shape in the larger cities, and high-school protests started erupting in the fall in cities from coast to coast, affecting nearly 20 percent of the nation's secondary schools by the end of the school year. So the Boulder NC directed that high-school organizing be "a large part" of chapter and RO programing, authorized the hiring of a full-time traveler for high schools, and proposed that the Los Angeles high-school underground, the *Free Student,* be made into "a high-school *New Left Notes.* "

With these two programs out of the way, the NC fell into another round of sectarian bickering between Progressive Labor and its opponents, typified by PL's attack on student drug use—it represented a hippie "do-your-own-thing" philosophy, it was "escapist" and "objectively counter-revolutionary"—and the regulars' assertion that telling college students they shouldn't smoke marijuana was like telling workers they shouldn't drink beer. But the fiercest battle came over a PL proposal, written by Jared Israel and other Boston PLers, for a Student Labor Action Project—SLAP—which had been presented at the June convention but postponed for lack of time. The SLAP program was simply an embodiment of PL's worker-student alliance:

> Behind SLAP . . . is the notion of worker-student alliance. This does not mean we give up student organizing. It means we realize that U.S. Imperialism is based on class exploitation, that to defeat it in the long run—indeed, even to win immediate victories against it— we must develop a class approach, build support for the working class in *all* struggles, defeat all anti-working class ideas, support workers' struggles, and launch anti-ruling class battles that concretely link workers and students in fighting their common enemy.

The SLAP idea found an unexpectedly sympathetic reception, reflective of the growing sense among SDSers that industrial workers would be necessary allies in any successful revolution (or at least of the sense that arguing *against* that notion was no longer politically effective in SDS councils); as Carl Davidson reported in the *Guardian,* "Nearly all degates accepted, as a political given, the necessity of building an alliance between students and workers." However, it also met serious opposition. There were those who would have voted against the dictionary if it had been written by Jared Israel, but there were also more substantial critics: some (especially chapter delegates) attacked its glaring neglect of *students'* interests, others (who had done actual working-class organizing) maintained that PL's unimpressive record in attracting workers to its party indicated its real misunderstanding of the working class, and others (including both members of the NO and the Motherfuckers) argued that SDS's role should be to win over high-school and working-class youths rather than to try to convince their elders. After several hours of wrangling, sometimes quite bitter, SLAP was defeated two-to-one. NO spirits soared.

The decisive defeat of SLAP plus the strong approval of the Election Day strike inspired the national leadership to a frenzy of activity in the days after the Boulder NC. NIC members were dispatched to campuses and the top officers scheduled Election Day appearances. In the three weeks before the election the NO spent, Klonsky later figured, "several thousand" dollars just in the Chicago office. A special WATS line was established in the NO for quick national communications. Some two hundred fifty thousand form letters, press releases, exhortations, and other election literature were sent out to chapters, individuals, and the news media. And fifty thousand copies of a special pre-election issue of *New Left Notes* were printed and distributed, the back page of which was an instant wall poster setting forth in sixty-point letters the SDS election platform in brief:

> THE ELECTIONS
> DON'T MEAN SHIT.
> VOTE WHERE THE POWER IS.
> OUR POWER
> IS IN THE STREET.

Alas, wherever SDS's vaunted power was, it was not in the streets. The operation was an abject failure. SDS, according to the *Guardian,* "failed to interrupt education by a strike at a single high school, college or university" and its "anticipated massive street actions were abortive at best." Campus actions were limited to a few small-scale boycotts, rallies usually numbering no more than several hundred students, and a few sparsely attended teach-ins;* particularly disappointing were the small turnouts at places like Berkeley, Columbia, Michigan, and Wisconsin, normally the Concords of campus activism. City-wide marches took place in some areas where the Regional Offices had made special efforts, but with the exception of Boston, where some four thousand turned out, none of the demonstrations drew as expected: only a thousand people marched in front of the White House in Washington (a hundred twenty of them were arrested), another thousand turned out for a rock-music rally in Chicago, less than a thousand participated in San Francisco and Los Angeles, and no more than six hundred joined the rally in New York (partly as a result of pre-emptive police arrests—effective, if illegal—of more than a hundred people in the hours before the event). Coverage in the overground media was virtually nonexistent—the NO charged afterward that there had been a deliberate news blackout so as to give the impression of national acquiescence to the elections—and most of America went blithely along without the slightest notion that the largest left organization in the land, so much ballyhooed in the previous months, had even protested the elections at all.

What had gone wrong? SDS went through much anguished soul-searching in the solemn days after the election fiasco. The NIC meeting in the middle of November was one of the somberest affairs to date. Certain deficiencies were obvious: three weeks was not enough time for mass national organizing; too much responsi-

---

*Among the campuses were American, Berkeley, Boston College, Boston State, Claremont, Columbia, Duke, Emmanuel, Georgetown, George Washington, Houston, Iowa, Kent, Los Angeles State, Maryland, Massachusetts, Michigan, Mount Holyoke, Newark State, North Carolina, Northeastern, Penn State, San Francisco State, Seattle, Southeastern Massachusetts, Temple Buell, Texas, Virginia, Virginia Commonwealth, Western Michigan, Wisconsin. SDSers were also involved in sizable demonstrations at West Texas State, San Fernando Valley State, and Brooklyn College, but these had nothing specifically to do with the election actions and occurred coincidentally.

bility had been given over to the Regional Offices, which turned out to be financially and operationally too weak to do much more than mobilize the already militant; too many organizers, carried away by the experience of Chicago, had spent their time trying to get media coverage rather than getting people into the streets; the withdrawal of Johnson, the beginning of peace talks in Paris, and a promised bombing halt in North Vietnam served to diminish the war as an issue and lessen general student activism; and many students, it seemed, were too truncheon-scarred after a year of militant confrontations to want to take the chance of going up against the police again in a case they saw as essentially hopeless and considerably remote from their own immediate concerns on campus. But obviously the election failure signaled something more than just that, something more even than similar strategic failures like the draft exams in 1966 or the Ten Days of Resistance in the spring. Underneath the mediaized success of SDS in the past months, serious problems were festering.

These problems took three shapes: factionalism and infighting on the chapter level, increased pressures from Progressive Labor, and ever widening distances between the national leadership and much of the membership.

The most immediate problem of the fall was the factionalism inside the most basic SDS units, the chapters. Chapter fights, which had begun to surface with the action-praxis debates in the spring, now became almost commonplace, occurring with more regularity and at more campuses than ever before. As Klonsky himself noted with some perturbation, there were "a lot of bullshit things that have been keeping chapters and regions disfunctional [sic], like personal conflict, action vs. education debates, dope or no-dope fights." Almost inevitably chapters suffered, some growing weaker, some dividing into contending camps, others disintegrating entirely.*

---

*Divisionitis, it should be noted, was a disease not peculiar to SDS during these months: it affected many other institutions, and for roughly the same reasons. Among the groups that experienced outright splits during this period were Liberation News Service (breaking into one group emphasizing culture and another more strictly political and more activist), the Boston Draft Resistance Group (splitting into PL and non-PL factions), the Student Mobilization Com-

Most of the infighting centered around the old confrontation vs. base-building issue, now brought to new heights by the conflict between those SDSers ready for the leap into revolution and those advocating what was called "consolidation,"· emphasizing education and recruitment, especially of the new crop of disgruntled McCarthyites. This produced splits with varying degrees of severity at almost every sizable chapter, including well-established ones like Berkeley, Columbia, and Wisconsin, and new and struggling ones like Kent State, American University, and North Texas State. It was as if SDSers, as they took their political tasks more seriously now, became more intolerant; as they saw themselves capable of exercising real national power, more righteous. Debate tended to become contentious and positions rigid, friendships would be formed and broken on the basis of whether this or that dogma was acknowledged, and the consentient and tolerant spirit of the early days of SDS gradually disappeared. Greg Calvert and Carol Neiman—now married—bemoaned the consequences:

> Sitting in an SDS gathering, which had once been a cross between an encounter group and a Quaker meeting, became a hellish agony when intellectualization and parliamentary manipulation had replaced a sharing of experiences and consensus decision-making. The anarchist style of earlier days had, by 1968, been replaced by rigid debates of organized factions who no longer talked about people's feelings and experiences but spoke in the pseudo-scientific language of Marxism-Leninism. It should have been clear to anyone in possession of their instinctual sanity that these Talmudic exchanges, ideological debates, and resolution-passing indicated symptoms of

---

mittee (taken over after an acrimonious battle by Socialist Workers Party sympathizers), and the Peace and Freedom Party (which grew a disgruntled offshoot, the Freedom and Peace Party). A number of free universities collapsed at this same time, as well as several remaining draft-resistance groups, and some local antiwar mobilization committees, all generally along revolution vs. consolidation lines. Unbridgeable political gulfs also destroyed at least two major left events of the fall, SDS's International Assembly of Revolutionary Student Movements held at Columbia in September (which disintegrated into more-revolutionary-than-thou shouting matches in a half-dozen different languages), and the *Guardian*'s twentieth-anniversary dinner in December (where such left-wing stars as Herbert Marcuse and H. Rap Brown were hissed and booed, and Bernardine Dohrn—who had openly shown her dislike of Marcuse during a sneering introduction—stalked off the stage before delivering her planned speech).

a deep malaise in the body politic of the New Left and were not part of an arena of meaningful confrontation.

The most notable of the chapter battles—indeed so representative that *New Left Notes* gave it lengthy coverage on the grounds that it was "typical of many SDS chapters throughout the country"—took place at Michigan. On the night of September 24 Michigan SDS held its first meeting of the term and some two hundred people packed into the smoky classroom. For a while everything seemed smooth and normal. The old proconsolidation leadership of the chapter presented its assessment of the campus, urged greater "education work" among the students to make them aware of the oppressive nature of the university and the society, and argued against any hasty confrontation that might alienate the general student body. As the presentation went on, however, some of the audience began hooting and hissing, and at length one man stood to denounce the discussion as "one long stream of bullshit." He derided the old leadership for its fiasco of the spring, when, after a long campaign, it had finally arranged for a student referendum on the issue of war research on campus only to suffer a humiliating defeat when the engineering students turned out in force to swing the vote against it. And he announced that a new SDS caucus, the Jesse James Gang, had been formed at the beginning of the term to push for "aggressive confrontation politics" in the style of Columbia and Chicago. "If you think the only thing to do with war research is to burn it up," he said, "and the only thing to do with bad classes is take them over, and the only thing to do about bullshit candidates is to run them out with your own lives, then let's talk." Many did.

Thus began the split in the Michigan chapter: on the one side most of the chapter veterans and some of the newer recruits, who formed themselves into something called the Radical Caucus, and on the other the Jesse James Gang, including several veteran activists like Bill Ayers, Terry Robbins, and Jim Mellen (an ex-M2Mer now connected with REP) and a number of underclassmen attracted to the politics of activism. For the next four weeks as the two factions faced each other in increasingly bitter meetings, tempers grew short, minor disputes turned into major hatreds, and matters of personality became differences of politics (and vice versa). The James Gang's patience with parliamentary debate, none too weighty to begin with, eventually vanished to the point where they began indiscriminately shouting and heckling ("communicating openly," they called it) at the chapter meetings. The Radical Caucus responded with cries of "brown-shirts" and "crazies," and soon began spreading the idea around campus that SDS was being taken over by a bunch of outside "power-grabbers." At one meeting early in October the James Gang won two key victories over the vehement arguments of the Radical Caucus, one to push for the student strike and rally on Election Day, the other to begin direct confrontations in the classroom around issues of class structure, ideology, and the politics of individual professors. Six days later, on October 14, the Radical Caucus in a private meeting voted to disaffiliate from SDS and set itself up as a completely separate SDS chapter: the first time in SDS history that it ever had two competing chapters on a single campus.

The James Gang rejoiced—"This particular movement," they said in *New Left Notes*, "is gaining a sense of itself, and learning from our own experience about growth . . . how liberating it can be"—but it was not long before they realized how disastrous it could be, too. It soon became apparent that the effect of the chapter fight had been to drive away many of the students initially interested in radical politics, to splinter the finite radical base from which any programs, confrontational or educational, could be launched, and thus unintentionally to weaken the SDS presence, and thereby the left, at Michigan. When the James Gang called for strikes on the day before Election Day, virtually the only classes it was able to turn out were those canceled by sympathetic teachers, and when it marched on the president's house that night it mustered only two thousand people (a considerable number of them anti-SDS athletes) out of twenty thousand students; its call for a sit-in at the president's office the next day drew barely four hundred people and ended in inconclusive disarray. Shortly thereafter the *Michigan Daily* accused the James Gang of practicing fascist tactics, chapter meetings dwindled to fifty people and fewer, and before the fall was over SDS in general had fallen into disrepute on the Michigan campus. And this at the very school which had been in many ways the fountainhead of SDS, where the original SDS activists had established their base, where for many years the largest chapter in the organization had flourished.

Such splits as these were exacerbated at many places by the second current problem, the all-out invasion of SDS by the Progressive Labor Party. PLers—concentrated chiefly in Boston, New York, and California, with some strength in Chicago and Michigan—were positively cyclotronic in their ability to split and splinter chapter organizations: if it wasn't their self-righteous positiveness it was their caucus-controlled rigidity, if not their deliberate disruptiveness it was their overt bids for control, if not their repetitious appeals for base-building it was their unrelenting Marxism.* Nowhere were they more successful than at Berkeley.

Progressive Labor had been gaining strength at Berkeley since the spring term, when with some skillful manipulation, repeated bloc voting, and day-and-night energy it managed to inject

*Two descriptions of PL tactics in this period are revealing. The first, from UCLA, is by William Divale, the Communist Party/FBI agent in the SDS chapter there: "Its plan was to break the chapter into four or five small committees, each of which would be virtually autonomous to make and proclaim policy in its own field of work. Now, at general chapter meetings, PL's strength was seldom more than one-third of the membership. But by segmenting SDS into bits and pieces, and in naming each piece's chairman—who inevitably would have been either a PLer or one of its sympathizers—PL almost certainly would have controlled the pieces and, in effect, the whole. . . . [Early in 1968] PL for the very first time managed to boost one of its own PL members to the chapter chairmanship. Thereafter, and right up to today [1970], UCLA's SDS chapter was wholly PL controlled." (*I Lived Inside the Campus Revolution,* Cowles, 1970, pp. 107, 110.)

Similar things were going on at Harvard. According to one observer, "In the fall of '68, PL was a minority at Harvard, but they had the initiative. . . . PL came up with the anti-ROTC program, and pushed it, working hard, with a disciplined caucus that bloc-voted at the general SDS meetings. The traditional SDSers did not work so hard, did not organize a disciplined caucus or bloc vote. Between September and December PL picked up practically a majority of the SDS membership, largely by talking, persuasion, and working harder. . . . They worked out a subtle tactic. When a leaflet had to be put out by SDS, PL would bring supporters to the executive committee, and would vote as many members as possible onto the leaflet committee. If there were any need for volunteers to work, PL members would volunteer first. The traditional SDSers did not coordinate their forces, and didn't have the intelligence to confront the PL strategy. Thus through most of the year most of the SDS leaflets that came out carried the PL line, and as a consequence SDS came to be viewed by quite a lot of the student body as a Maoist-dominated group, when actually the Maoists did not have a real majority of SDS support, or of sympathizing SDS support." (A letter to the author from a Harvard SDSer.)

its politics into the chapter both in general sessions and on the various committees the chapter was broken into. Regular SDSers were somewhat dilatory in combatting PL influence and some chose to drop out altogether rather than bother with internecine battles—the New Left was supposed to embody harmony, after all, not acrimony—and it was not until the fall that they found a way to counterattack. Then the regulars, over the bitter objections of the PLers, committed the chapter to a sit-in at Sproul Hall to protest a decision by the California regents not to give credit for a course being taught by Eldridge Cleaver, Minister of Information of the Black Panther Party and then a Presidential candidate of the Peace and Freedom Party. The sit-in was a disaster, with 122 people arrested and very little student support engendered; and the regulars (with help from other campus political groups) followed it with a building takeover that proved equally unpopular, ending up with 80 more arrests and a widespread feeling that such suicidal tactics had no more place in the protest armory.* In the wake of this errant misadventure, the chapter was plunged into an angry series of recriminations and renewed factionalism, but PL came up smelling like roses—red roses. Within a month PL and its sympathizers had effectively taken over the chapter and the regulars subsequently walked out, "fed up with the phony ideological discussions with PL," forming a new group, the Radical Student Union, which no longer even bothered to call itself an SDS chapter. At the fountainhead of student activism, SDS became nothing more than another sect.

PL's influence also operated on the national level, not only in national meetings (like the June convention) but inside the National Office itself, producing no end of trouble for the leadership trying to guide the organization into some overt form of revolution. PLers resisted and ignored policies they didn't like, generally working to sabotage the Election Day demonstrations, for example, when they themselves couldn't direct them and select the speakers. PLers also barraged the NO with articles for *New Left Notes,* a problem which the national officers generally solved

---

*Among those participating in the takeover were two SDS alumni who had independently gravitated to Berkeley to continue their activities, Tom Hayden and Al Haber.

with the undemocratic expedient of refusing to publish them, ultimately forcing PL to start its own student publication, *Fight to Win.* PL's work-in pamphlet, submitted to the NO in the early fall, was also withheld from publication, though in this case the NO came up with the excuse that it couldn't publish anything that wasn't signed, for the PLers had left their articles in it anonymous so as to be able to return to the factories next summer. "PL paranoia," as it became called, even resulted in the firing of the staff printer, Al Camplejohn, for "political and office security reasons" and on the grounds that he was a "PL agent" in the NO. Finally, there was an embarrassing defection to PL among the national officers: Fred Gordon, who had not been part of the original NO clique and who found himself ostracized by most of the national collective as soon as he moved to Chicago, apparently was befriended by a few local PLers and this in time grew to open PL sympathy; though he was not a member of the party, so far as is known, he gradually became an effective spokesman for its policies and a useful opponent of any moves to purge it from SDS. Relations between Gordon and the NO became so bad that in December he wrote a brief piece in *New Left Notes* to complain that the national leadership was "anticommunist"—this was PL's way of saying anti-PL—and that the literature program had suppressed both worker-student alliance views and a pamphlet he himself had written; he denied, however, the rumor then common in SDS that he was being "held captive" in the Chicago office.

The open enmity now between PL and the SDS regulars, and the obvious growth of PL power in both chapters and national meetings, prompted the NO to try various schemes to stifle and possibly eliminate PL from the organization. During the fall it approached members of the left wing of the Communist Party in the hopes that their long-standing opposition to PL and their superior knowledge of Old Left ideological debates could be used to blunt PL's effects at national meetings and perhaps drive it from the organization voluntarily. NO allies Les Coleman and Howard Machtinger, a 1966 Columbia graduate now at the University of Chicago, established ties with the Chicago-area Black Panther Party and campus black student associations, both known to oppose PL, with the idea of building up anti-PL strength in area chapters. There was even considerable talk in the air about a merger of SDS with the left-wing Communists and the National Mobilization Committee to form an entirely new group which would outlaw PL from the start; Dohrn labeled this talk "pure and simple trash" in a *New Left Notes* article in December, but it certainly had wide currency in the organization and represented the thinking of at least some SDS veterans. No one doubted now that SDS faced a very difficult challenge in the months ahead; as San Diego SDSer Jim Prickett noted unhappily: "The general malaise in SDS is apparent to all; people who barely know each other write fearful letters about the dangers of an upcoming split in the organization."

All this turmoil was compounded by the third major problem, the intensification of the old distance ailment brought on by the determined plunge into revolutionary politics. The people in and around the NO, and the national leadership in general, were unabashedly on the side of the actionists, had developed ideologies generally couched in Marxist terms, and saw themselves as allies of Third World freedom fighters and black revolutionaries; they were joined by most of the Regional Office staffs, the action factions, some of the veterans, many of the more hippie-identified street people, and a number of younger recruits coming to SDS after bellicose high-school careers. Out in the chapters, however, there were many others not so convinced of the successes of confrontation, nor so taken with the Marxist themology: the consolidation factions, many of the nonideological veterans of the early New Left days, others whose identification was more with radical life styles and culture than with radical politics, and a large number of the younger collegians only recently weaned from liberalism. The gulf was wide, but bridgeable, and many in SDS councils appealed for a period of moderation, going slow, or "evening out" as it was called: NICer Morgan Spector, for example, argued that "we should be as prepared to burn our little Lenin Library as to refer to it." But in the flush of a conscious dedication now to revolution, such appeals were generally ignored and the NO had the power to see that they did not swerve the organization from its path.

As a result, SDS did not effectively win over the audience of potential radicals on the campus, did not even succeed in holding on to many of those who participated in the initial meetings of the fall. At a time when many young people wanted some explanations for the failure of electoral politics, SDS was led by people who had long since given up caring about elections and were trying to organize for revolution. To students just beginning to be aware of their own radicalization and their potential role as the intelligentsia in an American left, SDS offered the wisdom that the only really important agents for social change were the industrial workers, or the ghetto blacks, or the Third World revolutionaries. For college students who swarmed into chapter meetings ready to take on their administrations for any number of grievances, SDS provided an analysis which emphasized "de-studentizing," dropping out, and destroying universities.* And for youths in search of an integrative ideology to supplant the tattered theories of corporate liberalism, SDS had only the imperfectly fashioned tenets of a borrowed Marxism and an untransmittable attachment to the theories of other revolutionaries; not even the serviceable explanations of an earlier day were available—*The Port Huron Statement,* for example, or Oglesby's *Containment and Change,* or the initial explorations of the new working class—having by now been assigned to the junkheap of history. It did not matter that the SDS leadership was in certain ways politically justified in its posture and far more sophisticated in its world view than the newcomers; what was important was that in organizational terms it simply failed to reach great segments of the membership or potential membership. And more than that, it failed to provide a radical politics for a subgeneration of militant students who were then forced to look elsewhere or, more often, chose not look at all. In coming months, and years, college and high-school youths would continue to turn to activism out of the inevitable condition of their lives and their society, but less and less were they guided by particular theoretic structures or worked-out politics, not even from the one political group on the left that had been able to fulfill this crucial function.

---

*This theme still figured prominently in SDS writing, as for example in an article by Mike Spiegel, Cathy Wilkerson, and Les Coleman in the October 7 *New Left Notes:* "Our strategy . . . must therefore be an attack on the entire institution of the university, a challenge to its purpose and its right to exist. Wherever possible, we must strive to shut it down—shut it down rather than 'reform' it because as long as society exists in its present form the university can only function to achieve [its] aims."

The accelerated distance problem had another effect, too. It meant that SDS was unable to achieve a unified political identity for itself, even the kind of loose identity it had managed to forge in earlier periods when, though embracing a multitude of tendencies, it stood for a certain shared analysis of America and the means of altering it. SDS now was a spectrum so vast as to be undefinable, almost more a state of mind than a political organization, more a flag of convenience than an umbrella. Any kind of self-proclaimed leftist, and there was an infinite variety these days, could call himself or herself an SDSer and join an SDS group without identifying with any ongoing tendency or having to learn the body of political thought stored up in the organization over the previous eight years. Any chapter (or faction within a chapter) could define for itself what "SDS" meant and act according to that definition without much regard for anybody else, certainly without any scrupulous attention to the resolutions out of the last NC or the latest article by the National Secretary. At any time in SDS history this might have proved dangerously disintegrative, but at a time when the leadership was hoping to forge a mass body of people committed to an all-out revolution it proved absolutely calamitous.

Not all the blame for the apparently sudden misfortunes of SDS should be laid to these three problems, critical as they were. Much of the crisis was brought on by the response of the very social institutions—the government, the cities, the universities— which felt themselves, or convinced themselves to feel, threatened by the growth of revolutionary politics and at last chose to launch a serious counterattack.

The atmosphere for the counterattack was set by both media and politicians. A time-to-crack-down theme was piped with increasing shrillness as the fall wore on, exemplified best by an article in the nation's largest-circulation periodical, the *Reader's Digest,* entitled "SDS: Engineers of Campus Chaos." This accused SDS specifically of violence, arson, rioting, looting, brawling, public fights, "anti-democratic tactics," and plotting the destruction of society itself; the organization was "subversive," a "totalitarian minority," inspired if not directed by Stalinist masterminds in Moscow, and readers were assured by no less than J. Edgar Hoover that, "to put it bluntly, they are a new type of subversive, and their danger is great." Hoover himself, testifying in Washington at the same time, proclaimed:

> The protest activity of the new left and the SDS, under the guise of legitimate expression of dissent, has created an insurrectionary climate which has conditioned a number of young Americans—especially college students—to resort to civil disobedience and violence. . . . The aim of the SDS attack is to smash first our educational structure, then our economic system, then, finally, our government itself.

Also in Washington the House Committee on Un-American Activities, acknowledging "persistent and growing demands" from Congressmen for legislative action against the New Left, saw fit to begin several days of elaborate hearings, with full TV and newspaper coverage, on what it called "subversive involvement" in the August Chicago demonstrations. SDS, said Committee Chairman Richard Ichord of Missouri, was one of the organizations in Chicago "determined to effect a general breakdown of law and order, preparatory to their long-range objective of seizing the powers of government"; among those subpoenaed were Rennie Davis and Tom Hayden, apparently on the assumption that they were SDS leaders, but no current officers were called to testify.* Similar inflated pronouncements on the dangers of SDS were being made elsewhere, by similar inflated people. In California Governor Ronald Reagan declared: "This is not just the hijinks of overenthusiastic students. This is insurrection. Organized society cannot back down without giving up our rights." And in Virginia the head of the State Board of Education urged the expulsion of all radicals from the campus—specifically SDS, the DuBois Clubs, and YSA—and proposed that the unlimited powers of the state be used to this end, for "like their heroes Che Guevara, Fidel Castro, and Ho Chi Minh, the only language student extremists understand is force." The speaker was Lewis Powell, four years later to take his seat as a Nixon appointee to the Supreme Court.

---

*Bernardine Dohrn was there, but as a legal co-counsel for Davis, Hayden, and Dave Dellinger, not (despite an erroneous report in *New Left Notes*) as a witness herself. Hayden's testimony forms the bulk of a book of his called *Rebellion and Repression* (Hard Times/Meridian, 1969).

All of this was capped by the climate of genuine fear and uncertainty engendered by an election race in which all three leading Presidential candidates exploited what was called the "law-and-order" issue, warning of black dissidents, student radicals, Communist agitators, unmanageable youths, and criminal malcontents who, it was held, were responsible for America's manifold problems. Campus militancy and student protest became key discussion points in the campaign and every candidate sought to show that he was firmer and fairer on the subject than the next man; both Democratic and Republican Vice Presidential candidates, as a matter of fact, first came into their own through their handling of the student issue, Edmund Muskie by his adroit put-downs of disrupters at college appearances, Spiro Agnew by his blunt and uncompromising denunciation of student protesters of every stripe.* Student militants themselves did little to diminish the impact of the law-and-order issue, picketing, heckling, and disrupting candidates whenever possible and gaining considerable publicity in the process. Ultimately it was Richard Nixon's particular manipulation of this issue which produced for him his narrow victory.

With the national mood thus primed, federal law agencies felt comparatively free to harass, intimidate, and ride herd on SDS and other campus political groups. The Army Intelligence operation, now directed by the former head of intelligence in Vietnam, "was moving at top speed," according to *The New York Times,* in receipt of more than a thousand reports a month on students and other radicals. The FBI, according to a former agent, issued "an order directing intensified investigations of student agitators and expanded 'informant penetration' of campus SDS groups";

*Typical of Agnew's performances was one at Towson State College in Maryland, the state in which he had risen to minor prominence as a hard-line antistudent governor. When he was repeatedly heckled during an address there he finally dispensed with his prepared remarks and shouted out into the audience, "How many of you sick people are from Students for a Democratic Society?" Nearly two-thirds of the audience of one thousand raised their hands. "All of you, good," said the candidate, "because I've done some research on that organization, and I know you'd like to overthrow the government. But on November fifth we'll put a man in office who'll take this country forward without you." Until then no one had known just what Agnew's areas of research interest were. (LNS, October 11, in *RAT,* November 1, 1968.)

presumably every major SDS group was watched and infiltrated, and undercover agents are known to have operated during this time at Chicago, Essex County Community College, Kent State, New Orleans Movement for a Democratic Society, Owego, and UCLA. The FBI also sought to deepen the factional crisis within SDS by writing anonymous letters designed "to play one faction off against another," and it regularly planted stories in sympathetic newspapers giving information from its dossiers to suggest that SDSers were conscious agents of "the Communist conspiracy."* The bureau also instructed all of its field offices to begin inquiries into the Chicago demonstrations, assigning 320 full-time special agents to the task, and before the fall was out the FBI had made no fewer than 1400 "investigations," visited more than 1000 people on campuses, and put taps on the phones of those against whom it was preparing the case that ultimately produced the Chicago "Conspiracy."†

Universities, too, moved in a concerted way to control or weaken radical groups on their campuses. The school year began with a special summit meeting of college presidents in Denver devoted to the single topic of how to handle student dissidents. Back at their desks, administrators beefed up campus police forces (many of which were allowed to carry arms for the first time), installed electronic security systems, removed important college records to secret safes, and established new offices for police liaison, legal advice, and the like; at a number of campuses administration officials are known to have opened up confidential files to local police and FBI agents seeking to spy on radicals. But the favorite administration tactic, despite the example of Columbia, was simply to call in the police and arrest demonstrators. At least

---

*Before the December National Council meeting in Ann Arbor at least one Detroit newspaperman was offered special FBI dossiers on SDS leaders so that he would print stories discrediting the NC in advance. (*Hard Times,* May 17, 1969.)

†Other federal agencies were no less diligent, though their attentions were not strictly on students. The Attorney General prosecuted more than fifteen hundred draft cases during 1968, a record number; the Department of Defense established a Civil Disturbance Directorate to handle campus and ghetto protests; and the federal drug authorities stepped up drug seizures by 155 percent over 1967 and brought the number of drug arrests of those under twenty-one to 774 percent more than in 1960.

twenty-one institutions summoned police and at least 1265 campus arrests were made—not counting those arrested for off-campus actions, including the two hundred or so arrested during Election Day demonstrations—almost three times as many arrests as were made in the spring (when the NSA figured 417, excluding Columbia).* And where police invasion and its threat were not enough, administrators banned SDS groups outright, for example at Colorado, CCNY, Illinois Institute of Technology, Texas, and Wisconsin (Oshkosh).†

Universities, however, had more at their disposal than just strong-arm tactics. Cooptation and melioration were also used in good measure at many campuses, especially those in the liberal

---

*Most notable instances of university repression occurred at Illinois in September, where police harshly arrested 240 students during a black-led sit-in; at San Fernando Valley State, in November, where more than 100 were arrested, 28 of whom were charged by administrators with felony offenses carrying up to thirty years in jail; at New York's City College, in November, where 170 were arrested trying to give sanctuary to an army deserter; at Oshkosh State, in November, where 98 students, the entire black population of the university, were arrested after a sit-in in the president's office and were summarily expelled from school; at Connecticut, in November and December, where 79 people were arrested and more than 150 injured in two separate battles with police called in to smash antirecruiter demonstrations; and at San Francisco State, from November to January, where 563 people were arrested during the student strike, 8 of them hospitalized for injuries.

†The role of the trustees, in whose name the college presidents were acting, should not be forgotten, and since these people were in great part conservative, old, rich, and remote they could be counted on to give general approval to sterner administrative actions. A 1968 survey by the Educational Testing Service gives some indication of trustee attitudes. According to the summary in *Protest!* (p. 383 ff.), trustees were shown to be "remote from most students" in almost every respect, to "qualify for 'Elite' and 'Establishment' labels so frequently pinned on them," and to hold political postures that in no respect resembled "that of any facet of the new left." Most of the trustees admitted to reading little or nothing on education or student protest, but over 80 percent felt that disruptive students should be expelled or suspended and more than 97 percent would refuse to let students have any voice whatsoever in any area of decision-making now handled by faculty, administration, or trustees. In addition, the survey indicated that nearly 70 percent had incomes over $20,000 and 16 percent (43 percent at the prestigious universities) over $100,000; almost 40 percent were executives in major businesses and 20 percent sat on the boards of top-ranking corporations; 73 percent were over fifty, 99 percent of them were white, and 82 percent described themselves as moderates or conservatives. "The gulf," it was concluded, "between the backgrounds, attitudes and beliefs of trustees and those of student activists is thus a very large one."

tradition; as Berkeley Chancellor Roger Heyns said that fall, "most campuses today have developed the skill and the will to breach their divisions, to keep things cool." On the one hand administrations could blunt the immediate effect of the protesters by making accommodations to satisfy student grievances (more students on committees, student-selected courses, liberalized social codes, upgraded food and housing facilities, appointment of ombudsmen and student aids), and on the other they could enhance the position of student moderates by giving them privileges and power (placing them on university committees, giving them access to administrative insiders, appointing them to well-funded and well-publicized study groups). Columbia, for example, was a model of this technique: it fired the president and dean who had been most disliked by the university community, appointed as acting president a longtime professional diplomat, abandoned construction of the unpopular gym, created a new academic senate giving students and faculty a voice for the first time in university affairs, dropped charges against the large majority of arrested students, established a new campus judiciary system, installed a "Director of Student Interests," agreed to move toward disaffiliating from both the IDA and ROTC, and created no fewer than fifteen campus committees involving moderate students in issues of campus reform. Largely as a result of this, student sympathy for SDS declined and the chapter fell into increasing factionalism: "Somehow," moaned SDSer Juan Gonzalez, "we were imprisoned by the past. We thought we could come back to the campus and the whole university would come falling down. It didn't."

The maneuvers both of the university and of the society at large had a real impact on campus activism in the fall. It did not by any means halt student protest or the further radicalization of campuses, because these were too inextricably a part of the era to be wiped out overnight merely by repressive punishment or moderative reform: there were at least seventy-four instances of major campus disturbances from September to January, ranging from the student strike at San Francisco State to the disrupting of the Saigon ambassador's speech at New York University, and including twenty-one sit-ins and buildings takeovers (plus one *campus* takover, at LeMoyne-Owen College in Tennessee), eleven locally based student strikes, and five destructive window-breaking demonstrations. But it was clear that both the number and intensity of demonstrations were reduced in the fall at most campuses; no matter how mild the protest, no one could be sure any longer about being able to make a political/moral point without getting thrown out of school, beaten into hospital, or packed off to jail. After years of demanding to be taken seriously, activists found that they were.

SDS chapters, the prime targets of most of this reaction, began to show the effects. Experience of course varied widely but in practically no instance were chapters prepared to deal with phone-tapping, daily surveillance, police infiltration, large-scale arrests, and administrative rigidity. As infiltration grew, fear and suspicion began to infest formerly easygoing organizations and the early SDS spirit of openness and honesty suffered the pall of secrecy and incipient paranoia. As arrests and jailings mounted, chapter resources, both of money and of time, tended more and more to be concentrated on raising bail and providing legal defense. As summary expulsions and other forms of university discipline became more commonplace, chapters found it increasingly difficult to attract large numbers of liberal students to campus demonstrations. And at a time when chapters already had troubles enough of their own, this kind of pressure had a steadily debilitating effect.

Political violence increased during the fall, partly as the result of the closing off of other avenues of protest and partly because of the growth of self-consciously revolutionary groups ready to follow Guevara's advice to "pick up the gun." The number of major incidents of presumably left-related bombing and arson, almost all symbolic, rose to forty-one, four times that of the spring. ROTC facilities were burned or bombed at Berkeley, Delaware, Oregon (twice), Texas, Washington University, and the University of Washington; this last was the most dramatic, causing an $85,000 fire in whose flames a group of students danced to the chant of

> This is number one
> And the fun has just begun,
> Burn it down, burn it down, burn it down.

Campus buildings were bombed at Bluefield State College, Georgetown, Michigan, NYU, and four California state colleges (Los Angeles, San Fernando Valley, San Francisco, and San Jose), for the most part without serious damage; in each instance the target was symbolic—a classified military research building at Ann Arbor, the administration offices at NYU—and one or more campus groups tried to broadcast the political reasoning behind the attack. The Detroit area experienced a rash of bombings during September and October, and Oakland and San Francisco city and government buildings were attacked five times during the fall.

SDS's relation to all of this was ambiguous. In general the national leadership—and of course the "consolidation" factions—frowned upon violence if it tended to alienate the bulk of students, though most of them would say at the same time that this would hardly be likely to happen with the bombing of a ROTC building. PL was especially loud in its scorn of violence outside the campus walls—trashing in the streets, for example—because this was thought to estrange the working class, and not a few others agreed. However, the style of SDS rhetoric and its avowed promulgation of revolution certainly did nothing to discourage political violence. A St. Louis SDSer, Michael Siskind, was the one responsible for the Washington University bombings and was sentenced to five years in jail. Various counterculture papers associated with SDS, like RAT in New York, published diagrams of how to make simple explosives. Copies of a non-SDS pamphlet called "Sabotage," giving instructions on bomb-making and fire-setting, apparently were scooped up with unabashed enthusiasm when they made an appearance at the Boulder NC. California SDSers Terry Cannon and Morgan Spector produced another pamphlet, more decorous, on "a strategy of total resistance" which also made the rounds of campuses. Probably many SDSers would have sympathized with the statement from the San Francisco State chapter, reprinted in New Left Notes, specifically defending student resistance to police on campus:

> Pacifism obfuscates the class nature of violence and is used by the ruling class to keep movements from winning. The ruling class uses any means necessary to keep people in their place, and we must use any means necessary including people's violence to defeat them.

Perceptibly, if slowly, the path toward violence was widening.

The people at the upper levels of SDS spent many gloomy days in the weeks before the December National Council trying to cope with the problems exposed by the abortive Election Day actions. It was a critical period for the organization, for it was faced with an absolutely crucial choice: whether to develop the unformed but original ideas born in the early days of resistance into a new kind of *Port Huron Statement* appropriate for 1968, or to link itself with the great Marxist tradition and adapt the pre-molded ideas of the most popular and successful ideology around. As Todd Gitlin saw it then, with his usual perception:

> *Either* the post-scarcity Left comprehends its own unprecedented identity as a social force, grasps its caused-ness, elaborates that identity into vision and program for its own trajectory on the campus and in youth ghettos, uses its reality as a strength from which to encounter anti-colonial and working-class energy and to devise common approaches; *or* it turns from its identity, throws the vision out with the narrowness of the class base, and seeks a historically pre-packaged version in which students or déclassé intellectuals are strictly appendages to really "real" social forces or are either the vanguard or the tail of the really real. *Either* it painfully accepts the reality of our class base and moves outward from there; *or* it denies the unprecedented possibilities by denying its own caused reality, and defines the student Left either as class-appendage or class-substitute. *Either* it takes itself seriously as a specifically post-scarcity and visionary force with revolutionary democratic vision; *or* it buys clarity on the cheap, taking refuge from the distinctness of metropolitan conditions in mirror-models of the underdeveloped socialism of Russia and the Third World. *Either* it accepts the awesome risk of finding new paths, *or* it walks the beaten trails, pugnacious and sad. A grave choice, where the stakes are immense and under the pounding pressure of the State there seems no time for placid reflection. Literally an existential choice.

SDS chose—not by referendum or by resolution, but more by osmosis and happenstance—the latter. In the haste to make itself revolutionary, to justify its revolutionism, to live up to the image it (and the press) was now creating, it chose the easier course, opting for what was at hand rather than what had to be constructed, for what was sanctioned by history rather than what was new and untried. The new-working-class theories, for example, so eagerly embraced a year and a half before, were now abandoned, still unshaped and untried, and the membership—the theoretically inclined membership, at any rate—rushed pell-mell into the comparative safety of one or another variety of Marxism.*

The choice of the national leadership was a variety that embraced wholeheartedly a class analysis of the traditional Marxist kind—workers against the rulers, proletariat against the bourgeoisie—and committed the organization to work among the classical proletariat, with the emphasis upon the youthful proletariat. A strange bird no doubt to emerge from the ashes of the election debacle, one with wings perhaps exhausted from overexposure and overuse, but a sturdy beast also and to it the SDS leadership tied all its plans for the year ahead. The formal enunciation of this final attachment to Marxism came with an article written by Mike Klonsky after long consultation with the theoretical heavies and featured in the issue of *New Left Notes* distributed at the National Council meeting.

"Toward a revolutionary youth movement" became a central document in SDS's final months. Klonsky began by trying to tip the whole balance of the student organization toward the working class:

> At this point in history, SDS is faced with its most crucial ideological decision, that of determining its direction with regard to the working class. At this time there must be a realization on the part of many in our movement that students alone cannot and will not be able to bring about the downfall of capitalism, the system which is at the root of man's oppression. . . .
>
> The main task now is to begin moving beyond the limitations of struggle placed upon a student movement. We must realize our potential to reach out to new constituencies both on and off campus and build SDS into a youth movement that is revolutionary.

The working-class identification was neatly meshed with the new attachment to street action born in Chicago, producing the

---

*Several last-ditch efforts were made by SDSers to defend and develop new-working-class theories in these months—for example, Greg Calvert and Carol Neiman in the *Guardian* (August 24 and 31, and September 7), Carl Oglesby in *Liberation* (July-August), Gordon Burnside in *New Left Notes* (August 15), and Bob Gottlieb, Dave Gilbert, and Susan Sutheim in a Movement for a Democratic Society pamphlet in October. But the effort was too little and too late.

idea of organizing among the *young* members of the working class:

> The notion that we must remain simply "an anti-imperialist student organization" is no longer viable. The nature of our struggle is such that it necessitates an organization that is made up of youth and not just students, and that these youth become class conscious. This means that our struggles must be integrated into the struggles of working people. . . .
>
> Because we can organize—as a student movement—around those contradictions which affect youth specifically, we can organize young working people into our class-conscious anti-capitalist movement. These young workers will (a) strengthen the anti-capitalist movement among the work-force, (b) provide an organic link between the student movement and the movement of working people, and (c) add to the effect that we will have as a critical force on older working people today.

Two means of implementation were offered: first, building "class consciousness in the student movement" by organizing in working-class colleges and high schools, allying with campus workers, attacking the privileged positions of students, and moving off campus into working-class communities; second, attacking the university's "institutional racism" by pressing for black and brown admissions, challenging racist teachers, and attacking campus police institutes and counterinsurgency centers.

   With this new theoretical underpinning—one which, incidentally, seemed to steal much of the thunder away from PL's association with Marxism—the SDS leaders came into the National Council meeting ready for supreme battle. They got it.
   The meeting, held in Ann Arbor from December 26 to 31 with perhaps as many as twelve hundred people, dissolved into one long battle between the myriad varieties of SDS regulars and the into-the-breach PLers. Whatever the issues, petty or grand, the plenary sessions debated them venomously, providing all the "hellish agony" the Calverts attested to, and the truly serious nature of the issues in this particular time made the debates all the more anguished. The three most important had to do with racism, women's liberation, and of course the "Revolutionary Youth Movement" proposal.

The racism resolution was introduced by PLers from San Francisco State and reflected a whole new campaign for PL to make racism into its major prism for viewing the way "the bosses" divide and exploit "the workers." PL's officially approved line was that racism was simply a device of the ruling class to oppress the working class and that blacks were strategically important only because they were the most exploited segment of the working class. The NO faction, following the traditional New Left line, greeted this position with the retort that racism was a malady inherent in all parts of the white world, *including* the white working class, and that blacks were important chiefly because their struggle for liberation was in fact the cutting edge of the revolution at this moment. The haranguing was bitter, heated, and lengthy, but ultimately when it became clear that the NO had no counter-proposal of its own to offer and the delegates were faced with the choice of coming out against racism or not, the PL proposal won by a narrow margin.

The same PL line was offered again during the debate over the resolution on women's liberation. PLers here argued that women were not a special category, really, just a specially oppressed part of the working class whose battles had to be fought as part of those of the class as a whole; most of the women, and the regulars, maintained that women were in a separate fix since their oppression came from men everywhere and not just the "ruling class." PLers repeated at increasing length their conviction that the basic "contradiction" in America was between the working class and the "bourgeoisie" and that any "contradiction" between men and women was secondary to that; the women replied that however secondary the "contradiction" may seem to PL, for women at this time it was the battle they certainly felt most acutely about. This time the dynamics of the convention worked against the PLers, since the NO forces had a concrete proposal on the floor (written in part by a man, Noel Ignatin, the Chicago SDSer close to the NO, and modified and presented by a women's caucus) and PL had none; the women's resolution was passed, affirming that the "oppression of women through male supremacy" was both qualitatively and quantitatively greater than the oppression of working people in general. (The resolution, however, did not suggest that women should go outside of SDS to join or form separate women's groups of their own, as a number of SDS women and feminist groups had been urging; it argued that inasmuch as women's liberation was "an integral part" of the battle against capitalism, women should remain in organizations primarily concerned with fighting that battle. This shortly became known as the "SDS position" in the women's movement, against which a variety of separatist groups were to array themselves in the coming year.)

But the sharpest fight of the NC came over Klonsky's proposal for a Revolutionary Youth Movement (RYM, pronounced "rim"), for the PL forces were perfectly aware that it was designed to undercut their influence in SDS and take away their exclusive identification with working-class politics. Led by Fred Gordon, Jeff Gordon (no relation), and San Francisco PL organizer John Levin, the PLers attacked the strategy at every point: it placed too much emphasis on youth and the "phony" youth culture and suggested that youths themselves would make the revolution; it invited more of the old resistance politics of street violence, leading to dangerous "wild-in-the-streets" attitudes; it exaggerated the importance of students over that of the working class, forgetting that students are really members of the bourgeoisie. Klonsky himself took on the burden of answering PL, and his defense of the proposal was impassioned and skillful. He began by acknowledging that some attacks on PL in recent months had been unprincipled, declared that the NO was not planning to expel PL ("PL has done a lot of good things in SDS, and don't think for a minute that when the Man comes down on PL, we won't stand beside them"), and argued that the RYM approach was really the best way to accomplish PL's stated goal of a union between students and workers; he adroitly defended the thrust of the RYM strategy, accused PL of not being sufficiently committed to the kind of action necessary for change, and upheld the role of youth and students in prodding others toward the revolution. It was by all accounts a winning performance, and Carl Davidson reported in the *Guardian* that it was "a decisive turning point in the NC." Shortly thereafter the RYM proposal passed, and SDS was formally set on a new path toward "class-consciousness" and working-class organizing, an acknowledgment of the victory of Marxist (and often pseudo-Marxist) ideas at the ideological levels of the organization, and of the final triumph of the "organize-the-left" tendency over the "organize-students" position within SDS. Davidson called it "the most most important change in its political thinking since the organization embraced the politics of anti-imperialism two years ago." The power of the resolution was muted somewhat by the fact that it passed by a very narrow margin—twelve votes, the chair announced—and individual chapters were therefore under little obligation to follow the RYM line unless they wanted to. Nonetheless, for those inclined in this direction already—and they included the national leadership, the action factions, and such future SDS strategists as Ayers, Dohrn, Jacobs, Machtinger, Mellen, and Rudd—the passage of the RYM proposal gave the national imprimatur to the kind of politics that would eventually become the basis of Weatherman.

After five days of rampageous political battles, lasting well into the early hours, setting delegate against delegate, producing despair and frustration and anger, the final session of the Ann Arbor NC should probably have come as no surprise. The ugliness and discordance of the scene, however, surpassed anything known in the organization before and left a bitter taste in the mouths of most SDSers that lasted for months to come. Carl Davidson caught it all:

> The chairman then moved into a fund-raising session, traditionally a time of merrymaking and song at SDS gatherings, while members are emptying their pockets of cash. This time the two opposing camps delivered volleys of chants back and forth. "Ho Ho Ho Chi Minh" came from the national collective supporters, answered by "Mao Mao Mao Tse-tung" from the other side.* When someone started singing "The Worker's Flag is Deepest Red," the student-worker alliance side of the room came up with "Don't use the red flag against the red flag" and "Defeat SDS's Khrushchev." The final blow came when the singing of "Solidarity Forever" was inter-rupted by the chant "Defeat False Unity." After that, everyone went home.

Such a stark and rapid change from the time, only a few months before, when Ayers and Robbins had felt the "new atmosphere of optimism and aggressiveness"—and it augured dark days ahead.

*The "Mao" chant in opposition to "Ho" represented PL's view that Ho was a sellout to the revisionist Russians for accepting aid while only Mao and China kept to the pure revolutionary path.

23

SPRING 1969

Dark days for national SDS, perhaps, but there was more to SDS than its national presence, more to the Movement than SDS, and the first six months of 1969 were illuminated by flashes of activism that swept across the nation like summer lightning.

On the campuses, protests were more frequent, more diverse, and more violent than even the previous year. The spring saw the longest and most violent student strike in American history, at San Francisco State, where black and "Third World" students, aided by white radicals and a large number of sympathetic faculty, boycotted classes for four and a half months, suffering 700 arrests and innumerable injuries in the process; the first open display of firearms by student protesters, at Cornell, where black students took over a campus building, armed themselves in self-defense, and later walked out brandishing rifles and bandoliers for press photographers; the first death at the hands of (presumably) protesters, at Santa Barbara, where a custodian was killed by a bomb he picked up on the patio of the faculty club; and the first white death at the hands of the state, at Berkeley, where police opened fire on a crowd of white demonstrators for the first time, killing one, James Rector, blinding another, and injuring at least a hundred.* All told, there were major protest demonstrations at nearly

*It was not the only student death that year: another black student was shot dead by police at North Carolina Agricultural and Mechanical College in May, and two Black Panthers at UCLA were killed, reportedly by an opposing black group, in January.

three hundred colleges and universities, in every part of the country, at a rate of nearly two a day, involving a third of the nation's students, roughly 20 percent of them accompanied by bombs, fires, or destruction of property, a quarter by strikes or building takeovers, and a quarter more by disruption of classes and institutional functions.

Elsewhere, protest movements blazed as never before. A GI resistance groundswell appeared, on the crest of which was the well-publicized mutiny trial of the "Presidio Twenty-Seven" for a sit-down protest at the San Francisco base, but which also included GI protests at more than a dozen army camps, the establishment of coffeehouses and GI newspapers (at least nineteen by June) in many of the basic-training towns, the development of campus and church sanctuaries for AWOL and deserting soldiers, and a 25 percent increase in the armed forces desertion rate over the previous year. The black and chicano movement took on new and more militant forms, especially on the campuses, where more than half the protests were led by blacks for black causes, but also off the campuses, with the emergence of the Black Panther Party on the national scene as an important influence both among ghetto blacks and radical whites, the growth of the Young Lords Organization in Chicago and New York, and the formation of the League of Revolutionary Black Workers among dissident blacks in the automobile plants of Detroit. Militance moved downward into the high schools, with 60 percent of secondary-school principals reporting student protests, an estimated two thousand demonstrations taking place from November to May, and radical high-school unions being formed in many of the larger cities of the country. And accompanying all this, a myriad of uncategorizable actions of the growing American left: street-fighting in Washington, Madison, Berkeley, a massive antiwar march on April 15 of 150,000 people in fifty cities from Washington to Pasadena, women's groups going after Wall Street, *Playboy* magazine, the New York City Marriage Bureau, and a dozen other targets, the spread of underground newspapers to more than a hundred cities, and the continuing growth of communes, collectives, and "free schools" across the land.

With it all, violence, political violence, escalated still another notch. There were at least eighty-four bombings, attempted bombings, and arson incidents on college campuses in the first six months of 1969, twice as many as in the fall, and another twenty-seven bombings and attempts in the nation's high schools. Total property damage in the nation's schools and college—"trashing," incidental wreckage, and vandalism, in addition to building destruction—amounted to $8,946,972 in the first eight months of the year, according to the American Insurance Association. In addition there were ten other major bombing incidents at off-campus targets associated with the white left; the most spectacular was a series of explosions in Denver from January 20 to 28 destroying four electric transmission towers of the Colorado Public Service Company, for which a federal grand jury indicted Denver SDS activist Cameron David Bishop and the FBI placed him on its ten-most-wanted list, a distinction which Bishop honored by going, and subsequently remaining, underground. There was no mistake: violence had become a real part of the lexicon of American left-wing politics.

SDS—SDS as catalyst, as progenitor—had clearly done its job well: protest was percolating into every part of the porous republic. But SDS—SDS the ongoing organization, the national presence—was no longer under any illusions that this meant its message was sweeping the country. It is true that the continual expressions of activism throughout the spring were encouraging signs that the left was on the move, and *New Left Notes* could be forgiven its Beatleoid jubilance in labeling its roundups of campus actions, "We made the news today, oh boy!" But as the national leadership worked itself out of the dark days of that winter, there was none of that earlier "optimism and aggressiveness," none of the hubristic gusto of "No class today, no ruling class tomorrow." The fall's multiplicity of troubles—infighting, PL factionalism, distance, repression—had produced a kind of bitter realism about what it is like to wage a serious war in the grown-up world of power. The people at the top levels of the organization no longer had the sense that the revolution was going to happen by itself, just because it was right—if it was going to come it would take a new and even more sustained effort, a new seriousness.

For the national leadership, the new seriousness meant a new way of operating, of confronting power, and it took the form of a search for a new discipline, new ideology, and new allies.

Discipline meant primarily that the NO would try at last to establish in the organization the principles of "collective leadership" at the top and "cadre responsibility" in the ranks, the sort of things people had been talking about ever since Greg Calvert's down-with-participatory-democracy article in December 1967. The NO began to take itself seriously as a "national collective," working out "collective positions" to which all leaders were expected to adhere, gathering around it like-minded people while weeding out those with PL sympathies, becoming almost a sect unto itself—to the point where Staughton Lynd, in an unusual criticism, warned that "both PLP and the national collective are working to recruit a revolutionary *cadre* out of SDS no matter what the cost to SDS as an organically evolving revolutionary *movement.*" Regional organizations, too, were held on a fairly tight rein, with Regional Office staffers and the several dozen travelers chosen from people who generally shared NO politics and who generally attended the more or less monthly NIC meetings where RYM strategy was hammered out; ROs with clashing politics—for example, the office in Philadelphia run by SDSers who styled themselves the "Labor Committee"* —were thrown off the roster and deliberately ostracized; while those sharing the RYM perspective—for example, the groups in New York, Michi-

---

*The Labor Committee was begun at the June East Lansing convention by a group of Columbia radicals influenced by an older ex-Troskyist named Lynn Marcus; the two most prominent younger members were Tony Papert and Steve Fraser, both of whom had been kicked out of PL in that spring for their "heretical" views on the working class. In the fall the group spread out, forming separate labor committees within SDS chapters in Philadelphia, Ithaca, Boston, Chicago, and the West Coast in addition to the central cell in New York. For a while the Labor Committee was tolerated, especially because it pushed a pro-working-class line within SDS in opposition to what it regarded as the mistaken ideology of PL and its "economism," or concentration on narrowly economic issues. But the New York group developed serious differences in the fall with the actionist leadership at Columbia SDS—chiefly over the Labor Committee's support for New York City school teachers on strike against community control of schools in black neighborhoods—and it was kicked out of the chapter, a move reaffirmed both by a regional meeting and the December National Council meeting. The Labor Committee continued to function, however, still calling itself part of SDS on the grounds that SDS was a nonexclusionary organization and the expulsion therefore invalid.

gan, Ohio, Washington, and Chicago—were allowed a considerable degree of autonomy and given whatever largesse in terms of
money, speakers, and literature the NO could afford.*

At the same time the theoretically inclined leadership—
people like Les Coleman, Don Hammerquist, Noel Ignatin,
Howie Machtinger, and Jim Mellen—set to work to fashion
the RYM ideas into a serious ideology that would both attract
militant students and dispel the PL challenge. The best expression of their work is found in a paper written by Bill Ayers
and Jim Mellen and passed by the National Council meeting in
March, a skillful refinement of the original Klonsky article.
The focus on youth, especially working-class youth, was still
central: "It is clear that SDS must begin to consciously transform itself from a student movement into a working class
youth movement . . . by emphasizing the commonality of the
oppression and struggles of youth, and by making these struggles class conscious." But to it were added two crucial exten-
sions, alliances with the black liberationists—"To recognize the
vanguard character of the black liberation struggle means to
recognize its importance to the 'white' movement"—and with
the Third World—"All our actions must flow from our identity as part of an international struggle against U.S. imperialism." And to make any of this serious, to transform SDS into
something that really could lead a revolutionary movement,
what was necessary was a commitment to discipline—

> In order for SDS to succeed at this task it will take tremendous
> self-consciousness and discipline from the membership. . . . Through
> collective political experience and study, cadre can be developed
> who can bring these things to SDS.

—and a dedication to action:

> The reactionary nature of pacifism, the need for armed struggle as
> the only road to revolution [are] essential truths which were not
> predominant within our movement in the past. . . . We [must]
> recognize the urgency of fighting white supremacy by building the
> material strength of the white movement to be a conscious, organ-

---

*The Washington RO, for reasons never explained, even went so far as to get
itself incorporated (the officers were Hank Topper, Andrew St. John, and Cathy
Wilkerson), carrying the new seriousness to the point of capitalist protection.

ized, mobilized fighting force capable of giving real support to the black liberation struggle.

Weatherman was now only a step away.

Partly as a result of this RYM analysis, but also because it saw outside alliances as a practical way to build up strength against PL, the national leadership worked hard to establish ties with revolutionary groups beyond the student movement. Chiefly through Bernardine Dohrn, now operating at peak energy, SDS established links with and gave support to the black movement, GI resistance groups, Third World revolutionaries, high-school unions, and even labor unions and strikes. During a single month at the beginning of the year, for instance, *New Left Notes* in successive issues carried front pages devoted to the tenth anniversary of the Cuban revolution, interviews with two Fort Hood GIs ("Revolution in the Army"), a report on high-school organizing in Denver, and plans for joint SDS–Black Panther Party celebrations of Huey Newton's birthday. The SDS leadership gave particular attention to the Panthers, developing a symbiosis in which SDS gained a strong ally against PL and a great cachet among young white radicals, and the Panthers gained a valuable buffer against the severe campaign of repression now being visited upon them; as Illinois Panther leader Fred Hampton acknowledged, "We work very close with the SDS, and they help us out in many ways, and we try to help them out in as many ways as we can." In fact SDS passed a special resolution at the March NC citing the Black Panther Party as "the vanguard force" in the black liberation movement, pledging its backing for the party and its "essentially correct program," and establishing local "defense committees" for money and propaganda in support of Panthers being jailed and tried. Internationally, SDS made ties with European student movements (it helped sponsor a trip to this country by German SDS leader Karl Wolff, who made a certain splash by walking out of a Congressional hearing in the middle of his testimony), with Vietnamese groups in both Paris and Hanoi (Dohrn had struck up several close friendships with Vietnamese women during a trip to Europe in the fall, giving one a ring from her own finger as a gesture of comradeship), and with the Arab guerrillas in the Middle East (Sue Eanet visited leaders of Al Fatah in the

spring and wrote an adulatory three-part account of the "Pales-
tinian liberation struggle" in *New Left Notes*).* But by far the
most important international turn was toward Cuba, to which
RYM adherents looked for inspiration and where SDS sent an
official delegation in honor of the tenth anniversary of the revolution in January; this visit in turn laid the groundwork for a scheme
to send Movement people to Cuba to cut sugar cane for the 1970
harvest, a project which eventually evolved into the Venceremos
Brigade, one of the most imaginative enterprises ever undertaken
by the American left.†

The national leadership, then, was clearly putting, or trying
to put, SDS through some major changes, as significant as anything in the organization's history. But whether it knew it or not,
it was fighting a battle not only against time but against power.

Power: in the end it came to that. Not with reform, when

---

*This last position received a good deal of flak from Jewish SDSers, several of
whom wrote to the paper with strangulating outrage. But as near as one can
figure out, "Jewish consciousness" was not high among SDSers or student activists generally, who were more likely simply to ignore their Jewish heritage or,
if committed revolutionaries, discard it as "bourgeois" baggage. It has been
estimated that no more than 5 percent of the Jewish college enrollment of 350,000
was involved in the New Left in 1969 (*New York Times Magazine,* June 15, 1969);
of the eleven national officers of SDS at this point, only two were Jewish (and
Dohrn half-Jewish). This suggests a change in the character of the organization's
leadership from the earlier days, as it spread out across the country from its
original Eastern strongholds.

†SDS was instrumental in creating the Venceremos Brigade during these
months. SDSers Julie Nichamin and Brian Murphy worked out the original
arrangements with the Cuban government; Bernardine Dohrn devoted considerable time during the spring organizing it at the Chicago end; and the initial
National Executive Committee of the Brigade included SDSers Karen Ashley of
the New York Regional Office, Arlene Eisen Bergman of the *Movement,* Gerry
Long of Chicago Newsreel, Connie Ullman (Long's wife) of the NO staff, and
Allen Young of Liberation News Service, in addition to Nichamin. Other SDSers
who played a leading role in the Brigade as it developed over the spring and
summer were Amy Ansara (Cambridge), John Buttney (Denver), Howie Emmer
and Rick Erickson (both from Kent State), John Fuerst (Wisconsin), Phoebe
Hirsch (Chicago), Jim Jacobs (REP), Mike Klonsky, Howard Machtinger, and
Diana Oughton. Ultimately SDS's own internal problems kept it from playing
a major role as an organization in the final working out of the project, but SDSers
were numerous among the 216 volunteers who made the first trip to Cuba in
November of 1969. The Brigade continued in operation well after SDS's demise,
sending three more contingents of several hundred Americans by the beginning
of 1972.

suasion and reason can suffice, not even with resistance, when fear and drama can avail—but with revolution, power is ultimate.

Aroused, the administrations of most institutions of higher education proved that they had, and were willing to use, considerable power to resist any significant alteration in their ways of governance or the character of their schools. Despite the enormous number of protests during these months, it appears that those which demanded major changes were successful less than 10 percent of the time, and even then the concessions were made without real shifts in the balance of power, as for example with the discontinuance of ROTC (twelve schools dropped it or made it extracurricular, seventy-seven granted lesser changes, usually making it voluntary). Worse than that. Some of the most ambitious protests, into which considerable time, money, effort, prestige, and hope were poured, were blunted or defeated outright, leaving SDS and its campus allies disillusioned and disarrayed. At Stanford, where after a long, carefully researched, and occasionally violent campaign SDS succeded in forcing the university to sell its $58-million-a-year defense research institute, it discovered that the facility was quickly bought up by others and simply carried on its business of war-making under a different management. At Berkeley, Wisconsin, Columbia, Michigan State, Kent State, Colorado, Chicago—the list could go on—demonstrations by SDS groups, for all their storm and publicity, ran up against intransigent administrations, immovable faculties, and resistant governments, ultimately producing factional splits, mistakes, exhaustion, and usually defeat.

The San Francisco State strike was perhaps the paradigm, a stark lesson in the dynamics of power. The students had the moral power of their cause against institutional racism and against police brutality, the support of a faculty union local which also went on strike, an organization which united blacks, chicanos, white radicals, and others under a single banner, and the courage and commitment of those who promised to wage a protracted guerrilla-style "war of the flea." Against this the university administration, led by a megalomaniacal S. I. Hayakawa and supported by a hard-line public, used the full power of the police (more than 700 arrests, countless beatings, and daily occupation of the campus), the courts (injunctions against demonstrations, costly trials, a legal embargo on the use of student funds by students), and its own authority (suspension of student publications, canceling of experimental courses, threats of dismissal for striking teachers). After nearly four months of battle, the strikers could no longer resist: they had been unable to build strong community support for their cause (despite major attempts in black areas and alliances with striking workers in nearby Richmond), they had been unable to interest the predominantly white student body in what was seen as a black issue hardly important enough to jeopardize their upward-mobile education, and they began to suffer fatigue (who, after all, thought it was going to take *this* long?), dissension, power plays, defections, and confusion in the ranks. Finally the teachers broke ranks and returned to classes, and the students reluctantly agreed to negotiations, out of which they wrested only the most face-saving crumbs and Hayakawa emerged a national hero. Todd Gitlin, who was there through it all, noted that "the strike, a didactic morality play with a cast of thousands, teaches that the enemy is not the police, not red tape, not fumbling administrators, but the State itself." And that in the war of the flea, the State owns the fly swatters.

Or, as the SDSers at the University of Chicago put it, after deciding to leave a building they had occupied for sixteen days without winning a single demand or realizing a single victory: "There will be no rational discourse between those with power and those with none."

And that was the nub of it: SDS was essentially without power, at least power sufficient for its revolution. True, the weapons it had held in the past—the capacity for disruption, unfavorable publicity, and embarrassment, for engendering guilt and awakening consciences, for creating sympathy, outrage, support, and commitment—were still at hand to be sure, but they were no longer adequate when the war to be waged was for the total dislocation of the society. And the one weapon SDS needed on its side above all others, the one without which political action of any kind was impossible, was the support of the students themselves, at least the important minds and talents among them, at least enough to make a visible and sustained campaign of protest. This, however, was a weapon slipping slowly from the SDS grasp. SDS was losing its campus base.

Part of the problem was a growing change in SDS's style. The paranoid temperament that had emerged in many chapters in the fall developed still further in the spring—not without cause, it should be added—often leading to a confusion of priorities and a paralysis of action: "Always looking over our shoulders," Todd Gitlin wrote in February, "we risk stumbling over our feet." Moreover, a sense of hardness and self-importance descended upon many who felt themselves to be revolutionary, all too often growing into a dogmatism, an impatient righteousness that scorned the winning of converts, even at the cost of making ene-mies. Seriousness hung like cigarette smoke over every gathering, and more-revolutionary-than-thou poses were struck as often as matches. Even the vaunted and sometimes exciting SDS demon-strations themselves as likely as not turned into harangues by the rebel rousers against their fellow students for their "narrow class interests" or "bourgeois values," or else drew unwary demonstra-tors into actions and politics beyond their comprehension, a pro-cess which SDSers saw as radicalizing but many others regarded as manipulation. A fair example of the deficiencies of this style is seen in this account (from someone sympathetic to SDS) of what happened at Columbia during this spring:

> SDS failed for a large number of reasons. . . . SDS isolated itself by *appearing* to be manipulative and by not dealing with the issue which primarily concerned students: restructuring . . . it *appeared* to be disrupting for disruption's sake. It continued to opt away from dealing with those issues which directly affected students' lives such as restructuring and the draft. (Restructuring may be a misleading issue and students may be naive; but at times in order to lead and expose it may be necessary to particpate [*sic*] in what one finds stupid. SDS was unable to do this, I fear, because many of its members were more concerned with appearing to be radical than with succeeding as radicals.) SDS members continued to talk in a rhetoric which many students saw as cant, irrelevant, and intellectu-ally embarrassing. . . . On top of everything else, SDS tended to be boring. It seemed to be repeating itself and was very predicta-ble. . . .
>
> The right mood was absent this spring, given that fact it might have been advisable to wait. But SDS did not wait. It didn't because it felt compelled to act in some way and disruption seemed the only course. . . .

SDS did not have to be contained; it contained itself. Buildings may have been occupied, but the normal processes of the university went on. As last year's events demonstrated, if power is in the people and you have the people, you can shut down an institution with very little force.

But without the people you are without the power.

Part of SDS's problem, too, lay with its failure to transmit its political ideas to large masses of students as it went headlong into revolution—it failed to make potential recruits or even sympathizers out of the liberals, and, worse, it failed to make true radicals, sophisticated connections-makers, out of the militants. Neither the disciplined style nor the RYM ideology of the national collective seemed to attract any great following on the campuses, and the kinds of political positions which surrounded them must have confused vast numbers of students (even SDSers) and repelled still others. SDS papers and pamphlets talked of "armed struggle," "disciplined cadre," "white fighting force," and the need for "a communist party that can guide this movement to victory"; SDS leaders and publications quoted Mao and Lenin and Ho Chi Minh more regularly than *Jenminh Jih Pao,* and a few of them even sought to say a few good words for Stalin;* SDSers even leveled

---

*Mike Klonsky, at a meeting in Atlanta, approvingly quoted from Stalin's essay on nationalities, a pre-Revolution work and written under Lenin's influence, but Stalin nonetheless. (See *Spartacist,* August-September 1969.) And a group close to SDS in California put out a paper explicitly defending Stalin: "Since the imperialists and their ideological running dogs, the Trotskyites, have not spared themselves in abuse of Stalin, since Khrushchev and his successors have found it necessary to outdo even the imperialists in the castigation of Stalin, in order to pull off their accommodation to imperialism and their initiation of capitalist restoration; we have the tendency to want to defend him, and so do. . . . We should judge Stalin by Marxist (materialist) and (working) class standards, rather than by the bourgeois criteria of his imperialist, Trotskyite, and revisionist assailants." ("The Red Papers," by three members of the Bay Area Revolutionary Union, Bob Avakian, Bruce Franklin, and Steve Hamilton; Avakian and Franklin had been SDS organizers in Bay Area campuses, Hamilton a part of the West Coast Resistance in its early days.) To be fair, however, it should be pointed out that other SDSers in good revolutionary standing criticized Stalin and even warned against uncritical "Stalinism" in the organization—as for example a letter from Christopher Hobson in *New Left Notes* which took pains to point out that the paper's recent articles on Greece, Cuba, and North Vietnam displayed "blindness to Stalinism as a general type" and made "one wonder about the conception of Socialism held by *NLN* and the National Office."

attacks against such old standbys as participatory democracy: Dohrn complained that it only led to meetings "where struggle is not allowed under the guise of 'respect for one another' and anti-authoritarianism" and Chicago SDSer Christopher Hobson added that it was in practice a "classless and non-revolutionary" concept. And with this went as if inevitably an increasingly sterile rhetoric, phrases borrowed from long-forgotten sectarian debates of middle Europe and pamphlets written when Lenin was young: "class struggle," "enslaved masses," "running dogs," "people's war," "principal contradiction," "exploitation of labor," "lackeys of the ruling class." Carl Oglesby, as sophisticated and committed a person as anyone in SDS, tells what effect SDS's new political hardness had upon him:

> For a long time I was baffled. Last fall [1968] the word began to reach me: It was being said that I had "bad politics." How could *that* be, I wondered, since I thought I had no politics at all. But by winter I conceded the point: no politics was the same as bad politics. So there followed a time in which I experimented with only the "mass line." Could Klonsky and Coleman be right? It didn't come to much. My mind and my instincts only became adversaries. By spring I had to deactivate, couldn't function, had to float. What I know now is that this did not happen to me alone. On every quarter of the white Left, high and low, the attempt to reduce the New Left's inchoate vision to the Old Left's perfected remembrance has produced a layer of bewilderment and demoralization which no cop with his club or senator with his committee could ever have induced.

Thus across the entire political spectrum of the campus, disenchantment with, and hostility to, SDS began to grow as never before. Conservative groups at many schools felt free for the first time to form their own groups in explicit opposition to SDS without general disapprobation, and at a number of schools—Cornell, Kent State, Columbia, Brooklyn, Berkeley, and Florida among them—open fights broke out between the two. Moderate students denounced SDS in a way that would have been unthinkable just two years earlier, and a certain fraternity-style chic became attached to making fun of SDSers and their troubles; for example, a cartoon booklet from Northwestern called "New Laugh Notes" (subtitled "Let the *Right* People Decide") pictured a busty Bernardine Dohrn lolling around the NO saying, "Let's raise the dues, I want to go to the Riviera," and showed a PLer hanging by a rope from a tree while SDSers beneath say, "Tomorrow we will give him a fair trial." And in fact SDS was no longer even the dominant leader of the militant students who were out doing the protesting. According to one poll of 232 major campuses during the spring,

> ... the striking finding about white student protests is that they were not dominated by the New Left. Students for a Democratic Society (SDS) and other organizations with identifiably radical views, commitments, and rhetoric, were active in less than half of the white protests, and in only 28 percent of all protests.

Nor was SDS succeeding, despite all the rhetoric, in establishing constituencies elsewhere, in building a new base among the "revolutionary youth" in the high schools, the army camps, and the factories to take the place of the crumbling campus base.

SDSers concentrated on high-school organizing as never before, and in such cities as New York, Los Angeles, San Francisco, Denver, Chicago, and Boston this became a high-priority program both for regional staffs and college chapters. And there is no question that SDS had an impact, both in bringing some of the new perspectives of the sixties into out-of-the-way schools where radicalism had never touched before and in providing assistance, information, and models in those schools where some of the students were already on the move. SDS organizers at this point, however, had as hard a time getting through to the high-school population as they did to the college one. A New York high-school activist complained:

> One SDSer went to the Seward Park Student Union meetings. She went to all their meetings. At first she just spoke a little and then more and more until she was running them. Before long the group was broken up and splitting into factions. This chick from the regional office of SDS just went in there and split them up. . . .

And:

> Brooklyn College SDS asked if they could send somebody to one of our meetings to present a proposal. We agreed and five Brooklyn College SDS kids came to the meeting. They got into a two-hour discussion among themselves about the definition of what a working

class is. They tied up the whole meeting and they didn't give a shit about what the kids there thought. . . .

It didn't take long for high-schoolers to react to this kind of "organizing": the response described by a high-school student in Madison, Wisconsin, seems to have been typical:

> Whenever SDS has come in to high schools we've either said, okay, you can help us in this way: give us your printing press and give us some paper, and that is it; or you can help us by giving us this information and getting us these pamphlets that we want. But we've stopped them coming into the high school and organizing for their own, and we've stopped them coming and speaking for the most part. We've kept them out of high schools because we don't want them there. The SDS of late hasn't been able to relate to high schools and many times they don't relate to their own ideas. They have certain ways of going about things, and it relates to college life and the college system, but it doesn't apply for high school.

As a result, SDS not only failed to attract significant numbers of those "working-class kids" who were regarded as essential for the Revolutionary Youth Movement, but it didn't even win over many of those militant students already in motion.

The army camps proved to be similarly unfertile ground for SDS. In the first place, few SDSers were really prepared to go into the army itself, where any serious organizing would have to be done, and so when GIs felt the need to organize some kind of national group they chose their own forms—the Movement for a Democratic Military, for example, and the American Serviceman's Union—rather than appending themselves to SDS and what they saw as a bunch of college kids. In the second place, the GIs, like the high-schoolers, were concerned with far different issues than the SDSers: their complaints stemmed from the immediate stifling conditions of their servitude, not the grander injustices of capitalism, and their oppositon to the war in Vietnam sprang from somewhat more concrete and frightening considerations than a theoretical opposition to imperialism. SDSers were instrumental in starting the Fort Dix Coffeehouse in New Jersey* and working with other GI coffeehouses in Texas, South Carolina,

*They included Fred Bogardus, a Princeton SDSer, Josephine Duke, from Columbia, Corinna Fales, a Newark ERAP veteran, Samuel Karp, a former Boston draft-resistance organizer, and Bob Tomashevsky, a long-time New York SDSer.

and Washington, and the NO put out a handsome fifty-page booklet on "GI counseling" edited by New England traveler Russ
Neufeld and intended for use by chapters near army bases. But for
the most part SDSers regarded the world on the other side of the
barracks gate as a conquered province.

Nor were the RYM practitioners able to make any significant
connections with young factory workers, despite considerable
rhetoric, and in some cases considerable work, in that direction.
SDSers tried to forge ties with workers through such techniques
as strike support in a dozen cities, primarily Boston, Chicago, Los
Angeles, New York, and San Diego, but though their help was
welcomed on the picket lines little was done in the way of establishing lasting relationships and alliances. SDSers from several
campuses in San Francisco, for example, were active in supporting
a union stike against Standard Oil in Richmond, picketing, leafleting, organizing campus boycotts, and passing a resolution for a
national Standard Oil boycott at the March National Council; the
strikers were responsive and union leaders grateful—"Student
support," the union head acknowledged in a *New Left Notes*
interview, "had a tremendous effect"—but when the workers settled and went back to work very little contact remained. Similarly
in Mahwah, New Jersey, where SDSers (chiefly from Columbia,
the New York RO, and Rutgers) joined a black wildcat strike at
a Ford assembly plant and helped to force the management into
a settlement, little common ground remained when the strike was
over, and no lasting student-worker contacts were established. All
that talk about how "our struggles must be integrated into the
struggles of working people" proved very hard to realize in
practice.

Campus support eroding, "revolutionary youth" unmoved—
and SDS was even losing some of the people who had heretofore
been in or close to the organization, committed radicals whose
numbers and energy had proved so helpful in the past. The most
serious defections came from the ranks of the women and the
alumni.

The separatist trend among SDS women grew considerably
stronger through the spring, despite the position of the December
National Council, as women increasingly felt that SDS's formal

acceptance of women's liberation was still unmatched by practice within the organization even after more than two years:

> We were still the movement secretaries and the shit-workers; we served the food, prepared the mailings and made the best posters; we were the earth mothers and the sex-objects for the movement men. We were the free movement "chicks"—free to screw any man who demanded it, or if we chose not to—free to be called hung-up, middle class and up-tight. We were free to keep quiet at meetings —or if we chose not to, we were free to speak in men's terms. . . . We found ourselves unable to influence the direction and scope of projects. We were dependent on the male elite for direction and recognition.

And if there was even one chapter which could put out a pamphlet, such as the one which appeared this spring saying, "The system is like a woman; you have to fuck it to make it change," then obviously SDS was not getting the message.

A variety of radical women's groups were now taking shape outside of SDS—the Feminists, Radical Feminists, Bread and Roses, Redstockings, WITCH—and their appeal to their SDS sisters was infectious: "You're always sucking off *other* people's oppression—why don't you dig your own?" Women indeed seemed to be looking for a place to talk about their own problems, find strength from other women, learn that their private agonies were in fact shared by others, and come to make connections between their individual oppression and the political system beyond: in short, looking more for a 1962-style SDS than the 1969 model. For a while the women's caucuses within SDS chapters served this purpose, but they were greeted with increasing hostility and insults, not just from the men who felt themselves threatened but also from the revolutionary elite of the organization who challenged their personalistic politics; as Bernardine Dohrn herself wrote in March:

> Most of the women's groups are bourgeois, unconscious or unconcerned with class struggle and the exploitation of working class women, and chauvinist concerning the oppression of black and brown women. . . . These women are flailing at their own middle class images. To focus only on sexual exploitation and the tyranny of consumption does not develop a mass under-

standing of the causes of oppression, and it does not accurately point at the enemy.

But here again the SDS leadership showed itself distant from much of the SDS membership, a gap which self-righteousness and invective did very little to close. More and more the feminists in SDS began to "get off the treadmill," form their own organizations, hold their own marches, and attend their own conventions, relating to SDS less and less.

As for the alumni, they partook of the movemental activism of the spring, but increasingly with organizations of their own making and in directions of their own choosing. SDS's evolving program simply had no place for the large number of alumni who had gone on, inevitably, to such "middle-class" jobs as teaching, social work, and journalism—and in fact the RYM ideology was set in terms which specifically scorned such professions as irredeemably "bourgeois." Ex-student radicals were therefore faced with the choice of supporting the Movement from the sidelines— hence the growing involvement in radical propaganda, underground newspapers, Newsreel, left research groups, printing shops, and the like—or getting on with the business of changing their own circumstances—hence the New University Conference, the proliferating "radical caucuses" within academic associations, the city-wide coalitions of professionals on the model of New York's Movement for a Democratic Society, and independent *ad hoc* groups like the Honeywell Project in Minneapolis and the Conservation Research and Action Project in Wisconsin.* SDS

---

*Here is a partial—very partial—roster of graduate SDSers in radical work at that time. Many worked on Movement propaganda: publications like the *Old Mole* in Cambridge (with Nick Egleson, Vernon Grizzard), the *Movement* in San Francisco (Arlene Eisen Bergman and Terry Cannon, with Mike James and Mike Davis in other bureaus), *RAT* in New York (Jeff Shero), the *Rag* in Austin (Thorne Dreyer); printing centers like the New England Free Press (Don McKelvey); *Leviathan* in New York and San Francisco (Kathy McAfee, Marge Piercy on staff, and Al Haber, Mike Goldfield, Ken Cloke as contributing editors); *Radical America* in Madison—still "An SDS Journal of American Radicalism" (Paul Buhle); and the *Guardian* (Carl Davidson and Peter Henig on staff, Clark Kissinger in charge of the Chicago bureau, Lee Webb and Marilyn Salzman Webb as the Washington bureau, and regular contributions from Todd Gitlin, Michael Klare, and Karen Wald). Broad-based organizing groups existed in numerous cities, among them the Union of Organizers in Chicago (with participation from Paul Booth, Mike Goldfield, Clark Kissinger, Staughton Lynd, Mel

might have found in these alumni an invaluable lode—they were people whose commitment to postgraduate radicalism was proven beyond a doubt, people whose politics was generally now just as "revolutionary" as the current SDSers,* and people who were often working in areas (high schools, welfare offices, hospitals) where they had intimate contact with just those poor, black, and working-class youth that the SDS leadership theoretically wanted to reach. Yet with the exception of a few joint conferences in smaller cities and occasional cooperative demonstrations, current SDSers made little effort to tap this lode and align with those who should have been their natural allies; far more often they were heard to speak of those "liberals" in NUC or those "wimps" at NACLA.

How ironic it all was: at precisely the time of the greatest explosion of the American left in all of the decade, SDS, its leading organization by every index—size, fame, geographical scope, energy—was gradually but unmistakably isolating and diminishing itself, losing its student constituency, its women, its alumni, failing to connect with the high schools, the soldiers, the workers. The SDS revolutionaries were on the barricades, but they had forgotten to look behind: their troops were no longer following.

McDonald, Sue Munaker, and Richie Rothstein) and the Movement for a Democratic Society in New York (Ted Gold, Ted Kaptchuk). On the academic side, there was NUC (Rothstein took over from Bob Ross as national secretary in June), and the Union for Radical Political Economics (founded by Barry Bluestone, Michael Zweig, and Al Haber). Tom Hayden and Todd Gitlin were working in the Bay Area, writing and organizing, the former close to the Bay Area Radical Union, the latter involved in the San Francisco State strike. Greg Calvert and Bob Pardun were both in Texas, still active in the Movement—the former had helped to establish a legal defense center for Texas radicals, and the latter was trying working-class organizing. Kim Moody and Steve Kindred were working for the International Socialists.

*For example, the preamble which NUC adopted at its first formal convention in June 1969 read: "The New University Conference is a national organization of radicals who work in, around, and in spite of, institutions of higher education. We are committed to struggle politically to create a new, American form of socialism and to replace an educational and social system that is an instrument of class, sexual, and racial oppression with one that belongs to the people." Or the statement to the Movement from Vernon Grizzard, in June: "Our goal should be to create revolutionary organizations based on a shared commitment to communism which can take into account an individual's strengths and weaknesses without constantly calling into question his ego." (*Liberation*, June 1969.)

As it turned itself into a political collective and engulfed itself
in revolutionary theories, the National Office functioned less and
less well as a secretariat for SDS. Correspondence and literature
orders piled up in boxes and pigeonholes became stuffed with
unanswered letters: somehow the minutiae of bureaucracy seemed
an insignificant contribution to the revolution. (Bernardine Dohrn
was apparently the most regular letter writer, though she showed a
notable disinclination to respond to the dozens of requests from
various gasoline companies for immediate payment on her numerous credit cards.) *New Left Notes* still came out regularly—now
blessed with another logo, this one with the clenched fist of revolution prominently displayed and the slogan ALL POWER TO THE
PEOPLE supplanting the three-year-old LET THE PEOPLE DECIDE—
but most other literature was hopelessly backlogged and even the
perennial "sds" pin was out of stock. The office itself began to
disintegrate, and landlord John Rossen, disenchanted both pro-
prietarily and politically (he shared few of the perspectives of the
RYM people), remembers that it became "a mess, an incredible
mess—they used the place like a garbage dump": books and clothes
everywhere, tattered signs and posters on the wall (one, a picture of
Christ with a rifle, was labeled "Dig It!"), dirt piling up on the floor,
broken furniture, malodorous unmade beds in the back room,
papers and pamphlets littering every horizontal surface.

It is very doubtful that any records were being kept about
anything any more—certainly none have survived—and so there
is no way of knowing with any accuracy the number of chapters
or national members. Mike Klonsky used the figure of 100,000
campus members when talking to the press, but there's no clue as
to how he arrived at that; other estimates ranged from 30,000,
according to one government committee, to 70,000, according to
the Associated Press, but both those are undoubtedly sheer
guesses, too. There is one source for the number of extant chapters, the Senate Committee on Government Operations, which
listed 304 chapters as of June—and since its operatives were said
to be investigating out in the field for more than a year, there is
some chance that the figure is approximately correct.* In any case,

*The list runs alphabetically by states. (The Senate Committee claimed it had
found 317 chapters, but it apparently didn't add very well—it listed only 304.)
Alabama: Alabama, Auburn; Arizona: Arizona, Arizona State (Phoenix,

Tempe); California: California Concordia, California State (Fullerton, Hayward, Long Beach, Los Angeles, Thornton, San Bernardino), Chico State, City College of San Francisco, Claremont, Cypress, East Los Angeles, El Camino, Fresno State, Harrett, Laney, Los Angeles City, Los Angeles Valley, Mt. San Antonia, Sacramento State, San Diego State, San Fernando State, San Francisco State, San Jose State, Santa Clara, Scripps, Southern California, Stanford, University of California (Berkeley, Davis, Irvine, Los Angeles, Santa Barbara); Colorado: Colorado College, Colorado State College, Colorado State University, Colorado University, Denver, Metropolitan State, Temple Buell, Wasson; Connecticut: Bridgeport, Connecticut, Hartford, Trinity, Wesleyan, Yale; Delaware: Delaware; Florida: Florida, Florida State, Florida Presbyterian, Miami-Dade, New College, Southern Florida, University of Miami; Georgia: Augusta, Emory, Georgia, Georgia State; Hawaii: Hawaii; Illinois: Bradley, Chicago, Chicago City, Eastern Illinois, George Williams, Hank Williams Chapter (Chicago), Illinois (Champaign-Urbana, Chicago Circle), Illinois Institute of Technology, Illinois State, Lake Forest, Loyola, MacMurray, Northeastern State, Northern Illinois, Northwestern, Roosevelt, Shimer, Southern Illinois; Indiana: DePauw, Indiana (Bloomington, South Bend), Indiana State, Notre Dame, Purdue; Iowa: Coe, Dubuque, Grinnell, Iowa, Iowa State, Luther, Northern Iowa, Parsons; Kansas: Kansas, Washburn, Wichita State; Kentucky: Kentucky; Louisiana: Fortier High School, Louisiana State, Loyola, McDonough High School, Movement for a Democratic Society (New Orleans), Northwestern Louisiana State, Tulane, West Jefferson High School; Maine: Maine; Maryland: Baltimore, Baltimore Junior College, Catonsville, Essex, Goucher, Johns Hopkins, Maryland (Catonsville, College Park), Towson State, Washington; Massachusetts: Assumption, Boston College, Boston State, Boston University, Brandeis, Brookline High School, Clark, Harvard/Radcliffe, Holy Cross, Massachusetts, Massachusetts Bay, MIT, New England Regional Office (Cambridge), Northeastern, Simmons, Smith, Tufts; Michigan: Central Michigan, Detroit, Eastern Michigan, Grand Valley State, Michigan, Michigan State, Muskegon County, Oakland, Wayne State, Western Michigan; Minnesota: Mankato State, Minnesota, St. Cloud, St. Olaf, Winona State; Mississippi: Mississippi State; Missouri: Fontbonne, Missouri (Columbia, Kansas City), Park, Southeast Missouri State, St. Louis, Washington University; Montana: Montana , Montana State; Nebraska: Nebraska; Nevada: Nevada; New Hampshire: Dartmouth, Franconia, New Hampshire, Plymouth State; New Jersey: Montclair State, Princeton, Rutgers (Newark, New Brunswick), St. Peters; New Mexico: Highlands, New Mexico; New York: Alfred, Brooklyn, *CAW* magazine, City College, Colgate, Columbia, Cornell, C.W. Post, Fordham, Harpur, Kingsborough, Long Island, Manhattanville, Movement for a Democratic Society (New York), Nassau, New Rochelle, New School for Social Research, New York Community, New York University (uptown, downtown), Niagara Regional Office (Syracuse), Orange County, Pace, Queens, Rochester, Sarah Lawrence, Siena, Skidmore, State College (Buffalo, Cortland, New Paltz, Oneonta), State University (Albany, Binghamton, Buffalo, Stony Brook), Syracuse, Up Against the Wall Motherfucker, Vassar, Wagner; North Carolina: Duke, North Carolina; Ohio: Antioch, Bowling Green, Case Western, Cleveland Draft Resistance Union, Cleveland State, Cuyahoga, Hiram, John Carroll, Kent State, Kenyon, Movement for a Democratic Society (Cleveland), Oberlin, Ohio State, Xavier; Oklahoma: Oklahoma, Oklahoma State; Oregon: Oregon, Oregon State, Portland State, Reed; Pennsylvania: Bucknell,

all the evidence suggests that through splits, defections, alienation, and distance SDS was actually losing old chapters and members and not gaining new ones—for the first time in its history.

Financial woes seemed to be a bit worse now than usual, a reflection of diminishing support. Clearly the organization was operating very close to the chest: it had only $600 in the bank in February ("WE'RE BROKE—SEND MONEY," shouted *New Left Notes* in inch-high letters), still only $550 in May ("The bail money that we've been forced to put out recently, added to our regular expense, has put us in bad financial straits," said the paper then, somewhat more plaintively), and by the end of the year it had managed to work itself more than $3,000 into debt (bank deposits amounted to $112,443, withdrawals to $115,587, and somebody was stuck with rubber checks). It was this kind of existence that no doubt led Mike Klonsky, responding to a request from the California Department of Education for reprint rights to SDS's 1966 "High School Reform" pamphlet, to ask for the immediate payment of one million dollars plus the withdrawal of criminal charges against Eldridge Cleaver and students at Valley State College and the declaration of May 25 as "a school holiday in honor of the founding of SDS"; the California Department of Education was apparently not moved to respond to the offer.

There is no sure way to know where SDS's funds *were* coming from, because the NO took it as part of its internal security to withhold such information. Klonsky in public always said that

---

Bryn Mawr, Carnegie-Mellon, Dickinson, Duquesne, Franklin and Marshall, Lehigh, Pennsylvania, Penn State, Philadelphia, Pittsburgh, Point Park, Scranton, Swarthmore, Temple, Villanova; Rhode Island: Brown, Rhode Island; South Carolina: South Carolina; South Dakota: Northern State; Tennessee: Le-Moyne-Owen, Memphis State; Texas: Austin High School, East Texas State, Houston, Midwestern, North Texas State, Rice, San Jacinto, Southern Methodist, Southwest Regional Office (Dallas), Stephen F. Austin State, Texas, Texas A & M, Texas Tech, Trinity, West Texas State; Utah: Middleburg, Utah; Vermont: Castleton, Goddard, Middlebury; Virginia: Falls Church High School, Fairfax High School, Old Dominion, Virginia, Virginia Commonwealth; Washington: Seattle, Washington, Washington State, Western Washington State; Washington, District of Columbia: American, Georgetown, George Washington, Howard; West Virginia: Marshall, West Virginia; Wisconsin: Lawrence, Marquette, St. Norbert, Wisconsin (Madison, Milwaukee), Wisconsin State (La Crosse, Oshkosh, Whitewater); Wyoming: Wyoming.

the money came simply from the membership (dues were still $5 a year), and no less an observer than J. Edgar Hoover conceded in April that he figured "nearly 60 percent" of SDS's funds came from "contributions, dues, sales of literature, benefits, advertisements, and its publication and fund drives," with "the majority of gifts . . . in the $10 to $50 range." Some additional funds also came from other left organizations—Resist (with alumni Dick Flacks, Florence Howe, and Paul Lauter among its advisers), the Chicago Peace Council (which shared the Rossen building with SDS), and a new dummy corporation called Cambridge Iron and Steel (headed by SDS veterans Michael Ansara and Daniel Schechter) each gave several hundred dollars to SDS during the spring.* And some undoubtedly came in from those SDS leaders who were born far on the other side of the poverty line (among them Bill Ayers, Les Coleman, Chip Marshall, Diana Oughton, and Mark Rudd), whose parents either supported their political work or at least did not halt the influx of family funds because of it. Only this is sure: wherever the money came from, there was never enough of it.

Something of the spirit and the troubles of the NO is suggested by the symbolic adversity that was visited upon the offices in the early morning of May 12. Chicago police, responding to a report of a shooting at the SDS National Office which they said was phoned into them by an unidentified "Mr. Brown," barged up the stairs at 1608 West Madison and demanded to inspect the premises. Klonsky, doing some fast talking, had just about convinced them that there had been no shooting and that their investigation was unwanted, when a truckload of firemen descended on the office, having responded to *another* anonymous phone call saying there was a fire raging in the place. Both cops and firemen now wanted to get into the office and the staffers inside just as steadfastly wanted them to stay out. Klonsky, again acting as the

---

*Cambridge Iron and Steel was begun with $25,000 which Harvard SDSer Mike Ansara wangled out of liberal Boston businessman Ralph Hoagland; its purpose was to funnel money into various activities with the aim of building a broad adult movement on the left, especially in the Boston area. CIS opened its bank account in February and during the next few months is known to have given $400 to the New York SDS office, $2000 to Liberation News Service, $3000 to the *Old Mole,* $5000 to the *Guardian,* and a few hundred dollars each to SDSers Linda Gordon, Beverly Kane, Sue Parker, and Ansara himself.

voice of reason, suggested that the fire chief alone be allowed in to inspect the premises, which that official finally agreed to, and he had just entered the door when the rest of his crew suddenly barged in behind and started shoving the SDSers aside. The youths shoved back—they were perfectly convinced that the whole scheme was a "pig" plot to destroy the national headquarters and steal the files—and the cops immediately joined the melee, seizing the opportunity to hand it to the pesky troublemakers. Very quickly five SDSers were arrested—Klonsky, Coleman, and Tim McCarthy of the NO staff, Ed Jennings of the Chicago Circle chapter, and Dave Slavin from the New York Regional Office—and dragged off to jail, where they were held on $12,000 bail on charges of "battery on an officer," "interfering with a fireman," and "inciting mob action." The money was raised during the night and the five were released before morning, but there was now no longer any doubt in the minds of all those around the NO that serious repression was going to come down and that they were going to be in the thick of it. *New Left Notes* responded in rhetoric characteristic of the time:

> It is clear that until the power to control the institutions of this society is in the hands of the people, the people will never have justice or freedom.
> Power to the People!
> DEATH TO THE PIG!

In January of 1969 the Progressive Labor Party issued a series of formal statements setting forth its official stand on the questions of nationalism in general and "black nationalism" in particular. These statements, which formed one of the cornerstones of PL's future development, were regarded with such special importance that their presentation and discussion occupied 40 percent of all the articles (14 out of 35) in the party's theoretical journal, *PL,* during 1969. The PL position—incidentally, similar to the PL racism proposal passed at the Ann Arbor NC, both presumably having been established at the same time—was based on a theory that PL had been evolving for several years that "all nationalism is reactionary" because it is based on national identity rather than class identity; as applied to the American situation, it made the assumption that the identity of the black population was also something which could be called nationalism and therefore was similarly reactionary. The party announced:

> The ruling capitalist class urges on the workers a nationalist ideology to replace their loyalty to the international working class. . . . It is in the class interests of U.S. imperialists to promote nationalist ideas among workers since it diverts them from loyalty to their own class. Nationalism is a bourgeois idea, which infects workers and prevents them from winning their freedom from the capitalist class.

Thus the whole black "nationalist" movement was seen as a danger, within which the most dangerous groups were the two most visible, the Black Panthers and the black student associations. The Panthers "ignore the working-class demands . . . don't attempt to organize Black workers . . . helped to serve the interests of downtown by not joining the side of the people . . . have not stressed political study and development . . . have no class outlook and believe they are out to fight a war against white people in general . . . [are] giving no political leadership." The black student groups "don't have a working-class orientation . . . are limited to securing a better deal for themselves from the schools and from the ruling class . . . are not aimed at defeating the system," and their demands for black studies departments with black administrators are "false and dangerous . . . founded on the illusion that under capitalism the university can serve the needs of Black workers and students, and that students can see to it that the university serves Black people by joining the administration."

At the same time the Progressive Labor Party reiterated its stand against the government of North Vietnam and the "revisionist" National Liberation Front for having agreed to negotiations with the United States instead of continuing to wage an all-out war:

> The People's War has beaten the US military machine in Vietnam, the negotiations process is turning this victory into a defeat for the revolutionary forces in Vietnam and in the world. . . . US imperialism, with the cooperation of the Soviet Union and the north Vietnam leaders, will use negotiations to achieve its goal of keeping a troop concentration based in Vietnam. . . . Negotiations, whether in Cambodia or Disneyland, are a setback for people's war. . . . EVERYONE KNOWS THAT THE ONLY WAY SOCIALISM CAN BE WON IS BY DRIVING OUT THE OPPRESSOR. And

this is what the Vietnamese people were doing so well until the
revisionists in Moscow and Hanoi agreed to sell them out to US
imperialism.

Simultaneously it renewed its attack on Cuba, which for PL had
been in disfavor ever since 1966 when Castro had begun attacking
China for economic blackmail and China had reciprocated with
charges of "revisionism" for accepting Russian aid:

> What the people of Cuba participated in was a bourgeois democratic
> revolution. . . . Castro has misused the great confidence bestowed
> on him by the people. He has taken the people into alliance with the
> most reactionary forces on earth. His one-man paternalistic rule
> smacks more of feudalism than socialism . . . [Castro's] is a "social-
> ism" whose policy towards its working class ranges through four
> choices: bribe 'em, starve 'em, chain 'em, replace 'em.

Neither position, of course, sat well with the large majority of
students. But PL was never one to let popularity interfere with
dogma.

That's PL in theory. What of PL in practice?

Naturally enough, PL and worker-student alliance supporters on the campuses found themselves in an awkward position
when the new line on black nationalism and black studies came
down; for until then they had generally supported black and Third
World demands which were now to be condemned as "bourgeois"
and "revisionist." Most PL groups made the switch without losing
a beat. At a dozen campuses—most notably San Francisco State,
Columbia, Brooklyn, Queens, and City College—PL and WSA
came out overnight against such black demands as open admissions, black studies departments, and the hiring of black professors; all that, they said, was anti–working-class "black power" and
capitalist "get-aheadism." At San Francisco State the turnaround
was most glaring, because there was PL, right in the middle of a
lengthy strike for which it had provided influential support and
after weeks of denouncing people who were against the black
demands as "racist," all of a sudden attacking these *demands* as
"racist" and trying to enlist students to their own cause of working-class solidarity. The two key PL figures in the black and Third
World organizations there, Bridges Randle and Hari Dillon, led

not only the turnaround but the subsequent invective: the strike leaders, they announced, were "right-wing, anticommunist (i.e., antirevolutionary), antiworking-class forces," "petty-bourgeois nationalists" and " 'Black Power' type reformists whose ideology is nationalism," and their demand for a black studies department was "national in form and ruling class in content," raised solely because the leaders "see a chance to get themselves some well-paying jobs as Black faculty." Needless to say, most of the campus was stunned by this sudden flip-flop, Randle and Dillon were subsequently dropped from their organizations, PL found itself in considerable disrepute among whites as well as blacks, and the strike itself suffered badly. But it is characteristic of the Old Left that reality should not be allowed to interfere with the carrying out of theory, at whatever cost.

But it wasn't only the black "nationalism" issue that set PL against its colleagues. PL was politically against Cuba, Castro, Guevara, guerrilla warfare, drugs, the youth culture, long hair, Marcuse, *RAT,* the North Vietnamese and NLF, peace negotiations, and women's liberation besides—practically the whole roster of what most political students, and most regular SDSers, were *for.* It is hardly any wonder that factionalism plagued SDS chapters now even more than in the fall, producing splits and dissolutions at Brandeis and Berkeley, Wayne State and Texas, Columbia and Michigan State, and many points in between. The *Old Mole,* whose people had been in many battles with PL in the Boston stronghold, summarized the turmoil this way:

> In the last year the Progressive Labor Party, a small self-appointed vanguard of the proletarian revolution, has become the center for all ideological and strategic debate inside . . . SDS. . . . In general, and particularly in its student work, it is unable to distinguish between its true enemy, the state and ruling class, and other groups on the left with whom it has political disagreements. It spends as much time attacking the one as the other. . . .
>
> Although it is nowhere set down as PL theory, sectarianism shows up so often in PL practice in the student movement as to be a guiding principle. Having decided that they are the vanguard of the revolution, the fact of their leadership becomes the chief goal. . . . Not only does the leadership by PL become the chief goal; it becomes the chief criterion for excellence. The work-study group in

Boston (factory work and discussions) was attacked by WSA. That
attack was not around differences in policy, but along the line that
since the organizers of the work-study were not in WSA, they must
have bad politics. . . .

We differ from PLP in our understanding of socialism, of
history, of culture, and therefore in our understanding of the dialec-
tics of the struggle for human liberation. These disagreements must
be debated, for they run to the heart of our battles and our goals.

Debated they were, and endlessly, wherever PL appeared.
The March National Council meeting in Austin, for example, was
another Donnybrook, as contentious and unpleasant as the one in
Ann Arbor, the only difference being that this time the NO came
prepared with its own proposals, its own selected speakers, and its
own supporters out in force: in the end PL's favorite items—
organizing May Day student-worker marches, the formal adoption of the worker-student alliance strategy, a denunciation of
drugs—were all defeated, whereas the NO's issues—support for
the Black Panthers, repudiation of PL's December racism program, a defense of Hanoi and the peace talks, and the new Ayers-
Mellen RYM proposals—were all duly passed. But the era of bad
feelings was clearly at its peak: NO people were castigated for
being "tools of the imperialists" when they spoke in favor of drugs,
PL was accused of "spreading lies" about the NLF and "working
objectively in the interests of the U.S. ruling class," and fist fights
between the two sides actually broke out on the floor.

But while the NO was winning its political debates—at least
these debates—PL was up to its own games. The two most interesting examples of how PL was operating during this climactic
spring were provided in the South and during the Harvard strike.

In the South, Progressive Labor saw as its chief target the
Southern Student Organizing Committee, an offshoot of SDS set
up in 1964 to carry on SDS-style politics with a slightly gentler
Southern accent. PL had begun its operations within SSOC at the
same time that it began infiltrating SDS itself (early in 1966) and
at one point in 1967 it loaded a SSOC convention and won approval for its own Southern Labor Action Movement project. This
scheme so repulsed the anti-PL leadership of SSOC that it shortly
sabotaged the project, proceeding then to change SSOC officially
from a membership organization to a service organization pre-

cisely to forestall any other such outside political interference—
and so PL set out to destroy SSOC from without. During 1967 and
1968 PL, with power bases in the New Orleans Movement for a
Democratic Society and the Austin SDS chapter, kept up a running attack on SSOC for being "liberal," "reactionary," and
"separatist" and for accepting operating money from liberal foundations.

SDS in its revolutionary phase had no special love for SSOC,
which had not made the same leap to Marxist ideology, but SSOC
was officially a "fraternal organization" and was jealous of its
"organizational hegemony in the South," so the national leadership left it alone until early in 1969. Then it became clear that PL
was successfully expanding its influence in the South because of
SSOC's moderateness and accordingly both Mike Klonsky and
NICer Bartee Haile made several Southern trips, searching out
people on the campuses who would ally themselves with RYM
against PL or would work to push SSOC leftward into the current
SDS camp. This campaign produced severe tensions within SSOC
—many staffers accused SDS of being "full of communists" and
railed against the "SDS carpetbaggers" and "Yankee meddlers"
—but there were enough pro-SDSers who accepted SDS's position
and began slowly to change SSOC's image.

But too slowly. PL saw the danger, mounted its forces, and
at the March National Council meeting it suddenly sprang a
resolution, signed by Fred Gordon and sixteen other SDSers close
to PL, denouncing SSOC as "one of the main tools of the ruling
class," calling for an end to SDS's fraternal relations, and proposing a strong new campaign to "build SDS in the South" in SSOC's
stead. The national collective was taken completely by surprise.
Klonsky made a last-ditch effort to postpone the challenge, but
with the realization that a public defense of the still-moderate
SSOC would be impossible and with the hope of supplanting it
anyway with a new RYM-oriented group, he finally capitulated
and gave the resolution his support. The NC voted overwhelmingly to discard SSOC and this effectively sounded the death knell
of that organization. Under continuing pressure from PL and with
its own ranks divided, SSOC voted at its June convention to
dissolve itself out of existence. PL had very neatly accomplished
its task: it had destroyed its main opposition in the South and

paved the way for its own ascendance as the dominant radical
organization on the campuses there.

Progressive Labor at Harvard was in quite a different position. PL had always been strong in the Boston area and was always
well represented in the Harvard/Radcliffe chapter—there are
some theories that only the sons and daughters of the aristocracy
have sufficient guilt to join disciplined parties laboring on behalf
of the working masses—and its task here was to gain control over
the chapter and push its politics onto the campus at large.

PL and its Worker-Student Alliance caucus began their serious push in the late fall of 1968 when by plain hard work and fancy
bloc voting they came to dominate most of the committees into
which the chapter, in a fit of "anti-elitism," had decided to split.
Regular SDSers, slow to respond to this sudden challenge, took
until the beginning of the year to establish their own bloc-voting
group, the New Left Caucus, and even then found themselves in
a minority. By early spring PL not only controlled two of the three
top offices and a majority on the executive committee, but had
committed the chapter to its own two pet projects, the elimination
of ROTC and an end to university expansion.

Neither of these issues attracted much attention on the campus, however, and PL efforts to mobilize the students were una-
vailing. When at last it looked as if the administration, despite
several avoidable blunders, would be able to ride through the
spring unmolested, PL decided to act. On April 9—defying a
chapter meeting the night before at which the New Left Caucus
and its allies won three separate votes explicitly rejecting an immediate building takeover—some thirty-five of the PL "cadre"
marched into University Hall, expelled the resident administrators, and took over the building. To New Left SDSers who objected, PL's reply was simple: "You're as bad as the administration—you have to be fought, too"; and when asked if it wasn't
more important to fight Harvard than their fellow SDSers, one
PLer answered: "No, you and the administration are the same
thing, and we will smash you both."

The building occupation itself did not succeed in galvanizing
any considerable student support (though several hundred SDSers
and other stray actionists did join PL inside), but the administration's decision to end it seventeen hours later with an onslaught

of local police and all the attendant brutality did do just that. Within hours Harvard students, prouder than most of the campus sanctuary and shocked by its bloody violation, had declared a student strike, and much of the university community was set to do all-out battle with the administration. Here was PL's chance at last: it could lead a popular strike, publicize and probably realize its demands, win over the student body, introduce people to its own radical politics, and widen the circle of those committed to revolution. PL welcomed the opportunity with folded arms: it decided to castigate the student "moderates" who had called the strike ("These guys are the enemy"), it denounced every effort by other students and the faculty toward a settlement as a "sell-out," it scorned all attempts by the New Left Caucus to build bridges to the student majority, it rejected a proffered alliance with a black student group on the grounds that it was "reformist," and it showed its general contempt for student opinion by choosing to continue with its own strike even after a massive student vote to return to classes. (Not that PL wrought any triumphs among their much-vaunted working class off the campus, either: despite a flurry of attempts to get Cambridge-area residents interested in the expansion issue, no links were made with any community groups, working class or otherwise, and one Cambridge block association in fact explicitly repudiated SDS and its cause.) Indeed, it seemed as if PL saw the crisis chiefly as an opportunity to attack— "smash" was the favorite word—the New Left Caucus: it issued leaflets dredging up old issues ("The right-wing of SDS plays to [the] bad aspect of student radicalism"), it repeatedly criticized the caucus's use of such tactics as guerrilla theater and rock bands for student propaganda ("creeping carnivalism"), it physically obstructed the caucus's attempt to hold a "mill-in" to confront the administration, and it turned the daily chapter meetings into what it called "struggle sessions" whose brawls and feuds would have made the Hatfields and McCoys seem blood brothers.

Because of the PL-created vacuum, the faculty and student "moderates" took control of the strike and forced the administration's retreat—helped in large part, ironically, by a group of ex-SDS graduate students—and the SDS chapter was isolated. PL's politics and strategies, and the inability of the New Left Caucus to circumvent them, had managed to give SDS a fixed reputation for inflexibility and dogmatism, and had destroyed SDS's chances at this opportune moment to become a major political group on campus. Instead the chapter was reduced to a shambles, its leaders spent and embittered (some to the point of dropping out of politics altogether), its ranks cut to perhaps half of what they were before the strike. PL, it is true, had succeeded in its two primary aims of consolidating its hold on the chapter—the WSA caucus was still strong enough in May to elect all its own people to the delegate positions for the upcoming National Convention—and of pushing its politics onto the campus, and from every indication that seemed to PL to be victory enough. But at what a price.

And still with all of this the screws of repression tightened —a stark display of power aroused.

The Nixon Administration which took office in January came on like—well, like gangbusters. It did not hesitate to carry out its law-and-order campaign promises—including those about unruly students—and to use the Department of Justice as a political arm of the White House to that end. Attorney General John Mitchell, Nixon's campaign manager in 1968, announced that the government intended to prosecute "hard-line militants" who crossed state lines to visit campuses and stir up trouble; Deputy Attorney General Richard Kleindienst, Barry Goldwater's field director in 1964, promised that the Administration would go after "radical, revolutionary, anarchistic kids" and take swift action to repress student radicals and "draft-dodgers." Kleindienst in fact singled out SDS for the department's special concern:

> If that or any group was organized on a national basis to subvert our society, then I think Congress should pass laws to suppress that activity. When you see an epidemic like this cropping up all over the country—the same kind of people saying the same kinds of things—you begin to get the picture that it is a national subversive activity. . . . If people demonstrated in a manner to interfere with others, they should be rounded up and put in a detention camp.

Various branches of the Department of Justice were instructed to step up their investigation and infiltration of militant and left-wing groups—most notably the FBI, but also the Law Enforcement Assistance Administration, the Community Relations Service, and a special thirty-man "campus rebellion" task force which Mitchell began to organize to carry out the "vigorous prosecution" of students who interfere with federally guaranteed civil rights or federally funded programs (that is, just about every university). And then to make known the kind of actions it had in mind, the department ordered the prosecution of eight people it determined were responsible for the troubles at the Chicago Democratic Convention, depending for its evidence of this "conspiracy" on a variety of infiltrators and informers and on unauthorized wiretaps which, though illegal, Mitchell justified on the grounds that they were being used against people he had determined on his own were going to "attack and subvert the government by unlawful means."*

Throughout the spring, the Administration kept up its pressure. Nixon began by warning that "this is the way civilizations begin to die," then demanded that college trustees, administrators, and faculties show more "backbone," declared that campus disorders were nothing less than "attempts at insurrection," and finally—at tiny and unaccredited General Beadle State College in South Dakota, probably the only campus Nixon could visit safely, and a wonder that his staff found it—he issued his government's ultimatum:

> We have the power to strike back if need be, and to prevail. . . . We have a Constitution that sets certain limits on what government can do but that allows wide discretion within those limits. . . . To challenge a particular policy is one thing: to challenge the government's right to set it is another—for this denies the process of freedom.

As his right-hand strong-arm man, Mitchell was given the job of driving this point home, and in a series of extraordinary appearances across the country he sounded the alarm:

*The defendants, formally indicted on March 2 and faced with ten years in jail and fines of $20,000 each, were Rennie Davis, David Dellinger, John Froines, Tom Hayden, and Lee Weiner of the Mobilization, Jerry Rubin and Abbie Hoffman of the Yippies, and Bobby Seale of the Black Panther Party. All had had contacts with SDS over the years, of course, and Davis, Hayden, and Froines had been SDS leaders at various times, but despite attempts to link SDS to the demonstrations, no present or immediate-past leaders of SDS were indicted. SDSers, including Staughton Lynd, were however among the 128 people convicted by Chicago courts under local laws for actions during Convention week.

The time has come for an end to patience. The time has come for us to demand, in the strongest possible terms, that university officials, local law enforcement agencies and local courts apply the law.

I call for an end to minority tyranny on the nation's campuses and for the immediate reestablishment of civil peace and the protection of individual rights.

If arrests must be made, then arrests there should be. If violators must be prosecuted, then prosecutions there should be.

It is no admission of defeat, as some may claim, to use reasonable physical force to eliminate physical force. The price of civil tranquillity cannot be paid by submission to violence and terror. . . .

Campus militants, directing their efforts at destruction and intimidation, are nothing but tyrants.

And he made it perfectly clear who he regarded as chiefly responsible for the tyranny: "The Students for a Democratic Society, despite a loose organizational structure, appears, through its local chapters, to carry out a national SDS policy keyed to widespread unrest among large segments of the otherwise peaceful student community." No government agent, police official, judge, lawmaker, or administrator could fail to get the message: the Administration wanted to see "reasonable" physical force used against SDS and its kind and would support any effort in that direction.

The FBI, for one, hardly needed the encouragement. Hoover had already determined, as he told the House in April, that the New Left was "a firmly established subversive force dedicated to the complete destruction of our traditional democratic values and the principles of free government," and that "at the core of the New Left movement in the United States is the Students for a Democratic Society." Accordingly, he was now assigning more than two thousand of the FBI's full-time agents to New Left investigations, paying (at roughly $300 a month) an unknown but at least equal number of informers, and soliciting information on activists and presumed activists from college administrators, campus police, ROTC units, banks, credit companies, and telephone companies; as one former agent has said, "There are hardly any limits on the bureau's activities in compiling political information, particularly about the new left." As far as SDS went, there seemed indeed to be no limits: *The New York Times* reported quite matter-of-factly in May that "the Federal Bureau of Investigation maintains lengthy dossiers on all of its important members and has undercover agents and informers inside almost every chapter."

But the FBI was not the only one operating in this area, only the most visible. No fewer than twenty federal agencies had now been geared to maximum surveillance, disruption, and harassment of the New Left, among them the army (with political dossiers on at least eighteen million civilians), the Civil Service Commission (with fifteen million names of "subversive activity" suspects), the Secret Service (with fifty thousand dossiers), the Department of Health, Education and Welfare (with two offices devoted to gathering intelligence on students), and even the Internal Revenue Service (with a file on practically everybody, plus a secret seven-man unit whose sole job was to spy on the finances of political organizations and their leaders), and, in the legislature, the House Internal Security Committee (with an admitted 754,000 cards of "subversives" on file). Every good-sized city now had its own Red Squad,* usually concerned with infiltrating and in some cases entrapping SDS groups, always devoted to elaborate surveillance of them; Philadelphia Police Inspector Harry Fox gave some idea of the extent of this in his testimony to the Senate:

> Police have now become "watch-dogs" and "observers" of vocal, subversive and revolutionary minded people. . . . They cover all meetings, rallies, lectures, marches, sit-ins, laydowns, fasts, vigils, or any other type of demonstration that has ominous overtones. . . . These officers know by sight the hard core men and women who lead and inspire demonstrations. They know their associates, family ties, techniques, and affiliations with organizations leaning toward Communism both on and off the Attorney General's list. They see them day in and day out recruiting, planning, carrying signs, and verbally assaulting the principles of democracy.

And state intelligence agencies were also in on the game to the point where Illinois State Police Superintendent James McGuire acknowledged that "our growing concern about subversives and militants, with their talk of armed revolution, has brought us to a temporary shift in emphasis away from the organized crime

*By 1969, the available figures of city Red Squad agents show that Boston had 40, Chicago 500, Columbus 14, Detroit 70, Houston 14, Los Angeles 84, and New York 123, and those were only the acknowledged operatives.

problem," and he added ominously: "I've never seen anything like the intensity of the current investigations in all my years in law enforcement."

As the spring wore on and campus battles became more frequent, the press and public began to loose an even greater outcry, as if student protest, only now in its second year of escalation, was something as execrable as the Vietnam war, in its fifth, as if the amount of damage done by demonstrators, perhaps $8 million at most, represented something more than what the American government admitted spending in Vietnam *every two hours*. The enormous publicity given to protests by the media—salivating over the violent few, somehow picturing the beaten and bloodied as aggressors, turning the picture of those Cornell students with unloaded rifles acquired in self-defense into the suggestion of gun-shooting killers on the loose in academia, and more—served to produce an unquestionable fear in the already jittered population.* "It is not easy to shake the indifference of the quiet majority in this country," wrote James Reston, voice of American respectability, "but the militants have achieved it," producing a "great pressure on the politicians from the middle class to get this movement under control." *Time* magazine, noting what it called "an enraged government and public," added that there was "a growing feeling throughout the nation that the rebels have at last gone too far. If there was one word that summarized the feelings of much of the U.S. toward the radicals last week, it was: 'Enough!' " As if in proof, the Gallup poll determined that 82 percent of the American public thought that student demonstrators should be expelled, and the Louis Harris poll determined that 52 percent of the public opposed demonstrations by students even if they were peaceful and legal.

*One ugly instance: the *Chicago Tribune* in its campaign against "student radicals" at one point listed the name of Dick Flacks among the University of Chicago professors who it said were really behind all the school's troubles, following which one unknown citizen invaded Flacks's office and beat him severely, causing multiple skull fractures and nearly severing his hand. Flacks, ironically, had just finished serving as one of the staff consultants for the "Skolnik Report" to the President's Commission on the Causes and Prevention of Violence.

To this last finding *New Yorker* analyst Richard Harris wryly remarked, "As usual, a position supported by more than half the people, even if it meant denying rights guaranteed under the First Amendment to some seven million citizens who happened to be students, was enough for Congress, and a move to impose strict federal penalties on students and teachers who disrupted college activities quickly gathered momentum in both houses." Four bills were introduced in the Senate, nineteen in the House, most of them concerned with cutting off federal funds to recalcitrant students and universities, one allowing administrators to go to federal courts for injunctions against disruptions, one suggesting the establishment of a Department of Youth Affairs, and one, from Senator John McClellan, subjecting student disruptors to penalties up to $10,000 fines and life imprisonment; as usual, the legislation was furious rather than sound and, since the federal government's actual power to prevent protests was nil, signified nothing except the appeasement of voters. Congressional committees quickly got into the act, too, with the Senate Subcommittee on Investigations going after SDS, the Panthers, SNCC, and the Republic of New Africa ("Testimony will disclose," Chairman John McClellan declared, "that they advocate the use of violence and disruption as a means of attaining their goals and that they and their supporters are dedicated to callous and cynical exploitation of issues and grievances in urban areas and on campuses"), and the House Internal Security Committee specifically investigating SDS ("In view of its probable membership strength and potential for acceleration of incidents," said Chairman Richard Ichord, "a serious threat is posed to the country's internal security").* And Congressional denunciations of SDS in particular, students in general, were as common as pork in a barrel; the pithiest came from Representative Elford A. Cederberg of Michigan—"The so-called Students for a Democratic Society is dedicated to the destruction of our democracy and should be called the Students for the Destruction of a Democratic Society"—and the most long-winded from Senator Russell Long of Louisiana (during Senate floor debate):

*The University of Missouri SDS group voted to rename itself the Richard Ichord Chapter of SDS after this latter distinguished alumnus, but the university refused to give it official recognition under that title.

They're about the most contemptible people I know of. They're the most overprivileged group in this country. Is the Senator familiar with the fact that the parents of these people have put up the money to pay all their expenses and buy soap for them? But they refuse to take baths. That they have put up the money to buy them razor blades? But they refuse to shave. That they put up the money to buy food for those children? And they spend it on marijuana. They are the most sorry, contemptible, overprivileged people in the world and I say those people are a good element for the Communists to move in on.

State legislatures followed suit. Something on the order of four hundred bills were introduced (more than a hundred in California, thirty in New York, twenty in Wisconsin) in thirty-nine states (all but Alaska, Arizona, Georgia, Hawaii, Kentucky, Maine, Mississippi, Nebraska, Vermont, Virginia, and Wyoming), and within months twenty states had enacted some kind of punitive measures against the colleges and their students. Indicative of the pervasive climate of anger then was the enactment of laws ordering the immediate expulsion of students who violate university rules (passed in Louisiana, Ohio, South Carolina, and Wisconsin), firing faculty members who violate rules (Louisiana, North Dakota), instituting criminal charges against those involved in sit-ins and takeovers (California, Colorado, Idaho, Illinois, Louisiana, Minnesota, North Dakota, Oklahoma, Tennessee, and Texas), and in one instance, giving police a license to kill on campus without legal reprisal (West Virginia). Rarely in the history of American legislatures have so many acted so quickly and with such force to control or eradicate an imagined social evil; one wonders what might happen to air pollution, for example, or dunken drivers, were it deemed possible to devote such purposive efforts to those public problems.

None of this quite remarkable vociferation was lost upon the administrators of the nation's colleges and universities, no matter how ivory their towers. The message was unmistakable: universities had better take strong measures to stop student protest or else the government would step in and do it for them. It was the one threat that universities feared most, challenging as it did their special position as strictly unaccountable bastions of privilege, and Harvard's Nathan Pusey, at his patrician best, acknowledged,

"Many of us, I think, are terribly afraid about that kind of reaction from outside the campus communities, and it is something that we ought rightly to be frightened by." With an alacrity rare among the dons of American education, presidents and deans descended upon Washington urging that no punitive legislation be enacted, thirty-nine top-ranking presidents signed a public statement promising future hard-line responses to disruptions, and professional education organizations like the American Council on Education and the American Association of State Colleges and Universities went on bended knee before Congressional committees to assure that universities could really take care of themselves.

And take care they could: once aroused, the academy displayed an ingenuity more infinite than the spider's. University admissions offices were told to screen out the "protest-prone" (Cornell's dean of admissions said bluntly, "It didn't help a candidate's chances any if he noted he was an active member of SDS");* university psychiatrists were encouraged to find and "treat" students active in politics ("The use of psychiatric counseling to control student dissidents takes place at many colleges and universities," one 1970 study reported); university scholarship offices were instructed to put pressure on activists who depended upon financial assistance from the school, and aid was actually withdrawn from protesters at no fewer than nineteen schools; university records offices furnished to the McClellan Committee the names and records of student activists, usually SDSers, and added a little "chilling effect" by making it known that they were doing so (among them were such prestigious institutions as the University of California, all branches, the City University of New

---

*The "protest-prone" could be identified with some precision—in fact, 81 percent accuracy—thanks to an elaborate study undertaken by the university-financed American Council on Education, underwritten by $100,000 from the government's National Institute of Mental Health. The ACE based its findings on a "data bank" it assembled containing detailed information on some 300,000 entering freshmen at 350 colleges and universities. (Astin and Bayer, published in an American Council of Education pamphlet, 1969, and in *Annals of the American Academy of Political and Social Sciences,* May 1971.) *New Left Notes,* incidentally, in its April 17 issue, warned that this survey was "part of the basis for infiltration of the movement" and "used to finger and destroy individuals and whole communities," and it recommended "counter-insurgency" against the " 'surveyor-pigs' " and a campaign to get students to refuse to participate.

York, Columbia, Cornell, and Harvard); and so on it went. Faculty members, aroused now as a result of finding themselves increasingly the targets of student attacks—including the disruption of classes, academic picket lines, threats, and even physical assaults—rallied to the administrators' cause under the banner of "academic freedom," which was, in fact, "professor power." Polls indicated that more than 80 percent of all faculty members disapproved of both the aims and methods of campus demonstrations and regarded them as "a threat to academic freedom," more than 76 percent favored the expulsion or suspension of disruptors, nearly half (46.8 percent) had decided that demonstrations were "created by left groups trying to cause trouble," and a quarter (25.2 percent) argued that there should be no demonstrations at all—so it was not difficult to enlist faculties on the side of campus law-and-order in these days.* In fact, in many places professors now took the lead in attacking student protesters: LID mentor Sidney Hook, for example, was instrumental in banding a number of conservative teachers into an anti-SDS "University Center for Rational Alternatives," and a hundred senior teachers at Columbia put out a much-publicized call for faculties to crack down on political militants—"demonstrate the will to act"—by a variety

*These figures are from a study by the Carnegie Commission on Higher Education, published in the *Chronicle of Higher Education* (April 6, 1970), covering 60,447 faculty members of all grades during the 1968–69 academic year. The survey described the teachers as liberal on nonacademic matters, though only 19 percent at this late date favored immediate withdrawal from Vietnam, 79.9 percent voted for either Humphrey or Nixon, and 53 percent defined themselves to the right of liberal (41.5 percent said they were "liberal" and only 5.5 percent characterized themselves as "left"). But, a survey analyst said, there was "a striking and clear shift toward a more conservative attitude where the faculty's immediate self-interest is involved"—for example, 66.1 percent opposed the abolition of grades, 77.6 opposed making all courses elective, 58.3 opposed university governance by faculty and students alone, 49.1 percent said that faculty unions would be "divisive," and 56.1 percent opposed relaxation of standards for admission of minority group students; 90.0 percent regarded themselves as successful, 89 percent thought their institutions were good places to be, and 88 percent rated their salaries as fair-to-excellent. As might be expected, the liberal arts faculties were most accepting of student activism, the agriculture teachers the least (by discipline, it went: sociology, social work, philosophy, religion, psychology, political science, anthropology, English, and history, all about 60 percent approving, down to business, home economics, engineering, physical education, and agriculture, all below 30 percent approving).

of methods including informing on them to the police and the administration.

The ultimate weapon of the university, however, as we have seen, was naked force, and administrators resorted to it now more than ever before. In the cool words of the American Council on Education investigators, "Major civil or institutional action (arrest, indictment, dismissal, or suspension) was taken against individual students at fully three-fourths of the institutions where there were violent protests; similarly severe punitive measures were taken against individual students at more than one-fifth of the colleges that had nonviolent disruptive protests." Police or National Guardsmen were called in on at least 127 campuses during the school year, sometimes for weeks on end, and more than four thousand people were arrested in campus protests from January to June. In addition at least one thousand students were expelled or suspended from school this spring—compared to 293 by the NSA's figures for the spring of 1968—making them instantly eligible for the draft and a possible future in Vietnam, a punishment ("signing a death warrant," as it was called) that until now administrators had been reluctant to mete out. Universities also went on to press charges in court for a variety of crimes ranging from trespassing to kidnaping, and punishment could often be severe: to take just a few examples, a Harvard PLer was given a one-year prison term for assault (actually, grabbing a dean by the arm), two San Francisco SDSers were given a year for three misdemeanor counts, seven Voorhees College students were given eighteen–to–twenty-four–month sentences for "rioting" in connection with a building takeover, a Washington University SDSer was given five years for attempted arson, and three San Fernando Valley State students were given one–to–twenty-five years (and eight others one year) for conspiracy, false imprisonment, and kidnaping for holding administrators temporarily captive during a takeover.

And with all this, university administrators were still being accused of laxness, not only by President Nixon, but by such as Tennessee Congressman Dan Kuykendall who attacked "spineless campus administrators," and columnist William Buckley—the only person still alive for whom the slogan "For God, For Country, and For Yale" went in ascending order—

who accused college presidents of being "made out of Cornell jelly."

SDS, as the Administration had declared, was the prime target for the national campaign of repression, for both university administrators, civil authorities, and government agents.*

On campus, punitive action (arrest, expulsion, withdrawal of aid) was taken against New Left organizations (chiefly SDS) in 76 percent of the spring's disruptive demonstrations, yet against other student groups only 37 percent of the time; and New Leftists were expelled or suspended twice as often as any other students. SDS was banned outright at half a dozen campuses (Arizona, Colorado, Florida Southern, Kent State, Maryland, and Saint Bonaventure), the March NC was kicked off the Texas campus despite an earlier signed contract ("We are not about to let the university be used by subversives and revolutionaries," the trustees announced), and the California Board of Education took steps to prohibit SDS from public high schools and junior highs (carried out throughout the system in the fall). SDS and pro-SDS faculty members were fired or suspended at City University of New York, Connecticut, Dartmouth, Harvard, Queensborough, San Francisco State, and Tulane (among others), and at Connecticut the administration even got a court injunction against one left teacher which forbade him from practically any overt activity—including the telling of falsehoods. Freelances, too, entered the fray: a Cuban exile threw a bomb into a meeting of the Columbia SDS chapter in January (it did not explode), an Army ROTC commander ordered the members of the Pershing Rifles Club in the "Big Ten" schools to spy on their fellow students in SDS, and conservative students at many schools took it upon themselves to disrupt SDS meetings and rallies with strong-arm tactics. And the ubiquitous FBI, with its agents, informers, and wiretaps, produced its own debilitating effects by methods somewhat more subtle; as one of its investigators said in May:

*That is, the prime target among whites. But it should not be forgotten that at the same time a far more severe repression was being enacted against the militant black groups, chiefly the Black Panther Party, who were victims of nothing less than a systematic drive of extermination and who suffered jailings and killings on a scale greater than anything visited upon SDS.

The S.D.S. can't be a dangerous organization as long as we know what they are up to. So we keep watching it. Nothing the S.D.S. does surprises us. If they are going to have a rally, then we know what kind of tactics they are planning and we are ready for them if they want to cause trouble.

Our inside information has caused S.D.S. to get more conspiratorial in a lot of places. They make their plans at the last minute now to fool us. But that doesn't leave them much time for getting the word around, and it causes them confusion and makes it harder for them to draw the kinds of crowds they used to get at their rallies.

We also find that the more conspiratorial S.D.S. becomes, the less they appeal to the hippies and people like that who think everything should be wide open and who are afraid of political secrets and secret political planning. I think the conspiratorial mood is hurting S.D.S. a lot.

Off the campus, SDS leaders were regular targets for municipal police, usually on wrung-in charges: in addition to the five arrested in the NO (and subsequently slapped with a ban to keep them from traveling), Mark Rudd and Columbia SDSer Peter Clapp were arrested in upstate New York (and faced the prospect of fifteen years in jail) for allegedly having two ounces of marijuana, Rudd was indicted by a grand jury for actions going back to the spring of 1968, Bill Ayers was arrested for assault in Michigan, Connie Ullman was arrested for vagrancy in Texas, and four members of the Labor Committee in Philadelphia were arrested for possession of explosives (a patently fabricated charge which it turned out was impossible to substantiate in court). In Denver in April a member of the Colorado State University SDS chapter, Susan Parker, was hauled before a grand jury investigating the January electric-tower bombings and because she refused to testify about her friendships she was put in jail on an indefinite sentence for as long as she declined to talk. The offices of the Michigan regional staff and the Radical Education Project in Ann Arbor were broken into on February 7, apparently by professionals, and addressograph plates, financial records, contact-card files, mail, and other SDS materials were stolen, though none of the valuable equipment or money in the office was touched, leading SDSers to the natural conclusion that the job was done by police or FBI. Five other ROs were vandalized, rifled, and damaged

during the spring. Things became so bad, in fact, that Mike
Klonsky, on national television—a CBS "Face the Nation" program on May II—went out of his way to charge that Mitchell was
"planning within the next ten days the 1969 version of the Palmer
Raids, that he has got it all mapped out, in over fifty cities in the
United States, trying to pick off so-called leaderships," Klonsky
presumably hoping that national exposure of the plan would forestall any escalation of the harassment and arrests. Perhaps it did
—at any rate no publicized raids occurred—but in the next few
days there was the invasion of the NO, police warfare at People's
Park, the killing of a black student at North Carolina A & M, and
grand-jury indictments delivered in New York, Memphis, Ithaca,
and elsewhere ("more than 400" in all, according to *New Left
Notes*), and that kind of official wrath was bad enough.

Repression proved to be ultimately very debilitating for SDS
both nationally and locally, exacerbating the paranoid style, wearing down individuals and eating into groups, tying up people in
courts, exhausting both finances and energy, forcing chapters to
give up some confrontational tactics, sending leaders into jail and
exile, and over the whole organization casting the dark realization
of what the stakes are in even an infant, proto-revolution. But its
effect was gradual and diffuse, like a slow poison, and its victims
initially skeptical and unimpressed, so very little was done to
combat or circumvent it: to the SDS leadership it seemed that a
few security precautions, some words of legal advice, and a
bloody-but-unbowed response would suffice. Accordingly, the
NIC sent out word that SDS offices should institute "night
watches," told chapters to outlaw tape recorders and burn notes,
and announced in May that "security considerations, which
should be in effect normally, MUST BE particularly emphasized
to all movement people now." The NO itself began what it called
"armed security," doubled its door locks (telling anyone coming
to the NO to call first), and made sure that no business of importance was carried on over the telephone (a wise precaution—
subsequent government publications revealed that the phone was
indeed tapped); Bernardine Dohrn had long since given up putting
anything down in her appointment book, the 1969 version of which
was thrown aside untouched. *New Left Notes* published several

warnings to SDSers about the power of grand juries, the dangers of talking to juries or FBI agents, and the ubiquitous penetration of undercover agents in campus chapters. Four New York SDSers (Kathy Boudin, Brian Glick, Eleanor Raskin, and Columbia law student Gustin Reichbach) prepared *The Bust Book* to give Movement people advice on how to avoid arrest and what to do when detained by the cops; it proved valuable (and necessary) enough that it was shortly picked up by Grove Press for overground publication. SDS even tried to use the courts in one instance—despite a conviction that they were hardly interested in SDS's welfare—by suing to block the Senate Investigations Subcommittee from subpoenaing chapter membership lists and records ("punishing, harassing, and intimidating," it said); predictably, the effort failed and the case was dismissed.

Perhaps one of the reasons for SDS's rather muted response was that in a curious way the leadership actually greeted the repression visited upon the organization more as a confirmation of its revolutionary power than as a peril to its functioning; as Mike Klonsky wrote in *New Left Notes:*

> The only reason SDS is being attacked so hard right now is because we have begun to learn the lessons of history while building our revolutionary youth movement.
>
> Our attack on white supremacy, which in practice over the last six months has helped shake the whole racist foundation on which this system of exploitation is built, has forced the racist power structure to move to crush us. We must respond by taking the issues to the people in a mass way and doing mass education around the fights that brought the repression down.

Obviously, if we weren't hurting them they wouldn't be resorting to such force. And when the force became increasingly blatant—arrests and jailings, gassings and beatings, shootings and killings, in New York, North Carolina, Chicago, Texas, Colorado, Berkeley—the revolution seemed increasingly imminent. And when the force seemed unable to *stop* the rising insurrection, on the campuses, in the high schools, in the army camps, and on the streets —well, then, what more natural than to feel, to hope, that it could even be triumphant? Certainly that was the mood of many people around the NO—despite the harassment, despite the factionalism,

despite the setbacks, despite the defections, the mood was confident, expectant. It was more than bravado, more than false courage, more than Mao-modeling, it was a wish attaining the stature
of a belief that led Jim Mellen, enunciating what all of the leadership was apparently thinking, to tell the students at Kent State:

> We are no longer asking you to come and help us make a revolution.
> We're telling you that the revolution has begun, and the only choice
> you have to make is which side you're on. And we're also telling you
> that if you get in the way of that revolution, it's going to run right
> over you.

It may have been delusory; but it was real. As spring turned into
summer, the question of power really seemed to be resolving itself,
at least in the minds of the SDS leadership, in favor of revolution.
The main preoccupation of the national collective and those who
felt themselves to be its allies was how to keep that revolution
going, how to mobilize the left into "a fighting force," how finally
to take that revolution to victory.

It is remarkable, really, what had happened to SDS. By now
both those who sided with the national collective and those who
favored Progressive Labor—and a number of various stripes in
between—were in general agreement on certain bedrock points:
you can't make a revolution with a loosely controlled organization
without substantial internal discipline . . . a dedicated cadre is
necessary in any revolutionary group . . . only a vanguard party,
or band, has the toughness and discipline to undertake the organization of masses of people, to withstand repression, to forge a
militant force, to lead the revolution. The points of disagreement
among these factions were many and in some cases crucial, but
they all tended to agree, if not necessarily consciously, that there
was no longer any need for something like SDS. All that had been
essential for SDS—a student constituency, membership in autonomous chapters, bases in the universities, a loose national structure,
the absence of rigid rules and internal discipline, freewheeling
debates and open disagreements, resistance to ideological prescriptions and space for a multitude of tendencies, political consciousness founded on the ability to make connections, and a
self-interest in one's own liberation as necessary for the liberation

of others—were no longer cherished, no longer protected: they were for the most part seen as impedimenta to the revolution. The shapers and movers of SDS no longer cared particularly for students—or for a democratic society. Something new was wanted, a new kind of organization for the new revolutionary job at hand.*

This, combined with the repression from above, the defections from below, and the factionalism within, wrote the death sentence for SDS. That sentence was read, amid much cacophony, at the June National Convention.

*One indication of the "something new" was this proposed version of a new preamble to the SDS constitution submitted by a group of University of Chicago SDSers: "Students for a Democratic Society is an organization of young people committed to the struggle for international socialist revolution.

"We stand together with the struggles of oppressed peoples throughout the world. We support the just demands of the black, Asian, and Latin peoples for self-determination. We are part of the international movement against imperialist exploitation and aggression. Within the United States, we stand together with the struggle of black and brown people for their liberation, and we believe that racism must be fought at every turn. We support and identify with the growing movement for women's liberation. We oppose capitalism as the source of racial and imperialist oppression and as a system of class exploitation.

"Our conception of socialism is revolutionary and democratic. We believe that the needs of the people can only be achieved when the people seize power in the state. The task of revolutionaries is to organize workers and all other oppressed peoples to fight to control production and the state. . . .

"Our activity as a movement is to build the struggles of young people against imperialist wars, and against education, training, and channeling designed to make us the agents or passive victims of oppression; we are part of the struggles of youth, black and brown people, women and working people for their liberation. We extend complete support and solidarity to popular struggles against oppression everywhere in the world." (*New Left Notes,* May 30, 1969.)

24

SUMMER 1969

Wednesday, June 18, 1969, was a gray, dank day in Chicago, perhaps nowhere grayer and danker than on South Wabash Avenue where some two thousand people were milling around in front of the Chicago Coliseum, a huge complex of ugly barnlike buildings which SDS had chosen as the site of its ninth annual convention. (The choice had been more or less forced: more than fifty colleges and universities, with an eye on Washington, had refused SDS permission to have the convention on their campuses. Some New England SDSers had found a college or two in that area that would agree to host the convention, but the National Office hardly wanted to hold deliberations in PL's home territory, so the Chicago site was selected instead, even though that meant postponing the convention a week and paying $440-a-day rental fees on the hall.) Some of those forgathered there were reporters from the major papers and wire services, trying to buttonhole any likely looking youth for a comment on what was going to happen (Abbie Hoffman told them grandly, "We have come to praise SDS, not to bury it"), more frustrated than usual because SDS wasn't letting them in the doors. There were also policemen of every type and jurisdiction, FBI agents with high-powered cameras in the third-floor windows of a vacant school across the street, out-of-town police agents in long hair and beards, regular Chicago cops in their baby-blues (the Coliseum was just a few blocks from the central police station), and Chicago Red Squad agents (whose ranks had been swollen to one thousand for this affair) in obviously unmarked cars, wearing obviously plain-clothes disguises, pretending obviously to be newspaper reporters as they took pictures of everyone who filed along the sidewalk ("This is America," retorted a police official when SDSers complained about the scrutiny; "people can take pictures without fear of harassment"). And there were the SDSers, perhaps twelve or fifteen hundred this first day, forced to mill about near the entrance of the Coliseum because of a wary registration desk which was set up to keep out suspect police agents and because of a "security check," the first one at a national SDS meeting, with NO trusties frisking all the delegates for knives, guns, cameras, tape recorders, and drugs, all of which were theoretically forbidden in the hall.

Slowly the delegates filed into the mammoth Coliseum, whose cement-block walls and echoing acoustics gave it less the atmosphere of a political convention than a roller-derby site, which in fact it usually was. Around the edges of the hall the various sects and groupuscules had set up tables to display their ideological wares and entice unwary delegates: Progressive Labor, the International Socialists, the Young Socialist Alliance, Communists, Spartacists, Wobblies, anarchists, Yippies, and assorted others. Adding to the paper barrage were pamphlets and mimeographed sheets from every tendency within SDS: the RYM people came with a series of exposés of PL's dangerous behavior, PL provided documents reaffirming its correctness, REP arrived with neat booklets setting out the RYM position and how it had worked in the past six months, the Bay Area Radical Union presented its "Red Papers" putting forth a pro-Maoist but anti-PL version of militant revolution, and New York anarchists offered Murray Bookchin's sprightly "Listen, Marxist" denouncing *all* of the other SDS tendencies. And to each of the delegates was handed the convention issue of *New Left Notes,* full of proposals and amendments, in which the pride of place went to an extraordinary article covering six solid pages with dense type (the longest article the paper had ever run), decorated with pictures of Marx, Lenin, Mao, and a recurring silhouette of armed guerrillas growing larger from first page to last. The title of the piece, cryptic for many, was "You don't need a weatherman to know which way the wind blows."

The "Weatherman" statement was the product of an unpublicized eleven-member committee (Karen Ashley, John Jacobs,
Jeff Jones, Mark Rudd, and Steve Tappis of the New York region,
Bill Ayers, Jim Mellen, and Terry Robbins of the Michigan-Ohio
area, and Bernardine Dohrn, Gerry Long, and Howie Machtinger
from Chicago), which the national leadership had established as
early as April to come up with some document to fight PL with
at the convention, and it had been further refined at a meeting of
two hundred RYM people (mostly from New York and the Midwest, with PLers uninvited) in Detroit in May. Most of the writing
was done by the New York City contingent and within that the
leading influence seems to have been John Jacobs ("JJ"), a man
who had the advantages of having once been through the theoretical thicket of PL, having been a major actionist at Columbia in
1968, and having been a Movement veteran, tracing his first arrest
back to 1966.

The title was taken from Bob Dylan's 1965 "Subterranean
Homesick Blues," where, along with "Look out kid" and "Keep
a clean nose" and suchlike, it is used as a piece of underground
advice to young Americans disaffected from the American system,
with the usual Dylanesque overtones of antiauthoritarianism and
youthful independence, both of special appeal to the SDSian soul.
But in the SDS context it means something more, an implied
repudiation of Progressive Labor and its from-on-high dicta to the
troops: you already know, the suggestion is, what is happening in
this country and what needs to be done to make a revolution, and
you don't need Milt Rosen to spell it out for you. (The very choice
of a counterculture quotation, the last thing in the world the PLers
would have approved of, is of course another repudiation.) Whereupon the statement then goes on to elucidate in intricate detail just
exactly which way the wind *is* blowing.*

---

*Various extended analyses of the "Weatherman" statement were forthcoming
in the months after its appearance, many of them hostile. Among them were
Andrew Kopkind, in *Hard Times,* June 30, 1969; Jack Weinberg and Jack
Gerson, in *IS,* an International Socialists publication, September 1969; Mike
Klonsky, in a REP pamphlet, "Documents on SDS and the Split," 1969; Conor
Cruise O'Brien, in *New York Review,* January 29, 1970; James Weinstein, in
Socialist Revolution, January–February, 1970; and Michael P. Lerner, in *Wea-
therman,* Ramparts Press, 1970.

"Weatherman" was written with two basic purposes in mind, and it is reasonably successful at fulfilling them. First, it tries to give a theoretical expression to the instincts that characterized those white youths who were moving toward a serious sense of revolution, the instincts born out of the whole decade of Movement activities and capped in the last year by the intoxicating dynamics of the action factions, the increasing identification with the black liberation movement, and the frustrations of powerlessness made evident in the spring's confrontations. Second, it tries to provide a shield of dogma that is impenetrable to all the ideological spears of Progressive Labor, and for this uses a peculiar mixture of categories borrowed from the Old Left, ideas about city-wide organizations borrowed from the Bell-Dohrn-Halliwell paper, and the basic premises of the original RYM statement of December and the refined (Ayers-Mellen) RYM position of March. This duality operates throughout.

The statement begins with a sweeping declaration that "the main struggle going on in the world today is between US imperialism and the national liberation struggles against it," and argues that the job of white Americans is to do anything they can in support of these struggles; here the instinct stems from the identification with the NLF, the Cuban revolution, and Third World guerrillas in general and a feeling that these forces seriously endanger America's world system—put forward in the teeth of PL's aloof criticism of "adventuristic" guerrillas and the "sell-out" Vietnamese. It then goes on to give unstinting approval to all "black liberation struggles," maintaining that blacks are so important in the revolution that they "could do it alone" if necessary and therefore assigning whites the secondary job to "support the blacks in moving as fast as they have to and are able to"; this instinct was born out of the ten-year-old identification of the Movement with black struggles, intensified by the "Lexington spirit" of the spring before, and heightened further by the recent close association with the Black Panthers—here meant as a counterthrust to PL's subordination of blacks within the working class as a whole and to its specific denigration of the Panthers. It argues, like the RYM statements before it, that youth (especially working-class youth) have a special part to play in aiding black and international liberation struggles, both because they have less of a stake in the imperialist society and because they are hurt most directly (through schools, the army, and unemployment) by imperialist oppression; the instinct stems from the experience of the previous decade in which it was the young who were responsible for the movements of protest and resistance and for the new counterculture—this position repudiating the PL analysis that youth culture is bourgeois and only the adult industrial proletariat can lead the revolution. It goes on to deny any real revolutionary role at this time for either the liberal professionals or the white working class, because they are bought off by short- or long-term "vested interests," because they want to take advantage of their racial position ("white-skin privilege," as it came to be called), or because they don't understand how their true interests would be served by a revolution; this instinct comes from the years of frustration of trying to awaken American liberals (prototypically, their own parents) and the concrete perception that the hard-hats were hardly even concerned with social justice, much less revolution— and this was set against PL's total commitment to the revolutionary role of the factory workers. It maintains that the task for American youth is to escalate its protest at home, showing solidarity with the world-wide "liberation forces" by opening another front in the anti-imperialist war, up to and including "the need for armed struggle"; this is the instinct generated by the success of confrontations over the years and compounded by the realization from the spring that in a battle of power there is a kind of power that does come out of the barrel of a gun—and it was set against PL's "base-building" slowness and its limitation of most current battles to picket lines and factory agitation. Finally, the statement declares that what is necessary in the creation of this supportive, white, young, military force is a "revolutionary party" based in cities and organized into collectives with "a cadre organization, effective secrecy, self-reliance among the cadres" and a "centralized organization"; the instinct here stems from the apparent inadequacies of past Movement organizations, including SDS, from a desire to avoid the present debilitating factionalism, and from a sense that a broad, loose organization like SDS was too vulnerable to repression—and here, at last, there is no real disagreement with PL except in deciding which people are to lead that "revolutionary party."

"Weatherman," in short, is a peculiar mix of New Left attitudes clothed in Old Left arguments, the instincts of the sixties ground through a mill of the thirties, the liberating heritage of SDS dressed up in leaden boots from the past.

There is much to criticize in "Weatherman." There is only a passing reference to "the woman question," no attempt to set out a program either short or long range, a total misreading of the centrality of blacks in the economic structure, a thoroughly romantic image of the toughness and heroism of "working-class kids," an unfounded overconfidence in the imminent collapse of the American system, and an utter confusion as to who is the "vanguard" for white youths to follow (blacks? Vietnamese? street kids?). The language is heavy with the sodden phrases of the Old Left now back in fashion ("revolutionary struggles," "oppressed peoples of the world," "achievement of a classless world," "capitalist exploitation," "enslaved masses," "proletarian socialist revolution"). The arguments are mostly scored off other ingroups, revolving about small points of difference about whether revolution comes in two stages or one, whether blacks are really a colony or not, exactly who constitutes the "petit bourgeoisie," whether it is good to have a "united front," and so on—matters which were, even to the majority of SDSers, esoteric arguments of sectarian irrelevance. And the lines of reasoning are tangled and elusive, seeming to mean one thing here and another there, leading even such a patient analyst as Carl Oglesby to say in exasperation, "Any close reading of the RYM's Weatherman statement will drive you blind."

But all of that is almost unimportant next to the two major defects of the statement—defects which, given the importance attached to the document and the identification with it by most of the national leadership, would prove quite important in the months ahead. The first problem is that it is really inaccessible to most people walking the land, young or old, educated or not, almost a polar opposite from *The Port Huron Statement* of exactly seven years before in its ability to excite and win people; and therefore it immediately creates a sense of distance, exclusion, and elitism, sins which were to beset its adherents over the whole next year. For all its talk about "the most important task" being "the creation of mass revolutionary movement," it really represents the culmination of the separation of the SDS leadership from the broad SDS membership, from the student constituency in general, and from most of the American left. The second difficulty is that it reduces the role of white American revolutionaries to fighting other people's battles, finding their own liberation only by tagging along after blacks and Third World guerrillas, being observers of an American revolution which comes about not through general social transformation by the bulk of its own people but through military defeat at the hands of the colonized people of color, aided perhaps by a few working-class youths in the wings. Not only are students no longer an agency of change, they are not even an object of change; not only do white middle-class college-educated people have no battles of their own to fight, they have no legitimacy as a stratum or validity as a force. *This* is where the "best minds of the generation" had come to.

The convention proper did not begin until just after two o'clock, when Assistant National Secretary Tim McCarthy called the gathering to order by hitting a rock on a table set up on the stage at one end of the dingy hall, and Mike Klonsky, wearing a cowboy hat, moved through a maze of wires to a microphone at the rostrum. The first order of business was to ratify the NO's decision to keep out representatives of the overground press unless they paid a $25 registration fee and agreed not to testify against SDS before Congressional committees (*New York Times* reporter Anthony Ripley had repeated details of his account of the 1968 convention in an appearance before the House Internal Security Committee only weeks before). But Ed Clark, a PLer from New Orleans who had been instrumental in the recent sabotage of SSOC, stood up and challenged Klonsky: there should be *no* members of the capitalist press in this hall, no matter what fee they pay—they distort and lie and we don't need them. Right there, at the start of the convention, PL threw down the gauntlet. There was some discussion, a vote was taken, and the PL position won handily, by perhaps three-to-two. Hearts among the RYM leaders must have dropped: PL and its WSA caucus, it suddenly seemed, had come in force and no doubt intended to make a bid for power.*

Now in fact PL probably had no more than a third of the fifteen hundred delegates under its control. It had worked hard, as usual, to rally its forces, chartering buses from New York and Boston and hiring a plane for some one hundred fifty people from the West Coast—PL leaders having been convinced that this time there would be an all-out attempt to purge it from SDS and determined to fight that at all costs. But there is no indication that PL was planning to try to take over the organization, nor would it have made much sense for them: SDS as it was, after all, provided by far the largest source of PL recruits, infinitely more fruitful than the vaunted factory lines, and it was far larger and more successful than anything PL could hope to produce under its own egis. That first vote was taken by the RYM faction to mean that PL was out for blood, but it more accurately reflected two other facts: that a large number of the delegates, perhaps a third, were committed to neither PL nor RYM and would vote with whichever position seemed best; and that many regular SDSers, especially veterans, had decided not to attend the convention, having been alienated by the distance and rigidity of the national collective over the previous year or simply put off by the succession of bitter and frustrating national meetings in the recent past.

Nonetheless, the NO regarded the press vote as an indication of a serious threat to its power, and that set the tone for much of the remainder of the convention. Two more battles shaped up that

*Accounts of the convention are necessarily somewhat imperfect, since tape recordings (even official NO ones) were forbidden for reasons of security and overground reporters were barred (and those who did sneak in were constrained from taking notes too openly). Only the underground press could write down the happenings with impunity, but more often than not its reporters were involved participants (Liberation News Service's Allen Young, for example, operated as a NO press spokesman, and the *Guardian*'s Carl Davidson was an open member of a "RYM II" group) and their accounts were also somewhat sketchy. Depending upon the police infiltrators and agents, with their hidden tape machines and trained memories, is no help either: the undercover agent of the Illinois Crime Investigating Commission who was present throughout the convention cribbed 99 percent of his official report from an article in the October issue of *Esquire* magazine written by Roger Kahn—who was never in the hall at all and relied for *his* information on oral reports given him at the end of each day by young friends inside.

very afternoon. First, Jeff Gordon, speaking for the PLers, protested that there weren't enough workshops on the NO's proposed agenda, to which Klonsky replied that the NO had decided workshops would only be "hunting grounds" for PLers to operate on new and innocent SDSers. No one thought much of that argument, and the vote was overwhelmingly for expanding the number of workshops. Then there came a battle over whether the convention would hear a speech from Chris Milton, a young man who had spent time with the Red Guards in China and was close to the RYM-lining Bay Area Radical Union, whom PLers castigated as a "deviant" who had been denounced by Peking. While this was going on the hall was suddenly in an uproar: the Ohio-Michigan contingent of perhaps fifty Weatherman supporters leaped on their chairs, whipped out copies of Mao's little red book, and in a mocking parody of the PL style began to wave the books back and forth and chant, "Mao, Mao, Mao Tse-tung, Dare to Struggle, Dare to Win," which rose in a reverberating roar through the cavernous hall until they all collapsed in laughter and self-applause at their little bit of anti-PL "guerrilla theater." PL, inevitably, took it with dead seriousness: this behavior, one PL spokesman took the microphone to complain, was "waving the red flag to oppose the red flag," a slogan which was immediately taken up by a PL contingent in the balcony and shouted back down to the Weathermen on the floor. (Even Abbie Hoffman, a master of guerrilla theater, was apparently confused by it all—"Through the conference," he later confessed, "I marvelled at how little I understand what was being said"—so one wonders what must have been going on in the minds of those for whom this was their first national meeting.) At the end it was somewhat anticlimactic when the delegates voted by a thin eight-vote margin to allow Milton to speak—a victory for the RYM forces, but not much of one, their first of the day, and gained only because most of the uncommitted delegates took the civil-libertarian "let's-hear-what-he-has-to-say" line.

The next day was devoted to workshops, for which the PLers showed themselves to be far better prepared than the RYM leaders, and to a general discussion of racism, at which both sides showed themselves to be implacable enemies—Jared Israel and Mike Klonsky ended up yelling at each other ("Klonsky's an authoritarian motherfucker," one NO supporter said during this debate, "but he's *our* authoritarian motherfucker"). RYM supporters met in caucus in the morning to decide how to go about holding off what they saw as the PL challenge, and there the first major disagreements with the new "Weatherman" line were aired, chiefly from a group of people around Mike Klonsky and Les Coleman, with allies in Noel Ignatin's Chicago Revolutionary League and Bob Avakian's Bay Area Radical Union; this group, which took a more traditional line than Weatherman, especially regarding the role of the working class and the dangers of "adventurism" by the youthful left, coalesced in the course of the convention to the point of issuing their own position paper from whose title, "Revolutionary Youth Movement II," they took the name RYM II. Their differences were submerged for the moment, however, in the shared desire to unite against PL.

The first opportunity to humiliate PL seemed to offer itself at that Thursday's evening session, when a small band of black and brown allies of SDS were scheduled to speak. First came a member of the Puerto Rican Young Lords Organization, then a representative of the chicano Brown Berets, and slowly the tempo of the attacks on "those who say all nationalism is reactionary" began to increase, and the PLers began to grow restive. Then came Rufus ("Chaka") Walls, the minister of information of the Illinois Black Panther Party, a somewhat older man, with dark wraparound glasses, flanked by arms-folded "bodyguards," and he lit into the PL "armchair Marxists" with all the macho rhetoric the Panthers had become famous for. He sneered at PL's claims of being a vanguard party and declared that the Panthers were the true vanguard because they had been out shedding blood and the white left hadn't even shot rubber bands yet. And then Walls began talking, quite unexpectedly, about women's liberation: we believe in women in the Movement, he said, we believe in the freedom of love and all that, we believe in "pussy power." Most of the fifteen hundred or so SDSers were stunned—enlightened or not, by the middle of 1969 you didn't go around *saying* things like that at Movement meetings. Cries of "Fight male chauvinism" were started all over the hall, picked up delightedly by the PL section on the left of the main floor. Walls paused: we've got some Puritans in the crowd, he went on, apparently misunderstanding

the source of the audience's discomfort, and then added out of the
blue, "Superman was a punk because he never even tried to fuck
Lois Lane." That did it. The chant swelled, from PLers who
sensed an unexpected reversal of fortunes, but from most others
as well: *"Fight male chauvinism,* FIGHT MALE CHAUVI-
NISM!" Walls, unable to continue, shrugged and walked off the
podium. The NO leaders, bewildered, quickly conferred. Then
Panther leader Jewel Cook took the microphone to try to pick up
the pieces with an all-out attack on PL. They aren't leading any
fights on the campus, he charged, like the Panthers are—you call
up Chairman Mao and ask *him* who's the vanguard party in the
U.S. The RYM people at last had a chance to cheer, but then Cook
continued. But you got to know, he said, that I'm with my brother
in this, I'm for pussy power myself—the "fight male chauvinism"
chant began again—and the brother was only trying to say to you
sisters that you have a strategic position in the revolution—the
chants were even louder now because everyone knew what was
coming, an old line of Stokely Carmichael's from the SNCC days
—the position for you sisters . . . is *prone!* "FIGHT MALE
CHAUVINISM, FIGHT MALE CHAUVINISM," the chant
was deafening, resounding off the cement-block walls and filling
the huge hall. "The house," reported the *Guardian,* "was in pan-
demonium."

The RYM strategy lay shattered. The Panthers had humi-
liated not PL but their own supporters, and in doing so had neatly
managed by a single stroke to turn to dross both of RYM's chief
theoretical weapons: its alliance with the vanguard Panthers and
its support for women's liberation. Klonsky rushed to the microphone to try to stem the rout, spoke feebly and without effect, and
cries for a "rebuttal" from PL drowned him out. Jared Israel, with
a clutch of PLers around him for support, rushed to the stage and
took the microphone, pounding home the wisdom of PL's "principled" stand on women's liberation and black struggles. Someone
proposed that there be a full-scale discussion of the Panthers'
sexism in the light of what had just happened, but RYMer Naomi
Jaffe effectively squelched the move with a declaration that
"women's liberation would not be used as a political football."
With that a desultory discussion of racism continued for a while

—enlivened by a few PL-RYM shoving matches in the back of the hall—but everyone knew that talk was meaningless now.

There was little sleep for the SDS leadership that night. Small knots of people gathered all over the convention floor, in nearby houses where delegates were being put up, and in the NO itself, over on the west side of town, to which most of the RYM leadership had repaired to lick its wounds—and, just in case, to spirit away the *New Left Notes* subscription lists, whatever membership files existed, and the SDS treasury, such as it was. At each place the topic was the same: was a split with PL imminent, and did RYM have enough votes at the convention to force it?

On Friday there was still no settlement of that issue. RYM forces did win a vote at the first plenary session over whether some non-PL Harvard delegates should be seated in lieu of some absent WSAers, but again the swing apparently came from the uncommitted delegates operating not from fixed politics but from common sense—and Lord knows that commodity could hardly be counted upon to provide victory in an all-out fight. The national leadership decided to bide its time.

That evening the first resolution was presented, a PL proposal called "Less Talk, More Action—Fight Racism" built principally around the issues of an end to university expansion and alliances with campus minority-group workers. Both Weatherman and RYM II spokesmen flailed at it, accompanied by choruses of "racist" and "bullshit" from time to time, Klonsky continuing to ridicule PL's position on black nationalism, Dohrn focusing on the necessity of "self-determination" for the black community. Suddenly Tim McCarthy took the microphone, announced that the Panthers had returned with an official statement, and asked the convention to give them the floor. Agreement was quickly provided. Jewel Cook once again came to the rostrum, and a hush fell on the gathering. Cook announced that he had a statement to read, approved by Chairman Bobby Seale and signed by the Panthers, the Brown Berets, and the Young Lords. It declared:

> After long study and investigation of Students for a Democratic Society and the Progressive Labor Party in particular, we have come

to the conclusion that the Progressive Labor Party has deviated
from Marxist-Leninist ideology on the National Question and the
right of self-determination of all oppressed people.

We demand that by the conclusion of the National Convention
of Students for a Democratic Society that the Progressive Labor
Party change its position on the right to self-determination and
stand in concert with the oppressed peoples of the world and begin
to follow a true Marxist-Leninist ideology. . . .

If the Progressive Labor Party continues its egocentric policies
and revisionist behavior, they will be considered as counter-revolutionary traitors and will be dealt with as such.

Students for a Democratic Society will be judged by the company they keep and the efficiency and effectiveness with which they
deal with bourgeois factions in their organization.

Whether the statement was entirely the Panthers' idea, a face-
saving retaliation for the humiliation of the night before, or
whether it was concocted with the concurrence of the SDS leadership as a way to force the PL split, is hard to say. The apparent
disarray with which the NO people reacted to the announcement
—the *Guardian* mentions "tactical blunders, utter confusion,
manipulation and unpreparedness"—suggests that it might have
been a surprise to everyone; yet the fact that it came at such an
opportune time for the regular SDSers and followed the emphasis
on the "self-determination" line by Dohrn, who was the SDSer
perhaps closest to the Panther leaders, allows the possibility that
it was planned the previous night by at least some of the NO
forces. In either case, it provided a dramatic moment for the
convention: every person in the hall recognized it as an inescapable ultimatum.

PLers, reacting immediately, began a chant of "Smash redbaiting, Smash redbaiting." Cook tried to go on with a few more
attacks on PL—"counter-revolutionary," "chickenshit," "they
act like pigs"—but the PL cries became ever more strident:
"Smash redbaiting, Smash redbaiting," "Read Mao, *Read Mao,"*
"Bull-*shit!* Bull-*shit!"* The NO supporters responded with the
Panther slogan, "Power to the people! Power to the people," and
with hardly a missed beat the PL delegates thundered back,
"Power to the *workers!* Power to the *workers!"* The cacophony
filled the Coliseum, rising with the passions and the angers on the

floor, fifteen hundred people caught in an acoustical tornado. The Panthers turned away, gave the finger to the women at the PL literature table near the stage, and stalked off from the bedlam they had created. As the sound slowly died, Jeff Gordon marched to the podium with a dozen of his heftiest colleagues, seized the microphone, and waited for quiet. Then in an eerie calm voice, and slowly, he said: "PL . . . will not . . . be intimidated out of SDS." Half the audience broke into cheers and applause. Gordon went on: PL has taken a principled stand in support of Third World liberation, it supports black self-determination in the United States, and it supports the Black Panther Party—though it also offers comradely criticism when it feels that this is needed. He was reasonable and firm, playing an avuncular role amid the tumult, taking the high ground of the offended but forgiving party—and it was effective.

The NO leaders—Klonsky, Dohrn, Rudd, and Robbins prominent among them—hastily gathered in a knot at the back of the stage, in heated discussion. Finally Rudd stepped to the microphone and proposed an hour's recess, both to let things cool off and to give the leaders a chance to figure out what to do next. But before the vote could be taken Dohrn wrenched herself away from Klonsky, who was trying to restrain her at the back of the stage, and marched to the rostrum, hair flying, jaw set. We're going to have to decide, she shouted into the microphone, whether we can continue to stay in the same organization with people who deny the right of self-determination to the oppressed—and anyone who wants to talk about that, follow me into the next room. She spun on her heel and marched off the stage down a corridor to the side. It may have been a planned performance, but if so there weren't many people in on the plan. Klonsky looked stunned and momentarily undecided, Rudd paused and stared into the crowd before following after, and RYM supporters throughout the hall only slowly and somewhat uncertainly got to their feet, maybe fifty at first, then slowly another fifty more. PL went into more chants: "Sit down, Sit down, Stay and fight, Stay and fight." A few dozen more people rose, and a procession out of the hall slowly took shape: "No split! No split! No split!" from the PL section. Finally, with perhaps two hundred in all, the RYM supporters crowded into the corridor at the front, now with their fists raised, and

shouting back, "Join us! Join us!" and "Two, three, many Vietnams." That last was an unconsciously ironic chant now, for there
was no longer any doubt what was happening in Chicago: two,
three, many SDSs.

The RYM caucus gathered in a smaller wood-floored arena
off the main hall and for the next three hours the NO leaders tried
to rally forces behind an all-out split. At midnight, nothing decided, the meeting broke until Saturday morning, when the process started over again; a long, rambling, often boring debate
ranging from grand political verities to minor tactical nit-picking,
with the heavies doing most of the talking, and the SDSers in
attendance ranging from five hundred to a thousand, many of
them going out to the main hall from time to time to participate
in the ongoing PL-run "plenary" session. For a long time there
was no agreement: everyone in the caucus was opposed to PL, all
right, but there was a lot of disagreement on how to do the
opposing. Some, unhappy with RYM politics to begin with and
bothered by the manipulative walkout, wanted to go back in and
join the PLers, try to get through the weekend, and go on as before
—what happens here doesn't really make much difference to the
thousands of people out on the campuses, and out there the PLers
are a tiny and unimportant minority anyway. Others favored
going back in and debating the PLers head-on, fighting it out on
the floor until one or the other gained a majority and won control
of the organization: dare to struggle, dare to win, they said, and,
besides, the credentials committee has figured that the non-PLers
were in a majority. Most of the SDS leadership, Weatherman and
RYM II alike, tended to favor the idea of expelling PL outright
and constituting the caucus as the "real" SDS. Finally, early
Saturday evening, with everyone growing weary and restive but
with the pro-expulsion stand gaining favor, Bernardine Dohrn
spoke once more, giving what reporter Andrew Kopkind described as "obviously the outstanding political speech of the whole
week." Pacing back and forth on the floor before the bleachers,
in raggedy-cuffed trousers and a faded man's shirt, she slowly
went through the history of the Movement in the past decade,
described the traditions that had made SDS into the leading organization in this Movement, and showed how PL stood outside this
tradition at every point; now, she said, when we are faced with a

greater task than ever before, it should be those who represent the true traditions who carry it on, unhampered by the "counter-revolutionaries" who simply stand in the way and want us to deny our decade-old allegiance to the blacks, the Vietnamese, the guerrillas, the youth of America. Expulsion, she argued, was the only answer, and directness the only means: we should simply go in there and tell PL that it is no longer a part of this organization. "We are *not* a caucus," she concluded. "*We are SDS.*" The die was cast. By a heavy margin, perhaps five hundred to one hundred, expulsion was agreed upon.

No one worried very much at that point about the legality of it all, the constitutional provisions that membership was "open to all who share the commitment of the organization to democracy as a means and as a social goal" and members could not be expelled except "by a two-thirds vote of the National Council." No one bothered much about the firmly entrenched and heretofore highly regarded principle that SDS was nonexclusionist. No one even protested much when the NO leadership decided that the expulsion question should not even be put to a vote of the unified plenary, on the grounds that it would mean "counter-revolutionaries having the right to 'vote' on their own counter-revolutionary nature."* Instead it was decided that a statement of principles should be drawn up explaining the reasons for the expulsion and simply dumped in the PLers' laps; accordingly, several of the RYM leaders, Bill Ayers and Dohrn prominent among them, set to work writing up the document. No one seems very clear about how the various items got included—one of them, for example, pledges SDS support to "the People's Republics of Korea and Albania," an allegiance that many people even in the anti-PL crowd found difficult to subscribe to—and since there wasn't time to supply mimeographed copies it is likely that most of the people in the caucus weren't precisely sure what they were agreeing to. Nonetheless, the official statement, written in the wooden RYM-speak characteristic of the deadest part of the Old Left tradition

*The new SDS leadership went on to say, with typical Weatherman logic: "Our task was not to vote: people saw clearly that our political position required action, that action alone would clarify the irreconcilable and antagonistic character of the differences in a way that no words could possibly have done." (*New Left Notes* [Chicago], June 25, 1969.)

(appropriate enough, considering the Old Left action being taken), declares:

> The Progressive Labor Party has attacked every revolutionary nationalist struggle of the black and Latin peoples in the U.S. as being racist and reactionary. For example, they have attacked open admissions, black studies, community control of police and schools, the Black Panther Party and their "breakfast for children" program, and the League of Revolutionary Black Workers.
>
> Progressive Labor Party has attacked Ho Chi Minh, the National Liberation Front of South Vietnam, the revolutionary government of Cuba—all leaders of the people's struggles for freedom against U.S. imperialism.
>
> Progressive Labor Party, because of its positions and practices, is objectively racist, anti-communist, and reactionary. PLP has also in principle and practice refused to join the struggle against male supremacy. It has no place in SDS, an organization of revolutionary youth.
>
> For all these reasons, which have manifested themselves in practice all over the country, as well as at this convention, and because the groups we look to around the world for leadership in the fight against U.S. imperialism, including the Black Panther Party and the Brown Berets, urge us to do so, SDS feels it is now necessary to rid ourselves of the burden of allowing the politics of the Progressive Labor Party to exist within our organization.

A little before eleven o'clock that Saturday night, with the statement drafted and approved, Klonsky went out to talk to Jared Israel and tell him that the caucus wanted to come back in and address the rump. Israel agreed, and both men pledged that there would be no violence. Israel made the announcement and the PLers suspended their meeting—they had been holding workshops and passing resolutions all the while the RYM people were out of the room—and waited, curious and apparently fearful of trouble ahead. Soon a column of women filed out of the caucus room and surrounded the base of the stage, hands stuck belligerently in jeans, faces unsmiling. Next a file of men, the NO's "security force," strode out and stood in a line in front of the women, arms folded across their chests, Panther-style. And the rest of the caucus marched in, slowly filing along the walls under the wary eyes of PL's own "security force" along the perimeters.

There was an eerie hush. Finally Klonsky, Rudd, and Dohrn came through the corridor and mounted the stage.

Dohrn was given the microphone. For the last twenty-four hours, she told the gathering, peering out over the podium into the smoky and ill-lit hall, the SDS caucus has been discussing principles; with that, she was off on another speech, twenty minutes of incisive invective, laying out every real or imagined sin of PL since its inception, quoting, citing, pinning, slashing, a performance so masterful that at least one person was convinced it must have been prepared days in advance. At last she paused. SDS can no longer live with people who are objectively racist, anticommunist, and reactionary. Progressive Labor Party members, people in the Worker-Student Alliance, and all others who do not accept our principles . . . *are no longer members of SDS.*

For a moment there was silence, and then the PLers started to giggle: a strange noise in this hall after all that had come before, a forced and awkward laughter of nervousness, the break of four days of tension. PLers quickly found their voices: "SHAME! SHAME! SHAME!" Dohrn glared down at the PLers and with a last shout into the microphone of *"Long live the victory of people's war"*—the slogan, from China's Lin Piao, was the closing line of the "Weatherman" statement—she stormed off the stage and led the walkout from the Coliseum. Hundreds, perhaps seven hundred in all, followed her, their fists raised, chanting a mélange of slogans—"Power to the people! Power to the people!" "Ho! Ho! Ho Chi Minh!"—out into the Chicago night.*

On the next day there were two SDSs—and a number of oddments in between. Many of the Old Left–style sects, such as the Labor Committees, International Socialist Clubs, and the Spartacists, stayed with PL-SDS, where they could debate traditional sectarian Marxism without interference from the traditional SDSers and their unorthodox and "anarchistic" tendencies. Other

---

*The estimates of how many people left the hall vary according to who is telling the story. Dotson Rader, a regular, claimed "nearly 1,000" (*Village Voice,* July 3, 1969), the *Guardian,* biased against PL, thought there were about 800 (June 28), PL's own *Challenge* reported 650 (July), *Newsweek* said 500 (June 30), the version of *New Left Notes* printed in Boston claimed "about one-third," or roughly 500 (June 30), and WSAer Jim Prickett estimated 400 (*Guardian,* July 26).

pre-formed groups—Yippie collectives, the Panthers, and the
Radical Union, for example—stayed with the SDS regulars. And
some, like a group of anarchists, left the whole thing, issued an
appeal for followers ("Tired of people throwing red books at each
other? Tired of the old rhetoric? Come breathe a breath of fresh
rhetoric!") and went over to the last remaining outpost of official
anarchism, the headquarters of the Industrial Workers of the
World on Chicago's north side.

In the Coliseum some five to six hundred people met: PLers,
WSA members, those who opposed the walkout on principle, and
those who were simply unhappy with the RYMers' behavior,
either before or during the convention. PLers were not particularly pleased with the split, fearful of now drying up the lake they
had been fishing in so successfully for the last three years, but at
the moment it seemed best to put as good a face as possible on the
whole affair and try to claim legitimacy for their side. Accordingly, they went ahead, asserting that they were the "real" SDS
—"There is only ONE S.D.S.: This meeting in the Coliseum is the
1969 National Convention of SDS. This attempt to split and destroy the student movement must and will be fought"—and held
a hypothetically ordinary meeting complete with amendments to
the constitution (to increase NC representation) and the passing
of resolutions (the PL racism proposal and a half-hearted
"women's liberation" proposal). Officers for the new year were
duly chosen, proposed by PLers and elected unopposed. John
Pennington (actually Elgar John Pennington III, but that would
hardly do in PL circles), twenty-four, a longtime PLer and Boston-area traveler for the party, became the new National Secretary; Alan Spector, twenty-three, a Wisconsin graduate who had
been a New England regional traveler and WSA supporter but not
a member of PL, was chosen as the new Education Secretary; and
Patricia Forman, twenty-five, a NYU graduate and WSAer from
San Francisco State, was elected Inter-organizational Secretary.*
With that, they decided to move their version of the National

*On the PL-NIC were Ed Galloway (Georgetown), Mike Golash (Columbia),
Fred Gordon, the outgoing Education Secretary, Jared Israel, Leslie Lincoln
(California, Irvine), Sandy Meyer (Illinois, Chicago Circle), Becky Reavis
(Texas), David Rossoff (Cornell), plus two alternates, Gordon DeMarco (San
Francisco State) and Jim Prickett, of a San Diego "Workers for a Democratic
Society."

Office to Boston and they all went home, happy in the feeling that, as Jeff Gordon told the delegates at one point, "we've just taken over the most important organization in America."

Meanwhile, in a Congregational Church on the west side of town, not far from the National Office, the regular SDSers met, their number estimated at nearly a thousand, swelled overnight by presumably reluctant but choiceless supporters of the national leadership. Little joined the regulars together, however, besides their detestation of PL—natural enough, given the traditionally loose character of SDS—and all attempts to forge a new organization with unified politics with which to fight the revolution were doomed to disaster: you can't go to the barricades with an umbrella. Instead, the regulars decided on two specific action proposals, one to co-sponsor a meeting with the Panthers in July to forge a "United Front Against Fascism," the other to hold a "mass action against the war" in the fall.

The lack of unity was underscored in the election of officers, where both the Weatherman and the RYM II group put up separate slates, though the politics of neither were discussed in any detail: Weatherman chose Mark Rudd for National Secretary, Bill Ayers for Education Secretary, and Jeff Jones for Inter-organizational Secretary. RYM II co-sponsored Jones, chose Bob Avakian for National Secretary, and put up Lynn Wells, a close Klonsky ally who had represented the left wing of SSOC, as Educational Secretary. After desultory debate, the Weatherman slate won by a fairly large margin, and into the national leadership came three of the most active and most dedicated SDSers, each of whom had long ago decided to give his life to the revolution.*

Mark Rudd, who had just turned twenty-two, was perhaps the best known, the media having made him almost into a per-

*The elections to the NIC followed the same pattern, assuring a solid victory for the Weatherman position. Elected on what was called a "unity slate" were Bob Avakian, Edward John ("Corky") Benedict (a graduate of Western Reserve, living in Cleveland), Bernardine Dohrn, Linda Evans (an ex-Michigan State student, living in East Lansing), Noel Ignatin, Mike Klonsky, Howie Machtinger, and Barbara Reilly (a German citizen in the U.S. for six years, living in New York), with Phoebe Hirsch (a New Yorker) as first alternate. (By July, Reilly had resigned from the NIC, presumably to avoid deportation problems rather than for political reasons, and she was replaced by Hirsch.) Avakian, Ignatin, and Klonsky were associated with RYM II, the rest with Weatherman.

sonification of SDS ever since the Columbia uprising; indeed, Rudd used this very fact in plumping for his election: "The Movement needs leadership," he said, "the Movement needs symbols, and my name exists as a symbol." He was quite good for the part, actually, tall, with large shoulders that gave him a kind of hulking posture, piercing blue eyes, a prominent lower jaw, and an over-all look of tough handsomeness, plus a thoroughly egocentric energy and a perpetually on-stage manner which the press liked to call "charisma." The second son of an upper-middle-class Jewish immigrant family in suburban Maplewood, New Jersey—his father was a real-estate operator and a lieutenant colonel in the army reserves—Rudd had an exemplary and undistinguished boyhood: Boy Scouts, good grades, well-liked. It was not until he got to Columbia in the fall of 1965 and began talking with the active students there ("They were the only people *doing* anything") that his politics grew: he began working for SDS in the fall of 1966, devoted more and more time during his junior year, and as we have seen, became chairman of the chapter on an action-faction platform in the spring of 1968. Since then he had dropped out of school to devote full time to SDS, based in the New York Regional Office but traveling across the country several times on fund raising and organizing tours, during which his blunt, profane style and his single-minded, humorless dedication attracted large audiences of students but did nothing to improve SDS's reputation for arrogance and rigidity.

Ayers, twenty-four, had also become a well-known figure—though within SDS circles rather than without—in the course of the last year, during which his good humor and enthusiasm had attracted attention both at national meetings and on the Ohio-Michigan campuses he traveled. Of only medium height, he gave off a kind of boyish air despite his age (he was generally known as "Billy") with his unkempt mop of light-brown hair, a wide-eyed look behind steel-rimmed glasses, and a soft, youthful face. Ayers was born in the wealthy suburb of Oak Park, Illinois, his father being the chairman of Commonwealth Edison Company of Chicago and a trustee of Northwestern, an eminent pillar of the Establishment whose generous allowances in later years, the son averred, were used "to finance the revolution." He had gone to the

University of Michigan for three years, during which he had been arrested at a draft board sit-in (the October 1965 affair that had called down the punitive wrath of Selective Service Director Hershey), but he dropped out of school after the spring of 1966 to devote himself full time to an Ann Arbor Children's Community School, a vaguely Summerhillian primary-school experiment started the year before. For two years he labored in the school—working with Diana Oughton, with whom he lived for much of the time, and Skip Taub, another Michigan SDSer—trying to make it politically and educationally successful; he served as director from 1967–68, and even ran for the local school board, a bid which failed because of reaction to his uncompromising politics. The school itself failed in the summer of 1968—the attempt to create new human beings in the bowels of the old system provoked only controversy among the rather conventional parents, and soon both support and money dwindled—leaving Ayers extremely bitter about the possibilities of peaceful change. That summer he worked in the National Office for a bit, became a leader of the activist Jesse James Gang at Michigan that fall, and devoted himself full time to SDS as a regional traveler.

Jeffrey Jones, twenty-two, was somewhat less flamboyant than the other two—his cool-headed chairing of the RYM caucus was one of the factors in his election—but he had been a committed organizer for just as long. Born in Philadelphia, he had gone to Antioch College in 1965, then quit after a year to work in the Movement, first serving as a regional organizer for SDS in the Midwest and then acting as an SDS representative (with Steve Halliwell and Cathy Wilkerson) at a meeting with the NLF in Cambodia in the fall of 1967. He was elected to the NIC the previous June as a New York City representative and worked out of that office for a while before going out to San Francisco State to lend a hand in the strike there during the early spring. An impressive sort of man with neat features and long straight blond hair sweeping to his shoulders, he became one of the leading public figures for SDS in the months ahead.

On Monday morning, June 25, it was all over. The country was then greeted by the curious spectacle of two "real SDSs" and no SDS—that is to say, two tight factional groups, neither recognizable to earlier SDSers as an SDS organization, and both excluding by design or inevitability the great bulk of ordinary SDSers on the campuses or in the streets. The *real* SDS could not stand up: it had been buried once and for all beneath the Chicago Coliseum.

"Weatherman"* was hardly more than another position paper when it was written, certainly not the foundation of an ideology nor the blueprint for a new youth organization. But out of the turbulence of the convention, during which Weatherman emerged both as the inheritor of the SDS tradition and the chief opposition to Progressive Labor, and then out of the buffeting experiences of the summer, when Weatherman tried to puts its principles into action, it grew into a new kind of political group, a self-conscious army of revolutionaries—ragtaggle and erratic, perhaps, but sincere and single-minded—a force unlike any ever seen before in America.

In the days after the convention, the Weatherman leaders— soon to be known, naturally, as the Weatherbureau—moved into the Chicago National Office and began overseeing the two major programs of the summer: the first, a series of city-based "action projects," as mapped out in the Ayers-Mellen paper at the Austin NC ("Weatherman" itself was devoid of programs), designed to propagandize and enlist working-class youths into the revolution; the second, preparations for the fall antiwar march, or "National Action," which was being billed as an "absolutely crucial" demonstration for SDS around the theme of "Bring the war home!" The three top officers were in Chicago, of course, but many of the other Weatherleaders stayed there, too (chief among them: Kathy Boudin, Bernardine Dohrn, John Jacobs, Gerry Long, Jeff Melish, Terry Robbins, Cathy Wilkerson), trying to forge themselves into a true "political collective" around Weatherman politics, giving

---

*Weatherman nomenclature is difficult. In general, during the first year of its existence, "Weatherman" referred to the politics and the group as a whole and "Weathermen" to the people, even the women, though gradually the term "Weatherwoman" came into use. It was not until sometime in 1970, however, that the sexism of "Weatherman" became abrasive and the term "Weatherpeople" (or "Weatherfolks") and "Weather Underground" came into more general use. There were also many neologisms, like "Weatherline," "Weatherleader," "Weatheraction," and so on.

SDS a truly homogeneous leadership that it had never really had since the earliest days.*

The city "action projects" were begun even before the convention, with SDSers renting apartments in bands of ten or a dozen in several medium-sized cities which were seen as appropriately "working class" in demography: about thirty people going to Seattle and fifteen to Denver in the West, some forty to Detroit, thirty to Cleveland, and twenty-five each to Athens and Columbus in the Midwest, and thirty to New York City (the Bronx and Queens) and half a dozen to Newark in the East—more than two hundred in all. Generally those attracted to the projects were college students from actionist SDS chapters on campuses where there had been some kind of major confrontation: Columbia, Wisconsin, Kent State, Colorado, Chicago, Seattle Community College. (Interestingly, if unexplainably, Weatherman and its summer projects seemed to attract very few people from California, even where campus disruptions had been large.) There were interesting similarities with the ERAP summer projects—about which the current people, alas, were ignorant—but these proved to be even more chaotic and wrenching, even more manic in their successes and failures, driving some people forever back into the arms of

*Some light might be shed upon the attitudes and tastes of these early Weathermen by the kinds of books later found in one of their apartments (shared by Long, Dohrn, Jacobs, Jeff Blum, Bob Tomashevsky, and Peter Clapp). Among them: *Alienation of Modern Man,* Fritz Pappenheim; *An Ordinary Laborer,* Wang Yuan Chien; *A Populist Reader,* George B. Tindall; *Beautiful Losers,* Leonard Cohen; *Billy Budd,* Herman Melville; *Caligari to Hitler,* Siegfried Kracauer; *Cat's Cradle,* Kurt Vonnegut, Jr.; *Economic & Philosophic Manuscript of 1844,* Karl Marx; *Flash and Filigree,* Terry Southern; *French Cinema,* Roy Armes; *Going Away,* Clancy Sigal; *Industry and Empire,* E. J. Hobsbawm; *Karl Marx,* T. O. Bottomore; *Let Us Now Praise Famous Men,* James Agee; *Marxism and the Linguistic Philosophy,* Maurice Cornforth; *Mexico,* Kate Simon; *The Magic Christian,* Terry Southern; *The Man Who Cried I Am,* John A. Williams; *The Negro and the First Amendment,* Harry Kalven, Jr.; *The Possessed,* Fyodor Dostoyevsky; *The Socialist Party of America,* David A. Shannon; *The Souls of Black Folk,* W. E. B. DuBois; *The Speeches of Malcolm X,* Archie Epps; *Toussaint L'Ouverture,* Aimé Césaire; and *Walden Two,* B. F. Skinner. (Cited by the Illinois Crime Investigating Commission in "Report on the SDS Riots," Senate hearings, "Extent of Subversion in the 'New Left,' " Part 4, p. 622.) It is possible, however, that none of these books was actually opened; Bill Ayers, for example, had announced with apparent pride during his nomination speech at the convention that neither he, Rudd, nor Jones had read a book in a year.

collegiate luxury, turning others into absolutely dedicated revolutionaries ultimately willing to die for their commitment.

The Columbus, Ohio, project seems to have been fairly typical of the Weatherman ventures that summer; it was, by their own account, " 'Weatherman' in practice." About twenty people from outside—four from Kent State (including the project leader, Howie Emmer, twenty-two), two from Penn State, and others from other Ohio colleges—moved into the city, joining a half-dozen other Ohio State and local high-school people already living there, renting three separate $60-a-month apartments in decidedly un-posh neighborhoods; something like a third of them were women, and their average age was twenty, the oldest twenty-four and the youngest eighteen. Several of them began by getting jobs in the area, but most people who didn't know the town found it difficult to get work and those who were employed generally quit as the summer wore on and their political work got heavier. Money seems to have been of no real concern: it took very little to keep them going, most of them had parents who were prepared to support them for the summer (at least two had wealthy parents), several were willing to chip in their own savings accounts, and some money apparently came from the Weatherbureau in Chicago.

At the beginning no one had any sure idea of just how they were supposed to carry out the Ayers-Mellen directive of "broadening our constituency to other sections of white working-class youth"; as one woman in the project, Lorraine Rosal, put it, revealingly: "All of us, both men and women, came off our campuses timid, physically afraid of moving in the streets, but more importantly psychologically afraid of the people." On July 4, a little more than a week after the convention, the putative revolutionaries tried marching with an NLF flag through a local park and passing out leaflets about the next American Revolution compared to the last one, but that action apparently won nothing but animosity and bewilderment from most of the holiday strollers; a similar propaganda assault at a fireworks display that night ended up in a shoving match with a bunch of local right-wingers that had to be broken up by the police. For the next two days the collectives talked over their July 4 actions, in a bout of navel-gazing that seems to have been typical of all the collectives across the country

—"criticism-self-criticism" it was called, in proper Maoist fashion —and it was agreed that something more had to be done. Just about then the word came down from the Weatherbureau that the fall's National Action should take top priority in organizing work, with the prime target being high-school-age people hanging around the summer streets or, in Weatherlanguage, "to develop cadre, 16 year old communist guerillas [sic], to build a city wide revolutionary youth movement to smash the pig power structure."

Accordingly, the collectives decided to concentrate their efforts on the poorer and tougher neighborhoods of Columbus. For days on end the SDSers would hang around the street corners and drugstores where teenagers were likely to gather, "rapping" with the local youths about the rich and the poor, how everyone should be equal, the need to have a revolution; at nights they would go to the hamburger joints and the schoolyards, acting tough and sure, talking about the need for militant action, about taking to the streets, "kicking ass," "getting us a few pigs," striving to find that resonant chord which the RYM theoreticians had assured them would be there in working-class kids. One night a small band of SDSers, operating under secrecy so stringent that not even other collectives were notified, made a nighttime raid on a high school to spray-paint the walls with slogans ("Off the Pigs," "Viet Cong Will Win" "Fuck U.S. Imperialism"), a commando action whose daring greatly impressed the people in the project but, when they bragged about it to the local teenagers, seemed to produce only genuine puzzlement or yawns. On another night the SDSers invited one group of youths they knew up to one of the apartments for beer, wine, a few cigarettes, and a display of three guns—a .22, a shotgun, and an M-1—which were the total armed might of the Columbus revolution and, as such, seemed pretty paltry to the high-schoolers. All of this effort proved to be notably unsuccessful; one of the SDSers, a local student who later dropped out of the organization, recalls:

> It was nice talking to them [the teenagers], and I wanted to talk to them, and they, you know, they agreed that there were a lot of things wrong. But the SDS plans for them was to get them to fight the police, you know, and to get them to attack the schools and whatever, go to Chicago, and it didn't make any sense, you know. These kids weren't going to do it. I mean they lived in the neighbor-

> hood, they wanted to stay out of trouble, and they wanted to make
> a living and just get along; and they have enough problems without
> getting themselves into more trouble. And the SDS line on them was
> all backwards, it was telling them to throw any chance they got
> away and fight, and fight even though they knew they were going
> to lose. You know, what you learn in SDS is that maybe you'll get
> killed, but the movement will grow, you know, and that's a helluva
> thing to go and tell a kid, I mean a kid who grows up on the street
> —he's gonna say you're crazy.

After a couple of weeks of this, the local kids finally did conclude
the SDSers were crazy, and the organizing effort collapsed one
night when half a dozen of them got into a fist fight with a bunch
of SDSers and chased them from the neighborhood, where they
were nevermore seen again.

But while the attempt at outreach was not notably successful,
there was an intensive ingrowth, and this was true for most of the
Weatherman projects. The more dedicated SDSers were determined to make themselves into true revolutionaries in the course
of the summer (the less dedicated played along for a while and
dropped out), and for them that meant it was as important to
abolish their old middle-class ideas and habits as to win over the
high-schoolers. They were trying to turn themselves into *new* men
and women, into what they called "good communists," people for
whom politics was all—"We have one task," Bill Ayers was to say,
"and that's to make ourselves into tools of the revolution." Operating beneath their quest was the wisdom of the insight, shared by
many Weathermen though not all, that the capitalist system operates not simply through obvious material and military ways but
infests daily lives and thoughts with a million ideas and patterns
which reinforce its power: not just racism and sexism and elitism,
but all the other elements of socialization ingrained since childhood—attitudes to property, privacy, material goods, family,
competition, collectivization, romantic love, homosexuality,
power, status, and all the rest. And though this insight did not
always shine through in practice—there was still a lot of arrogance
and impatience in these actionists—the attempt was made at every
commune: "The fight to destroy the shit in us," as one woman
wrote, "is part of building a new society." They threw themselves
into Mao and Marx, they practiced karate and survived on brown

rice diets, they tried abstinence (off and on) from drugs, alcohol, even pets. Accustomed property feelings had to be rooted out, so that no one felt attached to "personal" belongings, and in many cases Weathermen reduced themselves to a single set of clothes. Individualism and selfishness had to give way to a collective spirit, and this meant totally: nothing, including an individual's desire to leave the apartment for a walk, was to be decided without group discussion. The desire for privacy also had to be uprooted, smacking as it did of individualism and self-centeredness, and in several collectives no one was permitted to be separated from another communard (this had its security advantages, too, of course). Attitudes to wealth and materialism had to be challenged, eventually to the point of requiring the Weathermen to donate their personal savings to the collective, a step many found difficult to take. Anything hinting of racism, national chauvinism, or liberalism had to be confronted collectively, dissected, and discarded. Male chauvinism, both in word and action, had to be purged, again through collective sessions often resembling group therapy more than anything else, and the Weatherwomen grew in strength at most projects over the summer as they banded together to oversee this purgation. And accustomed sexual relations were to be scrapped in favor of a freewheeling partner-swapping that would allow people to concentrate on their particular jobs in the revolution rather than on the comforts or needs of any one other individual.

This last aspect of collective life—"smash monogamy" it was called in Weatherlanguage—attracted a good deal of attention both inside and outside the collectives, and because it was such a dramatic shift, with couples (even married couples) being separated and in some cases new partners selected with spin-the-bottle arbitrariness, it stands as symbolic of much of what Weatherman was trying to do. In many ways it was mechanical and stifling, as with the Columbus couple who were told they had to live separately and found after a while that they were behaving far more selfishly and cruelly apart than they had together; they eventually dropped out and went back together to fight the revolution their own way. "Very often," some Weathermen later wrote, "we failed to see how the strength that could come from a very close loving relationship between two people could be a very revolutionary thing." And yet for many people, and many collectives, the end of monogamy turned out to be truly liberating. A pair of New York Weathermen noted:

> The results of ending monogamy in our collective were amazing. Women, who for years had been silent or someone's girlfriend, in two or three weeks became strong political leaders. Women grew incredibly close to each other and used that closeness as a source of revolutionary strength.

And a Weatherwoman, reflecting a sense that seems to have been shared most particularly by the women in the Weathercollectives, has written:

> Our monogamous relationships broke up because we simply didn't need them any more. We began not to have to identify ourselves through men and could become total human beings. Women began digging one another, jealousy and competition were not necessary any more because our point of existence was the revolution and the old way of life became intolerable to us. . . . We do not view ourselves as sex objects but as part of the revolution. Sex isn't something to happen isolated from daily work. Destroying the one man, one woman relationship was perhaps the most liberating thing that happened to us. We could speak at meetings without being uptight or being on an ego trip and most important we were upfront at demonstrations along with men. We became self reliant and don't have to protect any one, we are forced to struggle and it makes life more meaningful. We changed because of the necessity of the times and dig the changes.

Naturally this kind of collective pressure, the attempt to make instant communists, took its toll. Especially racking, apparently, were the "criticism-self-criticism" discussions, sometimes so brutal and probing that in some collectives they were given the name "Weatherfries." One woman left the Columbus project in August, frantic and nerve-shattered, unable to take this version of the communal life: "I had to ask group permission even to go upstairs to read a book. I'm a private sort of person, but was never allowed to be alone. I broke under the pressure." Another Columbus man chafed under the collective discipline:

> I mean if you say something, just happen to say something that somebody might construe as being racist or imperialist, well, right

away, call a meeting, everybody in the collective has got to sit down
and we have to discuss this. And I want to go out to my mother's
to see if I got any mail out there or to do my laundry, we have to
have a meeting about that, you know.

He dropped out of the project with such a vengeance that he ended
up "confessing" everything to the Columbus police on a tape
recording later used by the House Internal Security Committee.
But it was not only the collective experience that caused difficulties in the Columbus project: there was also the haunted effect of
knowing you are being watched by the police every day (the
Columbus agents apparently made no secret of it), the distrusts
and enmities that develop in any group where strangers are
thrown together, and the gnawing feeling of uncertainty that came
with the failure of the project to live up to its hopes. And then the
fact that all but two of the Weathermen ended up the summer
having been arrested, several with high bonds and court cases and
possible jail terms in front of them, could hardly have been a
source of much comfort. Under these kinds of pressures, many
Columbus Weathermen of June went back to being students by
September. Of the two dozen people originally in the project, only
half a dozen went on to the fall's National Action.

But they were the committed ones, molding themselves into
the new men and women, the cadre who were the backbone of
Weatherman. Lorraine Rosal wrote after a summer in Columbus:

> The political polarization that has occurred through these struggles
> has been the basis for our organizing success. Every day it becomes
> clearer that struggle is the only way to build a fighting move-
> ment. . . .
>
> We have rejected our programmed bourgeois roles as the bas-
> tion of conservative forces in the home, on the job, and in the
> community; we have attacked our being used as a surplus labor
> force for imperialist, racist dogs; we have attacked our role as
> chattel, scabbing on the international liberation struggle. Instead,
> we have accepted a new role—a role of dignity—a role as members
> of a women's army, fighting not just for our own liberation, but for
> the liberation of all the people.

"Struggle is the only way to build a fighting movement": this
was the sampler over the Weatherman bed. Struggle . . . action
. . . confrontation . . . fighting: Weatherman made the summer into

a time to test itself, prepare itself, steel itself. Out of the action factions, convinced that power was not in broad support but in pinpointed militance, the Weathermen came with a determination for action. On every front.

Some actions were mild: attempts to leaflet and speak to rock concerts in Detroit and New York, impromptu speeches during the intermissions of such movies as *Che!* and *Easy Rider,* an official booth set up at the Woodstock Festival in upstate New York in August (though, truthfully, no one seems to have any memory of what went on at that booth). Others were more violent: there were fist and chair-leg fights with Progressive Labor–WSA forces in New York on July 7 when PLers, trying to crash a RYM meeting at NYU, started a minor brawl broken up by guns-drawn police; in Boston on July 16 when Weathermen, taking the battle into enemy territory, tried to exclude PLers and found themselves with another fight on their hands, this time with one WSAer wielding a broken bottle; in Oakland in mid-July when PLers and SDSers clashed at least twice in a park outside the Black Panthers' United Front Against Fascism convention (according to PL two Weathermen were hospitalized, according to *New Left Notes* [Chicago] ten PLers were hospitalized). There were confrontations between Weathermen and cops in several cities, usually staged by the former so as to give themselves a "tough" reputation among the street kids they were trying to impress—in Denver in August when six Weathermen were arrested resisting police who tried to break up a march on a local IDA project; in Seattle in August when fights between Weathermen and hostile youths at a local beach turned into fights against *police* and hostile youths, resulting in the arrest of some sixty people; in Milwaukee in September when Rudd and other SDSers scuffled with police at a teen-age hamburger hangout; and in Detroit on September 27 when police tried to arrest John Jacobs for leading a march of sixty Weathermen through downtown streets and were surprised when the young people, both men and women, turned on them and fought back with rocks, feet, fists, and a chain, creating a brief melee in which several police were roughed up, one suffered a broken wrist, eleven Weathermen were arrested, and one severely beaten. There were even internecine battles within the Movement —Weathermen stormed the stage of a Student Mobilization Committee convention in Cleveland in August to push and publicize their militant National Action politics; members of the "Motor City" collectives broke up an antiwar meeting in Detroit the same month, again urging their "kick-ass" tactics for the fall; and SDSers and other miltants broke out of the march lines and took over the stage during a Hiroshima Day demonstration in New York, after which Jeff Jones proceeded to harangue the assembled marchers and the entire Movement for insufficient toughness.

But the tactic of choice for the summer was the invasion of classrooms and schools—"jailbreaks," in Weatherlingo—and these took place in Akron, Boston, Chicago, Columbus, Detroit, Flint, New York, and Pittsburgh, with the two most dramatic in Warren, Michigan, and Pittsburgh. In Warren, a Detroit suburb, on July 31, ten women from the Motor City collectives descended on Macomb County Community College—chosen because its students were held to be "working class"—and invaded a classroom where students were taking final examinations. They barricaded the door and started lecturing the thirty bewildered students about imperialism, racism, sexism, and the upcoming National Action in what must have been fairly incomprehensible terms ("They rapped about . . . how the Vietnamese women carry on armed struggle together with Vietnamese men against US imperialism," according to *New Left Notes*), and shoved one older man into his seat when he started to complain and pummeled another man when he tried to escape (*New Left Notes* proudly told of "attacking the men with karate," but the victim himself said it felt more like biting and scratching). But the women failed to prevent the teacher from slipping out a back door and calling the police, so all but one of them were trapped and arrested in the parking lot as they were making their getaway. Despite the arrests and bail of $6500, however, despite the generally hostile reception from the Macomb students, *New Left Notes* proclaimed the women heroic warriors: "Women's liberation will come when women exercise real power as is done in Vietnam and in the Macomb college classroom."* The Pittsburgh action took place four weeks later,

*The "Motor City Nine" were Rachel Bishop, Ellen Borison, Lynn Garvin, Elizabeth Gilbert, Ann Hathaway, Lenore Kalom, Karen Latimer, Charlotte Marchant, and Karen Selin; the tenth woman was later identified as Denise Ryan. Of note is the fact that one of the women, Rachel Bishop, was a black, one of the few in all SDS at this point, certainly one of the few in Weatherman.

on September 4, when a contingent of some seventy-five women moved into the city, some of them casing the South Hills High School, thought to be a typical working-class school in a working-class city, and others going into the local American Friends Service Committee offices where they kept six of the workers hostage while they ran off leaflets for the "jailbreak." During the lunch hour they descended en masse on the school, and while one group outside distributed leaflets and papers another group stormed into the building itself, and at least some of them apparently raised their shirts over their heads exposing their breasts, which seems to have made a major impression on the male school administrators. Gathering outside with an NLF flag, one woman standing atop a car near the school entrance, the Weatherwomen began an impromptu rally trying to make instant recruits for the National Action. It didn't take long for the first two policemen to arrive, but when they tried to break up the demonstration they were set upon and pelted by the women, and it took the arrival of eight squad cars of reinforcements to send the women running; most escaped, but twenty-six were arrested, including NICer Linda Evans, Cathy Wilkerson, and New York SDSers Naomi Jaffe and Eleanor Raskin. Again *New Left Notes* saw a triumph: "The kids at the school know that what really happened was that women, speaking in support of the Vietnamese, black and brown struggles and against the pigs, the teachers, and the courts came to their school, fought the pigs, and won."

In fact there was never any noticeable evidence that these school invasions had this, or any other intended, effect. They seemed to have inspired more hostility than warmth, more puzzlement than respect. But such was the state of self-centeredness and self-intoxication of the Weathermen by now that the action became more important than the reception.

There were other factors, too, contributing to the growth of Weatherman attitudes that summer, most especially the split with the Black Panthers, the further rift within SDS itself, and the international contacts made with Cuban and Vietnamese revolutionaries.

The Panther split grew out of the United Front Against Fascism conference, July 18–20, in Oakland, called by the Black

Panther Party to try to mobilize white support against the very real and escalating campaign of repression waged against them by the government. It was an awkward affair to begin with, since its convening was really a confession by the Panthers that they had failed to build an effective popular base in their own black communities and had to depend upon the white left for aid and comfort in a time of crisis; it was made more awkward by the Panther's open dependence upon the discredited Communist Party, which was obviously footing most of the bill, and their rigid and authoritarian handling of the meetings. But the worst of it was that the whole conference was called to consider, and ended up approving, a Panther campaign for community control of the police, and the Weathermen felt that they simply couldn't go along: community control in black areas, yes, the NIC told the Panthers the day after the conference, but community control in white areas "not only undermines the fight against white supremacy" but would only lead to white vigilante bands, and that they couldn't support. This dissent, coupled with fairly common criticism of the conference by Movement whites, seems to have really enraged the Panthers and, as at the Chicago SDS convention, they struck out harshly in hurt response. Early in August Chairman Bobby Seale and Chief of Staff David Hilliard let fly at SDS, Seale denouncing them as "a bunch of those jive bourgeois national socialists and national chauvinists," and Hilliard added:

> We don't see SDS as being so revolutionary. We see SDS as just being another pacification front. . . . SDS had better get their politics straight because the Black Panther Party is drawing some very clear lines between friends and enemies. And that we're gonna make it very clear that we're not going to be attacked from any of those motherfuckers. . . . We'll beat those little sissies, those little schoolboys' ass if they don't try to straighten up their politics. So we want to make it known to SDS and the first motherfucker that gets out of order had better stand in line for some kind of disciplinary actions from the Black Panther Party.

This was not exactly the kind of fraternalism SDS thought it had been establishing with the Panthers, not the sort of unity it thought had emerged from the June convention. SDS was in a difficult position, being publicly denounced by the group that it had declared was both the "vanguard" and (in an issue of *New Left Notes* even then on the press) the "model for all who will fight"—the group it had even purged its ranks to accommodate —and this was made all the more difficult when Bobby Seale was arrested for murder three days later and white sympathies for the Panthers soared even further. Publicly the NIC confined itself to a small item in *New Left Notes,* a reprinting of its original stand on community control, plus a few bitter remarks toward the Movement papers that made much of the disagreements; privately, however, SDSers were hurt and stung, tending to agree with *Guardian* columnist Julius Lester that "the contempt shown SDS in this instance cannot be said to exemplify the conduct and attitudes one has a right to expect (and demand) from anyone claiming to be revolutionary." In the minds of many, the Panthers could no longer be counted upon as friends or allies, and it seemed clear to many of the Weathermen that they would have to go out and do the job themselves, an attitude that would eventually grow into an unspoken conviction that it was really Weatherman that was the vanguard of the revolution, after all.

The split within SDS ranks only increased this sense of isolation and commitment. As Weathermen evolved their politics and carried out their actions over the summer, major segments of the old SDS, including those among the leadership, found it impossible to go along. The most serious break was with the RYM II faction. As early as July, Mike Klonsky and several other people associated with the RYM II paper had begun voicing their doubts about Weatherman's direction, Noel Ignatin wrote a scathing indictment of "Weatherman" (expressing "profound, total and unresolvable disagreements"), and finally Klonsky formally resigned from the National Action Committee in Chicago and moved back to California. Klonsky's differences were aired in the August 29 *New Left Notes,* where he accused Weatherman of paying too little attention to the working class, destroying potential blue-collar support by the "arrogance" and "militancy" of such actions as the Macomb College raid, and displaying a "sectarianism and adventurism" about the National Action that had alienated most people, even in the Movement, and would turn it into a "big flop." Mark Rudd and Terry Robbins, speaking for the Weathermen, fired back an uncompromising—indeed, an unfriendly—reply, defending their plans for a militant demonstration and asserting that they would never compromise their politics just to gain Movement support. The result was that by the end of the summer those who leaned toward RYM II—chiefly the Avakianites in California, the REP collective in Detroit, Ignatin and his Revolutionary League in Chicago, Lynn Wells and the former "left wing" of SSOC in the South, and SDS alumni like Carl Davidson and Clark Kissinger—simply decided to go their own way and organize their own separate demonstration in Chicago in October.

The final determinant of Weatherman's character over the summer was its contact with the Cubans and Vietnamese, concrete experiences of the Third World revolution it had been so highly touting. NICer Linda Evans made a journey to Hanoi in July, along with six other antiwar activists,* in order to bring home three captured U.S. pilots whom the North Vietnamese had released in honor of America's Independence Day. The experience of being in a country resisting American imperialism—"to see how they are carrying out a People's War," as companion Norm Fruchter said afterward—was as profound on Evans as it had been on every other previous traveler, and she returned to Chicago full of enthusiasm for the way the Vietnamese were "winning total victory." A week later a contingent of Weathermen† returned from an intensive eight-day meeting in Cuba with representatives of North Vietnam and the new Provisional Revolutionary Government of South Vietnam full of the same enthusiasm, only coupled with the additional elation of seeing the Cuban society at work. The messages from the Vietnamese were two, both grist for the Weathermill: first, in the words of a man from the People's Liberation Armed Forces, that "the U.S. can never escape from the labyrinth and sea of fire of peoples' war" and was suffering a total defeat in Vietnam; second, that American revolutionaries had the job of building the American Movement to the point where it could put invincible pressure upon the government for

*Rennie Davis of the Mobilization Committee, Norm Fruchter, John Douglas, and Robert Kramer of Newsreel, Grace Paley of Resist, and James Johnson of the Fort Hood Three.
†Including Bo Burlingham, Peter Clapp, Bernardine Dohrn, Dianne Donghi, Ted Gold, Jeff Melish, Diana Oughton, and Eleanor Raskin.

withdrawal. To the Weathermen, this meant that the collapse of
the U.S. government was imminent, perhaps a matter of months
rather than years, that the "duty of every revolutionary is to make
the revolution," and that Americans had to go back and fight in
the "mother country" as vigorously as the Vietnamese and the
Cubans in the Third World. People from other sections of the
Movement who made the trip with the Weathermen (and for the
most part ended up in bitter disputes with them) recall that on the
boat going back the Weathermen were going around promising to
"kick ass" once they got back—which could hardly have been
what their hosts had in mind in urging the expansion of the
American Movement. But the Weathermen were not to be swayed
from their vision; as Ted Gold put it, in an article for Liberation
News Service which apparently reflected the passions of all the
Weathermen who had made the trip:

> As people who are located inside the monster, revolutionary Ameri-
> cans are in a position to do decisive damage to the U.S. ruling class's
> plans to continue and expand its world rule. The upcoming U.S.
> defeat in Vietnam will be a vital blow to those plans; we must aim
> to do everything we can to speed up that effect.

And in every Weatherman collective that message was taken to
heart.

By the end of the summer, Weatherman was moving full
speed toward a new style of revolutionary politics. In Cleveland
on the August 29–September 1 weekend some three hundred people gathered for what was billed as a Midwestern "National Action Conference" but actually was more like Weatherman's first
national convention, at which they hashed over their summertime
experiences and worked to mold themselves into a unified force for
the upcoming assault in October. It was by every account a high-
strung event, a release and a foretoken, a mix and match of youthful excitements, the first time in months that like-minded SDSers
could get together without the hassles of sectarian infighting—and
day by day the people gathered got steadily more intoxicated on
the sense of fellowship, liberation, and commitment. Discussions
were abnormally intense, an extension of the criticism-self-criticism spirit of the summer collectives; people displaying even

casual signs of sexism, racism, chauvinism, and the like were subjected to harsh and occasionally brutal group discussions. Everything was political, and all politics was directed toward making better revolutionaries. "Cleveland," wrote two New York Weathermen, "was a mind-fuck . . . seventy-two hours of nonstop political struggle."

Women, having asserted themselves with rare strength in the collectives, played an especially strong role in Cleveland, too, meeting for the most part by themselves, trading experiences of the summer, eventually coalescing with such purposiveness that they planned the Pittsburgh jailbreak right then and there as a national Weatherwoman's action. The overwhelming consensus was that the fight against monogamy was important and that it had proved to be a crucial lever, the collectives the fulcrum, in moving aside the immense bulk of male supremacy. One woman reported later:

> In Cleveland we began to see concrete examples of how monogamy politically weakened women. One woman told how she and her boyfriend were working in a Weatherman summer project together. She contributed very little and sort of hung around. When her boyfriend went to jail for a month she assumed some leadership of the summer project. Her fears about herself diminished, yet immediately upon his return she retired into the background again. Most of the women present had been through similar experiences. We then realized that if we were to become revolutionaries these relationships had to be broken because people had to become self reliant to do what has to be done to fight the state.

That weekend many couples who had survived the summer, including a few married couples, made the decision to live in separate collectives for the six weeks remaining until the National Action.

The emergence of the Weatherbureau as a unified and powerful political force also became evident in Cleveland. There was no more worry about whether there should be leaders or an "elite" at the top of the organization, the issue that so colored the early years of SDS; now the assumption was that a revolutionary organization had to be hierarchical, that orders had to come from the top, and that the people at the top should be strong and assertive. A pair of Weathermen later said:

It was in Cleveland that the Weatherbureau . . . firmly established
its leadership of the organization. That leadership existed on many
levels. . . . [On one occasion] Rudd asked a group of us why we
thought the Weatherbureau was leadership. People gave various
answers, none of which satisfied Mark. "The reason we lead this
organization," said Mark, "is that we're right more often than
anyone else. Because we try and work out a correct understanding
of what has to be done and then implement that understanding."

It was logic which seemed to persuade the participants:

> Leadership was a totally important concept for Weatherman. We
> were among the first white radicals to understand that strong lead-
> ers were good leaders, that leadership was seized, not granted, that
> being a leader meant doing it first, taking the most risks, being most
> open about yourself, fighting pigs hardest, building cadre most.

So much for participatory democracy.

But the high point of the weekend was a speech by Education
Secretary Bill Ayers, full of his infectious enthusiasm and of the
optimism which the national leadership was feeling, apparently
genuinely, about the October demonstrations. He used the occasion to dispel the criticism that had been made from a variety of
quarters about the Weathermen's plans, especially that they were
acting like "a bunch of adventurist fools":

> If it is a worldwide struggle, if Weatherman is correct in that basic
> thing, that the basic struggle in the world today is the struggle of
> the oppressed people against US imperialism, then it is the case that
> nothing we could do in the mother country could be adventurist.
> Nothing we could do because there is a war going on already, and
> the terms of that war are set. We couldn't be adventurist while there
> is genocide going on in Vietnam and in the black commu-
> nity. . . .

We have been attacked, he went on, specifically by Klonsky, for
"fighting the people" instead of serving the people:

> The more I thought about that thing "fight the people"—it's not
> that it's a great mass slogan or anything, but there's something to
> it. What's true about it is that we've never been in a struggle where
> we didn't have to fight some of the people. . . . There's a lot in white
> Americans that we do have to fight, and beat out of them, and beat
> out of ourselves. And that part of it is true—we have to be willing

to fight people, and fight things in ourselves, and fight things in all white Americans—white privilege, racism, male supremacy—in order to build a revolutionary movement.

Ultimately, as Ayers saw it, the National Action would be successful if people felt confident about it:

> What we have to communicate to people is our strength, and to show people our strength we have to show them the strength of fighting on the side of the worldwide movement. . . . That's the image of Vietnam, it's that strength, that confidence, and that's what we have to bring to our own constituency. . . . We can't project that phony kind of image that you join the movement because you get a dollar more an hour, you join it cause you get *New Left Notes,* some bullshit—though that's a good thing, not a bad thing. You join the movement because you want to be part of that worldwide struggle that's obviously winning, and you win people over to it, and you win people over by being honest to them about the risks, by being honest to them about the struggle, by being honest to them that what they are getting into is a fight: it's not a comfortable life, it's not just a dollar more, it's standing up in the face of the enemy, and risking your life and risking everything for that struggle. But it's also being on the side of victory, and that's the essential thing we have to show people. . . .
>
> Strategically, in the long run, it's our overwhelming strength that we have to play off of and that we have to win people to, and we have to communicate to people, and that's the only way people are going to come to understand the reality of the fact that we can, and will, and beginning in October are going to bring that war home in Chicago.

An extraordinary speech: Ayers managed to justify for the Weathermen their recklessness, arrogance, self-righteousness, and isolation, in the strongest and most persuasive terms.

The Progressive Labor Party's third annual summer work-in caused an enormous storm in the business community beforehand, helped on by dire warnings from the FBI, but it actually seems to have taken place with virtually no effect at all.

The National Association of Chain Drug Stores, the New York Commerce and Industry Association, and the National Association of Manufacturers all issued alarms to their members, and the NAM distributed four thousand copies of a special

"Checklist for Plant Security" specifically to protect them against SDSers. Local chambers of commerce replicated the warnings, the businessmen in Berkeley, for example, sending out memos against SDS's "insidious plan to disrupt our economy," and the Long Island Association of Commerce and Industry alerting its members that "the militant left-wing Students for a Democratic Society (SDS), responsible for most of the violence and anarchy on the nation's campuses, are planning to invade industrial plants and other business organizations this summer for the purpose of disrupting operations and conducting intense propaganda campaigns among employees." All of the business press—the *Wall Street Journal, Business Week, U.S. News, Barron's,* and the trade journals—carried articles or editorials steeling their readers to the summer's onslaught: *Barron's* predicted "intimidation, sabotage, and violence," and *Industry Week* ran glossy two-page advertisements for its treatment showing a young man with bandoliers and rifles, a young woman with a burning Molotov cocktail, and the headline, "These kids worked up a wild new act for Industry. It's a riot." A variety of unions also denounced the work-in, including teamsters, carpenters, brewery workers, auto workers, and machinists; one labor paper declared:

> We don't think the SDS is made of the stuff of which the Commies were made a generation ago. Those were real working-class stiffs. The SDS is only made up of arrogant, big-mouthed, so-called intellectual bumpkins. They never toil, just look for trouble.

And a Congressman from Texas, James M. Collins, announced that he had a list of twenty-four defense plants which SDS was planning to infiltrate (where this could have come from is a mystery), which the FBI put sufficient faith in to set up a special watch at all defense installations for the summer.

All of this thunder preceded only the merest summer sprinkle. Apparently none of these high-powered bulwarks of American industry was aware of the difference between PL and SDS, and assumed that when PL announced its work-in plans it was speaking for SDS and, moreover, the "SDS" of rioting and subversion which the press had created. In fact, however, PL had no intention of trying sabotage or disruption or rioting: the purpose of the work-in was to give students, especially the young ones brought into the Worker-Student Alliance groups, some factory-line experience so that they would be better WSAers and eventually easier recruits to the party. The work-in manual did suggest that if everything went as hoped the students could talk to workers about "the CLASS perspective," but in general, as PL's *Challenge* put it,

> The main emphasis of the work-in is not to organize or preach to the working class, but to get a deeper understanding of the problems workers face, their ideas, and their power in struggle. While doing this, students will also talk to workers about racism, the student movement, the war, etc. . . .
>
> The work-in is not a self-cultivating missionary experience. It is a key part of the strategy of building a worker-student alliance. This strategy flows from seeing that the exploitation of workers is the basis of this imperialist society.

Moreover, there were certainly no more than a thousand people involved in the whole affair, and they were concentrated mostly in New York, Boston, and Chicago—hardly enough of a force to "disrupt our national economy," even if they'd wanted to.

Naturally, then, the work-in had very little impact on the captains of industry. *Business Week* reported that not one single SDSer was ever found by the personnel departments or union bureaucrats, and added, "Across the country, the story was much the same: If SDS infiltrated plants, it was done so subtly that nobody noticed it—and nothing happened"; the Associated Press, similarly, took a sixteen-city survey in September and found the universal response: "no problems." In fact, the only time SDSers were noticed is when they made themselves obvious, largely during various strike-support efforts (in Atlanta, Chicago, Milwaukee, New York, Seattle, and Washington, D.C.), and these were projects outside of the work-in proper. Whatever else may have gone on that summer, there was certainly nothing in the 1969 work-in to cause businessmen any sleepless nights.

By the beginning of the fall the new shape of Weatherman was clear. A small group of people, perhaps no more than two or three hundred, finally dedicated themselves to the revolution in a wholehearted way: they were making themselves into new people, organized and living collectively, rooting out most of what they had been brought up to believe, accepting the necessity of violence, producing their answer to the problem of revolutionary power. Certain tendencies that had only been hinted at in the "Weatherman" document itself were now solidified into beliefs: the primary attachment to Third World revolutionaries, the sense of the immi-

nent collapse of the American state, the unwillingness to depend
upon other sources in the society (either liberal or working-class),
and the allegiance to violence. If the job of the revolutionary is to
make the revolution, that's what the Weathermen, in their own
particular way, were trying to do.

At the same time, much was hampering their success. The
summer's purgatory had produced in many Weathermen a dedication and commitment which turned very easily into arrogance and
belligerence, which the Weathermen in their attempts to communicate power did not try to dispel. The process of forging
instant revolutionaries through collective life and confrontational
actions proved too abrasive for many originally sincere and hopeful people. Others felt, as one man put it in Cleveland, that he
knew his "hang-ups" about living with one woman were bourgeois
but just now he wasn't willing to get rid of them simply for the
sake of being "a good communist." The emphasis on violence
bothered a number who had been brought up in pacifist ways, but
even many of those who were willing to accept political violence
thought that fighting with teen-agers on Detroit beaches or running through the streets of Chicago into tear gas and billy clubs
was hardly the best way to display it. In short, Weatherman was
estranging people—people who tried it, people within the same
organization, people close to it within the Movement—even as it
took shape.

Which bothered the Weathermen, at least professedly, not at
all. They had no real use any longer for a student movement—
except as an area of potential recruits—and little more for a left
movement. They were themselves the vanguard of a revolution
which was inevitable, and though they welcomed those who
wanted to fight they cared little for trying to make themselves into
a broad national organization. Whatever SDS had been was no
longer of interest to them—Mark Rudd said at one point, "I hate
SDS, I hate this weird liberal mass of nothingness"—for the old
SDS was too loose an organization and too undisciplined, too
diverse in its politics and preparedness, too susceptible to infiltration and subversion, too varied in its willingness to operate mili-
tantly. SDS was not, in short, an organization with which you can
realistically fight a revolution. Weatherman was—or thought itself to be.

25

FALL 1969-SPRING 1970

"Bring the war home"—that phrase, which John Jacobs and other Columbia SDSers had begun using during the May days of 1968, became the theme of the Weathermen's National Action in Chicago, emblazoned in two-inch-high letters on the cover of *New Left Notes,* superimposed on gummed stickers, used for captions and headlines on an immense variety of pamphlets and posters which began to emerge from the National Office in the weeks after the Cleveland meeting. What it meant was simple:

> When we move with the people of the world, against the interests of the rulers, we can expect their pigs to come down on us. So we're building a fighting force to struggle on the side of the Vietnamese, the blacks, and oppressed people everywhere. There's a war we cannot 'resist'. It is a war in which we must fight. We must open up another front against US imperialism by waging a thousand struggles in the schools, the streets, the army, and on the job, and in CHICAGO: OCTOBER 8-11.

It was not a slogan or a politics that seemed to attract many people: as Jeff Shero pointed out that fall, "While most want to end the war, SDS offers the unprepared a new war at home." But it seemed to sum up all that the Weathermen had become over the summer, convinced despite the chaotic nature of their actions that militant confrontation was still the correct component for the left in the equation of power. One Weatherman explained it thus:

The primary purpose, and the stance, of our organizing could not possibly be to "turn people on," or to have them like us, or to make them think that we are nice, but to compel them to confront the antagonistic aspects of their own life experience and consciousness by bringing the war home, and to help them make the right choice over a period of time, after initially shaking up and breaking through the thick layers of chauvinism-racism-defeatism. If being "arrogant," "pushy," "hard," if putting some people up against the wall, helps to create that tension and the requisite fluidity and space, then we ought to be "arrogant" and "hard."

And as the school year began, Weatherman continued its up-against-the-wallism. Weatherleaders, with Rudd the most visible, scoured the country trying to drum up support for the National Action by haranguing student audiences, engaging PLers and others who disagreed with them in bloody fist fights, coming on with macho toughness. Rudd's appearance at Columbia on September 25 was typical, involving skirmishes between regulars and PLers, two separate meetings with guards at the doors, and Rudd's usual pitch to the regulars about how they should all be in Chicago on October 8. Rudd, in heavy boots, workshirt, leather jacket, and cloth cap, gave off vibrations of restless energy during his speech, pacing back and forth at audience level in front of an unused podium, brandishing a chair leg he had used in the PL battle, yelling at the students there for being soft and "wimpy," and bragging of how he was preparing for the revolution ("I've got myself a gun—has everyone here got a gun? *Any*one? No?! W-e-ll, you'd better fuckin' get your *shit* together"). After some fifteen or twenty minutes of this, Paul Rockwell, a short, stocky non-Weatherman SDSer, got out of his seat and moved toward the front of the room, declaring that Rudd had had his turn and now he wanted to speak. Rudd took two menacing steps toward Rockwell, hulking over him, but Rockwell just barreled ahead, slammed Rudd against the podium, pushed Rudd's fists away, and turned to face the audience. Rudd's face was a picture of stunned fear, all his rhetoric having done nothing to overcome his ingrained middle-class unfamiliarity with, and anxiety about, violence; he stood there a moment, shrugged, then slunk off to join his friends to one side. The macho mood was dissipated; no one seemed to have joined the Weatherranks that night.

Nor were Weatherman's continued "jailbreak" and confrontation actions any more successful. Seven high schools in all were raided in the four weeks before the National Action, including Erasmus Hall in Brooklyn, where the invaders bound and gagged two teachers while "rapping" to their classes, and English High School in Boston, where a teacher was punched around with some viciousness and the students the next day organized a "Down With SDS" march through the streets. A band of twenty Weathermen—led by Eric Mann, a long way now from his NCUP days —invaded the Harvard Center for International Affairs, whose work included counterinsurgency research for various branches of the government, and ran screaming through the building, smashing windows, shoving secretaries, kicking and hitting professors, dumping over typewriters and files, pulling out telephones, and then running away before police could make arrests; five, however, were subsequently arrested and tried, and Mann was given a two-year jail sentence for assault and battery. In Cleveland a band of Weathermen tried to disrupt the Davis Cup tennis matches in Cleveland Heights in September, ending up with sixteen arrested and no disruption achieved. And in Chicago, when the Conspiracy trial opened at the end of September, Weathermen were among the crowd of two thousand doing battle with the police and a dozen (including Dohrn, Joe Kelly, Howie Machtinger, Russ Neufeld, and Bob Tomashevsky) were arrested on charges ranging from "mob action" to assault on a policeman.

Still, Weatherman, flush with the expectation of rising revolutions, approached the National Action—or, as it was increasingly being called, the "Four Days of Rage"—with optimism. True, not one Movement organization except YAWF actually offered support; Fred Hampton spoke for the Panthers when he called Rudd "a motherfucking masochist" to his face and proceeded to deck him with a single blow—but the Weatherleaders were counting on "the kids" to come anyway. A Weatherwoman working with youths in Denver predicted that "hundreds of them are ready for Chicago"; the "National Action Staff" in Chicago announced that "all over the country, from Detroit to Houston, from Miami through the cities in Ohio and on to Denver, Colorado, people are digging on the action—and digging on SDS"; and Mark Rudd in a TV interview in Columbus said, "We're gonna have a huge action in Chicago in October where we

get together thousands and thousands of young people to Chicago
to fight back, to fight the government, to fight their agents, the
police."

What must it have felt like, then, in the early evening of
Wednesday, October 8, 1969, standing in the darkness on a light
rise at the south end of Lincoln Park, gathered around a small
bonfire to ward off the chill of a Chicago fall, waiting for the
thousands of revolutionaries to appear, and finding yourself in the
midst of a tatterdemalion band of no more than two hundred
people? One man, looking nervously around, must have spoken
for all: "This is an awful small group to start a revolution."
Obviously, whatever the Weathermen had been doing, it wasn't
the right way to recruit a Red Army: probably no more than six
hundred people showed up in Chicago throughout the four-day
period, only half of whom regarded themselves as Weathermen
"cadre"—that is, members of a collective or "affinity group" that
had prepared for the demonstrations—while the rest were either
hangers-on who were close to but not in Weatherman or had
simply been drawn by the chance to "tear apart pig city." And as
near as one can tell, the large majority of these six hundred were
disaffected college students and former SDSers, *not* "street kids"
from the working class won over by Mark Rudd's militance;* in

*Facts and figures on the 287 people who were arrested during the National
Action were compiled by the Illinois Crime Investigating Commission (later
published by the Senate Internal Security Subcommittee, Part 4, June 10, 1970),
and they probably give a fair picture of the demonstrators as a whole. They
indicate that the summer's high-school recruiting was a failure: only twenty
high-schoolers were arrested, nine from the Chicago area, and only two dozen
other nonstudents who might have been street kids, half of them from Chicago.
National outreach was also a failure: at least 30 percent of the people came from
Illinois, most of them centered around the Chicago Weatherbureau, another 17
percent from three nearby states (Michigan, Wisconsin, Indiana), and the only
other states with significant percentages were those with strong collectives already established (New York, Ohio, Washington, Colorado, and Maryland, in
that order). The campus appeal had been negligible: more than half the demonstrators were nonstudents, and university contingents of half a dozen or more
came only from Purdue, Wisconsin, Seattle Community College, Columbia,
Reed, and Kent State, all of which had experienced fairly sizable confrontations
in the spring. Ages ranged from fifteen to thirty-seven (one fifty-one-year-old
man was arrested, but he turned out to have been a counterdemonstrator), with
a little over two-thirds between eighteen and twenty-three, twenty-eight under
eighteen and thirteen over thirty. All but eleven were white.

fact, one nineteen-year-old laborer who did take part in one action ended up in jail with this succinct reaction: "The guys in here are war-monguls. They all want a revolution and they are all with S.D.S. They are all fucking crazy."

But those whom Weatherman *had* persuaded to show up came prepared for something more than the ordinary peace march. Most were wearing helmets (army surplus, motorcycle, construction, even football), gas masks, goggles, gloves, heavy boots, leather or denim jackets, shirts taped at the sleeves (against gas), jock straps and cups or padded bras, first-aid kits, emergency phone numbers written in ink on their hands—and, generally hidden, such things as sticks, lead pipes, chains, blackjacks, rolled pennies, Mace, and at least one can of oven-cleaning spray.

There they stood, cold, with the adrenalin of fear and excitement, as the night darkened. It grew colder; cadre were sent out to break up the park benches and wooden railings for firewood. A group of perhaps a hundred, many in gleaming white motorcycle helmets, marched in from one side, shouting slogans, giving "Battle of Algiers" war whoops, and spirits rose for a time. Around nine, Bernardine Dohrn spoke through a bullhorn to the crowd, reminding them that the rally was called on the second anniversary of Che Guevara's death, a fact out of which she tried to inspire revolutionary fervor—but, for those who remembered how Guevara had died, at the head of a tiny band without friends in a foreign territory he didn't know and surrounded by hostile police and soldiers, the evocation of his name was probably something less than cheering right then. The contingent from YAWF showed up, with three orange banners. Another speaker, who did not announce his name, took the bullhorn to give the standard speech about imperialism, fighting in the belly of the monster, building a Red Army, and the chant came up from the waiting cadre, "Build a people's army, fight a people's war." Someone tried to lead one of the Panther chants—"Rev-o-*lu*-tion's beg-u-u-*un! Off the pig!* Time to *pick* up the gu-u-*un! Off the pig!*"—but after a time that faded. Another Weatherman group of perhaps two dozen marched across the grass, in two files, military style, NLF banners held high. The time dragged slowly by; more people went out to break up benches for the fire. Someone shouted that everyone should be facing away from the fire so that their eyes wouldn't become unaccustomed to the darkness, and people turned around, a little awkwardly, staring into the night and at the small knots of bystanders and police who had come to look at them. At about ten, Tom Hayden, in old tennis shoes and with his shirt hanging out, the first-generation SDSer having come to try to establish a link with these third-generation SDSers, took the bullhorn to tell them that the Conspiracy people he represented supported the National Action and welcomed any means to "intensify the struggle to end the war"—though ending the war was hardly what the Weathermen were concerned with now—but he spoke only briefly, as if perceiving the generation gap, the incredible gulf that separated the beginning of SDS from its end.*

A few more chants, some more wood on the bonfire. Suddenly, at about about 10:25, one man, probably Jeff Jones, stepped from the crowd and shouted, "I am Marion Delgado."† It was the code word that everyone had been waiting for, the final signal from the Weatherbureau about what the night's action, heretofore a top secret, would be. The speech was brief: The area to the south of Lincoln Park is called the Gold Coast, that's where the rich people, the pigs of this city, live, and that's where Marion Delgado would like to go; Judge Hoffman—the man presiding at the Conspiracy trial—lives down there at the Drake Hotel, a big fancy pig

---

*In the next several days, Hayden came to have doubts about the Weathermen's particular intensification of the struggle, and six months later he would say: "There was something wrong with what had happened in Chicago. To us revolution was like birth: blood is inevitable, but the purpose of the act is to create life, not to glorify blood. Yet to the Weathermen bloodshed as such was 'great.' . . . Their violence was structured and artificial, because in their heads they were part of the Third World. They were alienated from their own roots. . . . They were not guerrillas swimming like fish among the people; they were more like commandos, fifth columnists, operating behind enemy lines." (*Ramparts,* July 1970.)

†Marion Delgado was a five-year-old chicano who had derailed a passenger train in Alameda County, California, in 1947, by placing a twenty-five-pound slab of concrete on the tracks, and a photograph of the boy recreating his crime had found its way to the National Office, where he was quickly taken up by the Weatherbureau as a kind of ironic folk hero and inside-joke symbol. The picture was used on the cover of an issue of *New Left Notes* in September, people began signing letters and notes with his name, and he was listed as the editor of *New Left Notes* in October. At least one of the telegrams sending bail money to jailed Weathermen after the National Action was signed with his name.

pen down on Michigan Avenue, "and Marion Delgado don't like him, and the Weatherman don't like him . . . so . . . *let's go get him,*" and with shouting and whooping the Weathermen stormed out of Lincoln Park, into the city streets, running at nearly top speed, pulling out their concealed pipes and sticks and chains, ready at last to tear up pig city.

Now the Chicago police had figured they were ready for the Weathermen. Throughout the park, their crew cuts and ties marking them plainly, were literally dozens of plain-clothes men, on the fringes of the grass were masses of unmarked police cars phalanxed by police, and in the surrounding area the city, canceling all days off, had mobilized no fewer than two thousand uniformed policemen. Each man there had a score to settle with the types who had provoked the police riot of the year before and had given the Chicago police a bad name; each man knew that the statue of a policeman in Haymarket Square, the only such monument erected to the constabulary in the entire nation, had been blown ten feet off its pedestal by a Weatherman bomb two days before; each man remembered the words of the head of the police sergeants' association in response to that bombing: "We now feel it is kill or be killed." The police were prepared—only, as usual, they were prepared for the last war: they had expected that the Weathermen would stay in the park to defy the eleven o'clock curfew, as the demonstrators did in 1968. This time the demonstrators stormed into the Gold Coast before the cops knew what was happening.

The crowd swarmed down the streets, shouting and ululating and trotting with a supercharged emotion and a flush of unleashed energy—"I saw and felt the transformation of the mob," a New York Weatherman, Shin'ya Ono, wrote later, "into a battalion of three hundred revolutionary fighters"—and then within moments they began the assault— *"Ho! Ho! Ho Chi Minh!"*— throwing rocks and bricks through the windows of posh apartment houses — *"Dare to struggle, dare to win!"*—smashing the windows of parked cars— *"Bring the war ho-o-o-o-me!"*—shoving pedestrians and bystanders out of the way— *"Off the pig!"*—even knocking aside (and in some cases pausing to pummel) the solitary policemen isolated within their sweep. "Each one of us," Ono said, "felt the soldier in us." Their courage fed on the noise, the almost tangible vibrations of the chants and yells echoing off the buildings on the narrower streets, sending a tingle up the spine, creating for moments on end the hynoptic sense of vast and unstoppable numbers, invincible and righteous power. Their adrenalin rose at the forbidden, musical sound of breaking glass: ten plate-glass windows in a bank went crumbling, a Rolls Royce had every window in it shattered, on one block every parked car got hit, the windows of the Astor Hotel, Mon Petit Restaurant, Park Dearborn Hotel, Lake Shore Apartments were smashed and splintered, and the windshield of a police car was instantly cobwebbed, the cops inside too startled to move. They swept down the streets and sidewalks, unmindful of the ashtrays and flowerpots rained on them by the more indignant apartment residents, pushing aside those citizens who tried to get in their way; one young man who tried to save the windows in his car was pushed roughly to the sidewalk, kicked in the groin by two Weathermen, and when the woman with him tried to intervene, she, too, was was shoved to the pavement.

The Weathermen swooped south in the direction of the Drake Hotel, and they had gone more than four long blocks before the police managed to set up a barricade, with patrolmen in riot gear standing two deep across an intersection, backed up by police cars and paddy wagons. The young warriors got within a half-block of the police line, quickly halted, veered east, and then continued the march, still moving at almost top speed. After a block they cut south again, and again found the police waiting. This time they decided to meet the enemy head-on, testing their rhetoric and their courage, and they ran straight at the helmeted lines—"Cha-a-a-a-a-arge!" "Ya-ya-ya-ya-ya-a-a"—flailing and swinging at the astonished police. A number of the Weathermen in the front ranks, including several of the leaders, broke through, whooping off to the south, but most proved no match for even the Chicago police—who at least had the advantage of being familiar with bodily assaults—and some thirty of them were eventually subdued and taken off to the waiting vans.

Now the Weatherforce was split, some still going south, some having turned around and headed east again, some taking a completely different route back to the park—and none of them, apparently, very familiar with the Chicago streets. The main battalion, perhaps one hundred strong, found its way east to the drive along Lake Michigan, the very heart of the Gold Coast, and the sounds of shouts and shattering glass continued to fill the night, mingled now with the whine of sirens and the incessant clang of a dozen burglar alarms. But by now the police were on the attack, covering the area in force with perhaps a thousand men in uniform and uncounted others in private cars and plain clothes, apparently out for a little off-duty revenge. When the police found an isolated group of demonstrators cut off from the main body they would barge in, using their heavy riot sticks, going after the knees and groins, trying for unprotected heads and faces, bashing the neck if the head was helmeted: "Bodies were just mangled," one Weatherwoman said later, "people were bleeding out of their mouths and their noses and their heads . . . it was vengeance." At least twice police ran their squad cars full speed ahead into running crowds, knocking bodies ruthlessly aside, heedless of injuries. The acrid smell of tear gas wafted through the streets. One patrolman attacked by three Weathermen pulled his pistol and fired into a young man's neck; several other police fired revolvers at a clutch of demonstrators trying to escape through a building under construction; one cop fired into a small band which quickly fled for cover, then he turned and found a helmeted man standing alone to one side, shot him point blank, and ran off; shotguns, though hardly regulation issue, were hauled out from police-car trunks, and presently two people, a man and a woman, lay bleeding from buckshot wounds. Bring the war home.

After a little more than a hour, the force of the Weather-attack was dissipated. The demonstrators ended up thoroughly splintered, much of the leadership having either been arrested or isolated, many of the cadre were in paddy wagons, and most of the leftovers moved stealthily in small groups back to their lodgings. Before midnight it was all over: twenty-eight policemen were injured, none seriously, at least six Weathermen were shot (only three taken into custody), an unknown number injured, and sixty-eight arrested, twenty-five of them women. Back at the park, when at last the night was quiet, only embers of the bonfire remained. A tall, hunched figure in a coat and tie suddenly emerged from the darkness, looked around as if bewildered, stood a moment, and walked quickly off: it was Mark Rudd, in "straight" disguise, a general who it seems had decided not to march with his troops.

After the spasm of the first day of rage, a day or two of quiet. There was one action, a "women's militia" march the next morning, begun with militant speeches and braver-than-thou songs, but it drew only seventy women and twice as many police and it never had a chance. The militia leaders, showing considerable bravery if not much military sense, charged into the police lines, fought and kicked the cops for three or four minutes while their followers stood around cursing and yelling, and then were subudued in hammerlocks and half-nelsons and hauled off to jail. The rest of the women, forced to carry their helmets in their hands and march in straggly single file, were herded off by the police to a nearby subway, their action ignominiously crushed, their Leila Khaleds and Rosa Luxemburgs lying frustrated inside. Thereafter all the planned Weatherman actions—a rock concert, a march on the Conspiracy courthouse, "jailbreaks" in the city's high schools—were canceled, and Weatherman retired for a little introspection.

RYM II filled the gap, but with demonstrations of such an orderly and peaceful nature that the Chicago police who surrounded each of them must have been quite dumfounded as to what the initials "SDS" really meant. With support from the Black Panthers and Young Lords, with Klonsky and Noel Ignatin acting as its chief spokesmen, and with a following of perhaps two hundred, RYM II held a peaceful rally in front of the Conspiracy courthouse, a rhetoric-only demonstration at an International Harvester factory, a quiet rain-soaked mobilization at Cook County Hospital, and a black-white-brown march through Spanish-speaking areas which drew some two thousand people, the largest crowd in all the four days. The speeches were earnest but for the most part subdued, in vivid contrast to those of the other faction, with much emphasis upon the working class, the oppression of black and brown, racism both institutional and individual, and the lack of responsiveness from the institutions of government; of imperialism and the Third World and monster's bellies there was very little. The lines between the two factions were so sharply drawn, in fact, that when a bunch of Weathermen were arrested in the crowd of a RYM II rally by police who said they recognized them from the Gold Coast melee, RYM II supporters refused to offer any resistance: the word was, they're not part of "our" Movement.

Meanwhile, the Weathermen tried to get themselves ready for the next battle in their private war, a daytime march through the downtown Loop area on Saturday. In long and crowded criticism sessions in the intervening days they hashed over the effectiveness of the Wednesday action, debating for hours on end whether it had been worth the injuries and arrests; many blamed the Weatherbureau for insufficient preparation and bad leadership, and a number declared their intention of dropping out altogether. They confronted their own justified fears about going up against the police again, for they knew that the police would be fully prepared this time for any violence, that the state of Illinois had mobilized twenty-five hundred National Guardsmen and issued them ammunition, and that the chances were very high indeed of being beaten and arrested—possibly even shot—if another confrontation took place. Still, it was the general feeling that the opening action of the Days of Rage had ultimately been worth the price and that to give up now would be a confession of defeat; as Shin'ya Ono put it:

> For us to return to the streets on Saturday meant that we were going to respond offensively to, rather than be cowed by, the enemy's escalation after his defeat of Wednesday night. . . . To go back on Saturday meant that we begin to feel and live the law laid down by Che. You either win or get offed. That's what a revolution takes. Such an obvious truth, yet so hard to really feel and live by.

So on Saturday, courage screwed to the sticking place and beyond, some two hundred Weathermen, all that was left now of the depleted Red Army, took to the streets once more for "the second battle of the white fighting force." (It did nothing to bolster them when, before the march, plain-clothes men arrested four Weathermen at the starting point, among them Mark Rudd, who had come disguised with a fake dime-store mustache looking every bit like Mark Rudd with a fake dime-store mustache.) Marching swiftly through the downtown streets under the watchful eye of a double row of police, the Weathermen suddenly broke from the approved line of march and surged into the Loop area, startling the crowds of Saturday shoppers, flailing again at store windows and parked cars, swarming disconnectedly through the stalled traffic, and, when the waiting police closed in, going after them with their chains and pipes and fists and, in one instance, spiked railroad flares. This time, however, the police were ready and they sealed off the marchers quickly, descended in full force, and proceeded to club and collar them without undue ceremony; beefy plain-clothes men, unidentifiable and unrestrained, assaulted anything wearing long hair and jeans, even running from one clutch of already-arrested demonstrators to another to get in a few extra kicks and jabs. Within fifteen minutes the brave and pathetic warriors were dispersed, more than half of them hauled into paddy wagons, bloody and bowed, the rest scattered along the city streets, heading for home. The toll: thirty-six policemen hurt (one with a broken nose, one a broken kneecap, the rest with minor wounds), nineteen windows broken, and 123 demonstrators arrested, most suffering one kind of minor injury or another; most serious of all, a city official, Assistant Corporation Counsel Richard Elrod, who delighted in joining the police on actions like this, was paralyzed from the waist down after he tried to tackle a demonstrator headfirst and apparently smashed into a wall instead. (Brian Flanagan, a twenty-two-year-old Weatherman from New York, was arrested and charged with attempted murder in connection with this accident and was immediately found guilty by the Chicago press; at a subsequent trial, however, he was acquitted and the true version of the event was established.)

Thus did the Weathermen announce themselves to the world. In the course of four October "Days of Rage" they had provided a whole new political stance for the white American Movement, a symbolic watershed, an event by which many people on the left, now and later, were to measure themselves and their commitment, a genuine act, however feeble, of revolution. They had initiated offensive action against the property and the protectors of a major American city, deliberately committing a series of crimes in the name of their cause. They had wrought thousands of dollars' worth of damage and expenses ($183,081.99, according to the Illinois Crime Commission which investigated the action, including $100,000 for the National Guard payroll, $35,000 in building damages, and $20,000 for Elrod's medical expenses) and inflicted injury on seventy-five Chicago policemen and officials. They had attracted the riveting attention of the city's and the nation's media, winning steady television coverage and headlines such as "Radicals Go On Rampage," "Gold Coast Damage Runs High," "Guard Called in Chicago As SDS Roams Streets," implanting the idea of Weatherman in the national consciousness, occupying overnight the left end of the political spectrum to the point where people like Richard Nixon and Hubert Humphrey could refer to it with the knowledge that good American citizens would be horrified.* And somewhere in the course of it—at the first charge into the police lines, or during the long hours of self-criticism and evaluation, or huddled in the jail cells in the aftermath—they had transformed themselves—those that stuck with it, anyway—into a truly dedicated band of revolutionaries:

> Chicago was key in the development of a national organization. What happened in the Movement center, where we slept, and in our political meetings was often as important as what happened in the streets. Real strength and unity came from struggling with our people from other collectives and different parts of the country. More than ever before we felt that, however weak we were, this was the beginning of the army and the party.

In the minds of the Weathermen, publicly at least, the whole thing had shown itself on balance to be a victory; the next issue of *New Left Notes* declared, in the characteristic extravagance of Weatherlanguage:

> We came to Chicago to join the other side . . . to do material damage to pig Amerika and all that it's about . . . to do it in the road—in the open—so that white Amerika could dig on the opening of a new front . . . to attack . . . to vamp on those privileges and destroy the motherfucker from the inside.
>
> We did what we set out to do, and in the process turned a corner. FROM HERE ON IN IT'S ONE BATTLE AFTER ANOTHER—WITH WHITE YOUTH JOINING IN THE FIGHT AND TAKING THE NECESSARY RISKS. PIG AMERIKA—

---

*It was about this time that the Xerox Corporation decided to change the name of its computer subsidiary from Scientific Data Systems—known widely as SDS —to Xerox Data Systems.

BEWARE: THERE'S AN ARMY GROWING RIGHT IN YOUR GUTS, AND IT'S GOING TO HELP BRING YOU DOWN.

But that is only half the picture. "Revolutionary" or not, if this was Weatherman's answer to the problem of power, perhaps it hadn't understood the question. The National Action was tactically foolhardy, the product more of guilt than of courage, and obviously a far cry from the true guerrilla warfare of hit-and-run, swimming-in-the-sea, stealth-in-the-night that the Weathermen professed to respect. It was nearly suicidal—"Custeristic" was the word the Panthers used—and sorely debilitating to the Weatherman organization: probably two hundred people in all were injured, some seriously, and at least that many arrested, including all of the top leaders except Bill Ayers, Terry Robbins, and Jeff Melish; the Weathercoffers, already depleted, were scraped to the bottom by the imposition of $2.3 million worth of bail bonds, $234,000 of which had to be supplied immediately in cash (most of which ultimately came from reluctant parents and impoverished friends); and on top of everything was the prospect of lengthy court appearances (in many instances without the services of able lawyers since so few wanted to handle the cases of these revolutionaries), and sentences of up to five years in jail, all added to the innumerable cases left over from the summer.* And it had not attracted the numbers expected, it had not drawn in the Chicago-area working-class and high-school youths, and it had not even kept the allegiance of some of those who originally attended— several people who started as Weathermen dropped out before the four days were over, either out of disagreement with the organization's style (one woman later wrote that Weatherman "was the most fascist organization I've come in contact with") or disagree-

---

*As it worked out, the longest sentence actually meted out was 112 days, and this to a Weatherman who had already spent that time in jail awaiting trail. Most of the sentences were for terms of less than a week or were purely probational, and many involved only fines, amounting in all to more than $35,000. However, it should be noted that these cases involved mostly the less prominent—about thirty Weathermen, including many of the leaders facing the stiffest charges, did not show up for their trials in Chicago and went underground as fugitives without ever receiving sentences. (Illinois Crime Investigating Committee Report, 1970.)

ment with particular actions (another wrote, "If I had to take sides, I would have fought against the Weathermen"). Much later, two New York Weathermen acknowledged sadly:

> We won very few people over to our politics. We were not yet capable of leading masses of kids. Our dogmatism and intolerance, though it came out of conviction, fucked over many sisters and brothers who are or will be strong revolutionaries. We were lazy. It was so easy to accept a political line from the Weatherbureau, rather than struggle to develop a politics of our own. We had succeeded in hardening ourselves—we could be critical of each other, we could fight for our ideas, we could fight pigs. But in all this hardening, we lost some of our humanity. We often confused our revolutionary hatred for the oppressors with bourgeois self-hatred and hatred for each other. Very often we lost sight of the deep love that had made us revolutionaries in the first place.

On October 10 a press release was issued from "SDS National Headquarters" in Boston putting forth the PL-SDS view of the National Action:

> SDS CONDEMNS WEATHERMEN PROVOCATEURS
> For the last two days a group of provocateurs claiming to be from SDS have attacked students and working people in Chicago. Wednesday night they broke windows of people's homes and cars and attacked cab drivers. . . . These actions are all the work of a group of police agents and hate-the-people lunatics who walked out of SDS at the June Convention because their ideas had been rejected. Led nationally by Mark Rudd, this gang calling itself SDS-Revolutionary Youth Movement-Weatherman has absolutely nothing to do with SDS. They have been running all around the country attacking people. NO SDS CHAPTER SUPPORTS THEM! . . .
> We want to build a movement that sides with the masses of American people against the boss class that runs this country. The bosses have used the tiny Weathermen gang of provocateurs as an excuse to call in 2500 National Guards. They want to do two things: smear and discredit SDS, smash the honest student movement which is beginning to involve thousands of students in allying with workers. The bosses want to take peoples' minds away from seeing the bosses as their enemy and focus on the student movement as a scapegoat, while at the same time carry through an attack in work-

ing peoples' living and working conditions. This is the oldest trick in the book. The facts cannot be hidden for long though. We have confidence that the vast majority of people will see through this trick and repudiate Weatherman and RYM II—who have nothing to do with SDS—and build a united movement of workers and students to fight against racism and imperialism.

The reaction on the campuses to what had now become of SDS—or, more properly, the shell of SDS—was made clear almost as soon as the universities reopened. Neither Weatherman nor PL-SDS seemed to inspire any great enthusiasm among the students—certainly the summer's work-in and the material out of the Boston NO did nothing to strengthen PL's position, and the glaring lack of response to the National Action indicated the failure of the Weathermen. PL was dismissed most often with the comment that it was, as the phrase had it, "irrelevant," while Weatherman was pinioned by the widely circulated remark of one Wisconsin SDSer: "You don't need a rectal thermometer to know who the assholes are." Faced with a decision of where to turn, many SDS chapters simply splintered, duplicating the factionalism of the national organization on a smaller scale, and others, without the luxury of a decision, simply collapsed within weeks for want of a guiding national presence. Several of the WSA-dominated chapters declared allegiance to the PL-SDS, a few groups made formal bows toward RYM II, but as far as is known no chapter formally allied itself with Weatherman (which, logically, would have entailed the abandonment of the chapter anyway and a move en masse into the collectives under Weather-bureau discipline). The most common response, however, was a-plague-on-both-your-houses, exemplified by the widely reprinted statement of the theretofore uncelebrated SDS chapter in Fayetteville, Arkansas:

> Fayetteville SDS declares itself independent of either National Office because we do not feel that either bureaucratic Stalinistic group represents the politics of our chapter. Both national offices represent a petty bourgeois constituency of SDS, and we feel that neither NO represents the rank and file membership of SDS or any other segments of any other substantial New Left group. . . .
> We feel that the people who will make a revolution do not need

a vanguard to tell them how to run either that revolution or the society which will emerge.

We do not believe that either of these bureaucracies have any understanding of, or respect for, the revolutionary traditions and heritages of the American proletariat. Rather than making a true revolutionary analysis of this society, they have distorted and dogmatized the revolutionary experiences of dissimilar societies.

Both NO's have degenerated all political discussion into the chanting of meaningless slogans and empty rhetoric.

Because of these and other basic disagreements, we of Fayetteville SDS feel that both of the so-called leaderships of SDS are a serious threat to the Movement and therefore we cannot align ourselves with either "SECT"!!!!

"All Power to the People!!!" / NO POWER TO THE STALINISTS.

Many chapters, like Fayetteville's, at first chose to keep the initials "SDS," feeling that it gave them some identification with the past or hope for the future.* But as the fall wore on and it became obvious that no new SDS was going to rise from the ashes of the old, most chapters or chapter remnants chose to continue their activism under some such rubric as the "Revolutionary Organizing Committee" or the "Independent Radical Caucus"; Boston's November Action Committee and New York's December 4 Movement were two of the most prominent of these.

The collapse of SDS on the nation's campuses had several important ramifications. For one thing, the lack of a single strong student group, even one as loose and at times as divided as SDS, meant that any sustained national action—a march or an antidraft campaign—would be much more difficult to mount, and the ten-

---

*One such, a fledgling group at Central Connecticut State College, in Bridgeport, even gained legal fame by so doing. At the beginning of the fall term it voted to be unaffiliated with either National Office but asked for official college recognition as "Students for a Democratic Society" because it hoped that would have a certain attraction among politically minded students. The college administration then forbade them to use that name because it had determined in its wisdom that any such group would be a pernicious influence on campus. A group of eight students thereupon sued the college in a case that went all the way to the Supreme Court (No. 71–452, *Healy* v. *James*), which decided in 1972 that the college had overstepped its powers and SDS should be permitted on campus—only if, however, it agreed to obey "reasonable campus rules." (*The New York Times,* June 26, 1972.)

dency for each local group to pick and choose among the various causes would be accelerated. There would generally be no pamphlets or literature tables, no newspapers to proselytize with, no buttons to sell, there would be no regional travelers giving advice, no Movement veterans dropping by, no national meetings for recurrent contacts and inspiration. There would be no outside sources of sustenance and direction, leaving individual groups to their own devices for strategy and targets, to their own resources for money and energy. There would be no national identity for the press to focus on, nothing to give the chapters that mediaized sense of being part of a single nation-wide force, nothing that the incoming freshmen would know and anticipate, even pick their college because of.

This in turn meant that the job of political transmission, of passing on political insights, connections, meanings, and ideology from one subgeneration to the next, was stymied and all but abandoned. True enough, SDS had increasingly faltered at this particular task over the last two years, as its arrogance, paranoia, and distance grew apace, but at least while there was an organization with regular publications and regular meetings there was always the inevitable transmission, even by osmosis. Now there was nothing—or, to say the same thing, a blattering cacophony of things. It was impossible, of course, to stop the activism of college campuses—that was a function of the role of the university in mid-twentieth-century America, of the young in the economy, of authority in the society, and that would not change—but now there was no easy way for that activism to be infused with *politics*, with the kinds of understanding that from the beginning SDS had worked so hard to project and transmit. A campus might explode with anger over a tuition increase, but there would be no common appreciation of how that connected with the role of the university in a corporate society; a lengthy campaign against ROTC or university investments might excite a college, but there would be little understanding of the links with imperialism; students across the land could get outraged at the perilous condition of the ecology without ever seeing the nature of the capitalist system and how it works to produce and prolong that peril. Without something like an SDS, there would be no ready political mooring; without a political mooring, activism goes adrift.

The rest of the school year played out this unhappy script. There was plenty of protest activity, more so than even the year before—though it was played down by the commercial press, victims of their own predictions about "the cooling of America" and, as usual, meliorists for a troubled time—reaching more than two-thirds of the campuses during the year and striking at a rate of more than one a day. If in nothing else, the year was noteworthy in establishing new marks for the largest number of faculty members ever arrested (forty-five, at Buffalo, in February) and the largest number of students ever arrested in a single sweep (eight hundred and ninety-one, at Mississippi Valley State, also in February). But the activity tended to be isolated, contained, single-issued, and could not be sustained or directed. In October there was an enormous campus outpouring for a liberal-organized Vietnam Moratorium Day, fully a third of the colleges and universities taking part in various local actions and many cities holding demonstrations besides—yet the Moratorium Committee, bewildered as to its constituency and direction, had no sense of how to keep the effort going and within a few more months it had collapsed. In November there was the largest peace march ever, again in Washington, with more than half a million souls in attendance, many from the campuses—yet it was followed by an awkward silence, an embarrassed realization that the mass-mobilization tactic had been used beyond endurance, and the New Mobilization Committee limped its way into the spring and died. In October Bobby Seale was bound and gagged in the courtroom of the Conspiracy trial and in December Illinois Panther Chairman Fred Hampton was murdered in his bed by Chicago police—but there was no mass protest on the campuses at all, no one to force the issue onto the white constituency, no one to call the rallies and make the connections and rouse the passions. In February, following the guilty verdict in the case of the Chicago Conspiracy,* there were scores of separate "TDA" ("The Day After" the verdict) outbursts across the country, in Boston, Washington, New York, Madison, Los Angeles, Berkeley, and Seattle—but these protests

---

*A verdict eventually overturned by the U.S. Court of Appeals, Seventh Circuit, on November 21, 1972, chiefly on the the grounds of Judge Hoffman's legal errors and "antagonistic" behavior.

had no coordination or unified political base, they erupted essentially where local conditions were ripe, and they were almost all done with and forgotten as fast as the tear gas could clear. In April there was an event called Earth Day, featuring local rallies and exhibits drawing attention to the earth's ecology, in which nearly half the campuses in the nation participated—yet no one oversaw the affair to make sure that it would be anything more than liberal hand-wringing, no one was able to go on from there to establish a radical national organization on ecology, and within a few months most student attention had turned elsewhere without having been made any the wiser. And the climactic event of the year, the student strike in May, produced (as we shall see) one of the most serious crises in the nation's recent history—but it was directionless and unorganized, and so devoid of radical politics that it was easily coopted into a liberal electoral exercise. All of this, in short, from moratorium to strike, was rootless and bootless activism, often painfully and obviously without politics, and adrift.

The void caused by the demise of SDS was thus apparent to everyone on the left, and it should not be thought that the school year lacked for candidates to fill it.

The first, by virtue of continuity if nothing else, was the PL version of SDS, and it plowed into the fall trying to look for all the world like the genuine article: *New Left Notes* came out, demonstrations were held, the NIC met and passed resolutions, and chapters which had had strong PL and WSA contingents went right ahead meeting and setting up tables as if nothing had happened. But there was very little impact, and no noticeable outreach. Very few chapters which were not already in the PL orbit joined now, and some WSA groups (especially in the South) even decided to go their own way, avoiding the PL hegemony and carrying out worker-student politics by their own lights; a number of the smaller and more parasitic WSA caucuses apparently disintegrated altogether when their larger SDS hosts ceased to function during the fall. PL-WSA strongholds continued in the Boston and New York areas, with pockets in Los Angeles and San Francisco and isolated groups at schools such as Chicago, Cornell, Duke, Florida State, Michigan State, Wisconsin, and Yale, but in none of those places was SDS any longer a power and in most of them the ranks were embarrassingly small. Chapters may have numbered as many as forty, at least at the start, but total membership was probably not more than three thousand at any time.

One of PL-SDS's failings was its notable inability to work out any attractive strategy of its own. Over the summer, the PL heavies had hatched the idea of the *campus* worker-student alliance (CWSA) which they saw as perfectly suitable for their new all-to-ourselves student front; having students join campus cafeteria workers and maintenance men in raising grievances and strikes seemed the ideal way to get them to understand the working class and without having to budge from the campus. It was a sorry flop. Aside from a few going-through-the-motions actions here and there—support for a fired dining-hall worker at Yale, agitation for increased wages for "painters' helpers" at Harvard, a rally for free parking for campus workers at Wisconsin—the CWSA idea had all the impact of a siphonless flea. The workers, who filled the most marginal and shaky of jobs anyway, saw little point in joining with student "agitators" and even less in taking risks to create alliances with transient allies; the majority of students found the problems of campus janitors very small pickings indeed and without any connections to their own lives and their own grievances. Though PL-SDS pursued the strategy doggedly through the year —livened here and there by a few anti-ROTC and antiracism fights—the CWSA line never did get off the ground and died a quiet death sometime over the next summer. PL-SDS almost, though not quite, died with it.

The second former SDS group that tried to fill the void was RYM II. Though no formal RYM organization had come out of the June conference, the general politics was represented in a number of cities, often by SDS old-timers who hoped that a new position midway between the Weatherman "crazies" and the PL "politicos" could be worked out. This hope led to a national conference in Atlanta in November, at which some three hundred people formally established the Revolutionary Youth Movement, a new organization devoted to building a "mass anti-imperialist youth movement"—in other words, a new 1968-vintage SDS— with a program of fighting racism and male supremacy, organizing in the high schools, and even (the ghost of Kissinger's Kamikazi Plan) organizing in the army. Such was the reactive mood of these ex-SDSers at this point, however, that they went out of their way to give the new organization an unwieldy structure and an ineffective set of officers that could not possibly develop into an "elite" or an "NO collective," an attempt to make amends for the past (without learning from it) that condemned RYM to inefficency, invisibility, and eventually disintegration. Such was the mood of the campuses, also, that any attempt simply to duplicate SDS faced an uphill battle, something for which RYM had neither the resources nor the talent nor the energy— nor, indeed, the politics. By the spring, except for a pocket here or there, RYM was dead.

Of the non-SDS candidates to fill the SDS gap, there were a number of sects—the National Caucus of Labor Committees, YAWF, a new Communist Party group called the Young Workers Liberation League, the Workers League, varieties of anarchists, a temporarily revived Youth International Party, the International Socialists, the Spartacist League (and, eventually, its youth group, the Revolutionary Marxist Caucus), and the Young Socialist Alliance. The YSA, the nine-year-old youth group of the Trotskyist Socialist Workers Party, fared the best of all these groups, in part because it was not very demanding in its membership requirements ("general agreement with the organization's program") and in part because it operated with a certain seriousness and discipline that seemed attractive after the *laissez-aller* of SDS (in December, for example, fifteen former SDS chapter heads announced they were joining YSA to escape SDS's "personality cliques, based on personal alliances rather than political orientation"). Still, the YSA could never shake off its Old Left heritage and its rather stuffy brand of Marxism, so its appeal to college students was definitely limited—even by its own inflated estimates, the YSA had only sixty chapters by the middle of 1970 and somewhere between 5,000 and 10,000 members, only 3,000 or so on the campuses.

Somewhat greater success was enjoyed by the antiwar group controlled by the YSA and SWP, the Student Mobilization Committee, and for a time it seemed that it might actually be able to take the place of SDS. Its politics was reductionist, concerned only with the war ("the SMC is open to all youth opposed to the war," ran its creed, "regardless of political belief or affiliation"), and its tactics were confined solely to organizing mass marches—but it was at least active and visible, and its membership in 1969 climbed to an estimated 20,000 people at more than a thousand schools and colleges. The critical point in SMC's development came at a conference it called in Cleveland in February 1970, when some 3500 people showed up, many of them independent radicals hoping to broaden SMC's politics, inject an imperialist analysis into its antiwar policies, and turn it into a multi-issue organization that could succeed SDS. But the YSA and SWP vigorously resisted any changes in what had been a very successful front group for them and by maintaining rigid control over the proceedings were able to beat back the challenge and keep the SMC to the narrow antiwar path. The independents eventually found their way into the multi-issued coalition that grew out of the defunct New Mobilization Committee over the summer—first called the National Coalition Against War, Racism, and Repression, later known as the People's Coalition for Peace and Justice—but there was no other student-oriented membership group for them to influence and all attempts at originating such an organization failed to get off the ground.

There was, in short, no formal organization on the left that could replace SDS in the life of the Movement: a testimony to the value of SDS and to the tragedy of its collapse. A plethora of political groups continued to operate on the campuses in succeeding years—the sectlets, socialist parties, single-issue committees, *ad hoc* coalitions, women's groups, homosexual organizations—but none had the life or depth of SDS, none could match the sweep it had even in its late faltering stages.

It was a time of significant depression for the radical and revolutionary studentry. "We've learned that the only thing that can work is a revolution," one bitter Cornell SDSer said, "and it looks like a revolution can't work." Splintered and in disarray, student leftists floundered: some dropped out, some went back to the books, a few turned to the simplicity of bombs, many found a solace in drugs, and those who continued political work concentrated on narrow organizing projects (food coops, day-care centers, rent strikes) or small local activist groups (women's liberation, gay liberation, "consciousness-raising," Marxist study). Having put so much of themselves into politics, and with so much frustration to show for it now, many former SDSers went into what they half-jokingly called "retirement"—leading private lives, coming out for a march or demonstration when it was called, but for the most part hanging back, looking inward. And it was no small thing: 30,000 or 50,000 or 100,000 SDSers had to reshape their lives in one way or another. For some, of course, it meant no more than one less meeting to go to or one less pamphlet to write; but for many it meant agonized rethinking, reassessment, rejuggling of their assumptions and their lives.

The League for Industrial Democracy, still living its half-life in the shadows of the anti-Communist left, issued a report in August of 1970 which declared that the New Left was dead. In a survey of fifty institutions and several thousand "campus leaders," the LID discovered that most students did not identify themselves with the New Left (only 8.5 percent, as compared with 30.5 percent who called themselves liberals, and 25 percent identified with "new politics"), did not regard Tom Hayden as highly as Michael Harrington, and were not members of the Students for a Democratic Society. The New Left, it said, had collapsed because it had not followed liberal politics: "By provoking the opposition of labor, the representative black groups, and the traditional liberals, the New Left destroyed its possibilities of becoming a mass movement." The result, it said, was a disintegration on the left and the rise of fragmented and competing organizations, turning the student movement into a force "with no shared sense of direction, and very often with profound and even bitter internal differences." The lesson of the report was that the time-honored tenets of the LID—moderation, anti-Communism, liberalism, mainstream politics—were the requisite goals for any new student movement.

In truth, it was much too late for all of that—but the LID still had not learned.

The failure of Weatherman to attract people to the National Action and to establish any base whatsoever on the campuses in the fall of 1969 served only to nurture their "vanguarditis," their conviction that if there was to be a serious attack upon the system they would have to start it themselves without waiting around for the peace-marching students or the job-hunting working-class kids or even the breakfast-feeding Panthers.

Weathermen with every passing week grew more and more

isolated, from the campuses, from the Movement, from the street kids, from America. In the collectives they cut themselves off from family—in Linda Evans's passport, for example, the space under "In case of death or accident notify . . ." bore only, "SDS, 1608 W. Madison, Chicago, Illinois"—and from friends—as Dotson Rader wrote upon seeing an old friend then in Weatherman, "He was like a young priest who had taken vows and was under discipline and who consciously steeled himself against the past." Their standard was to see the Weatherlife as all, and it was on this basis that new members were specifically recruited:

> The issue was whether or not the potential cadre had the "guts" to carry out armed struggle, to be a *real* revolutionary, to be a *Weatherman.* Are you revolutionary enough to smash your closest relationships? Are you revolutionary enough to give away your children? This style of "struggle" came to be known as "gut-check." It was an important form of "struggle" within the organization on every question.

The life style of the collectives grew inward, too. People going through daily self-criticism sessions (which had, apparently, mellowed after Chicago to emphasize more supportiveness and less venom) got to know each other in a special, almost selfish way. Reorganization of sexual lives reinforced this inwardness, and whether or not the new everyone-sleep-with-everyone patterns were healthy, they certainly gave those within the collective a shared sense that no one on the outside could know; homosexuality, for example, especially among the women exploring a new sexual freedom but also among the men, broke down barriers in a surprisingly swift and effective way. The shared drug experience —a good deal of marijuana for relaxation, special group sessions with LSD, hashish, and in some cases barbiturates—also helped to draw people together, to establish new connections both personal and political. "We're moving, dancing, fucking, doing dope," one Weatherman flyer said that fall, "knowing our bodies as part of our lives, becoming animals again after centuries of repression and uptightness." The continual concern, the so-called paranoia, about official repression and harassment—born of the knowledge that in fact phones were tapped, letters opened, doors watched, cars tailed, rooms bugged, and trusted friends likely to be planted by the FBI—exaggerated the insularity.* And shot through everything else was the growing development of a special politics, a politics very much in flux from one week to the next, very much in the experimental stage, but informed by one singular idea: "Once you really understand the need for the revolution, it becomes part of you and your whole life makes sense for the first time."

Not everyone could take this kind of life, of course, not everyone liked the top-down discipline urged by the Weather-bureau, not everyone agreed with the go-it-alone isolationism. A number of people, even among those who had been in it from the summer, dropped out: some went back to more conventional Movement work (several to the Venceremos Brigade), some carried on Weatherpolitics apart from the collectives and the discipline of Weatherman itself, and others repudiated Weatherman and organized antithetical groups emphasizing outreach and non-violence (the Seattle Liberation Front, for example, was organized by several ex-Weathermen specifically as a counterthrust to Weatherman). But as these people left, the hard core became harder, and new people were continually added—a woman from the Chicago Conspiracy office, a man who had been in a WSA caucus, a high-school dropout bored with his factory job; one newcomer explained what it was like:

> It struck me, at a meeting I went to, that they were a family. A big, very tight family. I wanted to be part of that. People were touching each other. Women together, men together. They were beautifully free. I felt that they were experiencing a whole new life-style that I really hadn't begun to understand. They were so full of life and energy and determination and love.

*To avoid infiltration and expose agents, collectives often administered what was known as the "acid test" to suspected informers, giving them LSD to see how they would react when their guard was down and their psyche opened up. One Weathercollective in Cincinnati thought it had tumbled to an infiltrator, one Larry Grathwohl, when he announced during a heavy two-day acid trip, "You're right, I AM a pig"—but it turned out that he was merely expressing a general guilt for having served in the army: "I'm a pig because of what I did in Vietnam; because I stood by and saw brutality of what was being done to innocent people," and he was accepted into the collective. A mistake. A few months later he fingered two New York Weatherwomen for the FBI. (*Liberated Guardian,* September 27, 1970, from *Berkeley Barb.*)

The logical result of what Weatherman was becoming that fall was for it to go "underground," abandon entirely the public ways that were the legacy from SDS and split into small secret cells operating each in its own way to bring the war home. It was an honored tradition, the tradition of the Maquis, the Fidelistas, the Vietnamese, the Tupamaros, and now for the first time it would be followed in modern America. "More than ever," wrote members of one New York collective, "we saw the necessity of moving to a higher level; armed struggle had to become a reality. Clearly our present form of organization (open collectives,) was not capable of carrying out higher levels of struggle." No one knew for sure what an underground life would mean—

> Should we all go hide in a basement and read about explosives until we were ready to get an aircraft carrier? Could an underground provide political as well as military leadership for the mass movement? What exactly is the relation between an underground and an overground?

—but there was a general conviction that it was the only real way to fight the revolution militarily and even a general surge of feeling that it stood a good chance of winning: "Out of the often tortuous months we spent in collectives, out of confronting the task of building an underground, we feel an incredible confidence and joy in being part of the final destruction of imperialism and the building of communism."

The National Council—or "National War Council," as it had become—was held in Flint, Michigan, over the Christmas holidays, Weatherman's last public fling before this inevitable journey underground, a farewell to the old Movement, a last appeal for comrades. It was without doubt one of the most bizarre gatherings of the decade.

Some four hundred people showed up—attendance was kept down because the Weatherbureau didn't let out where the site would be until mid-December, but still the numbers were an indication that Weatherman had not grown substantially in the last six months—of whom perhaps two to three hundred were official "cadre" and the rest infiltrators, the curious, and assorted hangers-on, quite a few as young as thirteen and fourteen, some (the reports have it) even accompanied by their mothers. The

"Giant Ballroom" in a black ghetto of Flint was decorated with huge semipsychedelic posters of Weatherheroes (Castro, Cleaver, Guevara, Ho Chi Minh, Lenin, Mao, Malcolm X), one wall was covered with alternating red and black pictures of Fred Hampton, one banner showed scores of bullets each bearing the name of some Weatherenemy (Alioto, Daley, the *Guardian,* Humphrey, Johnson, Nixon, Reagan, even Sharon Tate, only recently murdered while eight months pregnant), posters showed a rifle with a high-powered sight labeled "PIECE NOW," and from the ceiling hung a huge six-and-a-half-foot cardboard machine gun. There was none of the usual National Council routine, no resolutions or programs, no workshops or formal plenaries, nor any opportunity to introduce any of these things—the Weatherbureau was in firm control of the affair and they wanted a happening, not a meeting:

> The war council was a frenzy, a frenzy in anticipation of the armed struggle they were calling for. Most Weatherpeople slept an hour a day; the rest was heavy, heavy rapping, heavy listening, heavy exercising, heavy fucking, heavy laughing, a constant frenzy-strain that went through the whole four days, all the time no flab, no looseness, no ease in anything that was done.

Daytimes were given over to informal, haphazard groups of people talking about the Weatherlife and about going underground, the nighttimes to chaotic mass meetings billed as "wargasms." The wargasms began with a group karate routine (sloppy, it was felt by most), then conventional exercises, then a few songs from the Weatherman songbook,* after which everyone burst into In-

---

*Some samples. To "White Christmas": I'm dreaming of a white riot/Just like the one October 8,/When the pigs take a beating/And things started leading/To armed war against the state.   We're heading now toward armed struggle,/With ev'ry cadre line we write./May you learn to struggle and fight/Or the world will off you 'cause you're white.

To the fifties' rock-'n'-roll "Oh, Donna": There once was a town, Chicago was its name,/Since we went there, it's never been the same,/Cause we offed that town,/Chicago, brought it down/To the ground,/Down to the ground.

To "Maria": The most beautiful sound I ever heard:/Kim Il Sung,/Kim Il Sung, Kim Il Sung, Kim Il Sung, etc.

To the tune of the Beatles' "Nowhere Man": He's a real Weatherman,/Ripping up the mother land,/Making all his Weatherplans/For everyone;/Knows just what he's fighting for,/Victory for people's war,/Trashes, bombs, kills pigs and more,/The Weatherman.

dian war whoops and ululations and settled down for speeches from the Weatherleaders. And these performances, by all accounts, were extraordinary. Bernardine Dohrn led off with a little story about how Weathermen behave: "We were in an airplane, and we went up and down the aisle 'borrowing' food from people's plates. They didn't know we were Weathermen: they just knew we were crazy. *That's* what we're about, being crazy motherfuckers and scaring the shit out of honky America." Mark Rudd's turn featured: "It's a wonderful feeling to hit a pig. It must be a really wonderful feeling to kill a pig or blow up a building." And "JJ" offered: "We're against everything that's 'good and decent,' in honky America. We will burn and loot and destroy. We are the incubation of your mother's nightmare." "The raps," according to one swept-up woman who went on to join the Weathermen, "were of such intensity that there was just nothing left to say." No doubt.

Something of the mind-set of the Weathermen during this period can be seen in the way the Weatherleaders in Flint talked about death, with a characteristic combination of ruthless if distorted logic and a sense of guilt so strong it had turned to rage. The Weatheranalysis held that whites were virtually useless in the world-wide confrontation going on, and except for a few brave street fighters like the Weathermen they all were corrupted, bought-off tyrants. Logically, then, the death of a white baby is a positive revolutionary action, and indeed the Weathermen actually held abstract debates at the "war council" about whether killing white babies is "correct," a Weatherman at one point shouting to the audience, "All white babies are pigs." From there it was only a step to Dohrn's ecstatic speech about the Charles Manson gang, the drugged and degraded children responsible for the recent Tate–La Bianca murders in Los Angeles: "Dig it: first they killed those pigs, then they ate dinner in the same room with them, then they even shoved a fork into the victim's stomach. Wild!" In later months Dohrn would come to regret this adulation (her account of the facts, incidentally, is wrong), not the least because Charles Manson was obviously a cruel master of a virtual harem where women were treated as objects with less value than cow dung; but at the time Manson seemed the perfect symbol of American values stood on their head, and this is what the Weathermen were after.

Amid all this wildness, there was very little in the way of real business transacted at Flint, but it was clear to all that the meeting marked a turning point; as one Weatherwoman remembered it:

> The War Council was a new beginning. A leap. A new era had begun. People were determined to destroy the State. The things that were talked about were things that people would be doing in the very near future—higher levels of struggle.

"Higher levels" meant two things to the Weathermen. First, it was decided that they would commit themselves to violence, to "armed struggle," giving up all notions of organizing a broad movement and just getting ahead with the business of destruction; in a packet handed out in the hall, Weatherleaders said:

> The notion of public violence is increasingly key. That is, planning, organizing, and carrying off public and visible violent action against the state. . . . We have to answer all the pig sounds about sabotage and terrorism being terrible, suicidal, and adventurous with what we have learned from the Vietnamese and from Black revolutionists:
>
> Any kind of action that fucks up the pigs' war and helps the people to win is a good kind of action.
>
> EVERYONE TALKS ABOUT THE WEATHER . . . Armed struggle starts when someone starts it. International revolutionary war is reality, and to debate about the "correct time and conditions" to begin the fight, or about a phase of work necessary to prepare people for the revolution, is reactionary. MAKING WAR on the state creates both the consciousness and the conditions for the expansion of the struggle, making public revolutionary politics, proving that it is possible to move and that there is an organization with a strategy.

Second, the Weathermen decided to break up the collectives into smaller groups—called variously cells, affinity groups, or, following the Latin American guerrillas, "focos"—and finally go underground. As they were to announce in the very last official publication out of the National Office:

> As the level of struggle has risen, a lot of people have felt the need for tighter and stronger forms, and now there are hundreds of collectives being built all over the country, chains of affinity groups linked together by strong leadership, discipline, and political coherence. A network of many collectives which can strike in coordinated ways and share resources, etc. And we are building an army, a centralized military organization that can lead the struggle.

On January 1, the self-styled Red Army went forth. Two hundred, perhaps three hundred, in a land of two hundred million. "Cuba started with 80 men at Moncada," they said, "Vietnam's General Giap started armed propaganda with 38 men"—but it was still a pathetically small band of people, isolated by intent as well as failure, taking the last desperate step they knew how to take to live their lives in such a way that it did not contradict their politics.

In New Haven, December 28–31, PL–SDS held its own National Council meeting, the first time it convened as a separate organization.* The NC gave formal endorsement to the campus-worker–student alliance strategy:

> We believe that an alliance of students with workers is the only way to oppose the injustices such as the Vietnam war and racism which America's rulers inflict on the people of this country and the world. . . . The group with whom we can now ally to implement a worker-student alliance strategy is campus workers. There are thousands of campus workers; they face the same administration boss which students face when they combat ROTC, expansion into the surrounding community, recruiters, etc.

There were also resolutions on women's liberation, community-college organizing, and support for the workers on strike against General Electric (the last of which was billed as "the most significant struggle against imperialism in the Movement's history"). The NC also came out against "nationalist black studies courses," ROTC, and open admissions; no resolutions were passed concerning the war, repression of the Black Panther Party, or students.

The Weatherman decision to turn to underground political warfare was perfectly consistent with the evolution of violence on the left in the decade of the sixties as we have seen it so far: from sit-ins and pickets, to marches and teach-ins, to confrontations and disruptions, to rock-throwing and trashing, and ultimately to

*Another National Council meeting, for the West Coast, was held January 30–February 2 in Los Angeles, attended by several hundred people. This unique solution to the problem of geographical distance was possible largely because PL operatives managed things so that both NCs endorsed the same general principles.

bombings and arson. Common to it all was a consistent New Leftist tradition of personal commitment, political militance, and moral righteousness, but the tactics changed dramatically as each method was tried, found wanting, and discarded, none being able to break through America's barriers of indifference and resistance, each eventually ignored or coopted or crushed by a Hydra-headed system. And as the issue came to be put in terms of raw power, active political violence—power at its rawest—seemed for many to be the only possible response of the left. Mike James, for example, addressing a Chicago audience, declared:

> Non-violent marches have their place, but they won't bring about the changes necessary for freedom. Capitalism won't crumble because of moral protest. It didn't in India, where only the color of the agents of the oppressors changed. Once again: revolution, liberation and freedom must be fought for. And that means we're dealing with power. They've got the guns, we've got the people. Right now they're stronger. The time will come when we'll have to use guns. Don't let that hang you up. Some of you say violence isn't human. Well, taking oppression isn't human; it's stupid. You only live one time, so you'd better make it good and make it liberating. The jerking of the brake may be violent, but sometimes the rolling of the wheel is more violent. For otherwise, the violence of liberation and the violence of oppression will only increase for those who follow. Violence, when directed at the oppressor, is human as well as necessary. Struggle sometimes means violence, but struggle is necessary, because it is through collective struggle that liberation comes. And life is nothing if it is not about liberation.

And the Weathermen themselves, in their first public communiqué after going underground, argued:

> All over the world, people fighting Amerikan imperialism look to Amerika's youth to use our strategic position behind enemy lines to join forces in the destruction of the empire.
>
> Black people have been fighting almost alone for years. We've known that our job is to lead white kids to armed revolution. We never intended to spend the next five or twenty-five years in jail. Ever since SDS became revolutionary, we've been trying to show how it is possible to overcome the frustration and impotence that comes from trying to reform this system. Kids know that the lines are drawn; revolution is touching all of our lives. Tens of thousands

have learned that protest and marches don't do it. Revolutionary violence is the only way.

This was not just rhetoric: the statistics indicate that it was being taken seriously. In the spring of 1968, when bombs were first used by the white left, there were ten bombing instances on campuses; that fall, forty-one; the next spring, eighty-four on campus and ten more off campus; and in the 1969–70 school year (September through May), by an extremely conservative estimate, there were no fewer than 174 major bombings and attempts on campus, and at least seventy more off-campus incidents associated with the white left—a rate of roughly one a day.* The targets, as always, were proprietary and symbolic: ROTC buildings (subject to 197 acts of violence, from bombings to window breakings, including the destruction of at least nineteen buildings, all of which represented an eight-fold increase over 1968–69), government buildings (at least 232 bombings and attempts from January 1969 to June 1970, chiefly at Selective Service offices, induction centers, and federal office buildings), and corporate offices (now under fire for the first time, chiefly those clearly connected with American imperialism, such as the Bank of America, Chase Manhattan Bank, General Motors, IBM, Mobil, Standard Oil, and the United Fruit Company).

But the violence wasn't all bombings and burnings. On the campuses this year there were more than 9,408 protest incidents, according to the American Council on Education, another in-

*It seems likely that even this figure may represent only a sixth of the actual number. It is based upon police reports and newpaper accounts as compiled by the Senate Investigations Subcommittee (Part 25, July and August 1970) and by the now-defunct *Scanlan's* magazine (January 1971)—but they pinpoint only some 862 incidents of bombing and attempted bombing in the period from January 1969 to April 15, 1970, whereas a more extensive survey by the Alcohol, Tobacco, and Firearms Division of the U.S. Treasury (Part 24, July 1970) shows at least 5,000 bombings and attempts during this period. This latter survey established that there were no fewer than 40,934 bombings, attempts, and threats (by admittedly "conservative" estimate) during these fifteen and a half months, and of the 36 percent it was able to attribute, something like 8,255 incidents were related to "campus disturbances." By extrapolation, we can figure that of the other 64 percent at least 13,000 incidents could be attributed to student activity, for a total of 21,000 incidents, or approximately 50 every day; of those, also by extrapolation, one can estimate some 2,800 were actual bombings, or approximately 6 a day for the entire period.

crease over the year before, and they involved police and arrests on no fewer than 731 occasions, with damage to property at 410 demonstrations, and physical violence in 230 instances—sharp evidence that the ante of student protest was being upped. Major outbreaks of violence occurred in November in Washington, when 5,000 people charged the Justice Department and had to be dispelled by massive doses of CN gas (this was the demonstration which Attorney General Mitchell and Weatherleader Bill Ayers both agreed, in totally separate statements with totally different meanings, "looked like the Russian Revolution"); at Buffalo in March when police clashed with students and twelve students were shot and fifty-seven others injured; at Santa Barbara in February, when students kept up a four-day rampage against the university, the National Guard, local police, and the Bank of America, more than 150 were arrested, two people were shot, and one student was killed; at Berkeley in April, when 4,000 people stormed the ROTC building, went up against the police, and kept up an hours-long assault with tear gas, bottles, rocks; at Harvard in April, when several thousand people took over Harvard Square, fought police, burned three police cars, trashed banks and local merchants; at Kansas in April, where students and street people caused $2 million worth of damage during several nights of trashing and demonstrations, forcing the calling out of the National Guard; and finally the massive confrontation of May.

Off the campuses, there were other forms of political violence. Attacks on police increased dramatically in 1969, with eighty-six policemen killed (up from the average of fifty-three a year heretofore) and a record of 33,604 assaults on cops (up from 16,793 in 1963), including sniper fire and bombings. Threats against public officials rose dramatically and in the course of fiscal year 1968–69 337 were arrested (and 269 convicted) for attempts or threats against government officials. And for the first time in recent American history, actual guerrilla groups were established, operating in secrecy and for the most part underground, each dedicated to the revolution and each committed to using violent means. There is no way to gauge the number of these groups operating in 1970, but of those whose existence is known there were, in addition to the Weathermen themselves, the New Year's Gang, the Quartermoon Tribe (Seattle), the Proud Eagle Tribe (Boston), the Smiling Fox Tribe (New York City), one unnamed group around Columbia University, the John Brown Revolutionary League (Houston), the Motherfuckers (now living in New Mexico), and various (generally unofficial) branches of the White Panthers and the Black Panthers; in addition, one nationally organized group of revolutionaries is known to have operated in the fall of 1969, led by blacks but with white members, and a *Newsweek* reporter in the fall of 1970 profiled a young white guerrilla warrior in California who estimated from his experience that there were some twenty groups actively training for revolution in various parts of the country.

It is important to realize the full extent of the political violence of these years—especially so since the media tended to play up only the most spectacular instances, to treat them as isolated and essentially apolitical gestures, and to miss entirely the enormity of what was happening across the country. It is true that the bombings and burnings and violent demonstrations ultimately did not wreak serious damage upon the state, in spite of the various estimates which indicate that perhaps as much as $100 million was lost in the calendar years 1969 and 1970 in outright damages, time lost through building evacuations, and added expenses for police and National Guardsmen. It is also true that they did not create any significant terror or mass disaffiliation from the established system, in part because violence is already so endemic in American society ("The United States is the clear leader among modern stable democratic nations," the President's Violence Commission declared in 1969, "in the rates of homicide, assault, rape, robbery, and it is at least among the highest in the incidence of group-violence and assassination") and in part because Americans generally cannot conceive of violence as a *political* weapon and tend to dismiss actions outside the normal scope of present politics as so unnecessary and inexplicable as to seem almost lunatic. Nonetheless, the scope of this violence was quite extraordinary. It took place on a larger scale—in terms of the number of incidents, their geographical spread, and the damage caused—than anything seen before in this century. It was initiated by a sizable segment of the population—perhaps numbering close to a million, judging by those who counted themselves revolutionaries and those known to be involved in such acts of public violence as rioting, trashing, assaults upon buildings, and confrontations with the police—and it was supported by maybe as much as a fifth of the population, or an additional 40 million people—judging by surveys of those who approve of violent means or justify it in certain circumstances. And, above all, the violence was directed, in a consciously revolutionary process, against the state itself, not against individuals, racial or ethnic groups, local businesses, or private institutions, as had been the pattern of American violence heretofore; for the first time since the Civil War, and over far more of the country, violence struck against the institutions of American government and those corporations and universities seen as complicit with those institutions, with an explicit aim of destroying or at least shaking that system. Political violence of the end of the decade, in other words, may not have brought about a revolution—but it was the closest thing to it that an ongoing society could imagine. Or perhaps endure.

The culmination of campus violence occurred in May, without doubt one of the most explosive periods in the nation's history and easily the most cataclysmic period in the history of higher education since the founding of the Republic.

On April 30, Richard Nixon announced that American troops, in contravention of international law and the President's own stated policy, were in the process of invading Cambodia, and within the hour demonstrations began to be mounted on college campuses. Three days later a call for a national student strike was issued from a mass gathering at Yale, and in the next two days students at sixty institutions declared themselves on strike, with demonstrations, sometimes violent, on more than three dozen campuses. That was remarkable enough, especially for a weekend, but what happened the following day proved the real trigger.

On May 4, at twenty-five minutes after noon, twenty-eight members of a National Guard contingent at Kent State University, armed with rifles, pistols, and a shotgun, without provocation or warning, fired sixty-one shots at random into a group of perhaps two hundred unarmed and defenseless students, part of a crowd protesting the war, ROTC, and the authoritarianism of the university, killing four instantly, the nearest of whom was a football field away, and wounding nine others, one of whom was paralyzed for life from the waist down. It took only thirteen seconds, but that stark display of governmental repression sent shock waves reverberating through the country for days, and weeks, and months to come. Clark Kerr, who knew a thing or two about campus protest, seemed shaken to his boots:

> The climax of dissent, disruption, and tragedy in all American history to date occurred in May 1970. That month saw the involvement of students and institutions in protests in greater number than ever before in history. The variety of protest activities—both violent and nonviolent—seemed to exhaust the entire known repertoire of forms of dissent.

The impact is only barely suggested by the statistics, but they are impressive enough. In the next four days, from May 5 to May 8, there were major campus demonstrations at the rate of more than a hundred a day, students at a total of at least 350 institutions went out on strike and 536 schools were shut down completely for some period of time, 51 of them for the entire year. More than half the colleges and universities in the country (1350) were ultimately touched by protest demonstrations, involving nearly 60 percent of the student population—some 4,350,000 people—in every kind of institution and in every state of the Union.* Violent demonstrations occurred on at least 73 campuses (that was only 4 percent of all institutions but included roughly a third of the country's largest and most prestigious schools), and at 26 schools the demonstrations were serious, prolonged, and marked by brutal clashes between students and police, with tear gas, broken win-

---

*Protests took place at institutions of every type, secular and religious, large and small, state and private, coeducational and single-sexed, old and new. Eighty-nine percent of the very selective institutions were involved, 91 percent of the state universities, 96 percent of the top fifty most prestigious and renowned universities, and 97 percent of the private universities; but there were also demonstrations with a "significant impact" reported at 55 percent of the Catholic institutions, 52 percent of the Protestant-run schools, and 44 percent of the two-year colleges, all generally strict and conservative schools which had never before figured in student protest in any noticeable way. Full details can be found in a study by the Carnegie Commission on Higher Education, "May 1970: The Campus Aftermath of Cambodia and Kent State."

dows, fires, clubbings, injuries, and multiple arrests;* altogether, more than 1800 people were arrested between May 1 and May 15. The nation witnessed the spectacle of the government forced to occupy its own campuses with military troops, bayonets at the ready and live ammunition in the breeches, to control the insurrection of its youth; the governors of Michigan, Ohio, Kentucky, and South Carolina declared all campuses in a state of emergency, and the National Guard was activated twenty-four times at 21 universities in sixteen states, the first time such a massive response had ever been used in a nonracial crisis. Capping all this, there were this month no fewer than 169 incidents of bombings and arson, 95 of them associated with college campuses and another 36 at government and corporate buildings, the most for any single month in all the time government records have been kept; in the first week of May, 30 ROTC buildings on college campuses were burned or bombed, at the rate of more than four every single day.† And at the end of that first week, 100,000 people went to Washington for a demonstration that apparently was so frustrating in its avowed nonviolence that many participants took to the streets after nightfall, breaking windows, blocking traffic, overturning trash cans, and challenging the police in an outburst which ended with 413

*Alabama, American, California (Berkeley, Los Angeles), Denver, Eastern Michigan, Illinois, Iowa, Jackson State, Kent State, Kentucky, Maryland (College Park), New Mexico, New York (Buffalo), Northwestern, Ohio, Ohio State, South Carolina, Southern Illinois, Stanford, Texas, Virginia, Washington, Wisconsin, and Yale.

†ROTC buildings were damaged or destroyed that month at Brooklyn Polytechnic, Buffalo, California (Berkeley, Davis), Case Western Reserve, City College of New York, Colorado College, DePauw, Hobart, Idaho, Indiana, John Carroll, Kent, Kentucky, Loyola (Chicago), Maryland, Michigan, Michigan State, Missouri, Nevada, North Carolina, Ohio University, Oregon State, Princeton, Rutgers, St. Norbert, San Francisco State, Seton Hall, Southern Illinois, Virginia, Washington University, Wisconsin, and Yale. One or more campus buildings, usually administration offices or those associated with military research, were damaged or destroyed at Alabama, Bowling Green, Bradley, California (Berkeley), California State (Fresno, Fullerton, Los Angeles City, Long Beach, San Francisco, San Jose), Cleveland State, Colorado State, Columbia, Fisk, Fordham, Illinois Wesleyan, Iowa, Livingston, Long Island, Marietta, Marquette, Miami (Ohio), Middlebury, Minnesota, Nebraska, New York State (New Paltz, Stony Brook), New York University, Northwestern, Northern Michigan, Ohio University, Penn State, Princeton, Richmond, Rockefeller, Rosary, Scranton, Southern Illinois, Southwest Missouri State, Valparaiso, Virginia Union, University of Washington, Western Illinois, and Wisconsin.

people arrested and which one Weatherman called worse than the Chicago National Action. The next day, a Sunday, George Winne, a student at San Diego State College, burned himself to death in protest against his nation and its war.

One other tragic event marked these violent days. On May 14, white police and state patrolmen in the city of Jackson, Mississippi, opened fire on an unarmed and unsuspecting crowd of black students from Jackson State College, killing two and injuring twelve. Another wanton murder by officials of the state, but this time, no doubt because the students were black, the country was most subdued in its reaction: *The New York Times,* which had given a four-column headline and fifty-one inches of copy to the Kent State killings, gave this story a one-column headline and six inches; the students, who had been outraged at Kent State, mounted protests this time at only some fifty-three campuses, most of them black.

The events of May had a profound effect upon the country, condensing and climaxing as they did the entire decade of student rebellion, providing for a brief time a clear look at the significant new position in society occupied by the American studentry. The Nixon Administration, which had been responsible for it all, reacted with cruelty at first (Nixon greeted the Kent State deaths with the remark that "when dissent turns to violence it invites tragedy," as if it were the students there and not the bastions of law-and-order who had turned to real violence); but the extent of the outbursts, accompanied by resignations and protest statements at all levels of the government, finally made the Administration aware of the crisis in the land and it was forced to commit itself to a revision of policy (early withdrawal of troops from Cambodia), to a humbling public apology for its inflated rhetoric, and to the appointment of two high-level investigations of student attitudes (one by Vanderbilt President Alexander Heard and the other by a Presidential Commission headed by former Pennsylvania Governor William Scranton). The media reacted first with bewilderment, victims of their own propaganda about the death of student protests, and then with blindness, acting out their role as social moderators: they generally overlooked the actual violence on the campuses—tossing off in a few paragraphs clashes that in other years would have rated front-page treatments, playing down the trashing of the capital, totally ignoring the incredible wave of bombings—to concentrate on Washington and the words out of official mouths, leaving the May insurrection as one of the great unreported stories of the decade. The public reacted, with encouragement from press and politicians, with a genuine sense of fear and alarm, made more ominous by its genuine lack of comprehension—resulting, for example, in a wanton and brutal attack by New York construction workers upon students marching peacefully at City Hall; in a Gallup poll for May which showed that campus unrest was regarded as the nation's leading problem (ahead of the war, racism, drugs, and crime); and in an outburst of antistudent, antiyouth sentiment manifested throughout the land but most dramatically demonstrated in Kent, Ohio, where every poll and paper showed that the overwhelming opinion, even among those with children in the May 4 demonstration, was that the Guardsmen should have shot every single student on the campus that day:

> When I reported home [one Kent State student has recounted] my mother said, "It would have been a good thing if all those students had been shot." I cried, "Hey, Mom! That's me you're talking about," and she said, "It would have been better for the country if you had all been mowed down."

The reaction of the students themselves was perhaps most interesting of all. Without the lead or participation of a strong radical student group such as SDS, without the sense of politics such a group might have transmitted, and consequently without a vision of how to effect real change at this unique point, most campuses turned toward the familiar path of electoral politics: a third of them engaged in letter-writing campaigns for dovish Congressmen and bell-ringing projects for antiwar petitions, a fifth sent representatives to pressure Congressmen in Washington, and hundreds mobilized people for mass marches in front of state and national legislatures. In this the students were of course encouraged by the instruments of the Establishment—newspapers, university administrations and faculties, political groups, and ultimately by the U.S. Congress itself, which passed legislation lowering the voting age in federal elections from twenty-one to eighteen (this eventually became the Twenty-sixth Amendment to the Constitution)—

and a dozen different electoral student groups were established with liberal funds (among them the Movement for a New Congress, Project Pursestrings, Campaign '70 Clearinghouse, Universities National Antiwar Fund). But either instinctively or analytically most students realized that within-the-system politics was no real answer to the evils that had prompted their protests, and it didn't take long for the electoral movement to dwindle: by the summer, only 12 percent of the colleges and universities could report any electoral activity among even 5 percent of their students, and by the fall less than 1 percent of the institutions gave students time off for electoral work (the so-called "Princeton Plan"). On November 3 the effect of the student vote was minimal.

But in spite of the comparative ease with which the protests were contained and channeled, in spite of the fact that no long-lasting effects emerged, there is no question that they were an expression of a profound dislocation in the American system, one made mainfest early in the sixties and continuing into the seventies. Not many people chose to listen to the words of the Presidential Commission which examined those events in detail, but its conclusions were wise and went far beyond the immediate circumstances:

> The crisis has roots in divisions of American society as deep as any since the Civil War. The divisions are reflected in violent acts and harsh rhetoric, and in the enmity of those Americans who see themselves as occupying opposing camps. Campus unrest reflects and increases a more profound crisis in the nation as a whole. . . . If this trend continues, if this crisis of understanding endures, the very survival of the nation will be threatened. A nation driven to use the weapons of war upon its youth is a nation on the edge of chaos. A nation that has lost the allegiance of part of its youth is a nation that has lost part of its future.

Four dead at Kent State, two at Jackson State: that brought the death toll of college students murdered at the hands of the nation's machinery of repression in the decade of the sixties to at least fourteen: Andrew Goodman and Michael Schwerner in Mississippi in June 1964, Samuel Hammond, Delano Middleton, and Henry Smith at Orangeburg, South Carolina, in February 1968,

Willie Ernest Grimes at North Carolina Agricultural and Technical State University in May 1969, James Rector in Berkeley in May 1969, Kevin Moran in Santa Barbara in April 1970, Allison Krause, Jeffrey Miller, Sandra Scheuer, and William Schroeder in Kent, Ohio, in May 1970, and Phillip Gibbs and James Earl Green in Jackson, Mississippi, in May 1970.* The lesson was unmistakable, and not lost upon most students: the government would go to any lengths, including killing, to repress the forces working for significant change in America, and from now on death had to be considered part of the stakes of student protest.

The corollary was equally frightening: the government would not take action against uniformed murder, no matter what the evidence and justification. The Kent State aftermath, watched bitterly by students across the land, attested eloquently to that. Despite evidence that the National Guardsmen had committed unprovoked and possibly premeditated murder, despite the finding of the Presidential Commission that the Guardsmen's acts were "unnecessary, unwarranted, and inexcusable," despite evidence that the Guardsmen subsequently conspired to lie to the police and FBI agents investigating the case, and despite pleas from officials of Kent State, a petition from 10,380 Kent State students, a formal appeal from twenty U.S. Congressmen, and editorial calls in many of the nation's newspapers, the federal government adamantly refused to authorize an investigation or convene a federal grand jury. Instead, the Portage County grand jury, made up of fifteen Kent area citizens, was allowed to be the sole official voice, and it completely exonerated the National Guard, put the chief blame for the deaths upon the administration of the university, and vociferously castigated the faculty, the Yippies, youth culture, and students in general. Ultimately it indicted neither the Guardsmen who fired into the crowd nor the state officials who ordered them to the scene, but rather twenty-four students and ex-students and one faculty member—"They blamed

*Three more were killed by police in July: in Lawrence, Kansas, Rick Dowdell and Harry Rice, freshmen at the University of Kansas, and in Milwaukee, Randy Anderson, of the University of Wisconsin at Milwaukee. One black man, Carl Hampton, was also killed by police in Houston in July, in a raid that left ex-SDSer Bartee Haile, then working with the Peoples Party II, seriously wounded.

us," one student said, "for getting in the way of the bullets." The charges proved to be so flimsy that only three students were found guilty of minor misdemeanors, one was acquitted, and the cases against the other twenty-one were dismissed for lack of evidence, but not until nineteen months and thousands of dollars later.

But of course by May 1970 there was no longer any doubt that the government intended to use any weapon at its disposal to contain student dissent. The Administration again set the tone. Nixon himself gave an unusual betrayal of his mind-set in an impromptu speech delivered just after ordering the Cambodian invasion in which he used a pejorative said to be the most Calvinistically emphatic in his entire vocabulary:

> You see these bums, you know, blowing up the campuses. Listen, the boys that are on the college campuses today are the luckiest people in the world, going to the greatest universities, and here they are burning up the books, storming around about this issue [the war].

Against this melody, the drone of Agnew rhetoric: "impudent snobs," "ideological eunuchs," "vultures," "arrogant, reckless, inexperienced elements," "political hustlers," and on and on, until the final warning, concentration camps:

> We cannot afford to be divided or deceived by the decadent thinking of a few young people. We can, however, afford to separate them from our society—with no more regret than we should feel over discarding rotten apples from a barrel.

Given these attitudes it was probably natural, but somewhat surprising, that the Administration with thinly disguised public scorn rejected both of its own Heard and Scranton reports when they failed to excoriate the students and absolve the government. Nixon followed this in the fall by writing an out-of-the-blue letter to nine hundred college presidents, telling them to restore "order and discipline" on the campuses or suffer the consequences (and enclosing an article reflecting his own views by one of the most virulent critics of the left, the LID doyen, Sidney Hook), and then proceeded to base the entire Republican campaign for that fall on whipping up public sentiment against youth and students.

The Administration simultaneously increased the federal ma-

chinery of repression, expanding by 300 percent its funds for local
law enforcement (including a national computerized information
network), enlarging its surveillance operations to the point where
The New York Times could report of federal files "on hundreds
and thousands of law-abiding yet suspect Americans," adding $20
million in 1970 for riot equipment and training for the National
Guard, and prosecuting more than four thousand draft-resistance
cases. Above all, it made the Department of Justice into the center
of the most elaborate and extensive operation against political
dissidence ever seen in this country.

The FBI continued to be the department's most active
branch. Despite Hoover's claim on November 19, 1970, that "we
have no special agents assigned to college campuses and have had
none," documents liberated from the FBI office in Media, Pennsylvania, four months later indicate that every single college in the
country was apparently assigned an agent and most of them had
elaborate informer systems as well. Even as tiny a bureau as the
Media one engaged in full-time surveillance and information-gath-
ering on every campus in its area, sixty-eight in all, ranging from
Penn State with its thirty-three thousand students down to places
like the Moravian Theological Seminary with thirty-five students
and the Evangelical Congregational School of Theology with
forty-one, and it used as its regular campus informers such people
as the vice-president, secretary to the registrar, and chief switchboard operator at Swarthmore, a monk at Villanova Monastery,
campus police at Rutgers, the recorder at Bryn Mawr, and the
chancellor at Maryland State College. As if that was not enough,
the FBI added twelve hundred new agents in 1970, mostly for
campus work, established a "New Left desk" (plus an internal
information bulletin called, without irony, "New Left Notes"),
and its agents were directed to step up campus operations:

> There was a pretty general consensus [reported an internal FBI
> communiqué] that more interviews with these subjects and hangers-
> on are in order for plenty of reasons, chief of which are it will
> enhance the paranoia endemic in these circles and will further serve
> to get the point across there is an FBI Agent behind every mailbox.
> In addition, some will be overcome by the overwhelming personali-
> ties of the contacting agent and volunteer to tell all—perhaps on a
> continuing basis. The Director [Hoover] has okayed PSI's [Poten-

tial Security Informants—i.e., campus informers] and SI's [Security Informants] age 18 to 21. We have been blocked off from this critical age group in the past. Let us take advantage of this opportunity.

And lest it be thought that these youthful informers and aging switchboard operators were all harmless molehills, it should be noted that the FBI reported that in fiscal year 1970–71 FBI informers supplied information which led to the arrests of at least 14,565 people.

At the same time the Department of Justice built up its Internal Security Division, a McCarthy-era leftover, into a full-scale national "Red Squad" for the investigation and prosecution of political dissidents anywhere in the country, and it acknowledged in the press that it was giving "top priority" to the new system. The division operated through two main agencies, separate but complementary. The Interdivisional Intelligence Unit was set up as the chief headquarters of all intelligence-gathering in Washington, combining for the first time the manifold files of the FBI, the Army, the Secret Service, the Narcotics Bureau, and other federal and local agencies. The Special Litigation Section was a team of eleven lawyers dispatched around the country to supervise and give information in cases involving the left and to operate federal grand juries for what were admitted frankly to be "investigative purposes" rather than judicial ones. This section instigated more than forty-five grand jury cases, including inquiries into SDS and the Weathermen in Boston, Brooklyn, Chicago, Cleveland, Detroit, Harrisburg, Kansas City (Missouri), Los Angeles, Manhattan, Seattle, Tucson, and Vermont;* it oversaw the

---

*These inquiries were considerably aided by a 1970 "use immunity" law passed by Congress which forced all witnesses either to answer grand jury questions about anything in their lives or be sent to jail for terms of up to eighteen months. Typical of the questions put to witnesses—not even defendants, mind you, or suspects—is this one by an Internal Security Division lawyer before the Tucson grand jury: "I want you to describe for the grand jury every occasion during the year 1970, when you have been in contact with, attended meetings which were conducted by, or been any place when any individual spoke whom you knew to be associated with or affiliated with Students for a Democratic Society, the Weatherman, the Communist Party or any other organization advocating revolutionary overthrow of the United States, describing for the grand jury when these incidents occurred, where they occurred, who was present and what was said by all persons there and what you did at the time that you were in these meetings, groups, associations or conversations." (*The Nation*, January 3, 1972.) Five witnesses who refused to answer such questions in Tucson were jailed.

operation of the conspiracy weapon again against the year-old White Panther Party (including ex-Jesse James Gang member, Skip Taub) in Detroit in October 1969, seven activists in St. Louis in the summer of 1970, and eight members of the Seattle Liberation Front (including four ex-Weathermen—Joe Kelly, Roger Lippman, Michael Justesen, Susan Stern—and three former Cornell SDSers—Jeffrey Dowd, Chip Marshall, Michael Abeles) in Seattle in May 1970.

Next to this, whatever the legislative branch of government could mount would have to be a poor second, but it did not seem to be reticent in trying. The Senate Internal Security Subcommittee subpoenaed the bank records and files of the SDS National Office, the New York Regional Office, Liberation News Service, the Institute for Policy Studies, and Cambridge Iron and Steel; the Senate Investigations Committee held hearings in the summer of 1970 to show that the Weathermen and the Black Panthers were primarily responsible for the spate of bombings in the nation; and the House Internal Security Committee continued its investigation of SDS, its chairman declaring in December 1969, "I doubt if there has been any organization which has been the subject of a more comprehensive and continuing review by any committee than has been SDS." As to actual lawmaking, the Congress showed its general commitment to repression by passing an Omnibus Crime Bill in 1969 which set up an intelligence system to coordinate for the first time local police reports from around the entire country, an Omnibus Crime Bill of 1970 which gave full largess to the FBI in any investigation of campus violence, and a District of Columbia Crime Bill in 1970 which provided for such heretofore forbidden measures as preventive detention and "no-knock" police raids on private homes. By the middle of 1970 there were no fewer than ten separate federal acts on the books aimed at punishing college protesters, chiefly by denying them federal money and grants, a penalty which was suffered by at least a thousand students in 1969 and 1970.

Given ample warning by the government, colleges and universities continued to expand their own operations. Undercover agents were discovered or acknowledged in 1969–70 on at least sixteen campuses—Berkeley, Colorado College, Harvard, Kansas, Kent State, Maryland, Minnesota, New Mexico, NYU, North Carolina, Northwestern, Ohio State, Texas, University of Washington, Wisconsin, and Yale—and that must have been only a small percentage, for, as *The New York Times* finally reported in the spring of 1971, "Undercover activity . . . has now become almost a permanent institution on the American college scene." Many state universities, including those in California, Iowa, Maryland, and Wisconsin, were endowed with special provisions giving their president greatly enlarged powers of campus repression; schools in at least thirty-two states by June 1970 were subject to state laws demanding that they punish student and faculty protesters. Most universities also increased (and often armed) their campus police forces during this period,* and adopted such other varied forms of control as identification cards, telephone taps (at perhaps a quarter of the campuses, according to one study), videotaping of demonstrations, wood-pellet bullets for riot control, closed-circuit television systems, and high-intensity spotlights along campus walks.

Repression is an ugly concept, conjuring up images of police states and totalitarian governments that Americans prefer not to think about, but a growing chorus of individuals and organizations (for example, the ACLU, Ramsey Clark's Committee for Public Justice, New York Mayor John Lindsay, even Senator Margaret Chase Smith) were warning now that repression was indeed on the way. But the thousands of young leftists harassed, arrested, beaten, shot, and jailed by this time needed no further convincing that repression, at least in its initial stages, existed in the United States by the middle of 1970. Even if the organizations of the left had been stable and powerful, even if they had been prepared for the intensity of the government's reaction, even if they had been psychologically set for a government willing to go to war against its own people, even then they would have had a difficult time holding together, advancing the Movement, pushing out new ideas, broadening the left. But they were not, and the repression in these years took a doubly heavy toll.

*Random examples: Columbia increased its force in 1970 from eighty to one hundred, Cornell from twenty-four to thirty-six, George Washington from twenty-six to fifty, Ohio State from thirty to sixty, Northwestern from three to twenty-five, Southern Illinois from twenty to seventy-five, and UCLA from nine to fifty-two.

Underground in America. During the first week of February 1970 the Weathermen began dropping out of sight, cutting themselves off totally, moving into apartments in out-of-the-way corners of large cities or cabins in the remote countryside. All earlier contacts, with family or Movement people, were severed. The last job, that of closing down the National Office, was left to Vickie Gabriner, a Cornell graduate and now a New York Weatherwoman. She phoned a friend, Pat Quinn, at the Wisconsin State Historical Society in Madison—long known as having one of the best collections of left and labor history material in the country, and the place where many of the earlier files of the NO had been stored—and she offered to turn over the complete contents of the NO if the society would come across with a quick $300. Quinn somehow finagled the money out of the Historical Society treasury, took a Society panel truck, and the next day appeared at the NO, handed over the money, and confronted an office that he says looked like "a garbage pit": piles of rubbish, papers scattered around, dirty clothes, sleeping bags, half-eaten food in various stages of decay, used rubbers, stacks of old newspapers, broken furniture, dust and dirt everywhere. Working quickly, since it was assumed that the Chicago Police had a stakeout on the office and would soon get around to wondering what was afoot, Quinn set to work to sweep up everything in sight; ultimately he loaded thirty-four large cartons with files, letters, an unwrapped Frisbee, Cuban posters, minutes of old NCs, miniature flags, long-unused chapter folders, tapes, magazines, anything at all inanimate, and packed them into the Society's truck waiting below. As soon as he was done and had gotten behind the wheel, two plain-clothes detectives suddenly appeared, threatened Quinn with arrest, and demanded that he turn over the contents of the truck. Quinn refused, arguing that the contents legally belonged to the sovereign state of Wisconsin whose servant he was, and he threatened to call the governor of the state if he was not released immediately. After much checking and scurrying, and lots of staring at the lettering on the side of the truck to determine if it was genuine, the police decided they were in the presence of an official, and nominally superior, branch of government and they let the truck and contents depart unmolested. So the last of SDS disappeared with the Weathermen.

Underground in America. On February 21, the Wilkerson townhouse cell set off three firebombs at the home of Judge John Murtagh, then presiding over the case of the New York "Panther Twenty-one." On March 6, the townhouse exploded, and six days later three New York City commercial buildings were bombed, presumably though not certainly by another Weatherman cell. On March 30, Chicago police raided an apartment on Kenmore Avenue and claimed to have uncovered a "bomb factory," stocked with dynamite and "subversive literature," for which they sought Dohrn and Jacobs, who are known to have stayed there, and Boudin and Wilkerson, who had not. And on May 21, just after the furor over Cambodia and Kent State was beginning to die down, Weatherman issued its first underground communiqué, promising an attack on "a symbol or institution of Amerikan injustice" within the next two weeks. Nineteen days later a devastating blast went off at the headquarters of the New York City police department, heavily damaging the second story, shattering windows throughout the building, causing seven minor injuries to policemen: this was Weatherman's first large and publicly acknowledged bombing.

Underground in America. Two separate grand juries, one in Chicago and one in Detroit, went after the Weathermen in their new habitat. On April 2, after a six-month investigation by the FBI and the U.S. Attorney's Office, a federal grand jury in Chicago indicted twelve of the top Weatherleaders for crossing state lines with the intention of inciting and participating in a riot —that was Title 18 of the United States Code, the same conspiracy law used against the Chicago Eight and the Seattle Seven—and for actually having committed one or more of forty different acts, including making inflammatory speeches and striking policemen; a total of fifteen counts was brought against the defendants, any one of which carried a penalty of five years in jail and a $10,000 fine.* Three months later, on July 23, a federal grand jury in

*Those indicted were national officers Mark Rudd, Bill Ayers, and Jeff Jones, and Kathy Boudin, Judy Clark, Bernardine Dohrn, Linda Evans, John Jacobs, Howie Machtinger, Terry Robbins (his body was still officially unidentified), Mike Spiegel, and Larry Weiss. Indicted as co-conspirators but not defendants were Corky Benedict, John Buttney, David Chase, Peter Clapp, Karen Daenzer, Dianne Donghi, Howie Emmer, Courtney Esposito, Brian Flanagan, Lynn Gar-

Detroit indicted thirteen Weathermen on additional conspiracy charges, this time stemming from the Flint National Council meeting, at which it was alleged that plots were laid to blow up police stations, corporate offices, and campus buildings in New York, Detroit, Chicago, and Berkeley; this time, however, the only overt act it was able to lay to the Weathermen, and none too convincingly at that, was an aborted bombing attempt at a police association building in Detroit on March 6.* In all, nineteen top Weatherpeople were indicted as defendants in three months—and though they were the objects of an extensive nation-wide search by FBI and local police, though Dohrn even made it on to the FBI's "most wanted list," though FBI and Red Squad agents were obliged to undergo regular refresher courses on the Weathermen's mug shots for at least the next six months, only three arrests were ever made (by the middle of 1972): Linda Evans and Dianne Donghi were fingered by Grathwohl in New York on April 15, causing him to blow his cover, and Judy Clark was spotted by an FBI agent at a movie theater in New York in December. The rest, with the exception of Robbins, lived and continued to carry on their revolution underground.

---

vin, Ted Gold, Ann Hathaway, Lenore Kalom, Samuel Karp, Mark Laventer, Karen Latimer, Jonathan Lerner, Chip Marshall, Celeste McCullogh, Brian McQuerry, Jeff Melish, Jim Mellen, David Millstone, Diana Oughton, John Pilkington, Roberta Smith, Susan Stern, and Cathy Wilkerson. This seems to be a fairly good estimate of the top leadership of Weatherman.

*Those initially indicted included five defendants on the Chicago list—Rudd, Ayers, Boudin, Dohrn, and Evans—plus Bo Burlingham, Dianne Donghi, Ronald Fliegelman, Larry Grathwohl (in fact an FBI informer), Naomi Jaffe, Russ Neufeld, Jane Spielman, and Cathy Wilkerson. A subsequent Detroit indictment (December 7, 1972) charged all of the above except Grathwohl and Spielman, plus John Fuerst, Leonard Handelsman (a Weatherman in Cleveland), Mark Real (a Kent State Weatherman), and Roberta Smith (a California activist); unindicted co-conspirators were Karen Ashley, Kirk and Paul Augustin, Clapp, David and Judith Cohen Flatley, David Gilbert, Gold, Linda Josefowicz, Michael Justesen, Laventer, Mark Lencl, Machtinger, Peter Neufeld, Oughton, Wendy Panken, Robbins, Robert Roth, Deborah Schneller, Pat Small, Spiegel, Marsha Steinberg, Robert Swarthout, and Joanna Zilsel. This indictment charged Weathermen with specific acts of constructing or transporting bombs in Cleveland, San Francisco, Tucson, and St. Louis, and with a fire-bomb attack on the home of a Cleveland policeman on March 2, 1970.

Underground in America. Dohrn issued another Weather-report in December 1970:

A growing illegal organization of young women and men can live and fight and love inside Babylon [the name for the United States then being used by the Black Panthers, borrowed from the old Baptist pulpit-thumpers as a symbol of high decadence and imperial evil]. The FBI can't catch us; we've pierced their bullet-proof shield. . . .

Because we are fugitives, we could not go near the Movement. That proved to be a blessing because we've been everywhere else. We meet as many people as we can with our new identities; we've watched the TV news of our bombings with neighbors and friends who don't know that we're Weatherpeople. We're often afraid but we take our fear for granted now, not trying to act tough. What we once thought would have to be some zombie-type discipline has turned out to be a yoga of alertness, a heightened awareness of activities and vibrations around us—almost a new set of eyes and ears. . . .

We are in many different regions of the country and are building different kinds of leaders and organizations. It's not coming together into one organization, or paper structure of factions or coalitions. It's a New Nation that will grow out of the struggles of the next year.

Underground in America: ten years after its first conference, after its first impact on the nation's campuses, after its first faint stirrings on the nation's left, SDS had come to this.

26

EPILOGUE: 1970-1972

By the summer of 1970, ten years after it had begun, SDS existed only in two bizarre distortions. Both continued on for several years more, each at its own games, each purporting to lead the revolution, but neither any longer had any connection with the organization which had given them birth.

Weatherman was to go on as an underground force in America and as a symbolic influence upon the left for another year or so, though with diminishing effect as time wore on. Underground life became wearying after months of work that seemed to bring the revolution no closer, shattering the earlier confident dreams. Some cells disintegrated, their members surfacing for more traditional political action if they were not wanted by the police, or living secret private lives in street communities and college towns if they were fugitives. Many other cells continued, with a membership of between one and two hundred people altogether, but they underwent changes too. More emphasis came to be placed on relating to the existing youth culture rather than denouncing it as somehow "bourgeois": Weatherman came to see it, Dohrn wrote later that year, "as the forces which produced us, a culture that we are a part of, a young and unformed society (nation)."* Those

---

*It was as a reflection of this new perception that the Weathermen in September 1970 designed and executed the escape of Timothy Leary, the high priest of the drug culture, from a minimum-security prison in San Luis Obispo, California, where he was serving a ten-year sentence for possession of marijuana. Weatherpeople helped Leary climb over the walls, kept him in hiding in several cities, and supplied the passport that enabled him to escape to Algeria.

groups which had chosen to emphasize personal development, trust, love, and communality came to be taken as models over the more militaristic and disciplined ones, and the growing role of liberated women in these "families" helped to emphasize the search for new styles of sexuality, intimacy, and openness. Ideas about leadership came to be altered, too, with the authoritarian hierarchy of the National Action period giving way to a more communal and open way of governing, downgrading the aggressive and dominating types who had assumed power before. ("We've learned from Fidel's speeches and Ho's poems," Dohrn wrote in December, "how leaders grow out of being deeply in touch with movements. From Crazy Horse and other great Indian chiefs we've learned that the people who respect their tribe and its needs are followed freely and with love.") The Weatherbureau, wherever it was, reflected these changes too, for Mark Rudd— whose macho style must have been impossible in one of these new intimate "families"—was demoted some time in 1970 and his name was no longer included among the leadership by October. The implicit sexism of Weather *man* now gave way to the locution "Weather Underground," the phrase with which the group's communiqués have been signed since December 1970, and to the general term "Weatherpeople."

Whatever its internal changes might have been, Weatherman was to go on to attract attention over the next two years largely through a series of dramatic and symbolic bombings and through the messages accompanying them. In October 1970 it announced a "fall offensive" during which "families and tribes will attack the enemy around the country" and then it proceeded to blow up the police statue in Chicago's Haymarket Square again, and bomb the Hall of Justice in Marin County, California, and the Long Island Court House in New York, both on behalf of political prisoners. (At the same time a half-dozen allied groups across the country, perhaps Weathercells or perhaps separate revolutionary groups also concerned with symbolic violence, launched attacks at government buildings. Damage from all this was said to be half a million dollars, media coverage was dramatic and extensive, and President Nixon intervened to order "a new crackdown" on those who would use bombs five thousand miles away from Vietnam.) On March 1 of the next year the Weather Underground set off a bomb in a toilet in the Capitol in Washington, making front pages everywhere and this time leading Nixon to denounce the "shocking act of violence that will outrage all Americans"; it was accompanied by a long, detailed, and thoroughly rational letter explaining that the act was taken in retaliation for Nixon's escalation of the war into Laos—a message almost totally ignored by the commercial media. On August 30, 1971, the Weather Underground bombed the Department of Corrections office in San Francisco after the shooting of black revolutionary leader George Jackson, and on September 17 it bombed the Department of Corrections offices in Albany in retaliation for the murder of twenty-eight prisoners at Attica Prison a few days before. On May 19, 1972, the Weather Underground set off an explosion in the Air Force section of the Pentagon, only days after Nixon had announced increased bombings of North Vietnam and the mining of its harbors. All told, eight major bombings, publicly admitted and defended, over the course of two years, each dramatic and specific, accompanied by an explanatory statement; with the exception of one person, Leslie Bacon, picked up for the Capitol bombing but later released, no one has ever been arrested, much less convicted, for any of them.

And thus would grow the Weathermyth. Whatever else the Weatherpeople might stand for, the fact that they continued to use symbolic bombings, continued to defy the authority of the state, and continued to run free, living underground, confounding the most massive police force in the world, gave them a certain stature. They were living evidence of young, white, armed revolutionaries in America, one pole of the possibilities of politics, and even if very few wanted to join up, many responded to their reverberations. Many political groups would measure themselves against the Weathermen in terms of politics, courage, commitment. Violence, straight-out political violence, became an issue in political meetings as never before. The meaning of Weatherman's attempts to create new men and women, if not exactly its means of doing so, sank into the consciousness of student activists. Women's groups, particularly, paid attention to the Weatherpeople's attempts to smash monogamy and reestablish sexual lives. And from time to time the Weathermen were even paid the flattery of imitation: small bands of quasi-Weathermen would take shape, living under their own discipline without direction from the official Weather Underground, surfacing with a bombing or a nighttime trashing and proclaiming themselves Weathermen even if no one in the original group had ever heard of them.*

And so the Weathermyth held on, for a few more years at least, even as Weatherman itself faded. Weatherman symbols—first a "W" on top of an "M" with a bolt of lightning passing between, later a crude rainbow with lightning running through—became familiar graffiti in every large city and college town . . . women marching in San Francisco in 1971 read a Weatherletter aloud and chanted, "Angela, Bernardine, Madame Binh, Sisters in struggle, gonna win" . . . Jerry Rubin dedicated a book to the Weather Underground in 1971, Abbie Hoffman regretted he hadn't given money to them instead of the Black Panthers, but "I didn't know their address" . . . Eldridge Cleaver announced, "When checking out the wretched of the imperialist earth, it is obvious the Weathermen as warriors of the people are a part of humanity's solution," and the Black Panther members on trial in New York, in defiance of their West Coast leadership, wrote: "We feel that the Weather underground fits truly in a revolutionary manner with Malcolm's 'whites who are really fed up,' 'like old John Brown,' and are showing it in a progressive and revolutionary manner" . . . a women's march on the Pentagon in April 1971 carried flags with the Weather rainbow and pictures of Bernardine Dohrn . . . a poet in the Chicago *Seed* wrote of "bernardine dohrn, alive, well, in amerika," with the words "Lightning and rainbows to all the Sisters" across a full-page photograph of her face . . . and a whole book, not very good but 519 pages long, was published presenting all the major documents by and about Weatherman in the first year of its life, a distinction few organizations could claim.

PL-SDS played out the illusion of being a mass student organization for the rest of the 1969–70 school year and would go on

---

*The New Year's Gang in Wisconsin, which carried out the bombing of the Army Math Research Center in Madison in August 1970—resulting in the death of a graduate student, the second victim of left violence in the decade—was one of these groups. Without any known connection to or sanction from the Weather Underground it regarded itself as a Weathercell and it even signed its bombing communiqué, "Marion Delgado."

to twist itself into a variety of odd forms thereafter, but there was little doubt that its deformed version of SDS was a failure.

The campus-worker-student alliance strategy, though a proven failure, was still made the central focus of chapter energies for many months, but its irrelevance to the lives of students only served to clinch PL-SDS's campus reputation as a remote organization off in a mad sectarian world of its own. The short-haired abrasiveness of these SDSers did nothing to overcome this, nor did their continuing opposition to such things as marijuana, the rock culture, and homosexual liberation. PL-SDS refused to join the general antiwar agitation—during the April 1970 antiwar marches, for example, it confined its role to storming the various speakers' platforms and trying to keep liberal politicians from speaking—and it avoided both campus issues of moment (tuition, student power) and national ones (racism, repression of the Panthers, complicity). When the uprisings came in the wake of the Kent State murders, PL-SDS was isolated, without a role to play or a constituency to lead, and on some campuses, notably in California, it was actually hostile to the student strike. By the end of the school year, PL-SDS was down to perhaps a dozen strong chapters, with a membership of not much above two or three thousand, its income had dwindled to less than $1500 a month (or $18,000, a sixth of what the old SDS had been operating on), its publications were almost at a standstill, *New Left Notes* barely coming out even once a month, and its scheduled national convention had to be postponed, and then canceled.

PL-SDS would continue to survive for at least the next two years, pumped up by the leadership and finances of the Progressive Labor Party, continually searching for some way to sell itself to the American studentry. Over the summer of 1970 it tried to adopt the war issue for a change, to become a left-wing SMC, and for a time it attended antiwar conferences pushing a hard anti-imperialist, no-negotiations line (pushing, in the case of one Boston meeting, to the point of all-out fist fights). When this scheme proved ineffective PL-SDS retreated for the 1970–71 school year to the old idea of the worker-student alliance, supporting local strikes, picketing on behalf of General Motors workers, marching in Washington against unemployment and low wages. This, too, inevitably, was a resounding failure and by the end of that school year PL-SDS was in pathetic shape: a number of former chapters (major ones like Columbia and Chicago among them) had broken from the national organization to go their own way, most groups outside the New-York-Boston-California orbit had disintegrated, once-strong chapters at places like Harvard and San Francisco State had become tiny study groups with only occasional flashes of activity, and the National Office, moved from Boston to Chicago, was in a state of what all acknowledged to be exhaustion. Normally such an organization would have died right there, but PL apparently decided to give it one last injection for the 1971–72 school year. It revived SDS as a broad, even reformist, student group, soft-lining and nonsectarian, avoiding the rhetoric and principles of socialism, class analysis, and the like, and open to anyone (in the words of a new constitution adopted in March 1972) willing to fight "against daily problems and their roots . . . against racism, imperialist wars, the subjugation of women and exploitation of every kind"; at the same time it guided that new SDS to concentrate almost exclusively now on the issue of racism— confined however to racism in classes and textbooks, since PL continued to believe that students would only get interested in narrow campus issues. Initially at any rate, most campuses received this newly furbished PL-SDS with indifference.

Whatever its twists and turns, PL-SDS would continue to suffer under the twin weights of its domination by a senior organization which thought of it chiefly as a recruiting grounds and its Old Left political heritage which prevented it from achieving either a style or a strategy that was attractive to broad numbers of students. Something called "SDS" would go on as long as PL felt it was getting its money's worth out of it, but it would have no relation to the organization that had borne those initials in the decade of the sixties.

Was this all that it had come to, then, this Students for a Democratic Society that had affected so much of the life of the sixties? Happily, no: though it achieved none of its long-range goals, though it ended in disarray and disappointment, it left a legacy, as suggested in the beginning, of deep and permanent worth. It shaped a generation, revived an American left, transformed political possibilities, opened the way to changes in the national life that would have been unthought of in the fifties; it was in good measure responsible for the changes in university governance, the liberation of campus life, the reordering of curricula, the aeration of American education; it played an important role in molding public opinion against the war in Southeast Asia and increasing public understanding of the imperialistic nature of that war, and in the corollary achievements of weakening the institution of the draft, lessening the overt role of universities in military research, and abolishing or transforming ROTC units at many campuses; and it directly affected the lives and consciousnesses of hundreds of thousands of university and high school students across the land, many in only initial and tentative ways, but many more in thorough and enduring ways, ways that will cling for the rest of their lives, producing at the very minimum a pool of people, many of them of the finest minds and talents, who have forever lost their allegiance to the myths and institutions of capitalist America and who will be among those seeking to transform this country, as SDS had always hoped, into "a democracy of individual participation, governed by two central aims: that the individual share in those social decisions determining the quality and direction of his life; that society be organized to encourage independence in men and provide the media for their common participation."

Whether from this legacy will evolve a new organization and a new leftward spirit to carry on the task that SDS began, only the future can tell. But it is certain that this is the place to begin.

ACKNOWLEDGMENTS

The author wishes to thank the following: Peter Agree, Maxime and Ruth Apfelbaum, Paul Axel, Bill Ayers, Donald Barthelme, Paul Booth, Jeremy Brecher, Jerome Breslaw, Robb Burlage, Byron Dobell, Douglas Dowd, Nick Egleson, Larry Fein, Henry Feldman, Tony Fels, Julie Fraad, Norm Fruchter, Betty Garman, David Gelber, Stephen Geller, Todd Gitlin, Michael Harrington, Peter Henner, John Herrick, John Edgar Hoover, John Hunter, Richard Ichord, Roger Kahn, Herschel Kaminsky, Sydney Levine, Patricia and Perry Mackey, Carlos Marichal, Steve Max, John McClellan, Don McKelvey, Lynn Nesbit, Jack Newfield, Jim O'Brien, Carl Oglesby, Grace Paley, Bob Pardun, Judy Pearlman, Jean Pohoryles, Thomas Pynchon, Patrick Quinn, Howard Rodman, Mark Rudd, Helen and William Sale, Daniel Schneider, John J. Simon, Victor Simpson, the Tamiment Library, Maria Varella, Vern Visick, Arthur Waskow, Lee Webb, Mark William Webber, Steve Weissman, Jim Williams, and the Wisconsin State Historical Society.

This book was made possible by a generous and absolutely vital grant from the Louis M. Rabinowitz Foundation.

ORGANIZATIONS

SDS—Students for a Democratic Society
        ERAP—Economic Research and Action Project
        JOIN—Jobs or Income Now
        MDS—Movement for a Democratic Society
        NAC—National Administrative Committee
        NC—National Council
        NCUP—Newark Community Union Project
        NEC—National Executive Committee
        NIC—National Interim Committee
        NO—National Office
        PEP—Political Education Project
        PREP—Peace Research and Education Project
        REC—Radical Education Center
        RIP—Research, Information, Publications
        RO—Regional Office
        RYM—Revolutionary Youth Movement
        T-O—Teacher-Organizer (institutes)

ASU—American Student Union
Campus ADA—Americans for Democratic Action
CP—Communist Party
FSM—Free Speech Movement
IDA—Institute for Defense Analysis
IS—International Socialists
IWW—Industrial Workers of the World
LID—League for Industrial Democracy
LNS—Liberation News Service
M2M—May 2nd Movement
Mobe—National (later New) Mobilization Committee to End the War
        in Vietnam
NACLA—North American Congress on Latin America
NCC—National Coordinating Committee Against the War in Vietnam
NCNP—National Conference for a New Politics
NSA—National Student Association
NSM—Northern Student Movement
NUC—New University Conference

PL—Progressive Labor (Party and Movement)
PYOC—Communist Progressive Youth Organizing Committee
REP—Radical Education Project
SANE—National Committee for a Sane Nuclear Policy
SLID—Student League for Industrial Democracy
SMC—Student Mobilization Committee
SNCC—Student Nonviolent (later National) Coordinating Committee
SPU—Student Peace Union
SSOC—Southern Students Organizing Committee
SWP—Socialist Workers Party
WSA—Worker-Student Alliance
YAWF—Youth Against War and Fascism
YPSL—Young People's Socialist League
YSA—Young Socialists Alliance

OFFICERS
AND MEMBERSHIP STATISTICS

1960–62:*

President: Al Haber

Vice President: Jonathan Weiss

Field Secretary: Al Haber (1960–62)

          Tom Hayden (1961–62)

Members:	250 (December 1960)
	575 (November 1961)
	800 (May 1962)

Chapters:	8 (December 1960)
	20 (November 1961)
	10 (May 1962)

1962–63:

President: Tom Hayden

Vice President: Paul Booth

National Secretary: Jim Monsonis

Field Secretary: Steve Max

Members:	900 (January 1963)
	(447 pd.)
	1100 (June 1963)
	(600 pd.)

| Chapters: | 9 (January 1963) |

1963–64:

President: Todd Gitlin

Vice President: Paul Booth

National Secretary: Lee Webb/Clark
                 Kissinger
Field Secretary: Steve Max

Members	1500 (October 1963)
	(610 pd.)
	1000 pd. (June 1964)

| Chapters: | 19 (October 1963) |
| | 29 (June 1964) |

1964–65:

President: Paul Potter

Vice President: Vernon Grizzard

National Secretary: Clark Kissinger

Members:	2500 (December 1964)
	(1365 pd.)
	3000 (June 1965)
	(2000 pd.)

| Chapters: | 41 (December 1964) |
| | 80 (June 1965) |

*There was no convention in 1961 and no election of new officers.

1965–66:

President: Carl Oglesby

Vice President: Jeff Shero

National Secretary: Jeff Segal/Clark
　　　　Kissinger/Paul Booth/
　　　　Jane Adams

Members:　10,000　(October 1965)
　　　　　　　(4000 pd.)
　　　　　15,000　(June 1966)
　　　　　　　(6000 pd.)

Chapters:　　89 (October 1965)
　　　　　172 (June 1966)

1966–67:

President: Nick Egleson

Vice President: Carl Davidson

National Secretary: Greg Calvert

Members:　25,000　(October 1966)
　　　　　　　(6000 natn'l.)
　　　　　30,000 (June 1967)
　　　　　　　(6371 natn'l.)

Chapters:　　265 (October 1966)
　　　　　(175 strong)
　　　　　247 (June 1967)

1967–68:

National Secretary: Mike Spiegel

Education Secretary: Bob Pardun

Inter-organizational Secretary:
　　　　Carl Davidson

Members:　35,000 (April 1968)
　　　　　?40,000–100,000
　　　　　　　(June 1968)

Chapters:　　265 (December 1967)
　　　　　280 (April 1968)
　　　　　350 (June 1968)

1968–69:

National Secretary: Mike Klonsky

Education Secretary:
　　　　Fred Gordon

Inter-organizational Secretary:
　　　　Bernardine Dohrn

Members:　?80,000–100,000
　　　　　　　(November 1968)
　　　　　?30,000–100,000
　　　　　　　(June 1969)

Chapters:　350-400
　　　　　　　(November 1968)
　　　　　?300 (June 1969)

1969-70:

National Secretary: Mark Rudd
Education Secretary:
　　　　Bill Ayers
Inter-organizational Secretary:
　　　　Jeff Jones

PL (Boston)
National Secretary: John Pennington
Education Secretary: Alan Spector
Inter-organizational Secretary:
　　　　Patricia Forman

CONSTITUTION OF THE STUDENTS FOR A DEMOCRATIC SOCIETY

(Adopted by the National Convention, June 1962, with major later additions and deletions noted.)

Preamble:
Students for a Democratic Society is an association of young people on the left. It seeks to create a sustained community of educational and political concern: one bringing together liberals and radicals, activists and scholars, students and faculty.

It maintains a *vision* of a democratic society, where at all levels the people have control of the decisions which affect them and the resources on which they are dependent. It seeks a *relevance* through the continual focus on realities and on the programs necessary to effect change at the most basic levels of economic, political, and social organization. It feels the *urgency* to put forth a radical, democratic program counterposed to authoritarian movements both of Communism and the domestic Right. [From 1965, "program *whose methods embody the democratic vision.*"]

Article I: Name
The name of the organization shall be Students for a Democratic Society.

[Article II: Affiliation (Dropped, 1966)
The Students for a Democratic Society shall be affiliated with the League for Industrial Democracy, Inc., a tax-exempt educational foundation concerned with the extension of democracy into all areas of social, political, and economic life.]

Article III: Membership
Section 1. Membership is open to students, faculty and others who share the commitment of the organization to democracy as a means and as a social goal.
Section 2. SDS is an organization of democrats. It is civil libertarian in its treatment of those with whom it disagrees, but clear in its opposition to any totalitarian principle as a basis for government or social organization. Advocates or apologists for such a principle are not eligible for membership. [From 1965, "to any *anti-democratic principle as a basis for governmental, social, or political organization.*"]

Section 3.　*Dues.* There shall be a national initiation of one dollar, supplemented by periodic dues, the amount and period of which shall be determined by the National Council. [From 1965, amount not specified.]

Section 4.　*Associates.* Individuals who do not wish to join the SDS, but who share the major concerns of the organization, may become associates with rights and responsibilities as defined by the National Council.

Article IV: Chapters and Affiliates

Section 1.　Any group of five or more members may apply to the National Executive Committee [from 1963, *"National Office"*] for a charter as a chapter.

Section 2.　A chapter may be chartered at any meeting of the National Council on recommendation of the National Executive Committee. It must be considered for chartering at the first meeting of the National Council after it has submitted a membership list, a constitution or statement of principles, and notification of elected National Council representative to the National Executive Committee. In the period between submission of the required information to the national office and the next National Council meeting, the chapter may be given a provisional charter at the discretion of the President. [From 1966, *"A chapter may be chartered by the regional council of the area in which it is organized, or by the National Council. The chapter shall submit a membership list, a constitution or statement of principles, and notification of officers or regional representatives. Chapters may be provisionally recognized by the President or appropriate regional officer pending the meeting of the National Council or regional council respectively."*]

Section 3.　Chapters are expected to operate within the broad terms of policy set by the National Convention and the National Council. Points of conflict should be referred to the National Council and a procedure established to make the issue public to the organization. In matters judged to be detrimental to the interests of the organization, the National Council shall have the power to cease whatever activity that has been brought into question. The matter shall be finally resolved by the National Council in meeting or referendum.

Section 4.　*Associated Groups.* Independent groups can affiliate as associates of SDS by vote of their membership and designation of a liaison representative to sit on the National Council with consultative vote. The representative shall be a member of SDS. Such association is provisional until the approval of the National Council. The form of the relationship shall be worked out in each case between the group and the National Council.

Section 5. *Fraternal Organizations.* National or regional organizations whose programs and purposes are consistent with the broad aims and principles of SDS can be invited by the National Council to be fraternal with the SDS and have a fraternal vote on the National Council. Such organizations shall appoint a liaison representative who shall be a member of SDS.

Section 6. SDS welcomes the opportunity to cooperate with other individuals and organizations in jointly sponsoring specific action programs and joint stands on specific issues. The National Council shall be empowered to determine specific cooperative activity. (Cooperation does not imply endorsement.)

[From 1966, *Regional Organization*

Section 1: *All or some of the chapters and/or members in a given geographical area may constitute themselves a region of SDS. New regions shall submit their constitutions and be recognized provisionally by the President pending the next regular National Council meeting. All disputes over regional boundaries shall be resolved by the National Council.*

Section 2: *Regions of SDS shall hold at least one membership convention each year and may establish regional officers as deemed necessary. Regional programs, staff, and offices shall be responsible to decisions arrived at by a democratically constituted regional council.*

Section 3: *While fundamentally responsible to their regional constituency, regions are expected to operate within the broad terms of policy set by the National Convention and National Council. Any points of conflict shall be finally resolved by the National Council.*

Section 4: *If one-third of the duly chartered chapters in the geographical area of a region so petition, the National Council shall immediately consider whether to declare the regional organization defunct and to prohibit it from speaking or acting on behalf of SDS.*]

Article V: Convention

Section 1. The SDS shall meet in convention annually, at a time and a place fixed by the National Council, with at least three months prior notice being given to all members.

Section 2. The Convention shall serve to debate major issues and orientation of the organization, to set program mandates to the national staff, and to elect national officers. The Convention shall not be the policy-making body on specific resolutions.

Section 3. *Representation.* Chapters shall elect Convention delegates on the basis of one delegate for every five SDS members in the chapter, each delegate to have two [from 1966, *"five"*] votes at the Convention. Individual SDS members shall have the right to attend the Convention with one vote each. [Dropped, 1966.] Delegates from associated and fraternal groups shall be elected by a procedure determined by the National Council. The National Council shall draft Convention rules, accreditation procedures, and other requirements.

Article VI: National Council

Section 1. The National Council shall be composed of (1) one representative elected from each chapter with five to twenty-five members, and one additional representative for each additional twenty-five members [from 1968, *"five members"*] or fraction thereof, in that chapter; (2) the seventeen National Officers; (3) elected liaison representatives from associated groups (with consultative vote); (4) liaison representatives from fraternal organizations (with fraternal vote); and (5) national staff (without vote). In all cases, NC members and liaison representatives must be members of SDS. [From 1964, *"No more than three members from one chapter or associated group may serve concurrently as National Officers."*]

Section 2. The National Council shall be the major policy making and program body of the organization. It shall determine policy in the form of resolutions on specific issues within the broad orientation of the organization; determine program priorities and action undertaken by the organization consonant with the orientation and mandates set by the convention; advise the National Executive Committee on financial matters; confirm committee chairmen, staff representatives to the

LID board; charter chapters, associated groups, and fraternal organizations. [From 1963, NEC dropped and additional budget responsibilities added.]

Section 3. The National Council shall meet at least two times [from 1963, *"four"*] a year. A quorum shall be 40 percent of the voting members. Chapter and liaison representatives may be represented by a designated alternate from that group.

[*Article VII: The National Executive Committee* (Dropped, 1963.)

Section 1. The National Executive Committee shall be composed of the seventeen officers elected by the convention with the chapter representatives on the National Council serving as alternates. No more than three members from one chapter or associated group can serve concurrently on the NEC. . . .]

[*Article VIII: Administrative Committee* (Dropped, 1963.)

Section 1. The Administrative Committee shall be located at the place of the national office and shall have as members all NEC members in the vicinity of the national office plus such other people as are approved by the NEC. . . .]

[From 1963, *National Interim Committee*

The President shall have the power to call a meeting of a temporary National Interim Committee, to be composed of the seventeen National Officers (from 1967, also "on a regular basis"), for emergencies only. Decisions of this body shall be subject to National Council approval.]

Article IX: National Officers and Staff

Section 1. The National Officers shall be the President, the Vice President, and fifteen other Officers, all to be elected at the Convention and to serve as members of the National Council. [From 1967, *"National Secretary, Education Secretary, and Inter-organizational Secretary"* and *"eight* other officers."] The Convention may on a year-to-year basis create other officers as seem necessary and shall designate their voting rights in the various bodies of SDS.

Section 2. The National Officers must have been members of the SDS at least two months prior to elections.

Section 3. The National President is the spokesman of SDS. He shall be responsible for carrying out organizational policy and shall convene the National Council. He shall be assisted by the Vice President, and in case of vacancy the Vice President shall assume his functions.

Section 4. The National Secretary shall be the chief administrative official of the organization, responsible to the President and the National Council. He shall be appointed by the NC for a stated period of time. The National Council may also create and fill additional positions of Assistant National Secretary to work under direction of the President and National Secretary. Other staff positions shall be created and filled by the National Secretary.

[*From 1967, "Section 3: The eleven National Officers are the spokesmen of SDS. They shall be responsible for seeing that organizational and political policies are carried out and shall convene the National Council. Political responsibility lies with the three Secretaries in consultation with the other officers. The three Secretaries shall work out of the national office. Important decisions in any one area which are made between meetings of the National Interim Council are to be made by the three national officers together. The officers shall be responsible to the Convention and the National Council.*

Section 4:   *The National Secretary shall have primary responsibility for the implementation of national programs approved by the Convention or National Council.*

Section 5:   *The Inter-organizational Secretary shall have primary responsibility for liaison with other organizations, both national and international, and for informing the membership about these groups. He/she shall not attend congresses, accept money, or establish formal relationships with organizations without the approval of the convention, the National Council, or, in emergency, the National Interim Council.*

Section 6:   *The Education Secretary shall have the primary responsibility for the functioning of the internal education program."*]

[*Article X: Relationship With the League for Industrial Democracy* (Dropped, 1966.)

Section 1.   The SDS shall be autonomously constituted, though its policy and functioning shall be within the broad aims and principles of the LID. . . .]

Article XI: Parliamentary Authority

In all cases not covered by this Constitution, *Robert's Rules of Order, Revised Edition* shall be the authority governing SDS business.

Article XII: Policy and Discipline

Section 1. Any member of the organization, including the Officers, may be expelled or relieved of duties by a two-thirds vote of the National Council. Due process shall be followed in all cases.

Section 2. Any two chapters, or one-third of the National Council, can initiate a national referendum on any question.

Section 3. All material sent out in the name of the organization shall have the approval of a majority of the National Council and shall have been submitted to all of the NC members.

Article XIII: Amendments

This constitution may be amended by one of three procedures:

a. by a two-thirds vote of the Convention in session on amendments introduced at the Convention, in which case the amendment will take effect at the following Convention;

b. by a two-thirds vote of the Convention in session on amendments introduced by distribution to the membership at least a month before the Convention, in which case the amendment will take effect immediately upon adoption;

c. by a two-thirds vote of the membership in referendum in which case the amendment will take effect immediately upon adoption.

APPENDIX
THE ROOTS: 1905-1960

On September 12, 1905, Harry W. Laidler, a junior at Wesleyan College and a young man with an interest in the left, attended a quiet meeting in a third-floor walk-up loft at 140 Fulton Street in New York City. "I found," he wrote,

> a group of some 100 men and women—writers, social workers, college students, members of organized labor and of various professions. They were intently listening to the message of the novelist and socialist, Upton Sinclair.
>
> He had gone through five years of college life at CCNY and four years of university education at Columbia, he said, but had been made scarcely aware during his college days of the existence of the world-wide labor and socialist movements, and of proposals to eliminate poverty and social injustices from our midst. It was only when by accident, he met Leonard Abbott, then an editor of *Current Literature,* and receiving a copy of a socialist magazine from him, that he came to the realization of the existence and significance of these movements and of the cooperative philosophy of life.
>
> "Why," he had asked himself, "was nothing like this taught me by my college professors?"
>
> "I decided that, since the professors would not educate the students," he continued, "it was up to the students to educate the professors."

That very night Sinclair asked those present to join him in forming an organization that would bring the message of socialism to American colleges, and everyone in the room agreed. And thus was born the Intercollegiate Socialist Society.

That began the history of what was to become, six decades later, the Students for a Democratic Society. Few people realized it in the sixties, when SDS seemed to have sprung full blown from the troubled brow of the decade, but in fact SDS was an integral part of a student movement dating back to the earliest years of the century and a direct descendant of the first successful student organization the country had ever known.

A measure of the importance of the new Intercollegiate Socialist Society was the stature of its sponsors, among them Clarence Darrow, prominent then as a legal champion of the criminal
underdog; Jack London, whom audiences even then tended to
admire for his immensely popular adventure books rather than his
thoroughgoing socialism; William English Walling, a wealthy patron of the left, author of numerous books and tracts on social
issues, and later a founder of the NAACP; Thomas W. Higginson,
who had made a considerable reputation many years before as an
abolitionist; James Graham Phelps Stokes, a Socialist Party activist and also a scion of one of the wealthiest families in America;
and of course Sinclair himself, already well known for his journalism and then at work on *The Jungle,* the book that was to make
him the most famous muckraker of the day.* Its first officers were
London, president, Sinclair and Stokes, vice presidents, and on its
executive board sat Harry Laidler, who was to continue his career
with ISS and its successors right down to the sixties.

Now all of these men were quite dedicated social reformers,
but they were from the upper end of the social and financial scale
and in their schemes to redress national ills were rather more
visionary than revolutionary; in common with much of the American left of the time, they saw the role of good socialists to be one
of education. What they envisioned for the ISS, therefore, was
quite modest: a loosely knit organization of campus "study clubs"
which would promote, as they said in their prospectus, "an intelligent interest in socialism among college men and women, graduate and undergraduate." Or, as London was to put it later that fall:
"We do not desire merely to make converts. . . . If collegians
cannot fight for us, we want them to fight against us—of course,
sincerely fight against us. . . . Raise your voices one way or the
other; be alive. That is the idea upon which we are working." And
a modest enough up-from-apathy idea it is, too.

It is of some importance that the founders of the ISS saw it
as a web of "study clubs" on different campuses, with a New York

---

*Sixty-three years later some of Sinclair's successors were rather confused about
his career: an SDSer writing in *New Left Notes* (October 25, 1968) maintained
that "early in this century Upton Sinclair resigned as president of Columbia
University because he considered the university system to be full of shit."

office in the center, for this organizational design remained with its successors into the sixties. It is also of some importance that they saw the target of this organization as being the universities, for never before had it been thought possible to spread a political message to people still in universities and draw a number of separate campuses together into a single political organization. That it seems so inevitable now only suggests a certain genius: for at universities are not only a corps of young, idealistic, and leisured people, but also dissatisfactions that mirror those of the society at large. Awaken these young people to the injustice and insensitivity of their universities, and you shortly have an army aware of the injustice and insensitivity of the society beyond, and probably prepared to act on them.

ISS president Jack London made this connection during the organization's first speaker's tour in the fall of 1905. First, the university:

> I went to the university. I found the university, in the main, practically wholly so, clean and noble, but I did not find the university alive. I found that the American university had this ideal, as phrased by a professor in Chicago University, namely: "the passionless pursuit of passionless intelligence"—clean and noble, I grant you, but not *alive* enough.

Then, the society:

> And the reflection of this university ideal I find [in] the conservatism and unconcern of the American people toward those who are suffering, who are in want. And so I became interested in an attempt to arouse in the minds of the young men of our universities an interest in the study of socialism.*

One reason that the connection was established at the start is that those who were guiding the organization were themselves of both worlds. Of all the early leaders of the ISS only one, Harry

---

*It is no accident that *The Port Huron Statement,* fifty-seven years after London, should make the same connections: "Look beyond the campus, to America itself. That student life is more intellectual, and perhaps more comfortable, does not obscure the fact that the fundamental qualities of life on the campus reflect the habits of society at large ... the desperation of people threatened by forces about which they know little and of which they can say less; the cheerful emptiness of people giving up all hope of changing things."

Laidler, was an undergraduate, and he seems to have been added more or less at the last minute. London was twenty-nine, Sinclair twenty-seven, Stokes thirty-three, Walling twenty-eight, and Darrow, the elder statesman, forty-eight, and none of them at the time had seen the inside of an ivy wall for half a decade. They were young enough to remember their own pallid university experiences, but it was natural for them to be equally aware of wider problems of the society in which they were now living. Whether the value of this perception is balanced by the disadvantages of having a leadership somewhat remote from the felt problems of those still in school is a real question and will continue to plague the organization into the future—but at the beginning, at least, it was no handicap. The ISS was the first student-oriented group to have a breadth beyond a single campus and a depth beyond a single issue, and it came upon the campuses in what was indeed an auspicious period. Its membership at the start was not large— by 1907 perhaps seventy-five members in a dozen chapters, all in the East (out of a student population of some two hundred thousand)—but within a decade it had grown to perhaps a thousand members at sixty-odd chapters from coast to coast. But membership was not really a criterion of its impact: enrollment was never made very much of, and campus chapters concentrated instead on holding study groups to talk about socialism and asking London, Laidler, or some other luminary to the campus every so often to stir it up. A better indication is the quality of those who joined: people like Morris Hillquit, Harry A. Overstreet, Laurence Seelye, Norman Thomas, and Alexander Trachtenberg in New York, Roger Baldwin, Heywood Broun, Walter Lippmann, and John Reed at Harvard, Babette Deutsch and Freda Kirchwey at Barnard, Edna St. Vincent Millay at Vassar, Paul Douglas and Joyce Kilmer at Columbia, Bruce Bliven at Stanford, William E. Bohn at Michigan, Ordway Tead at Amherst, Karl Llewellyn at Yale. Still better, the results: as John Reed later said,

> The result of this movement upon the undergraduate world was potent. All over the place radicals sprang up. . . . The more serious college papers took a socialistic, or at least a progressive tinge. . . . It made me, and many others, realize that there was something going on in the dull outside world more thrilling than college activities.

But the ISS also had inherent weaknesses. For one thing, it confined itself to an educational role, trusting to the Socialist Party to take all the political action, and so in many places it degenerated rather drearily into just another campus seminar for people who wanted to hear their own voices. For another, it had no criteria for membership—nonsocialists in fact were as welcome as socialists, the only test apparently a vague allegiance to "human right and human gain"—and in the long run suffered that familiar organizational problem of a group whose arms are so wide open that entrance and egress are equally easy.

And so when the initial decade of receptivity to socialism (1905-1915) withered in the heat of the first World War, the ISS was not strong enough to last. National sentiment was harsh upon the socialists, originally because the American Socialist Party opposed the war (the only Socialist party in the West to do so) and later because the Russian Revolution inclined much of the nation to regard anyone to the left of Hoover as a flaming Bolshevik. On campuses, many students fell prey to that mindless chauvinism that seems an inevitable concomitant of war and participation in ISS meetings dwindled to a small hard core, while a number of prowar university administrations made things difficult for the ISS chapters. By 1920, little remained of the ISS beyond an office in New York and a few unshakable adherents.

After the war, the ISS began to pick up again, but now with a different face. In the early twenties, with the fears generated by the Russian Revolution and a mood of mini-McCarthyism gripping the country, repression both organized and spontaneous came down upon the Left, and a shift away from that political position seemed in order. (The Socialist Party itself made things easier by falling apart, first losing its left wing to the new Communist Party in 1919, and then losing its head to factionalism in 1925.) So in 1921 the ISS changed its name to the League for Industrial Democracy—because, as a later LID pamphlet was to maintain, "students wanted a more inclusive name than 'socialist,' because they believed there were several alternative approaches to a cooperative commonwealth," and because they wanted a name "that would not necessitate innumerable explanations to students and administrators of the non-connection of their society with the

Socialist party." This was only the first of the organization's long series of moves away from the left and toward the position, later solidified into a dogma, of support for the reformist end of the capitalist spectrum. The new LID made no mention of socialism, and embraced "all believers in education for strengthening democratic principles and practices in every aspect of our common life."

In its new guise the LID managed to hold on, if never exactly to flourish. Robert Morse Lovett, Florence Kelley, John Dewey, and Roger Starr all served as presidents for brief times, Stuart Chase (in this period an influential reformist author) and Reinhold Niebuhr served as treasurers, and the executive directors and essential powers were Harry Laidler and Norman Thomas. Though most of the LID membership itself was now well beyond college age and the concerns of the group shifted during the twenties from campus to workshop, an Intercollegiate Council of the LID was formed to continue work among students. Campus members during these years included Sidney Hook, Darlington Hoopes, Max Lerner, Will Maslow, Talcott Parsons, Walter Reuther (president of the Wayne University chapter and a lifelong patron of the LID), Clarence Senior, William Shirer (at Coe College in Iowa), Irving Stone, and Frank Trager.*

But the twenties were not propitious years for student action. A National Student Federation of America was formed in 1926 but soon faded, and a National Student Forum made only a brief appearance. The LID clung on with a New York headquarters (financed by well-to-do men of the left, but now increasingly finding labor support) and some twenty-odd campus chapters (it claimed twenty-three in 1927), but the membership was small,

---

*The latter-day conservatism of these figures is at once noticeable, and it is from such slender reeds that theories about radical-in-your-twenties-conservative-in-your-fifties are built; it should be noted, however, that there was very little radical about the LID during these years, and all that happened with most of these men was that their conservatism simply became more pronounced as the years went on. An interesting contrast can be made with, for example, people prominent in the National Student League, which was the left/Communist group of 1931–35 —people like Harry Magdoff, Muriel Rukeyser, Felix Morrow, James Rorty, and Sherwood Anderson—whose radicalism lasted despite their years (though it should be noted that some NSL members, like Theodore Draper and Nathaniel Weyl, became good conservatives).

interest fluctuated greatly from year to year and campus to campus, and no coherent national policies or campaigns were ever
successfully formulated. (An LID-led Student Committee to Aid
Sacco and Vanzetti was established in 1927, but never gained a
following, the fate of the shoemaker and the fishpeddler apparently proving beneath the interest of the college population of the
Great Boom.) In the mid-twenties an antiwar pacifism had a
certain collegiate vogue, and at the City College of New York a
full-scale anti-ROTC movement grew, eventually leading the New
York *World* to talk about a "student revolt." But far from producing anything like the antiwar movement of the sixties, this early
activity was confined largely to New York City schools and even
there in large measure to the sons and daughters of (often leftist)
European immigrants.

It was not until the stock-market crash and the following
depression that the LID began to evolve into a vital student organization. The LID was in a particularly advantageous position to
gain campus support in those years when the concept of "the
working class" began to be revived among students, both because
of its ties to organized labor and because of its earlier work in the
late twenties in trying to build student support for unionism.
Then, too, perceiving through the rubble of the thirties that something did seem to be amiss with the capitalist system after all, the
LID began to discard its reformism and sound like it was serious
about social change; the student program of 1934 "expresses the
urgency of a new social order that will root out unemployment,
war, insecurity and injustice," which it sees as coming about
through "those students who desire social change of a revolutionary character [throwing] in their lot with the working class." On
individual campuses it moved out from the seminar room to the
picket lines, for the first time infusing its educational role with the
lifeblood of a little action. In 1931 it organized a group to work
among West Virginia coal miners and picketed mineowners'
homes in Philadelphia, Chicago, Boston, and New York. In 1932
the Columbia LID helped that campus hold the nation's first
student strike, in support of a student-newspaper editor deposed
by the administration, and the CCNY chapter renewed the fight
against ROTC; that year also LID organized a United Youth

Conference Against War, and led a march on Washington by the Association of Unemployed College Alumni.

Along about this time a fissure in the LID began to appear. The elders were middle-aged now—Laidler, still the guiding light, was forty-six in 1930—and more static, more New Dealish, more slice-of-the-pie-ish, while the collegians were more active, more radical, more uncompromising, and more Marxist. In the spring of 1931 several of the New York members, regarding the LID as hopelessly old fashioned and irredeemably moderate, called for "revolutionary student action" and broke away from the parent group to form a New York Student League. A year later this grew to become the National Student League, which in the next few years asserted itself as the most militant group on the student left. The NSL's view of the LID it left behind was put well that fall by its executive secretary, Donald Henderson, who had been on the LID Board of Directors:

> Its theory of education is the typical academic one of learning through discussion alone rather than through struggle and action. . . . Its conferences are usually held under circumstances which make it impossible for any but the higher income group students to attend even if they cared to; its dinners are graced with dress suits and evening gowns; and its policies are as shifting and opportunistic as are required by a disintegrating middle class.

Initially the LID response was to dismiss the NSL and all its works as Communist, the start of a tradition of redbaiting that was to become quite hoary by the mid-sixties. But then, hoping to fight fire with fire, the LID decided to establish its own rival campus division, turning one of its defunct projects, formed in 1928 as the Intercollegiate Student Council, into the autonomous Student League for Industrial Democracy.*

SLID turned out to be rather more of a problem child than its parents had anticipated. It did promote the virtues of socialism in contrast to the NSL's claims for Communism, but it soon came to believe that there was room enough on college campuses for both philosophies and both groups: "The Socialist and Commu-

---

*It was known then usually as "the Student L-I-D," the unfortunate acronym "SLID" not coming in until the fifties, but for consistency's sake we'll refer to it as SLID.

nist movement[s]," it argued in 1934, "must have groups on the campus whose function it is to serve their respective programs there. At the moment, the Student L.I.D. and the N.S.L. represent those tendencies. . . ." And it went on to urge fraternity for the moment—"on student matters joint action is clearly essential and possible"—and raise the possibility of a merger eventually—"It may be that an amalgamation of all radical groups on the campus may result." That year it did make a temporary alliance with the NSL, over the objections of the LID itself, to sponsor a Student Anti-War Week during which an estimated 25,000 students struck classes for an hour, the first widespread expression of student activism the country had ever seen.* The following April the two groups joined again in leading a student strike, drawing between 150,000 and 185,000 (by their own estimates) out of classes to protest inadequate domestic policies and the threat of war abroad; Joseph Lash, a SLID leader, said the "feeling of solidarity" thus created "marked the crystallization of the student movement in America."†

On its own, SLID soon showed that its socialism meant more than simple pot shots at the system. In 1934 it began a series of summer schools "to train Students for the Radical Movement" with a "thorough grounding in the theory and principles of Marxism" and in order to "solidify the alliance between students and workers by the interchange of experience and knowledge." Its "Declaration of Principles" that same year enunciated a class-war line ("In America . . . the class struggle goes on constantly"), a rudimentary anticapitalist analysis ("We regard war as an aspect of capitalist expansion and rivalry. . . . To abolish it, imperialist

---

*The strike call in many ways is prophetic of the 1970 strike sentiments: "We choose a strike for several reasons: Because it is the most effective and dramatic form of protest against the war preparations now in progress; because it is in a sense a 'fire drill' for the only form of mass action which promises to be effective against a summons to war in the future; because polls and convocations and conferences are played out, and can be dismissed as 'surface scratching' when the strike cannot; because of the publicity which a strike brings, publicity which will not only go far to impress the American people with the seriousness of our purpose, but which will reach foreign shores, there strengthening the hand of the anti-war movement." (SLID pamphlet, undated, c. 1933.)

†From this there grew, in the fall of 1935, an organization with the prophetic title of National Committee for the Student Mobilization. *Plus ça change . . .*

ambitions must be rooted out"), and a militant strategy for change ("Students who desire social change of a revolutionary character must throw in their lot with the working class [which] at times ... means defiance of power and authority"). SLID even published a bulletin called *Revolt* for a time, but that one was too much for the LID elders and after a few issues its title was transmuted to *Student Outlook*. By 1935 SLID was able to claim chapters on 125 campuses, heavily based in the East but including also—no mean feat—groups at Utah, Colorado, and San Diego.

It was that same year that the NSL avidly wooed SLID to join it in a united front of student leftists, and SLID finally succumbed. Though there was much anguish within SLID ranks, right-wing pacifists arguing with revolutionary socialists, proto-Trotskyists battling with liberals, the dominant opinion eventually held that the threat of war abroad and "fascism" at home was so great that a united student movement was essential, even if it meant that SLIDers had to give up their most valuable attributes, an annual budget from the LID and the prestige of affiliation with a respected adult group. At Christmas week of 1935, against the seasoned advice of practically all those in the LID, SLID agreed to cut its ties and join with the NSL in a new student organization to be known as the American Student Union.

The American Student Union was the most active student movement to date, and, with a claimed membership of 20,000 (12,000 paid, it said) in 1939, the most widespread. But it had a curious life. For its first two years it was quite militant. It enthusiastically supported the pledge of the Oxford Student Union not "to fight for King and country in any war" and turned that into its own battle cry, "We refuse to support any war which the United States government may undertake." It led demonstrations and marches at a number of universites, and in 1936 led what would now be called a "mill-in" at City College which was successful in reinstating a fired teacher. Its student slates won election to student governments at several Eastern colleges.*

*The spectrum of ASU membership went from Julius Rosenberg to Hal Draper to James Wechsler to Daniel Bell, and included one Jerry Voorhis, who had he been more adept at conventional mainstream politics might have spared us the Presidential fate we now endure.

But the ASU's militance had no staying power. Although SLID and the NSL were supposedly equal partners, and though SLID leader Joseph Lash was Executive Secretary of the ASU, the organization moved increasingly closer to the Communist Party line and thus shared its same deflated fate. The ASU, like the Communist Party (and for that matter the LID), had no programmatic power and never was able to enlist its 20,000 students into anything resembling overt political action. Visions of mass strikes or worker-student coalitions remained just that; talk of the "power of the working class" and "smashing the ruling class" never got beyond words. Just as the Communist Party misunderstood American realities, so did the ASU, and after a few years of hard-line talking both began to flounder around in a miasma of bewilderment.

Nor did their attachment to Marxism prove to be of any help. In a world which seemed on the verge of collapse, with economic disintegration and political frenzy at home and chaos and war in Europe, it was natural for the student activists to turn to a doctrine that seemed both to explain that collapse and to separate them from the system that had created it; that doctrine, as it was to be in a later period of chaos, was Marxism. Marxism was the common coin of both SLIDers and NSLers, as it was of many of their elders, and, however imperfectly understood, it was spent in enormous quantities in one long meeting after another. Somehow, though, Marxism failed to explain American events satisfactorily, and all the attempts at redoing Marx to provide this explanation produced division rather than agreement, sects rather than a united vanguard. Marxism succeeded in producing a historically learned, backward-looking, rigid set of intellectuals. What was happening here was American studentry's first runaway into somebody else's theory, somebody else's explanations, and it didn't work.

The ASU, in other words, was absorbed into the bankruptcy of the Communist Party, a party whose underpinnings were so insecure that Roosevelt's blunt-edge liberalism could cut them right out from under. Having no truly revolutionary program to put forth, having not even a fundamental distaste for America and its ways, the ASU (like the Communist Party) found itself falling more and more in the orbit of the New Deal. By 1937 the ASU had become a pale front of a pale Communist Party, and its most vociferously held ideas differed little from FDR's: in fact, Roosevelt himself wrote a letter of "hearty greetings" to the 1937 ASU convention. That convention dropped the Oxford Pledge in favor of support for the Communist Party's "collective security" stand, preparing for war in Europe. The next year the ASU dropped its anti-ROTC plank and supported much of the New Deal. The New Deal had clearly won the day in America, and the ASU, thoughts of "revolution" and "socialism in one country" far behind, welcomed the victory. Student power, insofar as it existed at all, was exhausted. The Hitler-Stalin pact in 1939 was its last gasp—as it was for most of the Communist Party itself—and in 1941, when no one was looking, the ASU declared itself for the war and passed out of existence.

The LID, however, endured. Its voice was a thin reed indeed, barely distinguishable in the late thirties and into the war years from those of countless other groups, and with each passing year more muted and more moderate. But it endured. The organization was kept alive largely through the efforts of a few onetime LIDers now in the New York clothing unions—especially the International Ladies' Garment Workers Union—many of whom were veterans of battles with Communists and others within their unions in the twenties and thirties. For these men the LID was seen as a helpful propaganda adjunct for the vigorously anti-Communist wing of the labor movement, a valuable political alternative between the Socialist Party and the Democrats, and a useful kind of old-age home for a number of dedicated social democrats (such as Harry Laidler) who spent their time as scholars *manqués* promoting social democracy in general and unionism in particular. Besides, it was a tax-exempt institution where a few thousand dollars could easily be sheltered, and it cost no more than $35,000 a year to keep it going anyway.

These years were instrumental in slowly squeezing the juice out of the LID's socialism until only a mealy kind of patriotic pulp remained, but to those in the LID the simple fact of its continued existence and continued identification with the triumphant United States government seemed only to confirm them in their course. And when they looked around after the war they congratulated themselves on having been against the SLID-NSL merger all along and decided that it was time for the LID, as Laidler told the fortieth anniversary dinner in 1945, "to develop again its college work with renewed vigor"—by which they really meant a new student division which would now be quieter, more apolitical, more "educational," and this time, by God, no joining up with the Communists.

The initial budget of the revivified SLID suggests the direction of the new group. Of the $6000 total, $2500 came from the People's Education Camp Society, otherwise known as Camp Tamiment, a Pocono vacation spot that attracted enough Manhattan secretaries during the summer to keep itself afloat during the rest of the year as a minor prolabor foundation. Another $1750 came from unions: $100 from locals of the International Ladies' Garment Workers Union, $500 from ILG headquarters, and $250 from the Dressmakers, one of whose top officers, Nathaniel Minkoff, was also an LID leader. The remaining $1750 of the budget came from individuals. This was not an enormous budget, and expenditures came to $5785, by what must have been a neat bit of bookkeeping, so there wasn't a lot left over. But in 1946 an anonymous $5000 legacy for student work dropped from the blue —possibly from the red-white-and-blue—and so LID was able to launch a new SLID that fall with what was, for them, a vengeance.

The first thing the LID did was to establish the position of "Student Secretary" (at different times called Field Secretary and National Secretary), who was to oversee SLID activities and travel to campuses to build up SLID support, but who would not himself be a student and who would be paid by and responsible to the LID rather than to the student group. Jesse Cavileer, then six years out of Syracuse and with a background in college religious organizations, was hired full time that fall as the first person in this post, beginning a succession that was to include, most notably, CORE founder (and later Nixon aide) James Farmer in the early fifties and, for a time, Gabriel Kolko, a SLID activist later to become one of the most important revisionist historians of the sixties.*

*Other Student Secretaries included Grace Mendelsohn, Richard Poethig, Dorothy Psathas, Irving G. Phillips, and James Youngdahl in the forties, and Mildred Perlman, Paula Goldberg, Susan Gyarmati, Robert Perlsweig, Evelyn Rich, Henry Christman, and Carol Weisbrod in the fifties.

The next thing was for SLID to trim its ideology as close to the bone as possible. Its adopted program proclaimed that "the SLID seeks to promote studies of student housing, employment opportunities, responsible and honest participation in student government, the development of student cooperatives, and the extension of student rights to participate in making college policy," and its activities were to consist solely of "bringing to the college campuses able and well-known representatives of government, labor, cooperatives and other social movements, to lecture on their respective subjects." Even so, there were few takers. Columbia and CCNY became the first two chapters, in November 1946, but there is no indication that either had more than a handful of members. By Christmastime, when SLID held its first postwar conference, there were said to be chapters at seven other schools.

The LID proceeded cautiously with SLID this time around, protecting it from the dangers of backsliding with all the liberal anti-Communism at its command. Laidler, still LID Executive Secretary, was inordinately proud of the membership clause he established for SLID:

> That membership in the LID be confined to those who believe in education for democracy in industry, in politics and in our cultural life; who believe in the democratic way of life as a means and as a social goal.
>
> By virtue of the democratic aims of the League, advocates of dictatorship and totalitarianism and of any political system that fails to provide for freedom of speech, of press, of religion, of assembly, and of political, economic and cultural organization; or of any system that would deny civil rights to any person because of race, color, creed or national origin, are not eligible for membership. Nor are those eligible whose political policies are wholly or largely determined by the policies laid down by the leadership of a foreign government.

This membership clause was formally adopted by the 1947 SLID convention, refined by the 1948 convention to add a provision against "all parties and/or factions based on Bolshevik principles" (the idea was to admit well-behaving Trotskyists), and, amazingly, remained a basic tenet of the organization's bylaws right up to 1962. The nervousness which permeates it seems rather quaint from this vantage point, but as in many things, SLID was to be slightly ahead of its time, and the time that was coming was McCarthy's.

SLID activities of the forties were negligible. Conventions were held in 1947 and 1948 at which national officers were elected,* and grand resolutions opposing or approving this or that national policy were passed, to no apparent purpose. Conferences were held on prejudice (in Detroit, in December 1947) and the economy (in Cleveland, in April 1948) with a parade of liberal-labor speakers, but the audiences were small and the results unnoticeable. In 1947 SLIDers attended the founding conference of the National Student Association—a group that was later to prove important for SDS—where, for a change, they were considered to be on the liberal wing, but they did not seem to gain much in the way of followers. Membership, in fact, was never more than a few hundred at most, despite more than 150 visits by SLID student organizers at college campuses from 1946 to 1948, and despite the fact that until the end of 1948 nonstudents were as welcome as students. SLID claimed four hundred members in 1947 and seven hundred in 1948, but most of that by all accounts was only on paper.† Chapters grew and collapsed with jerry-built rapidity, and never extended very widely despite a special provision that they could be as autonomous as they chose, even to the point of taking action contrary to official SLID policy. Things grew so bad, in fact, that the 1948 convention considered disbanding altogether, referring to the LID itself the question of whether it really was a necessary association since other student groupings did exist. The LID Board, pondering the issue, assured them that they must be important, and after some consideration determined that it was because, while other organizations were concerned with immediate actions, SLID had its sights set on long-range issues and broad policies.

The assurance, however, convinced few. In 1949 the new SLID reached its nadir: it had five breathing chapters at most,

---

*John Roche, later Lyndon Johnson's Apologist-in-Residence at the White House, was Vice-Chairman in 1947–48.

†André Schiffrin, a SLID leader of the fifties, has noted that the standard practice was that "figures were inflated by leaving people on membership lists, allowing older, part-time students to stay on 'at large,' etc." (*Radical America*, May-June 1968.)

only one of which was outside New York City, it had no permanent Student Secretary, and there was not enough interest among
the membership even to hold a convention.

The question is inevitable: Why *did* the LID want to keep its
student branch alive, at a cost of maybe $5000 to $6000 a year and
with no visible returns? The answer is nowhere to be found in
official LID records, but in part it has to do with a feeling of the
LID elders that if new blood was to come from anywhere—that
is to say, if the shaky parent organization was to survive at all—
it would have to come from the college campuses. Moreover,
having a college-oriented division fit perfectly into the LID's image of itself as an educational group and allowed it to propagandize to hungry audiences in a way that would have been virtually
impossible with adults. Finally, campus politics was an area
which, surprisingly, was virtually untouched by other organizations—though there were religious groups (YMCA, YWCA,
United Christian Movement) and a few political ones (Students
for Democratic Action, the Student Federalists, the Young People's Socialist League), no single national organization dominated,
and the LID therefore felt it could move into this area with
relative ease.

The LID therefore worked to keep SLID alive, even through
the particularly arid period of the fifties. Gabriel Gersch, SLID
chairman in 1951, said at the time: "The average student nowadays
is not only hostile to any form of socialism, but is indifferent to
most political questions. . . . The hysteria that is spreading in
America has reached the college campus." For survival, therefore,
what more natural than to drop the idea of socialism on the one
hand, and to join the hysteria, albeit decorously, on the other.
That is the history of SLID in the fifties.

The 1951 convention began things by adopting a preamble to
its constitution which is a triumph of the innocuous:

> The Student League for Industrial Democracy is a non-partisan
> educational organization which seeks to promote greater active
> participation on the part of American students in the resolution of
> present-day problems. It is hoped that such participation will con-
> tribute to their awareness of the need for the establishment in the
> United States of a cooperative commonwealth in which the princi-

ple regulating production, distribution, and exchange will be the supplying of human needs, and under which human rights will be protected and extended.

The 1953 convention managed to go this one better by adopting a constitution, the constitution that was to be the basic organizational document right up to Port Huron, which never once mentions the word "socialism," much less anything "radical," "left," or "revolutionary." By 1955 SLID is calling itself "a national *liberal* campus group, educating for increased democracy in every aspect of our life." In 1958 it holds a conference to ask, "Where are we, as young *liberals,* going?" And even in 1959, when it begins a new publication aimed at the now post-McCarthy generation, it is careful to include as its editorial statement: "The Student League for Industrial Democracy has served as a meeting point for students of *liberal* inclinations since 1905."

What is happening here obviously is the immurement of the radical tradition in America. Though many of the SLID members in these years were children of onetime socialists and former LIDers—else how would they have heard of this minute organization, much less think of joining it?—they had lived to see their parents' earlier ideology defamed and discredited, without much protest and often with *mea culpa* assistance. Socialism was for many of them something both outworn and out of step, communism was unquestionably a domestic and foreign danger, indeed radicalism of any kind was hopelessly out of date. If there was any reason to question that, they had only to look at the shamefaced radicals of the thirties for whom the most heroic act of the fifties was considered to be taking the Fifth Amendment before Congressional committees: had there been anything noble in the tradition of the past, surely they would have heard. André Schiffrin, a SLID leader of the fifties, reports the attitude of those days:

> It seemed impossible to make common cause with the left that had been active in the thirties and had fallen into the rationalizations and evasions of the forties and fifties. . . . It was difficult then, it still is difficult now for me to think of anyone aged, let us say, 40 to 55, who represents something on the American Left one would respect.

The result was that "only a few of us in SLID thought of ourselves as socialists of any kind. Most of our members were liberals."

One measure of the remove from socialism is the content of the series of summer institutes which SLID sponsored from 1953 to 1959 at Camp Three Arrows, near Peekskill, New York, the summer home of a number of ex-socialists with ties to the LID. The original meeting was designed, so its flyer said, "to stimulate thinking on the issues of the day, develop leadership, and provide an opportunity for us to meet fellow SLID-ers, exchange ideas, and have fun"—quite a change for the organization that in the thirties ran *its* summer camps "to train students for the radical movement," and to do it with Marxism, besides. The first year there were meetings on "the East-West conflict" and civil liberties, a few years later they were debating "How Should America React to the New Soviet Line?" and "Public Relations and Public Opinion," in 1957 the theme was "Bureaucracy, Corruption and Democracy," the next year "Work and Its Discontents." Hardly the stuff of which student activism is made.

As SLID's commitment to liberalism increased, so did its anti-Communism. In addition to the exclusionism of the constitution itself, SLID continued to purify its ranks and its line. The 1950 convention affirmed that the constitution should continue to exclude "Bolsheviks," but SLIDers that year were also forbidden to join a socialist coalition called the Student Federation Against War which included "Trotskyists" and "fellow travelers." The next year a bitter battle took place over the politics of a SLID chapter at CCNY led by Bogdan Denitch, a young Trotskyist whom the LID Board regarded, it said, as "a clear and present danger"; it urged the SLID convention to expel him, a move which the student group rejected, for reasons of obstreperousness rather than politics, but the pressure continued until Denitch took his whole chapter out the next year.*

Four years later the SLID convention showed faint signs of uppiness—it came out for the "eventual" abolition of the Attorney General's list of subversive organizations and after long debate rejected the idea then popular among LID elders that Com-

---

*It was a process so sordid that one SLID executive committee member resigned, accusing the LID of "utter disregard for democratic process when it no longer suited their purpose" and arguing that the student group had to be given "freedom from 'parent' group control"—attitudes that were to be echoed after the Port Huron Convention.

munist Party membership was *ipso facto* proof of a teacher's professional incompetence—but it still passed a resolution forbidding any SLID member anywhere from "cooperation, nationally, locally or internationally . . . with any whose actions or programs would bar them from admission in SLID," a roundabout way of saying Communists. In a SLID publication of 1955 SLID leader André Schiffrin attacked Communists as "unscrupulous machiavellians," and three years later a SLID "International Bulletin" echoed: "LID members are very likely to be agreed on the following crucial governing position: . . . that specifically Communist doctrine is anti-humanistic, Communist techniques are vicious, and Communist societies are unjust, and Communism cannot be countenanced by morally sensitive people." And this vehemence two years after poor Joe McCarthy had been censured and forgotten.

SLID, in short, began to play what Michael Harrington, then head of the Young Socialist League, calls "a pro-American, Cold War, State Department kind of role." It was decidedly middle-of-the-road, even conservative. Looking back, Schiffrin in 1968 tried to rescue for SLID a role as "representing the far left in the universities" and "reasserting the existence of dissent," but neither is accurate. SLID was never as left as such "national" groups as the Young Socialist League (or its successor, the Young People's Socialist League), as various permutations of the Communist Youth League, nor, later on, as any of the local groups that began to surface in California, Wisconsin, and elsewhere in New York. Nor, if it was dissenting, did anyone become aware of this—what little campus dissent there was then and what grew in the late fifties was independent of SLID.

For the fact is that even after adopting its Eisenhoweresque positions of liberalism and anti-Communism, SLID was hard-pressed to get many followers. Membership crises were recurrent, and throughout the fifties the number of paid-up members probably never got beyond a hundred—with perhaps another hundred occasional hangers-on—at no more than a dozen campuses altogether. The *New Republic* in 1951 estimated a membership of 150 in six colleges (though the SLID student secretary that year claimed 600 in twenty). Two years later a young fieldworker from

the Columbia School of Social Work named Bernard Cornfeld—
the same man who was in later years to find a somewhat more
profitable career as an international financier—spent a summer
investigating SLID for an M.S. thesis and noted that though the
SLID lists showed five hundred members, most were neither paid-
up nor active. The atmosphere, he concluded,

> ... is one of discouragement.... The present function of the Student
> League for Industrial Democracy is not . . . visibly productive.
> . . . While it is not a topic of general discussion, there is a feeling
> among the staff as well as the membership of some considerable
> misgivings about Student League for Industrial Democracy's pre-
> sent function.

The following year, according to Schiffrin, the "total active membership was in the dozens," and "the Yale chapter that we started
that year was the first real SLID campus group at the time," the
national organization being "a mere ephemeral business in many
ways." In 1958 a grand total of thirteen students showed up for
the annual convention.

Aryeh Neier, SLID president in 1957–58 and later an LID
executive (before going on to become executive director of the
American Civil Liberties Union), tried then to account for the
obvious collapse of SLID: "The fears engendered by the
McCarthy headline hunting may not have resulted in mass hysteria on the college campus but they did result in a degree of
overcautiousness on the part of the college student who decided
to play it safe and never sign or join anything." The LID, acknowledging that "the liberal tradition, in its old terms, has little to offer
to the new generation," appointed study commissions to try to
explain it all. But the simple fact was that SLID didn't *do* anything. A meeting there, a speaker here—even, once, after the
Russian invasion of Hungary in 1956, a call for national action that
seemed to be answered because its anti-Communism coincidentally matched the campus temperament of that moment. But nothing sustained, nothing with a vision, nothing to capture the
idealistic fervor that lies within every student generation.

By the end of the fifties SLID seemed to be on its last legs:
funds were drying up, interest was waning, membership was de-
clining, and the purposes and directions were blurred and uncer-

tain. The LID, its mentor, was similarly shriveled: Harry Laidler, the last link to the early days, retired in 1957, and debts were now running at about $6000 a year, on a budget of less than $40,000. Somber days indeed seemed in the offing.

Little could anyone have imagined what the sixties were to hold.

NOTES

General Note

The primary source for most of the material relating specifically to SDS—letters, internal memos, minutes of national meetings, NO files, "worklist" mailings, bulletins, and the like—is the SDS archives in the Wisconsin State Historical Society, Madison, Wisconsin; all references to "archives" indicate this source, and any material not otherwise specified as to source can be presumed to be found here. I cannot be more precise than "archives," however, for the material lies ajumble in more than seventy-five boxes and there is as yet no formal compilation of the contents; but I do have copies in my possession of most of the important documents from the archives and would be happy to share them with legitimate researchers. Some additional material, especially relating to the League for Industrial Democracy and the early years of SDS, is also available in the files of the Tamiment Institute Library of New York University in New York City.

Important sources for much of SDS's history are the *SDS Bulletins*, published from the fall of 1962 to the fall of 1965, copies of which can be found in some of the major university libraries as well as the archives; and the SDS newspaper, *New Left Notes* (NLN), files of which also exist in some of these libraries and in the Tamiment Library.

The following is a list of books (referred to in the notes by the authors' last names, with page citations) which contain considerable material on SDS:

Adelson, Alan, *SDS: A Profile*, Scribner's, 1971.
Calvert, Greg, and Nieman, Carol, *A Disrupted History: The New Left and the New Capitalism*, Random House, 1971.
Cohen, Mitchell, and Hale, Dennis, editors, *The New Student Left*, Beacon, 1966 and 1967 (revised).
Ferber, Michael, and Lynd, Staughton, *The Resistance*, Beacon, 1971.
Foster, Julian, and Long, Durward, editors, *Protest! Student Activism in America*, Morrow, 1970.
Gitlin, Todd, and Hollander, Nanci, *Uptown: Poor Whites in Chicago*, Harper and Row, 1970.
Goodman, Mitchell, *The Movement Toward a New America*, Pilgrim Press/Knopf, 1970.
Jacobs, Harold, *Weatherman*, Ramparts, 1970.
Jacobs, Paul, and Landau, Saul, *The New Radicals*, Random House, Vintage edition, 1966.
Keniston, Kenneth, *Young Radicals*, Harcourt, Brace and World, 1968.
Long, Priscilla, editor, *The New Left*, F. Porter Sargent, 1969.
Luce, Phillip A., *The New Left*, David McKay, 1966.
Newfield, Jack, *A Prophetic Minority*, New American Library, Signet edition, 1966.
Potter, Paul, *A Name for Ourselves*, Little, Brown, 1971.

Powers, Thomas, *Diana: The Making of a Terrorist,* Houghton Mifflin, 1971.
Rader, Dotson, *I Ain't Marchin' Anymore,* Paperback Library, 1969.
Thayer, George, *The Farther Shores of Politics,* Simon and Schuster, 1967.
Teodori, Massimo, editor, *The New Left: A Documentary History,* Bobbs-Merrill, 1969.
Wallerstein, Immanuel, and Starr, Paul, editors, *The University Crisis Reader,* two volumes, Random House, Vintage edition, 1971.

In addition, two events in which SDS figured prominently received book-length coverage:
Columbia 1968—

Avorn, Jerry L., and members of the *Columbia Daily Spectator, Up Against the Ivy Wall,* Atheneum, 1969.
Grant, Joanne, *Confrontation on Campus,* Signet, 1969.
Kahn, Roger, *The Battle for Morningside Heights,* Morrow, 1970.
Crisis at Columbia, Report of the Fact-Finding Commission (Cox Commission) Appointed to Investigate the Disturbances at Columbia University in April and May 1968, Vintage, 1968.

Harvard 1969—

Eichel, Lawrence E., Jost, Kenneth W., Luskin, Robert, and Neustadt, Richard E., *The Harvard Strike,* Houghton Mifflin, 1970.
Kelman, Steven, *Push Comes to Shove,* Houghton Mifflin, 1970.

Finally, committees of the U.S. Congress have investigated SDS and released their findings—often very inaccurate, so a grain of salt is necessary—in a series of official publications:

"Riots, Civil and Criminal Disorders," hearings before the Permanent Subcommittee on Investigations of the Committee on Government Operations, U.S. Senate, Parts 18–25, 1969–70.
"Extent of Subversion in the 'New Left,' " hearings before the Subcommittee to Investigate the Administration of the Internal Security Act and Other Internal Security Laws of the Committee on the Judiciary, U.S. Senate, Parts 4–9, 1970.
"Report on the SDS Riots," by the Illinois Crime Investigating Commission (ICIC), April 1970, reprinted in the above series, Part 4 (page numbers in the notes refer to the Senate version, not the original).
"Investigation of Students for a Democratic Society," hearings before the Committee on Internal Security, U.S. House of Representatives, Parts 1-A through 7-B, 1969.
"Subversive Involvement in Disruption of 1968 Democratic Party National Convention," hearings before the Committee on Un-American Activities, U.S. House of Representatives, Parts 1–3, 1968.

"Interview" in the notes refers to interviews with the author, most of which are on tape. "AP" is Associated Press, "LNS" is Liberation News Service, "REP" is Radical Education Project.

1. A Decade of Defiance

Pages 3–5: SOURCES FOR ELEVENTH STREET EXPLOSION, New York newspapers, March 7–21; Bernardine Dohrn, "New Morning—Changing Weather," Weather Underground communiqué, December 6, 1970 (var. reprinted, including "Outlaws of Amerika," by Liberated Guardian Collective, July 1971, and *Liberation,* November 1970); "Riots, Civil and Criminal Disorders," Part 24, pp. 5378 ff.; Mel Gussow, *New York,* March 5, 1971; Sale, *Nation,* April 13 (reprinted in Jacobs, p. 470) and May 4, 1970 (letter); Jacobs, pp. 484 ff.; Powers, Chs. 1, 9. **Page 9:** ROTC figures, D. Park Teter, *Change,* September 1971; Ralph Blumenthal, N.Y. *Times,* May 28, 1971. **Page 10:** "never in history," Edward Kern, *Life,* October 17, 1969. Chinese on Movement, Edgar Snow, *Life,* July 30, 1971. **Page 11:** "radical, and indeed," Richard Flacks, *Journal of Social Issues,* No. 1, 1971. On the number of revolutionaries, see e.g., Daniel Yankelovich, Inc., *The Changing Values on Campus,* Simon and Schuster, Washington Square edition, 1972, pp. 63, 64, 68, 75, 107, 121, and notes for Chs. 21 and 25.

REORGANIZATION

2. Spring 1960

Page 15: SLID material, Tamiment. **Page 16:** "We sense a growing," editorial, *Venture* (SLID, New York), April 1959. **Page 18:** Footnote, most figures obtainable from current annual almanacs; also, for divorce rates, U.S. Census Report, N.Y. *Times,* February 2, 1971; for alcoholism, nine million figure from George Washington University survey, reported by Jane E. Brody, N.Y. *Times,* March 5, 1970, fifteen million figure from House Commerce Committee hearings, December 3, 1970; for drugs, Lawrence K. Altman, N.Y. *Times,* August 13, 1970; for crime, annual FBI reports, esp. 1970 report, N.Y. *Times,* August 13, 1970, and 1972 report, *Time,* October 23, 1972. **Page 19:** Evidence on national doubts includes various national polls (e.g., periodic Gallup polls, regularly reported in N.Y. *Post* and elsewhere; Roper Poll in N.Y. *Times,* July 9, 1971; American Institute for Political Communication survey, N.Y. *Times,* March 7, 1972; Trendex poll, *Wall Street Journal,* November 16, 1971; Albert H. Cantril and Charles W. Roll, Jr., *Hopes and Fears of the American People,* Universe Books [N.Y.], 1971); "Year-end Report," National Committee for an Effective Congress, December 26, 1967; *Newsweek,* special issue, July 6, 1970; Andrew Hacker, *The End of the American Era,* Atheneum, 1970; William L. O'Neill, *Coming Apart,* Quadrangle Books, 1971; George Reedy, *The Twilight of the Presidency,* World, 1970; reports by various presidential commissions headed by Milton Eisenhower (Violence), Nicholas Katzenbach (Crime), Otto Kerner (Race), and William Scranton (Campus Unrest), and by the National Goals Research Staff; and Richard Nixon, "State of the Union," January 22, 1970, and interview, *Washington Star-News,* November 9, 1972. For attitudes of youths, see esp. Daniel Yankelovich, Inc., *The Changing Values on Campus,* Washington Square Press, 1972. "at all levels," "Year-end Report," op. cit. **Page 20:** Feuer, *The Conflict of Generations,* Basic Books, 1969, p. 528. Population statistics, U.S. Bureau of the Census, *Statistical Abstracts,* 1968–1970, and "Characteristics of

American Youth, 1970" (1971). Estimates of youth market, from *Wall Street Journal*, April 27, 1971, and "Selling the American Youth Market," AMR International, Inc. (N.Y.), 1969. On youth consciousness, and youth as a class, see esp. John and Mary Rowntree, *International Socialist Journal*, February 1968 (excerpted in Teodori, pp. 418 ff.), *Socialist Revolution*, May–June 1970, and Richard Flacks, *Youth and Social Change*, Markham (Chicago), 1971. **Page 21:** Erik Erikson, his corpus, but esp. *Identity: Youth and Crisis*, Norton, 1968, and *Daedalus*, Winter 1970. University enrollments and other educational statistics, *Projections of Educational Statistics to 1977–78*, National Center of Educational Statistics, Office of Education, Washington, D.C. (1968 edition). **Page 22:** Figures on knowledge industry, Fritz Machlup, *The Production and Distribution of Knowledge in the United States*, Princeton University, 1962, and statistics in N.Y. *Times* Education Supplement, January 10, 1972; see also Peter F. Drucker, *Age of Discontinuity*, Harper, 1969. Kerr, *The Uses of the University*, Harvard University, 1964, and Harper Torchbook, 1966, pp. 87–88. **Page 23:** Figures on civil-rights action, Newfield, pp. 36 ff., and Howard Zinn, *The New Abolitionists*, Beacon paperback, 1965. Human Rights Conference, reported by Haber and Carol Weisbrod, *Venture*, Vol II, No. 1, September 1960. **Page 24:** "I wish," letter to Nathaniel Minkoff, April 15, 1961. "I know," letter to Trager, March 11, 1961. **Page 25:** "In its early," *Venture*, September 1960, reprinted in Cohen and Hale (1967), p. 34. **Page 27:** ibid.

3. *Fall 1960–Fall 1961*

Page 28: Hayden, quoted in Newfield, p. 96. **Page 29:** "national coordination," *Venture*, September 1960. Kaminsky, interview. **Page 31:** "backbiting," letter to Trager, March 11, 1961. Minkoff, letter to Haber, March 28, 1961. **Page 32:** "I am president" and "I would be free," letter to Trager, March 11, 1961 William Haber letters, March 24, 1961, and May 4, 1961. **Page 33:** Haber memo, May 9, 1961. **Page 35:** Booth comments, interview. Membership figures, internal memo, September 1961, Tamiment. **Page 36:** Hayden wrote and SDS mailed four letters from the South, expanded into "Revolution in Mississippi," SDS, December 1961, excerpted in Cohen and Hale (1967), pp. 68 ff. "In more danger," ibid. Garman, interview. "A Letter to the New (Young) Left," reprinted in Cohen and Hale (1967), pp. 2 ff. **Page 38:** "reflection on our total," Hayden letter, mimeograph, December 5, 1961. Most of the Ann Arbor conference papers were later published as pamphlets by SDS. **Page 39:** Booth, interview. Garman, interview. **Page 40:** Booth, interview. Hayden, mimeographed letter (Convention Document #3), undated (spring 1962).

4. *Spring 1962*

Page 42: Hayden, ibid. Hayden's initial thoughts are from mimeographed letters (Convention Documents #1–3), undated (spring 1962). **Page 43:** "We must have," "Student Social Action," SDS pamphlet, 1962, reprinted (with errors) in Cohen and Hale (1967), pp. 272 ff. **Page 44:** "not much letter-writing," anonymous minutes of SDS-LID meeting, July 6, 1962. For Chapel Hill meeting, mimeographed minutes (Burlage's copy), and Harlon Joye, *Common Sense* (published by FDR Four Free-doms Club, New York), spring 1962. **Page 46:** Membership figures and "varying degrees," minutes of Chapel Hill meeting. "I've lost all," letter to Burlage, April 18, 1962. "SDS screws up," letter to Burlage, May 16, 1962. LID finances, Harry Laidler papers, Tamiment. **Page 47:** Thomas, quoted by Harrington, interview. Burlage, letter to Haber and Hayden, May 26, 1962. "SDS figures," mimeographed "Appeal Statement" from SDS to LID, July 12, 1962. **Pages 49–56:** *The Port Huron Statement* was first mimeographed and later printed as a pamphlet by SDS, available in most major libraries; small portions have been reprinted in Cohen and Hale (1967), pp. 292 ff., Jacobs and Landau, pp. 150 ff., and Teodori, pp. 163 ff. **Page 54:** " 'Observer' status," SDS "Appeal Statement," op. cit. **Pages 55–57:** The 1962 constitution is reprinted in the appendix; earlier versions are in the archives. **Page 58:** Harrington, interview. "Hagan was" and "We were," Booth, interview. **Page 59:** Max, interview. Ross, quoted in Newfield, p. 96.

5. *Summer 1962*

Page 60: Feuer, *The Conflict of Generations,* Basic Books, 1969. **Page 61:** Rony, memo to LID Executive Board, July 12, 1962. Hearings summons, SDS "Appeal Statement," op. cit. **Pages 61–64:** Quotations from extensive handwritten notes taken by one of the SDSers, possibly Hayden. **Page 64:** "ultraleftists," etc. quoted in Newfield, p. 114. **Page 65:** Ross, in Newfield, p. 98. Max, interview. Booth, interview. Hayden, in Newfield, p. 108. **Pages 65–66:** apartment meeting, from Max and Booth, interviews. **Page 66:** SDS "Appeal Statement," op. cit. **Page 67:** Taylor, *Students Without Teachers,* McGraw-Hill, 1969, p. 40. **Page 68:** Hayden, on letter from Haber to Burlage, undated (July 1962). **Page 69:** Franklin, letter to Burlage, August 1962. **Page 70:** Taylor, *Students Without Teachers,* p. 41.

REFORM

6. *Fall 1962–Spring 1963*

Pages 73–74: Missile crisis reaction, from Max, interview; Monso-nis memo, October 30, 1962; and *SDS Bulletin,* No. 2, fall 1962. **Page 73:** Max, interview. **Page 74:** "That's one," letter to Burlage, October 1962. "We're all," memo, October 27, 1962. **Page 75:** Monsonis on class, *SDS Bulletin,* March-April 1963. "I'm gradually," memo to SDS NEC, Octo-ber 30, 1962. **Page 76:** McKelvey, interview. "A real martyr," Booth, interview. Haber, "Dear Friends" letter with Barbara Jacobs, December 15, 1962. **Page 77:** McKelvey, letter to Burlage, February 7, 1963. Monso-nis, memo to NEC, October 30, 1962. "The LID," memo, October 4, 1962. Financial figures, from worklist mailings, February, March, and April 1963. **Page 78:** Haber, Haber-Jacobs letter, op. cit. **Page 79:** Max, interview. Gerson, letter in worklist mailing, May 20, 1962. Membership figures, worklist mailing, January 17, 1963. **Page 80:** Davis, worklist mailing, March 25, 1963. Pruitt, worklist mailing, February 18, 1963. **Page 81:** Haber-Jacobs letter, op. cit. Jacobs letter, January 7, 1963 (misdated 1962). **Page 84:** Burlage, letter to Max, undated, fall 1962. **Pages 84–85:** Potter, speech reprinted as "The University and the Cold

War," SDS, 1963. **Page 86:** For Brandeis conference, Shelly Blum, *Common Sense*, May 1963; Monsonis, *SDS Bulletin*, March-April 1963; quotations are from Blum. **Page 87:** Gitlin, interview. Piedmont student, quoted in Newfield, p. 87. "Bill Westbury," Keniston, p. 109 (ellipses in original); "Clarkson" is presumably Hayden. **Page 88:** Brecher, interview. Ireland, letter to NO, November 1962. **Page 89:** On middle-class origins, see e.g., Hayden, in Irving Howe, editor, *The Radical Papers*, Doubleday, 1966, p. 362. **Page 90:** Newfield, interview. **Pages 91-92:** *America and the New Era*, mimeographed and later published as a pamphlet by SDS, 1963; reprinted in *NLN*, December 9 and 16, 1966; excerpted in Teodori, p. 172. **Page 93:** Gitlin, interview. **Page 94:** Flacks, *Psychology Today*, October 1967. Kissinger, *NLN*, June 10, 1968; full article reprinted in "Riots, Civil and Criminal Disorders," Part 18, pp. 3383 ff.

7. *ERAP: Fall 1963-Spring 1964*

SOURCES FOR ERAP IN GENERAL, Cohen and Hale (1967), pp. 125–213; Gitlin and Hollander (a full report of the Chicago project); Tom Hayden, in Howe, *The Radical Papers*, op. cit., pp. 350 ff. and *Rolling Stone*, October 26 and November 9, 1972; Newfield, pp. 101 ff.; Potter, pp. 136 ff.; *Thoughts of Young Radicals*, Pitman/New Republic, 1966 (especially the pieces by Flacks, Gitlin, Tom Hayden, Casey Hayden, and Andrew Kopkind); *Studies on the Left*, Spring-Summer 1964, Winter, Spring, Summer, and Fall, 1965, January-February and March-April, 1966 (articles by Jessie Allen, Ronald Aronson, Connie Brown, Norm Fruchter, Robert Kramer, James O'Connor, Dan Schechter, Hamish Sinclair, James H. Williams); Todd Gitlin, *International Socialist Journal*, No. 24, 1967 (excerpted in Teodori, pp. 136 ff. and *NLN*, June 26, 1967; Joanne Grant, *National Guardian*, January 2, 1965; Jack Newfield, *Village Voice*, August 5, 1965; Staughton Lynd, *Liberation*, July 1969; Richard Rothstein, *Radical America*, March-April 1968 (reprinted with some changes, in Long, pp. 272 ff.); a series of *ERAP Bulletins* published in 1964 and 1965; "We Got to Live Here" and "Troublemakers," Newsreel films, 1965. The Wisconsin Historical Society has a large collection of ERAP material. **Page 95:** Axelrod, quoted in Samuel H. Baron, *Plekhanov*, Stanford, 1963, p. 15. **Page 96:** Hayden letter to Reuther, March 29, 1963. Hayden report, *SDS Bulletin*, March-April, 1963. **Page 97:** *America and the New Era*, op. cit. **Page 98:** Gitlin, "New Chances: The Reality and Dynamic of the New Left," mimeographed paper, November 1969, author's file. **Page 99:** Ray Brown, "Our Crisis Economy," SDS pamphlet, fall 1963. **Page 100:** Gitlin, in Cohen and Hale (1967), p. 126. **Page 101:** Hayden quotations, in order, from *The Radical Papers*, op. cit., p. 364; ibid, p. 362; ibid., p. 363; *Thoughts of Young Radicals*, op. cit., p. 41. "a new harmony," Keniston, p. 122. **Page 102:** Hayden, letter to Gitlin, August 2, 1963. **Page 103:** Chabot, "interim report" to NO, November 6, 1963. **Page 104:** Max, memo to Gitlin, November 23, 1963. **Pages 104-5:** For Chester organizing, Carl Wittman, *SDS Bulletin*, March 1964; Larry Gordon, *SDS Bulletin*, January 1964; Michael Ferber, *Liberation*, January 1964. **Page 105:** Webb, interview. "An Interracial Movement of the Poor?" SDS pamphlet, 1963, reprinted in Cohen and Hale (1967), pp. 175 ff.; italics in original. **Page 106:** Booth, interview. Brecher, interview. Webb, interview. **Page 107:** Hayden-Haber debate, mimeographed minutes; *SDS Bulletin,* February and March, 1964; *SDS Discussion Bulletin,* spring 1964; Booth, Brecher, and Webb interviews. **Page 108:** Gitlin, interview. Webb, interview. **Page 109:** "blitzed," letter to NO, May 27, 1964. **Page 110:** *Davis,* ibid. McKelvey, letter, undated (spring 1964). Haber, *SDS Bulletin,* March 1964. **Page 111:** Williams, interview. Gitlin, *SDS Bulletin,* May 1964. **Page 112:** Max, interview. **Page 115:** Ferry–Muste–Stone letter, *Guardian,* June 27, 1964, and elsewhere.

8. *Fall 1963–Spring 1964*

Page 116: This photograph reprinted in *NLN,* June 10, 1968. **Page 118:** Gitlin, interview. Webb, interview. Ryan, letter to Gitlin, October 1, 1963. Membership figures, worklist mailing, October 23, 1963. **Page 119:** Call for Vietnam demonstration, *SDS Bulletin,* October 1963, and Max memo, October 11, 1963. **Page 120:** Booth speech and the demonstration, *SDS Bulletin,* November 1963. **Page 121:** "We can't afford," memo, April 1964; "Think about dough," letter to Gitlin, May 1964. **Page 122:** "a strange," NC minutes. Max, memo, April 1964. **Page 124:** Williams, *SDS Bulletin,* May 1964. **Page 125:** Literature list, *SDS Bulletin,* June 1964. Flacks, letter to NO, February 15, 1964. Taylor–Reisman letter, printed, May 1, 1964. **Page 126:** "are usually," Kissinger, memo, undated (fall 1963). Flacks, letter to NO, op. cit. **Page 127:** Kissinger, to Kahn, June 30, 1964; to LID, August 14, 1964. **Page 128:** Minkoff, letter to Kissinger, September 3, 1964. Kissinger report, *SDS Bulletin,* July 1964. McKelvey, *SDS Bulletin,* January 1964.

9. *ERAP: Summer 1964–Summer 1965*

Page 131: Webb, interview. NCUP song, from *ERAP Bulletin,* summer 1965. **Page 132:** Williams, interview. Smith, letter to NO, November 1964. Mankiewicz, quoted in *ERAP Bulletin,* 1964. Davis, *SDS Bulletin,* September 1964. **Page 133:** Hayden, in *The Radical Papers,* op. cit., p. 361. **Page 134:** Webb, interview. **Page 135:** Davis, *SDS Bulletin,* op. cit. **Page 136:** "There is no," *Challenge,* July 1964. Epton, quoted in Newfield, p. 119. ERAP membership estimates, Max–Williams memo, January 6, 1965. **Page 137:** Booth, interview. "SNCC organizers," report written for *SDS Bulletin,* spring 1965, unpublished. **Pages 138–39:** Rothstein, "By the winter" and "in isolation," in Long, p. 282, 286. **Page 140:** Kopkind, *New Republic,* June 19, 1965, reprinted in *Thoughts of the Young Radicals,* op. cit., p. 1. "The [SDS] kids," Lee Webb, interview. **Page 141:** "The organizers," Dave Muhly, "A Failure to Think About," *Movement,* June 1968. **Page 143:** Harrington, *Thoughts of the Young Radicals,* op. cit., p. 71. Egleson, *ERAP Newsletter,* July 23, 1965. Gitlin, "New Chances," mimeographed paper, November 1969, author's file. **Page 144:** Hayden, in *The Radical Papers,* op. cit., p. 360; see also *Rolling Stone,* op. cit. **Page 145:** Levenson, *Paper Tiger* (Boston), May 1, 1968. Rothstein, in Long, p. 274. **Page 146:** ibid., p. 278. **Page 147:** Kopkind, *Thoughts of Young Radicals,* op. cit., p. 10. **Pages 147–49:** For JOIN experience, esp. Gitlin and Hollander, and "In Poverty," Chicago

Daily News, July 3, 1965. **Page 148:** "See, like it," Gitlin and Hollander, pp. 424–25. **Page 149:** NCUP estimate, Newfield, *Village Voice,* op. cit. **Page 150:** Brecht, "To Posterity," *Selected Poems,* Harcourt Brace, 1947.

10. Fall 1964
 Page 151: Potter, SDS Bulletin, October 1964. **Page 152:** *PREP Newsletters,* edited by Flacks, appeared in May 1963, January, April, and May 1964. "Bobbsey twins," from Arthur Waskow, interview. **Page 153:** "What grassroots," letter to Kissinger, October 10, 1964. "its potential," memo, undated (December 1964). South Africa demonstration plans, Gitlin, interview. **Page 154:** Davis, worklist mailing, February 23, 1965. Williams, interview. **Page 155:** PEP position, from Max, Williams, and others, "Report of the Committee on the Establishment of the Political Education Project," fall 1964; see also 1964 convention resolution, *SDS Bulletin,* July 1964. Webb, interview. **Page 156:** Habers, "Taking Johnson Seriously," written for a planned but never realized SDS magazine, *New Era,* fall 1964, unpublished. "the Johnson landslide" and Kissinger, mimeographed minutes of PEP meeting, November 6–7, 1964. Williams, interview. **Page 157:** Williams, interview. Booth, interview. Williams, interview. Max, interview. "Regretfully," Max, worklist mailing, February 23, 1965. **Page 158:** For December NC, Kissinger, *SDS Bulletin,* January 1965; elaborate mimeographed minutes; Flacks, letter, worklist mailing, January 30, 1965. **Page 159:** Williams, interview. Hayden–Brown debate, minutes, and Booth, interview. **Page 160:** M2M statement, archives, and quoted in Ferber and Lynd, pp. 50–51. **Page 161:** Brecher, interview. **Page 162:** Boston PREP, mimeographed letter, Chuck Levenstein, Pat Hammond, Dave Smith, Jean Cormack, undated (fall 1964). **Pages 162–67:** SOURCES FOR BERKELEY include Bettina Aptheker, *The Academic Rebellion in the United States,* Citadel, 1972; Hal Draper, *The New Student Revolt,* Grove, 1965; Lewis Feuer, *The Conflict of Generations,* Basic Books, 1969, pp. 436 ff.; Max Heirich, *The Beginning: Berkeley 1964,* Columbia, 1970; Jacobs and Landau, pp. 59 ff.; Seymour Martin Lipset and Sheldon S. Wolin, editors, *The Berkeley Student Revolt,* Doubleday Anchor, 1965; Michael V. Miller and Susan Gilmore, editors, *Revolution at Berkeley,* Dell, 1965; Michael Rossman, *The Wedding Within the War,* Doubleday, 1971; Steven Warshaw, *The Trouble at Berkeley,* Diablo (Berkeley), 1965; Sheldon S. Wolin and John H. Schaar, *The Berkeley Rebellion and Beyond,* New York Review/Vintage, 1970, pp. 19 ff.; Paul Booth, "A Strategy for University Reform," SDS pamphlet, 1965; A.H. Raskin, N.Y. *Times Magazine,* January 11, 1970; John R. Seeley, *Our Generation* (Montreal), May 1968; and a number of sociological/psychological studies, including Jeanne Block, Norma Haan, and Brewster Smith, in *Understanding Adolescents,* James F. Adams, editor, Allyn and Bacon, 1968; Paul Heist, in *Order and Freedom on the Campus,* O.W. Knorr and W.J. Minter, editors, Western Interstate Commission for Higher Education (Boulder); Paul Heist, "The Dynamics of Student Discontent and Protest," mimeographed paper, Center for Research and Development in Higher Education, Berkeley; Joseph Katz, *No Time for Youth,* Jossey-Bass (San Francisco), 1968; Joseph Katz, in *Psychological Development and the Impact of Col-*

lege, Katz and associates, editors, Stanford Institute for the Study of Human Problems, 1967; Edward W. Sampson, *Journal of Social Issues,* July 1967; William A. Watts and David Whittaker, *Journal of Applied Behavioral Science,* Vol. 1 (1965) and Vol. 2 (1966), and three studies in the Lipset and Wolin book, by Hanah C. Selvin and Warren O. Hagstrom; Glen Lyonns; and Robert H. Somers. **Page 164:** Somers survey, in Lipset and Wolin, op. cit., p. 549. Berkeley Center study, by Paul Heist, in *Order and Freedom on the Campus,* op. cit. **Page 166:** Seeley, in *Our Generation,* op. cit. Kerr, *The Uses of the University,* Harvard, 1964, and Harper Torchbook, 1966, p. 68. **Page 168:** Kissinger, both comments from letter to Potter, October 8, 1964. **Page 170:** PREP on Vietnam, minutes, November 1964. **Pages 170–72:** Vietnam debate reconstructed from careful minutes by Carol Stevens, mimeographed by NO, and Booth and Gitlin, interviews. **Page 172:** Booth, letter, January 18, 1965.

11. Spring 1965

Page 174: Booth, interview. Pre-march preparations, *SDS Bulletins* and worklist mailings, January, February, March, 1965. **Page 175:** Membership figures, *SDS Bulletin,* March 1965. **Page 176:** N.Y. *Times* article, by Fred Powledge, March 15, 1965. **Page 177:** Harrington, interview. **Page 178:** Kissinger, letter to Potter, October 8, 1964. On LID and Rustin, see Dave Dellinger, *Liberation,* May, and Staughton Lynd, *Liberation,* June–July 1965. "has developed," letter to PREP by Robert C. Angell, April 7, 1965. **Page 179:** Gilmore, et al., and *Post* editorial, N.Y. *Post,* April 17–18, 1965. Cox–Peretzes letter, mimeograph, April 27, 1965, copy at Institute for Policy Studies, Washington, D.C. **Page 180:** SDS vote and Kissinger comment, worklist mailing, March 21, 1965. **Page 181:** march call printed by SDS, reprinted in *Nation, Guardian,* and *Studies on the Left.* **Page 182:** PREP Executive Committee, worklist mailing, March 10, 1965. **Pages 183–85:** For teach-ins, Louis Menashe and Ronald Radosh, *Teach-ins: U.S.A.,* Praeger, 1967. **Page 185:** Gitlin, interview. **Pages 185–193:** For Washington March, *SDS Bulletin,* May 1965; *Guardian,* April 24, 1965; *Liberation,* May and June–July, 1965; *Studies on the Left,* May 1965. **Page 185:** estimate of colleges, SDS memo, April 25, 1965. **Page 186:** Stone and Greuning, quoted in *Liberation,* May 1965. **Page 187:** Lynd, quoted in *Guardian,* op. cit. Gitlin, interview. Potter speech, excerpted in *Guardian,* op. cit., later published in full as an SDS pamphlet, May 1965; excerpts in Teodori, pp. 246 ff. **Page 189:** Smith, *Guardian,* op. cit. **Page 190:** Lynd, *Liberation,* June–July, 1965. **Page 191:** Price, *Guardian,* op. cit., Mann, quoted, ibid. N.Y. *Times,* April 18, 1965. **Page 192:** N.Y. *Herald Tribune,* April 18, 1965. Baron, letter to LID, April 20, 1965. LID Board, memo, April 30, 1965. McDowell, letter enclosed with Harrington reply, May 1965. **Page 193:** "We are, de facto," quoted by Raymond R. Coffey, *Chicago Daily News,* May 17, 1965. Information on the NC, and Kissinger quote, worklist mailing, April 25, 1965. **Page 194:** "before the Kissinger," "Summary of National Council Meeting," mimeographed, undated (April 1965). **Pages 194–96:** Oglesby biography, from interview, and Roger Vaughan, *Life,* October 18, 1968; quotations, ibid. **Page 198:** "the Woodlawn ghetto" and "Crush imperialism," worklist mailing, May 1, 1965. **Page 199:** Oglesby, quoted in Booth, "Working Papers," mimeographed, undated (May 1965).

12. Summer 1965

Pages 203–11: For the Kewadin convention, Jacobs and Landau, pp. 27 ff., 174 ff.; *Guardian,* June 26, 1965; mimeographed "working papers" for the convention; Booth, Brecher, Shero, and Webb interviews; Max, *Viewpoint* (SDS-LID, New York), summer 1965, mimeographed by NO, December 1965. **Page 204:** Webb, interview. Booth, interview. **Page 205:** Newfield, p. 87. Haber, "Non-exclusionism," SDS paper, December 1965, excerpted in Teodori, p. 218. **Page 206:** Shero, interview. **Page 207:** Max, op. cit. **Page 208:** Max, ibid. **Page 209:** "Everyone felt," Brecher, interview. Shero biography and quote, interview. **Page 211:** "If I'd wanted," Paul Pipkin, convention working paper, June 1965; other quotations, letters to NO. Haber, "Non-exclusionism," op. cit. **Page 212:** Overstreet, letters to Harry Laidler, Laidler papers, Tamiment. Laidler, letter to Overstreet, July 13, 1965, Tamiment. LID Board of Directors, statement, June 22, 1965. **Page 213:** Kahn, letter to NO, June 29, 1965. **Page 214:** Gitlin, interview. Weissman, *NLN,* February 4, 1966. Flacks, "Some Problems, Issues, Proposals," working paper for 1965 convention, excerpted in Jacobs and Landau, pp. 162 ff. **Page 215:** Booth, letter to Brecher, January 18, 1965. **Page 216:** Booth, interview. **Page 216:** SDS articles, in *Nation,* May 10, *New Republic,* June 19, *Reporter,* May 6, *U.S. News,* May 10 and 17, all 1965. NO letters, 1965, archives. **Page 217:** "Clark has found," note from Sam Bennett, October 1965. **Page 218:** Kissinger, "There's a Change Gotta Come!" mimeographed paper, December 1965. **Pages 218–19:** Rosen, report to the March 1968 PL convention, reprinted in "Build a Base in the Working Class," PL pamphlet, June 1969; see also PL Constitution, Jacobs and Landau, pp. 187 ff. **Page 219:** map, *National Vietnam Newsletter,* August 26, 1965. **Page 220:** Booth, interview. Willis, quoted by AP, August 5, 1965, reprinted in *SDS Bulletin,* Vol. 4, No. 1, undated (fall 1965); see also Ferber and Lynd, p. 22. **Page 221:** Brecher, interview. Booth, interview. **Page 222:** Haber, letter to NC, September 5, 1965.

13. Fall 1965

Page 223: Description of NO from Newfield, p. 85; Thomas Brooks, N.Y. *Times Magazine,* November 7, 1965; "Studying a Student," N.Y. *Herald Tribune,* November 7, 1965; Shero interview. **Page 224:** N.Y. *Herald Tribune,* op. cit. Shero, interview. **Page 225:** "Participatory democracy," quoted by Pardun (attributed to "ex-staff members here in Austin") in "Organizational Democracy," mimeographed paper for "Rethinking Conference," December 1965. Kissinger, "There's a Change Gotta Come!" op. cit. Bennett, memo to NO/NAC, January 1966. **Page 226:** Gitlin, "Proposal for a Mission to North Vietnam," *National Vietnam Newsletter,* August 26, 1965. Kissinger, ibid. "All right," minutes of NC. **Page 227:** Webb and Booth, "The Anti-War Movement: From Protest to Radical Politics," mimeographed by SDS, fall 1965, reprinted in *Our Generation,* May 1966. NC report and quotations, worklist mailing, September 15, 1965. Antidraft program, worklist mailing, October 5, 1965. **Page 228:** Dodd, "The Anti-Vietnam Agitation and the Teach-In Movement," Senate Internal Security Committee report, October 13, 1965. **Page 229:** Stennis, *Congressional Record,* October 15, 1965. **Page 230:** Katzenbach, *Guardian,* October 23, 1965, and *SDS Bulletin,* October 21, 1965. *Guardian,* op. cit. *Playboy,* Nat Hentoff, March 1966. **Page 231:** Hershey, quoted in *New Republic,* October 8, 1966. Senate reaction, *Congressional Record,* October 18, 1965. Reston, N.Y. *Times,* October 16, 1965. Johnson, statement, October 17, and in *Guardian,* op. cit. *SDS Bulletin,* October 21, 1965. "If you are," "Super Late News," ibid. **Page 232:** Booth, worklist mailing, November 2, 1965. **Page 233:** "Build, Not Burn," mimeographed and distributed by SDS, reprinted in *Liberation,* December 1965, excerpted in Newfield, p. 107. **Page 234:** Booth, "National Secretary's Report," to December NC, mimeograph, December 10, 1965. SDS reaction and McEldowney telegram, NO files. **Page 235:** Calvert: *NLN,* February 13, 1967. M2M, *Free Student,* November 27, 1965. Shero, minutes of "Rethinking Conference," December 1965. McEldowney, telegram, op. cit. **Page 235:** M2M statement, *Free Student,* op. cit. **Page 236:** Gordon, ibid. **Page 237:** Oglesby, *Guardian,* November 20, 1965. *New Republic,* October 30, 1965. **Page 238:** Harrington, interview. Feldman, *LID News Bulletin,* Fall 1965. **Page 239:** Haber, letter to NO, in worklist mailing, October 12, 1965. **Page 240:** "Acting under the instructions," press release, Tom Kahn and Paul Booth, October 4, 1965, LID files. **Page 241:** SDS march call, printed by SDS, reprinted in *Liberation,* December 1965. **Page 242:** *Guardian,* December 4, 1965. Oglesby, "to show their 'responsibleness,' " introduction to "Trapped in a System" (a reprint of the speech), REP pamphlet, January 1969. **Pages 242–44:** Oglesby's speech, SDS pamphlet, 1965; *NLN,* January 27, 1966; *Monthly Review,* January 1966; Teodori, pp. 182 ff. **Page 244:** Just, *Washington Post,* December 9, 1965. **Page 245:** Thomas Brooks, N.Y. *Times Magazine,* November 7, 1965; *Newsweek,* November 1, 1965; Jack Newfield, *Nation,* November 8, 1965. Membership and chapter figures, mimeograph, distributed at December NC. **Page 249:** Eisen, *Activist* (Oberlin), March 1966, reprinted in Cohen and Hale, p. 306. Gitlin, *NLN,* February 4 and 11, 1966. **Page 250:** "We must be planning," NC statement, *NLN,* January 21, 1966. **Page 251:** Garvy, letter to NO, c. January 1966. "We can't even," handwritten minutes, NO files. For "freedom draft," worklist mailings, November 2 and 17, 1965, *NLN,* January 21, 1966. **Page 252:** women's statement, *NLN,* January 28, 1966.

14. Spring 1966
Page 254: For April NC, *NLN,* April 15, 1966, and minutes, NO files. Draft exam, NO files. **Page 255:** Booth, interview. Lynd, *Liberation,* April 1966. **Pages 256–63:** For Chicago rank crisis, Vern Visick, "A Short History and Analysis: The Rank Protest of 1966–67," mimeographed paper for Divinity School, University of Chicago, October 25, 1967; *NLN,* May 13 and 20, 1966. **Page 256:** "We feel," "the transformation," and "To rank," from SAR documents, quoted in Visick, op. cit. **Page 257:** "You're not," Visick, op. cit. **Page 258:** "Despite," Visick, op. cit. Flacks study, *Journal of Social Issues,* July 1967; see also C. Weiss-

berg, "Students Against the Rank," M. A. thesis, Department of Sociology, University of Chicago; Flacks, in Foster and Long, pp. 134 ff. **Page 260:** On rank protests, see May and June issues of *NLN;* Ferber and Lynd, pp. 38–41; Richard E. Peterson, in Foster and Long, pp. 59 ff. **Page 261:** *Viet Report,* February, March–April, and June–July, 1966. Ramparts, April 1966. SOURCES FOR UNIVERSITY COMPLICITY include Richard J. Barber, *The American Corporation,* Dutton, 1970; Seymour Hersh, *Chemical and Biological Warfare,* Bobbs-Merrill, 1969; Clark Kerr, *The Uses of the University,* Harvard, 1964 and Harper Torchbook, 1966; Michael T. Klare, *War Without End,* Random House, Vintage, 1972, esp. Chs. 3–5; Michael W. Miles, *The Radical Probe,* Atheneum, 1971, esp. Ch. 3; James Ridgeway, *The Closed Corporation,* Random House, 1968; David Horowitz, *Ramparts,* May 1969; Michael Klare, "The University-Military-Police Complex," North American Congress on Latin America, 1970, and his periodic column in the *Guardian,* "The War Game," 1968 and 1969; Allen Krebs, "The University," REP pamphlet, 1968; Martin Nicolaus, "The Iceberg Strategy," REP pamphlet, November 1967, reprinted in Goodman, p. 325; *Viet Report,* January 1968; *Student Mobilizer,* April 2, 1970; College Press Service, December 1970 (e.g., *Daily Cardinal* [Wisconsin], December 4–5); and various pamphlets by students at individual major universities exposing complicity on that campus. **Page 262:** sit-in use, Peterson, in Foster and Long, pp. 59 ff. **Page 263:** M2M, *Free Student,* May 1966. Gordon, letter to NO, copied verbatim, *NLN,* February 18, 1966. Murphy, NO files. **Page 264:** PL rules, see Newfield, p. 110. "A few Progressive Labor," *NLN,* May 6, 1966. **Pages 264–69:** SOURCES FOR FREE UNIVERSITIES, chiefly Paul Lauter and Florence Howe, *The Conspiracy of the Young,* World, 1970, and issues of *NLN,* spring and summer 1966. **Page 266:** "to establish protest," quoted in Lauter and Howe, op. cit., p. 108. "We wanted," quoted ibid., p. 92. **Page 267:** Craven, letter in an SDS "Free University" mailing, mimeograph, undated (June 1965). Free University of Pennsylvania, Lauter and Howe, op. cit., pp. 104 ff.; *NLN,* February 11, 1966. **Page 268:** Davidson, "The Multiversity: Crucible of the New Working Class," SDS pamphlet, 1967, widely reprinted, including Wallerstein and Starr, Vol. II, pp. 108 ff. **Page 269:** "There is only," letter from Paul Burke, *NLN,* July 15 & 22, 1966. **Page 270:** Silbar and Israel, *NLN,* June 24, 1966. **Page 271:** membership survey, *NLN,* March 18, 1966. **Page 272:** Booth, interview. Kissinger, "NICNAC" mailing, January 1966, mimeograph. **Page 273:** *NLNs*—Hayden, January 21, Chavez, March 25, Oglesby, April 1 and 8, Flacks, August 12, all 1966. Sinyavsky-Daniel statement, *NLN,* March 11, 1966; vote, March 25. **Page 275:** Hoover, testimony before House Appropriations Subcommittee, February 10, 1966. "debug" advertisement, NLN, April 8, 1966. Informers: Divale, *I Lived Inside the Campus Revolution,* Cowles, 1970; Kirk, "Investigation of SDS," Part 5; Taft, *New Republic,* March 25, 1967. Hoover, "Hoover Defends," N.Y. *Times,* May 5, 1966; see also Peter Kihss, N.Y. *Times,* April 9, 1966. **Page 276:** Conus Intel, see Richard Halloran, N.Y. *Times,* January 18, 1971. June NC, *NLN,* June 24, 1966. **Page 277:** Flacks, *NLN,* August 12, 1966. Stein, letter to NO, mimeographed, undated. NAC on Booth, *NLN,* May 13, 1966.

15. Summer 1966
Pages 279–92: For convention, *NLN,* August 24, September 9 and 23, 1966; *Guardian,* September 17, 1966. **Page 279:** *Nonpareil,* quoted by P. Boyd Mather, *Christian Century,* October 12, 1966. **Page 280:**"Revolt," *Guardian,* op. cit. Kleiman, *NLN,* November 4, 1966. Kissinger, *NLN,* June 10, 1966. "boomed up" and "Clear Lake," Paul Buhle, *NLN,* September 23, 1966. **Pages 280–81:** Convention resolutions, *NLN,* September 23, 1966, and minutes, copy from Lee Webb. **Page 282:** Shero, minutes. Weissman, interview. Webb, interview. **Page 283:** Egleson, *Liberation,* April 1970. Dellinger, *Liberation,* May–June 1967. Davidson, quoted by Calvert, *NLN,* September 9, 1966. **Page 284:** Calvert, "bumming" and "some of us," *Liberation,* May 1969, reprinted in Goodman, pp. 585 ff. and Wallerstein and Starr, pp. 247 ff. **Page 285:** Webb, interview. Maher, *NLN,* August 24, 1966. **Page 286:** Booth, NLN, October 1 and September 9, 1966. **Page 287:** Max, letter to Williams, September 1966, from Williams. **Page 288:** Jahn, *NLN,* October 1, 1966. On REP's formation, *NLN,* March 25, April 15, and May 13, 1966; Teodori, pp. 399 ff. Quotations are from Al Haber, "Radical Education Project," *NLN,* March 25, 1966, a later and longer version of which is in "Riots, Civil and Criminal Disorders," Part 18, pp. 3439 ff. **Page 289:** REP finances, *NLN,* December 23, 1966. **Pages 290–92:** Davidson's paper, *NLN,* September 9, 1966; reprinted by SDS, 1966; reprinted in Wallerstein and Starr, Vol. II, p. 98. **Page 293:** Silbar, *NLN,* October 28, 1966. The best source of university population statistics is "Projections of Educational Statistics to 1977–78," National Center for Educational Statistics, Office of Education, HEW, Washington, D.C., 1968 and regularly revised. Estimates of activists, John L. Horn and Paul D. Knott, *Science,* March 12, 1971; Kenneth Keniston, *Journal of Social Issues,* July 1967; Peterson, in Foster and Long, p. 78. **Page 296:** Calvert, *NLN,* September 9, 1966. **Page 297:** Shero, interview.

16. Fall 1966
Page 298: Shero, interview. **Pages 301–2:** For Berkeley 1966, *NLN,* December 12, 1966; James Petras, *Liberation,* February 1967; Sheldon S. Wolin and John H. Schaar, *New York Review,* February 9, 1967, reprinted in Wolin and Schaar *The Berkeley Rebellion and Beyond,* New York Review/Vintage, 1970. **Pages 303–4:** *NLN,* December 23, 1966; other accounts of the McNamara incident, Eichel et al., pp. 32–35, and Kelman, pp. 51 ff. **Page 304:** letter to N.Y. *Times,* November 20, 1966. **Page 305:** *PL,* October-November, 1966. **Page 306:** Simensky, letter to NO, December 1966. Calvert, letter to Simensky, January 1967. Chapter list, *NLN,* October 28, 1966. **Page 307:** Brandeis constitution, author's file. Form letters, undated (December 1966). **Page 308:** Davidson, *NLN,* February 3, 1967. Calvert, *NLN,* September 23, 1966. **Page 309:** Calvert, November 25, 1966. **Page 310:** Davidson, *NLN,* February 3, 1967. Baum and Faber, *NLN,* September 2, 1966. "Road to Revolution II," *PL,* February-March 1967; reprinted in *Revolution Today: U.S.A.,* Progressive Labor Party, 1970. **Pages 311–13:** SOURCES FOR EARLY DRAFT WORK, *NLN*s, fall 1966 and spring 1967, esp. March 27, 1967; Ferber and Lynd, Chs. 2–8; Paul Lauter and Florence Howe, *The Conspiracy of the*

Young, op. cit., pp. 127 ff.; Alice Lynd, editor, *We Won't Go*, Beacon paperback, 1968; Norma Sue Woodstone, *Up Against the War*, Tower, 1970; *Liberation*, May 1969. **Page 311:** "our man," *NLN*, October 28, 1966. **Page 312:** "return our draft," quoted in Ferber and Lynd, p. 51. "cooperate in any way," ibid., p. 50. **Page 313:** Spritzler, *NLN*, December 9, 1966. Berkeley NC, reported in *NLN*, January 13, 1967, and *Guardian*, January 7, 1967. **Page 314:** Calvert, minutes, *NLN*, January 13, 1967. Draft statement, *NLN*, ibid.; *Guardian*, January 7, 1967; Ferber and Lynd, p. 60. **Page 315:** Calvert, *NLN*, January 13, 1967. **Page 316:** Ibid.

17. Spring 1967
Pages 317–318: Calvert, "In White America," speech reprinted in *Guardian*, March 25, 1967, REP pamphlet, spring 1967, and Teodori, pp. 412 ff. **Page 319:** Davidson, *Guardian*, March 23, 1968. Henig, *NLN*, January 20, 1967. SSS document of July 1, 1965, reprinted in Lauter and Howe, op. cit., pp. 184 ff., and Wallerstein and Starr, Vol. I, pp. 195 ff. **Page 320:** Calvert, *Liberation*, May 1969; reprints cited supra. Segal, *NLN*, March 27, 1967. **Page 321:** Statement signers, *NLN*, ibid., and Ferber and Lynd, pp. 63 ff. **Page 322:** Calvert to SSS, letter, *NLN*, February 13, 1967. **Page 323:** For April 15, see Ferber and Lynd, pp. 68 ff.; J. Anthony Lukas, *Don't Shoot—We Are Your Children*, Random House, 1971, p. 323; commercial press. "powerful resistance," call, *Liberation*, May 1969, and Ferber and Lynd, p. 72. Jezer, in Alice Lynd, editor, *We Won't Go*, Beacon, 1968, p. 7. **Page 324:** Wicker, N.Y. *Times*, May 3, 1967. Segal-Jezer, Ferber and Lynd, p. 64. Lynd, *Liberation*, May 1969. Smith, *Guardian*, April 8, 15, 22, 1967. **Page 325:** Davidson, quoted April 8. Calvert, ibid. N.Y. *Times*, May 7, 1967. **Pages 325–29:** For spring campus actions, *NLN*, *Guardian*, campus and commercial press. **Page 327:** Murphy, *NLN*, February 27, 1967. **Pages 328–29:** for administration spying, Frank Donner, *Playboy*, March 1968; James Ridgeway, *New Republic*, March 25, 1967; FBI files from Media, Pennsylvania, office, in *WIN*, March 1972. **Page 329:** "in regular contact," quoted in Donner, op. cit. **Pages 330–31:** for CIA–NSA, see *Ramparts*, February 1967, and Todd Gitlin and Bob Ross, *Village Voice*, July 6, 1967, reprinted as an SDS pamphlet, August 1967. **Page 330:** Hayden's suspicions, from Garman, interview, and *Rolling Stone*, October 26, 1972; Booth's and Potter's, from Booth, interview. **Page 331:** Egleson, *NLN*, February 27, 1967. **Page 332:** Scott, letters, compiled by Ayers in 1969, NO files. **Page 333:** "Vietnam Work-In," "Thousands of," *PL*, July-August 1967. **Page 335:** "the largest demonstration," *Guardian*, April 22, 1967. Calvert, office memo, undated (January, 1967). Rader, Rader, p. 20. **Page 336:** Davidson, *NLN*, March 27, 1967. For T-Os, see *NLN*s, April, May, June, 1967. **Page 337:** brochure, undated (c. May 1967), archives and author's file. **Page 337:** Oglesby and Richard Shaull, *Containment and Change*, two separate essays, the first by Oglesby. **Page 338:** "Praxis" sections in *NLN*, February 13, March 27, April 13, August 7, 1967. Wilkerson, *NLN*, February 13, 1967. Gottlieb-Tenney-Gilbert, *NLN*, ibid., and May 22, 1967. **Page 339:** Calvert, "In White America," op. cit. **Page 340:** NO operation and "visited approximately," *NLN*, June 26, 1967. **Page 341:** Fite, *NLN*, ibid. Davidson, *NLN*, February 3,

1967. **Page 342:** "Current Financial," *NLN,* February 20, 1967. Jacobsen, *NLN,* June 26, 1967. "extremely low" and "provide enough," ibid.

18. Summer 1967
   Page 344: Lynd, *Liberation,* May 1969. Kopkind, *New York Review,* September 28, 1967. Kenneth Keniston, p. 142. Bardacke, *Steps,* op. cit. Freudiger, *NLN,* June 26, 1967. Zweig, quoted by Paul Hofman, N.Y. *Times,* May 7, 1967. **Page 345:** Johnson, *NLN,* June 26, 1967. **Page 346:** Hayden, *Rebellion in Newark,* Vintage, 1967, pp. 68–69. **Page 347:** " 'Movement people,' " *NLN,* October 2, 1967. **Page 348:** Conus Intel information, Richard Halloran, N.Y. *Times,* January 18, 1971. **Page 349:** *Time,* January 6, 1967. *Nation,* June 19, 1967. *Daedalus,* Summer 1967. *Teachers College Record,* Columbia University, 1967. *Playboy,* August 1967. **Page 350:** *Journal of Social Issues,* July 1967. Katz, *The Student Activists,* Office of Education, Washington, D.C. ACADEMIC STUDIES OF ACTIVISTS include Philip G. Altbach and Robert Lauter, editors, *The New Pilgrims,* McKay, 1972; Joseph Axelrod et al., *Search for Relevance,* Jossey-Bass (San Francisco), 1969, with a good bibliography; Foster and Long (esp. chapters by Alexander Astin, Leonard Baird, Richard Flacks, Foster, and David Westby and Richard Braungart); Theodore Roszak, *The Making of a Counter Culture,* Doubleday and Anchor, 1969; Edward E. Sampson, Harold A. Korn, et al., *Student Activism and Protest,* Jossey-Bass, 1970; *Annals of the Academy of Political Science,* May 1971; *Journal of Social Issues,* July 1967; Alexander Astin, *Guidance,* Fall 1968; Richard Flacks, *Psychology Today,* October 1967; Norma Haan, Brewster Smith, and Jeanne Block, *Journal of Personal and Social Psychology,* Vol. 10, No. 3, 1968; Jeffrey K. Hadden, *Psychology Today,* October 1969; John L. Horn and Paul D. Knott, *Science,* March 12, 1971; Kenneth Keniston, *Change,* November-December 1969; Larry C. Kerpelman, *Journal of Counseling Psychology,* Vol. 16, No. 1, 1969; Seymour Martin Lipset, in Daniel Bell and Irving Kristol, editors, *Confrontation,* Basic Books, 1969; Kathleen Ranlett Mock, "The Potential Activist," mimeograph, from the Berkeley Center for Research and Development in Higher Education, 1968; Sophia F. McDowell, Gilbert A. Lowe, Jr., and Doris A. Dockett, *Public Opinion Quarterly,* Fall 1970; Stanley J. Morse and Stanton Peele, *Journal of Social Issues,* No. 4, 1971; William A. Watts and David Whittaker, *Sociological Education,* Vol. 41, 1968; Watts, Steve Lynch, and Whittaker, *Journal of Counseling Psychology,* Vol. 16, No. 1, 1969; David Westby and Richard Braungart, *American Sociological Review,* Vol. 31, October 1966; and articles listed previously under Berkeley 1964. **Page 350:** "activism . . . is," R.S. Berns, quoted in Axelrod, et al., op. cit., p. 112. **Page 351:** Davidson, *NLN,* February 3, 1967. **Page 352:** Davidson, ibid. **Page 355:** Habers, "Getting by With a Little Help from Our Friends," REP conference July 1967, REP pamphlet, 1967; reprinted in Long, pp. 289 ff. **Page 357:** Adams, *NLN,* January 20 and April 17, 1967. **Page 358:** For the convention, detailed handwritten minutes, NO files; *NLN,* July 10, 1967; Egleson, interview. **Page 359:** O'Brien, *NLN,* August 15, 1967. *Times* article, May 7, 1967, op. cit. **Page 360:** Calvert, "I felt," "Was a," *NLN,* May 22, 1967. "really a," minutes. **Page 361:** Waskow, interview. **Pages 362–64:** Resolutions,

NLN, July 10, 1967. **Page 364:** Schlesinger, N.Y. *Times,* May 6, 1967. **Page 365:** Booth, interview. **Page 367:** Spiegel, quoted in *Life,* October 18, 1968. **Page 368:** Pardun, taped interview with Shero, for author.

19. Fall 1967
　Pages 369–74: For Wisconsin, *NLN,* October 23 and November 6, 1967; Durward Long, in Foster and Long, pp. 246 ff.; James Ridgeway, *New Republic,* November 4, 1967; Patrick Quinn, interview. **Page 369:** "From Tuesday," handout, author's file. **Page 372:** "There was no," *NLN,* November 6, 1967. **Page 374:** "A demonstration earns," ibid. **Pages 375–77:** For Stop the Draft Week, *NLN,* November 6; Ferber and Lynd, p. 140 ff.; Goodman, pp. 476–85; and *Movement,* November 1967. **Page 376:** Wald, *NLN,* November 6, 1967. Bardacke, in Goodman, p. 478. **Page 377:** Halliwell, *NLN,* November 27, 1967. **Page 378:** "It was the first," anonymous SDSer, interview, Columbia, November 1967. **Page 379:** N.Y. *Times,* November 16, 1967. **Page 380:** Kazin, *American Scholar,* Autumn 1969. Demonstration surveys, in Foster and Long, the first by Peterson (pp. 59 ff.), the second by Foster and Long (pp. 81 ff. and pp. 419 ff.). The sixty "largest and best-publicized" demonstrations, author's compilation from *NLN, Guardian,* campus and commercial press, and "Riots, Civil and Criminal Disorders," Part 18, pp. 3671 ff. **Page 381:** Davidson, *NLN,* November 13, 1967. "Survey," Foster and Long, op. cit. **Page 382:** Dow figures on protests, *Newsweek,* December 1, 1969. "We pick this week," Wisconsin handout, op. cit. Indiana information and quotation, Foster and Long, pp. 306 ff. **Pages 383–86:** SOURCES FOR PENTAGON, *NLN,* October 30, 1967; *Liberation,* November 1967; *WIN,* October 30, 1967; Ferber and Lynd, pp. 135 ff.; Norman Mailer, *The Armies of the Night,* NAL, 1967; Rader, pp. 60 ff.; "No Game," Newsreel film, 1968. **Page 384:** *East Village Other,* November 1, 1967. "SDS played," in "Riots, Civil and Criminal Disorders," Part 20, p. 4304. Calvert, quoted in Ferber and Lynd, p. 139. **Page 385:** "An SDS girl," Mike Goldfield, *NLN,* October 30, 1967. **Page 386:** N.Y. *Times,* Richard Halloran, January 18, 1971. Goldfield, op. cit. Rosen, report to 1968 PL convention, "Build a Base in the Working Class," op. cit., p. 25. **Page 387:** Davidson, *NLN,* November 13, 1967, reprinted in Wallerstein and Starr, Vol. II, p. 129. **Page 388:** Spiegel, *NLN,* December 4, 1967. Tax figures, "Riots, Civil and Criminal Disorders," Part 18, p. 3515. **Page 389:** Calvert, "in the resistance," *Liberation,* May 1969; "I think that," *Movement* (San Francisco), December 1967. Veneziale, *NLN,* September 25, 1967. **Page 390:** Davidson, ibid. **Page 391:** Oglesby, "Notes on a Decade Ready for the Dustbin," *Liberation,* August-September 1969, italics in original; reprinted in Goodman, p. 737, and William Slate, editor, *Power to the People,* Tower, 1970; excerpted in Wallerstein and Starr, pp. 300 ff. Davidson, *NLN,* November 13, 1967. **Page 392:** Halliwell, *NLN,* October 2, 1967. "advance their," NAC minutes, *NLN,* September 4, 1967. **Page 393:** "some type of tear," *NLN,* October 2, 1967. Calvert, *NLN,* December 18, 1967. "the many liberal," Mike Meeropol, *NLN,* December 4, 1967. **Page 394:** "In case you," Al Spangler, *NLN,* October 16, 1967. Spiegel, *NLN,* December 4, 1967. **Page 395:** Weissman, interview. **Page 396:** Rosen, "We have to have," "Build a Base in the Working Class,"

op. cit., p. 49. **Page 397:** Rosen, all from ibid.: "In the past," p. 21, "Without real base-building," p. 20, "We reject," p. 27. Gordon, *NLN,* November 13, 1967. Levin, *PL,* November-December, 1967. **Page 398:** Shero, interview. **Page 399:** Southern caucus, *NLN,* January 22, 1968. "We, as people," minutes. **Page 400:** Calvert-Davidson, *NLN,* December 4, 1967. **Page 401:** PL proposal, *NLN,* February 12, 1968 (ellipsis in original). Jaffe-Gottlieb-Fuerst, original copy in author's file; *NLN,* January 8, 1968. **Page 402:** Spiegel, *NLN,* ibid. **Page 403:** "There is something," Elaine Plaisance, *NLN,* January 29, 1968.

20. Spring 1968
Page 404: Dohrn's diary has been reprinted verbatim, including illegibilities, in "Extent of Subversion in the New Left," Part 4, pp. 243 ff. **Page 405:** Pearson, June 14, 1968, *Chicago Daily News* and elsewhere. **Page 406:** Minutes of January 26 meeting, "Subversive Involvement in Disruption of 1968 Democratic Party National Convention," Part 1, pp. 2284 ff. Johnson, "all aspects," in "Johnson and Clark," N.Y. *Times,* April 17, 1971. DOD surveillance, Richard Halloran, N.Y. *Times,* January 18, 1971. SSS directive, *NLN,* November 20, 1967 .**Page 407:** FBI surveillance, *WIN,* March 1972, and *NLN,* January-June, passim. Penn State estimate, *NLN,* February 12, 1967. Texas surveillance, Frank Donner, *Playboy,* March 1968. **Page 408:** Fuerst, *NLN,* January 15, 1967. *NLN,* February 5, 1967. For SDS regional meeting, Alice Widener, "Student Subversion," U.S.A. (New York), 1968; also letters to NO from David Gilbert, February 25, and Steve Halliwell, undated (c. March), 1969; documents from the meeting appear in "Riots, Civil and Criminal Disorders," Part 20, pp. 4289 ff. **Page 409:** "where the museum," ibid., p. 4290. "a procession," Widener, op. cit., p. 66. *Firebomb,* quoted, ibid., p. 65. **Page 411:** Davidson, *NLN,* February 12, 1968. "She was an overwhelming," quoted by Lindsy Van Gelder, *Esquire,* April 1971. Gottlieb-Piercy, "Movement for a Democratic Society," REP pamphlet, 1968, reprinted in Teodori, p. 403. **Page 412:** For NUC, see issues of *NUC Newsletter,* May 24, 1968–May 1972; N.Y. *Times,* July 10, 1968; Goodman, p. 711; Bob Ross, *Guardian,* June 28, 1969. **Page 413:** NUC program, "Riots, Civil and Criminal Disorders," Part 20, p. 4474. **Pages 413–14:** Information on Dohrn, chiefly *Esquire,* op. cit. **Page 415:** NC on "defections," minutes, and Morgan Spector, *NLN,* May 20, 1968. SDS ad, *Ramparts,* February 1968. NO estimate, archives. **Page 416:** Dorhn-Jaffe, *NLN,* March 18, 1968, reprinted in Teodori, p. 355. **Page 416:** NO chapter estimate, telegram to Bobby Hutton rally, *NLN,* April 15, 1968. **Page 418:** SOURCES FOR BLACK STUDENT PROTEST, Robert L. Allen, *Black Awakening in Capitalist America,* Doubleday Anchor, 1969; Stokely Carmichael and Charles Hamilton, *Black Power,* Vintage, 1969; Harry Edwards, *Black Students,* Free Press, 1970; Irving Louis Horowitz and William H. Friedland, *The Knowledge Factory,* Aldine (Chicago), 1970, pp. 185 ff.; James McEvoy and Abraham Miller, editors, *Black Power and Student Rebellion,* Wadsworth (Belmont, California), 1969; Michael Miles, *The Radical Probe,* Atheneum, 1971, Ch. 4; Jack Nelson and Jack Bass, *The Orangeburg Massacre,* Ballantine, 1970; Jerome Skolnik, *The Politics of Protest,* Ballantine, 1969, Chs. IV, V; *Report of the*

President's Commission on Campus Unrest, Avon 1971, Ch. 3; Durward Long, Foster and Long, pp. 459 ff. Forman, *NLN,* March 4, 1968. Oglesby, from minutes; Ferber and Lynd, p. 180; and interview. **Page 419:** NC proposal, mimeograph, NO files, and *NLN,* April 8, 1968. Lynd, *Liberation,* May 1969. **Page 420:** Calvert, ibid. Davidson, reply to Calvert, *Liberation,* June 1969. Calvert, op. cit. **Page 420:** Calvert, from NO memo, May 1968. "We knew," anonymous SDSer, Columbia, interview. **Page 421:** New York Resistance, *WIN,* November 15, 1969. **Page 422:** college population drafted, N.Y. *Times,* December 1, 1968. **Page 423:** Lippmann, *Washington Post,* March 24, 1968. **Page 424:** Figures on "civil disorders" and troops, Skolnik, op. cit., pp. 172–73. Hoover, testimony before House Appropriations Committee, April 17, 1969. Skolnik, op. cit. NO summons, *NLN,* April 8, 1968. Campus response, figures from Durward Long, in Foster and Long, pp. 459 ff. "She was really," quoted in *Esquire,* op. cit. **Page 425:** Keniston, p. 248. 1966 survey, Foster and Long, p. 176. **Page 427:** Bombing incidents, author's compilation based on *NLN, Guardian,* commercial press, Congressional testimony, esp. "Riots, Civil and Criminal Disorders," Part 18. **Page 428:** Davidson, *NLN,* February 12, 1968. Calvert, *NLN,* March 25, 1968. "We can't succeed," *NLN,* May 13, 1968. Pardun, interview. **Pages 430–46:** SOURCES FOR COLUMBIA, in addition to those listed in the introduction (all 1968 unless noted), *NLN,* April 29, May 6, 13, 27, June 10, and September 23; *Guardian,* May 4, 11, 18, and June 1; *Campaigner* (Labor Committees), December; *Columbia College Today,* Spring; *Life,* May 10; *LNS,* mailings April and May; *Movement,* June and November, March 1969; *Ramparts,* June; RAT, May 3; Daniel Bell and Roger Starr, in Bell and Irving Kristol, editors, *Confrontation,* Basic Books, 1969; *Crisis at Columbia,* daily *Spectator* reproductions; Lewis Feuer, *The Conflict of Generations,* Basic Books, 1969; Steve Halliwell, in Long, p. 200; Simon Michael Kunen, *The Strawberry Statement,* Random House, 1969; Mark Rudd, in Gary R. and James H. Weaver, *The University and Revolution,* Prentice-Hall, 1969; Wallerstein and Starr, esp. Vol. II, pp. 160 ff.; *Who Rules Columbia?* published by NACLA; Daniel Calahan, *Commonweal,* June 7; Tad Crawford, *National Review,* June 4; Stephen Donadio, *Partisan Review,* Summer, and *Commentary,* September; Richard Goldstein, *Village Voice,* May 2; Marvin Harris, *Nation,* June 10; Dotson Rader, *Evergreen Review,* August, *New Republic,* June 8, and with Craig Anderson, *New Republic,* May 11; Dankwart A. Rustow, *New Leader,* May 20, 1968; Paul Spike, *Evergreen Review,* August; Diana Trilling, *Commentary,* November; "The Columbia Revolt," Newsreel film, 1968. **Page 433:** Gilbert, letter to NO, February 10, 1968. Rudd, *Movement,* March 1969. Kaptchuk, quoted in Avorn, p. 31. Rudd, *Movement,* op. cit. **Page 435:** "The Issue," International Werewolf Conspiracy, quoted in Teodori, p. 370. **Page 436:** Rudd, "I resign," quoted in Avorn, p. 81. **Page 437:** Papert's talk in Low, Kahn, pp. 177–79, written for Kahn by Papert himself. **Page 439:** Ford and other grants, Avorn, p. 283. **Page 439:** "This was the first," Rader, p. 107. "the satisfaction of acting," Doug Dornan, *Liberation,* May 1971. **Page 440:** Rudd, *Movement,* March 1969. "Doesn't the university," quoted in Avorn, p. 106. Greeman, "In a Crisis the Center Falls Out: The Role of the Faculty in the Columbia Strike,"

REP pamphlet, 1968. **Page 441:** Oglesby, "Notes on a Decade," *Liberation*, August–September, op. cit. *Fortune*, editorial, June 1968. Kirk, "Face the Nation," May 5, 1968, excerpted in *NLN*, May 13, 1968. **Page 442:** "prime mover," *Newsweek*, May 20, 1968. "intellectual arrogance," *Time*, May 24, 1968. "single-minded fervor. . . . classic," Kenneth Crawford, *Newsweek*, May 27, 1968. *Times*, "rule-or-ruin," April 29; "to turn once again," May 5; "any society" (quoted in *Reader's Digest*, October 1968); "even most sympathizers," Section IV, May 26, all 1968. **Page 443:** *Barron's*, May 20, 1968. *Fortune*, op. cit. HUAC report, see N.Y. *Times*, May 6, 1968. **Page 444:** FBI, "anonymously," from Media files, reported in N.Y. *Times*, April 8, 1971. "Domestic war room," Richard Halloran, N.Y. *Times*, January 18, 1971. Survey, 72 percent, Foster and Long, pp. 419 ff., esp. p. 441. **Page 445:** Major demonstrations, author's compilation from *NLN*, *Guardian*, campus and commercial press, NO figures (archives), and "Riots, Civil and Criminal Disorders," Part 18. "College student," Peterson, in Foster and Long, p. 59. NSA survey, N.Y. *Times*, August 27, 1968, and Foster and Long, p. 434 (there misdated 1969). *Protest* survey, Foster and Long, esp. p. 472. ETS survey, Foster and Long, pp. 59 ff. **Page 447:** Gonzalez, quoted in Avorn, p. 260. Davidson, *Guardian*, November 16, 1968. "something on the order," Peterson, in Foster and Long, p. 78. National membership of 7,000 estimated from NO records of 1967–68 school-year dues ($20,000), extrapolated for twelve months, and *NLN* circulation (according to NO figures) of more than 6,700. **Page 448:** *Chicago Tribune*, May 19, 1968. Finances, NO files, and, e.g., *New York* magazine, October 11, 1968. **Page 449:** Davidson, *NLN*, June 10, 1968. Hayden, *Ramparts*, June 15, 1968. Mann, *Movement*, November 1968. **Page 451:** Dohrn exchange, Anthony Ripley, N.Y. *Times*, June 16, 1968, and *Guardian*, June 22, 1968.

21. Summer 1968
    Pages 455–70: SOURCES FOR THE 1968 CONVENTION, *NLN*, June 10 and 24, 1968; *Guardian*, June 22; Richard Anthony and Phil Semas, *New Republic*, June 29, 1968; Bruce Detweiler, *Village Voice*, June 27, 1968; Jeff Gordon, *PL*, October 1968; Tom Milstein, *Dissent*, September–October 1968; minutes; interviews. **Page 455:** "movement which," "Perspectives on Class Organizing," Columbia SDSers, *NLN*, June 24, 1968. "the destruction," by Morgan Spector and Susan Jankovsky, ibid. "professional revolutionaries," Bell–Dohrn–Halliwell, "Program Proposals," mimeograph, a part quoted in Calvert and Nieman, p. 878. "Throughout the convention," Don Newton, Los Angeles *SDS Regional Newsletter*, undated (1968). **Page 457:** "our movement," Neil Buckley, "Burning Questions for Our Movement," mimeographed position paper, June 1968, author's file. Survey on "revolutionaries," see Daniel Yankelovich poll, fall 1968, for *Fortune* magazine, in *The Changing Values on Campus*, Washington Square Press, 1972, p. 64, where 5 percent (or 368,000 out of 7,369,000 enrolled students) "strongly agree" on the need for "a mass revolutionary party" and 14 percent "partially agree"; and campus poll in *Playboy*, September 1970, where 15 percent (or 1,170,000) assert the need for revolution. **Page 458:** Pardun, interview. Hayden, *Ramparts*, June 15, 1968. **Page 459:** Buckley, "Burning Questions," op. cit.

Page 460: Bell–Dohrn–Halliwell, op. cit. **Page 461:** Pardun, interview. **Page 463:** Segal proposal, *NLN,* June 10, 1968. Pardun, quoted in *Time,* June 21, 1968. **Page 464:** Gordon, *PL,* October 1968, p. 110. **Page 465:** Pardun, *Guardian,* June 22, 1968. "audible gasp," Milstein, *Dissent,* op. cit. Bell performance and quotations, *Guardian,* June 22, and minutes. **Page 466:** Gordon, *PL,* October 1968. **Page 468:** Klonsky's previous publications include *NLN,* March 20, 1967, and March 18, 1968; for an account of his arrest with Eanet, *NLN,* November 27, 1967. Klonsky, "I think," *NLN,* March 18, 1968. **Page 469:** Klonsky, "Having been," version quoted in *New Republic,* June 29, 1968. **Page 470:** Rosen, speech to PL convention May 1968, in "Build a Base in the Working Class," PL pamphlet, June 1969. **Page 471:** PL National Committee, "Improve Our Basebuilding,"ibid. **Page 472:** PL pamphlet, "SDS Work-in 1968: Towards a Worker-Student Alliance," published by SDS, spring 1969. "We are convinced," ibid., p. 31. Bilazarian, speech to November election rally, Boston, in PL's *New England Regional Newsletter,* December 1968; for other writings on WSA, see Hilary Putnam, in Long, p. 318; Jeffrey Gordon, *PL,* February–March 1967; John Levin, *PL,* November–December 1967; various issues of PL-SDS's *"New Left Notes"* (Boston) in the fall of 1969 (e.g., Fred Gordon, "Build the Campus Worker-Student Alliance," *"NLN"* September 20, 1969, reprinted in Wallerstein and Starr, p. 296). **Pages 472–77:** SOURCES FOR THE DEMOCRATIC NATIONAL CONVENTION, *NLN,* March 4 and 25, July 29, August 5, September 9 and 16, 1968; *Guardian,* August 3, 17, 24, and 31, September 7, 1968; *Liberation,* October 1968; *Ramparts,* September 28, 1968; Richard Harris, *Justice,* Dutton and Avon, 1970; Abbie Hoffman, *Revolution for the Hell of It,* Dial, 1968; Norman Mailer, *Miami and the Siege of Chicago,* Signet, 1968; Potter, pp. 31 ff.; John Schultz, *No One Was Killed,* Big Table (Chicago) and Follett paperback, 1969; David Lewis Stein, *Living the Revolution,* Bobbs-Merrill, 1969; *Rights in Conflict* (the Walker Report), Dutton and Bantam, 1968; Ellen Willis, *New American Review,* April 1969; Misha S. Zaks, Patrick Hughes, Jerome Jaffe, and Marjorie B. Dolkart, "Young People in the Park," mimeograph, Northwestern University Medical School; "Subversive Involvement in Disruption of 1968 Democratic Party National Convention," Parts 1–3 (Hayden's testimony there later appeared in Hayden, *Rebellion and Repression,* Hard Times/Meridian, 1969); and several books on the subsequent conspiracy trial, esp. Peter and Deborah Babcox and Bob Abel, editors, *The Conspiracy,* Dell, 1969; Jason Epstein, *The Great Conspiracy Trial,* Random House, 1970; Hayden, *The Trial,* Ramparts, September 1970, and Holt, Rinehart and Winston, 1970; Mark L. Levine, George C. McNamee, Daniel Greenberg, editors, *The Tales of Hoffman,* Bantam, March 1970; John Schultz, *Motion Will Be Denied,* Morrow, 1972. **Page 473:** Mobilization call, mimeographed, also *Guardian,* August 24, 1968. Klonsky, *NLN,* August 5, 1968. **Page 474:** NIC, "educating and making," *NLN,* July 29, 1968. August 11 letter, signed by Wayne Heimbach, Jo Horton, Hamish Sinclair, Mike Klonsky, NO files. Oglesby's "Open Letter," reprinted in Teodori, p. 445. On demonstrator statistics, see Walker, esp. p. 92. Klonsky in Grant Park, quoted by Oglesby, "Notes on a Decade," *Liberation,* August–September 1969. "Handwriting on the Wall," #4, reprinted in *NLN*, September 9, 1968. Injured and arrested, Walker, op. cit. **Page 476:** "every survey," see John P. Robinson, *Public Opinion Quarterly*, Spring 1970. *Challenge*, September 1968. **Page 477:** Klonsky, *NLN*, September 9, 1968 ("Why Oglesby," unattributed).

22. *Fall 1968*

Page 478: Robbins and Ayers, *NLN*, October 7, 1968 (ellipses in original). For SDS growth, NO files; LNS, "SDS Membership Mushrooms," October 18, 1968, part reprinted in *Guardian*, October 26, 1968; *Guardian*, November 16, 1968, and January 4, 1969; Jack Gerson, *Movement*, November 1968; *Newsweek*, September 30, 1968. **Page 479:** "Across the country" *NLN*, October 7, 1968. **Page 479:** "I got my," *NLN*, ibid. Archibald, "we can't" and "just stopped," LNS, op. cit. Davidson, *Guardian*, November 16, 1968. **Page 480:** *Newsweek*, op. cit. *Life*, October 18, 1968. *Look*, October 1, 1968. Yankelovich survey, in *Fortune*, special issue on "American Youth," January 1969, subsequently published in book form by Time, Inc.; this survey expanded and compared, in *The Changing Values on Campus*, Pocket Books, 1972. **Page 481:** Klonsky, anonymous interview, copy in archives. **Page 483:** Rudd at Kent State, reported in James A. Michener, *Kent State: What Happened and Why*, Random House, 1971, p. 99. Dohrn–Jacobs–Jones, "Boulder and Boulder," mimeograph, and *NLN*, October 18, 1968. **Page 484:** "No class today," *NLN*, ibid. "organize in the high school," ibid. Kleiman, "High School Reform: Towards a Student Movement," SDS pamphlet, February 1966. **Page 485:** Widener, "Student Subversion," published by U.S.A. (New York), 1968, p. 34. High school protests 20 percent, see Congressional survey, "Protests Found," N.Y. *Times*, February 23, 1970. SLAP, printed in *NLN*, June 24 and October 7; responses by Les Coleman, October 18 and December 18, by Jim Prickett, December 4, and by Jared Israel, December 18, all 1968; SLAP also reprinted in "Riots, Civil and Criminal Disorders," Part 18, p. 3620, and *PL*, October 1968. "Behind SLAP," the Boulder version, *NLN*, October 7, 1968. **Page 486:** Davidson, *Guardian*, October 26, 1968. "THE ELECTIONS," *NLN*, October 25, 1968. **Page 487:** *Guardian*, November 16, 1968. NIC meeting, minutes, and *NLN*, November 19, 1968. **Page 488:** Klonsky, *NLN*, October 25, 1968. **Page 489:** "Sitting in," Calvert and Nieman, p. 140. **Page 490:** Ann Arbor report and "typical of many," *NLN*, November 11, 1968. (On the Ann Arbor meeting, see also Powers, pp. 77 ff.) **Page 491:** "This particular," *NLN*, November 11, 1968. **Page 492:** Some of the Berkeley story is in a document prepared by the "legal affairs staff" of California Governor Ronald Reagan, Printed in "Riots, Civil and Criminal Disorders," Part 22, pp. 5079 ff.; also, *Guardian*, October 5 and November 2, 1968, and February 15, 1969; *Movement*, April 1969. **Page 493:** "fed up," *Movement*, April 1969. **Page 494:** "political and office," NO memo, archives; see also Israel, *NLN*, December 18, 1968. Gordon, *NLN*, ibid. Dohrn, *NLN*, ibid. **Page 495:** Prickett, *NLN*, December 11, 1968. Spector, *NLN*, May 20, 1968. **Page 497:** *Reader's Digest*, October 1968; "To put it bluntly," is originally from his February 23, 1968, House testimony. **Page 498:** "The protest activity," September

1968, quoted in "Investigation of SDS," Part 1-A, p. 6. HUAC hearings, October 1, 3, 4, and December 2, 3, 4, 5, 1968, in "Subversive Involvement in Disruption of 1968 Democratic Party National Convention," Parts 1–3; Ichord, Part 1, p. 2239. Reagan, quoted in LNS package, December 1968. Powell, quoted by Davidson, *Guardian*, November 23, 1968. **Page 499:** "was moving," Richard Halloran, *N.Y. Times*, January 18, 1971. "an order directing," Robert Wall, *New York Review*, January 27, 1972. **Page 500:** "to play off," article on Wall, N.Y. *Times*, January 13, 1972. **Page 501:** Police arrest figures, from *NLN, Guardian*, and testimony in "Riots, Civil and Criminal Disorders," throughout, esp. Part 18, pp. 3679 ff. **Page 502:** Heyns, *Newsweek*, September 30, 1968. Gonzalez, quoted by Randy Furst, *Guardian*, October 12, 1968. "Seventy-four instances," based again on *NLN, Guardian*, campus and commercial press, plus a survey by the Senate Investigations Subcommittee, in "Riots, Civil and Criminal Disorders," Part 18, pp. 3669–3712. **Page 503:** Bombing incidents, similarly based. "This is number," quoted by Andrew Kopkind, *Hard Times*, November 1, 1968. **Page 504:** "Pacificism obfuscates," *NLN*, December 23, 1968. **Page 505:** Gitlin, "New Chances: The Reality and Dynamic of the New Left," mimeographed paper, November 1969, author's files; for additional analysis, see James Weinstein, *Socialist Revolution*, July–August 1972. **Pages 506–7:** Klonsky's "Toward a revolutionary youth movement," *NLN*, December 23, 1968; revised, *NLN*, January 8, 1969; reprinted in a REP pamphlet, spring 1969; *Guardian*, January 18, 1969; and Wallerstein and Starr, p. 216. **Page 508:** PL racism resolution, *NLN*, January 8, 1969, and *PL*, February 1969. Women's liberation resolution, ibid.; and *Guardian*, January 18, 1969; see also Ignatin's earlier version, *NLN*, December 23, 1968. **Page 509:** RYM debate described by Davidson, *Guardian*, January 11, 1969, including Klonsky, "PL has done." **Page 510:** Davidson, both quotations, *Guardian*, op. cit.

23. Spring 1969
   Pages 511–12: SOURCES FOR CAMPUS PROTEST, SPRING 1969, *NLN* and *Guardian*, which kept good track; Alan E. Bayer and Alexander W. Astin, *Educational Record*, Fall 1969; Roger Rapoport and Laurence J. Kirshbaum, *Is the Library Burning?*, Random House, 1969; "Student Protests 1969," Urban Research Corporation (Chicago), 1970 (summarized in advertisement and article, N.Y. *Times*, January 14, 1970), later printed, hoked up, as *Right On!*, Bantam, 1970; "Campus Tensions: Analysis and Recommendations," Report of the Special Committee on Campus Tensions, American Council of Education (Washington), 1970; report of the Brock Campus Tour, *Congressional Record*, June 24, 1969, reprinted in the *AAUP Bulletin*, September 1969; "Riots, Civil and Criminal Disorders," Part 18, pp. 3669–3712. **Page 511:** For San Francisco State, *Challenge*, February 1969; *Movement*, December 1968, January, February, March 1969; Bill Barlow and Peter Shapiro, *An End to Silence*, Pegasus, 1971; Kay Boyle, *The Long Walk at San Francisco State*, Grove, 1970; Arlene Kaplan Daniels and Rachel Kahn-Hut, *Academics on the Line*, Jossey-Bass (San Francisco), 1970; Foster and Long, pp. 271 ff.; Dikran Karaguezian, *Blow It Up!*, Gambit, 1971; Art Seidenbaum, *Confrontation on Campus*, Ward Ritchie (Los Angeles), 1969;

Robert Smith, Richard Axen, De Vere Pentony, *By Any Means Neces-
sary,* Jossey-Bass (San Francisco), 1970; John Summerskill, *President
Seven,* World, 1971; John H. Bunzel, N.Y. *Times Magazine,* November
9, 1969, and Bell and Kristol's *Confrontation,* op. cit.; Edwin C. Duerr,
Educational Record, Spring 1969; Nathan Hare, *Ramparts,* July 1969; A.
J. Langguth, *Harper's,* September 1969; Martin Nicolaus, *Movement,*
February 1969 and *New Left Review,* March–April 1969; Dorothy
Rabinowitz, *Commentary,* June 1969; "Crisis at San Francisco State,"
Journalism Department of San Francisco State, Insight Publications
(San Francisco), 1969; "Strike at Frisco State" by the Research Organiz-
ing Cooperative, San Francisco, undated; "On Strike," Newsreel film,
1969. For Cornell, *Cornell Reports,* published by the administration, esp.
June 1969; *Movement,* July 1969; Cushing Strout and David I. Grossvo-
gel, *Divided We Stand,* Doubleday 1970 and Anchor 1971; Michael Thel-
well, *Ramparts,* July 1961; Allan P. Sindler, "A Case Study of a University's Pattern of Error," paper to American Political Science
Association, September 1969; "Guns on Campus: Student Protest at
Cornell," Urban Research Corporation, 1970; "Black Determination—
Crisis at Cornell," Newsreel film, 1969. For Berkeley, *Ramparts,* August
1969; Goodman, pp. 505–13; Sheldon S. Wolin and John H. Schaar, *The
Berkeley Rebellion and Beyond,* New York Review/Vintage, 1970; Todd
Gitlin, *Hard Times,* May 26, 1969; Todd Gitlin and John Simon, *Liberation,* July 1969; "People's Park," Newsreel film, 1969. **Page 512:** Sources
for protest figures, Bayer and Astin, op. cit.; "Student Protests 1969," op.
cit.; and "Riots, Civil and Criminal Disorders," Part 18, op. cit. Black
protest figures, "Student Protests 1969," op. cit. High-school protests, 60
percent estimated by National Association of Secondary School Principals, 2,000 demonstrations by Columbia University faculty research
group, both in *Guardian,* May 17, 1969. Bombing figures, author's compilation based on "Riots, Civil and Criminal Disorders," Part 25, pp. 5757
ff., and *Scanlan's,* January 1971. **Page 513:** American Insurance Association, quoted in preface, *Scanlan's,* op. cit. **Page 514:** Lynd, *Liberation,*
June 1969. **Page 515:** Ideological work, *NLN,* 1969, e.g., "Smash the
Military" and Howie Machtinger, January 22, Don Hamerquist, January 29, Anne Goodman and Sue Eanet, and Bob Tomashevsky, February
12 (misdated February 5), Bernardine Dohrn, March 7 (misdated 1968),
Les Coleman, March 20, Jim Mellen, May 13; and two additional papers
by Les Coleman, in "Revolutionary Youth Movement," REP pamphlet,
undated (June 1969). Ayers–Mellen, "Hot Town: Summer in the City,"
NLN, April 4, 1969; reprinted in REP pamphlet, op. cit.; and Jacobs, p.
29. **Page 516:** *NLN* issues, January 15, 22, 29, and February 5, 1969.
Hampton, quoted by *Chicago Sun-Times,* May 25, 1969. NC resolution
on BPP, *NLN,* April 4, 1969; mimeograph pamphlet, SDS 1969; *Guardian,* April 19, 1969; *New Left Review,* July–August 1969; Wallerstein and
Starr, Vol. II, p. 226; and "Riots, Civil and Criminal Disorders," Part
18, p. 3340. Dohrn gave her ring to Pham Thanh Van, a delegate to the
Paris Peace conference, see "Report on the SDS Riots," Illinois Crime
Investigating Committee (ICIC), p. 577. **Page 517:** Eanet, *NLN,* Febru-
ary 28, March 7 and 13, 1969. Oglesby wrote of the Cuban visit, *NLN,*
January 29, 1969, and *Life,* February 14, 1969. SOURCES FOR THE VEN-

CEREMOS BRIGADE, *NLN*, January 15 and June 18, 1969; *Newsweek,* April 6, 1970; *RAT,* March 30, 1971; Sandra Levinson and Carol Brightman, *Venceremos Brigade,* Simon and Schuster, 1971; Julie Nichamin, *Movement,* February-March 1970; and sections from "Report on the SDS Riots," ICIC, esp. pp. 623 ff. **Page 518:** Less than 10 percent, see "Student Protests 1969," op. cit. For San Francisco State, supra. **Page 519:** Gitlin, *Guardian,* December 7, 1968. Chicago SDSers, *NLN,* February 21, 1969. **Page 520:** Gitlin, *Guardian,* February 1, 1969. "SDS failed," David Osher, *WIN,* June 1969. **Page 521:** "armed struggle," e.g., Klonsky, "Looking Back and Looking Ahead," "disciplined cadre" and "white fighting force," e.g., Ayers-Mellen, "Hot Town," "a communist party," Les Coleman, "Notes on Class Analysis," all in "Revolutionary Youth Movement," REP pamphlet, undated (June 1969). **Page 522:** Dohrn, *NLN,* special issue, "International Woman's Day," March 7, 1969. Hobson, *NLN,* May 30, 1969. Oglesby, "Notes on a Decade," *Liberation,* August–September 1969, reprints supra; see also Staughton Lynd, *Liberation,* March–April 1969. Northwestern booklet, in "Report on the SDS Riots," ICIC, pp. 753 ff. **Page 523:** "The striking finding," "Student Protests 1969," op. cit., p. 15. For high-school organizing, *NLN,* January 29, February 21, March 13 and 20, May 1, 1969; College Press Service dispatch December 1969 (e.g., in *Daily Cardinal,* Wisconsin, December 12, 1969); *Movement,* February and March 1969; *Socialist Revolution,* March–April 1970; REP pamphlet, "Revolutionary Youth Movement," op. cit.; "SDS Plans for America's High Schools," a report of the House Internal Security Committee, December 12, 1969; Diane Divoky, *How Old Will You Be in 1984?,* Avon, 1969; Goodman, pp. 79 ff., 266 ff.; Marc Libarle and Tom Seligson, *The High School Revolutionaries;* Tom Seligson, *To Be Young in Babylon,* Paperback Library, 1971; J. Edgar Hoover, *PTA Magazine,* January–February 1970; Al Hornstein, *Leviathan,* June 1969; Nicholas Pileggi, N.Y. *Times Magazine,* March 16, 1969; Dotson Rader, *Partisan Review,* April 1970; and "The Jackson Twins," McNaught Syndicate comic strip, February–April 1970. "One SDSer" and "Brooklyn College," Rob Cohen, *Scanlan's,* March 1970. **Page 524:** "Whenever SDS," *Daily Cardinal* (Wisconsin), December 12, 1969. For GI organizing, chiefly Bob Tomashevsky, *NLN,* February 12, 1969, and "Investigation of SDS," Part 7-B; also Andrew Stapp, *Up Against the Brass,* Simon & Schuster, paper, 1970, and Larry Waterhouse and Marian Vizard, *Turn the Guns Around,* Delta, 1971. **Page 525:** "GI Counseling," printed by NY Regional SDS, distributed by SDS, spring 1969. For factory organizing, Ira Perelson, *NLN,* February 12, and Jeff Jones, *NLN,* April 24 (misdated April 29), 1969; "Revolutionary Youth Movement," REP pamphlet, op. cit.; *Fifth Estate,* May 30 and June 6, 1969; *Guardian,* throughout the spring; Goodman, pp. 530 ff.; Russell W. Gibbons, *Nation,* September 8, 1969; "Oil Strike," Newsreel film, 1969. "Student support," *NLN,* April 24, 1969. SOURCES FOR WOMEN'S MOVEMENT AND SDS, *NLN,* February 28 and special issue, March 7, 1969; Robin Morgan, *Sisterhood Is Powerful,* Random House, 1970, esp. the introduction and Marge Piercy, pp. 421 ff.; Pamela Allen, *Guardian,* October 5, 1968; Kathy McAfee and Myrna Wood, *Leviathan,* June 1969; Marcia Salo and Kathy McAfee, *Leviathan,* May 1970; Marcia Stamberg, *Guardian,* March 22 and 29, April 19, 1969. **Page 526:** "We were still," Sue Munaker, Evelyn Goldfield, Naomi Weisstein, in Long, p. 236. "The system is like," quoted by Davidson, *Guardian,* June 7, 1969. Dohrn, *NLN,* March 8, 1969. **Page 529:** Rossen, interview. Membership figures, Klonsky, on CBS's "Face the Nation," May 11, 1969; "30,000," "Riots, Civil and Criminal Disorders," Part 18, p. 3394; AP, June 15, 1969, AP files, New York; James O'Brien (*Radical America,* July–August 1972) has estimated 60–100,000. **Page 531:** "WE'RE BROKE," *NLN,* February 12, 1969. "The bail money," *NLN,* May 20, 1969. Bank deposits, "Report of the SDS Riots," ICIC, p. 655. Klonsky, letter, November 30, 1968. **Page 532:** Hoover, testimony to House Appropriations Subcommittee, April 17, 1969. On Cambridge Iron and Steel, see *PL,* August 1969, and "Report on the SDS Riots," ICIC, pp. 663 ff. Police raid, *NLN,* May 13, 1969, and NO files; it was predicted by Klonsky on "Face the Nation," op. cit. **Page 533:** *NLN,* May 13, 1969. **Page 534:** "The ruling capitalist," *PL,* February 1969, p. 9. on BPP, ibid., pp. 30 ff. "don't have . . . system," ibid., p. 14; "false and dangerous . . . administration," *PL,* August 1969, p. 39. "The People's War . . . war," editorial, *PL,* June 1968; "EVERYONE . . . imperialism," *Challenge,* February 1969. **Page 535:** "What the people," Jake Rosen, *PL,* November 1969. **Page 536:** Randle-Dillon, *PL,* May 1969. *Old Mole,* "PLP: A Critique," REP pamphlet, c. June 1969. **Page 537:** For Austin NC, minutes; *NLN,* April 3, 1969; Adelson, p. 234; "Riots, Civil and Criminal Disorders," Parts 18, 20, 22, passim. SOURCES FOR SSOC, in addition to its own pamphlets and newspaper, *New South Student, NLN,* February 18, March 4 and 18, April 25, June 6, 1966, May 22, 1967, and April 24, May 1, 13, 20, 1969; *Guardian,* June 21 and 28, 1969; J. Anthony Lukas, *Don't Shoot—We Are Your Children!* Random House, 1971, pp. 117 ff.; Ed Clark, *PL,* November 1969; Harlon Joye, *Transaction,* September 1970. **Pages 539–41:** SOURCES FOR HARVARD, *NLN,* April 17, *Hard Times,* March 21, 1969; *New Leader,* April 28, 1969; *Old Mole* (Cambridge), April and May, 1969; *RAT,* April 18, 1969; "Harvard's Student Strike," Urban Research Corporation, 1970; "How Harvard Rules," published by Africa Research Group and *Old Mole,* 1969; Michael Holroyd, *Atlantic,* August 1969 (and letters, October); Kenneth Keniston, *New York Review,* September 24, 1970; David Papke, *Commonweal,* October 3, 1969; "Riots, Civil and Criminal Disorders," Parts 21 and 22; and books listed in introduction. **Page 539:** "You're as bad," Eichel et al., p. 83. "No, you and," *Old Mole,* "PL: A Critique," op. cit. **Page 540:** "These guys," *Harvard Crimson,* March 11. "The right wing," PL leaflet, quoted in Kelman, p. 139. **Page 541:** On the role of the Justice Department, see esp. Richard Harris, *Justice,* E.P. Dutton and Avon, 1970. Kleindienst, quoted by Elizabeth Drew, *Atlantic,* May 1969. **Page 541:** "campus rebellion" task force outlined to Congress May 13, reported by AP, June 13, 1969. Mitchell on wiretaps, "attack and subvert," Harris, op. cit. (Avon), p. 129. Nixon, "this is the way," press statement, March 22, 1969; "backbone," speech to U.S. Chamber of Commerce, April 29, 1969; "attempts at insurrection," speech, June 3, 1969; "We have the power," speech, June 3, 1969. **Page 543:** Mitchell, "The time," speech to Detroit Bar Association, May 1, 1969; "The Students for," testimony to

House Special Education Subcommittee, May 20, 1969. Hoover, testimony April 17, 1969, op. cit. "There are hardly," Robert Wall, *New York Review,* January 27, 1972. N.Y. *Times,* Barnard L. Collier, May 5, 1969. **Page 544:** For surveillance files, chiefly Wall, op. cit.; Frank Donner, *New York Review,* April 22, 1971; and Richard Harris, op. cit. Fox, "Police have now," quoted by Donner, *New York Review,* op. cit. McGuire, "our growing," quoted by Harris, op. cit. (Avon), p. 126. **Page 545:** Reston, N.Y. *Times,* May 4, 1969. *Time,* May 9, 1969. **Page 546:** Harris, *New Yorker,* November 22, 1969, and op. cit. (Avon), p. 175. Federal legislation, *Congressional Quarterly,* May 9, 1969; "Legislative Response to Student Protest," Urban Research Corporation, 1970. McClellan, "Riots, Civil and Criminal Disorders," Part 18, p. 3307. Ichord, "Investigation of SD," Part 1-A, p. 2. Cederberg, *Congressional Record,* April 24, 1969. **Page 547:** Long, ibid., June 5, 1969. State legislatures, "Legislative Response to Student Protest," op. cit.; Harris, op. cit.; "Campus Violence," N.Y. *Times,* September 1, 1969; AP, June 1, 1969, AP files. **Page 548:** Pusey, quoted in Eichel et al., p. 347. Additional university reaction and presidents' statement, see "Campus Unrest," testimony before House Education Committee, June 16, 1969; also Theodore Hesburgh, *Reader's Digest,* May 1970. "It didn't help," *Newsweek,* May 5, 1969. "The use of psychiatric," Irving Louis Horowitz, *Change,* January–February 1970. Aid loss, see Alexander Astin and Alan E. Bayer, *Educational Record,* Fall 1969. **Page 549:** Faculty response, *Chronicle of Higher Education,* April 6, 1970, and Stephen Cole and Hannelore Adamsons, *Public Opinion Quarterly,* Fall 1970. **Page 550:** ACE, Astin and Bayer, op. cit.; they add that "these figures are probably understatements." Figures on university force, ibid., and AP, June 16, 1969, AP files. Punishment figures, "Spring Protests 1969," op. cit. **Page 551:** "We are not," quoted in *NLN,* March 20, 1969. **Page 552:** "The S.D.S. can't," quoted in "S.D.S. Scores," N.Y. *Times,* May 5, 1969. **Page 553:** "more than 400," *NLN,* May 20, 1969. "security considerations," *NLN,* May 13. Phone tap, see "Report on the SDS Riots," ICIC, op. cit. **Page 554:** *The Bust Book, What to Do Until the Lawyer Comes,* Grove, 1970. Klonsky, *NLN,* May 20, 1969. **Page 555:** Mellen, quoted by Terry Robbins and Lisa Meisel, *NLN,* April 29, 1969.

24. Summer 1969

Pages 557-79: For the 1969 Convention, *NLN,* June 18 and 25, July 8, 1969; *"NLN"* (Boston), June 30, 1969; *Guardian,* June 28, July 5, 12, 19, 26, 1969; *Ramparts,* September 1969; REP pamphlets, "Documents on SDS and the Split," and "Debate Within SDS," both 1969. *Sparticist,* August–September 1969; Roger Kahn, *Esquire,* October 1969; Barry Kalb, *New Republic,* July 5, 1969; Andrew Kopkind, *Hard Times,* June 30, 1969 (reprinted in Jacobs, p. 15); Larry David Nachman, *Nation,* November 24, 1969; Dotson Rader, *Village Voice,* July 3, 1969; James Weinstein, *Socialist Revolution,* January–February 1970; interviews with Peter Henner, Booth, anonymous SDSers. **Page 557:** Hoffman, AP, June 18, 1969, AP files. **Page 558:** "This is America," *Newsweek,* June 30, 1969. **Pages 559–63:** "Weatherman" statement, *NLN,* June 18, 1969; reprinted by REP, summer 1969; Jacobs, p. 51; Wallerstein and Starr, Vol. II, p.

260. **Page 562:** Oglesby, "Notes on a Decade," *Liberation,* August-September 1969. **Page 565:** Hoffman, *Woodstock Nation,* Vintage, 1969, p. 55. "Klonsky's an authoritarian," quoted by Kopkind, *Hard Times,* op. cit. **Page 567:** *Guardian,* June 18, 1969. **Page 568:** "Less Talk, More Action" proposal, *"NLN"* (Boston), June 30, 1969. "After long study," *NLN,* June 25, 1969. **Page 569:** "tactical blunders," *Guardian,* June 18, 1969. **Page 571:** Kopkind, *Hard Times,* op. cit. **Page 572:** Dohrn, quoted in Kopkind, ibid. "counter-revolutionaries," Rudd-Jones-Ayers, *NLN,* June 25, 1969. **Page 573:** RYM statement, "1. We support," ibid. **Page 575:** "Tired of people," quoted in *New Republic,* op. cit. "There is only," *"NLN"* (Boston), June 30, 1969. PL's proposals, ibid. **Page 576:** "we've just taken," quoted in Adelson, p. 243. RYM "unity principles," *NLN,* July 8 and *Guardian,* July 5, 1969. "Mass action" proposal, *NLN,* June 25, 1969. **Page 577:** Rudd, "The Movement," *Guardian,* June 28. "They were," quoted by Lee Baxandall, in Goodman, p. 355. "to finance," quoted in Powers, p. 60. **Page 579:** "absolutely crucial," Jeff Jones, *NLN,* July 8, 1969. **Page 581:** For Columbus, *NLN,* August 1 and 23; James Michener, *Kent State: What Happened and Why,* Random House, 1971, esp. pp. 147 ff.; "Investigation of SDS," Parts 6-A and 6-B. " 'Weatherman' in practice," Lorraine Rosal, *NLN,* August 23, 1969. Rosal, ibid. **Page 582:** "to develop cadre," "Investigation of SDS," Part 6-B, p. 2000. "It was nice," ibid., Part 6-A, p. 1907. **Page 583:** Ayers, *NLN,* September 12, 1969 (misdated August 29). "The fight to destroy," anonymous, *RAT,* February 6, 1970. **Page 584:** One view of collective life, and "very often," anonymous Weathermen, *Defiance #2,* Paperback Library, March 1971, p. 9. **Page 585:** "The results," ibid., p. 12. "Our monogamous," *RAT,* op. cit. "I had to ask," Michener, op. cit., p. 149. "I mean if," "Investigation of SDS," Part 6-A, p. 1911. **Page 586:** Rosal, op. cit. **Page 587:** For summer violence, *Guardian,* commercial press, and "Investigation of SDS," Parts 6-A, 6-B, 7-B. **Page 588:** Macomb College action, see ibid., Part 6-B, and *NLN* (as *Fire Next Time*), August 16, 1969. "Women's liberation," *NLN,* ibid. **Page 589:** Pittsburgh action, "Investigation of SDS," Part 6-B, and *NLN,* September 12, 1969. "The kids," *NLN,* ibid. **Page 590:** NIC statement and UFAF coverage, *NLN,* July 24, and August 23, 1969. Seale and Hilliard, *Black Panther,* August 9, and *Guardian,* August 16, 1969. **Page 591:** "model for all," *NLN (Fire Next Time),* August 16, 1969. Lester, *Guardian,* August 23, 1969. Ignatin, "Without a Science of Navigation," in "Debate Within SDS," REP pamphlet, undated (September 1969). **Page 592:** Fruchter, quoted by LNS, in *Daily World,* August 21, 1969. "winning total," ibid. "the U.S. can never," quoted by Davidson, *Guardian,* August 30, 1966. **Page 593:** Gold for LNS, quoted by Rod Such, *Guardian,* March 21, 1970. Sources for Cleveland meeting, NLN, September 9, 1969; *Defiance #2,* op. cit.; Shin'ya Ono, *Leviathan,* December 1969 (reprinted in Jacobs, p. 227 ff.). **Page 594:** "Cleveland was," *Defiance #2,* op. cit., p. 7. "In Cleveland," a N.Y. Weatherwoman, *RAT,* February 6, 1970; reprinted in Jacobs, pp. 321 ff. **Page 595:** "It was in" and "Leadership was," *Defiance #2,* op. cit., pp. 7–8. Ayers, *NLN,* September 9, 1969; reprinted in Jacobs, p. 183. **Pages 596–98:** SOURCES FOR 1969 WORK-IN, *"NLN"* (Boston), June 30, July 30, August 26, September 20, 1969; *Business Week,* August 30, 1969;

Chemical and Engineering News, July 7, 1969; *Industry Week* (preview issue, undated, fall 1969); Paul Booth, *Ramparts,* September 1969; Russell W. Gibbons, *Nation,* September 8, 1969; "Riots, Civil and Criminal Disorders," Part 18; "Investigation of SDS," Part 7-B. **Page 597:** "the militant left-wing," Long Island Association pamphlet, May 12, 1969, author's file. *Industry Week* ad, *Advertising Age,* July 28, 1969. "We don't think," quoted by Gibbons, op. cit. Collins, "24 Defense Firms," *Washington Post,* June 6, 1969. **Page 598:** *Challenge,* August 1969. *Business Week,* op. cit. AP, September 6, 1969, AP files. **Page 599:** Cleveland man, see Ayers speech, *NLN,* op. cit. Rudd, quoted in *Esquire,* August 1970.

25. Fall 1969–Spring 1970
    Page 600: "When we move," *NLN (Fire Next Time),* c. September 20, 1969. **Page 601:** "The primary purpose," Shin'ya Ono, *Leviathan,* December 1969. Rudd at Columbia, and quotations, author's observations. **Page 602:** Pre-Chicago Weatheractions, in *NLN, Guardian,* Shin'ya Ono, op. cit., "Investigation of SDS," Part 7-B, "Report on the SDS Riots," ICIC. Hampton story, *People's Tribune,* Los Angeles, March 1970. "hundreds of them," *NLN,* August 28, 1969. "all over the country," *NLN,* August 23, 1969. Rudd, "Investigation of SDS," Part 6-B, p. 2142. **Pages 602–1 5:**SOURCES FOR CHICAGO NATIONAL ACTION, *NLN,* October 21, 1969; *Guardian,* October 18; LNS dispatch, October 1969; Chicago papers, October 7–12, 1969, and *Chicago Tribune Magazine,* November 23, 1969; Tom Thomas, "The Second Battle of Chicago," pamphlet published at Grinnell College, 1969 (excerpted in Jacobs, p. 283); Jason Epstein, *The Great Conspiracy Trial,* Random House, 1971, pp. 3 ff.; Jonathan Black, *Village Voice,* October 16, 1969; James K. Glassman, *Atlantic,* December 1969; John Kifner, N.Y. *Times Magazine,* January 4, 1970; Andrew Kopkind, *Hard Times,* October 20, 1969 (reprinted in Jacobs, p. 283); Ono, op. cit.; "Report on the SDS Riots," ICIC; notes, scraps, and trial documents, NO files; and author's observations. **Page 603:** "This is an awful," Thomas, op. cit. **Page 604:** "These guys in here," "Report on the SDS Riots," p. 450. **Page 606:** "and Marion," Thomas, op. cit. "We now feel," LNS dispatch (from *RAT,* October 29, 1969). "I saw and felt," Ono, op. cit. **Page 608:** "Bodies were just," interview in *RAT,* October 29, 1969; one police attack was photographed, *Chicago Tribune Magazine,* op. cit. Rudd at Park, personal observation. **Page 609:** The RYM II–Weatherman story, from Mary Moylan, *Hard Times,* April 20, 1970. **Page 610:** Ono, op. cit. **Page 612:** headlines, *Chicago Tribune,* October 9, *Chicago Daily News,* same date, N.Y. *Times,* October 10, 1969. "Chicago was key," anonymous Weathermen, *Defiance #2,* March 1971, p. 15. *NLN,* October 21, 1969. **Page 613:** "was the most fascist," "Report on the SDS Riots," p. 485. **Page 614:** "If I had," ibid., p. 494. "We won very," *Defiance #2,* op. cit., p. 16. PL-SDS, "Investigation of SDS," Part 7-B, p. 2554. **Page 615:** Fayetteville letter, *RAT,* August 27, 1969; excerpted in *Guardian,* September 13, 1969. **Page 618:** Statistics on protest activity 1969–70, Alexander W. Astin, *Educational Record,* Winter 1971; "Student Protest, Part II," Urban Research Corporation (Chicago), 1970; study by the Urban Institute (Washington, D.C.)

for President's Commission on Campus Unrest, reported by N.Y. *Times,*
November 4, 1970. **Pages 619–20:** For PL-SDS, *"NLN"* (Boston), fall
and spring, 1970, sporadic; *Sparticist,* April–May 1970; issues of "Revolu-
tionary Marxist Newsletter" (Sparticist youths) from February 1970 on;
Bob Leonhardt, *PL,* February 1970; Adelson, passim. **Pages 620–21:** For
RYM II, *Revolutionary Youth Movement,* RYM II newspaper for
Chicago National Action, undated (c. September 1969); *Guardian,*
November 22, December 20, 1969; *Militant,* October 17, December 12,
1969; "Debate Within SDS, RYM II vs. Weatherman," REP pamphlet,
September 1969. On the Atlanta meeting, *Guardian,* December 20, 1969.
Page 621: For YSA, see various issues of *The Militant,* organ of its
parent Socialist Workers Party; *Guardian,* January 17, 1970. "personality
cliques," *Young Socialist* (YSA), December 1969. Membership estimates,
Washington Post, December 11, 1969; College Press Service (CPS 47–1),
January 1970; *Militant,* August 7, 1970. **Page 621:** SMC membership
figures, *Guardian,* January 17, 1970, and SMC handout, mimeograph, fall
1969. SMC conference, *Militant,* February 27, 1970; *Guardian,* February
28, 1970; *Campaigner* (Labor Committees), May–June 1970; N.Y. *Times,*
February 16, 1970; *WIN,* April 1, 1970. **Page 623:** LID report, "The State
of the Student Movement—1970," August 1970. **Page 624:** Rader, in
Defiance #1, Paperback Library, October 1970, p. 206. "The issue was,"
Inessa, Victor Camilo, Lilina Jones, Norman Reed, in Jacobs, p. 436.
"We're moving," Weatherman pamphlet, "Looks Like We're in for
Nasty Weather," November 1969. **Page 625:** "Once you really," printed
letter from Weatherbureau, undated (fall 1969), author's file. Seattle
Liberation Front on Weatherman, Michael Lerner, *Liberation,* July
1970. "It struck me," interview, "December 1969: Weatherman Goes
Underground," *Scanlan's,* January 1971. **Page 626:** "More than ever"
and "Should we all," *Defiance #2,* op. cit., p. 20. "Out of the often,"
ibid., p. 21. **Page 626:** For Flint meeting, AP, December 31, 1969; LNS,
January 1970, in *Guardian,* January 10, 1970, Jacobs, p. 341; *Great Speckled Bird* (Atlanta), January 1970; *Philadelphia Free Press,* January 12,
1970; *RAT,* January 7 and February 24, 1970; *Seed* (Chicago), January
1970; "Report on the SDS Riots," ICIC, pp. 571 ff. **Page 627:** "The war
council," Tibor Kalman, *RAT,* op. cit. Weatherman songbook, excerpts
in *Philadelphia Free Press,* op. cit., and Jacobs, p. 351. **Page 628:** Dohrn,
"We were," and Jacobs, LNS, op. cit. Rudd, *Great Speckled Bird,* op.
cit. "The raps," *Scanlan's,* op. cit. "All white babies," *Great Speckled
Bird,* op. cit. Dohrn, "Dig it," LNS, op. cit. **Page 629:** "The War
Council," *Scanlan's,* op. cit. "The notion of public," Weatherbureau
packet, and Jacobs, pp. 444–46. "We are behind," *NLN* (as *Fire*), January 30, 1970, and Jacobs, pp. 450–51. **Page 630:** "Cuba started," Weatherbureau's printed invitation to Flint, December 1969, author's file. "We
believe" and "the most significant," AP, December 31, 1969, AP files; see
also *"NLN"* (Boston), January and February 5, 1970. **Page 631:** James,
quoted in "Report on the SDS Riots," ICIC, p. 606. "All over the
world," Weatherman communiqué No. 1, var. reprinted, underground,
and in a collection, "Outlaws of Amerika: communiqués from the
weather underground," Liberated Guardian Collective, July 1971. **Page
632:** Bombings 1969–70, author's compilation, based on commercial

press, *Guardian, Scanlan's* (January 1971), and "Riots, Civil and Criminal Disorders," Parts 24 and 25, esp. pp. 5757 ff. ROTC violence, author's compilation; FBI release, July 14, 1970, says 281 attacks. ACE figures, in *Educational Record,* Winter 1971. **Page 633:** Mitchell, quoted by his wife, N.Y. *Times,* November 22, 1969; Ayers, by John Kifner, N.Y. *Times Magazine,* January 4, 1970. Police killings, from FBI, in N.Y. *Times,* August 27, 1970. Assaults, from FBI, in *U.S. News,* May 25, 1970. Threats against officials, N.Y. *Times,* April 4, 1970. **Page 634:** *Newsweek,* Karl Fleming, October 12, 1970. Numbers initiating violence estimated from those claiming to be revolutionary and in favor of violence in surveys by Daniel Yankelovich, *The Changing Values on Campus,* op. cit., and *Playboy,* September 1970, plus polls by Gallup, Harris, and others, spring 1970, indicating between a third and a half of all students participated in protests; Harris, in *Report of the President's Commission on Campus Unrest,* Avon, May 1971, found that 58 percent of students—4,136,000—participated in May 1970 demonstrations, at least a quarter of which were violent. **Page 635:** Numbers supporting violence estimated from Yankelovich, op. cit., indicating between 20 and 35 percent of students justify violence, and polls indicating number in favor of violence for social change: Gallup, fall 1970 (44 percent), Cornell study (N.Y. *Times,* October 27, 1969, 20 percent), President's Commission (80 percent), and University of Michigan (20 percent). **Pages 635–640:** SOURCES FOR MAY 1970, *Guardian,* May 9, 16, 23, 30, June 6, 1970; *National Strike Information Committee Newsletter* (Brandeis), spring 1970; *Change,* July–August 1970; *New York Review,* June 18, 1970; Jeremy Brecher, *Liberation,* June 1970 (later published as a pamphlet by *Root and Branch,* Boston); *Report of the President's Commission,* op. cit.; Michener, *Kent State: What Happened and Why,* op. cit.; Richard E. Peterson and John A. Bilorusky, *May 1970: The Campus Aftermath of Cambodia and Kent State,* Carnegie Commission on Higher Education, 1971; I.F. Stone, *The Killings at Kent State,* New York Review/Vintage, 1971; Stuart Taylor, Richard Shuntich, Patrick McGovern, Robert Genther, *Violence at Kent State,* College Notes and Texts (New York), 1971. **Page 636:** Kerr, in *May 1970,* op. cit., p. xi. Figures from Peterson, ibid. **Page 637:** Bombing figures, *Scanlan's,* January 1971, and "Riots, Civil and Criminal Disorders," Part 25, p. 5781 ff. **Page 638:** Nixon, White House statement, May 4. **Page 639:** Kent reaction and "When I reported," Michener, op. cit., pp. 413 ff. Student reaction figures, Peterson, in *May 1970,* op. cit. **Page 640:** President's Commission, op. cit., pp. 1, 5. **Page 641:** "They blamed," LNS, October 1970. **Page 642:** Nixon, impromptu speech at Pentagon, May 1, 1970. Agnew, speech, October 30, 1969. **Page 643:** N.Y. *Times,* June 28, 1970. Hoover, House Appropriations Subcommittee. Media files printed in full in *WIN,* March 1972. "There was," ibid., p. 28. **Page 644:** Internal Security Division information and "top priority," *Newsweek,* May 31, 1971. Special Litigation Section information and "investigative purposes," *Ramparts,* December 1971; Thomas Powers, *Atlantic,* October 1972. **Page 645:** "I doubt if," Ichord, "Investigation of SDS," Part 7-A, p. 2185. Legislation, see Richard Harris, *Justice,* op. cit., and President's Commission, op. cit. **Page 646:** N.Y. *Times,* March 28, 1971. State laws, President's Commission,

op. cit.; *Newsweek,* December 7, 1970. Campus police forces, N.Y. *Times,*
September 15, and *Wall Street Journal,* September 4, 1970. Wiretap
study, N.Y. *Times,* March 29, 1971. **Page 647:** Quinn, interview. **Page
648:** Weatherman communiqués collected in "Outlaws of Amerika," op.
cit. **Page 649:** Dohrn, ibid., and *Liberation,* November 1970.

26. Epilogue: 1970–1972

For Weatherman Underground, sources are skimpy, of course, the
best being their own communiqués (esp. Dohrn, op. cit.; also *RAT,* 1970
passim, esp. June 26 and November; *Liberated Guardian,* 1970 through
1972, esp. March 11 and October 14, 1971 and March 1972; Eric Mann,
Defiance #2, op. cit., pp. 126 ff.; Russ Neufeld, *Nation,* May 17, 1971;
and Jacobs, pp. 453 ff. **Page 651:** Dohrn, "as the forces," communiqué,
op. cit. **Page 652:** "We've learned," ibid. Weathermessages, issued from
May 1970 to May 1972, were: "Declaration of War," May 21, 1970;
Number 2, accompanying the New York police headquarters bombing,
June 10, 1970; "Don't Look for Us, Dog, We'll Find You First," after the
Detroit indictments, July 25, 1970; "Rosemary and Tim are Free and
High," after the Leary escape, September 15, 1970; "Fall Offensive:
Guard Your Children, Guard Your Doors," October 5, 1970; "Message
to Brother Dan," responding to criticisms from the Reverend Daniel
Berrigan before his arrest by the FBI, October 8, 1970; "New Morning
—Changing Weather," December 6, 1970; "We Attacked the Capitol,"
February 28, 1971; "Dear Mrs. Bacon," a reassuring letter to the mother
of the woman arrested for the Washington bombing. May 1, 1971; Num-
ber 10, after George Jackson's murder, August 30, 1971; "Oswald's
Office," after the Attica slaughter, September 17, 1971; Number 12, in
connection with the bombing of the Pentagon, May 19, 1972. **Page 653:**
Seed (Chicago), January 1970. **Page 654:** Rubin, *We Are Everywhere,*
Harper, 1971. Hoffman, *WIN,* September 1, 1971. Cleaver, *Berkeley Tribe,*
November 7, 1969. New York Panthers, in *East Village Other,* February
23, 1971, and *Liberated Guardian,* February 25, 1971. *Seed,* March 1971.
Book, Jacobs. **Pages 654–55:** For PL-SDS, chiefly *"NLN"* (Boston),
Challenge, and *PL,* 1970–72; Adelson book. **Page 656:** March 1972 con-
stitution, author's file. **Page 657:** "a democracy," *Port Huron Statement.*

Appendix.

SOURCES FOR LID AND PREDECESSOR, chiefly the files in the Tami-
ment Library, esp. Harry Laidler papers, and "Twenty Years of Social
Pioneering," LID pamphlet, 1925; "Handbook of the Student League for
Industrial Democracy," SLID pamphlet, 1934; *The League for Industrial
Democracy: Forty Years of Education,* LID, 1945; issues of *SLID Bulle-
tin, SLID Newsletter, SLID Voice, Student Outlook,* and facsimile repub-
lications of *Student Advocate* and *Student Review.* **Page 675:** Laidler,
Outlook (SLID), Summer 1950. **Page 676:** London, in "Handbook," op.
cit. (copy in author's file). **Page 677:** London, ibid. **Page 678:** Reed,
quoted in Feuer, *The Conflict of Generations,* Basic Books, 1969, p. 346.
Page 679: For the history of the left during and after the war, see esp.
James Weinstein, *The Decline of Socialism in America,* 1912–25, Knopf,
1967, and Vintage, 1969. "students wanted," "Handbook," op. cit. **Page**

680: "all believers," "LID Principles," c. 1923, Tamiment. **Page 681:** 1934 program, in "Handbook," op. cit. **Page 682:** Henderson, *Student Review,* July 1932. "The Socialist," "Handbook," op. cit. **Page 683:** "feeling of solidarity," Joseph Lash, "Campus Strikes Against the War," LID pamphlet, 1934. Declaration of Principles, "Handbook," op. cit. **Page 684:** For ASU, see *Student Advocate;* also Feuer, op. cit., pp. 369 ff. **Page 687:** SLID budget figures, Tamiment. **Page 688:** "the SLID seeks," 1946 SLID Program, Tamiment. membership clause, Laidler, "Interim Report," November 30, 1946. **Pages 690–95:** For SLID in the 1950s, André Schiffrin, *Radical America,* May–June 1968. **Page 690:** Gersch, *SLID Voice,* October 1951. Constitution, Tamiment. **Page 691:** "a national *liberal,"* *SLID Voice,* March-May 1955, my italics. "Where we are," call to conference, "The Silent Generation Speaks," July 7–13, Madison, Wisconsin, my italics. "The Student," Venture, Vol. 1, No. 1, April 1959. Schiffrin, op. cit. **Page 693:** Schiffrin, *SLID Voice,* August-October 1955. "LID members," Francis B. Randall, SLID *International Bulletin,* November 1958. Harrington, interview. Schiffrin, *Radical America,* op. cit. *New Republic,* October 29, 1951. **Page 694:** Cornfeld, M.S. thesis, Tamiment. Schiffrin, *Radical America,* op. cit. Neier, "Report from the President," Fall 1957.

INDEX

Note: Colleges and universities where there were SDS chapters are not listed separately in the index. For individual institutions, see pages listed under CHAPTER LISTS, CHAPTER ACTIONS, and CAMPUS DEMONSTRATIONS.

ABOUT THE AUTHOR

KIRKPATRICK SALE has been a writer and editor for fifteen years. He is the author of more than a hundred magazine and newspaper articles for such publications as *The New York Times,* the *San Francisco Chronicle, Change, Dissent, Evergreen Review,* the *Nation,* the *New Leader,* and the *Village Voice.* He has been a teacher of history at the University of Ghana and has written a book on that country. He now lives with his wife and two daughters in New York City.